Financial
INFORMATION FOR DECISIONS
Accounting
2ND EDITION

Robert W. Ingram
Ph.D. and C.P.A.
Ross-Culverhouse Chair in Accounting
University of Alabama
Tuscaloosa, Alabama

SOUTH-WESTERN College Publishing

An International Thomson Publishing Company

To Erin, Shea, and Chris, my most valuable assets.

Sponsoring Editor: Elizabeth A. Bowers
Developmental Editor: Sara E. Bates
Production Editor: Peggy A. Williams
Production House: Matrix Productions, Inc.
Cover and Interior Designer: Joseph M. Devine
Internal Illustrations: Rick Moore
Marketing Manager: Steven W. Hazelwood

AO77BA
Copyright © 1996
by South-Western College Publishing
Cincinnati, Ohio

ISBN: 0-538-85134-1

2 3 4 5 6 7 8 9 KI 3 2 1 0 9 8 7 6 5

Printed in the United States of America

Library of Congress Cataloging-in-Publication Data

Ingram, Robert W.
     Financial accounting : information for decisions / Robert W. Ingram.
 -- 2nd ed.
        p.   cm.
     Includes bibliographical references and index.
     ISBN 0-538-85134-1
     1. Accounting--Decision making.   2. Managerial accounting.
 I. Title.
 HF5635.I484   1995
 658.15' 11--dc20   95-9261
                                                                      CIP

I(T)P
International Thomson Publishing
South-Western College Publishing is an ITP Company.   The ITP trademark is used
under license.

Preface

How to Make an A in this Course
(For Students Only)

I am going to let you in on some trade secrets instructors seldom tell students. That's why this section is labeled, "For Students Only." If instructors find out I have revealed these secrets, I'll probably get a lot of mail.

Getting good grades is not a matter of luck. That's not the secret. Also, it is no secret that doing assignments (on time), going to class (regularly), getting enough sleep and exercise, eating properly, and studying throughout the semester (instead of just at exam time) will improve your grades. But, this is hard work. So, what you want is a way to get good grades and not work so hard, right? Well, pay attention—the secret is to work smarter! That's not the same as being smarter, which is a matter of luck. Here's how you work smarter.

Step 1: Determine why this course is important for you. First, figure out why you're taking this class. What are your goals for the class? Do you care about this course? Do you have a strong motivation to learn about accounting? Perhaps being an accountant comes on your list of career options just below sweeping up at McDonalds. Maybe your goal is to make lots of money. Or, maybe you're just in college to have a good time until you inherit the family fortune. In any case, this course is designed for you. One of the surest ways to have a million dollars is to start with ten million and not know anything about accounting and business management. If you don't inherit wealth, you're not likely to get it without speaking the language of business. Accounting is the language! Maybe you just want to get a good job, but you're pretty sure you don't want to be an accountant. Fine! This course isn't going to make an accountant out of you. It will help you understand some of the "mystical rituals" of accounting that non-accountants often find confusing. Whatever type of management position you have in any organization, you can be pretty sure you're going to have to work with accountants and with accounting information. You should know they can have a major effect on your life. Many organizations use accounting information to evaluate their employees for salary and promotion decisions. You should understand how to interpret this information. You may even learn accounting isn't what you think. Whether you grow to love or hate accounting, decide what you can get out of this course that will be useful to you.

Step 2: Find out what your instructor expects of you in the course. Next, check out your instructor. If you're lucky, your instructor is sensitive, warm, caring, has a good sense of humor, is witty, loves teaching, and wants you to do well in the course. If instead, your instructor is more normal (and less perfect), remember, I'm OK, you're OK, and the instructor is still the instructor. And, as the instructor she/he has power over your life. So, find out what she/he expects from you. What are her/his goals for the course? What does she/he want you to know or be able to do once you complete the course? Perhaps, she/he will tell you (good sign), but if not, ask. You should say: "Professor Whatever-Your-Name-Is (it would be wise to use the right name) what's the lowdown on the layout for this course?" This is education jargon for "what are your goals for this course?" This may catch her/him off guard, so give her/him a minute or two to think. You may even have to wait until the next class meeting to get your answer. Make sure you and your instructor understand each other's goals. Some accounting instructors expect all their students to become accountants. If you have one of these, make it clear. Tell your instructor: "I don't plan to be no ac-count*ant*!" (Make sure you add the *ant*, or you may get fast agreement.) Find out what's in this course for you.

Step 3: Find out how you will be graded. Now, find out how you will be graded. How does the instructor test? Is she/he one of the picky types: "What is the third word on the fifth line on page 211?" Or, does she/he go in for the broader, thought questions: "Explain how accounting was instrumental in negotiating the third treaty of Versailles in 1623." Does she/he go in for multiple guess, or are short answers her/his cup of tea? I expect my students to be able to interpret financial statements. If students come to the exam expecting picky questions from the text, they're likely to be very disappointed. Whatever the method, you need to know what is expected of you and how these expectations translate into grades. Occasionally, you'll find an instructor whose stated expectations don't agree with how she/he tests and grades. That's why you need to find out about both expectations and grades. If they don't seem to be consistent, you'll have to determine what the instructor really expects.

Step 4: Emphasize learning what's important. Figure out what you need to do to accomplish your goals and meet the instructor's (real) expectations. A major lesson you should learn, if you haven't already, is "what you take from a course (and almost anything else) depends on what you bring to it." Your attitude is important. If you decide something is worth learning, you'll probably find a way to learn it. Not because you're supposed to learn it, but because you want to. "Wanting to" is the biggest part of working smarter. Wanting to learn will go a long way toward helping you get a good grade. Unfortunately, it may not be enough unless what you want to learn is also what your instructor wants you to learn. Therefore, you need to make sure you and your instructor are on the same wave length. If you're not, talk it over. Find out why the instructor has a different outlook. You may change your opinion about what's important. Determine how to focus your efforts. Not everything in this book or course is equally important. Focus on what's most important to you and to your instructor.

Step 5: Communicate with your instructor. Try to remember your instructor is a person. Even the author of this book is a person. I belong to a wife, two teenagers, and a dog. There are a few instructors around who enjoy treating students like peasants. Luckily, most of us really want to see you do well, but we need your help. Instructors don't know everything. In particular, we can't read your mind. You need to let your instructor know if you're having problems understanding the material you're expected to learn, figuring out what the instructor expects of you, or figuring out how to prepare for tests and other assignments. Talk with your instructor about problems you're having with the class. Remember, your instructor really is human.

This is your class. You paid for it. OK, maybe it was your parents, or somebody else who put out hard, cold cash for you to take this course. Don't let anybody keep you from getting your money's worth. Working smarter means determining what's important and focusing your attention and efforts on these things. Then, don't be distracted from your goals. If you run into problems, deal with them. If you don't understand something in class or in the book, ask questions. If you're afraid of asking dumb questions in class, remember: looking dumb in class is better than looking dumb on an exam. If you think you may be missing key points, talk with your instructor. If you want to learn, you can.

That's it. Give it a try. I think you'll find the course more enjoyable and the experience more rewarding. Of course, you might also try doing assignments, going to class, getting enough sleep and exercise, eating properly, and studying throughout the semester. They usually help, even though they are hard work. Finally, there's no guarantee you'll make an A in this course. But remember, what you take from class depends on what you bring to it.

Best wishes to you, not only in this course, but throughout life.

Rob Ingram

A side note:

To aid you in the learning process, basic concepts are indicated by margin icons. The concepts and their respective icons are shown below.

| Transformation Process | | Control of Accounting Systems | |
| Reporting Rules, Standards | | Cash, Cash Flow | |

Decisions, Decision Making, Analysis, Understanding

Time, Accrual Accounting

Organizations, Management, Professionals

International

Financial Reports

Stockholders

Accounting Information Systems

Obligations, Valuation, Contracts

Accounting, Processing Accounting Information

Effect of Business Activities (Risk and Return, Efficiency and Effectiveness, Business Results)

Computer Processing/ Applications

Preface

To the Instructor

This book is an introduction to financial accounting. It introduces the reader to concepts of accounting and financial reporting. These concepts are essential to understanding how decision makers use accounting information. Since the purpose of the book is to help students learn how to use accounting information, emphasis is on analyzing and interpreting the information rather than on information preparation. Very little attention is given to such preparation.

Two primary concepts explain accounting information in the book. The first of these is the transformation process in which organizations create goods and services. Accounting measures, records, and reports economic activities in the transformation process. A major philosophy of the book is students cannot understand accounting unless they first understand how organizations operate. The second concept is the need to measure performance in distinct time periods. Accounting measurement and reporting rules focus on timing differences between when events occur that create or use resources and when cash is received or paid. A second major philosophy of the book is students must understand the relationship between accrual and cash flow measures in order to interpret accounting information.

This edition retains the conceptual basis and most of the content of the first edition. Some substantive modifications have been made, however. Students and faculty who have used the first edition have provided useful feedback about areas of confusion and difficulty with this edition. I have modified several chapters to improve readability and comprehension. Most of these changes were minor or involved updates for changes in GAAP, and, for more recent examples, from annual reports and other resources. Major changes have been made to Chapter 4, "Processing Accounting Information," Chapters 8–10 on financing activities, and Chapter 14, "Analysis of Operating Activities."

Chapter 4 has been streamlined to eliminate much of the detail about computerized accounting systems. The general concepts of computer systems are discussed. A new Chapter 8 has been added to the book. This chapter, "Determining Value," introduces the present value concept and demonstrates its application to the valuation of assets, including stocks, bonds, notes, plant assets, and companies. Later chapters refer to and build on these concepts. Chapter 9, "Financing Activities," describes basic accounting treatment for debt and equity. Major concepts are discussed, but some of the details of pensions and foreign currency adjustments have been omitted. The section in Chapter 11 on investing in financial instruments has been revised to conform with SFAS 115.

The analysis chapters, Chapters 10, 12, and 14, have been modified to integrate the material better. My goal in these chapters, and a major purpose of the text, is to guide students into business decisions that involve financial accounting information. The second edition contains a more systematic approach to this process than did the first edition. Chapter 14 is a capstone chapter that ties the concepts of earlier chapters, back to Chapter 1, together. The chapter illustrates how the accounting measurement and reporting system and the value model can be used to evaluate risk and return attributes. Students should complete the book with an understanding of how investors and other decision makers use accounting information in pricing securities and making decisions about company value. These concepts are applied to actual company data to illustrate the link between accounting information and value.

Many exercises, problems, and cases have been modified and updated. New exercises and problems have been added to most chapters. Supplemental materials also have been revised. A computer assisted instruction (CAI) package has been added to the available set of materials. This software package can be used by students to provide self-paced learning of the accounting cycle. Accounting majors, or prospective majors, can use this material to learn the traditional bookkeeping process.

My goal in revising the book has not been to produce the perfect financial accounting book. The perfect book will never exist. Instead, I hope to continue to improve the book so that it better meets the needs of students and instructors. Toward this end, I welcome comments and suggestions. These will provide a basis for continued revision and improvement.

Acknowledgments

I gratefully acknowledge the assistance of those whose suggestions have become part of this text. Though numerous people, including former mentors and colleagues, have played an important role in shaping my thinking about financial accounting and instruction, those who made special contributions to this text through reviewing and diary keeping include:

Claudia Gilbertson   *Anoka–Ramsey Community College*

Elaine Harwood   *Boston College*

Cynthia Jeffrey   *Iowa State University*

Robert J. Kirsch   *Southern Connecticut State University*

Tina Mills   *Miami University*

Paula Morris   *Kennesaw State College*

Douglas Sharp   *Wichita State University*

Ronald Strittmater   *North Hennepin Community College*

George Violette   *University of Southern Maine*

Karen Walton   *John Carroll University*

Gerald P. Weinstein   *John Carroll University*

Michael Welker   *Drexel University*

I also gratefully acknowledge the assistance of those at South-Western Publishing Co. who have been instrumental in developing this text.

About the Author

ROBERT W. INGRAM

Robert W. Ingram is the Ross-Culverhouse Chair in the Culverhouse School of Accountancy at the University of Alabama. He teaches courses in financial accounting and has been actively involved in course curriculum development. He has served as Director of Education for the American Accounting Association, as a member of the Accounting Education Change Commission, and as editor of *Issues in Accounting Education*, a journal dedicated to accounting education research.

Professor Ingram is a Certified Public Accountant and holds a Ph.D. from Texas Tech University. Prior to joining the faculty at the University of Alabama, he held positions at the University of South Carolina and the University of Iowa, and a visiting appointment at the University of Chicago. His research, which examines financial reporting and accounting education, has been published widely in accounting and business journals. He is recipient of the National Alumni Association Outstanding Commitment to Teaching Award and the Burlington Northern Foundation Faculty Achievement in Research Award at the University of Alabama. He has also received the Notable Contribution to Literature Award of the Government and Nonprofit Section of the American Accounting Association, and the Award for Excellence and Professional Contributions of the Alabama Association for Higher Education in Business.

Professor Ingram is married and has two children. He and his family enjoy sports, travel, reading, music and art. They live contentedly in Tuscaloosa, Alabama.

Brief Contents

SECTION I
The Accounting Information System

SECTION II
Analysis and Interpretation of
Financial Accounting Information

APPENDICES

GLOSSARY

INDEX

Contents

SECTION 2
ANALYSIS AND INTERPRETATION OF
FINANCIAL ACCOUNTING INFORMATION

9 Financing Activities   377

10 Analysis of Financing Activities   429

11 Investing Activities   469

Section
I

The Accounting
Information System

Chapter
1

Accounting and Organizations

CHAPTER
Overview

This book introduces basic concepts of accounting. It will help you understand why accounting information is important, how accounting information is produced, and how you can use this information in making decisions about organizations. Accounting describes economic events that occur in organizations. Therefore, to understand accounting you need to understand organizations. This chapter will introduce the purposes of organizations, how they achieve their purposes, the types of decisions made in organizations, and the role of accounting information in making these decisions. **Once you have completed this chapter, you should understand that accounting is a system that produces information for making decisions about organizations.**

Major topics covered in this chapter include:

- An illustration of the accounting process.
- The purposes and functions of organizations.
- Decisions made in organizations.
- The role of accounting in making decisions about organizations.

CHAPTER
Objectives

Once you have completed this chapter, you should be able to:

1. Identify the purpose of accounting.
2. Explain why accounting is an information system.
3. Compare major types of organizations.
4. Explain how organizations contribute to society.
5. Explain why markets are important.
6. Explain why owners invest in businesses.
7. Explain why accounting information is useful to investors.
8. Identify financing activities and the types of decisions they require.
9. Compare forms of business ownership.
10. Identify investing activities and the types of decisions they require.
11. Identify operating activities and the types of decisions they require.
12. List the steps in an organization's transformation process.
13. Define accounting.

INFORMATION FOR DECISIONS

All of us make decisions. Most of the time, unless our decisions are purely emotional, we use information to help us make our decisions. *Information* **includes facts, ideas, and concepts that help us understand the world.** The proper use of good information usually results in better decisions. To use information, we must be able to interpret it and understand its limitations. Poor information or the improper use of information often leads to wrong decisions.

As an example, assume that you wish to drive from Summer Town to Snowshoe City. The drive will take several hours and require several turns on unfamiliar secondary roads. Therefore, you use a map to provide information to help guide you along the way.

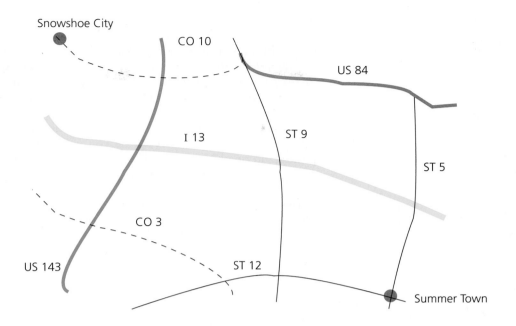

Why is the map useful? The map can help you plan your trip. You have selected a primary goal: arrive at Snowshoe City. You may have other goals as well, such as getting there as quickly as possible. Or, perhaps you wish to stop at various points along the way. The map provides information about alternative routes so that you can select the one that is shortest, fastest, or most scenic. Using the map along the way helps you make decisions about where to turn or stop. It helps you determine how far you have traveled and how far you have left to go. It helps you decide whether you are on the right road or where you made a wrong turn. It helps you decide where you are, how you got there, and where you are going.

Accounting provides information to help in making decisions about organizations. This information is like an organizational map. **Accounting information helps decision makers determine where they are, where they have been, and where they are going.** Rather than measuring distances in miles or kilometers, accounting measures an organization's activities by the dollar amounts associated with these activities. Thus, **the primary measurement unit for accounting information is dollars** in the U.S. or the local currency for other countries.

To illustrate, suppose you decide, as a summer job, to start a business at the beach selling sunglasses, swimwear, and suntan products. You will operate out of a small stand, appropriately named The Beach Shack, which you can rent from a nearby hotel that owns the beach property. Important questions you might ask include: Is this a good business opportunity? How much money should you expect to make? Are you making as much money as you expected?

Consider the primary components of your business. What will you need to start and run a business? You will need merchandise to sell. Therefore, you will have to purchase this merchandise from suppliers. You will need a place to operate your business and someone to sell the merchandise. You will need money to pay for your merchandise, the rent for your stand, wages, and any miscellaneous costs such as a business license and advertising.

As an initial step in deciding whether to start the business, you might consider how much you can expect to sell. You discuss the venture with some other business operators and determine that a small stand such as yours usually will sell about $7,000 of merchandise each month for June, July, and August.

Next, you might consider how much money you will need to operate your business. Assume you determine the merchandise that you can sell for $7,000 will cost you $3,500. Also, you decide you will need some part-time helpers to keep the stand open 10 hours a day, seven days a week. Therefore, you determine you will need the following each month:

Merchandise to sell	$3,500
Rent for stand	500
Wages	1,200
Miscellaneous	200
Total	$5,400

Also, you might consider how much you expect to make from the business. If you expect to sell $7,000 of merchandise and your costs will be $5,400, you should expect to make $1,600 from the business each month or $4,800 ($3 \times $1,600) for the summer.

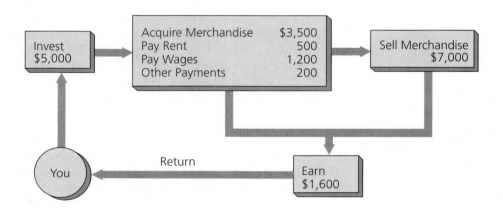

You should consider whether this appears to be a good business for you. Suppose you have $5,000 to invest in the business to purchase an initial stock of merchandise and to pay rent, the first week's wages, and miscellaneous costs. Would investing your money in the business be a good idea?

If you earn $4,800 from your investment, you will earn a rate of return on your investment (profit/amount invested) of 96% = $4,800/$5,000 for the summer. You would receive $4,800 of income in addition to the $5,000 you invested. Thus, at the end of the summer you would have $9,800. This is a much higher return than you could expect from investing the $5,000 in a savings account. On the other hand, you are also investing much of your time in the business. You plan to work 50 hours each week. If you don't start the business, you could work at some other job. For example, you might work at a fast food restaurant that pays $5 an hour. If you worked 50 hours a week at the restaurant, you could earn $3,000 ($5 × 50 hours × 12 weeks) for the summer. In addition, you would not be risking your $5,000 investment and could earn some interest from savings.

The information about costs and earnings cannot make your decision for you. You must consider whether you want to work on the beach instead of in a restaurant, how certain you are about the amount you can earn from your business, and how much risk you are willing to take. Investing in a business is always risky. *Risk* **is uncertainty about an outcome**, such as the amount of profit you will earn. Suppose the summer turns out to be unusually cold and wet. If you sell less than you expect, your earnings also will be less. You could even lose money. Are you willing to take the risk? Accounting can help with these decisions by providing information about what you should expect. You have to evaluate the information and make a decision.

Accounting is a way of looking at a business. It measures the activities of a business by the dollars it receives and spends. It helps decision makers determine where they started. For example, you will start by investing $5,000. It helps determine where you should end up. You expect to earn $4,800 from your investment. It helps determine whether your expectations are being met. For example, suppose you sold $6,000 of merchandise during June instead of the $7,000 you expected to sell. Like a map, accounting can help you determine that you are not where you want to be. It can help you determine what went wrong and, in some cases, what you might change to get back on the proper route.

Accounting provides a model of a business by measuring the business activities in dollar amounts. Underlying this model is an information system. This system provides a process for obtaining facts that can be converted into useful information. Understanding the system and its processes will help you understand the information provided by accounting.

THE ACCOUNTING PROCESS

Objective 1
Identify the purpose of accounting.

The purpose of accounting is to help people make decisions about economic activities. Economic activities involve the allocation of scarce resources. People allocate scarce resources any time they exchange money, goods, or services. These activities are so common that almost every adult in our society uses the accounting process to assist in decision making.

Learning Note

The terms "money" and "cash" often are used interchangeably. In everyday speech, money refers specifically to paper bills and coins. Cash is a broader term that includes checks, bank accounts, and other resources that are easily converted to money. A general term for money and items easily converted to money is "financial resources."

Accounting Records

To illustrate a simple accounting system, we can examine a checking account. Suppose you decide to invest in The Beach Shack. You open a checking account for the business at the First Beach Bank and deposit $5,000 in the account.

With your checks and deposit slips, you have a check register similar to the example in Exhibit 1-1. The register helps you manage and control your money by keeping track of amounts you deposit or withdraw, the source of the deposits, the recipients of the checks, the dates of these events, and the amount available in your account.

Exhibit 1-1   The Beach Shack Check Register

Date	Check Number	Activity	Deposits	Checks	Balance
June 1		Deposit by Owner	5,000.00		5,000.00
1	1	Beach Supply Co. (merchandise)		3,500.00	1,500.00
1	2	Beach Hotel (rent)		500.00	1,000.00
1	3	Sun City (license)		100.00	900.00
7		Sales Receipts	1,500.00		2,400.00
7	4	Wages		300.00	2,100.00

(Other transactions for June are omitted.)

Summary Reports

If you wanted to know how much you spent in June for your business and for what purposes, you could summarize the information from the check register to help you understand these activities. For example, you might prepare a summary similar to Exhibit 1-2.

Exhibit 1-2

The Beach Shack Checking Account
Summary of Deposits and Payments
For June

Beginning cash balance		$ 0
Cash deposits:		
Deposit by owner	$5,000	
Sales receipts	6,800	
Total cash deposited		$11,800
Cash payments:		
Merchandise	$5,200	
Rent	500	
Wages	1,200	
License	100	
Total cash paid		7,000
Excess of deposits over payments		4,800
Ending cash balance		$4,800

Observe that the summary of deposits and payments provides information about cash received and paid in June. For example, you can determine that

$5,200 was paid for merchandise and that $6,800 was received from customers in June. However, you cannot determine from this information if all of the merchandise purchased in June was sold to customers in June. Also, you cannot determine if customers owe you money for merchandise they bought but have not paid for.

The bank provides you with a statement that reports your checking account activities for the month. The statement lists deposits you made with the bank and checks you wrote that the bank paid during the month. The bank provides this report so you can verify the accuracy of the information you have recorded in your check register and the accuracy of the bank's information about your account. You verify the accuracy by comparing your check register with the bank statement.

Steps in the Accounting Process

Some of the most important steps in the accounting process occur in this example of a checking account. In a checking account, you are accounting for money held by a bank for your use. The basic information unit in an accounting system is an account. **An *account* is a record of increases and decreases in the dollar amount associated with a specific resource or activity.** All information you record in your check register involves one account, your cash account with the bank. The register helps you keep track of the increases, decreases, and balance in your checking account.

The information in your check register summarizes the activities of your checking account. You record information in the register when an event occurs that increases or decreases the money in your account. **A *transaction* is an event that increases or decreases an account balance.** Transactions identify changes in resources and activities that affect resources. For example, when you write a check to pay for merchandise, you exchange money from your checking account for the merchandise. This event is a transaction you record in your check register by noting the amount of the check and the reduction in your cash balance.

The bank maintains an account for each of its customers. Each time a customer deposits money or writes a check, the bank records the transaction in the customer's account. The account balance is the amount available for use by the customer. The monthly bank statement summarizes the transactions recorded by the bank for the customer's account.

The activities associated with a checking account provide an example of a typical accounting process. This process includes four basic steps that include:

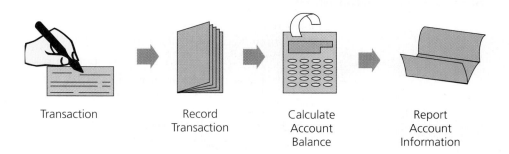

Transaction   Record Transaction   Calculate Account Balance   Report Account Information

Step	Example
1. A transaction occurs.	1. Purchase merchandise.
2. Record the transaction in the proper accounts.	2. Record payment in check register.
3. Calculate account balance.	3. Subtract check amount from balance.
4. Summarize and report transactions periodically to serve a specific need.	4. Prepare summary of checking account activities for the month.

Objective 2
Explain why accounting is an information system.

A *system* **is a set of interrelated activities or processes that work together to achieve a goal. Because accounting involves recording, summarizing, and reporting economic information used in making decisions, it is an information system.**

Uses of Accounting Information

The decisions made by users of an accounting information system determine the type of information reported by the system. A check register and a bank statement are examples of accounting information. They exist to help the depositor. Information about your checking account can help you understand how you have used your money. How much did you spend for rent last month? It can help you plan for future expenditures. Can you afford to purchase additional merchandise? It can provide assurance that you have the amount of money you think you have. Accounting information helps people make decisions.

This book explains accounting for business organizations. **An** *organization* **is a group of people who work together to develop, produce, and/or distribute goods or services.** Business organizations sell these goods and services to customers. Some organizations, for example social or religious organizations, provide services to their members or other recipients. Accounting provides information for managers, owners, members, and other stakeholders who make decisions about organizations. *Stakeholders* **include those who have an economic interest in an organization and those who are affected by its activities.**

The next section of this chapter discusses the purpose of organizations and the role of accounting in organizations. Before proceeding, test your understanding of what you have read by solving the following self-study problem.

SELF-STUDY PROBLEM 1-1

The following list contains transactions for the checking account of Garcia's Deli at the Central National Bank for April 1996:

April   1   Paid rent of $800 to Northside Real Estate Co.

        5   Deposited customer receipts of $1,000.

        7   Withdrew $70 for miscellaneous supplies from an automatic teller machine.

     12   Purchased food for $300 from Miller's Wholesale Grocery.

     14   Deposited customer receipts of $950.

April 17   Withdrew $50 for miscellaneous supplies from an automatic teller machine.
       20   Paid the company's car payment of $200 to Citizens Loan Co.
       21   Deposited customer receipts of $725.
       25   Paid utility bill of $160 to City Light and Water.
       27   Purchased food for $340 from Wang's Grocery.
       28   Purchased supplies for $280 from Restaurant Supply Co.
       28   Deposited customer receipts of $875.
       30   Transferred $500 (by check) to savings account at First Savings and Loan.

The beginning balance in Garcia's Deli's checking account was $1,450. Check numbers should be recorded sequentially beginning with 346.

Required

1.   Record each transaction as it would appear in Garcia's Deli's check register. Use the format provided below.

Date	Check Number	Check Issued to/ Deposit Received from	Amount of Deposit	Amount of Check	Balance

2.   Prepare a summary report of cash deposits and payments for April.
3.   List the steps in the accounting process associated with the checking account.

The solution to Self-Study Problem 1-1 appears at the end of the chapter.

THE PURPOSE OF ORGANIZATIONS

Objective 3
Compare major types of organizations.

Many types of organizations exist to serve society. Why do these organizations exist? Most exist because people need to work together to accomplish their goals. The goals are too large, too complex, or too expensive to be achieved without cooperation. All organizations provide goods and/or services. By working together, people can produce more and better goods and services.

Organizations differ as to the types of goods or services they offer. *Merchandising* (or *retail*) *companies* **sell to consumers goods that are produced by other companies.** Grocery, department, and hardware stores are examples. The Beach Shack is a merchandising company. It purchases merchandise from a supplier and sells the merchandise to customers. *Manufacturing companies* **produce goods that they sell to consumers, to merchandising companies, or to other manufacturing companies.** Examples include automobile manufacturers, petroleum refineries, furniture manufacturers, computer companies, and paper companies. *Service companies* **sell services rather than goods.**

These companies include banks, insurance companies, hospitals, colleges, law firms, and accounting firms. Some companies may be a combination of types. For example, gas stations are retail and service companies. Restaurants are both manufacturing and service companies.

Types of Organizations

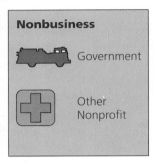

Organizations may be classified by whether or not they attempt to earn a profit. Profits result from selling goods and services to customers at prices greater than the cost of the items sold. **Organizations that sell their goods and services to make a profit are business organizations.** *Governmental and nonprofit organizations*, **sometimes referred to as nonbusiness organizations, provide goods or, more typically, services without the intent of making a profit.** *Nonbusiness organizations* include civic, social, and religious organizations. Some types of services are provided by both business and nonbusiness organizations. Examples include education and health care services. Though the products are similar, the goals of the organizations providing these services are different. Nevertheless, all organizations need accounting information for decision making.

Transformation of Resources

A common purpose of organizations is to transform resources from one form to a different, more valuable, form to meet the needs of people. Resources include: natural resources such as minerals and timber, physical resources such as buildings and equipment, management skills, labor, financial resources, legal rights such as patents and trademarks, information, and the systems that provide information. The transformation process combines these resources to create goods and services. Transformation may involve making goods or services easier or less expensive for customers to obtain, as in most merchandising and service companies. Or, it may involve physically converting resources by processing or combining them, as in manufacturing companies. Beach Shack transforms resources by obtaining merchandise and making it available to customers when they need it while they are on the beach.

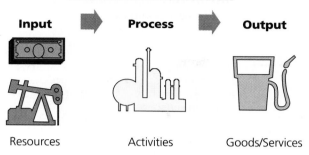

Transformation of Resources

Input ➡ Process ➡ Output

Resources   Activities   Goods/Services

Organizations are created because many transformations are too difficult or too expensive for individuals to accomplish without working together. By combining their managerial skills, labor, and money, individuals create organizations to provide benefits that otherwise would be unavailable. These benefits occur when an organization transforms resources from a less desirable form or location to a more desirable form or location. **The transformation, if it meets a need of society, creates value because people are better off after the transformation than before.** For example, a company that manufactures shirts creates value because the shirts are more useful to those who purchase them than would be the material from which the shirts are made or the cotton or synthetic fibers used to make the material.

To improve its welfare, a society must encourage organizations to increase the value they create. Because resources are in scarce supply, a society should attempt to use its resources wisely. **A major purpose of accounting information is to help decide how to get the most value from scarce resources.**

Creation of Value

How can a society determine how to use its resources? Decisions about using scarce resources wisely are not easy. Because society is made up of many individuals, disagreement often exists as to how resources should be used. In our society and many others, markets are the means used to promote the wise use of many resources.

Markets exist to allocate scarce resources used and produced by organizations. **A *market* is any location or process that permits resources to be bought and sold.** Competition in a market determines the amount and value of resources available for exchange. The more valuable a resource is in meeting your needs, the more you are willing to pay for it as a buyer, or the more you want for it as a seller.

The price paid for a resource in a competitive market is an indication of the value assigned to it at the particular time the buyer and seller negotiate an exchange. For example, when you buy a car, you exchange money for the car. The amount of money is a measure of the value you place on the car. Thus, the price of goods and services in a market is a basis for measuring value. **Accounting measures the increase in value created by a transformation as the difference between the total price of goods and services sold and the total** cost of resources consumed in developing, producing, and selling the goods and services.

What value results when you purchase a car? The amount you pay for the car is an indication of the value you expect to receive from owning it. But, resources were consumed in producing the car and making it available to you.

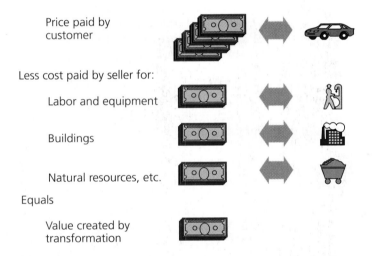

Price paid by customer

Less cost paid by seller for:

Labor and equipment

Buildings

Natural resources, etc.

Equals

Value created by transformation

The total cost of these resources, such as metals, plastics, rubber, fabric, machinery and labor used in the manufacturing process, the cost of money to acquire other resources, and the cost of transportation to the dealer, is the cost of resources consumed in making the car available to you. The increase in value from the transformation that produced the car is the difference between the price you pay and the total cost of the resources consumed.

For example, if you pay $12,000 for a car and the total cost of producing the car and making it available to you is $10,000, the value added by the transformation is $2,000. The difference between the price you pay and the total cost of the car to the seller is profit for the automobile manufacturer and the dealership, or more precisely, for the owners of those firms. *Profit* **is the difference between the price a seller receives for goods or services and the total cost to the seller of all resources consumed in developing, producing, and selling these goods or services during a particular period.** Thus, profits are the net resources generated by the sales events (resources received from the sales minus resources used in making the sales).

Learning Note

A "period" is an important concept in accounting. A period may be any length of time used to measure the effects of transactions. Common periods include months, quarters, and years. An accounting period often is called a fiscal period, because it may not coincide with a calendar period. For example, a company's fiscal year might begin on July 1.

Several markets are important in our economy. Markets exist for resources used by organizations. Organizations compete in **financial markets** for financial resources. Investors choose where to put their money to work by selecting among competing organizations. Organizations compete in **supplier markets** for other resources needed to produce goods and services. Competition in these markets determines the costs of materials, labor, equipment, and other resources available to organizations. Organizations compete in **product markets** (markets for goods and services). These markets determine the prices of goods and services available to customers. From the perspective of organizations, financial and supplier markets are input markets; markets for goods and services are output markets. All of these markets allocate scarce resources.

An Illustration of Creating Value

Exhibit 1-3 reports profit earned by The Beach Shack in June. **An *income statement* measures profit by subtracting the cost of resources consumed from the prices of goods or services sold for a period of time.** Other terms for profit are net income and net earnings. Net income of $1,600 represents the difference between the price of the goods sold to customers and the total cost of resources consumed in providing those goods.

Exhibit 1-3

The Beach Shack
Income Statement
For June

Revenues from merchandise		$6,800
Expenses:		
Merchandise sold	$3,400	
Rent	500	
Wages	1,200	
License	100	
Total cost		5,200
Net income		$1,600

The sales prices of goods sold are known as **revenues.** The costs of resources consumed in producing the goods sold and in making them available to customers are known as **expenses.** ***Net income*** **(or *net earnings*) is the difference between revenues and expenses for a period:** Net Income = Revenues − Expenses. Of course, a business venture may not produce net income. It may result in a net loss. **A** *net loss* **occurs when expenses are greater than revenues for a period.**

Observe that the income statement reports the cost of resources consumed, not resources purchased. Only part of the merchandise purchased was sold during June. The cost of merchandise sold during June was $3,400, though $5,200 of merchandise was purchased (see Exhibit 1-2). The Beach Shack still had $1,800 of unsold merchandise on hand at the end of June. Also, observe that revenues include only resources earned during a period. The Beach Shack earned the $6,800 of sales it made to customers during June. It did not earn the initial $5,000 investment by the owner. It is important to distinguish between resources earned and consumed and other amounts received or paid. This income statement reports results of activities that occurred during June. These results can be compared with expected results. Thus, The Beach Shack had sales of $6,800, compared with expected sales of $7,000. The cost of merchandise sold during June was $3,400, rather than the expected amount of $3,500.

Investment by Owners

Objective 6
Explain why owners invest in businesses.

Businesses earn profits (net income) by providing goods and services demanded by society. **Owners invest in a business to receive a return on their investments from profits earned by that business.** By investing in a business, owners are foregoing their money's use for other purposes. In exchange, they expect to share in a business's earnings. *Return on investment* **is the amount of profits earned by a business that could be paid to owners.** Return on investment often is expressed as a percentage: Profit ÷ Amount Invested.

Profits represent net resources that have been earned through sales transactions. A business may distribute profits to its owners. Alternatively, owners (or managers acting on their behalf) may decide to reinvest profits in a business to acquire additional resources. The business can use the additional resources to earn more profits by expanding its size or by expanding into new locations or product lines. Either way, the owners are better off. They receive cash from their investments if profits are withdrawn, or they own a business that is more valuable if profits are reinvested.

The income statement for The Beach Shack indicates the company earned $1,600 during June. As the owner, you may choose to withdraw some or all of this amount for personal use. It is your return on investment. Alternatively, you might choose to reinvest a portion of this profit to enlarge your company by buying a larger amount of merchandise for sale in July. Or, you might decide to open a second store if you are optimistic about future sales.

Your return on investment for June was $1,600 or 32% (= $1,600/$5,000) relative to your initial investment. If you withdraw more than $1,600 from your account, the additional amount withdrawn is a return *of* investment, not a return *on* investment. It is a return of a portion of the amount you originally invested. For a company to maintain its capital (the amount invested by its owners), it must pay a return to owners from profits the company has earned. Otherwise, the company is reducing its capital by returning a portion of owners' investments to them.

The amount of return you receive from a company depends on the success the company has in earning a profit. If you are the primary owner of a business, success depends primarily on your ability and effort. If you invest in a large company, success depends largely on the abilities and efforts of those who manage the business. When you invest in a business, you have no guarantee it will be successful. You are taking a risk that you may not receive a return on your investment, that the return may be smaller than you expected, or even that you might lose your investment. *Risk* **is uncertainty about the return that will be received.**

Why invest in a business if the investment is risky? If a business is successful, its owners can expect to earn a higher rate of return on their investments relative to a safer alternative such as a savings account. By investing $5,000 in The Beach Shack, you expect to earn $4,800 from your investment. If you invested your money in a savings account, you might expect to earn $100 for the same period (assuming an annual interest rate of 8%).

To earn profits and pay returns to owners, businesses must operate effectively and efficiently. **An** *effective business* **is one that is successful in providing goods and services demanded by customers.** Effective management involves identifying the right products and putting them in the right locations at the right times. **An** *efficient business* **is one that provides goods and services at low costs relative to their selling prices.** Managers must control costs by using the proper mix, qualities, and quantities of resources to avoid waste and to reduce costs. The risk of owning a business is lower if it is effective and efficient than if it is ineffective or inefficient. Efficient and effective businesses are competitive in financial, supplier, and product markets.

The Beach Shack will be effective if you select merchandise desired by customers and if your location is one that places you in proximity with your customers. The company will be efficient if you can purchase merchandise at a sufficiently low cost so that you can sell it profitably and also pay rent, wages, and other costs.

The Market for Investors

Businesses must compete, not only for resources and customers, but also for investors. Business owners expect to receive a return on their investments. Investors choose among alternate investments by evaluating the amount, timing, and uncertainty of the returns they expect to receive. Businesses that earn high profits and are capable of paying returns have less difficulty in obtaining investors than other businesses. A business that cannot earn sufficient profits will be forced to become more effective and efficient or to go out of business.

Objective 7
Explain why accounting information is useful to investors.

The accounting information system is a major source of information investors use in deciding about their investments. **Accounting information helps investors assess the effectiveness and efficiency of businesses.** It helps them estimate the returns that can be expected from investing in a business and the amount of risk associated with their investments. Financial, supplier, and product markets create incentives for businesses to provide products society demands. These market forces help ensure that scarce resources are used to improve society's welfare. Markets help allocate scarce resources to those organizations that can best transform them to create value.

You will profit from your investment in The Beach Shack if you provide products demanded by customers and provide them at competitive prices that are sufficient to cover your costs. If you believe you will be unable to create a profit from your investment, you will choose to invest in an alternative rather than The Beach Shack. Thus, as a part of society, you make a decision to invest when you believe the return will be sufficient to compensate you for your investment. Your decision depends on whether you believe you can provide society, as customers, with products it wants and at prices it is willing to pay.

SELF-STUDY PROBLEM 1-2

John Bach owns a music store in which he sells and repairs musical instruments, and sells sheet music. The following transactions occurred for Bach's Music Store during December 1995:

1. Sold $8,000 of musical instruments that cost the company $4,300.
2. Sold $1,400 of sheet music that cost the company $870.
3. The price of repair services provided during the month was $2,200.
4. Rent on the store for the month was $650.
5. The cost of supplies used during the month was $250.
6. The cost of advertising for the month was $300.
7. The cost of utilities for the month was $200.
8. Other miscellaneous costs for December were $180.

Required

1. Determine the profit (net income) earned by Bach's Music Store for December by preparing an income statement.
2. Explain how the income statement measures value created by Bach's Music Store.

The solution to Self-Study Problem 1-2 appears at the end of the chapter.

DECISIONS IN ORGANIZATIONS

Many types of decisions are made in organizations. Accounting provides important information to make these decisions. In this section, we will consider three organizational activities that use accounting information for decision making: financing, investing, and operating activities.

Financing Activities

Objective 8
Identify financing activities and the types of decisions they require.

Organizations require financial resources to obtain other resources used to produce goods and services. They compete for these resources in financial markets. *Financing activities* **are the methods an organization uses to obtain financial resources from financial markets and how it manages these resources.** Primary sources of financing for most businesses are owners and creditors. The following sections consider these sources.

Objective 9
Compare forms of business ownership.

Business Ownership. Businesses may be classified in two categories: those that are distinct legal entities apart from their owners and those that are not distinct legal entities. **A** *corporation* **is a legal entity with the right to enter into contracts, the right to own, buy, and sell property, and the right to sell stock.** Resources are owned by the corporation, rather than by individuals.

Corporations may be very large or fairly small organizations. Small corporations often are managed by their owners. The owners of most large corporations do not manage their companies. Instead, they hire professional managers. These owners have the right to vote on certain major decisions, but they do not control the operations of their corporations on a day-to-day basis. One reason most large businesses are organized as corporations is that they typically have greater access to financial markets than other types of organizations.

Corporations often are owned by many investors who purchase shares of stock (certificates of ownership) issued by corporations. **Each share of** *stock* **represents an equal share in the ownership of a corporation.** An investor who owns 10% of the shares of a corporation owns 10% of the company and has a right to 10% of the return available to stockholders. *Stockholders*, **or shareholders, are the owners of a corporation.**

Shares of stock often are traded in stock markets, such as the New York, London, and Tokyo stock exchanges, that are established specifically for this purpose. These markets facilitate the exchange of stock between buyers and sellers. Therefore, unlike other businesses, ownership in many corporations can change easily, simply by buying or selling shares of stock. Major corporations, such as General Motors, Exxon, or IBM, have received billions of dollars from stockholders.

Proprietorships **and** *partnerships* **are business organizations that do not have legal identities distinct from their owners. Proprietorships have only one owner; partnerships have more than one owner.** For most proprietorships and partnerships, owners also manage their businesses. In fact, in a legal sense, the owners are the businesses. Owners have a major stake in the business because often much of their personal wealth is invested in it. The amount of a proprietor's personal wealth and his ability to borrow limits the size of a proprietorship. If a proprietorship is profitable, profits earned by the proprietor can be reinvested and the business can become fairly large.

Partnerships can include several partners; therefore, the money available to finance a partnership depends on the money available from all the partners. New partners can be added, making new money available to the business. While most partnerships are small, large businesses (with as many as a thousand or more owners) sometimes are organized as partnerships.

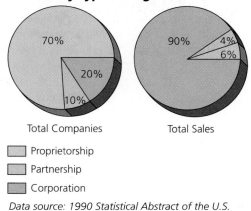

Percentage of Companies and Volume of Sales by Type of Organization

Total Companies

Total Sales

Proprietorship
Partnership
Corporation

Data source: 1990 Statistical Abstract of the U.S.

Management of Corporations. Exhibit 1-4 provides an organizational chart for a typical corporation that describes the formal organization structure among its managers.

Exhibit 1-4   Corporate management functions

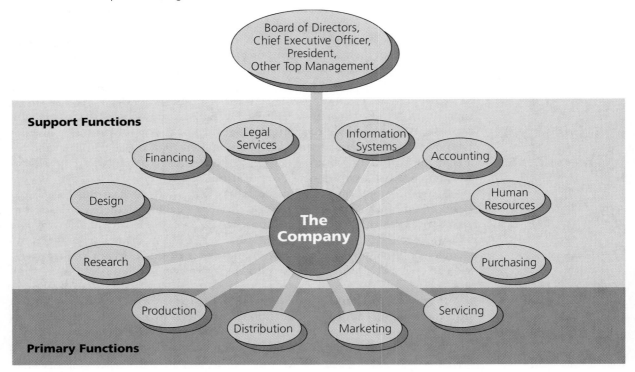

A **board of directors** oversees the decisions of management and is responsible for protecting the interests of stockholders. Normally, the board is appointed by management with the approval of stockholders. Top managers often serve on the board along with outside directors who are not part of the corporation's management. The **chairman of the board** often holds the position of **chief executive officer** (CEO) with the ultimate responsibility for the success of the business. The **president**, as **chief operating officer** (COO), is responsible for the day-to-day management of a corporation. In some cases, the president also may be the CEO. The company may appoint any number of **vice-presidents** who are responsible for various functions in the organization. The titles and roles of these managers will vary from corporation to corporation. Along with the CEO and president, the vice-presidents constitute the top management of a corporation. Together, they make planning decisions and develop company goals and policies.

Functions performed within a corporation may be separated into support and primary services. Support services assist the primary functions by providing information and other resources necessary to produce and sell goods and services. Primary functions are those actually involved in producing and selling goods and services. These functions include distribution of goods and services to customers and servicing the goods and services to meet customer needs.

Among the support services are research and development, product and production design, finance, legal services, accounting, purchasing, and human resources. The **chief financial officer** (CFO), who also may be the **treasurer**, is responsible for obtaining financial resources and managing a corporation's cash flows. If these positions are separate, the treasurer is responsible primarily for managing and protecting a corporation's cash. The **controller**, as the chief accounting officer, is responsible for accounting and financial reporting, developing and maintaining the accounting information system, and reporting to tax and regulatory authorities.

Primary functions involve the operation of production, distribution, and sales facilities. Plant managers oversee production for specific product lines or geographical locations. These managers often have their own staffs at the divisional or plant level. For example, divisional or plant level controllers exist in many corporations. Research, design, and development staffs also exist at the divisional or plant level in some organizations.

Corporations may be organized by functions such as those described in Exhibit 1-4. Other corporations are organized primarily by region or product line. For example, multinational companies may be organized into North American, European, or Pacific divisions. Functional areas, such as development and production, report to regional or product managers. Many corporations are finding advantages in changing from a traditional organizational structure to teams of managers working together on specific projects. Thus, the idea for a new product may be the responsibility of a team of employees from a company's functional areas, such as engineering, accounting, and marketing. Together, the team decides on a design for the product and on a production process to create efficiency and product quality.

An important function of top management is creating an organization's structure. Structure determines the functional areas, divisions, and other components of an organization; also, it establishes relationships among managers and employees of these components. Thus, it affects how information flows through an organization, lines of authority and responsibility, and how components of an organization will work together to accomplish its goals.

The distinction between managers and employees is not always clear; therefore, the term "manager" is used broadly in this book to include those in an organization who make decisions affecting the organization's transformation process. Many levels and types of managers exist in many large organizations. Some of these managers are supervisors of departments and divisions of the organization. Others play key roles in developing, designing, producing, distributing, and marketing an organization's products. Others provide and analyze information to assist other managers. The term "employees" will refer primarily to those who perform duties in an organization but do not have major decision-making responsibility.

Advantages of Corporations. Several advantages exist for a corporate form of organization over proprietorships or partnerships. Corporations have **continuous lives** apart from those of their owners. If a proprietor or partner sells her share of a business or dies, the business ceases to exist as a legal entity. The new owner of the business must reestablish the business as a new legal entity. Most corporations, however, continue unchanged if current owners sell their stock, donate it to charity, give it to relatives, or otherwise dispose of their shares.

Shareholders normally are not liable personally for the debts of a corporation. This is a characteristic known as **limited liability**. If a corporation defaults on debt or enters bankruptcy, its owners may lose a portion or all of their investments in the company. But, they are not obligated to repay creditors from their personal wealth for losses incurred by the creditors. Proprietors and partners are personally liable for the debts of their companies and could be required to use their personal wealth to repay their creditors. A proprietorship or partnership is not a separate legal entity apart from its owners.

Shareholders of most corporations do not manage the company. They elect members of the board of directors who then hire **professional managers** to run the corporation. Investors can own part of a corporation or parts of many corporations without having to participate in the day-to-day decisions of running the companies. Many Americans own stock in corporations through personal investments and retirement plans and, thus, are not required to commit large amounts of their personal time to corporate concerns.

Shareholders do not have the right of mutual agency. *Mutual agency* **permits a partner to enter into contracts and agreements that are binding on all members of a partnership.** Shareholders cannot enter into contracts or agreements that are binding on a corporation unless they are managers or directors. Therefore, investors in a corporation do not have to be concerned about the abilities of other stockholders to make good business decisions. In contrast, bad decisions by one partner can result in the personal bankruptcy of all partners in a partnership.

By selling shares to many investors, a corporation can obtain a large amount of financial resources. The ability to **raise large amounts of capital** permits corporations to become very large organizations. Thus, corporations can invest in plant facilities and undertake production activities that would be difficult for proprietorships or partnerships.

Disadvantages of Corporations. Several disadvantages exist for the corporate form of ownership. Most **corporations must pay taxes on their incomes**. Corporate taxes are separate from the taxes paid by shareholders on dividends received from the company. Some corporations, especially smaller ones, are not taxed separately. Another disadvantage is **corporations are regulated** by various state and federal government agencies. These regulations require corporations to comply with many state and federal rules concerning business practices and reporting of financial information. Corporations must file many reports with government agencies and make public disclosure of their business activities. **Compliance with these regulations is costly.** Also, some of the **required disclosures may be helpful to competitors**. Partnerships and proprietorships are regulated also, but the degree of regulation normally is much less than for corporations.

Owners of corporations usually do not have access to information about the day-to-day activities of their companies. They depend on managers to make decisions that will increase the value of their investments. On the other hand, managers' personal interests sometimes conflict with the interests of stockholders.

This problem produces a condition known as moral hazard. Moral hazard arises when one group, known as agents (such as managers), is responsible for serving the needs of another group, known as principals (such as investors). *Moral hazard* **is the condition that exists when agents have superior information to principals and are able to make decisions that favor their own interests over those of the principals.**

Without disclosure of reliable information, corporations would have difficulty in selling stock, and investors would be unable to determine whether managers were making decisions that increased stockholder value or were making decisions that took advantage of the stockholders. Accounting reports are major sources of information to stockholders to help them assess the performance of managers. For example, an income statement helps owners evaluate how well managers have used owners' investments to earn returns for the owners. **Moral hazard imposes costs on corporations because managers must report to stockholders and, generally, these reports are audited.** An audit verifies the reliability of reported information.

The size of many corporations makes them difficult to manage. An individual manager cannot be involved directly with all the decisions made in operating a large organization. Top-level managers depend on lower level managers to make decisions and to keep them informed about a corporation's operations. This process is costly because coordination among managers may be difficult to achieve. Moral hazard exists among managers and employees, not just between managers and investors. Corporate goals and policies provide guidance for manager decisions; but, communicating goals and policies and providing incentives for managers to implement them often is difficult and expensive. Employees and lower level managers may not report reliable information about their activities to higher level managers if the information is not in their best interests. Multinational corporations, in particular, are complex and difficult to manage. Distant locations for facilities and differences in language and local custom can cause special problems.

Creditors. In addition to money provided by owners, businesses (and other organizations) may borrow money. Money may be obtained from banks and other financial institutions, or it may be borrowed from individual lenders. **A lender or *creditor* is someone who loans financial resources to an organization.**

Most organizations depend on banks and similar institutions to lend them money. Corporations often borrow money from individuals or other companies. Exhibit 1-5 describes the amount of money several large corporations have received from owners and creditors. The amounts and proportions of financing from owners and creditors vary greatly across companies.

Creditors loan money to organizations to earn a return on their investments, just as do owners. Creditors, however, usually loan money for a specific period and are promised a specific rate of return on their investments. Usually, this is a fixed rate (say 10%). In contrast, owners invest for a nonspecific period (until they decide to sell their ownership rights) and receive a return that depends on the profits earned by the business.

The success of a business determines whether or not creditors will receive the amount promised by the borrower. When a business fails to generate sufficient cash from its revenues to pay its expenses and to pay its creditors, they may not receive the amount promised. Therefore, creditors evaluate the probability an

Exhibit 1-5   Financing Arrangements of Selected Corporations

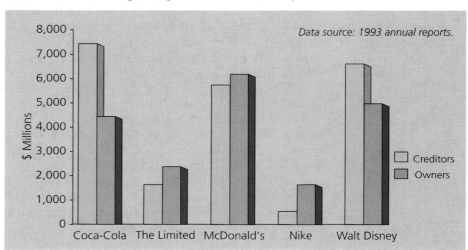

organization will be able to repay debt and interest. Risk is a concern of both creditors and owners. Exhibit 1–6 illustrates financing activities.

Exhibit 1-6   Components of Financing Activities

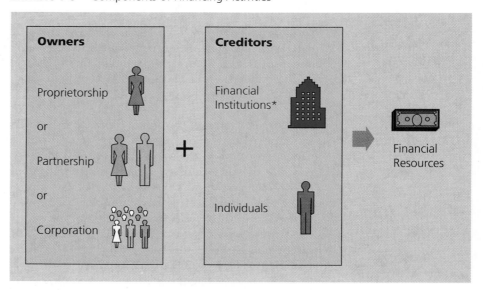

★The term "financial institutions" refers to banks, savings and loans, etc.

Financing Decisions. Financing decisions involve choices about when and where to obtain financial resources and about the amount needed. A corporation must decide how much stock and debt to issue, when they should be issued, and to whom they should be issued to obtain favorable prices. These decisions depend on the business's need for money and on its ability to repay owners and creditors for their investments.

Financing decisions are made by owners, creditors, and managers. Owners and creditors need to know how managers are using their money and how much risk they are taking. Managers decide how much money a business needs, how much return they will pay to investors, how they will invest capital, and the probable effect of financing arrangements on the profitability and survival of an organization. Questions answered by financing decisions include:

How much financing does an organization need?
Where should an organization obtain its financing?
When should an organization obtain financing?
How will capital be used?
What effect will financing have on profitability and survival?

As owner of The Beach Shack, you must decide how much money you will need and how to obtain the money you will need for your business. If you have sufficient money to start the business, you may decide not to borrow. If you lack the money you need, you may have to borrow. If you decide to borrow, you will have to make enough money to repay your loan and interest.

Investing Activities

Managers use capital from financing activities to acquire other resources used in the transformation process. Having the right mix of resources is essential to efficient and effective operations. The wrong set of resources or having resources in the wrong place or at the wrong time can lead to disastrous results.

Investing activities **involve the selection and management of resources that will be used to develop, produce, and sell goods and services.** Resources include supplies, insurance, land and natural resources, buildings, equipment, information systems, people, legal rights such as patents and trademarks, and other resources necessary for an organization to produce goods and services. Organizations compete in supplier markets for these resources. Exhibit 1-7 illustrates investing activities.

Objective 10
Identify investing activities and the types of decisions they require.

Exhibit 1-7   Components of Investing Activities

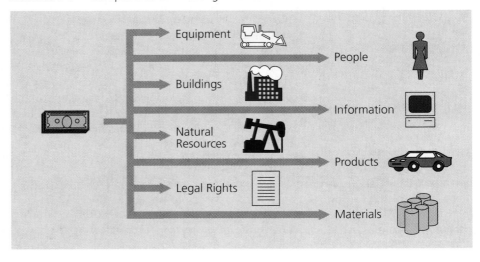

Many manufacturing companies require large investments in buildings and equipment to develop, produce, transport, and market their products. Exhibit 1-8 identifies the amount some large corporations have invested in resources. Some companies are much larger than others based on the amount of investment.

Exhibit 1-8   Amounts Invested in Resources by Selected Companies

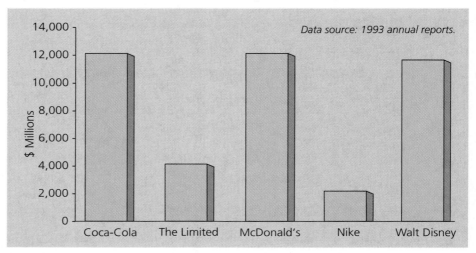

Learning Note   Don't confuse investments made by owners and creditors (financing activities) with investments made by managers (investing activities).

Investing Decisions. Managers decide how much to invest in resources and the types of resources to acquire. Often these decisions involve large amounts of money and have a major effect on the future of an organization. These decisions affect future profitability, future supply of goods and services, and future return to owners and creditors.

In making investing decisions, managers need information for predicting the demand for goods and services. They need to know which products will be demanded, when they will be demanded, how much will be demanded, and the prices customers are willing to pay. This information is useful for determining the types of resources needed to produce the goods and services demanded by customers. In addition, managers need information about the current availability of resources and how resources are being used. They need to know how much can be produced, when to produce, what can be produced, where it can be produced, and how costly it is to produce. Managers evaluate alternate ways of acquiring resources; for example, resources may be purchased or they may be leased or rented.

Examples of questions answered by investing decisions include:

What resources should an organization acquire?
How much of each type of resource should be acquired?

When should resources be acquired and replaced?
Where should resources be placed?

One of your tasks as owner and manager of The Beach Shack is to determine the types and amounts of resources your company will need. You must select the items that you will sell or obtain any equipment you will need to transport or display this merchandise.

Operating Activities

Objective 11
Identify operating activities and the types of decisions they require.

Operating activities **involve the use of resources to design, produce, distribute, and market goods and services.** Operating activities include research and development, design and engineering, purchasing, human resources, production, distribution, marketing and selling, and servicing. Organizations compete in supplier and labor markets for resources used in these activities. Also, they compete in product markets to sell the goods and services created by operating activities. Exhibit 1-9 features components of operating activities.

Exhibit 1-9   Components of operating activities

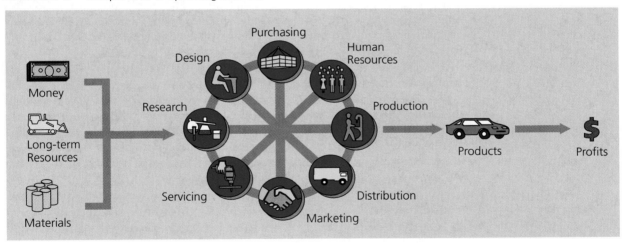

These activities often exist as individual departments or divisions of an organization. Each division may have its own manager who is responsible for decisions in that division. Not every organization needs each of these activities. For example, merchandising and service organizations generally do not require engineering and production. Often, some activities are combined in a division. For example, distribution, marketing, and servicing may be combined in a single division with one manager.

The following sections consider each component of a company's operating activities.

Research and Development. **Research and development activities create new products and update old products or production processes.**

Many companies operate in a highly competitive environment and must keep up with rapidly changing technology and consumer preferences. Examples include pharmaceutical and computer manufacturers. This environment demands that organizations search continuously for ways to improve their products, for new products that meet consumer needs, and for ways to reduce the cost of products. Service companies engage in research and development when they identify new services.

Design and Engineering. Design and engineering activities determine the design of products, production facilities, production processes, and distribution systems. Equipment and labor requirements, manufacturing and assembly processes, and other features of the way goods are produced and distributed have a major effect on product costs and marketability.

Purchasing. Purchasing activities involve acquiring and managing the materials and supplies needed for production or sale. Materials used in manufacturing must be purchased in the appropriate amounts and at the right times to ensure availability. Materials are expensive to acquire and store, but, production cannot occur unless the proper materials are available in the quantities needed. Purchasing decisions involve obtaining the proper types, qualities, and quantities of materials to minimize purchase, storage, and production costs. This function also is important in merchandising companies. Purchasing controls the selection and acquisition of goods that are available for resale and also is important in service organizations such as hospitals.

Human Resources. In addition to materials, labor is a primary factor in producing and selling goods and services. **Human resource activities involve obtaining the needed amount of human resources with the appropriate skills.** Primary functions involve hiring, firing, and training employees, as well as coordination of payroll and employee benefits such as retirement and health care. Salary negotiations and maintaining employee satisfaction also may be important responsibilities of the personnel function.

Production. Production activities involve the manufacture and assembly of goods for sale. Decisions must be made to schedule the production process so labor, materials, and equipment are available when needed. The appropriate mix of these factors is necessary to ensure the required quantity and quality of goods can be produced. Production decisions affect the cost and quality of products. Most companies monitor the production process closely to ensure quality and cost control.

Production activities exist in a simplified form in many service organizations. The production of services involves primarily human labor. Skills are applied in providing for specific consumer needs, such as information, repair, or maintenance. Facilities may be important in providing the services, but materials are not placed into production to create physical goods for sale.

Distribution. Distribution is a key activity in many merchandising companies whose primary transformation function is putting goods in an appropriate location for the convenience of customers. It is also important to many manufacturing and service companies. **Distribution activities involve getting the right goods to the right location at the right time.** Because transportation is costly, decisions must be made about how goods will be shipped, when they will be shipped, and how much will be shipped. Distribution activities are especially important for companies that operate in global markets. Goods often must be shipped from countries where they are produced to other countries where they are sold.

Marketing and Selling. **Marketing and selling activities involve making potential buyers aware of products and selling them to customers.** Providing information for potential buyers through promotion, advertising, and personal contact is essential for most businesses. Managers decide how to reach buyers effectively and how to present the company's products to create sales. Decisions involve the amount and type of advertising and sales force to use, the types and amounts of credit and discounting to give to different buyers, and the determination of consumer needs and demands. Therefore, selling involves more than the actual sale of goods and services. It involves careful monitoring of consumer needs and tastes. This information, in turn, is important in guiding the research and manufacturing efforts of the company to produce the amount and types of goods and services demanded by customers.

Servicing. The sale of goods and services is not the final step in the transformation process for many organizations. **Servicing products often continues after the sale.** Servicing activities involve the assistance provided to buyers after goods have been sold. Companies provide warranties on many products that require the company to repair and replace defective merchandise. Additionally, manufacturers or sellers often provide service for merchandise after the warranty period. Some organizations provide installation and training for products they sell. For example, computer companies often contract to install computer systems and to train employees to use them. Computers, automobiles, and other high-technology products require periodic maintenance after the sale.

Creation of Profits. In summary, this section has described the operating activities observed in most organizations, though not all activities will exist in every organization. The profitability of a company depends on its success in selling its products and controlling its costs. Profits are a measure of a company's ability to manage its capital and resources. How a company operates depends on the particular strategies management chooses for the organization. These strategies may involve providing goods and services at lower costs than competitors or providing goods and services that differ from those of competitors. Differences may be observed in product performance, quality, or features. Exhibit 1-10 describes sales, profits or losses, and returns on investment for several large corporations.

Operating Decisions. Producing and distributing the right set of products efficiently is critical to the success of a business organization. Having the wrong products or producing the right products inefficiently often leads to serious financial problems.

Exhibit 1-10   Operating Results of Selected Companies

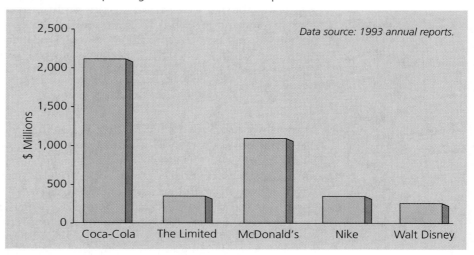

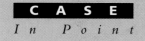

C A S E
In   Point

One of the most serious difficulties faced by the U.S. auto industry arose in the mid 1970s. Fuel shortages and high gas prices stimulated a demand for small, fuel-efficient cars. U.S. automakers had little experience in designing, manufacturing, or selling small cars. Foreign automakers, who had a lot of experience with small cars, imported their cars to the U.S. to meet the demand. The U.S. industry lost much of its competitive advantage and is only beginning to regain it. The loss resulted from an inability to react quickly to a changing economic environment.

Questions answered by operating decisions include:

Research and Development: How can new products be made or existing ones be improved?

Engineering: How should products be designed and produced?

Purchasing: What quantity and types of resources should an organization acquire that will be used to produce goods and services?

Personnel: How many and what types of employees are needed? What kind of training do employees need? How should they be compensated?

Production: How should production activities be scheduled? Should production occur in domestic or foreign locations?

Distribution: How should goods be shipped and stored so they are available to customers when needed?

Marketing and Selling: What activities are necessary to promote and sell goods and services?

Servicing: What types of installation, repair, and maintenance services should be provided to customers for the goods they purchase?

As owner, you will have to make operating decisions for The Beach Shack. Among these are where to get merchandise at the best price, what mix of quality and cost to include among your merchandise, how to handle defective merchandise, how to advertise or promote your business, whom to hire to assist in selling your goods, and how much to charge for your products.

SUMMARY OF THE TRANSFORMATION PROCESS

Objective 12
List the steps in an organization's transformation process.

Decisions made in financing, investing, and operating activities require information. The accounting information system is designed to meet certain information needs, particularly those involving the financial effects of the transformation process. **The** *transformation process* is a cycle that begins with the **acquisition of capital from owners and creditors.** This capital is **invested in facilities, equipment, people, and other resources** needed to create goods and services. Organizations use these resources in **developing, producing, distributing, and selling goods and services.** Selling goods and services results in the **inflow of additional financial resources** so the cycle can continue.

While the flow of resources typically is from financing to investing and operating decisions, information often follows the reverse path. For example, decisions about how much and what kind of products are demanded by customers are necessary before products can be designed. These decisions are necessary to plan production and distribution activities. The number of units produced affects the need for materials, labor, and equipment used in the production process. The need for materials, labor, and equipment determines the need for financing to provide money for these resources. Thus, planning often begins with expectations about the sale of goods and services and works backward to determine the resources and activities needed to produce the goods and services. Make sure you have a good understanding of how organizations transform resources into goods and services as illustrated in Exhibit 1-11.

Exhibit 1-11   A Summary of the Transformation Process

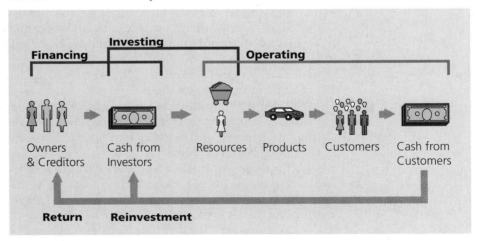

Accounting information provides a summary of the transformation process, much like a map provides a summary of a geographic location. Exhibit 1-12 illustrates the transformation process for The Beach Shack for June using accounting information.

Exhibit 1-12   The Transformation Process for The Beach Shack

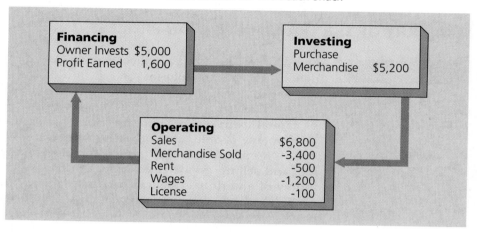

DEFINITION OF ACCOUNTING

Objective 13
Define accounting.

What role does accounting play in an organization's transformation process? *Accounting* **is an information system for the measurement and reporting of the transformation of resources into goods and services and the sale or transfer of these goods and services to customers.** Accounting uses the prices and costs of resources to measure value created by the transformation process and to trace the flow of resources through the transformation process. By tracing the flow of resources, managers and other decision makers can determine how efficiently and effectively resources are being used.

This chapter began by illustrating the accounting process as one of identifying, measuring, recording, summarizing, and reporting transactions. The accounting system in organizations also contains these steps. Transactions occur any time an organization acquires financial or other resources, uses the resources, or sells goods and services. The effects of these transactions are measured by their prices (or costs) and are recorded in individual accounts for each type of resource or activity. The account balances are summarized periodically and are reported to owners, creditors, managers, and others who make decisions about an organization. Accounting for organizations is much more complex than keeping a checking account because the number of events and accounts is much larger. Also, decisions about when to record events in a checking account are fairly simple. You should record a check when you write it. Decisions about when to record events in an organization's accounts are not so simple, as we will see in a later chapter.

Businesses account for financing, investing, and operating activities that are components of their transformation processes. They record:

1. capital invested by owners,
2. loans from creditors,
3. investments in land, buildings, equipment, and other resources,

4. the use of resources to develop, produce, and sell goods and services, and
5. financial resources from the sale of goods and services.

Accounting exists to serve the needs of those who make decisions about organizations. To understand accounting, you should first understand the purposes and functions of organizations. Also, you should understand the sociopolitical and economic environment in which organizations exist. This environment shapes organizations and affects the information needs of decision makers. Exhibit 1-13 illustrates the relationships among an organization, its accounting information system, and its environment. The organizational environment is a complex interrelationship between internal and external decision makers.

Structuring decisions determine the components of an organization and how they work together to accomplish the organization's goals. For example, key structuring decisions are how to organize and motivate employees to accomplish activities. Structuring decisions establish an organization's transformation process and information systems. Accounting information measures attributes of the transformation process within the organization's structure. Managers use this information to make decisions about the organization's structure and transformation process. This interrelationship of internal decision makers, organizational structure, transformation activities, and internal measurement and reporting defines the organization as a unique entity.

Exhibit 1-13   Accounting and the Organizational Environment

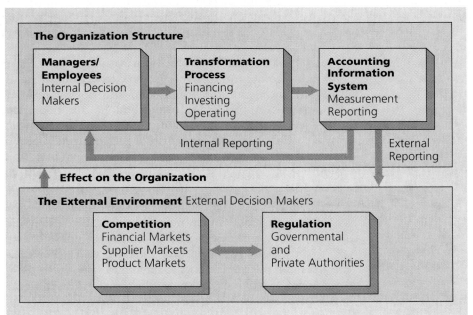

The organization operates within a larger external environment. External decision makers, who include participants in competitive markets and regulators, also use accounting information to make decisions that affect the organization. Organizations compete for financial resources provided by investors. They compete for other resources: materials, technology, human skills, equipment, and so forth. Also, they compete with other organizations to sell their goods and services. Regulators supervise organizational activities to protect the interests of investors, employees, suppliers, competitors for products, and society in general. Governmental agencies, such as the Federal Trade Commission, regulate business practices. Private organizations establish accounting and reporting requirements that are enforced by government agencies. Chapter 7 discusses organizations that regulate accounting.

This book emphasizes accounting and financial reporting for corporations. Moral hazard from the separation of owners and managers has created a strong regulatory environment for corporations. This environment oversees the development of accounting and reporting requirements for corporations. This book will examine this environment and the resulting requirements in detail. While accounting is important in other forms of organizations, owners normally manage these organizations; therefore, the formal regulation of reporting by managers to owners is unnecessary. Accounting information reported by managers to owners and other external decision makers is the subject of financial accounting. This information also is used by managers. Though managers have access to information that extends beyond that reported to external decision makers, internal and external decisions are related. Therefore, this book will consider internal and external decisions that rely on financial accounting information.

The modern multinational corporation is a complex entity. Many familiar corporations, Coca-Cola, IBM, and McDonald's to name a few, maintain headquarters in the U.S. They rely on U.S. markets for a major portion of their financing, but their production, marketing, and distribution facilities are spread throughout the world. These companies compete in a global market. Information is a critical resource for internal and external decision makers in both U.S. and foreign economies.

Accounting serves the information needs of a wide variety of decision makers who are internal and external to organizations. Chapter 2 will examine the accounting information system and how it provides information to decision makers. Appendix A, at the end of this book, summarizes some important sources of accounting information.

SELF-STUDY PROBLEM 1-3

G. Galileo, a manufacturer of small optical instruments, owns Galileo Glassware. Galileo invested $7,500 in the business and borrowed $2,500 from a local bank. With this investment, he purchased a small building and some equipment. He develops and designs the instruments he sells, purchasing materials from local hardware and specialty stores and has two assistants to help him fabricate and assemble the instruments. Galileo advertises in professional journals. He produces most of his instruments to fill special orders from customers to whom he ships the products.

Required

1. Identify each stage of the transformation process that occurs for Galileo Glassware.
2. What prices and costs are likely to be associated with each stage of the transformation?

The solution to Self-Study Problem 1-3 appears at the end of the chapter.

Summary of Important Concepts

1. The accounting process:
   a. Accounting is an information system for recording, summarizing, and reporting the financial effects of economic events to help in making decisions.
   b. The account is the basic unit of accounting information. The effect of transactions are recorded in accounts.
   c. The typical accounting process includes: (1) the occurrence of an event to be accounted for, (2) the recording of the effects of the events in accounts, (3) the calculation of account balances, and (4) the summary of the recorded events of a period and the reporting of those summaries.

2. Organizations:
   a. Organizations exist to benefit society by transforming resources from one form to another form that is more valuable in meeting the needs of people.
   b. Because most resources are in scarce supply, society attempts to use its resources to create the greatest benefit for its members.
   c. Markets provide a way for people to express their perceptions of the value of goods and services by the products they purchase and the prices they pay. The increase in value created by a transformation process can be measured by the total price of the goods and services sold less the total cost of resources consumed to produce them.
   d. Owners invest in a business to receive a return on their investments from business profits. Businesses that operate effectively and efficiently normally will earn greater profits.
   e. Businesses that are not profitable will have difficulty attracting investors and will be forced to change their behavior or to go out of business. Therefore, markets make financial and other scarce resources available to organizations that can best transform them to maximize their value for society.

3. Organizational decisions:
   a. Managers, owners, and creditors require information for assessing the effectiveness and efficiency of an organization, to ensure the protection of their interests, and to evaluate investment risk and return on investment.
   b. The transformation process involves the conversion of financial and other resources into goods and services. This process can be divided into financing, investing, and operating activities.
   c. Financing decisions are decisions an organization makes about how it will obtain financial resources. Businesses obtain capital from owners (proprietors, partners, or stockholders) and from creditors.
   d. Investing decisions involve choices managers make about resources an organization uses to produce goods and services for its customers.
   e. Operating decisions involve choices managers make about how resources will be transformed into goods and services. Decisions are made about the development and design of products, the purchase of materials, the selection and training of employees, the production process, and the distribution, marketing, and servicing of products.

4. Accounting's role in decision making:
   a. Accounting is an information system for measuring and reporting the transformation of resources into goods and services.
   b. Accounting information is used by internal and external decision makers who have a stake in an organization's activities.

DEFINE *Terms and Concepts Defined in This Chapter*

account
accounting
corporation
creditor
effective business
efficient business
financing activities
governmental and nonprofit
  organizations
income statement
information
investing activities

manufacturing companies
market
merchandising companies
moral hazard
mutual agency
net earnings
net income
net loss
nonbusiness organizations
operating activities
organization
partnerships

profit
proprietorships
retail companies
return on investment
risk
service companies
stakeholders
stock
stockholders
system
transaction
transformation process

SOLUTIONS

SELF-STUDY PROBLEM 1-1

1. Check Register

Date	Check Number	Check Issued to/ Deposit Received from	Amount of Deposit	Amount of Check	Balance
April 1		Balance			1,450
1	346	Northside Real Estate Co.		800	650
5		Customer receipts	1,000		1,650
7		Cash withdrawn		70	1,580
12	347	Miller's Wholesale Grocery		300	1,280
14		Customer receipts	950		2,230
17		Cash withdrawn		50	2,180
20	348	Citizens Loan Co.		200	1,980
21		Customer receipts	725		2,705
25	349	City Light and Water		160	2,545
27	350	Wang's Grocery		340	2,205
28	351	Restaurant Supply Co.		280	1,925
28		Customer receipts	875		2,800
30	352	First Savings and Loan		500	2,300

2.

Garcia's Deli
Summary of Cash Deposits and Payments
For April 1995

Beginning cash balance			$1,450
Deposits:			
Customer receipts		$3,550	
Cash payments:			
Rent	$800		
Food	640		
Car payment	200		
Supplies	400		
Utilities	160		
Transfer to savings	500		
Total cash paid		2,700	
Increase in cash for April			850
Ending cash balance			$2,300

3.   The steps in the accounting process include: (1) Horatio receives money or checks and deposits them in his account. He writes checks to exchange money for goods and services. (2) Each transaction is recorded in Horatio's check register. (3) His cash balance is calculated by adding or subtracting the effect of each transaction. (4) The transactions are summarized and a report is prepared to tell Horatio how he spent his money during April and how much money he has at the end of the month.

SELF-STUDY PROBLEM 1-2

1.

Bach's Music Store
Income Statement
For December 1995

Revenue from goods and services sold:		
Musical instruments	$8,000	
Sheet music	1,400	
Repair of instruments	2,200	
Total revenue		$11,600
Expenses from resources consumed:		
Cost of instruments sold	$4,300	
Cost of sheet music sold	870	
Rent	650	
Supplies used	250	
Advertising	300	
Utilities	200	
Miscellaneous	180	
Total expenses		6,750
Net income		$4,850

2. The value created by a transformation of resources is the difference between the total price of the goods and services sold and the total cost of the resources consumed in producing these goods and services. This difference is net income, or profit, for the seller.

SELF-STUDY PROBLEM 1-3

1. The stages of the transformation process are:
   a. Galileo financed his business by investing his own money and by borrowing from a bank.
   b. Financial resources were invested in a building and equipment and used to acquire other resources for the business to operate.
   c. Galileo operates the business. Operations involve:
      (1) Development of instruments.
      (2) Design of the instruments.
      (3) Purchase of materials and supplies for manufacturing the instruments.
      (4) Hiring employees to help with production.
      (5) Manufacture of instruments.
      (6) Marketing and sale of instruments.
      (7) Distribution of instruments to customers.

2. The prices and costs associated with the transformation include:
   a. A cost is incurred in borrowing money for use in the business.
   b. A cost is incurred in the purchase of buildings and equipment.
   c. Operating costs include: materials and wear on building and equipment used in development, engineering, and production activities; wages of assistants; advertising; and distribution of products.
   d. The price of the instruments sold provides income for Galileo.

EXERCISES

1-1. In your own words write a short, yet complete, definition for each of the terms listed in the *Terms and Concepts Defined in This Chapter* section.

1-2. At the beginning of February, F. Mertz had $200 in his checking account. The following events occurred during February:
   a. Wrote a check for payment on auto loan, $90.
   b. Deposited payroll check from employer, $325.
   c. Wrote a check for groceries, $50.
   d. Wrote a check for rent, $187.50.
   e. Wrote a check for clothing, $30.

Complete the following table for each event and then prepare a short report describing the changes in Mertz's cash account for February.

Transaction	Amount of Check	Amount of Deposit	Balance
Balance on February 1			$200

1-3. Assume that you have a friend, Alice Kravitz, who has no knowledge of accounting. She asks you to explain the purpose of accounting and to provide a brief description that will help her understand the accounting process. Draft a short memo to Alice that will help her understand the purpose of accounting and the accounting process.

DATE: (today's date)
TO: Alice Kravitz
FROM: (your name)
SUBJECT: Inquiry about accounting.
(your response)

1-4. Identify primary attributes of each of the following types of organizations and list an example of each:
a.   Merchandising   d.   Governmental
b.   Manufacturing   e.   Nonprofit
c.   Service

1-5. The processes involved in making a particular pair of cotton slacks include:
a.   Cotton is planted, grown, harvested, and shipped to a textile manufacturer. The cost of the cotton associated with the slacks is $4. This amount of cotton is sold to the manufacturer for $4.50.
b.   Raw cotton is processed into cotton fabric. The cost of producing the fabric for the slacks, including the cost of the raw cotton, is $12. This fabric is sold to a garment manufacturer for $16.
c.   Cotton fabric is cut and sewn to produce a pair of slacks. The cost of making the slacks, including the cost of the fabric, is $24. The slacks are sold to a retailer for $30.
d.   The cost of making the slacks available for sale, including the cost of the slacks, is $34 for the retailer. The retailer sells the slacks for $56.

How much profit is earned at each step in the production and selling process? How much total profit is earned by those involved in making and selling the slacks? Why are customers willing to pay the costs and profits earned by those involved in this process?

1-6. A. Doubleday makes baseball gloves by hand. He buys leather for $75 a yard. Padding costs $6 a pound; thread and other materials cost $9 for a month's supply. He pays $300 a month rent for a small shop where utilities average $150 a month. Shipping costs are about $4.50 per glove. In an average month, Doubleday produces and sells 6 gloves. Each glove requires a half yard of leather and a half pound of padding. What is the average cost of a glove made by Doubleday? How much profit does Doubleday earn on each glove if he sells them for $450 each? How much profit does Doubleday earn each month, on average?

1-7. Mario's is a restaurant specializing in Italian food. During October, Mario's recorded the following revenues and expenses:

Sales to customers	$9,750
Cost of food products	2,875
Cost of building and equipment	2,188
Cost of employee labor	1,875
Maintenance and utilities	1,000

Prepare an income statement for Mario's Restaurant for October.

1-8. Stop 'n' Chew is a fast-food restaurant. During January, Stop 'n' Chew recorded the following revenues and expenses:

Sales to customers	$2,200
Cost of food products	1,050
Cost of building and equipment	625
Cost of employee labor	500
Maintenance and utilities	300

Prepare an income statement for Stop 'n' Chew for January.

1-9. Pam Lucas is a high school student who delivers papers to earn spending money. During May, she received $450 from customers in payment of their subscriptions for the month. She paid $300 for the papers she delivered. In addition, she paid $45 to her parents for use of their car to deliver the papers, and she paid $30 for gas. Prepare a statement to compute the amount of net income Pam earned from her paper route in May.

1-10. On January 1, 1995, S. Clemens invested $4,000 in a savings account. At the end of January, the account balance had increased to $4,020. The balance at the end of February was $4,040.10. The balance at the end of March was $4,060.30. The increases occurred because of interest earned on the account. What was Clemens's return on investment in January, February, and March? What was the total return for the three months?

1-11. M. Twain invested $7,500 in Sawyer Rafting Co. in 1996. At the end of the year, Twain's investment was worth $8,625 because of earnings during the year. Sawyer paid Twain $1,500 at the end of the year. What was Twain's return on investment for 1996? What was his return of investment for the year? Did Sawyer Rafting Co. maintain its capital as a result of these events? Explain.

1-12. Flips and Slips are two companies that are identical with respect to the products they sell. They are owned by various individuals and are located in different parts of the same city. During September, Flips sold $24,000 of goods, while Slips sold $18,000. Flips produced $8,000 of profit, and Slips produced $2,000. Compare the efficiency and effectiveness of the two companies.

1-13. Spits and Hives are two companies that compete in the same market with the same product, a brand of steak sauce. The companies are the same size and sell to the same grocery retailers. Both products are sold by the retailers at the same price. During 1997, Spits sold 400,000 bottles of its sauce at a profit of 10 cents per bottle. Hives sold 325,000 bottles at a profit of 15 cents a bottle. Which company was more effective? Which was more efficient? Which company was more profitable?

1-14. You have a choice of investing in either of two companies, Lewis or Clark. Both companies make the same products and compete in the same markets. Over the last five years, the operating results for the two companies have been:

	Lewis	**Clark**
Sales revenue	$4,500,000	$5,625,000
Net income	$412,500	$675,000
Return on investment per dollar invested	$.045	$.075

Which company is more efficient? Which is more effective? In which company would you invest? State the reasons for your answers.

1-15. A. Ladin Lamps produces and sells specialty lamps to retail stores. During the latest year, the company sold 30,000 lamps at an average price of $80 per lamp. The production and distribution costs per lamp were $30, on average. Other expenses for management salaries and facilities were $1,200,000 for the year. Total investment in the company is $3,000,000. How much profit did A. Ladin Lamps earn for the year? Describe the steps you went through to get your answer. Suggest some changes A. Ladin could make to improve its profitability.

1-16. Refer to exercise 1-15. If A. Ladin increased its average price by $1 per lamp, how much would its profit increase? If it increased its sales volume by 2,000 lamps, how much would its profit increase? If it reduced its average production and distribution cost by $1 per lamp, how much would its profit increase?

1-17. Identify each of the following as describing corporations, proprietorships, and/or partnerships:
a. Distinct legal entity separate from its owners.
b. More than one owner.
c. Ownership by stockholders.
d. Controlled by a board of directors.
e. Company changes legal identity when it is sold.
f. Limited liability.
g. Mutual agency.
h. Access to large amounts of capital.
i. Direct taxation of profits.
j. Moral hazard usually is not a major problem.

1-18. Ann Moore is considering opening a small retail store to sell knives and other kitchen utensils. She has a small amount of money to invest and wants to maintain as much control over the business as she can. She has asked you to help her decide how to finance her business. Describe the primary issues you would suggest Ann consider.

1-19. Amen Hotep has started a small business making sundials. He has asked you to help him design a system to record cash received and paid by his business. Cash receipts are deposited daily in a bank account and payments are made by checks written against the account. Develop an information system you would recommend to Amen. Demonstrate how the system functions using the following transactions:

April	1	Cash balance	$500
	3	Cash received from customers	300
	4	Cash paid for rent	450
	5	Cash paid for supplies	225
	7	Cash received from customers	670
	8	Cash paid for taxes	180

1-20. B. Taylor owns a small business selling homemade pickles. She maintains a checking account with a local bank and keeps a record of her deposits and checks in a check register. Each month B. receives a bank statement describing the transactions in her account. She looks at the statements and then throws them away each month. She thinks it is a waste of the bank's money to prepare and mail the statements each month since she already has a record of her checking account transactions in her register. She asks you why the bank goes to the trouble of sending her the statements. How would you respond?

1-21. Porky's is a major corporation in the pigskin industry. The company has decided it needs an additional $1,000,000 in financing to build a new plant. What are the major sources of financing available to Porky's? What issues should company management consider in deciding on the type of financing to use?

1-22. H. Ferrari has obtained $5,000 from savings and a bank loan to start an automobile garage. Identify the types of resources Ferrari will need for his business. How might he choose to pay for these resources?

1-23. Prepare a table to describe the major operating activities you would expect in each of the following organizations: (a) Chrysler Corporation, (b) Wal-Mart, (c) Humana, a for-profit community hospital. The table should be organized so it is easy to understand.

1-24. Sandy Dune overheard some friends from your accounting class discussing the "transformation process." She is curious about what this term means and how it applies to organizations and accounting. Explain to Sandy your understanding of the transformation process and why it is an important concept in accounting.

PROBLEMS

PROBLEM 1-1   Summary Information About a Checking Account

Orville W. had the following checking account activity during February: Orville made deposits of $1,000 from salary and $300 from royalties on inventions. He wrote checks of $250 for house payment, $150 for food, $62 for clothing, $50 for entertainment, $45 for utilities, $37 for flying lessons, $100 for insurance, $125 for car payment, and transferred $250 to savings. The beginning balance in his checking account was $290.

Required   Prepare a report in good form, following the example of Exhibit 1-2, to describe Orville's financial activities for February. What would be the source of the information described in this report? Why might this information be useful for Orville? Describe some decisions Orville might make using this information.

PROBLEM 1-2   Information from a Bank Statement

At the end of February, Orville W. received the following statement from his bank:

Orville W.		
Bank Statement		
For February		
Beginning balance		$ 350
Deposits received:		
Feb. 17	$1,000	
Feb. 24	300	
Total deposits		1,300
Checks paid:		
Feb. 2	$ 60	
Feb. 5	250	
Feb. 8	150	
Feb. 9	62	
Feb. 13	50	
Feb. 16	22	
Feb. 19	37	
Feb. 22	100	
Feb. 25	125	
Total checks		(856)
Ending balance		$ 794

Required   What information is contained in the bank statement that is not available to Orville from his summary in Problem 1-1? Why are some of the numbers in the bank statement different from those in Orville's summary in Problem 1-1? Why is this information useful to Orville?

PROBLEM 1-3   A Basic Accounting System

Go-for-Broke Co. is a financial institution that lends money to individuals to purchase personal items such as furniture, appliances, and vacations. Once a loan application is processed, a check is written to approved applicants. The loan recipient then makes a payment to the company each month to repay the loan and to pay interest.

Required   Describe an accounting system that Go-for-Broke might use in its financial activities with its customers. Include in your description a discussion of the accounts, events, and reports that would be part of the process. What would be the primary purpose served by accounting reports prepared by the company? Illustrate your accounting system with example transactions for a customer. Prepare example reports for the customer.

PROBLEM 1-4   Developing a Cash Plan

Mary Antoinette is planning to start a new business as a hair stylist. She has saved $4,000 to invest in the business. She expects to receive $1,600 each month, on average, from sales to customers. She expects that she will need cash to pay the following items each month, on average: rent, $400; supplies, $200; utilities, $150; other, $100. She will need to purchase $6,000 of equipment to start the business; in addition, she thinks she will need $1,000 to cover initial operating costs. A local bank has agreed to consider a loan to help Mary start her business and has asked her to develop a plan that describes her expected cash receipts and payments for the first year. The plan should show how much cash she will need for the business, how much she will need to borrow, and how she expects to pay back the loan. Monthly payments will be required to pay off the loan and interest. The bank will charge $10 per year in interest for each $100 borrowed until the loan is repaid at the end of the year. Mary has asked you to prepare a plan for her to submit to the bank.

Required   Prepare a plan for Mary. Describe any assumptions you make.

PROBLEM 1-5   Determining Net Income and Return on Investment

Henry Pontiac owns a small car dealership. He rents the property he uses, buys cars from a manufacturer, and resells them to customers. During July, Henry sold 12 cars that cost him a total of $96,000. The total amount he received from the sale of these cars was $120,000. Other costs incurred by Henry for the month included rent, $2,250, utilities, $900, insurance, $525, maintenance of property and cars, $300, advertising, $270, and property taxes and business license, $180.

Required   Provide an income statement that describes the amount of net value created by Henry during July. How much profit did the company earn for July? What can Henry do with the profit he earned? Assuming he invested $750,000 in the dealership, what was the return on his investment for July expressed as a percentage of his investment?

PROBLEM 1-6   Determining Prices and Return on Investment

Tesla Electric Co. produces electricity. It is investor owned, the only electric utility in the geographic area that it serves, and is regulated by a public service commission. The commission has determined that the rate the company should charge its customers should be sufficient for investors to earn a 10% return on investment. At the end of 1996, the total investment in the company was $1,000,000. The commission considers rate requests from the company each January based on prior year costs and anticipated levels of production. The company expects to produce 20,000,000 kilowatt hours of electricity during 1997 at a cost of $2,000,000.

Required (a) What amount of profit should Tesla be permitted to earn during 1997? (b) How much total revenue would the company require to earn the profit? (c) What amount would the company charge its customers per kilowatt hour in order to earn the revenue and profit? Show all work in good form.

PROBLEM 1-7 Making Financing Decisions and Maintaining a Check Register

Part A. B. Ross wants to start a business making flags. She has calculated she will need $62,500 to start the business. The money will be used to rent a building, purchase equipment, hire workers, and begin production and sales. Ross has $12,500 in savings she can invest in the business.

Required What alternatives does Ross have for obtaining the additional $50,000 she needs for her business? What information will be important in determining the amount and kind of financing that will be available to Ross? What decisions will Ross have to make in deciding on which sources of financing to use?

Part B. B. Ross started the Ross Flag Co. on September 1 with an investment of $12,500 from savings and $50,000 borrowed from Independence Bank. The money was deposited in a checking account in the name of the company. During September, Ross wrote checks for the following purchases for the company:

Date	Check	Amount	Payee
9/3	101	$ 625	Gina Washington (for rent)
9/5	102	15,000	SingSong Sewing Machine Co.
9/12	103	28,750	Fulton Fabric Co.
9/18	104	500	City (for business license)
9/22	105	250	City (deposit on utilities)
9/25	106	4,500	Franklin Construction Co.
9/30	107	2,500	Tyler Jefferson (for wages)
9/30	108	625	Independence Bank (for interest)

Required Complete the check register for Ross Flag Co. for September, using the following format. Remember to record the deposits.

		CHECK REGISTER ROSS FLAG CO.			
Date	Check Number	Check Issued to/ Deposit Received from	Amount of Deposit	Amount of Check	Balance

PROBLEM 1-8 Accounting for Cash

Ross Flag Co. received cash for goods sold of $9,750 during October. The beginning cash balance for October was $5,925. The company made cash payments during the month, as follows:

Employee salaries	$1,500
Fabric	2,250
Utilities	900
Shipping	600
Interest	375

Required Prepare a schedule that calculates the company's net change in cash for the month of October. Explain why this information might be useful to managers and creditors.

PROBLEM 1-9 Identifying Financing, Investing, and Operating Activities and Reporting Cash

The following events occurred as part of the activities of the town of Teapot Dome during June:

Borrowed $75,000 from local bank
Received $122,700 in property taxes from taxpayers
Received $48,600 in sales taxes from businesses
Received $18,000 for fees and licenses
Paid $64,500 to employees for salaries
Paid $31,500 for new equipment
Paid $12,300 for maintenance and repair
Paid $6,900 for utilities
Paid $3,750 for supplies
Paid $6,300 for interest

Required (a) Identify the financing, investing, and operating decisions associated with these events. (b) Prepare a schedule reporting Teapot Dome's cash received and paid in June. Assume that the town's cash balance at the beginning of the month was $19,050.

PROBLEM 1-10 Activities in the Transformation Process

Businesses can be divided into three general categories based on the types of products they provide: merchandising, manufacturing, and service.

Required For each type of business, describe how the transformation process makes use of the following activities: (a) financing, (b) investing, (c) research and development, (d) design and engineering, (e) purchasing, (f) personnel, (g) production, (h) distribution, (i) marketing, (j) servicing. If any category of activity is not used, explain why not.

PROBLEM 1-11 Cash Flow in the Transformation Process

Required Prepare a chart containing the major components of the transformation process. Use arrows to show the flow of cash through the process and the exchange of cash with external parties at each stage of the process. Make the chart as simple and easy to understand as you can.

PROBLEM 1-12   **Ethics and Moral Hazard**

As manager of a retail electronics store, you purchased 200 Whizbang portable radios from a wholesaler in a going out of business sale. These units cost $80 each, about half of the normal cost of other brands you sell for $260. You expected to sell these units at the regular price and earn an above-normal profit. After your purchase, you discovered the units were poorly constructed and would probably last about a third as long as other major brands.

Customers often ask you for a recommendation when considering the purchase of a radio. If you tell them the truth about the Whizbang model, you may have difficulty in selling these units, even if you offer a steep discount.

Required   What should you tell a customer who asks about these radios? What are the short-run and long-run implications for your company's profits if (a) you conceal the quality of the units and sell them at their regular price or (b) reveal the quality problem? If you were to choose alternative b, what options might you consider in an effort to minimize the effect of these units on your profits?

PROBLEM 1-13   **Ethics and Moral Hazard**

You manage an auto service store. One of your major services is brake replacement. You purchase replacement parts at an average cost of $15 per set. Each set contains parts for four wheels and will repair one car. You charge an average of $45 per car for replacing worn brakes, including an average labor cost of $6. Your current volume for brake replacements is about 750 jobs per month. A new vendor has contacted you with an offer to sell you replacement parts at an average cost of $11.25 per set. After checking on the quality of these parts, you find that their average life is about two-thirds of that of the parts you are currently using.

Required   What are the short-run profit implications of using the $11.25 brakes instead of the $15 brakes? What are the long-run profit implications? What ethical issues should be considered in choosing which brakes to use?

PROBLEM 1-14   **The Transformation Process**

You are considering opening a shop in a nearby mall that will sell specialty T-shirts. T-shirts will be produced for customers on order, containing designs and words selected by customers. You will need $10,000 to acquire materials and supplies and $15,000 for equipment and facilities to begin operations. You have accumulated $5,000 in savings and will need to borrow the remainder. A local bank has agreed to consider a loan and has asked for a summary plan to demonstrate the performance you expect from your company and your ability to repay the loan. You will pay $5.50 for T-shirts and will sell them for $15. The cost of paint and supplies will be $0.50 per shirt. An examination of similar stores at other malls indicates you should be able to sell an average of 1,000 shirts per month. Rent for your store will be $800 per month. Utilities will be $150 per month, on average. Wages will be $2,800 per month. Interest on the loan will average $180 per month. The loan will be repaid in monthly installments of $400. All transactions are for cash.

Required   (a) Identify the major financing, investing, and operating activities that will be part of your business. (b) Develop a plan describing the expected performance of your company for the first year of operation. The plan should show the initial financing and investing activities that will be needed, and it should show the expected results of operating activities and the use of cash to pay the bank.

PROBLEM 1-15   Multiple Choice Overview of the Chapter

1. The basic purpose of accounting is to:
   a.   minimize the amount of taxes a company has to pay.
   b.   permit an organization to keep track of its financial activities.
   c.   report the largest amount of net income to stockholders.
   d.   reduce the amount of risk experienced by investors.

2. The four primary steps in the accounting process are listed in random order. In what chronological order do these steps really occur?
   A.   A summary is prepared of the events of the period.
   B.   A transaction occurs.
   C.   An account balance is increased or decreased.
   D.   The effect of an event is recorded.
       a.   C, B, D, A
       b.   A, B, C, D
       c.   D, C, B, A
       d.   B, D, C, A

3. A primary purpose of all organizations in our society is to:
   a.   make a profit.
   b.   minimize the payment of taxes.
   c.   provide employment for the largest number of workers possible.
   d.   transform resources from one form to another.

4. Mustafa Co. is a manufacturer of pharmaceuticals. Which of the following events would ordinarily be expected to create value for the company?

	The firm sells shares of its own stock	Raw materials are converted to finished products and sold
a.	Yes	Yes
b.	Yes	No
c.	No	Yes
d.	No	No

5. Which pair of terms describes the same thing?
   a.   net income, profit
   b.   financing activities, operating activities
   c.   partnership, proprietorship
   d.   revenue, net income

6. Tammy Faye invested $2,000 in a partnership. One year later, the partnership was sold and cash from the sale was distributed to the partners. On that date, Tammy received a check for her share of the company in the amount of $2,250. What was Tammy's return on investment?
   a. $ –0–
   b. $ 250
   c. $2,000
   d. $2,250

7. Sternberg Enterprises developed a new type of roller skate that is very popular because of its high quality and reasonable price. Sternberg is losing money on the product, however, because several key production personnel recently resigned and replacements are not as skilled. Which of the following terms properly describes the firm?

	Effective	**Efficient**
a.	Yes	Yes
b.	Yes	No
c.	No	Yes
d.	No	No

8. Which of the following is an investing activity?
    a.   A manufacturer borrows from creditors.
    b.   A service firm pays a return to its stockholders.
    c.   A retailer sells goods to a not-for-profit agency at cost.
    d.   A government agency purchases a new mainframe computer system.

9. Which of the following is not an operating activity?
    a.   Merchandise is sold to customers.
    b.   Utility bills are paid.
    c.   Merchandise is shipped to customers.
    d.   Equipment for use in manufacturing is purchased.

10. The term "transformation process" refers to:
    a.   a repetitive cycle of financing, investing, and operating activities.
    b.   the conversion of materials into goods for sale.
    c.   procedures designed to reduce a company's risk.
    d.   training methods by which unskilled workers become efficient and effective.

C A S E S

CASE 1-1   Understanding the Transformation Process

A. Lincoln Co. is a designer and builder of log homes. Financing is provided by owners and creditors, primarily banks. The company owns buildings and equipment it uses in the management, design, transportation, and construction process. It purchases logs and other building materials from other companies. These materials are shipped by the sellers. Homes are designed for customers. Logs are cut to the dimensions called for in a design and shipped to the customer's building site with other materials for assembly. Lincoln employs design engineers, construction and assembly workers, maintenance personnel, and marketing and service personnel, in addition to its management and office staff. The company is in charge of the construction process until the home is completed and ready for occupancy. The company warranties the completed home for one year after completion to be free of defects from materials or construction.

Required   Discuss the stages of the transformation process for A. Lincoln Co. and provide a chart describing the flow of resources through the transformation process. Note the events in the transformation process that will result in money flowing into or out of the company in exchange for other resources.

CASE 1-2   Financing, Investing, and Operating Activities as Part of the Transformation Process

Refer to the information provided in Case 1-1.

Required List decisions Lincoln's managers would make at each stage of the transformation process involving the acquisition, use, or disposal of resources.

PROJECTS

PROJECT 1-1 Organizations and Their Purposes

Different types of organizations exist in our society, including: service organizations, retail organizations, manufacturing organizations, government and nonprofit organizations. Identify the names of three organizations that fit into each type. Prepare a table listing (a) the type of organization, (b) the name of the organization, (c) the primary purpose for which the organization exists, (d) major resources the organization consumes in carrying out its purpose, and (e) the goods and services the organization produces in carrying out its purpose.

PROJECT 1-2 Organizations and Their Purposes

Visit your library and locate where corporate annual reports are kept. Most university libraries receive annual reports either in their published form or on microfiche or in computer readable format. Select a corporation whose name begins with the same first letter as your first name. Consult the most recent annual report you can find for this company. Read through the annual report and identify the following information: (a) the year covered by the annual report, (b) the major products or services sold by the organization, (c) the primary resources consumed by this organization in producing goods and services, (e) the amount of net income earned by this company during the year covered by the report as described on its income statement. (Be sure to determine if that number is expressed in thousands, millions, or billions of dollars.)

PROJECT 1-3 Financing, Investing, and Operating Activities

Assume you are trying to explain to a friend what is meant by the following terms: financing activities, investing activities, and operating activities. Write a short explanation of each term so it can be understood by someone who has not studied accounting. Provide examples of each type of activity to illustrate the decisions managers make about the activities in an organization that your friend is likely to be familiar with. Show your description to a friend who has not had accounting and ask her/him to write a brief note indicating any problems with understanding your description.

PROJECT 1-4 Financing, Investing, and Operating Activities

The purposes of this project are to (1) familiarize you with your college library and several periodicals that are widely read by managers, and (2) to have you identify examples of financing, investing, and operating decisions that managers make. Review Appendix A of this book, then:

a. Go to the current periodical room of your college or university library and locate the following newspapers and magazines: *The Wall Street Journal, Barron's, Business Week, Forbes,* and *Fortune.*

b. Find an example of an operating, an investing, or a financing decision discussed in an article in a recent issue of one of these periodicals.

c. Write a brief summary of your reading that includes the name of the periodical, the date of the issue, the name of the article, its page number, and the type of decision discussed.

d. Briefly describe the decision you identified in the article.

PROJECT 1-5   Identifying Revenues and Profits

Several publications available in most college libraries list financial information about major corporations. Review Appendix A of this book. Then, examine one of the listed publications, such as *Fortune, Value Line,* or *Moody's Industrial Manual.* Select 10 U. S. corporations and prepare a table listing each corporation, its revenues (net sales), and net income for the most recent year available. Compute the ratio of net income to revenues. Rank the firms from most to least efficient and effective.

Chapter
2

Information in Organizations

Chapter 1 described an organization as a transformation process. This process converts resources into goods and services that are sold to customers or distributed to recipients. Chapter 1 examined decisions owners, creditors, and managers make about organizations. Chapter 2 considers the information used by decision makers in greater detail. The need for information occurs from the interaction among those who provide resources and services to an organization. Also, this chapter describes major components of information systems. Several information systems may exist in an organization, each serving a different purpose. Accounting is a particular type of system that provides information about economic consequences of the transformation process. This chapter considers features of the accounting system. After reading this chapter, you should understand that accounting is an information system for measuring, summarizing, and reporting the economic consequences of an organization's transformation process. This information is used by decision makers to form and evaluate contracts that identify the rights and responsibilities of the decision makers.

Major topics covered in this chapter include:

- Information needs of external and internal decision makers.
- Primary functions of information systems.
- Components of an accounting information system.
- Processing information in an accounting system.

Once you have completed this chapter, you should be able to:

1. Explain why contracts affect the need for information about organizations.
2. Explain why risk and return are important to investors.
3. Explain how debt and equity financing affect risk and return.
4. Discuss the effect of compensation on managers' decisions.
5. Identify uses of accounting information by managers, employees, suppliers, customers, and governmental agencies.
6. Identify the purpose of generally accepted accounting principles and audits.
7. Define financial accounting.
8. Define managerial accounting.
9. Identify the primary activities in an information system.
10. Explain the purpose of a management information system.
11. Explain the purpose of an accounting information system.
12. Identify activities in an accounting information system.
13. List the types of accounts included in an accounting information system.
14. Define assets, liabilities, and owners' equity.
15. Define revenues and expenses.
16. Explain the relationships among contracts, transactions, and accounting information.

INFORMATION FOR DECISION MAKERS

As discussed in Chapter 1, the purpose of accounting is to provide information for decision makers about an organization's transformation process. The value of accounting information is determined by how well it meets the needs of those who use it. Accounting information describes economic consequences of the transformation process. It is concerned with measuring financial resources used to acquire other resources, the conversion of resources into goods and services, and the prices of goods and services sold to customers. Information needs arise within the organizational environment as depicted in Exhibit 2-1.

Exhibit 2-1   Accounting and the Organizational Environment

Information needs of decision makers arise from the many relationships that occur among an organization's stakeholders: managers, investors, suppliers, employees, customers, and government authorities. Many of these decision makers are participants in the transformation. They compete in markets for resources, or they regulate these markets. They exchange resources or services with an organization as part of its transformation process.

Contracts **are legal agreements for the exchange of resources and services.** They provide legal protection for the parties to an agreement if terms of the agreement are not honored. Contract terms establish the rights and responsibilities of the contracting parties. Contracts are "give and get" relationships. Each party to the contract expects to receive something in exchange for something given. For example, a contract by an employee to provide labor to a company involves the giving of labor services by the employee in exchange for wages and benefits. Contracts with proprietorships and partnerships are between the owners/managers and other contracting parties. In contrast, because corporations are legal entities, contracts can be formed with the corporation as one of the contracting parties. Managers make contracts on behalf of corporations and their owners.

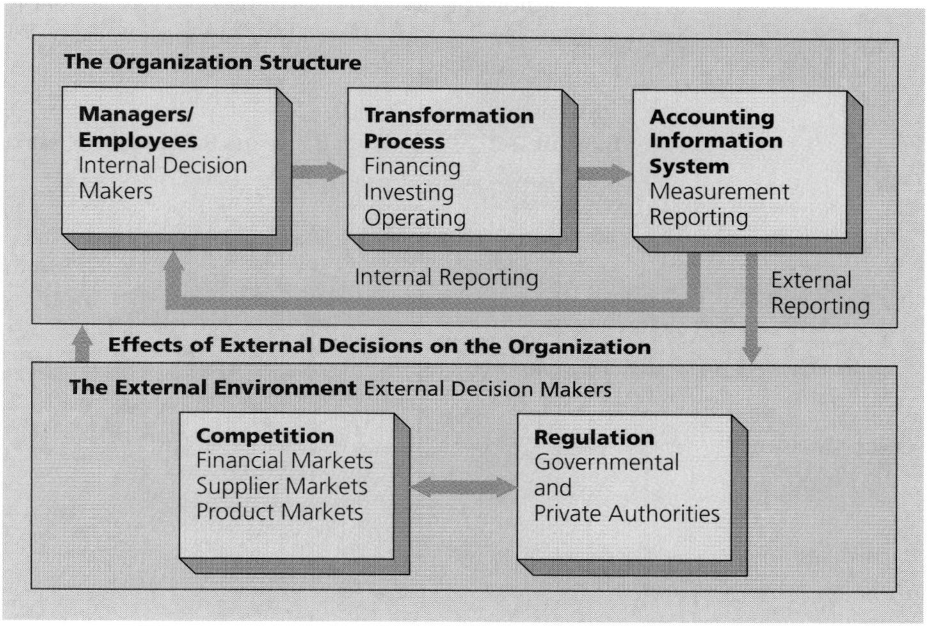

Objective 1
Explain why contracts affect the need for information about organizations.

Contracts are enforceable only to the extent contracting parties can determine whether the terms of the contract are being met. Assume you and I sign a contract that calls for you to invest $1,000 in my company, and I agree to pay you 10% of the amount my company earns each year. Unless you have reliable information about my company's earnings, you cannot determine whether I am paying you the agreed amount. Therefore, you probably would not agree to the contract. Contracts require information contracting parties accept as reliable and sufficient for determining if terms of the contract have been met. **Accounting information is important for forming and evaluating contracts.**

Exhibit 2-2 identifies examples of exchanges among stakeholders for which contracts and information about organizations are important. The following sections discuss these exchanges.

Exhibit 2-2   Examples of Exchanges Requiring Information

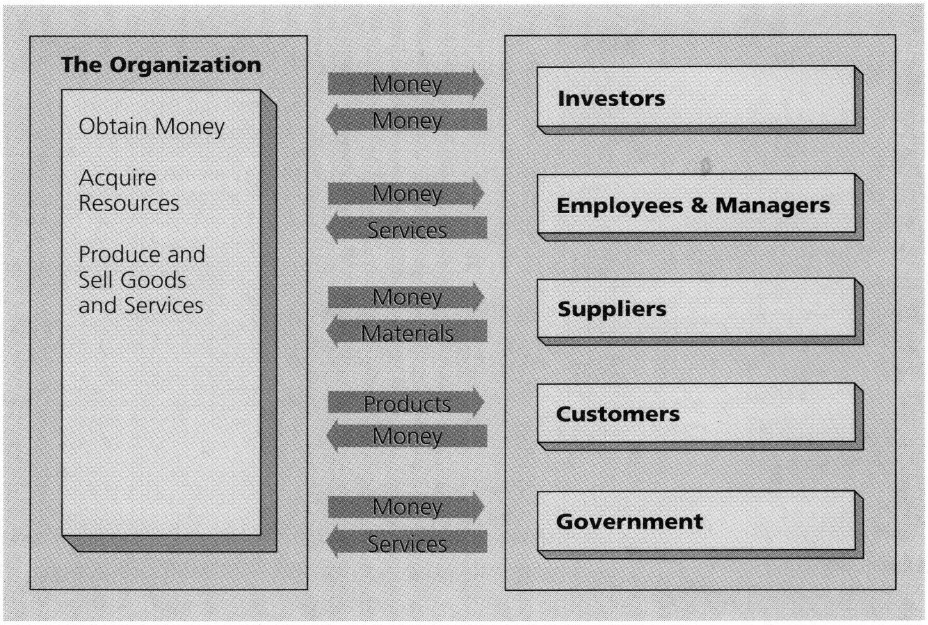

Risk and Return

Contracts are formed to identify rights and responsibilities. These rights and responsibilities establish how risk and return will be shared among contracting parties. Information about risk and return is needed to determine contract terms. Chapter 1 defined return on investment as the amount of profits earned by a business that could be distributed to owners. Risk results from uncertainty about the amount and timing of return. Exhibit 2-3 contains the returns of two investments (A and B) over several time periods. Which investment is riskier? Returns for investment A are relatively stable and predictable; they are growing at a steady rate. Returns for investment B are less predictable. Investment B is riskier than A, though it may produce higher returns over time than A.

Exhibit 2-3   An illustration of Risk and Return

	Returns	
Time Period	Investment A	Investment B
1	$6	$10
2	6	12
3	7	7
4	7	3
5	8	8
6	8	11

Management decisions about financing, investing, and operating activities affect risk and return for an organization's stakeholders. An organization's external environment also affects risk and return. Competition and regulation affect the cost and availability of resources used in the transformation process, as well as the demand for a company's goods and services and their prices. Competition and regulation vary across companies and time because of different market conditions, types of products and production processes, and changing political and social concerns. For example, concern about product safety can change a relatively stable market into a very uncertain market.

Objective 2
Explain why risk and return are important to investors.

Those who invest in a company expect to earn returns from their investments. At the same time, they must evaluate the risk inherent in investing in the company. What should they earn if the company does well? What might happen if the company does poorly? Risk and return are related in most situations; investors expect to earn higher returns from riskier investments. The higher returns compensate them for accepting higher risk, but actual returns may differ from expected returns. Therefore, riskier investments may actually result in higher or lower returns than less risky investments. On average, however, higher return should be associated with greater risk; otherwise, investors will not participate in risky investments. Accounting information helps investors predict risk and return associated with investments. The following sections consider the risk and return evaluations made by those who contract with an organization.

Evaluating Exchanges

Investors. Owners and creditors are *investors* **in an organization.** They contract with managers to provide financial resources in exchange for future returns. They need information to decide whether to invest in a company and how much to invest. **Accounting information helps investors evaluate the risk and return they can expect from their investments. Also, it helps them determine whether managers are meeting the terms of their contracts.**

Objective 3
Explain how debt and equity financing affect risk and return.

Financing decisions are a major source of risk in a company. *Debt financing* **results when a company obtains financial resources from creditors.** *Equity financing* **results when a company obtains financial resources from owners.** Decisions to use debt or equity financing affect a corporation's risk and return. Obtaining resources from creditors often increases the risk of a company. A company has a legal obligation to pay creditors interest on their loans and to repay the amount borrowed. *Interest* **is a return earned by a creditor. The**

amount borrowed is the *principal* **of a loan.** Interest is an amount paid to a creditor in addition to repayment of the principal. If a company does not earn sufficient profits, it may be unable to make these payments, and creditors can force a company into bankruptcy. Bankruptcy is a legal status in which a company is largely controlled by and for its creditors. Creditors also may require a company to liquidate its resources to repay its debts.

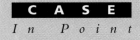

R. H. Macy & Co. declared bankruptcy in 1992. The company operated 251 stores throughout the U.S. Less than six years earlier, the company's management had purchased the company by issuing large amounts of debt. They used the proceeds of the debt to buy out the owners in a "leveraged buy-out," or LBO. The recession of the early 1990s resulted in declining profits for the company, which was unable to generate sufficient cash from its sales to pay interest and maturing principal on its debt. In late 1991 and early 1992, Macy's earnings, before interest and taxes were deducted, dropped to about half of the amount for the preceding year. After considering the effect of interest expense, the company incurred a large loss with little hope of recovery in the near future.

Adapted from The Wall Street Journal, January 28, 1992.

If a company is forced to liquidate (sell all of its noncash assets), creditors are paid amounts owed them before stockholders receive any payments. On the other hand, if a company is profitable, stockholders normally earn higher returns than creditors because stockholders have a right to share in a company's profits. Creditors receive only the amount of interest agreed to when debt is issued. Consequently, investors and managers choose between risk and return.

Assume a company has $300,000 of debt and $500,000 of stock outstanding. Creditors agreed to lend the company money at 10% interest per year. Consider the three scenarios presented below:

	Scenario 1	Scenario 2	Scenario 3
Income before interest	$100,000	$50,000	$ 0
Interest	(30,000)	(30,000)	(30,000)
Net income	$ 70,000	$20,000	$(30,000)

In scenario 1, the company earns $100,000. After paying interest (and disregarding taxes), the company earns net income of $70,000. Thus, while creditors earn a 10% return, stockholders earn a 14% return ($70,000/$500,000). In scenario 2, stockholder return is only 4% ($20,000/$500,000), and in scenario 3, it is − 6% (− $30,000/$500,000). Creditor return is less risky than stockholder return, but the potential for higher (and lower) returns exists for stockholders, relative to creditors. Also, the risk to the company and its stockholders increases as its debt increases. If the company were to incur losses, as in scenario 3, for several periods, it might be unable to pay amounts owed to creditors. The more debt a company has outstanding, the more cash it must generate to make these payments. If a company is unprofitable, it may have difficulty generating the cash it needs.

Objective 4
Discuss the effect of compensation on managers' decisions.

Managers. Owners generally do not manage large corporations. Instead, they hire managers who operate the businesses for them. Managers contract with owners to provide services in exchange for salaries and other compensation. Owners, or directors who represent them, need information to determine how well managers are performing and to reward managers when they do well. To provide incentives for managers to perform well, owners may offer managers bonuses when a company is profitable. **Accounting information provides a means for owners and managers to determine the amount of compensation managers will receive.**

Compensation arrangements also encourage managers to present their companies' performances in the best light. Often, compensation is linked to profits and other accounting information, giving managers incentives to report numbers that will maximize their compensation. The combination of management control over information and manager incentives to make their companies look good provides an ethical dilemma for managers. Sometimes, they must choose between the best interests of the company and their own best interests.

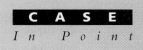

Suppose you are the manager of a company. You are paid a salary of $80,000 a year. In addition, you will receive a 50% bonus ($40,000) if the company's profits exceed $500,000 for the year. You have worked hard during the year and the company has done well. However, your calculations suggest the company's profits will be only $450,000. The company owns some stock in another company that was purchased for $100,000. The market value of the stock is now about $200,000. By selling the stock, you will generate an additional after-tax profit of $65,000. The company will pay $30,000 of additional taxes and about $5,000 in fees associated with the sale. If you sell the stock, you will probably repurchase it (or similar stock) again because it has been valuable to the company. What is the best decision for you as manager? What is the best decision for the company? What would you do?

Objective 5
Identify uses of accounting information by managers, employees, suppliers, customers, and governmental agencies.

Managers' investing and operating decisions have a direct effect on the risk and return of those who contract with a company. Managers decide which resources to acquire, when to acquire them, and how much to pay for them. The value of a resource to a business depends on the contribution the resource is expected to make in earning future profits.

Each investment in a resource involves decisions about risk and return associated with the investment. An organization is a portfolio (collection) of individual resources. In combination, the risks and returns on the investments in these resources help determine the risk and return on investment of the organization as a whole. One task of management is to select a portfolio of resources that will yield a desired amount of return at a level of risk managers and owners find acceptable. Investments in proven technology and established products generally are less risky than investments in new technology or products. Investments in resources in some countries are riskier than those in other countries because of their political and economic environments. **Accounting information is useful for identifying the types and locations of an organization's resources.**

Operating activities transform resources into goods and services. A major purpose of accounting is to measure costs associated with the flow of resources through the transformation process. Accounting also measures resources obtained from selling goods and services. The profits earned by a corporation from its operating activities are a major determinant of risk and return. **Information about the results of operating activities is used to estimate, compare, and manage companies' risks and returns.**

Employees. Employees have a major effect on a company's risk and return. Wages and quality of work directly affect product quality, sales, costs, and profits. Companies evaluate the cost and productivity of their employees. They compare employee performance with management expectations, examine changes over time, and compare different divisions with each other. **Accounting information helps managers assess employee performance.**

Employees negotiate for wages, benefits, and job security. Compensation is affected by a company's performance and financial condition. Labor unions and other employee groups use accounting information to evaluate a company's ability to compensate its employees. Like other contracting parties, employees evaluate risk and return in an employment relationship. If a company does well, employees expect to be rewarded. If it does poorly, they may face lay-offs, wage and benefit cuts, and loss of jobs. **Accounting information helps employees assess the risk and return of their employment contracts.**

Suppliers. An organization purchases materials, merchandise, and other resources from suppliers. These resources are a major cost for most companies. Careful negotiation of prices, credit, and delivery schedules between management and suppliers is required. If a company cannot obtain quality materials when they are needed, it may incur major losses from idle production, waste, lost sales, and dissatisfied customers. If a supplier goes out of business or cannot fulfill its commitments, a company may have difficulty obtaining needed resources. **Accounting information helps companies evaluate the abilities of their suppliers to meet their resource needs.**

Suppliers often sell resources to companies on credit. These suppliers are creditors who are financing the sale of resources to a company in anticipation of future payments. Usually, these loans are for short periods of 30–60 days, though longer financing sometimes is arranged. When a company declares bankruptcy, it often owes large amounts to suppliers. Suppliers may have difficulty collecting these amounts or may be unable to collect them. Therefore, suppliers evaluate the risk they are taking in selling on credit to other companies. Terms of these sales, including prices and payment schedules, are affected by a seller's perception of risk associated with these sales. **Suppliers often use accounting information about their customers to evaluate the risk of a buyer's not being able to pay for goods and services acquired.**

Customers. A company is a supplier to its customers. Thus, it evaluates customers in the same way it is evaluated by suppliers. Managers decide the terms of sales by evaluating the risk and return associated with the sales. Riskier customers normally receive less favorable terms. For example, a customer with good credit can purchase a house, car, appliances, and other goods on more favorable terms than can a customer with bad credit.

Customer decisions to buy products often are affected by their perception of quality and dependability, as well as price. These decisions also may depend on the financial reputation of the seller. Will the company be in business in the future when maintenance, repair, or replacement is needed? Will it be able to honor warranties? Are its profits sufficient to invest in new technology and maintain quality products? **Accounting information is used to assess the risks of buying from specific companies and selling to specific customers.**

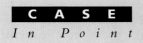

In 1991, several major airlines, including Eastern and Pan Am, abruptly ceased operations after periods of financial distress. Aircraft were grounded and most employees were discharged. Many thousands of customers held reservations and prepaid tickets and were inconvenienced by the events. Many other potential customers had been wary of the airlines because of their ongoing financial problems over the prior months. The refusal of these potential customers to purchase tickets from these airlines was one problem leading to the demise of these companies.

Governmental Agencies. Organizations are required to provide information to governmental agencies. Governments require businesses to purchase licenses for selling goods and services and to pay fees and taxes for various government services. Often these amounts are determined by the amount of sales or profitability of an organization. Governments collect information about organizations as a basis for economic forecasts and planning at the local, state, and national levels. Businesses are required to report information to state and federal authorities that regulate business activities to ensure fair trade, fair treatment of employees, and fair disclosure to investors.

Businesses report information to taxing authorities at various levels of government. Reports are required for filing sales, property, payroll, excise, and income taxes. The amount of these taxes is determined by how much a company sells, the costs it incurs, and amounts paid to employees. **Governmental agencies use accounting information to make taxation and regulatory decisions.**

Financial Accounting

Objective 6
Identify the purpose of generally accepted accounting principles and audits.

Because of concerns about information reliability and moral hazard, managers of major corporations prepare accounting information for investors and other external users according to specific rules called generally accepted accounting principles (GAAP). *GAAP* **are standards developed by professional accounting organizations to identify appropriate accounting and report-**

ing procedures. GAAP establish minimum disclosure requirements and increase comparability of information from one period to the next and among different companies.

Learning Note

GAAP apply only to information prepared for use by external decision makers. Because managers control information available inside an organization, accounting standards such as GAAP are not necessary for this information.

Accounting information reported to investors by most corporations must be audited. **An *audit* is a detailed examination of an organization's financial reports.** It includes an examination of the information system used to prepare the reports, and involves an examination of control procedures organizations use to help ensure the accuracy of accounting information. The purpose of an audit is to evaluate whether information reported to external decision makers is a fair presentation of an organization's economic activities. Standards (GAAP) for the preparation and reporting of information help ensure the reliability of accounting information. The auditors, who are independent certified public accountants (CPAs), examine this information to confirm it is prepared according to GAAP. To be a CPA, a person must pass a qualifying exam and meet education and experience requirements. CPAs are independent of the companies they audit because they are not company employees; rather, they are hired by corporate investors. Also, they should have no vested interests in the companies that might bias their audits.

Objective 7
Define financial accounting.

Accounting information prepared for use by external decision makers is financial accounting information. *Financial accounting* **is the process of preparing, reporting, and interpreting accounting information that is provided to external decision makers.** As a primary source of information for investors, this information is important for the financing activities of organizations. It also may affect the decisions of suppliers, customers, and employees.

Learning Note

Managers, as internal decision makers, use financial accounting information in addition to managerial accounting information. They are also concerned about the effect of financial accounting information on the decisions of other stakeholders.

Many corporations must report audited financial accounting information to governmental agencies. Corporations whose stock is traded publicly in the U.S. report to the Securities and Exchange Commission (SEC). This agency examines corporate financial reports to verify their conformance with GAAP and SEC requirements. A corporation whose stock may be listed on stock exchanges in more than one country must report to local authorities in each of those countries. Because countries do not use the same GAAP, reporting may involve preparation of separate reports for the investors in the different countries. In the U.S., banks and other financial institutions, defense contractors, hospitals, and many other organizations also report accounting information to governmental agencies.

Managerial Accounting

Objective 8
Define managerial
accounting.

Managers need information in addition to that provided to external decision makers to evaluate the efficiency and effectiveness of their companies. *Managerial* **(or** *management*) *accounting* **is the process of preparing, reporting, and interpreting accounting information for use by an organization's internal decision makers.** Managers develop accounting systems for internal use to meet their own decision needs. These systems often are separate from the systems used to report financial accounting information. Managerial accounting is used by managers to make planning and control decisions.

Planning **decisions require managers to identify goals and to develop strategies and policies to achieve these goals.** Planning decisions involve choices about which goods and services a company will provide, where a company will locate its facilities, what technology it will acquire, and how it will expand into new markets. These decisions determine the structure of an organization. Managers estimate the profitability of alternate strategies and the risks associated with these alternatives.

Control **decisions require managers to evaluate the accomplishments of their organization and to make changes if the organization is not meeting its goals.** These decisions focus on how well the company is implementing the strategies and policies developed in the planning process. In addition, they require evaluation of employees who have responsibilities for accomplishing an organization's goals. Evaluations motivate employees to make decisions consistent with an organization's goals.

Planning decisions are future oriented: What do managers want to happen in the future? Control decisions are past and present oriented: What has the company accomplished and what changes should be made to improve performance? Planning decisions often are long-run decisions: What objectives exist for the next five years? Control decisions are more immediate: Are objectives being met now? If not, what can be done to improve the situation?

Planning and control decisions are made about financing, investing, and operating activities. Managers plan for a company's financial resource needs and decide how these resources will be invested. They evaluate how financial resources were used and the success of the investments they have made. They plan for new products, product design, and the acquisition of materials and labor to produce products. They plan for the production, distribution, marketing, and servicing of goods and services. Control decisions evaluate these activities. Control of costs is a major management task affecting a company's efficiency.

Accounting and Information Needs

The accounting information system should be adaptable to provide the information demanded of an organization. Specialized accounting systems often are necessary to provide information for different needs of managers, for reporting to investors, for tax planning and reporting, and for reporting to other governmental authorities. These systems work together to meet the needs of those who make decisions about an organization. Decisions managers make in an organization are not independent of decisions made by investors, customers, suppliers, and others. Information reported to external parties affects internal decisions. Fi-

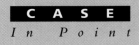

C A S E

In   Point

Assume that you own a business that processes film for customers. Your current store is located in a mall. You have invested in state-of-the-art equipment that has the capacity to process 1,000 rolls of film a day. Currently, you are processing an average of 500 rolls a day.

In your planning decisions you want to identify a strategy to increase your processing volume to take advantage of your unused capacity. One strategy would be to open small stores in different locations around town where customers could drop off their film. Twice daily, the film would be picked up from the outlets and delivered to the processing location in the mall. Once processed, the film would be returned to the outlets on the next trip.

This strategy should increase the number of customers because they would not have to take their film to the mall. Also, it would increase the visibility of your business in different parts of town. Whether this is a good strategy depends on how much additional business you can create and on how much additional cost will be necessary to open the outlets and transport the film.

Thus, the planning process depends on weighing the relative benefits and costs that you anticipate if you adopt this strategy. The control process becomes important once you decide on a strategy. Success will depend on how well each outlet performs its mission. You must evaluate each outlet you open. Is it creating sufficient business? Is the film being delivered on time? How expensive is the outlet to operate? How well are employees serving customers? By answering these questions, you may decide some outlets should be closed or moved, or some personnel should be replaced. You may decide the entire strategy is unsuccessful and you should look for an alternative, or you may decide the strategy is successful and you need to enlarge your operations. Planning and control work together. Through planning, you decide what to do. Through control, you decide how well you have done and what to do differently to improve performance.

nancial accounting provides a window for those external to a company to view the consequences of decisions made by managers. Thus, management decisions are the primary concern of both financial and managerial accounting.

Accounting information can be divided into financial and managerial components:

Financial accounting includes general purpose and specialized reporting to external decision makers. General purpose reports are provided to investors, customers, suppliers, employees, and others with a need for information about a company's overall performance. Specialized reports are prepared for tax and regulatory authorities who have a need for specific information, and often are prepared using different accounting rules from those for general purpose reports. Managerial accounting serves numerous needs of internal decision makers. This information is reported in a wide variety of formats and can be designed for specific needs that arise within an organization.

SELF-STUDY PROBLEM 2-1

R. Floorshine is a manufacturer of shoes. The company operates as a corporation and has issued shares of stock to its owners and debt to creditors. It has purchased and leased buildings and equipment. It purchases materials on short-term credit and converts the materials into shoes. The shoes are sold to retail stores, also on a short-term credit arrangement.

Required

Identify the primary exchanges and contracts between the company and those who interact with R. Floorshine. Describe the primary information needs associated with these exchanges and contracts.

The solution to Self-Study Problem 2-1 appears at the end of the chapter.

INFORMATION SYSTEMS

Objective 9
Identify the primary activities in an information system.

To meet the many information needs of internal and external users, organizations develop systems to collect, process, and report information. Exhibit 2-4 illustrates the primary activities in an information system.

An information system identifies and collects data from appropriate sources and converts the data into information that can be used in making decisions. Data are individual facts or symbols that can be converted into useful information.

The purpose of an information system may be to change data to make them more useful before they are received by users or to make information more accessible to users. For example, sound or visual images may be converted by microphone and camera to signals stored on compact disks or tapes. When the disks or tapes are played on appropriate equipment, the signals are converted back to sounds and images. The storage devices make the information more useful by preserving it until it is needed.

Computers are a familiar type of information system. Data are entered through a keyboard into a processing unit. The processing unit converts the data into signals that can be displayed on a monitor or printer or that can be stored until needed. An important aspect of this type of system is that data are transformed into information by the computer. Software is used to rearrange the data, to summarize it, or to tabulate it, so the output is useful information.

Exhibit 2-4   Primary Activities in an Information System

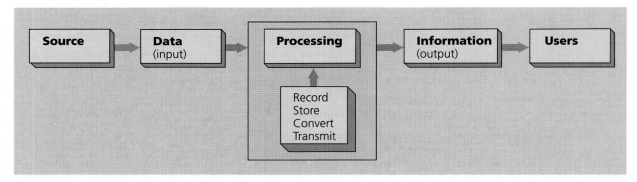

The ability to store and manipulate data before they are output is an important attribute of many information systems. One part of an information system that plays an important role in permitting the storage and manipulation of information is a data base. **A** *data base* **is a physical or electronic arrangement of data that allows the data to be retrieved and manipulated systematically.** Telephone directories and dictionaries are common types of data bases. If you need to find someone's phone number or the meaning of a word, you can look it up in the data base because information is stored in an alphabetical format. An accounting data base might be a computer file containing information about amounts owed to individual creditors.

Management Information Systems

Information systems designed to meet the needs of managers are a source of information to be reported to investors, creditors, government authorities, and others with whom managers interact. A management information system provides information managers need to operate an organization. In theory, a management information system might be designed so it receives input from all parts of an organization. The system stores the input in a data base, which then provides information for many decisions of internal and external users. In reality, such comprehensive management information systems are not found currently in most organizations. New technology probably will make them more common in the near future.

Exhibit 2-5 presents a model of a comprehensive management information system. In this system, each part of an organization provides input into the data base. For example, marketing provides data about the number of units and dollar amount of sales of each type of product for each geographical location. Personnel provides information about the number of employees in different divisions and the amount of wages and benefits earned and paid. From this comprehensive data base, data are converted into information in the form of schedules and reports that are provided to internal and external users. Computers provide a means for organizations to link managers so information can flow among divisions. To illustrate, a computerized system could allow production to obtain information about the number of units to produce to meet sales orders, purchasing could determine the quantity of materials to order to meet manufacturing requirements, and so forth.

Exhibit 2-5   A Comprehensive Management Information System

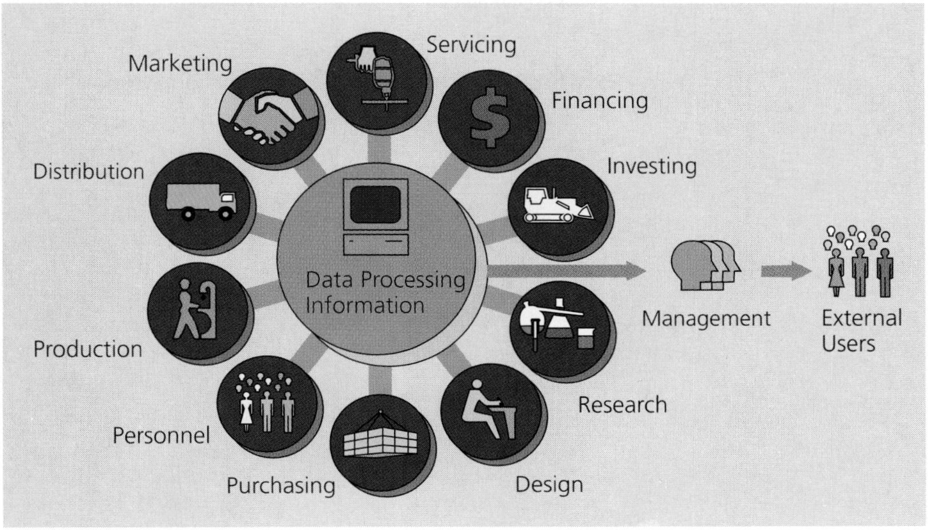

Instead of one comprehensive management information system, organizations normally maintain several information systems (or subsystems) that serve different purposes. Each subsystem is part of the total management information system. Thus, separate information subsystems may exist for marketing, production, and personnel. Each subsystem collects input from activities occurring in that part of the transformation process. The subsystem stores these data and converts them to information as needed to meet the requirements of the particular managers of that division. Periodically, data from each division are converted into reports and provided to other parts of an organization or to top management.

Objective 11
Explain the purpose of an accounting information system.

Whether comprehensive or not, the management information system provides information about the types, quantities, locations, and uses of resources from the time they are acquired until they are consumed, sold, or discarded as part of the transformation process. **The** *accounting information system*, **a specific subsystem of the management information system, is responsible for: (1) identifying the resources of an organization, (2) tracking the transformation of resources into goods and services sold to customers or provided to recipients, (3) determining the costs of resources used by an organization, and (4) reporting information about these activities to internal and external users.**

The Accounting Information System

Objective 12
Identify activities in an
accounting information
system.

Like other information systems, the accounting system is a process in which data are input, recorded and stored in a data base, converted into summaries and tabulations, and transmitted as schedules, reports, and other types of information to users. Primary inputs to the accounting system are (1) costs of resources acquired and used by an organization, (2) prices of goods and services sold by an organization, and (3) management policies affecting these activities. Exhibit 2-6 illustrates the activities that occur in an accounting information system.

Exhibit 2-6   The Accounting Information System

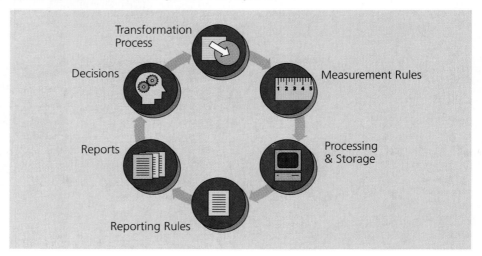

The source of data for the accounting information system is an organization's transformation process. The financing, investing, and operating activities of an organization are sources of data about resources that are acquired, transformed, and consumed.

Measurement rules are criteria that determine which attributes of the transformation process enter the accounting system. They identify data collected by the system. For example, the system records the cost paid for equipment when it is purchased, but it usually does not record the price the equipment could be sold for unless it is actually sold. The cost of equipment is recorded in the accounting system but not its size, or weight, or color. Measurement rules are designed to select those attributes of the transformation process important to users of the system. GAAP are a primary source of measurement rules for general purpose financial accounting information. Government authorities determine rules for tax and regulatory requirements, while managers develop their own measurement rules for management accounting information.

The transformation process activities measured by the accounting system are recorded in one or more accounting data bases where they may be stored and processed. **Accounting data bases often are books or computer files con-**

taining accounts in which an organization's transactions are recorded, summarized, and stored.

Each transaction is recorded by identifying the accounts affected by an event along with the amount of the transaction. Assume a company purchased equipment for $500. An account for the equipment would be increased by $500, and an account for cash would be decreased by $500. Each transaction is separated into two parts. Often these parts identify an exchange between a company and customers, suppliers, investors, and others. For example, a company receives equipment and gives up cash.

Recording a transaction is similar to recording a check in a check register. The date, purpose, and amount of a transaction are recorded. Data bases permit account data to be summarized in a variety of ways. An organization can determine how much money it spent in a particular period, the purposes for which money was used, as well as the other resources it acquired, when they were acquired, and how they were used. Users can obtain different types of information from the data base depending on their needs.

Reporting rules are criteria that determine the information that will be reported by an information system. Reporting rules determine which data from the data base will be presented for specific uses and the format of the presentation. Some users may need information about which products were sold and how much was sold in different locations or periods. Other users may need more general information about the total amount of sales for a company. GAAP also provide reporting rules for general purpose financial accounting information. Government authorities determine reporting rules for tax and regulatory information, while managers determine rules for reporting managerial accounting information.

Reports provide the information output by the accounting system. Reports may be available in a variety of forms, such as on paper or on a computer screen. The frequency of reports and amount of detail they contain will vary depending on the needs of users.

Users make decisions after evaluating reported information. Users employ decision rules to interpret information. For example, an investor might decide she will sell her stock in a company if profits reported by the company decline for three years in a row. The investor compares information about profits reported by the company with the decision rule and decides whether to sell or to continue to own the stock. Decision makers use accounting information to evaluate risk and return.

An important step in the system described in Exhibit 2-6 is the link between decisions and the transformation process. User decisions affect the organization. If investors decide not to buy stock in a company or if creditors decide not to lend it money, it may have difficulty obtaining the financial resources it needs to operate or to stay in business. If customers are concerned about the continued existence of a company, they may decide not to buy its products.

SELF-STUDY PROBLEM 2-2

N. Bonapart is purchasing manager for a company that sells suits. On April 12, Bonapart received the following weekly report for the suits purchased from one of the company's suppliers:

Merchandise Report
April 12, 1995

Fabric Type	Usual Order Quantity	Unit Cost	Last Order Date	Actual Number on Hand	Desired Number on Hand
Wool	12	$120	Feb. 15	5	10
Cotton	20	80	Mar. 2	8	15
Synthetic	25	75	Mar. 10	20	15

Bonapart immediately ordered another 12 wool suits and another 20 cotton suits from the manufacturer.

Required

1. What information did Bonapart consider in making his decision?
2. How does the Merchandise Report assist him with the decision? Does this report appear to meet his information needs for the decision he made?
3. What effect does the information in the report and Bonapart's decision have on the future of the company?

The solution to Self-Study Problem 2-2 appears at the end of the chapter.

PROCESSING ACCOUNTING INFORMATION

Objective 13
List the types of accounts included in an accounting information system.

This section describes the accounting data base in more detail. To understand the accounting system, you must understand how the system categorizes and stores data. As discussed in Chapter 1, an account is the basic unit for recording data in the accounting system. It contains a record of when an event occurred, the dollar amount of the increase or decrease in the account, and the balance of the account. Accounts are categories for storing data. The number of accounts will vary depending on the complexity and information needs of an organization.

The accounting information system in a business organization contains five types of accounts to record the transformation process:

1. Assets
2. Liabilities
3. Owners' Equity
4. Revenues
5. Expenses

These types of accounts capture all the transactions occurring in a company's transformation process. Accounts are like a filing system. A separate file exists for each account. The accounts are arranged by type to make them easy to locate and to make reports easier to prepare, as illustrated on page 69.

Assets, Liabilities, and Owners' Equity

Objective 14
Define assets, liabilities, and owners' equity

Assets **are resources purchased by an organization or otherwise under its legal control and available for its use in the future.** Included under the

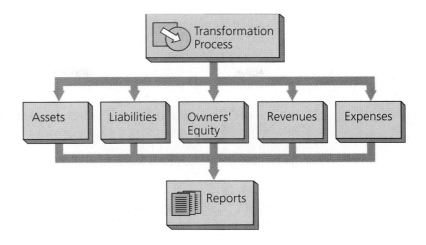

asset category are accounts for financial resources such as CASH and AC-COUNTS RECEIVABLE. *Accounts receivable* **are amounts of cash to be received in the future from credit sales to customers.** Assets also include accounts for physical resources such as INVENTORY (merchandise for sale), MATERIALS, SUPPLIES, EQUIPMENT, BUILDINGS, LAND, and NATURAL RESOURCES, and accounts for other resources that provide legal rights of value to an organization, such as PATENTS and TRADEMARKS. Asset accounts are increased when assets are acquired and are decreased when they are consumed or sold.

Learning Note	Account titles are shown in capital letters in the first few chapters to make them easier to identify.

Liabilities **are obligations owed by an organization to its creditors.** *Owners' equity* **is the amount of investment made by owners in a business.** Both direct investments and retained earnings are part of owners' investment. **Owners' equity for corporations usually is called** *stockholders'* **(or** *shareholders'***)** *equity*.

Some liability and owners' equity accounts result from financing activities. The balances of these accounts indicate the amount invested by creditors and owners in an organization. A separate account is used for each major source of financing. A liability account is increased when creditors provide money to an organization, and decreased when an organization repays amounts to creditors. Liability accounts include NOTES PAYABLE for amounts borrowed from banks and other lending institutions and BONDS PAYABLE for amounts borrowed by selling bonds. *Notes payable* **are contracts with creditors that affirm the borrower will repay the amount borrowed plus interest at specific dates. A** *bond* **is a certificate of debt issued by an organization.** Most bonds can be traded in securities markets. The balances of these accounts increase when a company borrows money and decrease when it repays money to its creditors.

Other liabilities are associated with operating activities. Examples include ACCOUNTS PAYABLE, amounts owed to suppliers; WAGES PAYABLE, amounts owed to employees; and TAXES PAYABLE, amounts owed to governmental authorities. Suppliers, employees, governments, and others become creditors of a company when they provide goods and services in exchange for future payments or benefits.

Owners' equity accounts are increased when owners invest money in an organization and when profits are reinvested. Various titles are used for owner investment accounts: PROPRIETOR'S CAPITAL for a proprietorship, PARTNERS' CAPITAL for a partnership, and CAPITAL STOCK or COMMON STOCK for a corporation. Profits earned by a proprietorship or partnership normally are recorded in the PROPRIETOR'S OR PARTNERS' CAPITAL accounts. **Profits earned by a corporation are recorded in an account normally called *RETAINED EARNINGS*.**

Learning Note

Capital refers to the investment in a company (liabilities and owners' equity) that equals the resources acquired from these investments (assets). Thus, a company's total capital is its total assets or its total liabilities and owners' equity.

An important relationship exists between assets and liabilities plus owners' equity. Liabilities and owners' equity provide financial resources to a business. Assets are resources acquired with the financial resources provided by creditors and owners. Therefore, a relationship exists between the amount of assets available to an organization and the amount of its liabilities and owners' equity.

The accounts included in the following illustration are examples of accounts for each category. Many other accounts could be listed. The right-hand side of this equation represents the claims of owners and creditors who provide resources to an organization. The left-hand side represents how managers have used investors' capital to acquire resources for the organization. **One of the primary accounting reports describes the relationship among assets, liabilities, and owners' equity. This report is called a *balance sheet* because of the balancing relationship (assets = liabilities + owners' equity).** Other names for the balance sheet are statement of financial position and statement of financial condition.

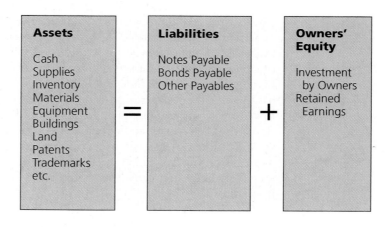

Amounts associated with asset, liability, and owners' equity accounts are for a *particular date*. A company may have assets of $500,000, liabilities of $200,000, and owners' equity of $300,000 on January 1, 1995. If an event occurs on January 2, 1995 that affects these accounts (for example, owners invest an additional $50,000), the account balances will differ between the two days. Accordingly, a report of assets, liabilities, and owners' equity for a company should identify the specific date of the report.

Revenues and Expenses

Objective 15
Define revenues and expenses.

As explained in Chapter 1, revenues result when a business creates resources by selling goods and services to customers. More technically, *revenues* **are increases in assets or decreases in liabilities from selling goods or services that constitute the primary operating activities of an organization.** To illustrate, the sale of merchandise for $1,200 results in the recognition of revenue of $1,200. The resource created is either cash or accounts receivable. Expenses result when an organization consumes resources in producing, selling, and delivering goods and services. More technically, *expenses* **are decreases in assets or increases in liabilities from producing and delivering goods or providing services that constitute the primary operating activities of an organization.** If the cost of merchandise sold is $800, the sale results in an expense of $800. The resource consumed is the merchandise from inventory delivered to a customer. Typical expenses include the cost of goods sold, wages, rent, insurance, utilities, and interest. Together, revenues and expenses measure the results of the operating activities of a business *for a period*.

Recall from Chapter 1 that an organization creates value when the total prices of goods and services it provides to its customers are greater than the total costs of the resources the organization consumed in producing and making available these goods and services. This created value is called profit, or net income. In the accounting system, profit is the difference between the amount of revenues and the amount of expenses a business records during a period. Thus, the profit earned by a business for a period can be expressed as follows.

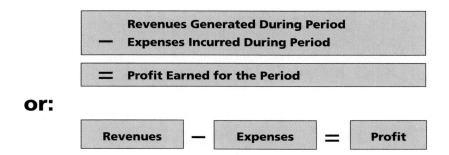

As discussed in Chapter 1, profit earned by a company for a period is reported on the income statement as net income. Revenues, expenses, and net income result from the operating activities of an organization for a fiscal period. A fiscal period can be any length of time: for example, the month of June, the first quarter of 1996, or the year ended September 30, 1995. When reporting revenues, expenses, and net income, it is important to know the fiscal period covered by the report. Reporting net income is something like reporting the score in a baseball game. You need to know the inning or if the game is over. Once a game is over, the score is reset to zero to start a new game. Net income is zero at the beginning of each new fiscal period. The amount at the end of the period is the score for the period.

Owners may receive cash payments from a business. This cash normally is a portion of the amount generated by a company's profitable operations. For corporations, these payments are called *dividends*. For proprietorships and partnerships, they are called *withdrawals*. The balances of PARTNERS' or PROPRIETOR'S CAPITAL and CASH are reduced when withdrawals are recorded. RETAINED EARNINGS and CASH are reduced when dividends are recorded.

Exhibit 2-7 describes relationships among types of accounts in a corporate accounting system.

Exhibit 2-7   Relationships Among Types of Accounts

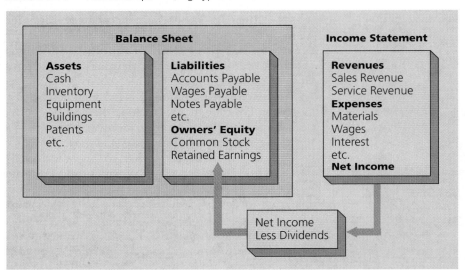

Net income measures the results of operating activities. The amount of net income not paid to owners increases the amount of retained earnings and is a source of financing used to acquire additional resources. These resources, in turn, are used in the operations of the organization to produce revenues. Thus, the five account categories used in the accounting data base record the results of the transformation process of an organization. A numerical example is useful to illustrate how the transformation process is reported by the accounting system.

An Illustration of an Accounting System

Assume you start a small merchandising business in a local shopping mall, selling electronic equipment. You invest $10,000 in the business from savings and borrow $40,000 by issuing a note payable to a local bank. These transactions occur on January 1. Because of these transactions, the following data would appear in the accounting data base after the events of January 1:

Assets =		Liabilities + Owners' Equity		+ (Revenues − Expenses)	
Cash	$50,000	Notes payable	$40,000	Sales	$0
		Investment by owner	10,000	Expenses	0
Total	$50,000	Total	$50,000	Total	0

On January 1, the only asset available to the business is cash. This resource resulted from the financing activities of the business. No investing or operating activities have occurred.

On January 2, you (a) purchase merchandise to sell and pay $20,000 in cash. This merchandise becomes an inventory of goods available for sale to customers. In addition, you (b) purchase equipment for $12,000 and (c) purchase supplies for $4,000. You pay cash for these items which leaves you with $14,000 of cash. Each of these three transactions exchanges one type of asset for another. The accounting data base would now contain the following data:

Assets =		Liabilities + Owners' Equity		+ (Revenues − Expenses)	
Cash	$50,000	Notes payable	$40,000	Sales	$0
	− 20,000 (a)	Investment by owner	10,000	Expenses	0
	− 12,000 (b)				
	− 4,000 (c)				
	14,000				
Inventory	20,000 (a)				
Equipment	12,000 (b)				
Supplies	4,000 (c)				
Total	$50,000	Total	$50,000	Total	$0

During January, you (d) sell at a price of $8,000 in cash, one-fourth of the inventory. The inventory sold had (e) a cost to you of $5,000. Because of the sales transaction, cash has increased by $8,000, and inventory has been reduced by $5,000. Therefore, the total amount of assets has increased by $3,000 to $53,000. Sales revenue of $8,000 has been recorded, representing the amount of the sale. Resources (inventory) amounting to $5,000 were consumed in the sale, resulting in an expense of $5,000. *Cost of goods sold* **is an expense representing the cost of inventory sold to customers.** The result of operating activities for January was net income of $3,000. Assuming you do not withdraw money from the business, the net income (f) is reinvested (as retained earnings) and becomes part of owners' equity. Both resources and finances have increased by $3,000 (assets = liabilities + owners' equity). This fact is apparent after net income has been added to retained earnings. After recording these transactions, the data base would contain the following:

Assets =		Liabilities + Owners' Equity		+ (Revenues − Expenses)	
Cash	$50,000	Notes payable	$40,000	Sales	$8,000 (d)
	− 20,000	Investment by		Cost of goods	
	− 12,000	owner	10,000	sold	− 5,000 (e)
	− 4,000	Retained earnings	3,000 (f)		
	8,000 (d)				
	22,000				
Inventory	20,000				
	− 5,000 (e)				
	15,000				
Equipment	12,000				
Supplies	4,000				
Total	$53,000	Total	$53,000	Net income	$3,000

Learning Note   Expenses are shown in the illustrations as negative values (−) because they represent decreases in net income. Thus, the third column in the above illustration identifies net income as revenues − expenses, and expenses are shown as negative values.

Exhibit 2–8 illustrates the flow of resources through the transformation process.

Exhibit 2-8   Accounting Information and the Transformation Process

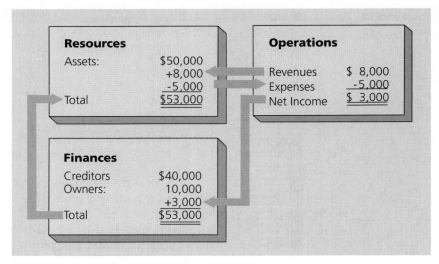

Note from the illustration that the three parts of the transformation process are interrelated. Investments by owners and creditors are used to acquire resources, and some of these resources are consumed in the operating activities of the business. Additional resources are generated from the sale of goods and services. The excess of resources generated from sales over resources consumed provides additional financing for the company. By identifying exchanges among contracting parties, amounts recorded in accounts are useful for determining whether the rights and responsibilities of those who contract with a company have been met. Also, these recorded amounts are a basis for formulating contracts that will affect the future allocation of scarce resources. The results of the transformation process can be summarized in the form of financial statements at the end of the fiscal period as shown in Exhibit 2-9:

Exhibit 2-9   A Financial Statement Summary of the Transformation Process

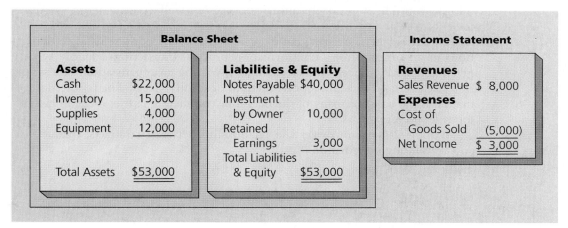

Balance Sheet		Income Statement
Assets	**Liabilities & Equity**	**Revenues**
Cash $22,000	Notes Payable $40,000	Sales Revenue $ 8,000
Inventory 15,000	Investment	**Expenses**
Supplies 4,000	by Owner 10,000	Cost of
Equipment 12,000	Retained	Goods Sold (5,000)
	Earnings 3,000	Net Income $ 3,000
	Total Liabilities	
Total Assets $53,000	& Equity $53,000	

Learning Note   Parentheses often are used to indicate subtraction in financial statements. Thus, cost of goods sold is shown in Exhibit 2-9 in parentheses to indicate that this amount is subtracted from sales revenue.

Revenues and expenses are accumulated during a fiscal period. Net income (revenues − expenses) is then transferred to retained earnings at the end of the period. Therefore, during a fiscal period:

Assets = Liabilities + Owners' Equity + (Revenues − Expenses)

After, net income is transferred to retained earnings at the end of a period:

Assets = Liabilities + Owners' Equity

because revenues and expenses have become part of owners' equity.

CONTRACTS AND ACCOUNTING INFORMATION

Objective 16
Explain the relationships among contracts, transactions, and accounting information.

Accounting provides information to help those who make decisions about organizations. These decisions result from contractual relationships among investors, managers, employees, suppliers, customers, and government agencies. Contracts specify services and resources each party to a contract is to provide and what each party can expect to receive in return. Contracts identify what is to be given and what is to be received. In other words, they identify how scarce resources will be allocated. Participants in these contracts need information to determine whether terms of the contracts are being met and to evaluate the risk and return they expect from contractual relationships. This information helps determine the terms of contracts and helps decision makers determine whether to participate in contractual relationships.

Information systems are an important mechanism for providing information needed by decision makers. They collect data, process them, and report resulting information. The accounting information system collects data about resources, their sources, and their uses. Data are stored in accounts classified as assets, liabilities, owners' equity, revenues, and expenses. The source of these data are transactions in an organization's transformation process. Transactions identify what is given and what is received in exchanges involving an organization. The system summarizes these data and reports them to decision makers. The reported information is the basis for many of the decisions contracting parties make in evaluating risk and return.

Exhibit 2-10 summarizes the relationship between contracts, transactions, and accounting information.

Exhibit 2-10   Contracts, Transactions, and Accounting Information

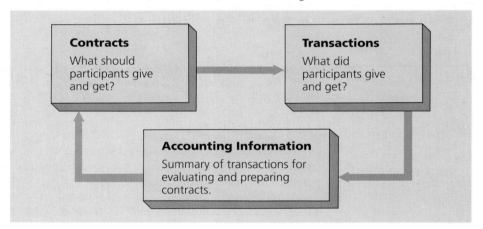

Contracts identify the rights and responsibilities of the contracting parties. Transactions identify actual exchanges among contracting parties and events resulting from their activities. Accounting summarizes the transactions and provides the parties information for evaluating whether contract terms have been met and for preparing future contracts.

The next chapter will examine how accounting measures exchanges and other events occurring in transactions. Accounting measurement rules provide a basis for forming and evaluating contracts.

SELF-STUDY PROBLEM 2-3

Harvey Benedict owns a restaurant called Eggs. He opened the restaurant in November by investing $20,000 from savings and borrowing $20,000 from a local bank. The following additional events occurred for Eggs during November:

1. Purchased equipment for $12,000.
2. Purchased food supplies for $9,000.
3. Sold $14,000 in meals for cash. The food used for the meals cost Eggs $6,000.
4. Paid the following expenses: employee wages of $3,000, rent of $1,000, utilities of $800, other expenses of $500.

Required

1. Use the format of Exhibit 2-8 to describe the data that would be contained in the accounting data base after recording transactions for November. Draw arrows to show the relationships among the accounts in the data base.
2. Identify the resources that are available to Eggs at the end of November. List each asset and the amount available.

The solution to Self-Study Problem 2-3 appears at the end of the chapter.

R E V I E W   *S u m m a r y   o f   I m p o r t a n t   C o n c e p t s*

1. Information needs of external and internal decision makers:
    a. Accounting provides information about the transformation of resources into goods and services.
    b. Managers interact with owners, creditors, suppliers, employees, governmental authorities, and customers as part of the transformation process. Exchanges and contracts among these parties require information to determine if the terms of the contracts are being met.
    c. Accounting assists investors by providing information for evaluating the risk and return expected from alternate investments.
    d. Managers have incentives to report information that reflects favorably on their performances. To limit management ability to manipulate reported information, managers prepare reports for external users that conform with generally accepted accounting principles. These reports are audited by independent accountants.
    e. Accounting measures the cost of resources used in the transformation process and compares the cost of resources consumed with the amount of resources created from the sale of goods and services.
    f. Managers make planning decisions in selecting strategies and policies for achieving organizational goals.
    g. Managers make control decisions when they evaluate an organization's operations to determine whether goals are being met and whether changes are needed to improve operations.

2. Primary functions of information systems:
    a. Management information systems help managers make decisions about an organization's operations. Also, it provides information managers report to other decision makers.
    b. The accounting information system is the specific part of a management information system responsible for (1) identifying the resources of an organization, (2) tracking the transformation of resources into goods and services sold to cus-

tomers, (3) determining the cost of resources used by the organization, and (4) reporting information about these activities to managers and external users.

3. The primary components of an information system are a data source; data; a process for collecting, storing, transmitting, and converting the data; information produced by the system; and decision makers who use the information.

4. Processing information in an accounting system:
    a. The source of data for the accounting information system is an organization's transactions. Measurement rules determine the types of data the system collects. Data are recorded in accounting data bases. These data are summarized and reported according to reporting rules that determine the content and format of reports. Users apply decision rules to determine how to interpret the information and make decisions. These decisions affect the organization.
    b. Transactions are recorded in the accounting data base in five account types: assets, liabilities, owners' equity, revenues, and expenses.
    c. Data recorded in accounts represent an organization's transformation process. These data identify exchanges and other activities useful for evaluating and forming contracts.

DEFINE   *Terms and Concepts Defined in This Chapter*

accounting information system	dividends	notes payable
accounts receivable	equity financing	owners' equity
assets	expenses	planning
audit	financial accounting	principal
balance sheet	generally accepted accounting	retained earnings
bond	principles (GAAP)	revenues
contracts	interest	stockholders' equity (shareholders'
control	investors	equity)
cost of goods sold	liabilities	withdrawals
data base	managerial accounting	
debt financing	(management accounting)	

SOLUTIONS

SELF-STUDY PROBLEM 2-1

1. **Exchanges and contracts between managers, owners, and creditors:** Owners and creditors exchange money with Floorshine for the right to receive cash in the future from the company. Contracts exist among managers, owners, and creditors. Managers contract with owners and creditors for money to acquire resources that will generate profits for the company and to employ the resources effectively and efficiently. Managers expect to be rewarded for their effectiveness and efficiency and owners and creditors expect a fair return on their investments. These contracting parties need information to assess how well managers have performed and to determine how much cash from the company's operations should be distributed

to each party. Managers, owners, and creditors decide whether the terms of contracts are being met. Companies hire independent auditors (CPAs) to examine the financial information provided by managers to owners and creditors to ensure its reliability.

2. **Exchanges and contracts between suppliers and managers:** Suppliers exchange goods and services with the company for the right to receive cash. Contracts between suppliers and managers require information to determine that the company receives the correct types and quantities of goods and services at the appropriate times. Also, information is needed to demonstrate the company has made timely payments for these goods and services.

3. **Exchanges and contracts between employees and managers:** Employees exchange labor services with the company for wages and benefits. Contracts between employees and managers describe the payments, benefits, and rights employees have negotiated with managers. Information is needed to demonstrate that labor services have been provided and employees have been treated fairly. The demands of employees for future wages and benefits depend, in part, on the profitability of the company. Employees and managers need information about the performance of the company to negotiate future contracts.

4. **Exchanges and contracts between customers and managers:** Customers exchange cash for goods and services provided by the company. Customers, such as retail stores, may receive the goods and pay for them later, say within 30 or 60 days. Managers expect to receive the payments when due. Contracts between customers and managers call for the delivery of goods to customers and payment to the company. Customers decide whether to continue to purchase the company's goods. The quality and costs of the goods and future prospects for obtaining the goods when needed are relevant information. Managers must decide whether to continue to extend credit to customers.

5. **Exchanges and contracts between governmental authorities and managers:** Governmental authorities monitor companies to determine if they are engaged in fair trade and labor practices. Managers provide information to demonstrate the company is conforming to governmental regulations. Governments provide services to companies in the form of police and fire protection, utilities, sanitation, and streets and roads. Companies pay taxes and fees for these services. Information is required to verify appropriate amounts of taxes and fees are being paid.

SELF-STUDY PROBLEM 2-2

1. Nap compared the actual number of suits of each type on hand with the minimum number of suits the company desires to have in stock.

2. The Merchandise Report provides information about the number of suits of each type on hand and the minimum number desired. This information is sufficient for Nap's decision and is available in a form that is easy to understand.

3. The decisions Nap makes determine when additional units will be ordered and how many units will be purchased to provide for future sales. This information system provides a means for the company to maintain an adequate amount of merchandise.

SELF-STUDY PROBLEM 2-3

1.

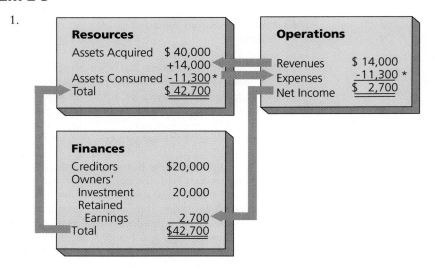

Resources

Assets Acquired	$ 40,000
	+14,000
Assets Consumed	-11,300 *
Total	$ 42,700

Operations

Revenues	$ 14,000
Expenses	-11,300 *
Net Income	$ 2,700

Finances

Creditors	$20,000
Owners' Investment	20,000
Retained Earnings	2,700
Total	$42,700

$11,300 = $6,000 supplies consumed + $3,000 wages + $1,000 rent + $800 utilities + $500 other expenses

2.

Cash from financing		$40,000
Cash from sales		14,000
Cash available in November		54,000
Cash used:		
for equipment	$12,000	
for supplies	9,000	
for wages	3,000	
for rent	1,000	
for utilities	800	
for other expenses	500	
Total cash used		(26,300)
Cash at end of November		27,700
Equipment acquired		12,000
Supplies acquired	9,000	
Supplies consumed	(6,000)	
Supplies at end of November		3,000
Total resources available at end of November		$42,700

EXERCISES

2-1. Write a short definition for each of the terms listed in the *Terms and Concepts Defined in This Chapter* section.

2-2.   Marjorie Morningstar has saved $5,000 that she would like to invest. She has been of-
fered two investment alternatives. One alternative is to purchase a five-year certificate of
deposit (CD) with a local bank. The CD will pay 7% interest annually. Another alternative is to purchase shares of a mutual stock fund. The earnings from the fund fluctuate
with stock prices and interest rates. The fund's return for the last five years has been: 8%,
3.5%, 9%, 6%, and 10%. Assuming the fund's return is expected to be about the same in
the next five years, compute the average annual return Marjorie should expect to receive.
Explain the concept of risk. Which investment alternative is riskier?

2-3.   Gazzooks Co. is preparing to raise $200,000 of additional capital for plant expansion. The
company currently has $200,000 of long-term debt and $400,000 of stock (80,000
shares) outstanding. The debt pays an annual return of 10% to creditors. The stock has
been paying an average return of about 14% to stockholders. The company has been advised that it could borrow the funds it needs at a 10% interest rate. To obtain the needed
money from stockholders, the company would need to sell 40,000 shares of new stock.
What factors should Gazzooks's management consider in making its decision? Assuming
the company expects to earn a 20% return on investment for the foreseeable future,
which form of financing would be most beneficial to current stockholders? Which form
would be most beneficial if the company fears a downturn in the economy and believes
it may earn only an 8% return on investment over the next few years?

2-4.   Read Exercise 2-3. If you were going to invest in Gazzooks Co. and you believed it was
likely to earn a return on investment of 20% per year, would you rather be a creditor or
stockholder? Would your answer differ if you expect the company to earn a return on investment of 8%?

2-5.   To encourage its managers to earn a profit for its stockholders, Plumtree Corp. pays a
bonus to top managers if the company earns at least a 12% return on investment each
year. The return is computed as the ratio of net income to total assets. To determine
whether a bonus will be paid, the board of directors requires management to submit an
income statement and balance sheet at the end of each fiscal year. Should the board and
stockholders be concerned about the reliability of the financial reports? What can they
do to make sure the reports faithfully represent the company's economic activities?

2-6.   Financing activities occur when organizations obtain financial resources to invest in
other resources and to engage in providing goods and services. Who makes financing decisions? List some factors that are important in making these decisions.

2-7.   Jean Roget does not understand the concept that an organization is a portfolio of individual resources. Explain to Jean why the selection of a portfolio is important to the success of a business. Use Wal-Mart as an example to explain the concept to Jean.

2-8.   Wendy Hu is considering two new products for her office products manufacturing business. One is a laser printer. Wendy has had numerous calls for the product, which will
compete with other known brands. The other product is a new computer projection
system that permits a presenter to display color computer images without the need of a
regular computer or projection system. The product would have little competition.
Wendy believes the market will be receptive to this product. What are some of the risks
inherent in the decision of whether to produce the two products?

2-9.   Identify each of the following as planning or control decisions:
   a.   Decision to buy a new production facility.
   b.   Decision to change the mix in a chemical compound used to produce a synthetic
        fiber to reduce the cost of the product.

c. Decision to replace a machine that is no longer serviceable.
d. Decision to retrain workers to enhance long-run productivity.
e. Decision to open retail stores in a foreign country.
f. Decision to count goods for sale to verify inventory records.
g. Decision to sell a production plant that is no longer profitable.
h. Decision to survey customers to determine their satisfaction with a company's products.

2-10. USX is a major manufacturer of steel. Identify a planning and a control decision USX managers would make concerning (a) financing, (b) investing, and (c) operating activities.

2-11. Vladimire Polyester owns a small men's clothing store. He buys from manufacturers and sells to customers. He employs a small sales force. His financing comes from operations and a loan from a local bank. He pays sales, payroll, and income taxes. He also pays for electricity, water, and telephone services to local utilities. List each of the parties involved in an exchange with Vladimire's store. For each, identify the resources or services that are exchanged. Also, briefly identify the type of information required to complete each exchange.

2-12. A telephone book is an example of an information system. How is the system designed to meet the needs of users? What limitations does the way a telephone book is organized place on its use?

2-13. Listed below are types of information available in a company's management information system. Identify those types that are likely to be provided by the accounting information system by writing "Yes" next to the item. Write "No" next to those that are not likely to be provided by the accounting system.
a. The cost of merchandise sold to customers.
b. The number of units of product 101A sold to customers on 12/24/97.
c. The number of customers who made purchases during April.
d. The dollar amount of sales for April.
e. The product styles available for sale.
f. The dates that sales are made to customers.
g. The number of machines used to produce product 12C.
h. The cost of the machines used to produce product 12C allocated to production in January.
i. The quality of goods produced in division B.
j. The cost of goods produced in division B.

2-14. Ink Co. is a small printing company owned and managed by B. Franklin. Franklin takes orders from customers and writes the pertinent information on an order form. One copy of the order form is given to the customer. Another copy is sent to the print shop where the job is completed. The shop operator writes a bill that lists the charges for materials and labor for the job. The bill is attached to the order and sent back to Franklin. Customers return for their orders and pay the amounts listed on the bills. The bills are marked PAID. A copy is given to the customer and a second copy is sent to the bookkeeper. The bookkeeper records the sale in the company's accounting records. Franklin deposits the cash or checks received from customers at a local bank. The bank deposit slip is sent to the bookkeeper for confirmation and to record available cash. Develop a simple diagram to chart the flow of documents and information through the system Ink Co. uses to process orders and record sales transactions.

2-15. K. Khan is owner of an import business, Khan's Imports. He wants to develop a management information system for his business. He is unclear about the particular role of an accounting system in a management information system. Explain to Khan the purpose of an accounting system and how it differs from other parts of a management information system.

2-16. Able Transportation Co. is a trucking company that delivers freight throughout the U. S. and Canada. One of the primary costs of the company's operations is gas used to fuel the trucks. Gas is purchased from commercial suppliers by truck operators. These purchases are accumulated and recorded to expense each month for each region based on the number of miles traveled in the region. The expenses are included in regional income statements prepared each month that top managers use to evaluate the performance of regional managers. Identify the components of the accounting information system represented by these events.

2-17. Louise McEnroe is a stockholder of National Concrete Co., a major supplier of building materials. Today, Louise received information that National Concrete sustained a major loss from operations during the most recent quarter and is expecting even bigger losses during the coming quarter. How can this information, available to Louise and other decision makers, affect the transformation process of National Concrete during the coming fiscal period?

2-18. Yashiko Takawa is a loan officer at a major bank. Hendrick Swindler recently applied for a small business loan for his dry cleaning company, Take 'Em to the Cleaners. As part of the application, Swindler was asked to provide an income statement and balance sheet for his company. These statements revealed impressive performance information. What concerns might Yashiko have about the information provided by Swindler? What actions might she take to relieve these concerns?

2-19. Dr. Ben Gazara is a general practitioner. Among his financial records is a list of patient charges and payments. An example record follows:

Patient: Ben Cartwright, One Ponderosa, Hollywood, CA 99931

Date	Charges	Payments	Balance Due
6/18/95	$150.00		$150.00
7/4/95		$150.00	0
9/23/95	437.50		437.50

How is this information system useful to Dr. Gazara's practice? What kinds of decisions could the system be used for?

2-20. Listed below are some of the accounts that appear in the accounting system of Hides, Inc., a manufacturer of leather goods. Indicate the type of account by writing asset, liability, owners' equity, revenue, or expense next to each account title.

a.	Accounts Receivable		i.	Cost of Goods Sold	
b.	Accounts Payable		j.	Interest Expense	
c.	Sales		k.	Notes Payable	
d.	Cash		l.	Retained Earnings	
e.	Leather Products		m.	Supplies Expense	
f.	Display Equipment		n.	Utilities Expense	
g.	Leather (materials)		o.	Wages Expense	
h.	Common Stock		p.	Wages Payable	

2-21. Balance sheet accounts for Fern's Florist are listed below at the end of a recent fiscal year. Prepare a schedule to demonstrate that assets = liabilities + owner's equity for the company.

Accounts Payable	$ 6,380
Accounts Receivable	4,150
Buildings	79,500
Cash	1,200
Equipment	12,750
Flowers and Plants	18,400
Notes Payable	61,000
Proprietor's Capital	47,820
Wages Payable	800

2-22. The following events occurred during December for Christmas Cookie Co.:
a. Consumed $60,000 of flour, sugar, and other ingredients for cookies sold.
b. Paid $97,500 for December wages.
c. Paid $24,000 for utilities consumed in December.
d. Sold $234,000 of cookies, receiving $187,500 of cash. The remainder was an increase in Accounts Receivable.
e. Consumed $15,000 of supplies and other items.
Prepare an income statement and a schedule showing resources acquired and consumed for December for the company.

2-23. Amora Mudala opened a music store in a local mall, selling CDs and tapes. She invested $60,000 in the business and borrowed $90,000 from a local bank. The following additional events occurred during April, the first month of operations:
a. Paid cash for equipment costing $37,500.
b. Purchased an inventory of CDs and tapes for $90,000 in cash.
c. Sold one-third of the CDs and tapes for a cash sales price of $60,000.
d. Paid expenses:

Employee wages	$7,500
Rent	12,000
Utilities	3,000
Interest	900

e. Recorded an expense for use of equipment for month of $750.

Use the following format to describe the data that would be contained in the accounting data base after recording these transactions for April.

RESOURCES: OPERATIONS:
Assets Acquired: Revenues:
Assets Consumed: Expenses:
Total Assets   Net Income

FINANCES:
Creditors:
Owner's Investment:
Retained Earnings:
Total Finances

2-24. Listed below are transactions for Perez Manufacturing Co. For each transaction, describe the phases of the transformation process that are involved and how each phase is affected by the transaction. Show expenses as negative amounts. The first transaction is described as an example.

a.   Juanita Perez invested $10,000 in the company.

	Assets		Liabilities and Owners' Equity		Revenues and Expenses	
a.	Cash	+$10,000	Owners' Investment	+$10,000		

b.   Sale of goods for $30,000 on credit (increase in Accounts Receivable).
c.   Purchase of raw materials for $45,000. Cash is paid.
d.   Payment of wages for services provided, $7,500.
e.   Paid back part of loan to a bank (Notes Payable), $1,500.
f.   Purchase of equipment for $4,000 on credit (increase in Accounts Payable).
g.   Paid utilities company for services consumed, $600.

2-25. Har-Mone Co. is a producer of perfumes and cosmetics. The following changes were recorded in the company's accounting records during October. For each item, describe the transaction that would have resulted in the record. The first item is described as an example.

a.   Cash increased $15,000; Owners' Investment increased $15,000.
     The owners invested $15,000 in the company.
b.   Accounts Receivable increased $22,500; Sales Revenue increased $22,500.
c.   Equipment increased $11,250; Cash decreased $11,250.
d.   Materials increased $13,500; Accounts Payable increased $13,500.
e.   Supplies expense increased $2,250; Supplies decreased $2,250.
f.   Cash increased $7,500; Notes Payable increased $7,500.
g.   Inventory decreased $6,750; Cost of Goods Sold increased $6,750.

2-26. Edgar Feinstein is considering an investment of $20,000 in either of two companies. Summary financial statement information is provided for each company below. From an analysis of the information presented, what advice would you give Edgar about which company to invest in?

	Arsino Chemical Co.	Basalt, Inc.
Balance Sheet:		
Assets	$3,000,000	$40,000,000
Liabilities	2,000,000	24,000,000
Equity	1,000,000	16,000,000
Income Statement:		
Revenues	$800,000	$4,800,000
Expenses	440,000	2,800,000
Net Income	360,000	2,000,000

PROBLEMS

PROBLEM 2-1   Risk and Return

Carlotta Icon is considering a major investment in the common stock of one of the companies listed below. She has asked your assistance in determining the comparative risk and return of these investments. Your extensive financial knowledge leads you to suggest that past earnings performance could be evaluated as a potential indicator of future performance. Comparative historical information is presented below for both firms.

(amounts in millions of dollars)	19A	19B	19C	19D	19E
USX					
Net income	$ 8	$ 9	$10	$11	$13
Total assets	61	59	68	73	70
TWA					
Net income	$42	$(5)	$13	$31	$(23)
Total assets	62	63	64	65	66

Required   Compute (a) return as the ratio of net income to total assets for each year for each company and (b) the average ratio of net income to total assets over the five years for each company. (c) Compare the returns for the two companies. Write a brief memo to Carlotta Icon describing your findings as to comparative risk and return of these two firms. (d) Which firm would you recommend to Carlotta? Why?

PROBLEM 2-2   Identifying Information Desired from the Accounting System

Tree-Top Airlines began as a small commuter line 10 years ago but has grown into the seventh largest airline in America with a strong regional route system. In addition, it has many routes to America's commercial centers and a few selected international routes. Tree-Top has a fleet of 300 planes and approximately 9,000 employees who (by company policy) must all be stockholders. The company grew rapidly after airline deregulation using a clever combination of long-term financing from banks and leasing companies and is now the largest employer in its home state. Its stock is widely traded on the American Stock Exchange. In light of the company's rapid growth, the controller is performing a detailed and complete reevaluation of the firm's accounting information system.

While the system has been updated and improved constantly through the years, the controller is concerned whether it is providing useful information to the appropriate parties.

Required   (a) Identify the parties that have an economic interest in Tree-Top Airlines. (b) For each party, identify the type of information that should be provided by Tree-Top's accounting information system.

PROBLEM 2-3   Compensation Arrangements for Managers

You are a member of the executive compensation committee of the board of directors of Fresh Catch Food Co. Your committee has been directed to investigate the feasibility of adopting an incentive compensation plan for the company's top-level management. Included in this group is the CEO, the president, the controller, and the vice presidents of finance, marketing, and manufacturing. The board of directors has requested that you consider the following options and prepare a recommendation for the full board of directors.

1. Year-end cash bonuses based on exceeding sales targets for the year

2. Year-end cash bonuses based on exceeding profit targets for the year

3. Free shares of company stock if the stock price goes up by a target amount over a three-year period

Related to your full-time executive position in another firm, you recently attended a seminar where it was claimed that executive compensation plans can sometimes affect the content of financial reports provided to owners. The chair of the executive compensation committee has asked you to write a brief memo to the rest of the committee describing the potential effects and problems you see in a compensation plan.

Required   Prepare that memo (in good form). Be sure to include examples where possible.

PROBLEM 2-4   Planning and Control Decisions

Connie Thompson is manager of the Long-Term Care Division of the Cooper County Health Department. With its $150 million budget, the division is responsible for provision of long-term care services (often in nursing homes) to the elderly and physically disabled. The division contracts with providers for nursing home care, adult day care, in-home visiting nurses, and a variety of other long-term care services. In her position of manager, Connie makes a variety of planning and control decisions on a daily basis. On a recent Tuesday morning, Connie sat at her desk with the following issues and decisions needing attention:

1. Two months ago, the child of a nursing home patient filed a complaint alleging mistreatment of his parent. An investigation revealed substance to the complaint and several remedial actions have been developed. Connie must decide which actions to require of the nursing home.

2. For nearly a year, a task force in Connie's department has been developing an experimental alternative to nursing home care. It will require a waiver of the federal Medicaid rules but has the potential to provide better quality care at a lower cost to taxpayers. Connie must decide whether to proceed with this initiative via a formal request to Washington, DC.

3. Budget problems caused the state legislature to reduce funding for a certain program. A citizens committee has recommended priorities to Connie for trimming the program. Connie must make and announce the final decision today.

4. Connie is contemplating engagement of a consultant to conduct an evaluation of her division. Such an evaluation would judge whether the goals and objectives of her unit are being carried out in an effective and efficient manner.

5. Connie's immediate superior has proposed moving a service unit currently located in another division to the Long-Term Care Division. The unit is not operating effectively, because of a variety of problems within the unit. Connie must provide a written recommendation to her supervisor by tomorrow about how this new unit could be integrated into the work of her division.

Required   (a) Discuss the differences between a planning decision and a control decision. (b) Specify whether each issue described above is a planning decision or a control decision. Briefly justify your answer.

PROBLEM 2-5   The Components of an Information System

The Church of Inner Peace is a local congregation of about 500 members and regular attendees. At each church service, an offering is taken. Nearly all contributions are by check. At the end of each service, the head ushers, Fred Westlund and Dale Chapetta, turn over the proceeds to the church treasurer, Margaret Gorsey. Margaret makes a confidential record of each identifiable contribution (for year-end tax statements to contributors), totals the amount received, and deposits it. The deposit slip is given to the church bookkeeper, Zenia Flowers. Zenia enters the deposit in the church's ledger each week. At the end of the month, Zenia summarizes all accounts and prepares a Statement of Contributions, Expenditures, and Cash on Hand. This document is distributed to members of the congregation.

Required   Prepare a diagram like the one in Exhibit 2-4 that shows the components of an information system. For each component of the system, identify the persons, documents, or events from the narrative above that correspond to the component.

PROBLEM 2-6   Entering Data into an Accounting Information System

Melocky Beach Co. sells a variety of trinkets and do-dads to tourists on the beach. Teenagers are paid 20% of the sales price to hawk the wares up and down the beach and are paid daily. The company was formed only recently and given approval by the local city council to operate this business. The following events are the first in the company's short history:

1. The company was formed when José Melocky contributed $1,150 to the firm.

2. The Bank of Acapulco loaned the firm $3,500 in exchange for the firm's one-year note payable.

3. Merchandise costing $3,000 was purchased on 30-day credit from Cabo Co.

4. Goods costing $750 were sold to tourists at prices totaling $2,250 in cash, and the teenagers were paid their commissions.

5. A payment of $1,000 was made to Cabo Co.

6. Goods costing $950 were sold for cash totaling $2,750, and the teenagers were paid their commissions.

7. A payment of $1,400 was made to the Bank of Acapulco. (Ignore interest.)

8. José Melocky withdrew $1,000 from Retained Earnings for personal uses.

Assume the company uses the following set of accounts:

Cash
Payable to Cabo
Sales
Retained Earnings
Inventory
Notes Payable
Cost of Sales
Investment by Owner
Commissions Expense

Required (a) For each event above, identify whether it is a financing activity, an investing activity, or an operating activity. (b) Determine how each event affects the accounting data base. Show the account balances that should appear in the accounting data base after each of the events above has been recorded. Event (1) is done for you as an example.

	Assets =		Liabilities + Owners' Equity		+ (Revenues − Expenses)
1.	Cash	1,150	Investment by Owner	1,150	

PROBLEM 2-7 Entering Data into an Accounting Information System

Randy had a hard time finding a summer job when he went home from college this summer, so he decided to go into business for himself mowing lawns. He had the following business activities during the month of June.

1. Used $150 of his own money and borrowed $525 from his father to start the business.

2. Spent $150 to purchase a used lawnmower, an additional $56.25 for a lawn edger, $37.50 for a wheelbarrow, and $18.75 for hand clippers and shears.

3. Bought a (very) used pickup truck for $600 from Bettis Motors. He made a $187.50 down payment and signed a note payable for the balance.

4. During the first two weeks, Randy performed $225 of lawnmowing services. Customers paid $150 of this in cash and promised the remaining payment the next week (use Accounts Receivable). He paid out $30 for gas, oil, and other supplies.

5. Collected the remaining amount of cash from prior lawnmowing.

6. During the last half of the month, Randy performed $382.50 of lawnmowing services. All but $37.50 was collected in full at the completion of each respective job. He paid out $56.25 for gas, oil, and other supplies.

7. Paid back one-half of the amount he had borrowed from his father.

8. Randy withdrew $75 from Retained Earnings for his personal use.

Randy knew from taking an accounting class at college that the following accounts would be needed to keep track of his business activities.

Cash
Note Payable—Dad
Sales Revenue
Accounts Receivable
Note Payable—Bettis Motors
Expenses
Equipment
Investment by Owner
Retained Earnings

Required   (a) Determine how each event affects the accounting data base. Transaction (1) is done for you as an example. (b) Prepare a financial report (as of the end of June) that lists the firm's resources and finances. List the resources on the left side and the finances on the right. Total each list to show that they are equal in amount. (c) Prepare a financial report that summarizes operations for the month of June. List revenues first and then expenses.

	Assets =		Liabilities + Owners' Equity		+ (Revenues − Expenses)
1.	Cash	675	Notes Payable—Dad	525	
			Investment by Owner	150	

PROBLEM 2-8   Reconstructing Events from Information in the Accounting Data Base

Horace and Hortense have just established a home-cleaning service. They charge $11.25 per hour per person and are usually paid by check upon completion of the job. For certain customers, they send a bill immediately and are paid promptly by return mail. Their out-of-pocket expenses are rather low; usually only cleaning supplies and transportation. They use a simple accounting system in which they update their account balances after each transaction. Listed below are their updated account balances after each of the ten transactions that occurred during their first week in business.

	Cash	Accounts Receivable	Supplies	Notes Payable	Investment by Owner	Retained Earnings	Sales Revenue	Expenses
a.	$ 75				$75			
b.	187			$187				
c.	−56		$56					
d.	225	$45					$270	
e.			−30					−$30
f.	−37		37					
g.	−120			−120				
h.	45	−45						
i.	300	37					337	
j.			−45					−45
k.	−375					−$375		
l.	37	−37						

Required Describe each of the firm's first ten transactions, and specify the amounts involved.

PROBLEM 2-9   Ethics and Accounting Systems

Charlie Clancy owns an appliance store that sells major appliances such as washers and refrigerators. Charlie obtained financing for his business from a local bank. In January of each year, the bank requires Charlie to prepare and submit an income statement and balance sheet for the past year. Charlie also prepares his personal income tax return at this time and includes the profits earned from his appliance business.

Charlie purchases appliances from a major manufacturer throughout the year. Because of inflation, the costs of the appliances to Charlie typically increase during the year. Often the units purchased at the end of the year cost 10% to 15% more than those purchased at the beginning of the year.

In preparing his financial statements for the bank, Charlie uses the costs of the earliest units from his stock in computing Cost of Goods Sold for the year. These costs are subtracted from revenues to compute net income on the income statement. The last units purchased are reported as part of Inventory on the balance sheet. In preparing his tax return, Charlie subtracts from revenues the costs of the most recent units purchased to compute taxable income.

Required   (a) What are the financial implications of the measurement rules Charlie uses for his financial statements and income tax return? (b) Are there ethical problems with Charlie's decisions about measurement rules?

PROBLEM 2-10   Ethics and Accounting Systems

(a) Henry Bradshaw owns a furniture store. In January 1997, Henry applied for a loan from a local bank because of a cash shortfall he has been facing. As part of the loan application, the bank required Henry to submit an income statement for the most recent year, ended in December 1996. Henry owes a sizable sum to a furniture manufacturer for merchandise he purchased and received in 1996. Much of the merchandise was sold in 1996. Henry delayed payment for the merchandise until January 1997. Also, he did not record an expense for the cost of the merchandise sold until January, though he recorded the sales as revenue in 1996.

Required   What are the financial and ethical implications of Henry's actions?

(b) Alley Smith is Budget Director for a midwestern state. The state has been facing a financial crisis. It is required by law to spend no more than the total revenues it collects during its fiscal year, which ends on September 30. State employees are paid on the last day of each month. The wages are recorded in the accounting system as an expenditure when paid. Because of the current financial crisis, the state is in danger of spending more than the revenues it expects to collect during the current year. To help solve the problem, Alley changed the state's accounting system in September of the current year so employee wages are not recorded until the first of the month. Therefore, September wages will be recognized in October of the next fiscal year.

Required   What are the financial and ethical implications of Alley's actions?

PROBLEM 2-11   Design and Use of an Information System

Carmen Miranda is owner of a company that manufactures wax fruit, Miranda Fruit Co. The fruit is sold to hat makers, florists, and novelty shops. The fruit is sold in lots of 100 and is manufactured in three sizes: small, medium, and large. Orders are received from customers by mail or phone. Customers indicate the size and quantity of product they desire. Orders are filled and shipped within 3 days. A bill is shipped with the order. Customers are expected to pay in full within 30 days of the billing date. Delinquent accounts are noted for a second billing. Those that are over 60 days old are marked so no additional orders are accepted until the account has been paid. The following account balances were outstanding at the end of March 1997:

Company	Amount	Due Date
Tropical Hats	$ 9,000	March 10
Penway Florists	4,000	April 4
Hurley Hats	12,000	April 12
Oscar's Novelties	7,000	April 20

Lots are priced at $100 for large, $85 for medium, and $75 for small. The following transactions occurred during April:

April   3   Received payment of $4,000 from Penway Florists.
7   Received order from Hurley Hats for 20 lots of large, 30 lots of medium, and 10 lots of small.
9   Shipped Hurley order with bill for $5,300.
10   Billed Tropical Hats for overdue account.
12   Received payment from Hurley Hats for $12,000.
18   Received order from Penway Florists for 10 lots of large, 25 lots of medium, and 40 lots of small.
19   Received payment of $7,000 from Oscar's Novelties.
21   Shipped order to Penway with bill for $6,125.
24   Received payment of $5,000 from Tropical Hats.
28   Received payment from Penway for total amount owed.

Required   Design a form as part of an information system Miranda Fruit Co. can use to keep track of its customers' orders and payments. Record data for each of the transactions for April using the form.

PROBLEM 2-12   Recording Transactions and Calculating Value

Assume that you began a small business by (a) investing $10,000 and (b) borrowing $30,000 from a bank. You (c) purchased equipment for $25,000 cash and (d) purchased merchandise for $12,000 on credit. During the first month of operations, your company (e) sold merchandise for $24,000 in cash. (f) Credit sales were $3,000. (g) The cost of merchandise sold during the month was $10,000. By the end of the month, (h) $8,000 had been paid to the supplier of the merchandise. In addition, you (i) repaid $300 of the amount borrowed from the bank. You (j) withdrew $800 from the business for personal use.

Required   (1) Prepare a simple accounting system and record the effects of the transactions (a–j) for the first month. (2) Prepare a schedule in good form to explain the amount of resources available to the company at the end of the month. (3) Prepare a schedule in good form to explain the amount of value created during the month.

PROBLEM 2-13   Multiple-Choice Overview of this Chapter

1. The value of accounting information is greatest when it:
   a.   has been obtained at low cost.
   b.   meets the needs of users.
   c.   supports expansion of the business into new products or markets.
   d.   reports favorable results allowing dividends and bonuses to be paid.

2. An investor is evaluating the potential investments described below. Past financial results of these two companies are judged to be indicative of future returns and risk.

Year	Ball Bearing Profits	Beach Ball Profits
A	$ 8	$ 3
B	9	22
C	10	7

   Which investment appears to have the highest return and highest risk from the information provided?

	Highest return	**Highest risk**
a.	Ball Bearing	Ball Bearing
b.	Ball Bearing	Beach Ball
c.	Beach Ball	Ball Bearing
d.	Beach Ball	Beach Ball

3. Which combination below correctly matches the type and audience of accounting information?

	Information prepared primarily for decision makers inside the firm	**Information prepared primarily for decision makers outside the firm**
a.	managerial accounting	managerial accounting
b.	financial accounting	managerial accounting
c.	managerial accounting	financial accounting
d.	financial accounting	financial accounting

4. The primary difference between a planning decision and a control decision is that:
   a. investors make planning decisions while management makes control decisions.
   b. planning decisions involve dollars while control decisions involve qualitative factors.
   c. planning decisions involve revenues while control decisions involve expenses.
   d. planning decisions are developmental while control decisions are corrective.

5. Accounting information is developed by an organization to assist its managers in dealing with which of the following?

	Suppliers	Government officials
a.	Yes	Yes
b.	Yes	No
c.	No	Yes
d.	No	No

6. Which of the following is a true statement concerning an information system?
   a. It must be computerized to function efficiently.
   b. It increases risk but decreases expected return.
   c. It eliminates the need for an audit.
   d. It creates information from data.

7. Management information systems supply information:

	Needed by managers for internal decision making	That managers must provide to persons outside the firm
a.	Yes	Yes
b.	Yes	No
c.	No	Yes
d.	No	No

8. The accounting information system used by Ombozzi Medical Supply keeps track of the cost of each inventory item, its purchase date, and its supplier. No record is kept of the transportation company that delivered the goods. These facts deal most closely with which component of the accounting information system?
   a. reporting rules
   b. transformation process
   c. measurement rules
   d. decision processes

9. Liability and owners' equity accounts usually arise from which type of activities?
   a. investing activities
   b. financing activities
   c. operating activities
   d. manufacturing activities

10. Expresso Delivery Service purchased a new delivery truck for $21,000 by making a $4,000 cash payment and giving a $17,000 note payable to the seller. How were each of the following affected when this event was recorded in the firm's accounting information system?

Assets	Liabilities
a. increased	increased
b. no change	increased
c. increased	decreased
d. decreased	increased

C A S E S

CASE 2-1   Designing an Accounting Information System

For about a year, Frank Poppa has been operating a hot dog stand in the parking lot of a major discount retailer in a suburban area. The stand appears to be a pushcart but is actually a small trailer which is towed from home each day. Frank cleverly designed the stand to include storage compartments, a propane gas cooker, insulated coolers for canned sodas, and plenty of space for condiments, napkins, and the like. What started out as a "weekend gig" to pick up a few extra bucks has turned into a full-time vocation. Frank soon found that on a hot summer day, he could easily take in more than $1,000 from sales of a full line of fancy hot dogs and cold sodas.

About four months ago, he decided to expand to more locations. He found that large discount retailers were quite happy to provide him adequate space near the front door because customers enjoyed the convenience and the stand helped build traffic for the retailer. Frank formed Poppa's Dogs Co. and negotiated contracts with several retailers to provide pushcart operations outside their stores. The contracts generally call for Poppa's Dogs to pay a location fee to the retailer plus 3% of the pushcart's sales.

Frank plans to be very careful when hiring the people necessary to operate the five new pushcart locations. He is confident he can assess good moral character and avoid hiring anyone who would take advantage of him. Frank will have to spend about $3,000 for each new pushcart and related equipment. In addition, he will have to finance an inventory of hot dogs, condiments, and sodas for each location. A local bank has agreed to provide financing.

Until now, Frank has maintained an informal accounting system consisting of an envelope full of receipts and his personal checking account. The system has served him O.K. so far, but he is finding that more and more he is getting his personal financial activities confused with those of his business. Frank is positive the business is profitable because he seems to have more money left at the end of the month than he did when he was working full time as an auto mechanic. He has decided he needs a better accounting system and has decided to consult with a CPA he knows to see what she might recommend.

Required   What information does Frank obtain from his current accounting system? What information should Frank be able to obtain from a new accounting system? Make recommendations to Frank regarding how he can improve his accounting system and identify a chart (list) of accounts that you would expect to find in Frank's new accounting system. For each account, identify whether it is an asset, liability, owners' equity, revenue, or expense.

CASE 2-2   Determining Measurement Rules for an Accounting System

(Read Case 2-1 before reading the additional information below.) In general, Frank expects the daily operations of Poppa's Dogs to go as follows. All carts will be parked at his home each evening. Each morning, operators will pick up a trailer and a supply of hot dogs, condiments, sodas, and a change fund. At the end of each day the trailers, remaining inventory, supplies, and the day's receipts will be returned to Frank. Operators will be paid each Friday.

Required   (a) Describe what a measurement rule is in relation to an accounting information system. (b) For each event that follows, recommend and defend a measurement rule. Also, specify what information this measurement rule would exclude from the accounting data base. (c) Identify two additional events that are likely for the company and construct a measurement rule to fit those situations.

1.   On Wednesday, June 5, 19A, five gallons of relish ($5.50) and five gallons of mustard ($3.86) were ordered on credit from Wallace Food Supply. The goods were picked up that same day at 4:00 p.m.

2.   On Thursday, June 6, 19A, a hot dog (Cajun style—$1.75) and can of soda (7 UP—$0.50) were sold for cash to Julie Wyndross at 11:15 a.m.

3.   On Friday, June 7, 19A, a new employee (Pat Carlucci) was hired to operate push-cart #6 at Home Center Discount Club.

CASE 2-3   Designing an Information System for Large Quantities of Data

Your client, Gary Gearshift, has unexpectedly obtained national publicity and is suddenly a hot property in the entertainment world with his music played on the Oilpan Flute. As his agent, you are arranging for a 3-cassette package of his "best loved favorites" to be marketed on late-night cable TV. After consultation with experts you reasonably expect that you will receive up to 1,000 telephone orders per day for approximately 30 days. After that, you expect orders to fade away to near zero.

Given the tremendous outpouring of national enthusiasm for this fad, you will charge a premium price ($45) and offer three easy monthly payments of $15 each. There will be a separate charge for shipping and handling ($6 due with the first installment) and 6% sales tax on each order (also due with the first installment). A deal has been made with a music production company to provide 3-cassette packages to you for $5 each. They can be ordered in batches of 500 and will be delivered in 7 days. You decide to build an accounting system to keep track of this venture.

Required   (a) List the information you would like the accounting system to provide you (e.g., total sales for each day). Briefly explain why the information is important. (b) Design an information system that will produce the information you need. Identify the components of the system (what are the primary inputs, processes, and outputs of the system?).

PROJECTS

PROJECT 2-1   Interviewing a Decision Maker

Select an organization in your community that interests you. This might be a business firm, a government agency, or some other not-for-profit organization. Make an appointment for an interview with the owner, general manager, or a department manager. Ask the decision maker how he or she uses financial information to make decisions in the job. Every organization and manager is different but, in general, you want to understand the types of decisions the manager has to make and whether financial information guides any of those decisions. Further, you want to learn how financial information affects decisions that need to be made. Ask the manager to give you some specific examples of decisions that were affected by financial information. Another way of addressing the issue is to ask which management decisions would be tougher (or riskier) to make if there were no financial information available to the decision maker. Write a short report from the information and examples you obtained in your interview.

PROJECT 2-2   Comparing Risk and Return

Go to the library and find the latest edition of *Moody's Industrial Manual*. From the alphabetical index, select three companies, including at least one that operates in the state where you are attending college. Estimate risk and return for each company for the most recent 10 years. Estimate return by computing the ratio of net income to total assets for each year. Prepare a graph of the returns for 10 years for the three companies. (You will need to use several different years' editions of *Moody's* to obtain the data you need.) Assume you are advising your instructor about potential investments. Write a memo evaluating the companies you have chosen. Include your graph and provide an assessment of the relative returns and risks of the companies. Recommend one for investment.

PROJECT 2-3   Compensation Contracts with Managers

Select three companies whose annual reports are in your library. Try to find one company whose name starts with the same letter as your first name, a second company (using the first letter of your middle name), and a third company (using the first letter of your last name). Find the most recent annual report for each of your three companies. In the back half of each annual report you should find the financial statements. After the financial statements will be several Notes to the Financial Statements. They generally include important information explaining specific items on the financial statements. Carefully read through these notes to find any information about executive compensation. Common forms of executive compensation that are disclosed in the notes include bonus plans, profit-sharing plans, and stock option plans. Make a photocopy of this information and label it with the company's name. If any of your three companies doesn't have disclosures about executive compensation, substitute another firm having the same first letter in its name. Examine the information in the notes. Write a memorandum to your instructor that compares and contrasts the practices of the three different firms. List any questions these disclosures bring to mind. Attach the photocopies to your memo.

PROJECT 2-4   Corporate Balance Sheets

Select three companies whose annual reports are in your library. Try to find one company that is a manufacturer, one that is a retailer, and one that is a utility. Find the most recent annual report for each of your three companies. In the back half of each annual report you should find the financial statements. Find the statement with the title Balance Sheet (often Consolidated Balance Sheet) or Statement of Financial Position. List the major resources reported for each company for the most recent year. Which resources appear to be most important for each company? Also, list the major liabilities and the total amount of stockholders' equity. For each company compute the ratio of total assets to total liabilities. Compare the ratios for the three companies. What reasons can you provide for why different companies rely on different types of resources and financing?

PROJECT 2-5   Planning and Control Decisions

Examine recent issues of business publications (the *Wall Street Journal*, *Business Week*, *Fortune*, etc.). Find three articles or news items that describe management planning decisions. Also, find three that describe management control decisions. Briefly summarize the decisions described in the articles. Note the publication, date, and page number for each article.

Chapter 3

Accounting Measurement

Chapter 1 described organizations as a transformation process, which is the primary source of data for the accounting system. Chapter 2 examined information needs of decision makers that affect the development of information systems, and introduced the accounting information system as illustrated below. This chapter examines some fundamental concepts of accounting measurement. These concepts guide the development of measurement rules in the accounting information system. The concepts determine which events in the transformation process are recorded by the accounting system and when they are recorded.

The Accounting Information System

Transformation Process

Decisions

Measurement Rules

Reports

Processing & Storage

Reporting Rules

Major topics covered in this chapter include:

- Accounting measurement of the transformation process.
- The importance of time in accounting measurement.
- The relationship between accrual and cash measurements.
- The purpose of accrual basis accounts.

Once you have completed this chapter, you should be able to:

1. Demonstrate the use of an accounting system to record financing, investing, and operating activities.
2. Summarize the information an accounting system provides about a transformation process.
3. Explain the implications of the going concern principle for the transformation process.
4. Explain the implications of periodic measurement for accounting information.
5. Explain why change in cash is not a valid measure of an organization's performance for a period.
6. Explain why cash flow from operating activities is not a complete measure of an organization's performance for a period.

7. Distinguish the accrual basis of accounting from the cash basis and explain why the accrual basis is used.
8. Reconcile cash and accrual measures of operating activities.
9. Identify information reported by an accrual basis accounting system.
10. Explain the purposes of different account types in an accrual accounting system.

ACCOUNTING FOR THE TRANSFORMATION PROCESS

Objective 1
Demonstrate the use of an accounting system to record financing, investing, and operating activities.

The accounting information system provides a means of recording, summarizing, and reporting an organization's transformation process. This process consists of (1) **financing activities**: the acquisition and management of financial resources, (2) **investing activities**: the investment of financial resources in other resources, and (3) **operating activities**: the use of resources to produce, sell, and distribute goods and services.

The complexity of an organization's accounting system depends on the complexity of the organization's transformation process. Factors such as the size of the organization, the number of geographical locations in which it operates, the number of different products it manufactures and sells, and the types of financing it uses affect the size and complexity of the accounting system. Thus, a small business, like a hair styling salon, requires a relatively simple accounting system, while a chain of Wal-Mart stores requires a relatively complex system. A multinational company like Ford Motor Company is extremely complex. Accounting systems may need to accommodate language, currency, and regulatory differences among countries. The information needs of decision makers increase with the size and complexity of an organization. An organization's accounting system becomes more complex as the information needs of decision makers increase.

Though some accounting systems are more complex than others, most accounting systems have similar objectives and use similar procedures. As a basis for discussion, consider the transformation cycle of a small business, Produce Transit Co., owned by Y. Lemon. The company contracts with a chain of grocery stores in Michigan to provide them with fresh produce from Florida. Lemon invests $2,000 from savings and borrows $1,000 from a friend to finance the business venture, agreeing to pay interest of $25 a week, beginning June 1, until the loan is repaid. With $3,000 available, Lemon rents a truck for one week for $500 and leaves for Florida on June 1.

On June 1, the account balances shown in Exhibit 3-1 represent the financial situation for Produce Transit Co. immediately after renting the truck but before leaving for Florida.

The company obtained $3,000 of financing but spent $500 for rent on the truck. In exchange for the cash, the company has a resource available for use (a truck) that was not available previously. The truck is represented in the accounts by PREPAID RENT because the company did not purchase the truck but rented it for one week. *Prepaid rent* **is an asset representing the cost of a rented resource to be consumed in the future.** For example, if you pay your apartment rent at the beginning of a month, you have an asset, prepaid rent. Note that

Exhibit 3-1

Produce Transit Co.
Account Summary
June 1, 1996

Assets =		Liabilities + Owners' Equity		+ (Revenues − Expenses)	
Cash	$2,500	Loan	$1,000	Revenues	$0
Prepaid rent—truck	500	Investment by owner	2,000	Expenses	0
Total	$3,000	Total	$3,000	Total	$0

Analysis of cash:
  Cash received: Investment by owner $2,000
                   Loan   1,000
  Cash paid: Truck rental   − 500
                   Total $2,500

in Exhibit 3–1 the amount of assets equals the amount of liabilities plus owners' equity.

Lemon returned to Michigan on June 6. He incurred the following costs as part of the trip:

Cost of produce $2,000
Food and lodging   220
Gas   280

On June 6, immediately before selling the produce, the company has an additional resource, $2,000 of produce. However, all of its cash has been consumed:

Cash received: Investment by owner $2,000
                 Loan   1,000 $3,000
Cash paid: Truck rental   − 500
                Food/lodging   − 220
                Gas   − 280
                Produce   − 2,000 − 3000
                Total cash $ 0

On June 7, Lemon sells the produce to the grocery chain for $3,500 and pays back the loan of $1,000 and interest of $25, leaving him with $2,475 in cash. After selling the produce on June 7 and repaying the loan plus interest, the company's financial condition would appear as illustrated in Exhibit 3–2.

Analysis of cash:
  Cash received: Investment by owner $2,000
                   Loan   1,000
                   Sales   3,500 $6,500
  Cash paid: Truck rental   − 500
                 Food   − 220
                 Gas   − 280
                 Produce   − 2,000
                 Loan repayment − 1,000
                 Interest   − 25 − 4,025
                 Total $2,475

Exhibit 3-2

Produce Transit Co.
Account Summary
For Week Ended June 7, 1996

Assets =		Liabilities + Owners' Equity		+ (Revenues − Expenses)	
Cash	$2,475	Loan	$ 0	Revenues	$3,500
Prepaid rent	0	Investment by owner	2,000	Expenses:	
Produce	0			Cost of goods sold	− 2,000
				Truck rental	− 500
				Food and lodging	− 220
				Gas	− 280
				Interest	− 25
Total	$2,475	Total	$2,000	Total (Net Income)	$ 475

Observe from Exhibit 3-2 that assets do not equal liabilities plus owners' equity. Net income has not been added to retained earnings yet. **During a fiscal period, the accounting equation ASSETS = LIABILITIES + OWNERS' EQUITY must be extended to include revenues and expenses:**

ASSETS = LIABILITIES + OWNERS' EQUITY + REVENUES − EXPENSES

In Exhibit 3-2 this equation contains the following amounts: $2,475 (assets) = $0 (liabilities) + $2,000 (owners' equity) + $3,500 (revenues) − $3,025 (expenses). If the revenue and expense account balances ($475 = $3,500 − $3,025) were transferred to retained earnings on June 7, the first two columns in the exhibit would be equal: $2,475 (assets) = $0 (liabilities) + $2,475 (owners' equity). This relationship can be illustrated as follows:

Assets =		Liabilities + Owners' Equity		+ (Revenues − Expenses)	
Cash	$2,475	Investment by owner	$2,000	Revenues	$3,500
		Retained earnings	475 ◄┐	Expenses	− 3,025
			└──────►		$ 475

The linkage between revenues and expenses and owners' equity is provided through reinvested profit (retained earnings). Retained earnings is increased by revenues and decreased by expenses for a period. Therefore, when examining account balances, it is important to know whether the revenue and expense account balances have been transferred to retained earnings. **If revenue and expense account balances have been transferred to retained earnings: ASSETS = LIABILITIES + OWNERS' EQUITY. If revenue and expense account balances have not yet been transferred to retained earnings: ASSETS = LIABILITIES + OWNERS' EQUITY + REVENUES − EXPENSES.** Organizations often do not transfer revenue and expense account balances until the end of a fiscal year. Thus, during a fiscal period, these balances normally are part of the accounting equation.

As of June 7, the company has earned $475 in net income after its sale of $3,500. The price of the goods sold is $475 greater than the total cost of all the resources consumed in making the goods available for sale. Lemon now has

$2,475 in cash and is $475 better off than before the venture. Because of the transactions associated with this transformation, Lemon's wealth has increased by $475. This fact is verified by the amount of cash available once all activities of the venture have been completed. The amount also is verified by the amount of net income earned from the venture. The net income figure is important because it clearly distinguishes the return *on* investment from the venture ($475) from the return *of* investment from the venture ($2,000). As explained in Chapter 1, return *of* investment is recovery by an owner of an amount invested in a business.

Objective 2
Summarize the information an accounting system provides about a transformation process.

The accounting system in this example described the economic consequences of the transformation from start to finish. It described the resources that were available during the transformation, and how the company obtained financial resources to acquire other resources. It measured the price of goods sold. It measured the costs associated with the transformation process, $3,025. It measured how well the business performed: Lemon received a return on investment of $475. These measures provide a basis for estimating future performance if Lemon chooses to continue the business.

In addition, the accounting system can be used to summarize the economic consequences of contracts the company formed with other parties.

Contracting Party	Given in Exchange	Received in Exchange	Contract Completed
Owner	Investment of $2,000	Return on investment of $475	Yes
Lender	Loan of $1,000	Repayment of loan plus interest of $25	Yes
Suppliers of:			
Truck	Use of truck	Rent of $500	Yes
Food and lodging	Food and lodging	Payment of $220	Yes
Gas	Gas	Payment of $280	Yes
Produce	Produce	Payment of $2,000	Yes
Customers	Payment of $3,500	Produce	Yes

This information is important for identifying the various participants in the transformation process and what they gave and received. Also, it is helpful to know all contracts have been completed. Anyone interested in contracting with the company in the future can use this information to evaluate the risk and return associated with the contract.

SELF-STUDY PROBLEM 3-1

On December 1, 1996, S. Claus signed a one-month contract with a toy manufacturer, Elves, Inc. Under the terms of the contract, Claus will deliver merchandise from Elves' Far North plant to locations throughout the U.S. On December 1, Claus signed a one-month lease on a sleigh and a team of reindeer for which he paid $1,500 from his savings. The lease is an investing activity. As an additional investment, he withdrew $3,500 from savings to cover his operating costs for the month. From these resources, he paid the following expenses in December:

Lodging	$ 750
Meals	600
Hay and oats	1,800

At the end of December, Claus was paid $5,000 by Elves, Inc. for providing delivery services.

Required

Complete the following account summary for S. Claus for December. Show the amounts of revenue and expense for Claus before the balances of these accounts are transferred to retained earnings for December.

S. Claus
Account Summary
For Month Ended December 31, 1996

Assets =	Liabilities + Owners' Equity	+ (Revenues − Expenses)
Cash	Investment by owner	Revenues
		Expenses
Total _____	Total _____	Total _____

The solution to Self-Study Problem 3-1 appears at the end of the chapter.

ACCOUNTING FOR INCOMPLETE TRANSFORMATIONS

Objective 3
Explain the implications of the going concern principle for the transformation process.

The Produce Transit Co. illustration is not typical of the activities of most organizations in two respects. First, the transactions were simpler and fewer than those observed in most organizations. Second, and more important for the current discussion, the illustration considered a transformation that began and ended during a short period. The transformation began with the investment on June 1 and ended a week later with the sale of the produce and repayment of the loan. The transformation began with cash and ended when all resources were converted back to cash. Most organizations are going concerns: their transformation processes are continuous, extending beyond the current fiscal period. **A** *going concern* **is an organization with an indefinite life that is sufficiently long so that, over time, all currently incomplete transformations will be completed.**

Consider a trucking company that owns many trucks and that continuously hauls produce to different parts of the country. Cash is invested in trucks and produce and is paid to employees. The company does not stop operations periodically to sell all its trucks and produce to determine how well it is performing. The company must evaluate its performance while its transformation process is still unfinished.

Managers, owners, creditors, and other decision makers need frequent information about how well a company is doing. Important questions need to be answered before a company knows the final results of all its current activities: How much money is available to pay bills and purchase resources? How much profit has the company earned? How much money can the company distribute to owners? Therefore, organizations report the results of their financing, investing, and operating activities periodically, even though they do not know all the results of these activities. Because the results are not fully known, managers must estimate the results they expect from the activities of a particular fiscal period. These estimates may not always be precise or accurate. They are better, however, than having no information until all results are known. For some companies, all the results cannot be determined for years after the period in which activities occur.

The accounting systems of most organizations report periodically the estimated results of financing, investing, and operating activities. *Periodic measurement* **occurs when the accounting system measures and reports the performance of an organization for particular fiscal periods so decisions can be made using timely information.** Managers often receive reports monthly, though more frequent reporting is common for purposes such as ordering materials, controlling production, and shipping goods.

The going concern and periodic measurement principles are important for the development of Generally Accepted Accounting Principles (GAAP). Accounting rules used to prepare reports for external users assume an organization is a going concern. If evidence exists that an organization is not a viable going concern, different accounting rules are used to measure and report its economic activities. Many corporations report summary information to their stockholders and other external users quarterly and prepare a detailed annual report. The choice of how often to report represents a tradeoff between the cost of providing the reports and the benefits users derive from timely information. Reporting frequency also results from a tradeoff between the timeliness and accuracy of information. For example, quarterly reports are more timely than annual reports, but they typically contain more estimates because some events cannot be measured until fiscal year end.

TIME AND ACCOUNTING MEASUREMENT

Major decisions in estimating the results of a transformation process are when to recognize the sale of goods and services and when to recognize the consumption of resources. Recognition occurs in accounting when transactions are recorded in the accounting system. The following sections describe alternate approaches for identifying when transactions should be recorded.

Cash Flows

One alternative for measuring the economic consequences of an organization's activities is by the amount of cash resulting from the transformation process during a fiscal period. *Cash flow* **is the amount of cash received (cash inflow)**

or paid (cash outflow) during a period. For example, assume you manage a business, A. Einstein Electronics. On May 1, 1995, owners invested $200,000 in the business, and the business borrowed an additional $100,000 from creditors. You used this financing to purchase equipment for $25,000, a building for $125,000, and land for $30,000. In addition, you purchased $75,000 of merchandise for sale, which left you $45,000 of cash. These transactions occurred during May. On May 31, the company's account balances would appear as illustrated in Exhibit 3-3.

Exhibit 3-4 reports cash received and paid for A. Einstein Electronics for May. Cash increased $45,000 for the company in May. This amount does not represent the results of operating activities, however, because no operating activities occurred in May. No goods were produced or sold. The $45,000 does not represent a return on investment to owners. It is simply the cash that remains from the owners' investments after other resources have been acquired. Therefore, the change in cash for a period is not, by itself, a valid measure of how much better off the owners of a company are from the company's activities for a period.

Exhibit 3-3

A. Einstein Electronics
Account Summary
For Month Ended May 31, 1995

Assets =		Liabilities + Owners' Equity		+ (Revenues − Expenses)	
Cash	$ 45,000	Loans	$100,000	Revenues	$0
Merchandise	75,000	Owners' investment	200,000	Expenses	0
Equipment	25,000				
Building	125,000				
Land	30,000				
Total	$300,000	Total	$300,000	Total	$0

Exhibit 3-4

A. Einstein Electronics
Cash Received and Paid
For Month Ended May 31, 1995

Cash received:		
Loans from creditors	$100,000	
Investment by owners	200,000	$300,000
Cash paid:		
Purchase of merchandise	$75,000	
Purchase of equipment	25,000	
Purchase of building	125,000	
Purchase of land	30,000	255,000
Increase in cash		$ 45,000

Cash Flows from Operating Activities

Objective 6
Explain why cash flow from operating activities is not a complete measure of an organization's performance for a period.

Another possible measure of performance is the amount of cash flow from operating activities, rather than the total cash flow for a period. Assume that during June, the first month of operations, you sell for $67,500 half of the merchandise you purchased. Of these sales, $50,000 was for cash and the remainder was on credit, with the cash to be received within 30 days. The company paid wages of $10,000 to employees and owed $3,000 of additional wages at the end of the month. The company paid other operating costs (e.g., utilities, licenses, insurance, and maintenance) amounting to $1,200. Exhibit 3-5 reports the cash flow from operating activities for A. Einstein Electronics for June.

Exhibit 3-5

A. Einstein Electronics
Account Summary
For Month Ended June 30, 1995

Assets =		Liabilities + Owners' Equity		+ Net Cash Flow from Operating Activities		
Cash	$ 83,800	Loans	$100,000	Cash received		$50,000
Merchandise	75,000	Owners' investment	200,000	Cash paid:		
Equipment	25,000			Wages	− $10,000	
Building	125,000			Other	− 1,200	
Land	30,000					−11,200
Total	$338,800	Total	$300,000	Total		$38,800

Cash has increased to $83,800 ($45,000 from May + $50,000 of cash sales in June − $11,200 of cash payments in June). This summary reports net cash flow of $38,800 based on the difference between the cash received from operating activities ($50,000) and the cash paid for these activities ($11,200) during June.

Does $38,800 represent a complete measure of performance for June? Consider the following problems related to Exhibit 3-5:

1. Sales of $17,500 made on credit have not been recognized. Customers owe this amount to the company, though cash was not received in June.
2. The amount of merchandise reported at the end of June is incorrect. Half the merchandise has been sold; therefore, the cost of merchandise available for sale at the end of June is $37,500, instead of $75,000. No cash outflow occurred for merchandise in June, though some merchandise was consumed. The cash outflow occurred in May when the merchandise was purchased.
3. The $3,000 owed to employees has not been recorded. The cash outflow will not occur until July, but an obligation for the payment exists in June, when employee services were received. The cost is related to services received by the company in June, not July.

These problems suggest reporting operating activities, as well as financing and investing activities, on a cash flow basis is not adequate. The issue is one of timing. Cash flows do not always occur at the same time goods are sold or resources are consumed as part of the transformation process. This limitation does not mean information about cash flows is unimportant to managers, owners, and others who provide and use cash. But, cash flow is not a complete indicator of a company's performance.

Individuals often use cash as a basis for measuring their financial conditions. When you and I make decisions about going to a movie, buying a car, or going on a vacation, we look at how much cash we have available. Cash is important to businesses and other organizations, as well. But, cash is not the primary measure most organizations use to evaluate their operating activities. The next section examines the accrual basis businesses use to measure performance.

The Accrual Basis of Accounting Measurement

Objective 7
Distinguish the accrual basis of accounting from the cash basis and explain why the accrual basis is used.

Instead of cash measurement, businesses typically use the accrual basis of measurement. Accrual measurement focuses on events that create or consume resources, in addition to cash flows. **The** *accrual basis* **of accounting measurement recognizes revenues when resources are created as part of an organization's operating activities. It recognizes expenses when resources are consumed as part of operating activities.** The following sections describe accrual measurement and compare it with cash measurement.

Sales and Receivables. In most situations, revenue is recognized when goods and services are sold. A sale is a contract between a company and a customer. A customer takes possession of goods or receives services. In exchange, the customer pays cash or agrees to pay cash in the future for these goods or services.

To illustrate the relationship between accrual and cash measures, consider A. Einstein Electronics again. The accrual measurement of the June sales transactions can be represented as:

Assets =		Liabilities + Owners' Equity	+ (Revenues − Expenses)	
Cash	$50,000	$0	Sales revenue	$67,500
Accounts receivable	17,500			

The accrual basis reports $67,500 of revenue for June because this is the price of the goods sold to customers during June. It is the amount of the contract between the company and its customers. The contract calls for customers to exchange $67,500 of financial resources for goods. Of this amount, $50,000 is a CASH asset. The remaining $17,500 is a receivable asset (indicating the right to receive cash in the future). ACCOUNTS RECEIVABLE represents the amount owed to an organization by its customers. The revenue account indicates how much current and future cash ($67,500) was generated and where it came from (sale of merchandise to customers). The assets indicate which resources were generated by the sale and their amounts, cash ($50,000) and future cash ($17,500).

Recognizing revenue and receiving cash may occur at the same time, as when goods are sold for cash. The critical event for purposes of accounting revenue recognition, however, is the sale, not the receipt of cash.

Cost of Goods Sold. The accrual basis recognizes $37,500 of expense for merchandise consumed from sales made in June. COST OF GOODS SOLD is an expense for the cost of merchandise sold to customers. This transaction can be illustrated as:

Assets =		Liabilities + Owners' Equity		+ (Revenues − Expenses)	
Merchandise	− $37,500	.		Cost of goods sold	− $37,500

Merchandise is reduced by $37,500, and net income is reduced by the cost of the merchandise that has been consumed, also $37,500.

The expense for merchandise is recognized in the period in which revenue from the sale is recorded. The accrual basis matches the expense with the revenue produced from the resources consumed.

Wages. The accrual basis recognizes wages for June as:

Assets =		Liabilities + Owners' Equity		+ (Revenues − Expenses)	
Cash	− $10,000	Wages payable	$3,000	Wages expense	− $13,000

The accrual basis recognizes $13,000 of WAGES EXPENSE because this is the cost of employee services consumed during June. Of this amount, $10,000 is cash paid to employees, a reduction in the balance of the cash account. The remaining $3,000 is a liability, WAGES PAYABLE. WAGES PAYABLE is an amount owed by a company to its employees for services they have already provided. This liability represents a contractual obligation of the company to pay cash in the future. Part of the wages earned in June is paid during the current period (CASH) and part will be paid in the future (WAGES PAYABLE).

Interest. A. Einstein Electronics pays interest on a loan at periodic intervals. The accrual basis records an expense for the interest each fiscal period. For example, if the loan requires interest payments of $3,000 every three months, the company records one-third of the interest as an expense of each of the three months. Therefore, A. Einstein would record $1,000 of INTEREST EXPENSE for June. *Interest expense* **is the cost associated with borrowing money during a fiscal period.** This $1,000 is owed to creditors because the company has used the creditors' money during June. *Interest payable* **is an amount owed to creditors for the use of the creditors' money during a fiscal period.** Like WAGES PAYABLE, INTEREST PAYABLE is a contractual obligation to pay cash in the future for a resource (use of borrowed money) that has been consumed. The transaction can be illustrated as:

Assets =		Liabilities + Owners' Equity		+ (Revenues − Expenses)	
	$0	Interest payable	$1,000	Interest expense	− $1,000

In this transaction, assets are not affected during the current period because cash will not be paid out for two more months. Net income has been reduced during June, however.

Depreciation. Two other accounts need to be considered, BUILDING and EQUIPMENT. These accounts are examples of fixed assets. *Fixed assets* **or** *plant assets* **are long-term, physical resources.** The company purchased the building for $125,000 and the equipment for $25,000. Because the business is a going concern, we assume the building will be used until it wears out or outlives its usefulness and has to be replaced. The same is true of equipment. Both assets are expected to last for several years. It is misleading to report the entire cost of the building or equipment as expense in the period in which they are purchased or in the period in which they are replaced. Instead, the accrual basis allocates a portion of the cost of these assets to expense during each fiscal period that benefits from their use.

For example, assume the building has a useful life of 25 years. The company might allocate $5,000 ($125,000/25 years) of the building's cost to expense each year or approximately $417 ($125,000/300 months) each month of this 25-year period. In the same manner, if the equipment has a useful life of 10 years, the company might allocate $2,500 ($25,000/10 years) of cost to expense each year or approximately $208 ($25,000/120 months) each month. **The process of allocating the costs of fixed assets to expense over the useful lives of the assets is known as** *depreciation*. Total depreciation for A. Einstein Electronics would be $625 for June. This transaction can be illustrated as:

Assets =	Liabilities + Owners' Equity	+ (Revenues − Expenses)
Accumulated depreciation − $625		Depreciation expense − $625

Depreciation expense **is the cost of fixed assets recognized as being consumed during a fiscal period.** Instead of reducing the building and equipment accounts directly, accounting normally uses an accumulated depreciation account. *Accumulated depreciation* **is the portion of fixed asset costs allocated to depreciation since the assets were acquired.** Accumulated depreciation is a contra-asset account. It offsets the asset account to which it relates. **A** *contra account* **is any account that offsets or reduces the amount of another account.** Thus, on its balance sheet, A. Einstein Electronics will report the cost of its fixed assets less the accumulated depreciation recognized for these assets. Some fixed assets, notably land, are not depreciated because it is assumed they will not wear out. As an example, A. Einstein Electronics would report the following information on its balance sheet at the end of June:

Equipment	$ 25,000
Building	125,000
Accumulated depreciation	− 625
Property, plant, and equipment	$149,375

The measurement of depreciation is an estimation procedure. The amount of depreciation recorded depends on assumptions about the lives of assets. The company assumed the building would last 25 years. Also, it chose to allocate an equal amount of depreciation expense to each month of the asset's life. A different assumption as to the building's life or a different allocation method would change the amount of depreciation expense and accumulated depreciation recorded each month.

Numbers such as $417 and $208 for depreciation expense appear to be very precise. Nevertheless, this precision is misleading because the numbers are the result of allocation decisions. Different allocation methods would produce different numbers. Because the amounts are estimates, it makes little sense to report numbers that make the amounts appear to be more precise than they are. Thus, accounting reports usually round amounts to hundreds, thousands, or even millions of dollars, depending on an organization's size.

Other Expenses. The final transaction for A. Einstein Electronics for June is the payment of other expenses of $1,200. The payment can be illustrated as:

Assets =		Liabilities + Owners' Equity	+ (Revenues − Expenses)	
Cash	− $1,200		Other expenses	− $1,200

The cash payment for expenses reduces the amount of cash available to A. Einstein Electronics. In this transaction, like many others in most organizations, a cash payment occurs at the time an expense is recorded. It is the use of resources, not the payment of cash that requires an expense to be recognized, however.

Product and Period Costs. Accrual accounting attempts to match expenses with revenues. Most revenues are recognized when goods are sold. Therefore, expenses directly associated with specific goods also are recognized when the goods are sold. For example, cost of goods sold for specific items of merchandise is recorded when this merchandise is sold. The expense is matched with the revenue from the sale. **Costs directly associated with specific goods are** *product costs*. **Product costs are expensed in the fiscal period the goods with which they are associated are sold.** Product costs are inventoried until the related goods are sold. Merchandise acquired by A. Einstein Electronics for $75,000 in May is an asset, merchandise inventory, until this merchandise is sold. At the time it is sold, the inventory account is decreased and COST OF GOODS SOLD is recognized. Manufacturing companies inventory the costs of goods produced until the goods are sold. These costs include the costs of labor, materials, and other resources that are part of the production process. For example, assume a company pays $100 for labor and $150 for materials that are used to produce a washing machine in September. The washing machine is sent to a warehouse and later sold to a retailer in December. The total manufacturing cost of $250 is recorded as an asset, inventory, in September. COST OF GOODS SOLD and a reduction in INVENTORY by $250, are recorded when the machine is sold in December.

Some costs cannot be associated directly with specific goods. Examples include management salaries, depreciation and insurance on office facilities, and advertising costs. *Period costs* **are costs not directly associated with specific goods. Period costs are reported as expenses in external accounting re-**

ports in the period in which they occur (in other words, the period
benefiting from the cost). Cash may be paid for these resources in a period
other than when they are consumed. For example, interest expense for A. Einstein Electronics is a period cost. It is recognized in June, the period benefiting
from the cost, though cash is not paid until August.

Managers may allocate certain costs differently for internal reporting and decision purposes than for external reporting purposes. GAAP require some costs,
for example, those associated with research and development, to be expensed
when they are incurred. Managers may treat these costs as product costs for planning or control purposes. Accounting procedures used in external reporting may
differ from those used in internal reporting.

Summary of Accrual Accounting. Exhibit 3-6 illustrates the result of recording all of A. Einstein Electronics' June transactions using the accrual basis.

Exhibit 3-6

A. Einstein Electronics
Accrual Basis Account Summary
For Month Ended June 30, 1995

Assets =		Liabilities + Owners' Equity		+ (Revenues − Expenses)	
Cash	$83,800	Loans	$100,000	Sales revenue	$67,500
Accounts receivable	17,500	Wages payable	3,000	Cost of goods	
Merchandise	37,500	Interest payable	1,000	sold	−37,500
Equipment	25,000	Owners' investment	200,000	Wages expense	−13,000
Building	125,000			Depreciation	
Accumulated				expense	−625
depreciation	−625			Interest expense	−1,000
Land	30,000			Other expense	−1,200
Total	$318,175	Total	$304,000		$14,175

Analysis of cash:		
Cash received:	Sale of merchandise	$50,000
Cash paid:	Payment of salaries	−10,000
	Payment of other expenses	−1,200
Net increase in cash		38,800
Beginning cash balance		45,000
Ending cash balance		$83,800

The accrual basis reports $14,175 of net income for A. Einstein Electronics
in June. Though an estimate, this amount is a measure of performance based on
the economic consequences of the company's operating activities in June. It is a
measure of how much better off the owners are as a result of the company's operating activities during June. Observe that the accounting process can become
complex very quickly. Even a few transactions result in a complex set of data that
must be organized carefully if it is to make sense to users.

Like the analysis for Produce Transit Co., the accounts for A. Einstein Electronics provide information about the status of contracts involving the company:

Contracting Party	Given in Exchange	Received in Exchange	Contract Completed
Owner	Investment of $200,000	Return on investment of $14,175	No, business is a going concern
Lender	Loan of $100,000	Interest earned of $1,000	No, interest and principal not yet paid
Suppliers:	Merchandise Equipment Building Land Other items	Payment of $75,000 Payment of $25,000 Payment of $125,000 Payment of $30,000 Payment of $1,200	Yes, cash owed to suppliers has been paid
Employees	Labor	Payment of $10,000 and right to $3,000 more	No, a portion of wages not yet paid
Customers	Payment of $50,000 and promise to pay of $17,500	Merchandise	No, a portion of sale not yet received

RECONCILING ACCRUAL AND CASH MEASUREMENTS

Objective 8
Reconcile cash and accrual measures of operating activities.

The relationship between accrual and cash measurements is critical to understanding accounting information. Exhibit 3-6 provides an analysis of changes in cash during June for A. Einstein Electronics. Changes in the cash account result from transactions that produce cash inflows and outflows. Several items recorded using the accrual basis, such as sales for credit and noncash expenses, cost of goods sold, depreciation, and interest, did not affect cash flows in June. Accrual and cash numbers provide different measures of operating activities for the month. These two measures can be reconciled, as in Exhibit 3-7.

This illustration indicates the timing of cash flows associated with revenues and expenses recorded in June. Net cash flow from operating activities for June was $38,800, corresponding to Exhibit 3-5, but some cash inflows associated with revenues recorded in June will be received in the future. Some cash outflows associated with expenses recorded in June were paid in May, and some will be paid in the future. Thus, while net cash flow from operating activities was $38,800 in June, the net result of all cash flows (past, present, and future) from revenues and expenses recorded in June is only $14,175. This amount is the company's net income for June. **The accrual basis attempts to measure the economic consequences of operating activities during the period in which they occur.** This accrual measure should approximate the cash flow that will result from these operating activities, once *all* of these cash flows occur. Therefore, it should provide a more accurate measure of the economic consequences of operating activities during a period than cash flows provide for the period.

Exhibit 3-7

A. Einstein Electronics
Reconciliation of Net Cash Flow from Operating
Activities and Net Income
For Month Ended June 30, 1995

	Cash Flow from Operating Activities for June			Net Income from Operating Activities for June		
	Past	**June**	**Future**	**Revenues**	**Expenses**	**Total**
Cash received for June sales		$50,000		$50,000		
Cash to be received for June sales			$17,500	17,500		
Total June sales						$67,500
Cash paid in June for resources consumed in June:						
Wages		−10,000			−$10,000	
Other		−1,200			−1,200	
Cash to be paid for resources consumed in June:						
Wages			−3,000		−3,000	
Interest			−1,000		−1,000	
Cash paid in past for resources consumed in June:						
Inventory	−$37,500				−37,500	
Depreciation	−625				−625	
Total resources consumed in June						−53,325
Net cash increase in June		$38,800				
Net income for June						$14,175
Net cash increase	−$38,125	+$38,800	+$13,500			$14,175

MEASURING THE TRANSFORMATION PROCESS

Objective 9
Identify information reported by an accrual basis accounting system.

The major purpose of an accounting system is to provide information about an organization's transformation process. With this information, users can measure the financing, investing, and operating results of the process. Exhibit 3-8 illustrates the scope of information available from the accounting system. The information in the exhibit includes all transactions related to the transformation process of A. Einstein Electronics for both May and June.

Exhibit 3-8

Summary of Transformation Process
A. Einstein Electronics

Income Statement
For Two Months Ended June 30, 1995

Sales revenue		$67,500
Expenses:		
Cost of goods sold	$37,500	
Wages	13,000	
Interest	1,000	
Depreciation	625	
Other	1,200	
Total expenses		53,325
Net income		$14,175

Statement of Cash Flows
For Two Months Ended June 30, 1995

Cash flow from operating activities:		
Sale of merchandise	$ 50,000	
Cash paid for expenses	− 11,200	
Cash paid for merchandise	− 75,000	− $36,200
Cash flow for investing activities:		
Purchase of equipment	− 25,000	
Purchase of building	− 125,000	
Purchase of land	− 30,000	− 180,000
Cash flow from financing activities:		
Loans from creditors	100,000	
Investment by owners	200,000	300,000
Net increase in cash		83,800
Cash balance, May 1		0
Cash balance, June 30		$ 83,800

Balance Sheet
June 30, 1995

Assets:		
Cash		$83,800
Accounts receivable		17,500
Merchandise inventory		37,500
Equipment	$ 25,000	
Building	125,000	
	150,000	
Less: Accumulated depreciation	− 625	149,375
Land		30,000
Total assets		$318,175
Liabilities:		
Wages payable	$ 3,000	
Interest payable	1,000	
Loans payable	100,000	
Total liabilities		$104,000

Owners' equity:		
Investment by owners	200,000	
Retained earnings	14,175	
Total owners' equity		214,175
Total liabilities and owners' equity		$318,175

Learning Note

Accounting rules require cash paid for merchandise, materials, and interest to be included as part of operating activities on the cash flow statement. Logical arguments can be made for including these as investing or financing (interest) activities. They are related directly to expenses on the income statement, however, and are included as operating activities for comparison purposes.

The information provided in this exhibit is typical of the financial statements reported by an accounting system. The economic consequences of transactions occurring in an organization's transformation process are summarized in accounts. Accounts are created as needed to capture information from transactions. As a group, the accounts form a data base in which information is stored until needed by users. Periodically, the account information is summarized and reported in a form that enables users to understand the transactions that occurred in the transformation process.

The income statement reports the costs of resources consumed in producing, selling, and distributing goods and services and the prices of goods and services sold during a period. The statement of cash flows reports the cash consequences of financing, investing, and operating activities during a period. The balance sheet reports the resources available for use in the transformation process and claims to those resources at a point in time. Observe that retained earnings are reported on the balance sheet after revenues and expenses for the current fiscal period have been transferred to this account.

Reports by large corporations to external users often summarize accounts by general categories. For example, "operating expenses" may be reported instead of individual expenses such as wages and depreciation. Corporations report additional information along with their financial statements to help readers understand and interpret the statements. Later chapters will examine this additional information.

Learning Note

Assets are the resources reported by a company. All other accounts provide information about where resources came from and how they were used. Students often have trouble interpreting some of these accounts. For example, revenues are not cash. Cash is an asset on the balance sheet. Revenues describe where some resources (including some cash) were obtained during a period: from customers. Net income and retained earnings also are not cash. These accounts provide information about the amount of resources generated from operating activities, but they are not resources themselves. An organization must have cash to acquire other resources and to pay its bills. It cannot pay for anything with revenues, net income, or retained earnings.

Both accrual and cash measures of the transformation process are useful. The accrual basis estimates the economic consequences of the transformation process during a period. The cash basis measures the net amount of cash provided by the transformation process during the period. Accrual basis measurements provide information about whether an organization's operations are sufficiently effective and efficient for long-run success. Cash basis measurements provide information about whether an organization is generating sufficient cash to meet its current obligations and survive in the short run. Either measure can be misleading when considered in isolation.

For example, a company may report a large amount of net income for a period. That income may result from a large amount of revenue that does not generate current cash inflow. Thus, the company may not have sufficient cash to meet its operating needs and pay its creditors. A profitable company can be forced into bankruptcy because of inadequate cash flow. On the other hand, a company may report a large amount of cash flow for a period because of collections on sales to customers from a prior period. Though cash flow may look good, net income may demonstrate the company is having difficulty selling its products. Both accrual and cash flow measures are important in evaluating a company's performance. A successful company normally will demonstrate good accrual and cash basis performance.

SELF-STUDY PROBLEM 3-2

N. Bates is owner and manager of Bates' Motel. He purchased the motel at the end of 1993. On January 1, 1995, the asset, liability, and owners' equity account balances for Bates' Motel were as follows:

Bates' Motel
Account Summary
January 1, 1995

Assets		Liabilities & Owners' Equity	
Cash	$ 4,200	Notes payable	$ 80,000
Supplies	7,300	Investment by owners	45,000
Furniture and equipment	19,500	Retained earnings	9,600
Buildings	93,600		
Accumulated depreciation	−5,000		
Land	15,000		
Total	$134,600	Total	$134,600

During 1995, the motel earned $88,000 from room rentals. Of this amount, $82,000 was received in cash by year end; $6,000 was accounts receivable from corporate clients. Expenses incurred during the year included: wages, $30,000; utilities, $8,400; supplies consumed, $5,300; depreciation on furniture and equipment, $2,000; depreciation on buildings, $3,000; interest on note, $7,000; and miscellaneous, $2,400. Other than depreciation and supplies consumed, all expenses were paid in cash when incurred, except that $1,500 of wages (of the

$30,000) were owed to employees at year end. Other cash payments included $2,200 for purchase of supplies and $10,000 paid on the principal of the notes payable. Bates withdrew $20,000 from the business during the year for living expenses.

Required

Prepare a summary of the transformation process for Bates' Motel for 1995 using the format of Exhibit 3-8.

The solution to Self-Study Problem 3-2 appears at the end of the chapter.

THE PURPOSE OF ACCRUAL BASIS ACCOUNTS

Objective 10
Explain the purposes of different account types in an accrual accounting system.

Each of the types of accounts in an accounting system plays an important role in accrual measurement. Each type of account provides information about economic consequences of an organization's transformation process and contractual relationships in the process. Also, these accounts link events together that occur in different fiscal periods. The following sections examine how accounts provide this link.

Assets, Liabilities, and Owners' Equity

The balance sheet reports accounts that represent resources and claims to those resources by creditors and owners. These resources and claims resulted from events occurring prior to the balance sheet date. Also, they provide information about future events that will occur.

Assets are resources available for future use by an organization to which it has a legal right. They may be resources purchased in the past that will be consumed in the future, such as merchandise, equipment, and buildings. Other assets, such as accounts receivable, represent legal rights to receive cash in the future. A company may invest cash in securities, such as stocks or bonds issued by other companies, with the expectation of receiving returns in the future. Cash is a financial resource that represents the legal right to purchase other resources. Therefore, assets consist of: (1) past cash outflows for resources to be used in the future, such as INVENTORY, BUILDINGS, EQUIPMENT, and PATENTS, (2) future cash inflows resulting from sales made by an organization, such as ACCOUNTS RECEIVABLE, (3) future cash inflows from INVESTMENTS held by a company, and (4) financial resources, such as CASH, currently available for use.

Liabilities represent legal obligations of an organization to provide cash or goods and services to external parties in the future. Some liabilities arise from financing activities. These liabilities, such as NOTES PAYABLE and BONDS PAYABLE, will be repaid in the future. Thus, these liabilities result from past cash inflows to an organization that will result in future cash outflows. Other liabilities include obligations to pay cash for resources acquired or consumed in the past, such as ACCOUNTS PAYABLE, WAGES PAYABLE, and INTEREST PAYABLE. Accounts payable are amounts owed to suppliers for merchandise, materials, and other resources purchased on credit. Liabilities also include *UN-EARNED REVENUES*, **which are obligations to provide goods and services in the future.** These liabilities arise when an organization receives financial resources from customers in exchange for goods and services to be provided in the future. An example is a publisher that sells magazine subscriptions. The publisher receives cash from customers in advance of publishing the magazine. The amount received is recorded as UNEARNED REVENUE. Revenue is not recognized for these goods or services until they are distributed to customers. At that time, UNEARNED REVENUE is decreased and REVENUE is increased. Thus, liabilities include (1) cash inflows in the past that will require cash outflows in the future, (2) resources acquired or consumed in the past that will require cash outflows in the future, and (3) cash received in the past for goods and services that will be provided in the future.

Owners' equity includes investments in an organization by owners and retained earnings. Owners of proprietorships and partnerships recover their investments when they sell their businesses. A corporation, however, is under no obligation to repay amounts invested by stockholders as long as it is a going concern. A corporation may choose, however, to repurchase shares of stock that it has issued. Thus, it may pay cash to owners for their stock. In addition, owners expect to receive returns on their investments. These returns may be in the form of cash payments from the organization or in the form of higher values for their investments, such as increases in stock prices. If returns are paid to owners as dividends (corporations) or withdrawals (proprietorships and partnerships), the owners receive cash directly from the company. Information about assets, liabilities, and owners' equity is reported on a company's balance sheet.

Revenues and Expenses

Revenues and expenses provide information about resources generated and consumed during a fiscal period. They report the economic consequences of transactions that help explain why resources changed from the beginning to the end of a fiscal period. Revenues result during the current period from the sale of goods and services to customers. Cash inflows associated with the sales may be received in past, current, or future periods. Similarly, expenses result from the consumption of resources during a period, irrespective of whether cash is paid for these resources in past, present, or future periods. Information about revenues and expenses is reported on a company's income statement; information about cash flows is reported on a statement of cash flows.

Accounts and Time

As a whole, an accrual accounting system provides information about revenues and expenses during a fiscal period for an organization that is a going concern. Also, it provides information about cash flows that occurred during the fiscal period. Asset, liability, and owners' equity accounts provide information about future cash flows, revenues, and expenses that will result from transactions that occurred in prior fiscal periods.

This information is necessary because the economic consequences of an organization's transformation process must be separated into distinct periods of time:

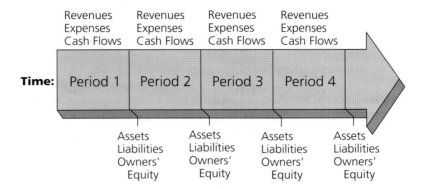

Separation into periods is necessary to report activities on a timely basis. Assets, liabilities, and owners' equity identify resources and claims to those resources at distinct intervals, the beginning and end of fiscal periods. Revenues, expenses, and cash flows identify events that change an organization's resources and claims to the resources during a period. Together, these accounts provide a dynamic picture of the economic consequences of the transformation process. They provide information about past events that created and consumed resources, affected claims to the resources, and created and consumed cash flows. They provide information about current resources and claims to the resources. And they provide information about expected future changes in resources, claims, and cash flows resulting from events that have already occurred.

How the accounting system functions to create and report this information is the subject of Chapter 4.

SELF-STUDY PROBLEM 3-3

The following are independent transactions:

1. An organization purchased supplies in February for $6,000 cash. $1,000 of the supplies was consumed in February; $2,000 was consumed in March.
2. An organization sells $10,000 of merchandise in March; $8,000 for cash and $2,000 on credit.
3. An organization buys $5,000 of merchandise in March and sells it during the month. It paid $1,000 for the merchandise in March. The remainder will be paid in April.
4. An organization consumes $3,000 of merchandise in March that was purchased in February. $1,200 was paid for the merchandise in February, and the remainder is paid for in March.
5. An organization borrows $20,000 from a bank in March. The loan will be repaid over a 10 year period beginning in April. Consider only the loan and repayment of principal.

6. An organization buys equipment priced at $7,000 in March and pays cash. $500 of the equipment value is consumed in March; the remainder will be consumed in the future.

Required

For each transaction, indicate the amount of revenue, expense, and cash flow that would result. Use the format provided below and place the appropriate amount in each box to indicate when the revenue, expense, or cash flow would be recorded. Transaction 1 is worked for you:

1.	Past	March	Future	Total
Revenues				
Expenses	− $1,000	− $2,000	− $3,000	− $6,000
Cash Received				
Cash Paid	− $6,000			− $6,000

The solution to Self-Study Problem 3-3 appears at the end of the chapter.

R E V I E W   *Summary of Important Concepts*

1. Transformation process:
   a. The accounting information system provides a means of recording, summarizing, and reporting an organization's transformation process.
   b. Together, assets, liabilities, owners' equity, revenues, expenses, and cash flows measure the outcome of an organization's transformation process.

2. Time and accounting measurement:
   a. Most organizations are going concerns: their transformation processes are continuous.
   b. Going concerns report results of their financing, investing, and operating activities periodically, even though all results of these activities are not fully known and must be estimated.
   c. Major decisions in estimating the results of a going concern are when to recognize the sale of goods and services and when to recognize the cost of resources consumed in providing goods and services.

3. Accrual and cash measurement:
   a. The accrual basis of accounting measures revenues when resources are created from sales and expenses when resources are consumed in operating activities, irrespective of when cash is received or paid.

b.   Revenues and expenses measure the results of an organization's operating activities on an accrual basis. Cash flows measure the cash provided by and used in an organization's operating activities, as well as by its financing and investing activities.

4.   Accrual basis accounts:
   a.   Assets measure the amount of resources available to an organization to be consumed in the future and the amount of cash expected in the future from revenues earned and other transactions in the current or prior periods.
   b.   Liabilities measure the amount of obligations owed by an organization that will be paid in the future for resources acquired or consumed in the current or prior periods.
   c.   Owners' equity measures the amount invested by owners in an organization either as direct investments or as retained earnings.

D E F I N E   *Terms and Concepts Defined in This Chapter*

accrual basis	fixed assets	plant assets
accumulated depreciation	going concern	prepaid rent
cash flow	interest expense	product costs
contra account	interest payable	unearned revenues
depreciation	period costs	
depreciation expense	periodic measurement	

S O L U T I O N S

SELF-STUDY PROBLEM 3-1

S. Claus
Account Summary
For Month Ended December 31, 1996

Assets =		Liabilities + Owners' Equity		+ (Revenues − Expenses)	
Cash	$5,350	Investment by owner	$5,000	Revenues	$ 5,000
				Expenses:	
				Lease	− 1,500
				Lodging	− 750
				Meals	− 600
				Hay and oats	− 1,800
Total	$5,350	Total	$5,000	Total	$ 350

SELF-STUDY PROBLEM 3-2

**Summary of Transformation Process
Bates' Motel**

**Income Statement
For Year Ended December 31, 1995**

Rent revenue		$88,000
Expenses:		
Supplies	$ 5,300	
Wages	30,000	
Utilities	8,400	
Interest	7,000	
Depreciation	5,000	
Other	2,400	
Total expenses		58,100
Net income		$29,900

**Statement of Cash Flows
For Year Ended December 31, 1995**

Cash provided by operating activities:		
Room rental:	$82,000	
Cash paid for expenses (Note 1)	−46,300	
Purchase of supplies	−2,200	$33,500
Cash used for financing activities:		
Payment of loan	−10,000	
Withdrawal by owner	−20,000	−30,000
Net increase in cash		3,500
Cash balance, January 1, 1995		4,200
Cash balance, December 31, 1995		$ 7,700

Note 1: Cash paid for expenses:		
Wages	$28,500	
Utilities	8,400	
Interest	7,000	
Miscellaneous	2,400	
Total cash paid	$46,300	

**Balance Sheet
December 31, 1995**

Assets:		
Cash		$ 7,700
Accounts receivable		6,000
Supplies (Note 2)		4,200
Furniture and equipment	$ 19,500	
Buildings	93,600	
	113,100	
Less: Accumulated depreciation	−10,000	103,100
Land		15,000
Total assets		$136,000

Liabilities:		
Wages payable	$ 1,500	
Notes payable	70,000	
Total liabilities		71,500
Owner's equity:		
Investment by owner	$ 45,000	
Retained earnings (Note 3)	19,500	
Total owner's equity		64,500
Total liabilities and owner's equity		$136,000

Note 2:		Note 3:	
Supplies on hand, beginning	$7,300	Retained earnings, beginning	$ 9,600
Supplies purchased	2,200	Net income, 1995	29,900
Supplies consumed	−5,300	Owner withdrawal, 1995	−20,000
Supplies on hand, ending	$4,200	Retained earnings, ending	$19,500

SELF-STUDY PROBLEM 3-3

2.	Past	March	Future	Total
Revenues		$10,000		$10,000
Expenses				
Cash Received		$8,000	$2,000	$10,000
Cash Paid				
3.				
Revenues				
Expenses		−$5,000		−$5,000
Cash Received				
Cash Paid		−$1,000	−$4,000	−$5,000
4.				
Revenues				
Expenses		−$3,000		−$3,000
Cash Received				
Cash Paid	−$1,200	−$1,800		−$3,000
5.				
Revenues				
Expenses				
Cash Received		$20,000		$20,000
Cash Paid			−$20,000	−$20,000
6.				
Revenues				
Expenses		−$500	−$6,500	−$7,000
Cash Received				
Cash Paid		−$7,000		−$7,000

EXERCISES

3-1. Write a short definition for each of the terms listed in the *Terms and Concepts Defined in This Chapter* section.

3-2. Compare and contrast the accounting systems of (1) a large retail company such as Sears and (2) a small local retail store such as Marvin's Men's Store. Consider the following attributes in your comparison: (a) number of accounts in the system, (b) relative number of decision makers and their information needs, (c) effect of locations and departments on the complexity of the system, and (d) the primary types of accounts included in the system.

3-3. Jerry Reed drives for a large moving company. The company contacts Jerry when it has a job for him and furnishes a truck for his use. Jerry picks up the truck, drives to the mover's home, loads, transports, and delivers the mover's belongings. He returns the truck to the company and receives his pay. Jerry is paid $4 per mile for the job. He is responsible for paying for his own gas, food, and lodging. Also, he must hire any helpers he needs to load and unload the truck. Jerry traveled 2,400 miles on a recent job. He paid $500 for gas, $116 for food, $204 for lodging, and $80 for helpers. How much did Jerry earn for the job? How much net cash did he receive? Was the amount he earned more or less than the net cash he received? Why?

3-4. Alice Ekberg makes wooden mailboxes in her garage. She makes a supply of boxes during the week. On the weekend, she rents a booth at a flea market near her home, where she sells her products. She paints the purchaser's name and address on a mailbox when it is sold. During a recent week, Alice paid $400 for wood and supplies she used to construct 20 mailboxes. On Saturday, she sold 10 of the boxes for $100 each. On Sunday, she sold 8 of the remaining boxes, also for $100 each. She had to pay $20 each day for rent for the booth. How much net cash did Alice receive on Saturday? How much on Sunday? How much did each box cost Alice (excluding rent)? How much did Alice earn on Saturday, Sunday, and for the week? What was her net cash flow for the week? Was the amount earned more or less than the net cash received? Why?

3-5. Refer to Exercise 3-4. How much additional cash will Alice have available to spend during the week following her sales from making and selling mailboxes? If she expects to sell the same number of mailboxes next week, how much should she earn next week? How many mailboxes should she make during the coming week? What will her net cash flow be for the coming week if she purchases materials to make the additional boxes she plans to sell at the same costs as last week and sells these for $100 each? She again will pay $20 rent each for Saturday and Sunday. Is the amount earned for the week more or less than the net cash received? Why?

3-6. Acorn Products Co. is a manufacturer of oak furniture. It began operations in 1994. During its first year of operations, Acorn paid $2,150,000 for wood and other raw materials for its products. From these materials, it produced 8,600 pieces of furniture. The average cost of raw materials for each piece was $250 ($2,150,000/8,600). During 1994, Acorn sold 7,000 pieces of the furniture it manufactured at an average price of $600 per piece. All sales were for cash. Assuming the total of other expenses incurred by Acorn during 1994 was $1,500,000, how much net income did Acorn earn in 1994? If other expenses were paid in cash, how much was Acorn's net cash flow from operations? Was the net income more or less than the net cash flow? Why? Which measure is a better predictor of next year's operating results? Why?

3-7. During its second year of operations, Acorn Co. (see Exercise 3-6) began with inventory of $400,000, representing 1,600 pieces of furniture. During 1995, Acorn paid $1,500,000 for materials, sufficient to produce 6,000 pieces of furniture at an average cost of $250 per piece. During the year, the company sold 7,000 pieces of furniture at an average price of $600 per piece. All sales were for cash. Other expenses amounted to $1,500,000, all paid in cash. How much net income did Acorn earn in 1995? How much net cash flow did it receive from operations? Was the net income more or less than the net cash flow? Why?

3-8. Meteor Transport Co. is a trucking company. It owns a large fleet of trucks that transport freight throughout the country. Some of these trucks cost hundreds of thousands of dollars and are operated for 15 years or more before being replaced. The company issues long-term debt to pay for most of its equipment. The company's fiscal year ends on June 30. The company prepares financial reports for each fiscal year that include estimates of its results of operations for the year. How do the operations of Meteor illustrate the periodic measurement and going concern principles of accounting?

3-9. South Plains Grain Co. began operations in January of 1995. It is investor owned, and provides storage facilities for farmers who grow wheat in the South Plains area. During 1995, the company issued $4,500,000 of stock and $3,000,000 of long-term debt. $7,200,000 of the capital was used to purchase land, construct grain silos, and purchase equipment for their operations. $2,100,000 of storage fees were paid by farmers. An additional $450,000 of fees were owed to the company at year end. $1,500,000 was paid by the company for wages, utilities, interest, insurance, and taxes during the year. An additional $300,000 was owed by the company at year end for resources consumed during the year. How much was South Plains' net cash flow for 1995? What was its net cash flow from financing, investing, and operating activities? Why is this information useful? Does this information provide an adequate measurement of the performance of the company for the current fiscal year? Does it provide a good indicator of cash flows that should be anticipated during 1996? Why or why not?

3-10. Oscar Wheatfield is a wheat farmer. He owns farm equipment and buildings that cost him $562,500 when he purchased them several years ago. He owes a local bank $375,000 for loans used to purchase these assets. In 1995, Oscar sold $600,000 of wheat he raised during the year. He incurred operating costs of $555,000 to produce the wheat. This amount included $33,750 of interest on the bank loans and $52,500 of depreciation on the plant assets. In addition, Oscar repaid $37,500 of the amount he owed on the loans. The sales and all operating costs but depreciation were for cash. How much net income did Oscar earn in 1995? What was his net cash flow for the year? Explain the difference.

3-11. Bernstein Piano Co. sold $111,250 of goods during September. It collected $37,500 from these sales plus $82,500 from sales of prior months. Complete the following table:

	Cash Flow for September	Cash Flow in Future	Sales Revenue for September
Cash from prior sales	?		
Cash from September sales	?	?	?
Total cash received in September	?		

3-12. Mercy Hospital paid $400,000 in wages during May. Of these, $48,000 were for wages earned in April. An additional $32,000 of wages were owed to employees for services provided in May. These wages will be paid in June. Complete the following table:

	Cash Flow for May	Cash Flow in June	Wages Expense for May
Cash paid for prior wages	?		
Cash paid for May wages	?	?	?
Total cash paid in May for wages	?		

3-13. Chin Construction Co. purchased $230,000 of materials during February. It owed $75,000 for material purchased during January. It paid the amount for January plus $120,000 of the amount purchased during February. $37,500 of the materials purchased in January were used in February along with $200,000 of the materials purchased in February. What was Chin's cash flow for materials in February? What was its expense for materials used in February?

3-14. Luna Pottery Works paid $137,500 for materials purchased in October. $93,750 of these materials plus $31,250 of materials purchased in September were used in goods sold during October. All materials available at the beginning of October were consumed during October. What was Luna's cost of goods sold for October? What amount of materials was left in inventory at the end of October?

3-15. George Carver borrowed $150,000 on January 1 to open a peanut processing plant. Interest on the loan is $4,500 each quarter. The first interest payment will be made on March 31. Complete the following table:

	January	February	March	Total for Quarter
Cash paid for interest	?	?	?	?
Interest expense	?	?	?	?

3-16. Pasteur Pharmaceutical Co. manufactures prescription drugs. The company recently purchased $450,000 of equipment. Cash was paid for the equipment on January 1, 1995. The company will depreciate the equipment over a three-year period at $150,000 each year. Complete the following table:

	1995	1996	1997	Total for 3 Years
Cash paid for equipment	?	?	?	?
Depreciation expense	?	?	?	?

Explain the difference between cash flows each year and the amount of depreciation expense recorded.

3-17. Ali Baba Rug Co. manufactures oriental rugs. It pays utility bills at the end of the month services are received. The company received the following bills for June, July, and August: $1,050, $1,275, $975. Complete the following table:

	June	July	August	Total for 3 Months
Cash paid for utilities	?	?	?	?
Utilities expense	?	?	?	?

When are cash and accrual basis measures different? When are they the same?

3-18. Complete the following table:

	Past Cash Flow	April Cash Flow	Future Cash Flow	April Revenues/ Expenses
Cash received for April sales		$180,000	$50,000	?
Cash paid for resources consumed in April:				
Merchandise	− $30,000	− $60,000	− $10,000	?
Wages		− 20,000	− 6,000	?
Equipment	− 40,000	0	0	?
Net cash increase in April		?		
Net income for April				?

Why was cash flow from operations in April different from net income in April?

3-19. Listed below are definitions for four types of assets:
a.   Financial resources available for use in future
b.   Cash paid in past for resources that will be consumed in future
c.   Goods and services sold in past that will result in future cash receipts
d.   Cash paid in past for resources that will yield future cash receipts and earnings

Place the letter (or letters) of the appropriate definition beside each of the assets below:
_____ Buildings   _____ Equipment
_____ Investments   _____ Accounts Receivable
_____ Supplies   _____ Patents
_____ Cash   _____ Inventory

3-20. Listed below are definitions for three types of liabilities:
a.   Financial resources received in past that will be repaid in future
b.   Merchandise and other resources and services acquired in past that will result in future cash payments

c. Financial resources received in past for goods and services that will be provided to customers in future

Place the letter of the appropriate definition beside each of the liabilities below:

_____ Notes Payable   _____ Accounts Payable
_____ Wages Payable   _____ Bonds Payable
_____ Unearned Revenues   _____ Rent Payable
_____ Interest Payable   _____ Insurance Payable

3-21. For each of the transactions listed below, indicate the amount of revenue, expense, and cash flow that would result. Use the format provided and place the appropriate amount in each box. Use a separate table for each transaction.

   a. $5,000 of supplies were purchased in August. $1,500 of the supplies were consumed in August and $2,500 were consumed in September.
   b. $15,000 of merchandise was sold in September. $6,000 of the sales were on credit.
   c. Merchandise that cost the seller $7,500 was sold in September. The seller paid $5,000 for the merchandise in August. The rest was paid for in September.
   d. $50,000 was borrowed in August. $2,500 will be repaid each month for 20 months beginning in September.
   e. $25,000 of equipment was purchased and paid for in August. $500 of the equipment value was consumed in September; the remainder will be consumed in the future.

	Past	September	Future	Total
Revenues				
Expenses				
Cash Received				
Cash Paid				

3-22. For each of the following transactions, indicate the amount of cash, other assets, liabilities, and/or owners' equity that would result. Provide your responses by completing the table provided below. Show revenues and expenses as additions or deductions to owners' equity.

   a. $20,000 of supplies were purchased in June.
   b. $6,000 of the supplies were consumed in June.
   c. $60,000 of merchandise was sold in June. $24,000 of the sales were on credit. The merchandise cost the seller $28,000.
   d. $200,000 was borrowed in June.
   e. Interest of $2,000 was incurred and paid in June.
   f. $100,000 of equipment was purchased in June.
   g. $4,000 of equipment value was consumed in June.

Transaction	Cash	Other Assets	Liability	Owners' Equity
a.				
b.				
c.				

Transaction	Cash	Other Assets	Liability	Owners' Equity
d.				
e.				
f.				
g.				

3-23. Sit and Sleep is a retail furniture store. At the end of the 1995 fiscal year, the company had a balance in accounts receivable of $97,500. During 1996, it received $592,500 in payments from customers, including the receivables from 1995. The balance in accounts receivable at the end of 1996 was $75,000. During 1997, it received $630,000 in payments from customers, including the receivables from 1996. The balance in accounts receivable was $90,000 at the end of 1997. How much revenue did Sit and Sleep earn from sales to customers in 1996? How much did it earn in 1997?

3-24. Complete the following table. Each column represents an independent situation. All receivables are collected in the year following sale.

	(a)	(b)	(c)
Cash received from customers for 1996	$300,000	$525,000	?
Sales revenue for 1996	$322,500	$480,000	$270,000
Accounts receivable at beginning of 1996	$67,500	?	$45,000
Accounts receivable at end of 1996	?	$105,000	$57,000

PROBLEMS

PROBLEM 3-1 The Effect of Transactions on Accounts

Z. Taylor Mortuary had the following account summary at April 1:

Z. Taylor Mortuary
Account Summary
At April 1

Assets =		Liabilities + Owners' Equity		+ (Revenues − Expenses)	
Cash	$ 2,800	Wages payable	$ 1,750	Revenues	$0
Equipment	17,450	Loan from bank	20,000	Expenses	0
Building	50,000	Owners' investment	27,500		
Land	12,000	Retained earnings	33,000		
Total	$82,250	Total	$82,250	Total	$0

The following transactions occurred during April:

a.   All amounts owed to employees at the beginning of the month were paid in full.

b.   Services were sold to customers for cash at prices totaling $3,295.

c.   The owners withdrew $2,750 from the business for personal use.

d.   Depreciation expense was recorded as follows: Equipment, $250; Building, $450.

e.   One month's interest (at a 12% annual rate) was paid to the bank.

Required   (a) Prepare a new account summary that incorporates April's transactions. (b) Prepare a separate explanation of changes in the cash account. (c) Discuss the return on investment that occurred during April.

PROBLEM 3-2 Determining Transactions from Changes in an Account Summary

A. Capone Correctional Facility is a private enterprise prison that contracts services to a Midwestern state. At the end of September, the organization had the following account summary:

A. Capone Correctional Facility
Account Summary
At September 30, 1996

Assets =		Liabilities + Owners' Equity		+ (Revenues − Expenses)	
Cash	$ 43,725	Accounts payable	$ 28,350	Revenues	$0
Supplies	65,700	Bonds payable	450,000	Expenses	0
Equipment	300,000	Owners' investment	1,050,000		
Buildings	1,350,000	Retained earnings	883,575		
Land	652,500				
Total	$2,411,925	Total	$2,411,925	Total	$0

During the month of October, a number of economic events occurred and were entered into the accounting data base. At the end of October, the company had the following correct account summary:

A. Capone Correctional Facility
Account Summary
At October 31, 1996

Assets =		Liabilities + Owners' Equity		+ (Revenues − Expenses)	
Cash	$ 58,725	Accounts payable	$ 28,350	Revenues	$810,000
Supplies	28,200	Bonds payable	0	Expenses:	
Equipment	297,000	Owners' investment	1,050,000	Supplies	− 37,500
Buildings	1,344,375	Retained earnings	883,575	Depreciation	− 8,625
Land	652,500			Wages	− 345,000
Total	$2,380,800	Total	$1,961,925	Total	$418,875

Required Identify the transactions that occurred during October. Also, prepare a separate analysis of the cash account detailing all changes.

PROBLEM 3-3 Preparing an Account Summary for a Fiscal Period

On March 1, Carl Caldwell started Caldwell Furniture Repair Co. He invested $2,000 of his own money, borrowed $16,000 from his father-in-law at 9% annual interest, and obtained an additional $3,000, 12% loan from Maxibank. He purchased $15,000 of tools and equipment (some new, some used), bought $5,200 of supplies such as paints, resins, and glue, and rented a shop at a local business park. He paid $3,600 in advance for the months of March, April, and May. During March he performed repairs totaling $7,600 and used up $2,400 of supplies. Of the repair services performed, 75% were paid for in cash by the end of the month and the balance was expected to be collected in April. Carl estimated that wear and tear on the equipment and tools during March was $250. On March 31, he owed $332 to the electric company and $78 to the water company for services consumed. Also on that date, he paid interest totaling $150 on the two loans.

Required (a) Prepare an account summary for Caldwell Furniture Repair for the month of March. (b) Prepare a separate presentation that details the changes in the cash account during March. (c) Is the transformation cycle complete or incomplete at the end of March? Explain your answer.

PROBLEM 3-4 Explaining the Difference Between Cash and Accrual Accounting

The accounting department at Klinger Realty sent the following financial reports to Robin Garrison, general manager. Attached was a note indicating that both sets of data are based on the same set of events that occurred during the quarter just completed. Robin was only recently promoted to this position and is not very knowledgeable concerning accounting information.

Klinger Realty
Results of Operating Activities
Third Quarter, 1995

	Cash Basis		Accrual Basis	
Cash receipts/revenues:				
Sales commissions	$300,000		$400,000	
Property management	210,000		165,000	
Total		$510,000		$565,000
Cash Payments/Expenses:				
Office employee wages	−53,000		−48,000	
Advertising	−10,000		−90,000	
Office supplies	0		−3,400	
Depreciation—office equipment	0		−1,800	
Rent	−6,000		−6,000	
Sales staff commissions	−150,000		−200,000	
Property managers' salaries	−116,000		−90,000	
Total		−335,000		−439,200
Net cash flow		$175,000		
Net income				$125,800

After reviewing this report, Robin is somewhat disturbed because she always thought accounting was an exact process. How, she wonders, can there be two different results from the same set of facts? Furthermore, how could they be so different? Which one is the "true" or "correct" report?

Required Assume you are called in to advise Ms. Garrison. Write a memo to her explaining why there can be two measures of operating results and why they differ.

PROBLEM 3-5 Preparing a Report of Net Cash Flow from Operations

Weintraub Water Products is a retailer of water sports products for backyard swimming pools. During August, the firm had the following operating activities:

Date		Event
Aug.	1	Bought $2,500 of goods for resale from Pinetree Wholesalers on credit.
	5	Paid $225 to the local newspaper for advertising that ran during July.
	6	Paid $500 rent for the month of August.
	9	Sold goods to customers for $3,650 on credit. These goods had cost the firm $1,800.
	10	Paid $1,500 to Pinetree Wholesalers for goods purchased August 1.
	11	Collected $2,600 from goods sold on August 9.
	13	Bought $4,600 of goods for resale from Stanley Co. Paid cash.
	16	Paid employees for their work so far in August, $575.
	19	Sold goods to customers on credit for $3,175. These goods had cost the firm $1,095.
	25	Collected $1,850 from the sales made on August 19.
	29	Paid $500 rent for the month of September.
	31	Employees had earned $600 of wages but would not be paid until September 1.

Required Prepare a report of net cash flow from operating activities.

PROBLEM 3-6 Preparing an Accrual Basis Income Statement

The Computer Den is a retailer of computer hardware and software. It had the following operating activities during the month of April:

Date		Event
April	1	Purchased $16,000 of inventory on credit from Big Byte Wholesalers.
	3	Paid $3,600 rent for the months of March and April.
	8	Sold goods to customers for $28,400. 40% was for cash with the balance on accounts receivable. These goods had cost the firm $17,200.
	11	Paid $12,000 to Big Byte Wholesalers for goods purchased April 1.
	14	Collected $15,400 from goods sold on April 8.
	17	Bought $46,400 of goods for resale from Tech-O Co. Paid cash.
	18	Paid April employee wages to date, $2,300.
	21	Sold goods to customers on credit for $24,700. These goods had cost the firm $16,380.
	22	Contributed $200 to the local United Way campaign.
	24	Collected $18,000 from the sales made on April 21.
	27	Paid $3,000 to the local newspaper for an ad campaign that ran during April.

April 30   Paid May's rent of $1,800.
       30   Employees had earned $2,400 of wages but would not be paid until May 1.

Required   Prepare an accrual basis income statement.

PROBLEM 3-7   Converting Net Income to Net Cash Flow

The following accrual basis information is available about Syria Corp. for 1996:

Total revenue from sales to customers	$ 45,000
Total expenses	− 34,500
Net income	$ 10,500

In addition, the following account information is known:

	Accounts Receivable	Accounts Payable
Beginning of year balance	$ 4,500	$ 7,500
End of year balance	10,500	4,500

Required   Determine (a) the amount of cash collected from customers during the year, (b) the amount of cash paid out for expenses during the year, and (c) the net cash flow for the year.

PROBLEM 3-8   Converting Net Cash Flow to Net Income

Mizzi Retail Co. reported the following cash flow information at the end of its first year in business:

Cash received from customers	$117,500
Cash paid out to suppliers of inventory	− 27,500
Cash paid out to employees	− 38,750
Cash paid out for advertising	− 6,250
Cash paid out for taxes	− 15,000
Net cash flow for the year	$ 30,000

Also known at year end was the following:

Amounts not yet collected from customers	$42,500
Amounts owed to suppliers	7,500
Wages owed to employees	11,250
Additional taxes still owed	5,000
Amount remaining in inventory	0

Required   Prepare an accrual basis income statement for Mizzi Retail's first year in business.

PROBLEM 3-9   Preparing Cash Basis and Accrual Basis Reports

Madison Remodelers has the following information available at the end of November concerning operating activities during the last three months:

	September	October	November
Remodeling services provided:	$136,500	$122,250	$96,000
Cash collections from customers:			
For services provided during September	67,500	45,000	24,000
For services during October		60,000	41,250
For services during November			48,750
Cash paid out:			
For goods/services used in September	−75,000	−22,500	−15,000
For goods/services used in October	−7,500	−60,000	−22,500
For goods/services used in November		−6,000	−56,250

In addition, during each month, $6,000 of goods and services were used in operations that were not paid for until December.

Required (a) Prepare a report of November's net cash flow from operations. (b) Prepare an accrual basis income statement for November.

PROBLEM 3-10   Revenue Recognition in Accrual Accounting

Daisy Political Consultants has been in existence for many years. During the month of November, the following events occurred:

a.   The owners contributed an additional $6,500 to the business to finance an expansion of operations.

b.   Consulting services totaling $11,000 were performed on credit during November and billed to customers.

c.   A loan in the amount of $25,000 was obtained from a wealthy campaign contributor.

d.   Expenses in the amount of $6,000 were incurred during the month. One-third had been paid for by month end.

e.   Cash of $18,500 was collected from customers for whom services had been performed during September and October.

f.   Services totaling $4,500 were performed for customers who had previously paid for the services during October.

Required   Daisy uses accrual basis accounting. For which of the events above should revenue be recorded in November? In each case, how much revenue should be recorded? If an event does not involve revenue, specify why not.

PROBLEM 3-11   Expense Recognition in Accrual Accounting

The local chapter of Special People, a social service organization, had the following economic events occur during the month of May:

a.   A luncheon honoring volunteers was held at a cost of $875. By month end the bill hadn't been received or paid.

b. New letterheads and envelopes were printed at a cost of $500 and paid for. The new items will not be used, however, until the old supply is exhausted sometime in June.

c. The executive director was paid her usual salary during May of $3,750.

d. Prizes, ribbons, and awards for events upcoming in July were delivered by the supplier who charged $9,375. The amount was paid in cash.

e. The electric bill for April totaled $155 and was paid in full.

f. Radio, TV, and newspaper advertising related to a special fundraising campaign ran during May. The $8,125 cost had been paid in April.

Required   Special People uses accrual basis accounting. For which of the events above should an expense be recorded in May? In each case, how much expense should be recorded? If an event does not involve an expense, specify why not.

PROBLEM 3-12   Distinguishing Among Types of Accounts

Bishop Auto Glass uses the following accounts when preparing its financial reports. Place a mark in the appropriate column to indicate the type of account.

	Asset	Liability	Equity	Revenue	Expense
a. Wages Payable					
b. Accounts Receivable					
c. Retained Earnings					
d. Buildings					
e. Supplies Used					
f. Inventory					
g. Cash Sales					
h. Marketable Securities					
i. Loan from Bank					
j. Land					
k. Owners' Investment					
l. Supplies on Hand					
m. Credit Sales					
n. Bonds Payable					
o. Advertising Paid in Advance					
p. Wages Earned by Employees					
q. Utilities Consumed					

PROBLEM 3-13   Ethics and Accounting Measurement

Hardy Rock is proprietor of a jewelry store. In January, he applied for a bank loan and was asked to submit an income statement for the past year, ended in December. Near the end of the prior year, Hardy had purchased merchandise for resale that cost him $60,000. He still owed $45,000 for this merchandise at year end. Half of the merchandise was sold during the Christmas holidays for $75,000. Customers owed Hardy $50,000 for these purchases at year end. Hardy included these transactions as part of his financial statements as follows:

Added to revenues	$75,000
Added to expenses	7,500
Added to net income	$67,500

Hardy reasoned that because he had sold half the merchandise in December, he should report it as revenue, though he had not received all of the cash from customers. Also, he reasoned that because he had paid $15,000 for the merchandise by year end and had sold half of the merchandise, he should report $7,500 of this amount as cost of goods sold.

Required What problems do you see with Hardy's reasoning? Is there an ethical problem with Hardy's treatment of these transactions? What should the effect of these transactions have been on net income?

PROBLEM 3-14   Ethics and Accounting Measurement

Nick Nash, Fred Ford, and Dick Dodge are partners in an automobile dealership, Riverside Chevrolet. Nick keeps the accounting records for the partnership. The other partners do not have much knowledge of accounting and depend on Nick for his expertise. The partners have agreed they will share equally in the company's profits at the end of each year. For fiscal 1996, the first year of operations, the company sold $6,600,000 of merchandise. Of this amount, $1,600,000 was still owed the company by customers at year end. The company purchased and paid for merchandise costing $3,400,000 during 1996. $1,000,000 of this merchandise remained in inventory at year end. The company purchased and paid for $1,200,000 of equipment during the year. The equipment should have a useful life of six years. Thus depreciation expenses would be $200,000 each year. Other expenses amounted to $580,000, all paid for in cash. Nick prepared the following income statement and distribution of profits for 1996:

Income Statement		
Revenues		$5,000,000
Expenses:		
Merchandise	$3,400,000	
Equipment	1,200,000	
Other	580,000	
Total Expenses		5,180,000
Net loss		$ 180,000
Distribution of net loss:		
Reduction in owners' capital:		
Dick Dodge		$ 60,000
Fred Ford		60,000
Nick Nash		60,000
Total distribution of net loss		$180,000

Dick and Fred were mystified by these results because they believed the company had been performing above their expectations. Nick assured his partners his numbers were correct.

Required   What problems do you see with Nick's financial report? How might Nick have used the information in his report to take advantage of his partners? Prepare a proper income statement and distribution of profits schedule for Riverside Chevrolet.

PROBLEM 3-15   Multiple-Choice Overview of the Chapter

1. Which of the following are part of an organization's transformation process?

	Investing activities	Operating activities
a.	Yes	Yes
b.	Yes	No
c.	No	Yes
d.	No	No

2. A going concern:
   a. need not prepare financial reports.
   b. should be expected to go out of business in the near future.
   c. need not concern itself with cash flow but should concentrate instead on generating net income.
   d. is assumed to have an expected life sufficiently long to complete any transformation cycles currently in process.

3. Tempel Mfg. uses accrual accounting. Each of the following events occurred during the month of February. Which one of them should be recorded as a revenue or expense for the month of February?
   a. Sales of $30,000 were made on credit. They will be collected during March.
   b. Collections of $10,000 were made from sales that occurred during January.
   c. Materials costing $18,000 were purchased and paid for. It is expected that they will be used during March.
   d. A bill in the amount of $8,600 was received from a supplier for goods purchased during January. It was paid immediately.

4. Zinsli Co. uses the accrual basis of accounting. Each of the following events occurred during July. Which one of them should be reported as an expense of July?
   a. Office supplies costing $800 were used up. They had been purchased and paid for during April.
   b. A new delivery truck was purchased on the last day of July. It was not put into use until August.
   c. On the third day of the month, $8,000 was paid to employees for hours worked during the month of June.
   d. Near the end of the month, August's rent of $1,500 was paid in advance.

5. Montvise, Inc. started operations during 1995. By year end, cash collections from customers totaled $153,000. In addition, the firm had accounts receivable from customers of $20,000. What amount of revenue should Montvise report on its 1995 income statement if it uses accrual accounting?
   a. $0
   b. $133,000
   c. $153,000
   d. $173,000

6. Periodic measurement requires that:
    a. the transformation process of an organization be measured and reported regularly.
    b. financial events be measured using a periodic chart of accounts.
    c. the life of a company should be long enough so that all incomplete transformation cycles can be completed.
    d. financial statements be prepared for owners at least every month.

7. The following information is available for two companies for the year 1996:

	Handle-Bar Mustache Co. *Cash Operating Statement* **For the Year 1996**	**Pencil-Thin Mustache Co.** *Accrual Income Statement* **For the Year 1996**
Receipts/Revenues	$50,000	$55,000
Payments/Expenses	38,000	31,000
Net Cash/Net Income	$12,000	$24,000

   Which of the following statements can be determined from the information provided?
    a. Pencil–Thin collected more cash from customers during 1996 than did Handle–Bar.
    b. Pencil–Thin was profitable during 1996, while Handle–Bar may have been profitable.
    c. Pencil–Thin is twice as profitable as Handle–Bar.
    d. Handle–Bar consumed more total resources during 1996 than did Pencil–Thin.

8. Which of the following accounts is a liability?

	Depreciation expense	**Accounts receivable**
a.	Yes	Yes
b.	Yes	No
c.	No	Yes
d.	No	No

9. On January 1, 19A, a company bought machinery for $15,000. The machinery was expected to last for five years and to be worthless at that point. The firm will depreciate the machinery $3,000 per year. At the end of the second year, the machinery is appraised to be worth $11,000 on the open market. How much depreciation did the company record on the asset for the first two years?
    a. $4,000
    b. $11,000
    c. $6,000
    d. $9,000

10. Using accrual-based measurement, expenses should be recognized when:
    a. a business owner recognizes that the firm is incurring too many expenses.
    b. resources are used rather than when they are paid for.
    c. cash is paid for resources.
    d. sufficient revenue is earned to offset the expenses.

C A S E S

CASE 3-1 Evaluating the Transformation Process

Provolone Pizza Company has just completed its first month in business. The owners, Charla and Pauline, had previously worked for a major pizza chain but were convinced they could offer a better product in a better atmosphere. They knew the importance of accurate financial records and hired a bookkeeper. Yesterday, the bookkeeper hand-delivered an account summary to the owners and promptly fell over dead. You have been retained by Charla and Pauline to interpret the following financial report and explain its significance.

Provolone Pizza Company
Account Summary
For First Month of Business

Assets =		Liabilities + Owners' Equity		+ (Revenues – Expenses)	
Cash	$ 2,240	Wages Payable	$ 180	Revenues	$4,000
Food Products	980	Advertising Payable	400	Expenses:	
Supplies	1,000	Loan from Bank	6,800	Store Rent	–800
Prepaid Rent	2,400	Owners' Capital	5,500	Food Products	–1,475
Equipment	5,100			Wages	–990
				Advertising	–1,430
				Interest	–40
				Supplies	–375
				Depreciation	–50
Total	$11,720	Total	$12,880	Total	–$1,160

Required   (a) Discuss whether the information provided by the summary could be helpful to the owners and, if so, describe how. If not, describe why not. (b) Identify at least 10 events that occurred as part of the transformation process during the firm's first month in business. For each event, identify the amount of cash involved. (c) Prepare an analysis of cash that explains how the cash balance changed during the period covered by the report. (d) Did Charla and Pauline make a good judgment when they decided to get into this business? Would you recommend they continue with the pizza business or discontinue it? What additional information would be helpful to you in making such a recommendation?

CASE 3-2 Evaluating the Results of an Organization's Transformation Process

Spivey Software Corp. has been in business for several years and is publicly traded on a major U.S. stock exchange. It is a wholesaler of a variety of commercial software applications including word processing, spreadsheet, and database applications. On January 1, 1996, the company's balance sheet appeared as follows (all amounts are in thousands of dollars):

Spivey Software Corporation
Balance Sheet
January 1, 1996

Assets		Liabilities & Stockholders' Equity	
Cash	$ 4,240	Wages payable	$ 640
Accounts receivable	7,800	Capital stock (owner's investment)	32,000
Inventory	15,200	Retained earnings	13,600
Buildings & equipment	12,000		
Land (for plant expansion)	7,000		
Total assets	$46,240	Total liabilities and stockholders' equity	$46,240

During the first quarter of the current year (January, February, March), the following events occurred.

a. New office furniture costing $500 was purchased on the last day of March. This was to be used in a new sales office that was scheduled to open April 1. The office furniture was paid for in cash.

b. Wages and salaries totaling $3,200 were paid. 20% of this amount was to liquidate wages payable that arose in the fourth quarter of the previous year. The company has a policy of not making wage or salary advances to employees.

c. All accounts receivable outstanding at January 1 were collected.

d. The company's advertising agency billed the firm $1,000 for a campaign that had run during the current quarter. The company is planning to pay the bill during April.

e. Sales were made to customers totaling $18,000. Of these sales, 60% was collected during the first quarter and the balance is expected to be collected during the next quarter. The goods that were sold had cost the company $13,000 when they had been purchased.

f. Dividends were declared and paid to stockholders in the amount of $1,500.

g. Inventory (software programs) costing $10,500 was purchased. 10% was paid for by the end of the quarter.

h. A three-year, $4,000, 12% loan was obtained from a local bank on the last day of the quarter.

i. New shares of stock were sold by the company for $2,000 in cash.

j. A new three-year lease agreement was signed and executed. The lease required that a $900 monthly rental be paid in advance for the first two quarters of the current year.

k. The accountants calculated that depreciation totaling $300 should be recorded for the quarter regarding the firm's buildings and equipment that had originally cost $16,870.

l. Sold the land that had been held for plant expansion for $7,000.

Required Did the company have a satisfactory first quarter? Prepare any summary documents you believe might help management (or interested external parties) better understand the effectiveness or efficiency of the firm's first quarter transformation process.

PROJECTS

PROJECT 3-1 Bibliographic Indexes for Business

The purpose of this assignment is to acquaint you with business bibliographic indexes in your library and to help you understand how cash flow and accrual basis accounting information is used. Bibliographic indexes list magazine, journal, or newspaper articles by topic. Using an index, you are to identify a published article, find it, copy it, and write a summary of it that will be discussed in class or turned in to your instructor. To begin, go to the reference area of your library and locate one or more of the following: *The Business Periodicals Index, The Accountant's Index, ABI/INFORM* (a computerized system). In one of the indexes, look up categories such as cash flow, cash basis accounting, cash management, and accrual basis accounting. Select two articles that appear to address examples of how cash flow (or cash basis) accounting information is used. Alternatively, you might look for articles that compare the usefulness of accrual and cash basis information. Read the articles and write a one-page summary.

PROJECT 3-2 Comparing Cash Versus Accrual Financial Reports

Under GAAP, a company must report the results of its operating activities on both the accrual basis and the cash basis. Users can then compare the amount of cash generated by operating activities to the amount of net income generated by operating activities. The purpose of this exercise is to locate and compare cash and accrual information in annual reports. The results of operating activities are reported in two separate places. Accrual basis information is reported on the income statement, while cash basis information is reported on the statement of cash flows. In this assignment you are to choose three companies. Choose one merchandising company, one manufacturing company, and one service company (e.g., utility, bank, or insurance). From your library's collection of annual reports, obtain the four most recent annual reports of each company you selected. Because each report contains two years' information, you will have at least five years of data. In each annual report, find the income statement and statement of cash flows. Prepare a schedule of information in the format below.

Results of Operating Activities

	From the Cash Flow Statement *Cash Flow from Operating Activities*	From the Income Statement *Net Income (or Operating Income)*
Company #1:		
19 ___	$_____	$_____
19 ___	$_____	$_____
19 ___	$_____	$_____
19 ___	$_____	$_____
19 ___	$_____	$_____
Total for 5 years	$_____	$_____
Average per year	$_____	$_____

Use the amount labeled "Operating income" if you can find it. If not, use "Net income" as an approximation. Start with the most recent year first and work backward. Continue similarly for the second and third companies. For each company, write a short description of how its cash flow pattern compares to its net income. Are they similar? Opposite? Do any trends emerge? If the cash flow is different from the net income (and it will be), explain how this can occur.

PROJECT 3-3 Identifying Cash Flows

Identify recent annual reports for five companies in five different industries. Find the statement of cash flows in each company's report. Make a list of the cash flows from operating, financing, and investing activities for each company. List the primary financing and investing activities identified in each company's report. Write a short report to accompany your lists that discusses how these activities appear to differ in importance across industries.

PROJECT 3-4 Cash and Accrual Measures

Assume you are trying to explain to a friend the differences between cash and accrual accounting. Write a short comparison of the two types of measurement. Provide examples of each to show how they differ when used to measure a common type of transaction. Show your comparison to someone who does not have much understanding of accounting and ask this person to write a brief note indicating any problems with understanding your explanation.

PROJECT 3-5 Unethical Behavior

Use an index of business periodicals (e. g., *The Business Periodicals Index* or *The Accountant's Index*) in the reference room of your library to identify articles about recent cases in which businesses or their managers have been accused or convicted of fraud. Find one of these articles that discusses how the fraud occurred. Write a brief summary of the article that includes a citation for the article. Explain the general effect the fraud had on the company's financial condition and on its financial statements. How were investors and others who had contractual relationships with the company affected by the fraud? What legal remedies (if any) were being sought for the fraud?

Chapter
4

Processing Accounting Information

This chapter examines the processing phase of the accounting information system. The chapter considers procedures accountants use to record, store, and summarize accounting data in a form that provides useful information for decision makers. The processing phase is the third stage of the accounting information system described in Chapter 2:

**The Accounting
Information
System**

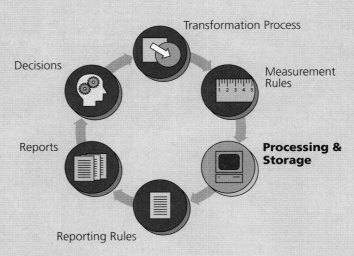

Transformation Process

Decisions

Measurement
Rules

Reports

Processing &
Storage

Reporting Rules

Also covered in this chapter are manual and computerized accounting systems. Both types of systems serve the same basic function: to convert data about economic events into information useful for decision makers. Therefore, all accounting systems require the analysis of events to determine transactions that should be recorded in the system. How transactions are recorded and how the system processes transactions differ, however, among systems. We will consider how transactions are identified and recorded and how accounting systems process data to create useful information. Also, we will consider controls used with accounting systems to increase their reliability and the accuracy of accounting information.

Major topics covered in this chapter include:

- The effects of transactions on accounting records and reports.
- Components and functions of accounting systems.
- Control procedures to improve the reliability of accounting systems.

Once you have completed this chapter, you should be able to:

1. Summarize the purpose of the processing phase of an accounting information system.
2. Explain what is meant by the term "double-entry bookkeeping."
3. Explain the purpose of the journal and the ledger.

4. Explain the purpose of debits and credits.
5. Explain the purpose of a subsidiary ledger.
6. Analyze transactions and determine their effects on account balances.
7. Explain the purpose of closing the books.
8. Summarize the steps in the accounting cycle.
9. Describe the components of a microcomputer accounting system.
10. Identify the modules of a large computer accounting system.
11. Identify the types of management decisions an accounting system facilitates.
12. Explain the purpose of accounting controls for accounting systems.

PROCESSING TRANSACTIONS

The processing phase of the accounting information system begins with identi-fying and recording transactions, which are events that occur within the transfor-mation process. The financial effects of transactions are recorded in the accounting system as increases or decreases in the balances of individual ac-counts. Account balances are stored in a data base. Reports for internal and ex-ternal decision makers summarize information from the data base.

Objective 1
Summarize the purpose of the processing phase of an accounting information system.

Transactions occur when an organization obtains financial resources, when it invests its financial resources in other resources, when it consumes these re-sources to produce goods and services, and when it sells goods and services. An organization's resources include financial resources (such as cash and securities), physical resources (such as buildings and equipment), services (such as human labor), or legal rights (such as patents). An organization obtains financial re-sources when it borrows from creditors and receives investments from owners; it invests in other resources when it purchases, borrows, or rents them. An organi-zation consumes resources when it uses them in the transformation process to produce goods and services. When the goods and services are sold to customers, an organization earns the right to receive additional financial resources. **The purpose of the processing phase of the accounting information system is to record resource acquisition and consumption activities in a sys-tematic form that can be summarized and reported.**

ACCOUNTING SYSTEMS

Systems for processing accounting information come in a variety of forms. These systems fulfill the purpose discussed in the previous section and lead to similar results. How they work may be quite different, however. Major differences de-pend on whether the system is manual or computerized.

Objective 2
Explain what is meant by the term "double-entry bookkeeping."

The traditional approach used to process transactions is known as *double-entry bookkeeping*, **a systematic method for recording transactions.** Double-entry bookkeeping involves a series of interrelated steps. The organiza-tion creates a set of accounting "books" to record and store the effects of transac-tions on accounts. For many centuries, these transactions were recorded manually in bound books or loose-leaf documents. The term "double-entry" comes from the requirement that each transaction be recorded in two or more accounts. A transaction identifies an exchange of resources or other event in which a "give and take" has occurred. The "give and take" process affects at least two elements of the accounting equation:

ASSETS = LIABILITIES + OWNERS' EQUITY + REVENUES − EXPENSES

This equation is critical to understanding how transactions are recorded in an accounting system. **A balance must be maintained at all times among the elements of the equation.** Therefore, if one element changes in the equation, some other element also must change to maintain the balance. Thus, the title "double-entry." The following section provides an example of transactions associated with an accounting system. We will use the transactions to illustrate double-entry bookkeeping.

An Illustration of an Accounting System

Round-O Tires is a small retail business selling automobile and light truck tires. Most of the company's sales are for cash, though it sells on credit to a few major business customers.

Objective 3
Explain the purpose of the journal and the ledger.

Round-O, like many businesses, records transactions using a journal and a ledger. **A *journal* is a book or computer file for recording transactions in the order in which they occur. A *ledger* is a book or computer file for summarizing account balances.** The journal and ledger are data bases for many accounting systems. Accounting systems almost always use at least one primary journal and one primary ledger, called the **general journal** and **general ledger**. Special journals and ledgers may be used for specific purposes. Transactions are recorded in the journal after being analyzed to determine which accounts are affected, the amount of the effect, and whether the transaction increases or decreases these accounts. Source documents provide a basis for determining the effect of transactions on accounts. *Source documents* **are records of specific transactions such as sales invoices, receiving notices, bills, and cash register receipts.**

Processing data in the accounting system involves the analysis of transactions, often from source documents, to determine their effect on the balances of individual accounts. *Transaction analysis* **is the determination of which accounts a transaction affects, the amount of the effect, and whether the transaction increases or decreases affected account balances.**

Sales and Inventory Transactions. Most of Round-O's transactions involve the sale of goods and services, collecting cash from customers, obtaining inventory, and paying suppliers.

When a customer makes a purchase, Round-O's sales personnel write a **sales receipt**, which describes the items or services sold, and lists the quantity and prices of the sales, and the date and customer's name. Cash sales are marked "Paid" on the sales receipt. For credit sales the customer's signature is required on the sales receipt.

Example of a Sales Receipt

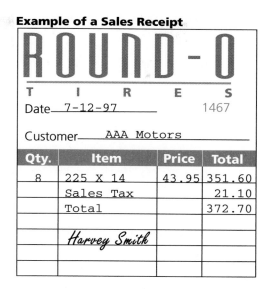

Exhibit 4–1 provides an example of a portion of a page from a journal. The first transaction records sales of tires for cash; the second records sales on credit.

Exhibit 4-1   An Example of a Journal

Date	Transaction	Debit	Credit
Oct. 3	Cash	1,300.39	
	Sales Tax Payable		73.61
	Sales Revenue		1,226.78
Oct. 3	Accounts Receivable	893.86	
	Sales Tax Payable		50.60
	Sales Revenue		843.26

The journal identifies the date of each transaction, the accounts affected by the transaction, and the amounts. Each transaction must be recorded in at least two accounts to preserve the balance of the accounting equation. We can illustrate this process as follows:

Assets =		Liabilities + Owners' Equity		+ (Revenues – Expenses)	
Cash	1,300.39	Sales Tax Payable	73.61	Sales Revenue	1,226.78

An increase in the asset CASH of $1,300.39 is balanced by an increase in SALES TAX PAYABLE of $73.61 and an increase in SALES REVENUE of $1,226.78. Note that Round-O collects 6% sales tax for local governments. These collections result in obligations to remit the taxes to government authorities, and thus, are recorded as liabilities.

The elements of the accounting equation can be thought of in the following way:

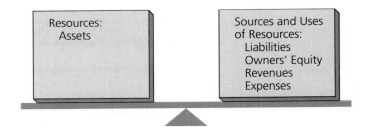

Assets are resources. Resources originate from those who invest in an organization (liabilities, owners' equity) and those who purchase its goods and services (revenues). Resources are consumed in payments to investors and in materials and services that are used to provide goods and services for customers (expenses). Thus, the balance between resources and the sources and uses of resources must always be maintained.

Traditionally, accountants have recorded transactions using debits and credits. **Debits and credits refer to increases and decreases in account balances.** *Debits* **are increases in asset and expense account balances and decreases in liability, owners' equity, and revenue account balances.** *Credits* **are decreases in asset and expense account balances and increases in liability, owners' equity, and revenue account balances.** In Exhibit 4-1, CASH was increased by a debit, while SALES TAX PAYABLE and SALES REVENUE were increased by credits. By convention, the left-hand side of the accounting equation (assets) is increased by debits, while the right-hand side (liabilities and owners' equity) is increased by credits. Revenues increase owners' equity and, therefore, are increased by credits. Expenses are an offset to revenues and reduce owners' equity. Therefore, they are increased by debits:

Assets =	Liabilities + Owners' Equity	+ (Revenues	− Expenses)
Debit +	Debit −	Debit −	Debit +
Credit −	Credit +	Credit +	Credit −

These rules preserve the mathematical relationship in the accounting equation. At the same time, they provide a check on the accuracy of recorded transactions. The total of debits recorded in the journal for any period should be equal to the total of credits. If debits do not equal credits, an error has occurred in recording one or more transactions for the period.

The mathematical relationship of debits and credits with the accounting equation is readily observable if the equation is transformed by moving expenses from the right-hand to the left-hand side:

ASSETS + EXPENSES = LIABILITIES + OWNERS' EQUITY + REVENUES

The left-hand side of the equation is increased by debit entries and the right-hand side is increased by credit entries:

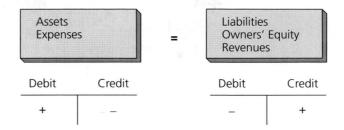

Recording transactions properly so debits are equal to credits results in maintaining a balance in the accounting equation.

Learning Note

The format shown above for debits and credits is referred to as the T-account format. It is a commonly used approach for demonstrating the effect of transactions on accounts. For example, the sales transaction of October 3 in Exhibit 4-1 could be represented as:

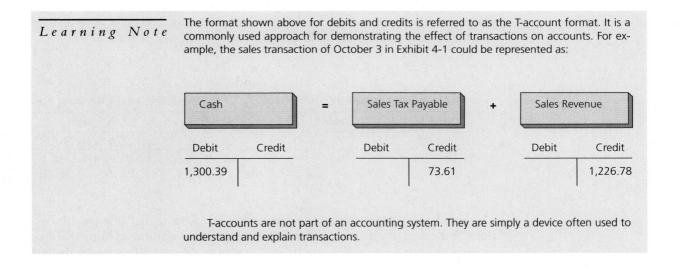

T-accounts are not part of an accounting system. They are simply a device often used to understand and explain transactions.

As illustrated in Exhibit 4-1, by convention, debit entries in a journal are recorded first and are followed by credit entries for each transaction. Credit entries are indented from the left-hand margin to make them easier to identify. An explanation might follow below the journal entry describing the event that produced the transaction.

A ledger provides a summary of transactions affecting individual accounts. Exhibit 4-2 illustrates a portion of Round-O's general ledger for the cash account.

A ledger page is maintained for each account. Accounts generally are numbered for ease of reference. **A** *chart of accounts* **is a list of account titles and numbers for an organization.** Often, assets are numbered from 100–199, liabilities from 200–299, etc. Account numbers may have subcodes to identify divisions, departments, or individual customers. For example, account 301-16 may

Exhibit 4-2   An Example of a General Ledger

Account: CASH

Date	Debit	Credit	Balance
Sept. 26	879.25		17,892.34
		578.91	17,313.43
27		490.18	16,823.25
	133.82		16,957.07
Oct. 3	1,300.39		18,257.46

identify an ACCOUNTS PAYABLE account (301) for Never-Wear Tire Company (16). Account 425-06-112 may identify utility expenses (425), at the North Dakota plant (06), in the maintenance department (112).

Increases in asset and expense accounts are recorded to the debit column of the ledger account. These debit entries increase the balances of the asset and expense accounts. Increases in liability, owners' equity, and revenue accounts are recorded to the credit column, as shown below for the sales revenue account.

Account: SALES REVENUE		Account Number: 401	
Date	Debit	Credit	Balance
Sept. 28			43,249.75
Oct. 3		1,226.78	44,476.53

An advantage of using two columns, one for additions and one for subtractions, is the ease of computing totals. Remember that, for most of history, bookkeepers did not have adding machines, calculators, or computers. Mathematical calculation was a mental activity. It is easier to add a column of debits and another column of credits and then compute the difference than it is to mix pluses and minuses in the same column. Adding columns to verify totals has been a routine part of bookkeeping. The debit and credit system is designed to help the bookkeeper maintain accurate records. Much of this advantage is lost in an age of computers. Debits and credits are still part of the language of accounting, but their importance for accounting systems is much diminished. Computers identify pluses and minuses, rather than debits and credits, and do not care about the order in which they occur.

The goal of this book is not to make you proficient in using debits and credits. Instead, a goal is to help you understand the effect of transactions on accounting reports. It is important that you be able to analyze transactions to determine their effect on financial statements. **A set of financial statements is a summary of transactions.** Therefore, to understand financial statements you should understand the underlying transactions. Our concern is that you understand which elements of the accounting equation are affected, how they are affected, and how the effects are observed in the financial statements. However, debits and credits are part of the language of accounting and business you should include in your vocabulary.

Credit Sales and Accounts Receivable. Credit sales are recorded to the accounts receivable and sales revenue accounts:

Assets =		Liabilities + Owners' Equity		+ (Revenues − Expenses)	
Accounts Receivable	893.86	Sales Tax Payable	50.60	Sales Revenue	843.26

Amounts received from credit customers are recorded to the cash and accounts receivable accounts:

Assets =		Liabilities + Owners' Equity	+ (Revenues − Expenses)
Cash	657.00		
Accounts Receivable	−657.00		

Observe that exchanging one asset for another preserves the balance in the accounting equation.

In addition to a general accounts receivable account, a company must maintain detailed records for amounts owed and paid by individual customers. This information often is maintained in an accounts receivable ledger.

Objective 5
Explain the purpose of a subsidiary ledger.

The accounts receivable ledger is a subsidiary ledger. **A** *subsidiary ledger* **contains accounts that are subcategories of a general ledger account.** By using subsidiary ledgers, a company can maintain detailed information separate from the summary record found in the general ledger.

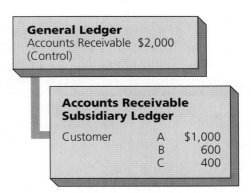

Cost of Goods Sold and Inventory. In addition to recording sales, Round-O must record the cost of inventory sold to the cost of goods sold and inventory accounts. This transaction reduces inventory and increases expense, thereby reducing net income:

Assets =		Liabilities + Owners' Equity	+ (Revenues − Expenses)	
Inventory	−1,076.12		Cost of Goods Sold	−1,076.12

Detailed records must be maintained for each inventory item showing the number and cost of units acquired, sold, and on hand.

Purchases and Accounts Payable. When the number of units in inventory becomes low, additional inventory is purchased. Round-O receives a purchase invoice from the supplier of the inventory. The purchase invoice identifies the costs of items and the amount owed the supplier. When the invoice is received, the purchase is recorded in the journal to the inventory and accounts payable accounts:

Assets =		Liabilities + Owners' Equity		+ (Revenues − Expenses)	
Inventory	8,460.93	Accounts Payable	8,460.93		

Round-O also must keep detailed records about the amount it owes to individual suppliers. Any payments are recorded to the accounts payable and cash accounts:

Assets =		Liabilities + Owners' Equity		+ (Revenues − Expenses)	
Cash	−5,794.68	Accounts Payable	−5,794.68		

Other Transactions. Round-O pays bills for utilities, advertising, and other expenses when they are received. Wages expense is recorded when employees earn their wages. Also, the company records PAYROLL TAX EXPENSE and PAYROLL TAXES PAYABLE for the amount that has to be distributed to the government.

Purchases of equipment and other assets are recorded to the appropriate asset account and to CASH or ACCOUNTS PAYABLE. Detailed records about individual assets also are maintained.

The following illustration summarizes transactions for Round-O:

Assets =		Liabilities + Owners' Equity		+ (Revenues − Expenses)	
a. Cash	1,300.39	Sales Tax Payable	73.61	Sales Revenue	1,226.78
b. Accounts Receivable	893.86	Sales Tax Payable	50.60	Sales Revenue	843.26
c. Cash	657.00				
Accounts Receivable	−657.00				
d. Inventory	−1,076.12			Cost of Goods Sold	−1,076.12
e. Inventory	8,460.93	Accounts Payable	8,460.93		
f. Cash	−5,794.68	Accounts Payable	−5,794.68		
g. Cash	−465.89			Utilities Expense	−465.89
h. Cash	−7,234.97			Wages Expense	−7,234.97
i.		Payroll Tax Payable	1,320.12	Payroll Tax Expense	−1,320.12
j. Equipment	2,047.39				
Cash	−2,047.39				
Total	−3,916.48	Total	4,110.58	Total	−8,027.06

Objective 6
Analyze transactions and determine their effects on account balances.

Note the **accounting equation is in balance after each transaction is recorded.** At any time, the column totals for transactions recorded for a period will demonstrate that the equation is balanced. Also, be careful to observe that transactions change account balances. **The amounts recorded are not the balances of the accounts but changes in the balances.** Therefore, after all the transactions described above have been recorded, the assets column reports a decrease in total assets of $3,916.48. This amount is the change in assets resulting from the transactions. It is *not* the amount of assets available after the transactions have been recorded.

Exhibit 4–3, on the next page, illustrates the effect of Round-O's transactions on its account balances. This exhibit provides the kind of information that would be obtained from a company's ledger. It identifies the account balances and changes in these balances during a period.

The transactions change the balances of Round-O's accounts. The equality, ASSETS = LIABILITIES + OWNERS' EQUITY + REVENUES − EXPENSES, is maintained before ($317,285.65) and after ($313,369.17) the transactions are recorded.

Summary of Transactions. Though many types of transactions occur in an organization, a few types of transactions account for most activity recorded in an accounting system. Exhibit 4–4 summarizes primary transactions between an organization and external parties. Other than adjustments (considered in Chapter 6), these are the types of transactions you will observe most often in a business.

Objective 7
Explain the purpose of closing the books.

Completing the Accounting Process. Account balances at the end of a fiscal period, such as those in Exhibit 4–3, are used to prepare financial statements. A final step in processing accounting information involves transferring revenue and expense account balances to owners' equity. Accountants refer to this process as closing the accounts or **closing the books**. A closing transaction adjusts each revenue and expense account so it has a zero balance at the end of a fiscal period, usually a fiscal year. For example, assume the sales revenue account for Round-O has a balance of $289,000 at the end of the 1996 fiscal year. This balance represents the company's total sales since the beginning of the fiscal year. The balance is eliminated by deducting $289,000 from the revenue account. This balance is added to an owners' equity account. For proprietorships and partnerships, this account usually is the OWNERS' CAPITAL account. For a corporation, it is the RETAINED EARNINGS account.

The balances of expense accounts are eliminated by deducting the balance from each account and subtracting it from OWNERS' CAPITAL or RETAINED EARNINGS.

Once these adjustments have been made, (1) the balances of all revenue and expense accounts are zero and (2) the balances of these accounts have been transferred to owners' equity. Therefore, once the books are closed, the accounting equation ASSETS = LIABILITIES + OWNERS' EQUITY is balanced because revenue and expense accounts are all equal to zero. When a company begins a new fiscal year, it accumulates new revenues and expenses for the new period.

Processing accounting information involves a cycle of activities for recording, summarizing, and reporting the activities in a company's transformation process. **The** *accounting cycle* **is the process of analyzing transactions, recording transactions in the journal and in ledger accounts, and**

Objective 8
Summarize the steps in the accounting cycle.

Exhibit 4-3   The Effect of Transactions on Account Balances

	Balances Before Transactions	+ or – Transaction Effects		= Balances After Transactions
Assets:				
Cash	$ 16,957.07	a. c. f. g. h. j.	+1,300.39 +657.00 −5,794.68 −465.89 −7,234.97 −2,047.39 −13,585.54	$ 3,371.53
Accounts receivable	24,305.91	b. c.	+893.86 −657.00 +236.86	24,542.77
Inventory	89,570.12	d. e.	−1,076.12 +8,460.93 +7,384.81	96,954.93
Property, plant, and equipment	186,452.55	j.	+2,047.39	188,499.94
Total assets	**317, 285.65**		**−3,916.48**	**313,369.17**
Liabilities:				
Accounts payable	20,410.33	e. f.	+8,460.93 −5,794.68 +2,666.25	23,076.58
Sales tax payable	8,100.47	a. b.	+73.61 +50.60 +124.21	8,224.68
Payroll tax payable	5,326.84	i.	+1,320.12	6,646.96
Notes payable	187,500.00			187, 500.00
Total liabilities	**221,337.64**		**+4,110.58**	**225,448.22**
Owners' equity	**87,532.14**			**87,532.14**
Sales revenue	**43,249.75**	a. b.	+1,226.78 +843.26 +2,070.04	**45,319.79**
Expenses:				
Cost of goods sold	−17,687.08	d.	−1,076.12	−18,763.20
Utilities expense	−2,590.10	g.	−465.89	−3,055.99
Wages expense	−12,399.26	h.	−7,234.97	−19,634.23
Payroll tax expense	−2,157.44	i.	−1,320.12	−3,477.56
Total expenses	**−34,833.88**		**−10,097.10**	**−44,930.98**
Total liabilities, owners' equity, revenues, and expenses	**$317,285.65**		**−3,916.48**	**$313,369.17**

Exhibit 4-4 Common Types of Transactions

Transaction	Source Documents	Accounts Affected		
		Assets	Liabilities and Owners' Equity	Revenues and Expenses
Sales for cash	Sales slips and invoices	+ Cash − Inventory		+ Sales Revenue − Cost of Goods Sold
Sales on credit	Sales slips and invoices	+ Accounts Receivable − Inventory		+ Sales Revenue − Cost of Goods Sold
Collections from customers	Checks and billing statements	+ Cash − Accounts Receivable		
Purchase merchandise or materials for cash	Purchase orders and invoices	− Cash + Inventory		
Purchase merchandise or materials on credit	Purchase orders and invoices	+ Inventory	+ Accounts Payable	
Payment to vendors	Bills and checks	− Cash	− Accounts Payable	
Other purchases for cash	Purchase orders and invoices	− Cash + Equipment or other assets		
Other purchases on credit	Purchase orders and invoices	+ Equipment or other assets	+ Accounts or Notes Payable	
Payment of operating expenses	Bills and checks	− Cash		− Expenses—Wages, Utilities, etc.
Borrow from creditors	Loan agreements	+ Cash	+ Notes or Bonds Payable	
Repay creditors	Checks	− Cash	− Notes or Bonds Payable	
Pay interest to creditors	Checks	− Cash		− Interest Expense
Investment by owners	Owner or stockholder agreements	+ Cash	+ Owners' Capital or Stockholders' Equity	
Payment of return to owners	Checks	− Cash	− Owners' Capital or Dividends	

preparing financial reports from the ledger account balances. Exhibit 4-5 summarizes the accounting cycle.

Exhibit 4-5 Summary of the Accounting Cycle

SELF-STUDY PROBLEM 4-1

Leonardo's is a retail store that specializes in artists' supplies. The following transactions occurred during May. Identify the effect of each transaction on Leonardo's accounts using the format below. Demonstrate that the accounting equation is balanced after all transactions have been recorded.

1.   Sold $300 of merchandise for cash.
2.   The merchandise sold in (1) cost Leonardo's $135.
3.   Sold $800 of merchandise on credit.
4.   The merchandise sold in (3) cost Leonardo's $320.
5.   Purchased on credit $3,400 of merchandise from suppliers.
6.   Paid $2,000 to suppliers for credit purchases.
7.   Paid $230 for utilities expense.
8.   Paid $690 to employees for wages.

Assets =	Liabilities + Owners' Equity	+ (Revenues − Expenses)
Total	Total	Total

The solution to Self-Study Problem 4-1 appears at the end of the chapter.

COMPUTERIZED ACCOUNTING SYSTEMS

Many organizations, even small ones, maintain their accounting records on computers in the U.S. and other industrialized countries. An advantage of a computerized accounting system is the journal and ledger functions are performed by the computer. Accounts are updated automatically. The computer can print transaction and account records. Also, it can prepare financial statements from the accounting records. Therefore, the amount of manual work is limited primarily to entering transactions on the computer. Fewer opportunities for error exist than with a manual system. A computer system normally is faster and less expensive than a manual system for all but very small organizations.

Microcomputer Systems

Objective 9
Describe the components of a microcomputer accounting system.

Within computerized systems, there are small systems that operate on a micro-computer as well as large systems that require mainframe computers or computer networks. Smaller companies often use accounting programs designed for personal computers. These programs provide accounting records similar to those provided by a manual bookkeeping system. For example, the program provides a sales invoice template. The template is an invoice with blanks for customer name, address, items purchased, and amounts. A computer operator completes the template on the computer with the name of the customer and a description of items purchased. The operator enters the quantity of each item purchased and the computer fills in the price from product pricing records stored on the computer. Appropriate taxes are determined by the computer program. The program automatically records the transaction to the appropriate sales and inventory accounts and updates inventory records and customers' accounts for credit sales. The operator can print a copy of the sales invoice for the customer. Exhibit 4-6 illustrates a sales invoice, which documents the items sold to the customer.

Exhibit 4-6   Example of a Sales Invoice

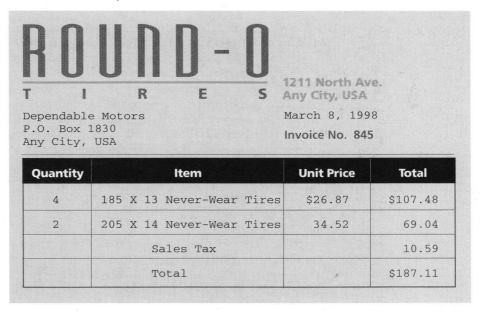

Quantity	Item	Unit Price	Total
4	185 X 13 Never-Wear Tires	$26.87	$107.48
2	205 X 14 Never-Wear Tires	34.52	69.04
	Sales Tax		10.59
	Total		$187.11

The sales invoice template is part of an **accounts receivable module** in the system. Other major modules usually include **accounts payable**, **payroll**, and **general ledger and financial statements**. These are the primary accounting activities, in volume of transactions, for most companies.

The accounts receivable module maintains customer records. It can be used to print reports of customer activity for a period, current amounts owed, and overdue accounts. Also, it is used to print periodic billing statements to customers. These statements are used to prompt payment from customers. Exhibit 4-7 provides an example of a billing statement.

Exhibit 4-7   Example of a Billing Statement

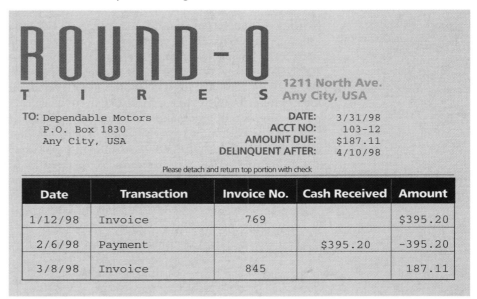

A purchase order template in the accounts payable module permits the operator to prepare a purchase order on the computer with the name of the supplier and a description of the items ordered. The operator prints a copy of the purchase order for mailing to the supplier. When a shipment and purchase invoice are received from the supplier, a template is completed for the items and amount of the purchase. The computer updates inventory and accounts payable accounts and records. The module permits an operator to prepare checks for operating expenses and other purchases, and can be used to print reports of current accounts payable balances.

A payroll module permits an operator to update employee records for hours worked during a pay period. The computer prepares payroll forms and prints checks for employees. The system also prepares payroll tax reports for government authorities.

The general ledger and financial statements module permits other transactions to be recorded for nonroutine transactions such as bank loans and owner investments. It prepares financial statements for various periods, such as the current month, the year-to-date, or the current fiscal year.

A computerized system may be fairly simple. One operator may enter all transactions and maintain the system. For larger organizations, several operators may be involved. Different operators may be responsible for different types of transactions: accounts receivable, accounts payable, payroll, and so forth. Their computers may be part of a network, so data entered at different work stations are maintained as part of one data base.

Large Computer Systems

In large companies, computerized accounting systems can become quite complex. Many employees may be involved in entering data in the computer. Separate departments often are used for accounts receivable, accounts payable, payroll, and the like. Computer operators are linked to a large mainframe computer, a (medium-sized) minicomputer, or a network of microcomputers. Operators may be in different geographic locations.

One of the advantages of a computerized accounting system is the ability it affords managers to access information about current activities. For example, a manager in a company's headquarters in the Northeast can query the system for sales information for a division across town or on the West Coast. Other advantages are a reduction in duplication of data and the ability to produce a wide variety of reports. Computer systems can share data bases; therefore, data entered in a system for one purpose can be accessed for other purposes. Computer data files can be manipulated to produce reports for different products, regions, customers, and time periods. Multinational companies use computer systems to link facilities throughout the world. These systems compile data from various locations and translate data measured in foreign currencies into dollars. Thus, these systems are major assets for large companies.

Objective 10
Identify the modules of a large computer accounting system.

Exhibit 4-8 depicts a large computerized accounting system. A large accounting system consists of several computer modules that interact with each other. Each module accesses one or more data bases. These data bases store information about customers, products, vendors, and other aspects of the business's activities. Each module also includes programs that manipulate and summarize information in the data bases.

Exhibit 4-8   Modules in a Computerized Accounting System

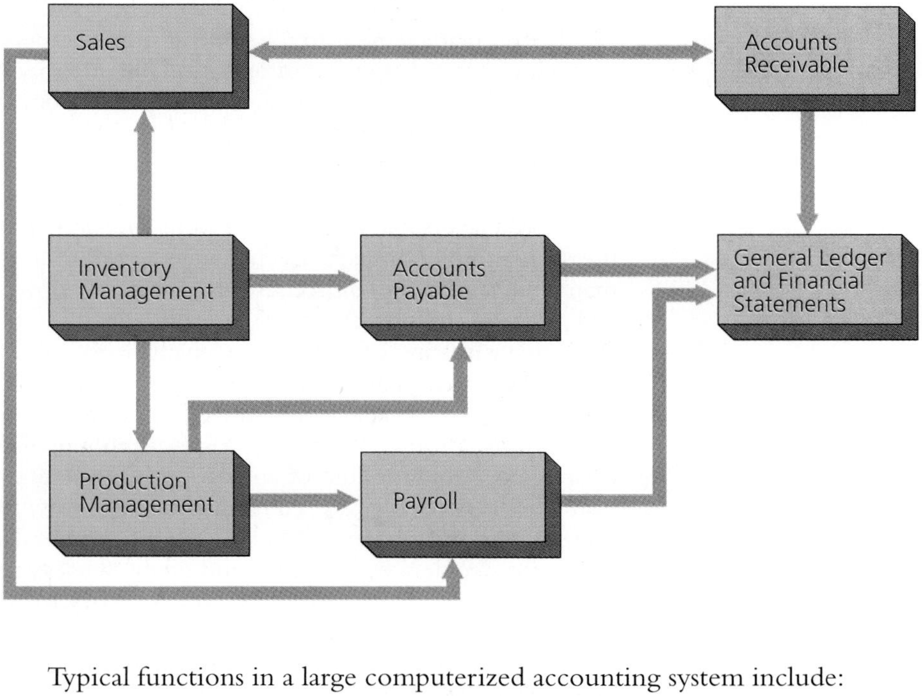

Typical functions in a large computerized accounting system include:

Sales: recording and analyzing sales transactions.
Accounts Receivable: recording customer information, billing, and cash receipts.

Inventory Management: recording inventory and purchasing information.

Accounts Payable: recording amounts owed and paid to suppliers.

Production Management: recording resource and cost information associated with manufacturing activities.

Payroll: recording employee information, hours worked, wages, and payroll taxes.

General Ledger and Financial Statements: recording transactions not recorded in other modules; preparing and analyzing financial reports.

THE ACCOUNTING SYSTEM AND MANAGEMENT DECISIONS

Objective 11
Identify the types of management decisions an accounting system facilitates.

An accounting system serves a variety of needs, providing information for internal and external decision makers. External decision makers receive reports prepared by the system. We will examine these in Chapters 5 and 6. The system serves various needs of managers. The design of an accounting system is important to facilitate effective and efficient operations within an organization. This section discusses some of the needs served by the modules of the accounting system we considered in the prior section.

The sales module is designed to facilitate the timely and accurate processing of customer orders. Prompt and reliable servicing of customer orders is necessary in competitive markets. Customers want fast service and delivery. Fast order processing increases customer satisfaction because of quicker response to customer demands. Customers need to know when they will receive their orders, so sales must interact with inventory management to identify available items or with production management to schedule customer orders for manufacturing.

Sales analysis provides information for identifying high demand and profitable products. It helps managers make pricing decisions. It helps managers decide which products to emphasize, which product lines to expand, and which products to eliminate. Also, it helps managers identify profitable territories and customers. Thus, managers can decide where to invest in additional marketing efforts. Managers need to predict future sales activity to determine how much to invest in production capacity and inventory. By anticipating fluctuations in demand, managers can control resources and cash flows to meet changing financial and market conditions.

The processing of accounts receivable and cash from sales provides information to help a company manage its cash flow. Management needs information to help it control cash and reduce the delay in collecting receivables. Also, managers need information to minimize losses from uncollectible receivables. The accounts receivable module of an accounting system assists in providing information about who owes a company money, how long receivables have been outstanding, and past experiences with a customer. Management uses this information to decide whether to extend credit, what type of credit terms to provide, and whether or not special actions are necessary to collect accounts.

Inventory management provides information to control inventory and costs associated with inventory. Managers determine the amount of inventory to maintain, and should protect it from theft and obsolescence. Too much or too little inventory is costly because sales are lost or cash is tied up in nonproductive resources.

Information about accounts payable helps managers control cash outflows. Managers want to delay outflows as long as they do not incur substantial costs from the delay. They do not want to pay high financing charges or late fees; they want to take advantage of discounts for early payment. Also, they want to maintain favorable relations with vendors. Managers use information from accounts payable to determine when to make payments and to monitor future cash requirements. Planning for cash inflows and outflows is an important management function. A company does not wish to maintain too much cash that could be invested in productive assets. On the other hand, it does not wish to be short of cash for meeting obligations and current operating needs.

Production is a primary activity in many organizations. The production process can be extremely complex. The accounting system can assist managers in controlling this process. Information on production costs and resource constraints can make a major difference in a company's profitability. Managers schedule production activities to make efficient use of available materials, labor, and equipment. Accounting systems can help managers plan for the efficient use of resources.

Payroll is a major expense in most organizations. Control over this expense and cash flows is an important activity. Accounting information helps managers monitor labor costs. It also provides for information needs of employees, labor unions, and tax and regulatory authorities.

The effective design of an accounting system involves trade-offs between costs and benefits. Computerized systems reduce the cost of information processing and reporting and increase the flexibility of the system to meet management needs. They can be very expensive, however. Hardware and software needed by the system may require a significant investment. Therefore, an organization must assess its information needs and determine the type of system that is best suited to meet those needs at a reasonable cost.

SELF-STUDY PROBLEM 4-2

Agnes Coates is the proprietor of a retail clothing store. She has been thinking about replacing her manual accounting system with a microcomputer system. She would need to purchase a computer and software. Agnes has asked you for some information.

Required

Write a short memo to Agnes explaining the advantages of a computerized system over those of a manual system. In addition, briefly describe the various components or modules that Agnes might acquire as part of her system and their functions.

The solution to Self-Study Problem 4-2 appears at the end of the chapter.

CONTROL OF ACCOUNTING SYSTEMS

A primary concern about any accounting system is its reliability. For accounting information to be useful, it must accurately measure economic events that affect an organization. A variety of difficulties can arise that result in unreliable infor-

Objective 12
Explain the purpose of accounting controls for accounting systems.

mation. For example, data may be recorded incorrectly in the accounting system. Errors may be made in source documents or as data are entered into the system. Deliberate errors may be made by managers or employees to cover mismanagement, fraud, or theft. Events may go unrecorded because of oversight or because of theft or misuse of resources. Programming errors in the system may result in improper processing of data, leading to erroneous reports. Events may not be recorded for the period in which they occur. Whatever the cause, unreliability is a serious problem in an accounting system.

To reduce the likelihood of error, omission, or misstatement, controls are built into accounting systems. These controls are part of an organization's system of internal accounting controls. *Internal control* **consists of procedures designed to protect an organization's resources and to ensure the reliability of its accounting records.** This section considers internal control procedures designed to ensure the reliability of accounting records. We will consider both manual and computerized systems. Other internal control procedures will be considered in Chapter 7.

Control of Manual Systems

Some of the most important internal control features of an accounting system are integral to the system itself. Many features of double-entry bookkeeping were developed to increase the reliability of the system. Debits and credits simplify the recording of transactions and provide a means for identifying errors if debits are not equal to credits. Comparing subsidiary ledger balances with general ledger account balances can detect errors in recording data. Therefore, one of the most important control features of a manual system is use of a double-entry system by a trained bookkeeper.

Manual systems most often are used by small, owner-managed companies. These systems are operated by one or a few employees. Therefore, control of these systems depends on the integrity and ability of these employees. The following internal control procedures can be helpful in maintaining a reliable accounting system:

1. Hire qualified employees. Bookkeepers and other office staff should have the necessary training and experience to meet job requirements. Employees must be honest and dependable.
2. Establish clear policies to define the authority and responsibilities of employees. Employees should understand their duties and the limits of their authority. Record-keeping responsibilities should be separated from physical control over cash, inventory, and other resources whenever possible.
3. Establish procedures for proper processing of transactions. Transactions should be authorized by the owner or appropriate manager who should sign checks, invoices, or other documents.
4. Use proper forms and prenumbered documents. Preprinted and prenumbered forms permit validation of all transactions. Proper forms reduce the opportunity for error through omission of data or failure to document transactions. Prenumbered forms permit the owner to determine that all transactions have been recorded.
5. Maintain control over documents and resources. Documents should be filed for future reference and later verification. They should be maintained in safe

locations for protection from unauthorized access or destruction. Cash should be deposited daily. Inventory should be stored in a safe location.

6. Accounting records should be independently verified. The cash account should be reconciled with bank statements. Inventory account records should be verified by periodic physical counts. An audit by an independent accountant is useful for verifying accounting records.

Control of Computer Systems

A computerized accounting system creates many internal control problems. Much of the documentation of a manual system is replaced by computer records. These records are subject to manipulation after they are created; therefore, they may not provide independent verification of transactions. Computers can make mistakes with the speed of light and are not capable of judging the reasonableness of their actions. Whether a check is written for $100 or $100,000 does not matter to a computer. Computerized data can be destroyed. Computer systems can fail, resulting in the loss of programs and data. Employees can change programs and erase data. Numerous examples exist of disgruntled employees who deliberately sabotaged computer systems, costing companies millions of dollars.

In addition to the types of internal control procedures described in the prior section, the following procedures often are used with computerized systems:

1. Control access to the system. An important safeguard is physical access to the computer. Control over the computer itself is important. Terminals and microcomputers should be protected from unauthorized use. They should not be accessible by unauthorized personnel. Passwords should be used to prevent access to the system and to specific data files and programs.

2. Identify responsibility for specific functions. Employee identification codes can be used to determine who processed certain transactions. Employees should have access only to those files and programs they need to perform their duties.

3. Substantial error checking should be built into the computer system. Programs should be designed to determine the reasonableness of data entered in the system and to check for mathematical accuracy and completeness. Data entered in one part of the system should be verified against data from other parts; for example, purchase invoices should agree with purchase orders. Limits should be placed on what the computer can do without special authorization; for example, a limit might be placed on the amount that can be printed on a check.

4. Computer programs should be checked carefully when they are installed. They should be rechecked periodically to determine that they are functioning properly. To illustrate, test transactions can be run through the system and outputs can be compared with expected results to verify the system's accuracy.

5. Data files should be backed up regularly, and copies should be secured. Extra copies of programs and documentation should be maintained, as well. Even access to backup computer systems may be necessary for some organizations.

6. Segregate duties among data-processing employees. Design and operation of computer systems should be separate functions. If employees who enter data

and process records do not understand how the programs are designed, they will have little opportunity to modify the programs for personal gain.

7. Document the system, programs, and operating procedures. Documentation of how the system works and the proper procedures to be used by employees is important. Documentation is needed when the system is modified to determine the appropriateness of changes. Documentation is useful when employees are trained for new duties. Finally, it is important when the system is audited to make sure the system is functioning properly. Reliable accounting information depends on reliable processing. Internal controls are important for ensuring the accounting system is processing data accurately.

SELF-STUDY PROBLEM 4-3

Deborah Stinger works in the systems development department of a major company. She helped develop the company's computerized accounting system. Occasionally, she fills in for one of the operators in the accounts payable department. This operator is responsible for processing checks to vendors for purchases made by the company. While filling in, Deborah created an account for a fictitious company, just to see if the system could be tricked into writing checks for nonexistent purchases. She added data to the company's vendor file and entered some phony purchase invoice numbers and data. The computer wrote the checks, and they were mailed to a post office box Deborah had opened. Over the last few years, Deborah has written over $80,000 in checks to her fictitious company.

Required

Identify some internal control deficiencies in the accounting system that have allowed Deborah to embezzle money from her company.

The solution to Self-Study Problem 4-3 appears at the end of the chapter.

REVIEW *Summary of Important Concepts*

1. The effects of transactions on accounting records and reports:
   a. Financial effects of transactions are recorded in the accounting system as increases or decreases in account balances.
   b. Debits and credits refer to increases and decreases in account balances.
   c. Double-entry bookkeeping requires each transaction be recorded in two or more accounts to maintain the balance in the accounting equation.
   d. Transactions are recorded in chronological order in a journal. A ledger provides a summary of account balances.
   e. Subsidiary ledgers provide details about transactions affecting a control account such as accounts receivable and accounts payable.
   f. Closing transactions transfer revenue and expense account balances to owners' equity.

2. Components and functions of manual and computerized accounting systems:
   a. Major differences in accounting systems depend on whether the systems are manual or computerized.

    b.   A computer provides the journal and ledger functions in a computerized accounting system.

    c.   A computerized accounting system consists of modules that work together to process transactions. Modules include sales, accounts receivable, inventory management, accounts payable, production management, payroll, and general ledger.

3.   Control procedures to improve the reliability of accounting systems:

    a.   Accounting systems include controls to reduce the likelihood of error, omission, or misstatement of accounting records.

    b.   By following good internal control procedures, such as hiring qualified employees, establishing clear policies and procedures, using proper forms and prenumbered documents, controlling access to documents and resources, and having accounting records verified, a reliable accounting system can be maintained.

    c.   Internal control procedures helpful when the accounting system is computerized include thorough check of the system at installation, control of access to the system, identification codes indicating function responsibilities and segregation of duties, built-in error checking, regular backup of data files, secure storage of backup copies, and documentation of the system, programs, and operating procedures.

    d.   Accounting systems facilitate effective and efficient operations within an organization by providing information for management decisions.

DEFINE *Terms and Concepts Defined in This Chapter*

accounting cycle	double-entry bookkeeping	source documents
chart of accounts	internal control	subsidiary ledger
credits	journal	transaction analysis
debits	ledger	

SOLUTIONS

SELF-STUDY PROBLEM 4-1

Assets =		Liabilities + Owners' Equity		+ (Revenues − Expenses)	
1. Cash	300			Sales Revenue	300
2. Inventory	−135			Cost of Goods Sold	−135
3. Accounts Receivable	800			Sales Revenue	800
4. Inventory	−320			Cost of Goods Sold	−320
5. Inventory	3,400	Accounts Payable	3,400		
6. Cash	−2,000	Accounts Payable	−2,000		
7. Cash	−230			Utilities Expense	−230
8. Cash	−690			Wages Expense	−690
Total	1,125	Total	1,400	Total	−275

SELF-STUDY PROBLEM 4-2

TO: Agnes Coates
FROM: I. Student
RE: Acquisition of computerized accounting system

I am pleased to respond to your request for information about the advantages of a computerized accounting system. In addition, I am providing a brief description of the primary components of a system you might consider for your business.

Several major advantages exist for a computerized system over a manual system. A computerized system provides many of the accounting functions automatically. Once an operator enters transaction data, the computer updates account balances. Financial statements and other reports can be prepared by the computer. Thus, less time is required to maintain the accounting records and prepare reports. Also, less opportunity exists for errors to be made after the data are recorded.

Major components of a small computerized accounting system include accounts receivable, accounts payable, payroll, and general ledger and financial statements modules. An accounts receivable module is used to record sales information, to keep track of customer accounts, and to record cash receipts. An accounts payable module is used to record purchases, to maintain supplier information, and to record payments to suppliers. A payroll module is used to maintain employee information, to prepare payroll checks, and to prepare payroll tax reports. A general ledger and financial statements module is used to record special transactions, to maintain ledger account data, and to prepare financial statements. Together, these modules provide for most accounting needs of a small business.

SELF-STUDY PROBLEM 4-3

Internal control deficiencies include lack of sufficient barriers to the accounting system that would prevent access by an unauthorized employee. Limitations on physical access, passwords, and employee identification numbers should have prevented Deborah from accessing the system. Deborah should not have authority to use the system. Another deficiency was the failure to separate systems development from computer operations personnel. Deborah was able to embezzle funds because she understood the computer programs that created master and transaction files. Computer operators normally do not have sufficient knowledge of the system to manipulate it in this manner. A third deficiency was the failure of the system to verify transactions or compare amounts from one part of the system to another. Use of sequentially numbered purchase orders should make it difficult for an employee to create fictitious data without the system's identifying a problem.

EXERCISES

4-1. Write a short definition for each of the terms listed in the *Terms and Concepts Defined in This Chapter* section.

4-2. For each of the types of transactions listed below, indicate whether it is a financing, an investing, or an operating activity, and indicate the effect of the transaction on net income and cash flows. The first item is provided as an example.

	Transaction	Type of Activity	Effect on Net Income	Effect on Cash Flows
a.	Purchase merchandise	Operating	None	Outflow
b.	Repay creditors			
c.	Sale of goods & services			
d.	Borrow from creditors			
e.	Sale of long-term assets			
f.	Investment by owners			
g.	Consume resources to produce goods			
h.	Pay return to owners			

4-3. The following transaction occurred for Pittman Co. on March 23, 1995: The company sold merchandise for cash, $5,000. Diagram the flow of information resulting from this transaction through an accounting system. Include the following items in your diagram, in the proper order: ledger, sales invoice, financial statements (balance sheet, income statement, statement of cash flows), journal.

4-4. For each of the situations below, indicate whether a debit or a credit entry is required by placing a check in the appropriate box.

		Debit	Credit
a.	to increase a liability account		
b.	to decrease an equity account		
c.	to increase a revenue account		
d.	to decrease a contra account to an asset		
e.	to increase an expense account		
f.	to decrease an asset account		
g.	to decrease a liability account		
h.	to increase an equity account		
i.	to increase a contra account to an asset		
j.	to increase an asset account		
k.	to close a revenue account		
l.	to close an expense account		

4-5. Complete the chart below by indicating whether the type of transaction would require a debit or credit entry in an organization's journal. Place an X in the appropriate box to indicate your response.

Transaction Type	Debit	Credit
Increase in cash		
Decrease in accounts payable		
Increase in sales revenues		
Decrease in equipment		
Increase in cost of goods sold		
Decrease in accounts receivable		
Increase in note payable		
Decrease in owners' investment		
Increase in inventory		
Decrease in cash		
Increase in wages expense		
Decrease in inventory		

4-6. For each of the accounts listed below, indicate whether you would expect the account to have a debit or a credit balance. Place an X in the appropriate column to indicate your answer.

Account	Debit	Credit
Cash		
Accounts payable		
Sales revenues		
Owners' investment		
Inventory		
Equipment		
Cost of goods sold		
Notes payable		
Wages expense		
Wages payable		
Buildings		
Accounts receivable		

4-7. Excerpts from the ledger of Merrylynn's Craft Store are provided below. For each excerpt, describe the type of transaction that would have produced the effects reported in the ledger at each date.

a. INVENTORY

Date	Debit	Credit	Balance
Jan. 1			24,000
Jan. 15		8,000	16,000
Jan. 23	4,000		20,000

b. ACCOUNTS PAYABLE

Date	Debit	Credit	Balance
Jan. 1			14,000
Jan. 10	6,000		8,000
Jan. 25		2,000	10,000

c. SALES REVENUES

Date	Debit	Credit	Balance
Jan. 1			0
Jan. 8		12,000	12,000
Jan. 19		6,000	18,000

4-8. Sweitzer's is a medical supply company. For each of the following events indicate in the box provided whether the balance of the listed account would increase or decrease as a result of the transaction:

Event	Account	Increase or Decrease
Cash is paid	Cash	
Land is sold	Cash	
Merchandise is acquired	Merchandise Inventory	
Merchandise is sold for cash	Merchandise Inventory	
Merchandise is sold on credit	Sales Revenue	
Wages are paid for month	Wages Expense	
Wages are paid for month	Cash	
Cash is received from a loan	Notes Payable	
Merchandise is sold on credit	Merchandise Inventory	
Merchandise is purchased on credit	Accounts Payable	

4-9. For each transaction of Park's Tree Service indicate how it affects the accounting equation. Use the format provided below.

a. On July 1, Chung Park invested $4,000 in the business.

b. On July 5, Chung borrowed $2,000 from a local bank for the business by signing a note.

c. On July 8, Chung purchased equipment for $5,000 cash.

d. On July 8, Chung purchased insurance for $300 for a one-year period.

e. On July 10, Chung completed his first job and received payment of $250.

f. On July 14, Chung signed a contract to provide services for a local community. The contract provides for specific services to be provided each month and for payment of $50 at the end of each month.

g. On July 18, Chung completed the services required by the contract for July and sent a bill to the community.

Assets =	Liabilities + Owners' Equity	+ (Revenues − Expenses)

4-10. For each transaction of Rose's Flower Shop indicate how it affects the accounting equation. Use the format provided below.

a. Purchased merchandise for sale on October 1 for $1,200 to be paid by October 30.

b. Sold merchandise for $300 cash on October 3. The merchandise cost Rose's $90.

c. Sold merchandise for $600 on credit on October 6. The merchandise cost Rose's $195.

d. Ordered $750 of merchandise on October 7 from a supplier.

e. $150 of the merchandise purchased on October 1 spoiled on October 9 and had to be trashed resulting in spoilage expense.

f. Paid $900 on October 9 to suppliers for merchandise purchased on October 1.

g. Received $450 on October 10 from customers for sales of October 6.

Assets =	Liabilities + Owners' Equity	+ (Revenues − Expenses)

4-11. A list of account balances for Marta's Vineyard is shown below. The balances include all transactions for the fiscal year except closing entries. Use the information provided to describe what the company would need to do to close its accounts for December. What is the purpose of this process?

Marta's Vineyard
Adjusted Trial Balance
December 31, 1996

Account	Balance
Cash	650
Inventory	2,800
Supplies	1,000
Prepaid Insurance	450

continued

Account	Balance
Equipment	3,550
Accumulated Depreciation	1,700
Interest Payable	150
Notes Payable	2,000
Investment by Owner	4,175
Sales Revenue	2,200
Cost of Goods Sold	900
Wages Expense	350
Utilities Expense	150
Depreciation Expense	50
Insurance Expense	100
Supplies Expense	75
Interest Expense	150

4-12. The following events occur as part of an accounting cycle. List the events in the order in which they should occur in the cycle.
   a. Record transactions to ledger.
   b. Prepare source documents.
   c. Record closing transactions.
   d. Prepare financial statements.
   e. Analyze and record transactions in journal.

4-13. Woody's Building Supplies uses a computerized accounting system on a personal computer. The system includes accounts receivable, accounts payable, payroll, and general ledger modules. What is the purpose of each of these modules? Give examples of transactions that would be recorded in each.

4-14. Explain the purpose of the sales and order-processing module of a computerized accounting system. What relationship does this module have with other modules in the system?

4-15. Primary source documents for an accounting system include: customer orders, sales invoices, purchase invoices, cash receipts, and cash payment. Explain why these documents are important to each of the following modules in an accounting system: sales, accounts receivable, inventory management, accounts payable, and production management.

4-16. Computerized accounting systems create special control problems for an organization. Common control procedures used by organizations include:
   a. Use of passwords to access terminals and program.
   b. Limits placed on amounts that the computer will accept for various transactions.
   c. Use of test transactions.
   d. Data and programs are backed up regularly.
   e. Separation of design from operation of systems.
   Explain the purpose of each control procedure.

4-17. The following are subsidiary accounts for Uptown Auto Parts:

Accounts Receivable	**Accounts Payable**
AAA Auto	Ford Motor Co.
Highway 20 Honda	General Motors Corp.
Fred's Garage	Honda Corp.
Macedonia Buick	Ted's Rebuilt Parts

Identify the purpose of these accounts. Explain how the subsidiary accounts are related to the accounts appearing on Uptown Auto Parts' financial statements.

4-18. Identify the events that would produce each of the following transactions:

Assets =		Liabilities + Owners' Equity		+ (Revenues − Expenses)	
a. Cash	600			Sales Revenue	600
Inventory	−225			Cost of Goods Sold	−225
b. Inventory	1,050	Accounts Payable	1,050		
c. Equipment	1,500				
Cash	−1,500				
d. Cash	3,750	Notes Payable	3,750		
e. Cash	−750	Accounts Payable	−750		
f. Cash	−150			Interest Expense	−150

4-19. Flushing Pipe Co. closes its books on December 31 each year. Explain what is meant by "closing the books" and why this procedure is part of Flushing's accounting process.

4-20. Harvey Hammer owns a hardware store. Harvey receives information from his bookkeeper each month that includes a chart of accounts, a list of journal transactions, ledger account balances, and financial statements. Harvey is bewildered by all of the information. The following list includes the kinds of information Harvey needs from the system. For each item, indicate which component of the system Harvey would use to obtain the information.
  a. Profits earned for the month.
  b. Transactions that occurred on June 22.
  c. The amount of cash available on June 10.
  d. A list of asset accounts included in the system.
  e. Total liabilities at the end of the month.
  f. The amount of cash paid to creditors during the month.
  g. Expenses for the month.

PROBLEMS

PROBLEM 4-1   Processing Accounting Information

Your college roommates are microbiology majors and have had little exposure to accounting. They've heard references to debits and credits and are vaguely aware that something called journals and ledgers are involved. In their view, accounting is record keeping and doesn't seem very important. They don't understand why anyone needs to know how accounting information is processed, unless you want to be a bookkeeper.

Required   Prepare an explanation for your roommates of why the processing function is an important and critical part of an accounting information system.

PROBLEM 4-2   Types of Accounts

For each of the accounts below, identify the type of account (asset, liability, owners' equity, revenue, or expense). Also, describe briefly the purpose for which each account would be used.

   a.   Prepaid Insurance

   b.   Retained Earnings

   c.   Accumulated Depreciation

   d.   Wages Expense

   e.   Commissions Revenue

   f.   Interest Payable

   g.   Supplies

   h.   Insurance Expense

   i.   Unearned Rent

   j.   Prepaid Advertising

   k.   Notes Payable

   l.   Cost of Goods Sold

   m.   Machinery

   n.   Owners' Capital

   o.   Accounts Receivable

   p.   Bonds Payable

   q.   Supplies Expense

PROBLEM 4-3   Recording Transactions

On March 1, 1995, Anita and Louise started the Appliance Rescue Co. They offer a complete line of appliance parts and repair services. Below are the transactions occurring during the first month of business.

   a.   The business was started by each partner contributing $2,500.

   b.   Each partner also contributed personal tools with a total value of $4,000.

   c.   The annual business license and permits totaled $125 and were paid in cash.

   d.   A used service truck was purchased by paying $1,500 down and signing a 3-year, 12% note payable for the $3,300 balance.

e. An inventory of repair parts was purchased on credit for $5,000.

f. A shop was rented for $400 monthly and the first month's rent was paid.

g. Advertising costing $300 was run in the newspaper. The bill had not yet come by the end of the month and had not been paid.

h. Services totaling $1,100 were performed during the month for cash.

i. Services totaling $1,750 were performed during the month on credit.

j. Parts costing a total of $1,000 were sold to customers for $1,550 cash.

k. Gas, oil, and maintenance on the service truck of $192.50 was charged to the company's credit card.

l. At the end of the month, Anita and Louise each withdrew $500 from the business for personal expenses.

Required   Below is a list of the company's accounts. Use them to record each transaction. Use the format illustrated.

Accounts Payable	Advertising Expense
Accounts Receivable	Cost of Goods Sold
Cash	Gas, Oil, & Maintenance Expense
Note Payable	License and Permit Expense
Owners' Capital—Anita	Owners' Capital—Louise
Repair Parts Inventory	Rent Expense
Tools	Sales Revenue
Truck	Service Revenue

Assets =	Liabilities + Owners' Equity	+ (Revenues − Expenses)

PROBLEM 4-4   Identifying and Recording Transactions

Bill Collector has worked for many years in the credit evaluation business and recently decided to open his own collection agency on August 1. Following are the events occurring during the first month of business.

Aug. 1   Bill started the firm by investing $11,875.
   3   An office suite was rented at $1,250 per month and the first month's rent was paid.
   5   Furnishings for the office were purchased on credit at a cost of $6,750.
   6   A $7,500 loan was obtained from a relative at 10% annual interest.
   7   Three employees were hired. They will start training next Wednesday.
   12   Bill arranged for promotional literature to be printed for distribution to potential clients. It was printed and distributed at a cost of $2,625 cash.
   23   Services provided to clients totaled $5,625. Of this amount, 40% was collected in cash, with the balance on accounts receivable.
   31   Utilities used during the month totaled $600 but have not been paid.
   31   Employee wages for the month were $4,000, of which 30% was still owed at month end.

Aug. 31   On this day, three more clients contracted for service that would begin during the following month. Bill estimated that these clients would generate $7,500 of billings per month. No cash has yet been received.

Required   (a) For each event, identify the accounts affected, the amount, and whether the effect was to increase or decrease the account. If no accounts were affected, write No Effect. Use the format shown below. (b) Provide a total for each account at the end of the month and demonstrate that assets = liabilities + owners' equity + (revenues − expenses).

Assets =	Liabilities + Owners' Equity	+ (Revenues − Expenses)

PROBLEM 4-5   Describing an Accounting System

Weiser Fruit Co. uses an accounting system that includes a journal, a ledger, and financial statements. Prunella Weiser, daughter of the owner, has recently completed college and is new to the company. Prunella majored in music and doesn't have much understanding of accounting. You have been asked to help her become familiar with the accounting system.

Required   Write a memo to Prunella describing briefly the purpose of each part of the system and how the parts work together to provide information for management and other users. Also, indicate your willingness to meet with her to discuss the system in detail and provide further information.

PROBLEM 4-6   Describing an Accounting System

On March 12, Barney Fife ordered a uniform from Ace Detective Uniform Co. On April 18, Barney received the uniform and a bill for $87.59. On April 26, Ace received a check from Barney.

Required   Trace the flow of information through the accounting system of Ace Detective Uniform Co. associated with these events. Identify source documents and transactions associated with the events in each of the following departments: sales, accounts receivable, inventory, and shipping.

PROBLEM 4-7   Evaluating an Accounting System

Angelo Sarcozzi is a vegetable grower. He buys seeds, plants, fertilizers, insecticides, and other products from local vendors. Most purchases are on credit. Angelo receives bills monthly and writes checks to pay his accounts. He owns his land and has borrowed to purchase a tractor and other equipment. Angelo sells his crops to local merchants at grocery stores and restaurants. Most of the sales are for cash; some are for credit. He records cash payments and receipts in his personal checkbook. He records noncash sales in a notebook, listing the customer, date, and amount of the sale. When he receives checks from these customers, he marks off the amount in the notebook.

Required   Evaluate Angelo's accounting system. What problems do you see with the system? What changes would you recommend to improve it?

PROBLEM 4-8   Ethical Issues in an Accounting System

Ethel Spikes works for Hard Rock Candy Co. She enters customer orders in the company's accounting system. The orders are written on prepared forms by the company's sales representatives (reps). The company employs ten sales reps, who work different territories. The reps are paid on a commission basis for sales made during the preceding month. Sales reports prepared by the accounting department supervisor are used to determine the commissions. Sales reps drop off the forms with the accounting supervisor each week. The supervisor then delivers the forms to Ethel. She enters the orders in a computer and prints out a sales report and sales invoices for each customer. These are picked up by the supervisor who delivers them to payroll and to shipping. The result of entering the orders in the accounting system is to increase accounts receivable and to increase sales revenue.

Ethel has discovered an interesting regularity in some of the orders. One of the sales reps always reports abnormally high orders from a particular customer. A few days after the end of each month, the rep submits a cancelation form for the customer to eliminate a large portion of the customer's order. The supervisor directs Ethel to record the cancelation by reducing accounts receivable for the customer and recording an increase in an operating expense account. Ethel doesn't know much about accounting. When she asked her supervisor about this procedure, she was told it was standard for this customer and not to worry about it.

Ethel smells a rat, however, and has considered discussing the matter with the vice-president for finance. But, she is concerned she may simply be making waves that will alienate her supervisor.

Required   Ethel has sought your advice, as a friend, about this matter. What would you recommend to Ethel? What problems do you see in Hard Rock's accounting system? How might these problems be solved?

PROBLEM 4-9   Economics of Accounting Systems

Oscar Grinch is president of the Sesame Garbage Can Co. Grinch is a notorious miser, who spends as little as possible on new technology, especially in support services. You were recently hired by the company to manage its accounting department. You were aware the company's system was antiquated before taking the job. But, soon after beginning work, you realized it was hopelessly outdated. The system relies on manual procedures that have been in place since the company was a small operation when first founded by Grinch.

You have contacted some vendors and have a good idea about the type of system that would meet the company's needs. A new computerized system would cost about $50,000 for hardware and software.

Required   Write a memorandum to Grinch explaining the benefits of a new system. Justify the cost of the system by identifying how it could improve the company economically.

PROBLEM 4-10   Analyzing and Correcting Accounting Information

Assume that you invested $1,000 in a business venture on January 1, 1995. At the end of the year, you received the following information about the venture, along with a check for $60 representing your share of the company's distribution of profits.

Dear (Your Name):
We are pleased to send you the enclosed check, representing your share of profits for the company for last year. As one of the 100 partners who invested $1,000 in the business, you are entitled to an equal share of the company's profits. The following events occurred during 1995:

1.   Equipment was purchased at a cost of $50,000.

2.   A 5-year lease was taken on a building at $12,000 per year. A payment ($24,000) was made for the first two years of the lease.

3. Merchandise was purchased at a cost of $40,000.

4. Eighty percent of the merchandise was sold during the year. $150,000 cash was received from the sale. Customers still owe $25,000, that should be collected during 1996.

5. Wages, utilities, transportation, and other costs of $30,000 were paid for in 1995.

    Accordingly, company profits were as follows:

Sales revenues	$150,000
Cost of merchandise	− 40,000
Cost of equipment	− 50,000
Cost of lease	− 24,000
Other costs	− 30,000
Net income	$ 6,000
Distribution per partner	$ 60

Required   (a) Assume depreciation expense on the equipment was $10,000 for the year. Prepare an analysis of each event (1–5) for the company describing the effect of the event on the company's assets, liabilities, owners' equity, revenues, and expenses. Include any related events that should affect the company's accounts. (b) Prepare a corrected income statement in good form.

PROBLEM 4-11   Multiple-Choice Overview of the Chapter

1. The processing phase of the accounting information system includes which of the following events?

	Deciding how to raise needed capital	Recording transactions
a.	Yes	Yes
b.	Yes	No
c.	No	Yes
d.	No	No

2. An important characteristic of a double-entry bookkeeping system is that:
    a. errors cannot occur.
    b. the total of debit entries must always equal the total of credit entries.
    c. it was developed in Great Britain during the Industrial Revolution.
    d. source documents are not needed if the double-entry system is used.

3. Office supplies were purchased for $900 on credit. Which of the following changes in account balances is the correct result of the transaction?

	Office supplies	Accounts payable
a.	Increased	Increased
b.	Increased	Decreased
c.	Decreased	Decreased
d.	Decreased	Increased

4. Which of the following is a true statement regarding the journal and ledger?
    a. Transactions are recorded in the ledger before being posted to the journal.
    b. Normal entries are initially recorded in the journal while closing entries are initially recorded in the ledger.

    c. Transactions are arranged chronologically in the journal but are recorded in separate accounts in the ledger.

    d. Account balances are easily determinable from the journal but more difficult to determine from the ledger.

5. The balance of the merchandise inventory account increased by $3,000 during February. Which of the following statements can be made as a result of this information?

    a. Credit sales for the month were $3,000 greater than cash received from customers.

    b. Purchases of inventory for the month were $3,000 less than the cost of merchandise sold for the month.

    c. Purchases of inventory for the month were $3,000 greater than the cost of merchandise sold for the month.

    d. Merchandise purchased for the month totaled $3,000.

6. All of the following are advantages of a computerized accounting system except:

    a. Journal and ledger functions are performed by the computer.

    b. It is easier to control than a manual system.

    c. It is faster than a manual system.

    d. Fewer opportunities for error exist than in a manual system.

7. Cash received by a company from customers would be recorded initially in a microcomputer accounting system in the:

    a. accounts receivable module.

    b. accounts payable module.

    c. payroll module.

    d. general ledger module.

8. An inventory report from an accounting system probably would provide all of the following information except:

    a. the amount of inventory purchased during a period.

    b. the amount of inventory sold during a period.

    c. the cost of each inventory item.

    d. the amount owed to the company by those who purchased inventory.

9. To protect its assets and accounting information, a company should:

    a. hire employees with college degrees.

    b. give one person sole responsibility for the accounting system.

    c. permit access to accounting records by top managers only.

    d. independently verify accounting records.

10. An effective accounting system should:

    a. increase customer satisfaction.

    b. eliminate the need to borrow money.

    c. improve a company's products.

    d. reduce the speed of cash inflows.

C A S E S

CASE 4-1 Developing an Accounting System

Peggy Sue is a close friend who has recently purchased a specialty store in a local mall. Peggy has little understanding of accounting. She has asked for your assistance in developing an accounting system. She needs information about her business to determine how well the business is performing. In a recent visit, she showed you the following documents that she uses to keep track of her business activities: (a) Sales receipts are written for each sales transaction. The sales receipt notes the items sold and the sales price. A copy is given to the customer, and another copy is placed in a box. (b) Cash or checks received from customers are placed in a cash register. Deposit slips are made out each day and the receipts are deposited in a local bank. (c) Peggy keeps a checkbook for the company. When bills are received from suppliers, or for rent, utilities, and the like, Peggy writes a check and fills out a check register that is maintained in the checkbook. Wages, interest on a bank note, and other expenses are paid by check, as well. (d) Index cards are maintained for each inventory item. As merchandise is received, the quantity obtained is noted on the appropriate card along with the unit cost. The index cards are updated weekly for merchandise sold by referencing the sales receipts for the week. (e) Receipts for equipment and other asset purchases are maintained in a file folder.

Required Recommend an accounting system for Peggy that would make use of the documents she is using. Describe the components of the system and how they can provide information for Peggy. Use some example transactions to demonstrate for Peggy how the system would work.

CASE 4-2 Correcting Errors

Hansel and Gretel Cook own a bakery, famous for its gingerbread. Neither is a trained accountant. They have devised a system for recording transactions that they believe is sufficient. Listed below are a series of transactions for a recent month. The transactions were recorded as shown in the table.

a. Received orders for goods. Payment of $1,000 to be made when delivered.

b. Placed an order for supplies of $600.

c. Shipped goods to customers and received $1,000 cash.

d. Received supplies and paid $600 cash.

e. Paid interest to bank of $400 cash.

f. Purchased equipment on credit for $6,000.

Assets =		Liabilities + Owners' Equity		+ (Revenues − Expenses)	
Orders Received	1,000			Sales	1,000
Supplies Ordered	600			Supplies Expense	−600
Cash	1,000				
Orders Shipped	−1,000				
Supplies Received	600	Accounts Payable	−600		
Cash Paid	400			Interest Paid	−400
		Accounts Payable	6,000	Equipment Expense	−6,000

Required Explain to the Cooks the misunderstanding they have about recording transactions. Correct the recording errors they have made.

PROJECTS

PROJECT 4-1   Developing and Analyzing Transactions

Develop a set of hypothetical transactions for a fictional company following the pattern of Problem 4-4. Create a minimum of ten transactions and identify the accounting effects of each.

PROJECT 4-2   Developing a Personal Accounting System

Develop an accounting system you could use to provide information about your economic activities. Write a short report describing your system. The report should include:

a.   a list of decisions the system should help you make.

b.   a list of source documents that would provide data for your system.

c.   examples of the system, demonstrating how it operates, including transactions for at least a week.

d.   example reports that help you with the decisions identified in part (a).

PROJECT 4-3   Identifying Components of an Accounting System

Visit a nearby business or talk with a business manager you know. Ask for a list of source documents that provide data for the accounting system. Ask for copies of any documents the manager can share with you. Also, ask the manager to describe how the business maintains its accounting records and for a chart of accounts for the business. Write a short report that summarizes your findings and that includes the examples you obtained.

PROJECT 4-4   Evaluating Accounting Systems

Assume you are an employee of a small business. The business has been using a manual accounting system, but your boss has decided to consider a microcomputer system. You have been assigned the responsibility of identifying the features of the system that need to be evaluated. Also, your boss wants you to identify at least three brands of computer systems and compare their costs and features. Research some commonly used types of accounting software, and write a short report for your boss. Include references to the sources of information you used in preparing your report. (Hint: Use a periodical index to identify some articles that evaluate accounting computer packages for use on personal computers.)

Chapter 5

Reporting Accounting Information

CHAPTER

O v e r v i e w

This chapter introduces the reporting phase of the accounting information system. The output of the accounting system consists of reports and schedules. For these outputs to be useful to decision makers, the reports must accurately summarize the transactions in the transformation process. Therefore, the system must measure the effects of transactions accurately. It must process transactions to produce reliable information. And, it must summarize the information in a form understandable to users.

This chapter discusses stages 4 and 5 of the accounting information system, reporting rules and reports:

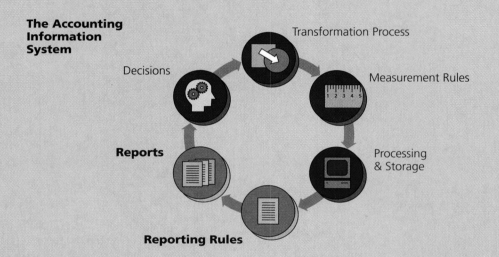

Reporting rules define how data are combined and summarized in preparing reports and schedules. Reports present information in a form consistent with reporting rules.

The form and content of reports from the accounting system depend on the needs of users. This chapter introduces some of the most common accounting reports, financial statements. The purpose of this chapter is to explain how financial statements report transactions that occur in an organization's transformation process. **Once you have completed this chapter, you should understand the purpose of financial statements.**

Major topics covered in this chapter include:

*   The purpose and content of financial statements.
*   Special attributes and limitations of financial statements.

CHAPTER

O b j e c t i v e s

Once you have completed this chapter, you should be able to:

1. Identify the primary financial statements issued by businesses.
2. Summarize the information reported on a company's income statement.

3. Explain reporting rules that determine the format of an income statement.
4. Summarize the information reported on a company's statement of stockholders' equity.
5. Summarize the information reported on a company's balance sheet.
6. Explain reporting rules that determine the format of a balance sheet.
7. Summarize the information reported on a company's statement of cash flows.
8. Explain reporting rules that determine the direct format of a statement of cash flows.
9. Discuss how financial statements work together to present a picture of a company for a fiscal period.
10. Explain why many corporations publish consolidated financial statements.
11. Identify some of the primary limitations of financial statements.
12. Discuss how financial statements relate to the transformation process and the time periods in which companies operate.

THE PURPOSE OF FINANCIAL STATEMENTS

Objective 1
Identify the primary financial statements issued by businesses.

Accounting information may serve general and specific purposes. Financial statements are the primary format organizations use to report general purpose accounting information to external decision makers. Most business organizations prepare three financial statements:

1. **an income statement**,
2. **a balance sheet**, and
3. **a statement of cash flows**.

Many corporations prepare a fourth statement, **a statement of stockholders' equity**, because of the variety and complexity of their ownership transactions. The following sections examine the purpose and content of these four financial statements. Information contained in financial statements and information accompanying the statements provide the subject for much of the remainder of this book. Specific-purpose accounting reports and other information used by internal decision makers is the subject of managerial accounting.

The form and content of financial statements have evolved throughout the twentieth century and continue to change to meet user needs. Financial statements are used by internal and external decision makers. The format and content of the statements used by managers to make financing, investing, and operating decisions often follow those of statements prepared for external users. Statements for internal use may be prepared in any form and with any content desired by management, however.

For many years the balance sheet was the primary financial statement reported to external users. It was designed to meet the needs of creditors who want information about resources available to pay debts and claims to these resources. The income statement developed to meet the needs of corporate investors who want information about earnings. Earnings information is useful for evaluating management decisions that affect dividends and stock values. The statement of stockholders' equity describes transactions affecting stock and the amount and use of retained earnings. A recent addition to external reports, the statement of cash flows provides information for creditors, investors, and other users to assess the ability of a company to meet its cash requirements.

Financial statements for general-purpose external reporting normally are prepared according to generally accepted accounting principles (GAAP). GAAP specify the format and content of the statements, though they permit managers to choose among alternate procedures in reporting some transactions. Chapter 7 provides a more extensive discussion of GAAP.

Income Statement

An income statement (sometimes called an earnings statement or a profit and loss (P&L) statement) reports an organization's revenues and expenses for a fiscal period. The income statement presents operating results on an accrual basis. It measures the amount of goods and services provided to customers and resources consumed in providing these goods and services.

Revenues and expenses result from the sale and consumption of resources for a fiscal period. Therefore, the income statement reports the results of these operating activities for a particular period such as a month, quarter, or fiscal year. For example, the income statement might report operating results for the month of July, the first quarter ending September 30, or the fiscal year ending June 30.

Statement of Stockholders' Equity

A *statement of stockholders' equity* **reports changes in a corporation's stockholders' equity for a fiscal period.** These changes result from profits earned during a period, from dividends paid to owners, and from the sale or re-purchase of stock by a corporation. This statement links the income statement to the balance sheet because it describes how much net income was reinvested as part of stockholders' equity.

Balance Sheet

A balance sheet reports the balances of the asset, liability, and owners' equity accounts at a particular date. Other names for the balance sheet are **statement of financial position** and **statement of financial condition**. These names are good descriptions of the statement because it reports the cost of resources available to an organization at a particular date and the sources of financing used to acquire those resources. In combination, the resources and financing are the financial position, or condition, of the organization at the report date.

Statement of Cash Flows

A *statement of cash flows* **reports events that resulted in cash inflows and outflows for a fiscal period.** The statement of cash flows and the income statement both report operating activities for a fiscal period, but these statements differ in two important ways. First, the cash flow statement reports financing and investing activities in addition to operating activities, while the income statement reports primarily operating activities. Second, the cash flow statement reports operating activities on a cash basis, while the income statement reports them on an accrual basis. The income statement provides an *estimate* of the cash flows that will result once all cash inflows and outflows associated with current period operating activities have been received or paid. The statement of cash flows reports *actual* cash flows received or paid during the current fiscal period.

The income statement and statement of cash flows reflect a trade-off in the value of information that can be reported from an accounting system. An income statement provides an estimate of how well an organization has performed when all events are completed that had, or will have, an economic effect on a company because of the current period's operating activities. Because the information reported is an estimate, it is not always precise. In contrast, the statement of cash flows is precise because it reports events that have been completed. But, this information normally is not as good a measure of current period operating results as that contained on the income statement. The statement of cash flows reports cash flows of the current fiscal period irrespective of when the activities occurred that caused the cash flows.

To illustrate, assume during October a company sells $30,000 of goods and services and collects $26,000 from customers. The $26,000 of cash inflow is a precise measure of cash received from sales during October. It is not, however, a complete measure of the amount of goods sold by the company to customers during October. Some portion of the $26,000 may represent sales made in prior months that were collected in October. Some portion of the cash from sales made in October may not be collected from customers until later months.

Information about cash flows is useful for decisions about an organization's ability to pay current obligations. Profitability, as measured by the income statement, is only one aspect of performance. An organization may be profitable but may not have sufficient cash to pay its debts. This situation may arise, for example, when a business is unable to collect on a large amount of sales made on credit. The sales are reported as revenues on the income statement when goods are sold. Yet, the cash is not available for use by the business until it collects the accounts receivable resulting from the sales.

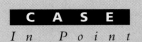

C A S E
In   Point

Having a popular product line and a large backlog of orders does not guarantee a company will have cash available to pay its bills on time. In one of the most famous cash flow shortages in American business history, Douglas Aircraft of California was forced into a 1967 merger with McDonnell Company of St. Louis. The merger formed the McDonnell Douglas Corporation.

At the time, Douglas Corporation's DC-8 and DC-9 aircraft had found an enthusiastic market with airlines and had accumulated a $3.2 billion backlog of orders. Douglas literally could not make its airliners fast enough. A severe shortage of skilled employees and jet engines disrupted production and raised costs sharply. Rather suddenly, Douglas needed additional cash of $350–$400 million to continue production. As word of the company's plight spread, its stock price plummeted from a 1966 high of $112 per share to $45 at the time of the merger.

Unable to raise the money from banks, Douglas was forced to merge with its old rival, McDonnell, which previously had attempted a takeover of Douglas. As part of the merger agreement, McDonnell provided $68.7 million of cash to Douglas. Douglas was then able to borrow another $300 million to restart its production lines.

FINANCIAL STATEMENT CONTENT AND PRESENTATION

Financial statements summarize account balances. This section illustrates financial statements that report typical business transactions. Assume you manage a company, Rockyfellow, Inc., that operates a small chain of gas stations. Exhibit 5-1 lists account balances for Rockyfellow, Inc. at December 31, 1997, the end of the fiscal year. The following sections illustrate how these data are reported in the company's financial statements.

Exhibit 5-1

Rockyfellow, Inc.
Account Balances
December 31, 1997

Account	Balance
Cash	$ 15,600
Accounts Receivable	22,430
Merchandise Inventory	43,500
Supplies	12,670
Prepaid Insurance	8,290
Equipment	93,070
Allowance for Depreciation—Equipment	22,350
Buildings	275,000
Allowance for Depreciation—Buildings	83,510
Land	36,810
Patents	32,000
Accounts Payable	24,790
Wages Payable	4,100
Interest Payable	11,250
Income Taxes Payable	2,400
Notes Payable, Current Portion	14,400
Notes Payable, Long-Term	177,600
Owners' Investment (Contributed Capital)*	125,000
Retained Earnings, 1/1/97	62,700
Dividends	5,000
Sales Revenue	186,230
Cost of Goods Sold	73,350
Wages Expense	42,700
Utilities Expense	6,430
Depreciation Expense	9,650
Insurance Expense	3,420
Supplies Expense	8,390

Interest Expense	10,300
Advertising Expense	7,120
Patent Expense	3,000
Income Tax Expense	5,600

Explained later in this chapter.

The Income Statement

The income statement reports the revenue and expense account balances and the net income for the period. Exhibit 5-2 illustrates a multiple-step income statement, which is a commonly used format.

Exhibit 5-2

Objective 2
Summarize the information reported on a company's income statement.

Rockyfellow, Inc.
Income Statement
For the Year Ended December 31, 1997
(Multiple-Step Format)

Sales revenue		$186,230
Cost of goods sold		73,350
Gross profit		112,880
Operating expenses:		
Wages	$42,700	
Utilities	6,430	
Depreciation	9,650	
Insurance	3,420	
Supplies	8,390	
Advertising	7,120	
Patent*	3,000	
Total operating expenses		80,710
Income from operations		32,170
Other revenues and expenses:		
Interest expense		10,300
Pretax income		21,870
Income tax expense		5,600
Net income		$ 16,270
Earnings per share of common stock*		$1.30
(12,500 shares outstanding)		

Explained later in this chapter.

Learning Note	Amount columns are used on financial statements to facilitate addition and subtraction. The number and format of columns is a matter of convenience. The objective is clarity of presentation.

In interpreting the income statement, it is important to remember revenues and expenses are measured on an *accrual basis*. Revenues indicate the sales price of goods and services sold during a period. They do *not* indicate how much cash was received from the sales during a current fiscal period. Expenses identify the cost of resources consumed in producing and selling goods and services sold during a period. They do *not* identify how much cash was paid for resources during a period. **Net income is not cash flow.**

As shown on the income statement for Rockyfellow, Inc., a **multiple-step income statement** is divided into several sections or steps. The usual sections include:

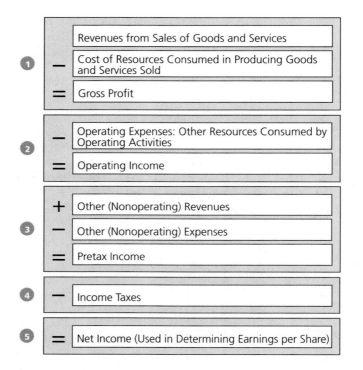

Gross Profit. The income statement reports *gross profit*, **which is the difference between the selling price of goods or services sold to customers during a period and the cost of the goods or services sold.** For a merchandising company, the cost of goods sold is the cost of the merchandise inventory sold during a period. For a manufacturing company, cost of goods sold includes the dollar amounts of materials, labor, and other resources that are consumed directly in producing the goods sold during a period. As explained in Chapter 3, these costs are product costs. Product costs are recorded as an asset (INVENTORY) until goods are sold. Then the costs are matched against the revenues generated from the sale by recording an expense (COST OF GOODS SOLD) during the same fiscal period as the sale.

Costs of services, rather than cost of goods, are important for service companies. **The** *cost of services sold* **is the cost of material, labor, and other resources consumed directly in producing services sold during a period.**

For example, the cost of nursing and other patient care costs in a hospital are costs of services. These costs cannot be inventoried and, therefore, are expensed in the period in which the services are provided.

Other Operating Expenses and Operating Income. The second section of a multiple-step income statement lists operating expenses other than cost of goods sold or cost of services sold. *Operating expenses* **identify costs of resources consumed as part of operating activities during a fiscal period in addition to those directly associated with specific goods or services. Most operating expenses are period costs because they are recognized in the fiscal period in which they occur.** Operating expenses include administrative and selling expenses incurred during a period. Salaries for managers and their support staffs who are not involved directly in producing goods and the cost of resources used by managers are operating expenses. These expenses include depreciation, taxes, and insurance on office buildings and equipment, and the costs of supplies and utilities consumed in operating these facilities. GAAP require most marketing and selling costs and research and development costs incurred during a fiscal period to be reported as operating expenses of the period in which they occur. Because identifying how much of these costs is associated with benefits of future periods is difficult to determine, GAAP require these amounts to be expensed to avoid an overstatement of profits during the current fiscal period.

The excess of gross profit over operating expenses is *income from operations*, **or** *operating income*. If operating expenses are greater than gross profit, a loss from operations results.

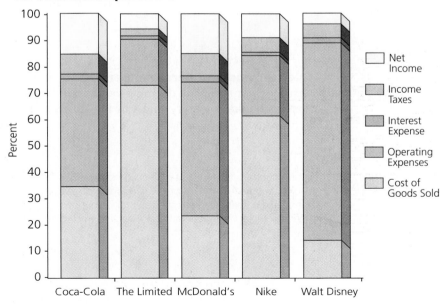

Expenses and Net Income as a Percentage of Total Revenues for Selected Corporations

Data source: 1993 Annual Reports

Other Revenues and Expenses. Revenues and expenses may occur that are not directly related to a company's primary operating activities. These are reported separately as *other revenues and expenses*. This category sometimes is labelled *financial revenues and expenses* because most items reported in this section result from financing activities. The largest item listed in this category often is interest expense on debt issued by an organization. This expense results from a financing activity rather than from an operating activity. **Borrowing money frequently is necessary for an organization's operations; however, except for financial institutions, it is not part of its operating activities.** Accordingly, other expenses and revenues are reported on the income statement after income from operations. This separate listing distinguishes them from revenues and expenses that result from operating activities.

Interest expense is reported as an operating activity on the statement of cash flows because it is an expense on the income statement.

Income Taxes. Most corporations pay income taxes on their earnings. **The amount of income tax expense is determined by applying tax rates required by current tax laws and regulations to the income earned by a company during a fiscal period.** Exhibit 5-2 reports Rockyfellow, Inc. incurred income taxes of $5,600 on pretax income of $21,870 in 1997.

Proprietorships and partnerships do not pay income taxes on their profits directly. Instead, those profits are treated as personal income of the owners. The owners pay income tax on a proprietorship's profits or on their share of the profits of a partnership.

Learning Note | Not all U.S. corporations pay income taxes on profits. Certain small corporations, known as Subchapter S corporations in the tax laws, are treated like partnerships for tax purposes. Thus, each stockholder is taxed on his/her share of the profits rather than the corporation's being taxed.

Net Income and Earnings per Share. Net income is the amount of profit earned by a company during a fiscal period. It represents an increase in owners' or stockholders' equity, and can be distributed to owners or reinvested in the company.

Learning Note | It is important to note that cash dividends and cash withdrawals are paid out of cash. Therefore, a company must have either current or past undistributed profits and sufficient cash available before it can pay dividends or before owners can withdraw money. Remember that net income does not guarantee a company will have favorable cash flows during a period.

GAAP require that corporate income statements prepared for distribution to shareholders and other external users present earnings per share as part of the statement. *Earnings per share* **is a measure of the earnings performance of each share of common stock during a fiscal period. In general, it is** computed by dividing net income by the average number of shares of common stock outstanding during a fiscal period.[1]

Single-Step Format. The income statement presented in Exhibit 5-2 is typical of the type of information reported by companies in their income statements. Nevertheless, the format and content of income statements vary in practice. An alternate format to that described in Exhibit 5-2 is a **single-step statement**. In this type of statement, all revenues, such as sales, service, and interest are grouped together in the first section of the statement and are added together to compute total revenues. All expenses, including cost of goods sold, operating expenses, and other expenses are grouped together as total expenses. Total expenses are subtracted from total revenues to compute net income. Exhibit 5-3 illustrates a single-step income statement for Rockyfellow, Inc.

Internally used income statements may be prepared in a variety of formats and may use different reporting rules from those described in Exhibits 5-2 and 5-3. The statements may be prepared for different divisions of a company, for different product lines, or for different regions. The type and amount of information included in a statement will depend on the needs of managers who use them. The format and content of these statements are not governed by GAAP.

Externally used income statements, especially those of large corporations, may be more or less complex than the ones presented in Exhibits 5-2 and 5-3. In addition, most corporations report income statements for the most recent 3 fiscal years in their annual reports. Some income statement information often is reported for the latest 5- or 10-year period in schedules accompanying the financial statements. Later chapters examine additional information that may appear on or accompany income statements.

Exhibit 5-3

Rockyfellow, Inc.
Income Statement
For the Year Ended December 31, 1997
(Single-Step Format)

Sales revenue		$186,230
Expenses:		
Cost of goods sold	$73,350	
Wages	42,700	
Utilities	6,430	
Depreciation	9,650	
Insurance	3,420	
Supplies	8,390	
Advertising	7,120	
Patent	3,000	
Interest	10,300	
Income tax	5,600	
Total expenses		169,960
Net income		$ 16,270
Earnings per share of common stock		$1.30
(12,500 shares outstanding)		

[1] Common stock is explained in Chapter 8. The computation of earnings per share can be quite complex. Chapter 13 will examine this computation in more detail.

SELF-STUDY PROBLEM 5-1

An income statement for IBM Corporation for a recent fiscal year is provided at the top of the next page. Use this statement to answer the following questions:

1. How much revenue did IBM earn from selling computers?
2. How much revenue did it earn from other operating activities?
3. How much revenue did it earn from nonoperating activities?
4. How much gross profit did IBM earn from the sale of computers?
5. How much gross profit did it earn from the sale of software?
6. How much expense did it incur for nonoperating activities?
7. Approximately how many shares of stock did IBM have outstanding during the year?
8. What were IBM's product costs for equipment and software sold for the period?
9. How much loss did IBM incur during the fiscal year?
10. How much cash did IBM receive from its operating activities during the year?

The solution to Self-Study Problem 5-1 appears at the end of the chapter.

The Statement of Stockholders' Equity

Recall that the statement of stockholders' equity provides information about changes in owners' equity accounts for a corporation during a fiscal period. Exhibit 5-4 provides an example of this statement for Rockyfellow, Inc.

Exhibit 5-4

	Contributed Capital	Retained Earnings	Total
Rockyfellow, Inc. **Statement of Stockholders' Equity** **For the Year Ended December 31, 1997**			
Balance at December 31, 1996	$100,000	$62,700	$162,700
Common stock issued	25,000		25,000
Net income		16,270	16,270
Dividends paid		(5,000)	(5,000)
Balance at December 31, 1997	$125,000	$73,970	$198,970

Objective 4
Summarize the information reported on a company's statement of stockholders' equity.

Stockholders' equity consists of two major divisions: contributed capital and retained earnings. *Contributed capital* **is the amount of direct investment by owners in a corporation.** It is the amount paid in to the corporation by stockholders for the ownership shares at the time the stock was sold by the corporation. The balance of contributed capital changes during a fiscal period when a corporation sells additional shares of stock. The balance also changes when the company buys its own shares back from stockholders and retires those shares so they cannot be resold.

International Business Machines Corporation
Consolidated Statement of Earnings
For the Year Ended December 31, 1993

(Dollars in millions except per share amounts)

Revenue:		
Hardware sales	$30,591	
Software	10,953	
Services	9,711	
Maintenance	7,295	
Rentals and financing	4,166	
		$62,716
Cost of goods and services sold:		
Hardware sales	20,696	
Software	4,310	
Services	8,279	
Maintenance	3,545	
Rentals and financing	1,738	
		38,568
Gross profit		24,148
Operating expenses:		
Selling, general and administrative	18,282	
Research, development and engineering	5,558	
Other	8,945	
		32,785
Operating loss		(8,637)
Other income, principally interest		1,113
Interest expense		(1,273)
Loss before income taxes		(8,797)
Income taxes (refunded)		810
Other adjustments		(114)
Net loss		$ (8,101)
Per share amounts:		
Net loss		$ (14.22)

Data source: IBM, 1993 Annual Report. Slight modifications in format have been made to the original.

Retained earnings is the cumulative amount of net income earned that has been reinvested in the corporation. It is the amount of profit that has not been paid out as dividends to stockholders. Retained earnings increases during a fiscal period by the amount of net income. It decreases by the amount of any net loss and by the amount of dividends paid or promised during a period.

Dividends are not reported on the income statement because they are not expenses. They are a distribution of net income to owners. **DIVIDENDS is a contra–owners' equity account.** It is a direct reduction in retained earnings and is reported on the statement of stockholders' equity.

The statement of stockholders' equity provides a link between the income statement and the balance sheet. The ending balances from the statement of stockholders' equity are the amounts reported as stockholders' equity on the balance sheet. Corporations typically provide a statement of stockholders' equity for the most recent three fiscal years in their annual reports.

The Balance Sheet

Objective 5
Summarize the information reported on a company's balance sheet.

A balance sheet reports the asset, liability, and owners' equity account balances for a company at the end of a fiscal period. Exhibit 5-5 provides a balance sheet for Rockyfellow, Inc.

Recall that the total amount of assets reported on the balance sheet at the end of a fiscal period must be equal to the total amount of liabilities and owners' equity (after the balances of revenue and expense accounts have been transferred to owners' equity). This relationship of assets = liabilities + owners' equity is the fundamental balance sheet equation.

Objective 6
Explain reporting rules that determine the format of a balance sheet.

Exhibit 5-5 provides a **classified balance sheet** in which assets and liabilities are separated by type. Also, the exhibit illustrates a **comparative balance sheet** because it provides information for more than one fiscal period. A balance sheet provides information for a particular date; thus, information for the beginning and ending dates of a fiscal period is useful for determining changes in balance sheet accounts during that period. GAAP require classified and comparative balance sheets in reports to external users. Supplemental schedules may disclose some balance sheet information for the most recent 5 or 10 years.

A balance sheet can be classified into eight primary sections, as illustrated below.

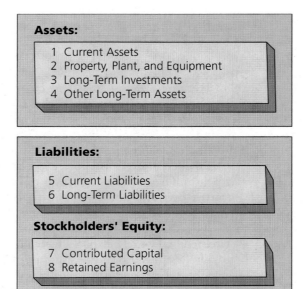

Exhibit 5-5

Rockyfellow, Inc.
Balance Sheet
December 31, 1997

	1997	1996
Assets		
Current assets:		
Cash	$ 15,600	$ 11,700
Accounts receivable	22,430	13,850
Merchandise inventory	43,500	44,450
Supplies	12,670	9,920
Prepaid insurance	8,290	5,950
Total current assets	102,490	85,870
Property, plant, and equipment:		
Equipment	93,070	79,570
Buildings	275,000	235,000
	368,070	314,570
Less: Accumulated depreciation	105,860	96,210
	262,210	218,360
Land	36,810	45,000
Total property, plant, and equipment	299,020	263,360
Other assets:		
Patents	32,000	35,000
Total assets*	$433,510	$384,230
Liabilities		
Current liabilities:		
Accounts payable	$ 24,790	$ 22,630
Wages payable	4,100	5,510
Interest payable	11,250	9,920
Income taxes payable	2,400	3,000
Notes payable, current portion	14,400	9,320
Total current liabilities	56,940	50,380
Long-term liabilities:		
Notes payable, long-term	177,600	171,150
Total liabilities	234,540	221,530
Stockholders' Equity		
Contributed capital	125,000**	100,000
Retained earnings	73,970**	62,700
Total stockholders' equity	198,970**	162,700
Total liabilities and stockholders' equity	$433,510	$384,230

Total assets = Total current assets + Total property, plant, and equipment + Other assets

**From Exhibit 5-4*

Current Assets. *Current assets* **are cash or other resources management expects to convert to cash or consume during the next fiscal year.** Most current assets are liquid assets. *Liquid assets* **are resources that can be converted to cash in a relatively short period.** In addition to cash, current assets include: (1) accounts receivable for which a company expects to receive cash during the next fiscal year, (2) inventory a company expects to sell during the next fiscal year, and (3) resources it expects to consume during the next fiscal year, such as supplies and prepaid insurance.

Learning Note — An organization's operating cycle is the period from the time cash is used to acquire or produce goods until these goods are sold and cash is received. The operating cycles of most organizations are less than 12 months. A fiscal year is the primary reporting period for these companies. Occasionally, a company's operating cycle is longer than 12 months. In such cases, which are rare, current assets are defined as those a company expects to convert to cash or consume during the next operating cycle.

Long-Term Investments. *Long-term investments* **occur when one company purchases the stock or bonds of another company.** Companies often invest in other companies to share in their earnings or to obtain access to resources, management skills, technology, and markets available to other companies. If management expects to hold these investments beyond the next fiscal year, they are classified as long-term investments.

Property, Plant, and Equipment. *Property, plant, and equipment,* **often called fixed or plant assets, are long-term, tangible assets that are used in a company's operations.** Unlike inventory, these assets are not intended for resale. U.S. GAAP require fixed assets, other than land, to be depreciated over their estimated useful lives. Depreciation allocates the cost of these assets to the fiscal periods that benefit from their use as a means of matching expenses with revenues. GAAP in some countries permit the immediate expensing of plant assets.

Other Long-Term Assets. *Other assets* **include noncurrent receivables, fixed assets held for sale, prepaids not expected to be consumed in the next fiscal year, and long-term legal rights such as patents, trademarks, and copyrights.** These types of assets may be listed on the balance sheet under separate headings if they constitute a significant portion of a company's assets.

Accounts and notes receivable a company does not expect to collect during the next fiscal year (or longer operating cycle) are not included among current assets. These items are reported in the Other Assets category. This category includes supplies, prepaid insurance, and similar assets that will not be consumed during the next fiscal period. Property, plant, and equipment items a company is not using currently but is holding for future use, disposal, or sale also are included in this category. For example, land held for a future factory site would be listed here.

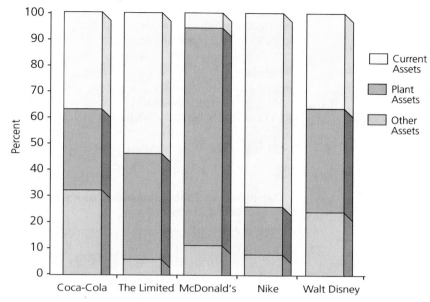

Current, Plant, and Other Assets as a Percent of Total Assets for Selected Corporations

Data source: 1993 Annual reports

Long-term legal rights resulting from the ownership of patents, copyrights, trademarks, and similar items are known as *intangible assets*, in contrast to tangible assets such as property, plant, and equipment. The cost of these assets is allocated over their estimated useful lives in a similar manner to the allocation of fixed asset costs. *Amortization* **is the process of systematically allocating a cost to expense over a period of time.** Intangible assets usually are amortized on a straight-line basis. That is, the cost of the assets is allocated to expense equally over the fiscal periods management expects will benefit from their use. This allocation attempts to match expense with revenue. PATENT EXPENSE, reported on the income statement in Exhibit 5-2, is the amortization expense for patents. Unlike fixed assets, an accumulation account, such as ACCUMULATED DEPRECIATION, normally is not used to record the cumulative amortization of intangibles. The amortization expense for a period is subtracted directly from the appropriate intangible asset account when the expense is recorded.

To illustrate, assume that on January 1, 1996, a company purchased a patent, giving that company the exclusive right to produce a product. The cost of the patent was $10,000, and it was expected to have a useful life for the company of 10 years. The amount of amortization expense for the patent would be $1,000 per year for the 10-year period. The balance of the patent account reported on the company's December 31, 1996, balance sheet would be $9,000. The balance on December 31, 1997, would be $8,000, and so forth.

Liabilities. A balance sheet separates liabilities into current and long-term categories. *Current liabilities* **are those management expects to pay during**

the next fiscal year (or longer operating cycle). *Long-term liabilities* **are those not classified as current liabilities.**

When long-term debt is paid in installments, the amount that will be paid during the next year is a current liability (such as NOTES PAYABLE, CURRENT PORTION in Exhibit 5-5). For example, assume a company issues $20,000 in long-term notes payable on January 1, 1995. The principal is to be paid in four equal annual installments. Therefore, $5,000 of the notes would be reported as a current liability on any balance sheets prepared prior to January 1, 1999. The remaining unpaid balance would be reported as a long-term liability ($15,000 in 1995, $10,000 in 1996, and $5,000 in 1997). There would be no long-term liability during 1998 because the final installment is paid at the end of 1998 and is classified as a current liability in 1998.

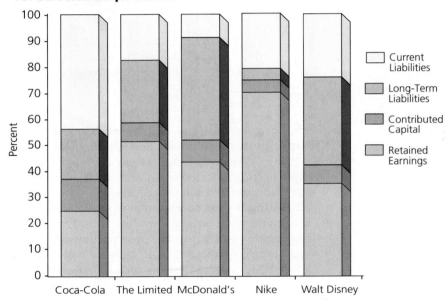

Liabilities and Stockholders' Equity as a Percent of Total Assets for Selected Corporations

Data source: 1993 annual reports

Working Capital. Financial statement users often are interested in the relationship between an organization's current assets and current liabilities. *Working capital* **is the amount of current assets minus the amount of current liabilities.** Rockyfellow, Inc.'s working capital for 1997 is $45,550 ($102,490 of current assets − $56,940 of current liabilities). Working capital often is expressed as a ratio. **The** *working capital ratio*, **or** *current ratio*, **is the amount of current assets divided by the amount of current liabilities.** Rockyfellow's working capital ratio for 1997 is 1.8 ($102,490/$56,940). Working capital is a commonly used measure of a company's *liquidity* **(having sufficient liquid assets to pay current obligations).** A large amount of working capital, or a high working capital ratio, often implies a company has satisfactory liquidity and will be able to pay its current obligations on a timely basis.

Stockholders' Equity.[2] The balances of stockholders' equity accounts on the balance sheet are the ending balances reported for these accounts on the statement of stockholders' equity (see Exhibit 5-4). These balances normally include the cumulative amount of contributed capital and retained earnings created by a corporation since its beginning.

Other Balance Sheet Formats. Like the income statement, the balance sheet may appear in a variety of formats in practice. Companies may use different reporting rules from those previously described. Some types of companies, many utilities for example, report fixed assets prior to current assets and report stockholders' equity prior to liabilities. Foreign companies often use formats that differ from those used in the U.S. Examples of various formats will be illustrated throughout this book.

The Statement of Cash Flows

Objective 7
Summarize the information reported on a company's statement of cash flows.

The purpose of the statement of cash flows is to identify the primary activities of a fiscal period that resulted in cash inflows and outflows. The statement describes the cash flow results of financing, investing, and operating activities for a company for a fiscal period. It explains the change in a company's cash balance. GAAP permit the statement of cash flows to be presented in either of two formats: the direct and the indirect. **The two formats differ only with respect to reporting operating activities.** Thus, the presentation of financing and investing activities does not differ between the two formats.

As illustrated at the top of the next page, the statement of cash flows contains three primary sections regardless of which format is used.

This chapter considers the primary content of the direct format. The indirect format will be examined in Chapter 6.

Exhibit 5-6 provides an example of the cash flow statement for Rockyfellow, Inc. using the direct format.

Objective 8
Explain reporting rules that determine the direct format of a statement of cash flows.

The direct format of reporting the statement of cash flows presents each major source and use of cash. Amounts of cash received from customers and amounts paid to suppliers for inventory, to employees for wages, and so forth, are listed on the statement. The cash balances reported in Exhibit 5-6 correspond with those of the comparative balance sheet in Exhibit 5-5. The statement of cash flows is divided into three sections corresponding to the three parts of the transformation process: financing, investing, and operating.

Operating Activities. Operating activities are transactions involving the acquisition or production of goods and services and the sale and distribution of these goods and services to customers. Cash flow from operating activities identifies cash received from the sale of goods and services. Also, it identifies cash paid for resources used to provide goods and services. An important relationship exists between the income statement and the operating activities section of the statement of cash flows. Both are based on the same set of activities. On the income statement, operating activities are measured on an accrual basis. On the cash flow statement, these activities are measured on a cash

---

[2]   More extensive coverage of stockholders' equity appears in Chapter 8.

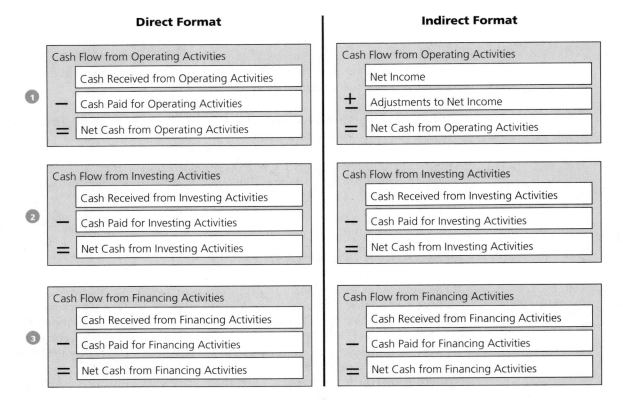

Direct Format	Indirect Format

Cash Flow from Operating Activities
- Cash Received from Operating Activities
- − Cash Paid for Operating Activities
- = Net Cash from Operating Activities

Cash Flow from Operating Activities
- Net Income
- ± Adjustments to Net Income
- = Net Cash from Operating Activities

Cash Flow from Investing Activities
- Cash Received from Investing Activities
- − Cash Paid for Investing Activities
- = Net Cash from Investing Activities

Cash Flow from Investing Activities
- Cash Received from Investing Activities
- − Cash Paid for Investing Activities
- = Net Cash from Investing Activities

Cash Flow from Financing Activities
- Cash Received from Financing Activities
- − Cash Paid for Financing Activities
- = Net Cash from Financing Activities

Cash Flow from Financing Activities
- Cash Received from Financing Activities
- − Cash Paid for Financing Activities
- = Net Cash from Financing Activities

basis. These amounts can be compared to determine timing differences between accrual basis recognition of revenues and expenses and cash flows for the period.

Current asset and current liability transactions normally result from the operating activities of a company, for example, from buying and selling merchandise. Therefore, cash flows associated with working capital items, such as the purchase of inventory, supplies, or prepaid insurance, and payment of wages, are part of the operating activities section of the statement of cash flows.

Learning Note   Interest is included as an operating activity on the cash flow statement because it appears on the income statement. Interest is the result of a company's financing activities rather than its operating activities, however.

Investing Activities. Investing activities are acquisitions or disposals of long-term assets during a fiscal period. Depreciation and amortization expenses are not cash flow items. These expenses are not listed either in the operating or investing sections of the statement of cash flows when the direct format is used. Cash flow occurs when fixed or intangible assets are purchased or sold, not when the costs of these assets are amortized.

Some transactions affect investing and financing activities without affecting cash directly. Assume a company borrows $300,000 from a bank to purchase a building; the transaction increases BUILDINGS and NOTES PAYABLE but

Exhibit 5-6

Rockyfellow, Inc.
Statement of Cash Flows
For the Year Ended December 31, 1997
(Direct Format)

Cash flow from operating activities

Receipts:		
Collections from customers		$ 177,650
Payments:		
To suppliers of inventory	$(70,240)	
To employees	(44,110)	
For utilities	(6,430)	
For insurance	(5,760)	
For supplies	(11,140)	
For interest	(8,970)	
For advertising	(7,120)	
For income taxes	(6,200)	
Total cash payments		(159,970)
Net cash flow from operating activities		17,680
Cash flow from investing activities		
Purchase of plant assets	(53,500)	
Sale of plant assets	8,190	
Net cash flow from investing activities		(45,310)
Cash flow from financing activities		
Proceeds from issuing common stock	25,000	
Proceeds from issuing long-term debt	32,000	
Payment of long-term debt	(20,470)	
Payment of dividends	(5,000)	
Net cash flow from financing activities		31,530
Net increase in cash		3,900
Cash balance, December 31, 1996*		11,700
Cash balance, December 31, 1997*		$ 15,600

From Exhibit 5–5

Note: Cash outflows are indicated on the statement by parentheses.

does not have a direct effect on cash. GAAP require such transactions to be disclosed in notes to the financial statements. Some companies list these items on the statement of cash flows below the cash flow items.

Financing Activities. Financing activities are transactions between a company and its owners or between a company and its long-term creditors. The financing activities section reports only the cash flow effects of transactions associated with long-term debt and investments by owners. Cash flows result when debt is issued or repaid and when stock is issued or repurchased. Payment of dividends also is a financing activity.

Other special items that do not fit into one of the three primary divisions of the statement also may appear on the statement. The effect of exchange rate changes (considered in Chapter 8) is an example of this type of item.

GAAP also require a schedule to reconcile cash flows from operating activities with net income when the direct format is used. This schedule is similar to the presentation of the statement of cash flows using the indirect format examined in Chapter 6.

SELF-STUDY PROBLEM 5-2

Listed below are account balances, cash receipts and payments, and other data for Lewy Pasture, Inc., a company that distributes pharmaceutical supplies, for the fiscal year ended October 31, 1997:

Accounts payable	$ 22,000
Accounts receivable	11,000
Accumulated depreciation	164,000
Buildings	412,000
Cash	16,000
Cash collections from customers	360,000
Cash from disposal of equipment	8,000
Cash from issuance of notes payable	60,000
Cash paid for acquisition of buildings	32,000
Cash paid for acquisition of land	5,000
Cash paid for acquisition of long-term investments	8,000
Cash paid to repurchase stock	35,000
Cash payments for income tax	11,000
Cash payments for insurance	9,000
Cash payments for interest	23,000
Cash payments for notes payable	30,000
Cash payments for supplies	10,000
Cash payments to employees	100,000
Cash payments to suppliers	154,000
Contributed capital	300,000
Cost of goods sold	146,000
Dividends (declared and paid)	17,000
Equipment	245,000
General and administrative expenses	96,000
Income tax expense	14,000
Income tax payable	6,000
Interest expense	25,000
Interest payable	14,000
Land	35,000
Long-term investments	35,000
Merchandise inventory	62,000
Notes payable, current portion	10,000
Notes payable, long-term	278,000
Prepaid insurance	7,000
Retained earnings, October 31, 1996	25,000
Sales revenue	357,000
Selling expenses	47,000
Supplies	13,000
Trademarks	13,000
Wages payable	18,000
Shares of common stock: 10,000	

Required

From the data presented above, determine the amount of each of the following items for Pasture's financial statements:

1. Gross profit
2. Income from operations
3. Net income
4. Earnings per share
5. Current assets
6. Property, plant, and equipment
7. Other assets
8. Total assets
9. Current liabilities
10. Working capital and working capital ratio
11. Total liabilities
12. Retained earnings, October 31, 1997
13. Total stockholders' equity
14. Total liabilities and stockholders' equity
15. Net cash flow from (for) operating activities
16. Net cash flow from (for) investing activities
17. Net cash flow from (for) financing activities
18. Net increase or decrease in cash

The solution to Self-Study Problem 5-2 appears at the end of the chapter.

USE OF FINANCIAL STATEMENTS

Financial statements are a primary source of accounting information for external decision makers. External users analyze statements to evaluate the ability of an organization to use its resources effectively and efficiently. By comparing changes in assets, liabilities, earnings, and cash flows over time, users form expectations about return and risk. Comparisons across companies help determine which companies are being managed effectively and provide the best investment opportunities.

Section 2 of this book describes methods of analyzing and interpreting financial statements in detail. The remainder of this chapter considers attributes of financial statements decision makers should understand when interpreting them.

Interrelationships Among Financial Statements

Objective 9
Discuss how financial statements work together to present a picture of a company for a fiscal period.

Taken as a whole, the financial statements describe the economic events that changed the financial condition of a company from the beginning to the end of a fiscal period. Information on the income statement and statement of cash flows explains changes in balance sheet accounts during a period.

For example, Rockyfellow, Inc. reported a beginning balance for accounts receivable of $13,850 and an ending balance of $22,430 (Exhibit 5-5). This increase of $8,580 can be explained by two other financial statement numbers. Sales revenue on the income statement was $186,230 for the period (Exhibit 5-3). The statement of cash flows reports cash of $177,650 collected from customers for the period (Exhibit 5-6). The increase in accounts receivable is the difference between sales for the period and the amount of cash collected from customers: $8,580 = $186,230 − $177,650.

The summary information presented in financial statements does not always provide sufficient detail to explain the change in every balance sheet account. Access to individual account balances would be necessary to provide a complete explanation. Nevertheless, the relationships among the financial statements are important. Balance sheets for the beginning and ending of a fiscal period reveal changes in the resources and finances of a company. The company's income statement and statement of cash flows reveal major events that caused these changes. **The relationship among financial statements in which the numbers on one statement explain numbers on other statements is called** *articulation*. You should remember a company's financial statements are not independent of each other. They work together to explain the events that changed the company's financial condition:

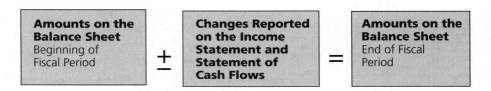

| **Amounts on the Balance Sheet** Beginning of Fiscal Period | + − | **Changes Reported on the Income Statement and Statement of Cash Flows** | = | **Amounts on the Balance Sheet** End of Fiscal Period |

Consolidated Financial Statements

Objective 10
Explain why many corporations publish consolidated financial statements.

Most large corporations publish consolidated financial statements. *Consolidated financial statements* **report the combined economic activities of two or more corporations owned by the same stockholders.** Most major corporations own a controlling interest in other corporations. If one corporation owns a sufficient number of shares of another corporation (generally more than 50%), it is able to control the management of the corporation it owns. **A corporation that controls another corporation is known as a** *parent corporation*. **A corporation controlled by another corporation is a** *subsidiary*. A subsidiary may be wholly owned (100% owned by a parent), or partially owned (less than 100%). Consolidated financial statements report the activities of a parent and its subsidiaries as though they were one company. A parent and its subsidiaries are sometimes referred to as a group. This term is particularly common in financial reports of European corporations. These reports refer to "group accounts" or "group financial statements" when referring to consolidated statements.

Consolidated statements combine the accounts of a parent and its subsidiaries for reporting purposes. Assume that Push Automotive Co. owns Slick Tire Co. and Sticky Brakes Co. At the end of fiscal 1997, the cash account for the three companies appears as follows:

Push Automotive	$180,000
Slick Tire	60,000
Sticky Brakes	40,000
Total cash	$280,000

The consolidated balance sheet for Push Automotive for 1997 would report a cash balance of $280,000.

All accounts cannot be combined in the same way as cash, however. For example, assume sales revenue for the three companies was as follows:

Push Automotive	$1,400,000
Slick Tire	500,000
Sticky Brakes	300,000
Total revenue	$2,200,000

The combined total represents the consolidated revenues of Push Automotive and its subsidiaries only if no sales were made *among* the three companies. Assume Slick Tire sold goods to Push that amounted to $300,000 of its sales. Sticky Brakes sold goods to Push that amounted to $180,000 of its sales. Consolidated revenues would be:

Push Automotive		$1,400,000
Slick Tire	$500,000	
Less intercompany sales	300,000	200,000
Sticky Brakes	300,000	
Less intercompany sales	180,000	120,000
Total consolidated revenue		$1,720,000

Intercompany sales must be eliminated from total revenues because these sales are not transactions with customers outside the consolidated business. Cost of goods sold would have to be adjusted, as well, for the costs associated with intercompany sales. Other accounts that require adjustments include intercompany payables and receivables. In addition, subsidiary stockholders' equity is eliminated because it is owned by the parent.

The consolidated statements represent the economic activities of a parent and its subsidiaries as though they were one business organization. Owners of a parent firm are also owners of the subsidiaries controlled by the parent. Therefore, consolidated statements provide information about the activities of a group of companies owned by particular stockholders. The stockholders should be concerned about the activities of both parent and subsidiaries because the value of the stockholders' investments is determined by the value of the consolidated business.

Some countries do not require consolidation of parent and subsidiary financial statements. Each company reports its own statements. When statements are not consolidated, investors have more difficulty in assessing the performance of a parent company.

Limitations of Financial Statements

Objective 11
Identify some of the primary limitations of financial statements.

In spite of the abundant information financial statements provide, their usefulness is limited by certain constraints of the reporting process. Some of these limitations include:

1. use of estimates and allocations,
2. use of historical costs,
3. omission of transactions,

4. omission of resources and costs, and
5. delay in providing information.

These constraints result primarily from costs associated with the reporting process. Information is a resource. It is costly to provide. Its value is determined by benefits derived by those who use the information. For information to be valuable, its cost must be less than the benefits it provides to users. Therefore, the amount and type of reported information is constrained by costs and benefits.

The following sections consider these limitations. Users should keep these limitations in mind when interpreting financial statement information.

Use of Estimates and Allocations. Many of the numbers reported in financial statements result from estimates and allocations. For example, depreciation and amortization represent allocations of asset costs to expenses over the estimated lives of the assets. These estimates often are imprecise because the amount of the asset consumed in a particular fiscal period is difficult to determine. Decisions about when to recognize revenues and expenses frequently require management judgment. Sometimes it is not clear when a revenue has been earned or when an expense has been incurred. For example, revenues earned on long-term contracts, such as those in the construction industry, are known with certainty only after the contract has been completed. But, if the contract takes several years to complete, determination of the revenue that should be recognized each year during the contract period requires management judgment. Different managers and companies may use different methods for recognizing certain revenues and expenses. Managers estimate the amount of credit sales that will be uncollectible, and determine when to recognize a loss from obsolete inventory or from plant assets that have experienced an unexpected decline in value. These subjective decisions and estimates mean accounting numbers are not as precise as they might initially appear. Precision is limited by the cost of obtaining precise information in a timely manner.

Use of Historical Costs. Financial statements report primarily the historical cost of assets and liabilities. *Historical cost* **is the purchase or exchange price of an asset or liability at the time it is acquired or incurred.** The recorded values of many assets are reduced over time by depreciation and amortization. They are not adjusted for changes in the purchasing power of money or for changes in the current value of the assets or liabilities, however. The purchasing power of money changes over time because of inflation; for example, a dollar in 1997 buys less than a dollar would purchase in 1980. The current value of an asset is the amount at which that asset, in its current condition, could be bought or sold at the present time. A building purchased in 1980 for $500,000 may be reported in the financial statements at a book value (cost minus accumulated depreciation) of $200,000 in 1997. This amount has not been adjusted for inflation. Suppose inflation has been 100% since the building was purchased; the current cost of that building in its 1997 condition would be about $400,000 (200,000 + [200,000 × 100%]). However, disclosure of current cost and the impact of purchasing power changes are not required by GAAP. Rather, financial statements report most assets and liabilities at their historical costs, adjusted for accumulated depreciation or amortization when appropriate.

Some countries such as the United Kingdom and the Netherlands permit financial statements to be reported using current values. Assets and liabilities are restated to approximate their market values at the end of a fiscal period.

Net income should provide financial statement users a reasonable estimate of the amount a company can distribute to its owners and maintain the company's capital. If economic conditions are stable, a company that maintains its capital should be able to earn profits indefinitely at approximately the same level as in the past. In reality, economic conditions are seldom stable across fiscal periods. Companies must contend with changing economic conditions such as variations in interest rates and inflation, changing markets and competition, variations in the price and availability of materials, plant assets, labor, and changing technology. **Therefore, the amount of net income reported by a company may overstate or understate the amount a company can distribute to its owners and still maintain its capital.** Numerous factors must be examined by users in interpreting a company's earnings and in forecasting its prospects for the future.

Omission of Transactions. Financial statements include the primary transactions that occur as part of a company's transformation process. Nevertheless, **a guarantee does not exist that all important transactions are fully reported in a company's financial statements**. Some transactions do not result from specific exchanges. They result when revenues or expenses are allocated to fiscal periods. Accountants and managers sometimes disagree about when certain activities should be recognized. Also, they may disagree about the amount that should be reported in the financial statements for these activities. The accounting profession has debated extensively such issues as how to recognize the costs of employee retirement benefits. Today, companies report certain liabilities, assets, and expenses associated with these items that were not reported 10 years ago. Undoubtedly, other issues will arise that will alter information reported in the financial statements.

The importance of information changes over time. Companies develop new financing and compensation arrangements. Reporting rules for these arrangements may not be covered by existing GAAP. If the arrangements become common such that new reporting rules would increase the benefits of information for users, GAAP may be created for transactions involving these new arrangements. GAAP are dynamic. They change as the needs of users and economic activities of organizations change. Chapter 7 examines the process used to establish GAAP.

Omission of Resources and Costs. Certain types of resources and costs are not reported in the financial statements. The value of employees is not an asset listed on most balance sheets. Nevertheless, a well-trained and stable work force and skilled managers may be the resource that adds most to the value of many companies. Without skilled labor and management, the remaining resources of a company often would have little value. Financial statements do not report these human resources. They are not owned by a company, and their values are difficult and costly to determine. A major portion of the value of many companies derives from their research and development activities that create new and improved products. The costs of these efforts are expensed when they are incurred each fiscal period even though they may have a major effect on the future earnings of a company. Such costs are expensed because of the difficulty and cost of identifying the timing and amount of future benefits a company will receive from these efforts. Nevertheless, the economic value of a company differs from the amount reported on its financial statements because of these measurement limitations.

Delay in Providing Information. Financial statement information is not always timely. Annual financial statements may lag actual events by a year or more; even monthly statements may lag events by several weeks. While such delays may not be a major problem for certain types of decisions, they may be critical for others. Users often need more timely sources. Managers, in particular, may need information on an ongoing basis to make effective decisions. Traditional financial statements are only one type of accounting information. Because financial statements are costly to produce and distribute, external reporting is limited to distinct fiscal periods. In addition to annual financial reports, major corporations provide quarterly reports to stockholders. As information technology reduces the cost of reporting, more frequent reporting to external users may become feasible.

Usefulness of Financial Statements

Though a variety of problems impair their usefulness, financial statements continue to be a primary source of information for managers and external users about a company's activities. But, these problems mean considerable care is needed to understand accounting information and to use it correctly in making decisions. Careful analysis of the information is necessary.

FINANCIAL STATEMENTS AND THE TRANSFORMATION PROCESS

Objective 12
Discuss how financial statements relate to the transformation process and the time periods in which companies operate.

The first five chapters of this book have examined the purpose and function of business organizations and the role of the accounting information system. Organizations transform resources into goods and services. The accounting information system identifies events associated with the transformation process. It includes these events in financial information that can be summarized and reported to decision makers.

Exhibit 5-9 illustrates the accounting information system as it represents the transformation process.

Financial statements and individual accounts originate within the transformation process. The balance sheet identifies sources of financing for a company and how the financing was invested in resources available to the company. The income statement identifies operating activities that provide additional financial resources and equity. These operating activities also require the consumption of resources. Their consumption is measured by expenses. Events from financing, investing, and operating activities affect a company's cash flows. The statement of cash flows identifies these events. Both investments by owners and reinvestment

Exhibit 5-9   Accounting Information and the Transformation Process

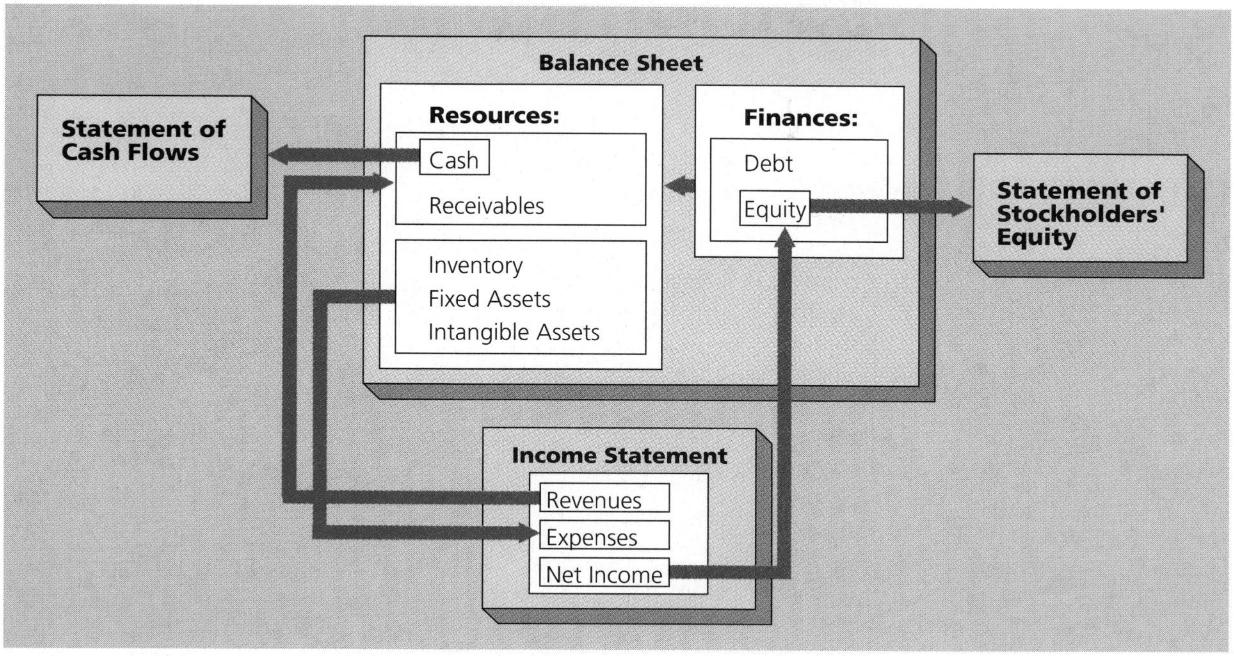

of profits affect stockholders' equity. These events are identified in the statement of stockholders' equity.

Transformation and Time

Two essential concepts must be mastered to understand accounting information. One of the concepts is the transformation process. Transactions associated with the transformation process are the basis for accounting information. Accounting information is meaningful only when it is a reasonable representation of an organization's transformation process. To interpret accounting information, you must understand the transformation process.

The second concept is the importance of time in measuring financial performance. A company's activities are separated into periods of time, fiscal periods. The events that occur in a company's transformation process should be associated with the periods in which they occur. But, many events extend to more than one fiscal period. Contracts often begin in one period and end in a subsequent period. Cash flows may occur in one period, while revenues or expenses may be recognized in another. Cash flows are reported on the statement of cash flows. Revenues and expenses are reported on the income statement. The balance sheet identifies resources and sources of financing for the resources. Resources and financing on the balance sheet result from past cash flows and operating activities and affect future cash flows and operating activities.

To understand accounting, you must understand that accounting information:

1. depicts the financial consequences of events occurring in financing, investing, and operating activities in the transformation process, and

2. recognizes the financial effects of these events in specific fiscal periods.

   Chapter 6 examines in detail the effect of fiscal periods on accounting information.

SELF-STUDY PROBLEM 5-3

A series of financial statement items is listed below:

1. Accounts Receivable
2. Inventory
3. Supplies
4. Prepaid Insurance
5. Buildings
6. Patents
7. Accounts Payable
8. Wages Payable
9. Interest Payable
10. Notes Payable
11. Contributed Capital
12. Retained Earnings
13. Dividends
14. Sales Revenue
15. Cost of Goods Sold
16. Depreciation Expense
17. Wages Expense
18. Interest Expense
19. Cash Collected from Customers
20. Cash Paid to Suppliers
21. Cash Received from Issuing Debt
22. Cash Paid for Equipment

Required

For each account, indicate the financial statement on which the account would appear. Then, identify the information provided by the account and the meaning of the account for an organization's transformation process. Use the format provided below. The first item is provided as an example:

Item	Financial Statement	Activity Reported
1. Accounts Receivable	Balance Sheet	Cash to be received in future from prior sales

The solution to Self-Study Problem 5-3 appears at the end of the chapter.

REVIEW   *Summary of Important Concepts*

1. Purpose and content of financial statements:
   a. Financial statements include the balance sheet, the income statement, the statement of cash flows, and the statement of stockholders' equity.
   b. The income statement reports the results of operations of a company for a fiscal period on the accrual basis. It reports information about the creation and consumption of resources in producing and selling goods and services, not about actual cash flows.
   c. Income statement formats vary, but typical statements are prepared using a multiple-step or single-step format.
   d. Corporations often report a statement of stockholders' equity. It describes the results of transactions that have changed the amount of contributed capital and retained earnings of a company during a fiscal period.
   e. A balance sheet identifies asset, liability, and owners' equity account balances at the end of a fiscal period. Balance sheets often classify accounts into current and long-term asset and liability categories. Comparative balance sheets report account balances for more than one fiscal period.
   f. The statement of cash flows reports the cash inflows and outflows associated with operating, investing, and financing activities of a company for a fiscal period. The statement may be presented in a direct or an indirect format.
   g. Two essential concepts describe the information reported by financial statements: (1) financial statements represent the transformation process of an organization for a fiscal period and (2) financial statements report the effects of transactions for specific periods.

2. Special attributes and limitations of financial statements:
   a. The interrelated financial statements, as a set, describe the financial impact of economic events of a company from the beginning to the end of a fiscal period.
   b. Consolidated financial statements report the economic activities of a parent and its subsidiaries as though they were one business entity.
   c. Limitations exist in financial statements that affect the usefulness of the information the statements report. Limitations include the need for estimates of financial results, the use of historical costs for representing asset values, and incomplete measures for some resources or transactions that might affect a company's value.

DEFINE   *Terms and Concepts Defined in This Chapter*

amortization
articulation
consolidated financial statements
contributed capital
cost of services sold
current assets
current liabilities
current ratio
earnings per share
financial revenues and expenses

gross profit
historical cost
income from operations
intangible assets
liquid assets
liquidity
long-term investments
long-term liabilities
operating expenses
operating income

other assets
other revenues and expenses
parent corporation
property, plant, and equipment
statement of cash flows
statement of stockholders' equity
subsidiary
working capital
working capital ratio

SOLUTIONS

SELF-STUDY PROBLEM 5-1

(Answers in millions)
1. Revenue from sale of equipment — $30,591

2. Other operating revenue:

Software	$10,953
Services	9,711
Maintenance	7,295
Rentals and financing	4,166
Total	$32,125

3. Other income — $1,113

4. Gross profit from sale of equipment:

Sales revenue	$30,591
Cost of goods sold	20,696
Gross profit	$ 9,895

5. Gross profit from sale of software:

Sales revenue	$10,953
Cost of goods sold	4,310
Gross profit	$ 6,643

6. Interest expense — $1,273

7. Number of shares outstanding ($8,101,000,000/$14.22) = 569,700,000 shares (approximately).

8. Cost of goods sold:

For equipment	$20,696
For software	4,310
Total	$25,006

9. Net loss — $ 8,101

10. Net cash from operations cannot be determined from the income statement.

SELF-STUDY PROBLEM 5-2

1. Gross profit:

Sales revenue	$357,000
Cost of goods sold	146,000
Gross profit	$211,000

2. Income from operations:

Gross profit		$211,000
General and administrative expenses	$96,000	
Selling expenses	47,000	
Total operating expenses		143,000
Income from operations		$ 68,000

3. Net income:

Income from operations		$ 68,000
Interest expense	$25,000	
Income tax expense	14,000	39,000
Net income		$ 29,000

4. Earnings per share:
   Net income ÷ shares of common stock ($29,000/10,000) = $2.90

5. Current assets:

Cash	$ 16,000
Accounts receivable	11,000
Merchandise inventory	62,000
Supplies	13,000
Prepaid insurance	7,000
Current assets	$109,000

6. Property, plant, and equipment:

Land	$ 35,000
Buildings	412,000
Equipment	245,000
Accumulated depreciation	(164,000)
Property, plant, and equipment	$528,000

7. Other assets:

Long-term investments	$ 35,000
Trademarks	13,000
Other assets	$ 48,000

8. Total assets:

Current assets	$109,000
Property, plant, and equipment	528,000
Other assets	48,000
Total assets	$685,000*

9. Current liabilities:

Accounts payable	$ 22,000
Wages payable	18,000
Interest payable	14,000
Income tax payable	6,000
Notes payable, current portion	10,000
Current liabilities	$ 70,000

10. Working capital and working capital ratio:

Current assets	$109,000
Current liabilities	70,000
Working capital	$ 39,000

   Working capital ratio ($109,000/$70,000) = 1.557

11. Total liabilities:

Current liabilities	$ 70,000
Notes payable, long-term	278,000
Total liabilities	$348,000

12. Retained earnings, October 31, 1997:

Retained earnings, October 31, 1996	$ 25,000
Net income	29,000
Dividends	(17,000)
Retained earnings, October 31, 1997	$ 37,000

13. Total stockholders' equity:

Contributed capital	$300,000
Retained earnings	37,000
Stockholders' equity	$337,000

14. Total liabilities and stockholders' equity:

Total liabilities	$348,000
Stockholders' equity	337,000
Total liabilities and stockholders' equity	$685,000*

15. Net cash flow from operating activities:

Collections from customers	$360,000
Payments for income tax	(11,000)
Payments for insurance	(9,000)
Payments for interest	(23,000)
Payments for supplies	(10,000)
Payments to employees	(100,000)
Payments to suppliers	(154,000)
Cash flow from operating activities	$ 53,000

16. Net cash flow from (for) investing activities:

Disposal of equipment	$ 8,000
Acquisition of buildings	(32,000)
Acquisition of land	(5,000)
Acquisition of long-term investments	(8,000)
Cash flow from (for) investing activities	$ (37,000)

17. Net cash flow from (for) financing activities:

Issuance of notes payable	$ 60,000
Repurchase of stock	(35,000)
Payments for notes payable	(30,000)
Payment of dividends	(17,000)
Cash flow from (for) financing activities	$ (22,000)

18. Net increase or decrease in cash:

Cash flow from operating activities	$ 53,000
Cash flow from (for) investing activities	(37,000)
Cash flow from (for) financing activities	(22,000)
Net decrease in cash	$ (6,000)

Note: Total assets = total liabilities + stockholders' equity

SELF-STUDY PROBLEM 5-3

Item	Financial Statement	Activity Reported
1. Accounts Receivable	Balance Sheet	Cash to be received in future from prior sales
2. Inventory	Balance Sheet	Cost of resources acquired in past to be used in future operations
3. Supplies	Balance Sheet	Cost of resources acquired in past to be used in future operations
4. Prepaid Insurance	Balance Sheet	Cost of resources acquired in past to be used in future operations
5. Buildings	Balance Sheet	Cost of resources acquired in past to be used in future operations
6. Patents	Balance Sheet	Cost of resources acquired in past to be used in future operations
7. Accounts Payable	Balance Sheet	Cash to be paid in future for resources acquired in past
8. Wages Payable	Balance Sheet	Cash to be paid in future for services used in past operations

continued

Item	Financial Statement	Activity Reported
9. Interest Payable	Balance Sheet	Cash to be paid in future for use of money borrowed in past
10. Notes Payable	Balance Sheet	Cash borrowed in past to acquire resources, to be repaid in future
11. Contributed Capital	Balance Sheet and Stockholders' Equity	Cash received in past from owners used to acquire resources
12. Retained Earnings	Balance Sheet and Stockholders' Equity	Profits earned from operations used to acquire additional resources
13. Dividends	Stockholders' Equity	Cash paid or promised to owners from results of operations
14. Sales Revenue	Income Statement	Cash received or to be received from past operations
15. Cost of Goods Sold	Income Statement	Cost of resources consumed in past operations
16. Depreciation Expense	Income Statement	Cost of resources consumed in past operations
17. Wages Expense	Income Statement	Cost of services consumed in past operations
18. Interest Expense	Income Statement	Cost of services consumed in past operations
19. Cash from Customers	Cash Flows	Cash received from sales
20. Cash to Suppliers	Cash Flows	Cash paid for resources acquired
21. Cash from Debt	Cash Flows	Cash received from creditors
22. Cash for Equipment	Cash Flows	Cash paid for resources acquired

EXERCISES

5-1. Write a short definition for each of the terms listed in the *Terms and Concepts Defined in This Chapter* section.

5-2. Listed below are typical accounts that appear on financial statements. For each account, identify the financial statement(s) on which it appears:
  a. Wages expense
  b. Wages payable
  c. Cash received from customers
  d. Common stock
  e. Dividends paid
  f. Accounts receivable
  g. Sales revenue
  h. Common stock issued during year
  i. Cash used to purchase equipment
  j. Inventory
  k. Net income
  l. Retained earnings
  m. Contributed capital

5-3. A list of information contained in financial statements is provided below. For each item, indicate which financial statement provides the information.
  a. Changes in a corporation's stockholders' equity for a fiscal period
  b. The dollar amount of resources available at a particular date
  c. Cash used for investing activities
  d. Accrual based operating results for a fiscal period
  e. The cost of resources consumed in producing revenues for a period
  f. The sources of finances used to acquire resources
  g. The effect of issuing stock on the amount of contributed capital during a period
  h. Cash received from operating activities during a period
  i. Revenues generated during a fiscal period

5-4. Both a company's income statement and its statement of cash flows provide information about operating activities during a fiscal period. Why are both statements included in the company's financial report? How can information in each statement be used by decision makers?

5-5. Johansen Co. sells, rents, and services ski equipment. Information about the company's financial performance for a recent fiscal period is provided below:
  Average shares outstanding, 10,000
  Cost of goods sold, $17,000
  Debt outstanding, $32,500
  General and administrative expenses, $6,000
  Income tax expense, $10,000
  Interest expense, $4,000
  Payments to owners, $15,000
  Rental revenue, $22,500
  Sales revenue, $39,500
  Selling expense, $13,500
  Service revenue, $11,500
  From the information provided, compute the following amounts for the period:
  a. Gross profit
  b. Operating expenses
  c. Income from operations
  d. Pretax income
  e. Net income
  f. Earnings per share

5-6. An income statement provides information about product and period costs. Distinguish between these types of costs. Classify each of the following as a product or period cost:
  a. advertising expenses
  b. wages for factory workers
  c. wages for management
  d. commissions for sales staff
  e. depreciation on factory equipment
  f. depreciation on office equipment
  g. materials used in production
  h. merchandise purchased for resale
  i. utilities used by management facilities
  j. utilities used by a factory

5-7. Adorondike, Inc. manages resort property. Use the following information to prepare a statement of stockholders' equity for the year ended September 30, 1995:
  a. The company paid $30,000 of dividends during the fiscal year.
  b. The company issued $300,000 of common stock during the year.

    c.   The company paid off $240,000 of long-term debt during the year.

    d.   Net income for the year was $90,000.

    e.   Contributed capital on September 30, 1994 was $525,000. Retained earnings was $105,000.

5-8. Differentiate between contributed capital and retained earnings. Identify events that affect the amount of contributed capital or retained earnings for a corporation.

5-9. Listed below are selected account balances for Navaho Rug Co. for June 30, 1997:

Accounts payable, $100,500
Accounts receivable, $84,000
Accumulated depreciation, $318,000
Buildings, $750,000
Cash, $34,500
Contributed capital, $900,000
Cost of goods sold, $840,000
Equipment, $450,000
Interest payable, $43,500
Land, $300,000
Merchandise inventory, $690,000
Notes payable, current portion, $60,000
Notes payable, long-term, $720,000
Prepaid insurance, $48,000
Retained earnings, $279,000
Supplies, $57,000
Trademarks, $45,000
Wages expense, $375,000
Wages payable, $37,500

Use this information to compute the following amounts:

a.   Current assets
b.   Current liabilities
c.   Property, plant, and equipment
d.   Total assets
e.   Long-term liabilities
f.   Total liabilities
g.   Stockholders' equity
h.   Total liabilities and stockholders' equity
i.   Working capital

5-10. The following information reflects cash flow and other activities of MaGoo Eyeglass Co. for three months ended March 31, 1996:

Paid for advertising, $150
Paid for equipment, $21,000
Paid for income taxes, $1,500
Paid for insurance, $100
Paid for interest, $225
Paid for utilities, $395
Paid to employees, $9,000
Paid to owners, $6,000
Paid to suppliers, $21,000
Depreciation expense, $6,500
Received from customers, $43,500
Received from issuing long-term debt, $10,000
Received from sale of land, $16,500

Use this information to answer the following questions:
a.   What was net cash flow from operating activities for the period?
b.   What was net cash flow from financing activities?
c.   What was net cash flow from investing activities?
d.   What was the net change in cash for the period?

5-11.   For each of items listed below, identify whether it would appear on the statement of cash flows as part of the computation of cash flow from operating activities, cash flow from investing activities, cash flow from financing activities, or if it would not appear at all. Also, indicate whether the item is added or subtracted in computing cash flow using the direct method of preparing the statement of cash flows:
a.   Purchase of plant assets
b.   Cash paid to suppliers
c.   Cash collected from customers
d.   Payment of long-term debt
e.   Net income
f.   Depreciation expense
g.   Payment of dividends
h.   Issuing stock
i.   Cash paid to employees
j.   Cash paid for income taxes
k.   Disposal of plant assets

5-12.   The following information is available for Hourglass Watch Co. for the first six months of 1995:

Cash collected from customers	$162,500
Cash paid to suppliers	56,250
Cash paid for utilities	10,000
Cash paid for insurance	15,000
Cash paid for equipment	43,750
Cash paid to employees	28,750
Cash paid for interest	3,750
Cash paid for dividends	2,500
Cash received from disposal of equipment	11,250

Determine the cash flow from operating activities for the six-month period.

5-13.   Listed below are account balances. For each item, indicate the future implications for cash flows and/or operating activities. Item (a) is provided as an example.

	Account Balance	Implication
a.	Accounts receivable, $10,000	$10,000 of cash should be received from customers during the next fiscal year.
b.	Accounts payable, $7,500	
c.	Inventory, $50,000	
d.	Notes payable, long-term, $100,000	
e.	Equipment, $80,000	
f.	Prepaid insurance, $22,000	
g.	Wages payable, $8,000	
h.	Unearned revenue, $13,000	
i.	Notes payable, current, $5,000	

5-14.   An income statement for Delta Airlines for a recent fiscal year is provided below:

Consolidated Statement of Income
For the Year Ended June 30, 1993

(In Thousands, Except Per Share Amounts)

Operating revenues:	
Passenger	$11,075,212
Cargo	697,437
Other	224,001
Total operating revenues	11,996,650
Operating expenses:	
Salaries and employee costs	4,797,910
Aircraft fuel	1,591,722
Passenger commissions	1,250,488
Depreciation and amortization	734,920
Aircraft rent	728,566
Passenger service	548,650
Aircraft maintenance materials and repairs	465,128
Facilities and other rent	355,628
Landing fees	262,534
Fleet restructuring	82,500
Other	1,754,043
Total operating expenses	12,572,089
Operating loss	(575,439)
Other income (expense):	
Interest expense	(238,829)
Less: Interest capitalized	61,948
Gain on disposition of flight equipment	64,843
Miscellaneous income	36,193
	(75,845)
Loss before income taxes	(651,284)
Income tax credits	236,536
Net loss	$ (414,748)
Loss per share	$(10.54)

Note: Modifications have been made to the statement for the purposes of simplifying the presentation.

Use this income statement to answer the following questions:
a.   What were Delta's main sources of revenues?
b.   What were its largest expenses?
c.   How much revenue did Delta earn from transporting passengers?
d.   How much revenue did it earn from other operating activities?
e.   How much revenue did it earn from nonoperating activities?
f.   How much operating income did Delta earn (or lose)?
g.   How much expense did it incur for nonoperating activities?
h.   Approximately how many shares of stock did Delta have outstanding during the year?
i.   How much profit did Delta earn during the fiscal year?

5-15.   Compaq Computer Corporation reported the following income statement in a recent year:

> **Consolidated Statement of Income**
> **For the Year Ended December 31**
>
> | In millions, except per share amounts | 1993 |
> |---|---|
> | Sales | $7,191 |
> | Cost of sales | 5,493 |
> | | 1,698 |
> | Research and development costs | 169 |
> | Selling, general, and administrative expense | 837 |
> | Other income and expense, net | 76 |
> | | 1,082 |
> | Income before income taxes | 616 |
> | Provision for income taxes | 154 |
> | Net income | $ 462 |
> | Earnings per share | $5.45 |
>
> *Note: Slight modifications have been made to the format of the statement for purposes of simplifying the presentation. Assume other income and expense is nonoperating.*

a.   What was Compaq's gross profit for the year?
b.   What was the amount of the company's product costs expensed during the year?
c.   What was its operating expenses?
d.   What was its operating income?
e.   What was its nonoperating income or expense?

5-16.   The Limited, Inc. reported the following information for 1994 (in millions):

Accounts payable	$ 250
Accounts receivable	1,057
Accrued expenses (payables)	348
Cash and equivalents	321
Contributed capital	319
Deferred income taxes (liabilities)	275
Income taxes payable (current)	93
Inventories	734
Long-term debt	650
Other current assets	109
Other current liabilities	16
Other long-term assets	248
Other long-term liabilities	61
Property and equipment, net (of depreciation)	1,667
Retained earnings, net of adjustments	2,124

Accrued liabilities are current liabilities. Deferred income taxes are long–term liabilities.

Use the information provided to prepare a balance sheet for The Limited, Inc. in good form.

5-17. Selected information reported by Disco Corporation included (in millions):

Contributed capital at June 30, 1995	$ 657
Retained earnings at June 30, 1995	1,536
Dividends	222
Net income	953
Common stock issued	243

Use this information to prepare a statement of stockholders' equity for Disco for the year ended June 30, 1996.

5-18. The following information was reported by Allied Products Corporation in a recent year (in thousands):

Proceeds from issuance of long-term debt	$13,057
Additions to plant and equipment	5,379
Proceeds from sales of businesses	30,957
Proceeds from sales of plant and equipment	1,986
Payments of debt	80,323

Calculate the net cash flow from financing and investing activities for Allied Products.

5-19. The following table provides cash flow information for three corporations for the 1993 fiscal year:

(in millions)	Chrysler	Ford	General Motors
Cash flow from operating activities	$3,052	$6,862	$14,656
Cash flow from (for) investing activities	938	(4,409)	457
Cash flow from (for) financing activities	(2,307)	(834)	(12,476)

Use the table to answer each of the following questions:
a. Which company had the largest amount of cash flow from operating activities? Which had the smallest?
b. Would you expect cash flow associated with investing activities to be negative? Why or why not?
c. In what ways does Ford appear to be different from the other two companies? What do these differences suggest about the companies?

5-20. Though U. S. companies report their plant assets at historical cost, some foreign companies report current values for their plant assets. For example, a recent annual report for Nestlé, a Swiss company, disclosed:
Tangible fixed assets are shown on the balance sheet at their net replacement values arrived at as follows:
— Land: market value prudently estimated.
— Other tangible fixed assets: replacement new value (the amount that theoretically would have to be invested in order to replace an asset by a similar new asset duly installed and rendering the same service) less the accumulated depreciation calculated on this value.
These amounts are recalculated each year.
Using this method, Nestlé reported plant assets of 14,867 million Swiss francs. The book value of these assets using historical cost would have been 10,616 million Swiss francs. What are some of the advantages and disadvantages of the asset valuation method used

by Nestlé relative to that used by U. S. companies? What implications does the use of current value have for Nestlé's return on assets and return on stockholders' equity?

PROBLEMS

PROBLEM 5-1   Identifying the Purpose of Financial Statements

Assume you are a financial manager with a U. S. corporation. A. Suliman is a recently employed manager in the Middle Eastern division of your corporation and a visitor to the U. S. He has little familiarity with U. S. financial reporting practices. Your boss has given you the responsibility of explaining financial reports to Mr. Suliman.

Required   Write a short report describing each of the four basic corporate financial statements for Suliman. Make sure you are clear about the purpose of each statement, its contents, and its relationships to the other financial statements.

PROBLEM 5-2   Preparing Financial Statements

Argyle Co. manufactures socks. A list of account balances for December 31, 1996, the end of the company's fiscal year, is provided below. Argyle had 10,000 shares of stock outstanding during the year.

Argyle Co.
Account Balances
At December 31, 1996

Account	Balance
Cash	$ 4,650
Accounts Receivable	16,350
Inventory	30,500
Supplies	7,700
Prepaid Insurance	3,550
Equipment	42,500
Allowance for Depreciation—Equipment	17,500
Buildings	170,000
Allowance for Depreciation—Buildings	105,000
Land	10,000
Patents	3,000
Accounts Payable	18,250
Wages Payable	3,450
Interest Payable	1,700
Income Taxes Payable	4,050
Notes Payable, Current Portion	2,500
Notes Payable, Long-Term	37,500
Owners' Investment	25,000
Retained Earnings, December 31, 1995	60,150
Dividends	15,000

continued

Account	Balance
Sales Revenue	$130,000
Cost of Goods Sold	62,500
Wages Expense	16,000
Utilities Expense	2,000
Depreciation Expense	1,050
Insurance Expense	1,500
Supplies Expense	2,300
Interest Expense	3,650
Advertising Expense	1,450
Patent Expense	400
Income Tax Expense	11,000

Required   From this list, prepare an income statement and a balance sheet for the fiscal year. Use the multiple-step format for the income statement. Include titles for each statement.

PROBLEM 5-3   Interpreting an Income Statement

Recent income statements are provided below for Microsoft Corporation:

Income Statements

(In millions, except earnings per share)

	Year Ended June 30		
	1993	**1992**	**1991**
Net revenues	$3,753	$2,759	$1,843
Cost of revenues	633	467	362
Gross profit	3,120	2,292	1,481
Operating expenses:			
Research and development	470	352	235
Sales and marketing	1,205	854	534
General and administrative	119	90	62
Total operating expenses	1,794	1,296	831
Operating income	1,326	996	650
Interest income—net	82	56	37
Other	(7)	(11)	(16)
Income before income taxes	1,401	1,041	671
Provision for income taxes	448	333	208
Net income	$953	$708	$463
Earnings per share	$3.15	$2.41	$1.64

Note: Slight modifications have been made to the format of the statement for purposes of simplifying the presentation.

Required   Ratios often are used to assess changes in financial statement information over time. Use the income statements to answer the following questions:

a.   What was the ratio of net income to net revenues each year?

b.   What was the ratio of cost of revenues (cost of goods sold) to net revenues each year?

c.   What was the ratio of operating expenses to net revenues each year?

d.   What was the percentage change in net income between 1991 and 1992, and between 1992 and 1993? (Hint: Divide the increase in net income from 1991 to 1992 by the net income for 1991.)

e.   Did Microsoft's operating results improve between 1991 and 1992? Between 1992 and 1993? Explain your answers.

PROBLEM 5-4   Limitations of Financial Statements

Markus O'Realius is considering the purchase of a business, Caesar Co. The potential seller has provided Markus with a copy of the business's financial statements for the last three years. The financial statements reveal total assets of $350,000 and total liabilities of $150,000. The seller is asking $300,000 for the business. Markus believes the business is worth only about $200,000, the amount of owners' equity reported on the balance sheet. He has asked your assistance in determining a price to offer for the business.

Required   Write a memo to Markus explaining why he should not interpret the balance sheet as an accurate measure of the value of the business. Describe limitations of financial statements that might result in the market value of the business being higher (or lower) than the financial statement amounts.

PROBLEM 5-5   Accounting Concepts

Latin Specialties is an import company, financed primarily by stockholders and bank loans. It imports handmade goods from Central and South America to the U. S., where they are sold to retail stores. The company's buyers contract with small companies for goods that the buyers ship to a central location in the U. S. The goods are inventoried and then redistributed as orders are received from retailers. The company receives a bill from the manufacturers along with the goods it receives. Payment is made each month. Bills are sent to retailers along with orders. Most retailers pay their bills each month, as well. From the time goods are shipped to the U. S. until cash is received from retailers can be several months.

Required   Explain how Latin Specialties' financial statements represent the company's transformation process. Consider the events and transactions in the transformation process and how they are described in the financial statements. In particular, consider the relationships the company has with investors, suppliers, and customers. How does the timing of the events in the transformation process affect the financial statements? Why is it important that time be considered in reporting accounting information?

PROBLEM 5-6   Interpreting a Balance Sheet

A recent balance sheet for The Walt Disney Company is provided on the next page.

Consolidated Balance Sheet
(in millions)

September 30	1993	1992
Assets		
Cash	$363.0	$764.8
Investments (marketable securities)	1,888.5	1,407.0
Receivables	1,390.3	1,179.3
Merchandise inventories	608.9	462.8
Film and television costs (a)	1,360.9	760.5
Theme parks, resorts, and other property, at cost		
Attractions, buildings, and equipment	6,732.1	6,285.3
Accumulated depreciation	(2,286.4)	(1,999.6)
	4,445.7	4,285.7
Projects in progress	688.2	440.1
Land	94.3	72.9
	5,228.2	4,798.7
Other assets	911.3	1,488.6
	$11,751.1	$10,861.7
Liabilities and Stockholders' Equity		
Accounts payable and other accrued liabilities	$2,530.1	$1,791.9
Income taxes payable	291.0	381.0
Borrowings (a)	2,385.8	2,222.4
Unearned revenues (a)	840.7	872.8
Deferred income taxes (a)	673.0	889.0
Stockholders' equity		
Common stock	876.4	619.9
Retained earnings	4,833.1	4,661.9
Adjustments	(679.0)	(577.2)
	$11,751.1	$10,861.7

(a) Noncurrent

Note: Slight modifications have been made to the format of the statement for purposes of simplifying the presentation.

Required   From the information provided, answer the following questions:

a.   What was the total amount of current assets for the company in 1992 and 1993?

b.   What was the total amount of current liabilities for 1992 and 1993?

c.   What was the amount of working capital, and what was the working capital ratio for 1992 and 1993?

d.   What were the amounts of noncurrent assets and noncurrent liabilities for 1992 and 1993?

e.   What was the amount of contributed capital for 1992 and 1993?

f.   What were the amounts of total assets, total liabilities, and stockholders' equity for 1992 and 1993?

g.   Did the company's financial position improve between 1992 and 1993?

PROBLEM 5-7   Ethical Issues in Financial Reporting

Morgan Beetlejuice is a regional sales manager for Green-Grow, Inc., a producer of garden supplies. The company's fiscal year ends on April 30. In mid-April, Morgan is contacted by the president of Green-Grow, B. Elzebulb. He indicates the company is facing a
financial problem. Two years ago, the company borrowed heavily from several banks to
buy a competitor company and to increase production of its primary products, insecticides and fertilizers. As a part of the loan agreement, Green-Grow must maintain a
working capital ratio of 1:2 and earn a net income of at least $2 per share. If the company
fails to meet these requirements, as reflected in its annual financial statements, the banks
can restrict future credit for the company or require early payment of its loans, potentially forcing the company into bankruptcy.

The president explains that this fiscal year has been a difficult one for Green-Grow.
Sales have slipped because of increased competition, and the rising prices of chemicals
have increased the company's production costs. The company is in danger of not meeting
the loan requirements. The company could be forced to make drastic cuts or to liquidate
its assets. The president informs Morgan her job could be in danger. The president asks
Morgan to help with the problem by dating all sales invoices that clear her office during
the first half of May as though the sales had been made in April. May is a month of
heavy sales volume for the company as retail stores stock up for the coming season. The
president believes the added sales would be sufficient to get the company past the loan
problem. He explains this procedure will be used only this one time. By next year, the
company will be in better shape because of new products it is developing. Also, he re-
minds Morgan her bonus for the year will be higher because of the additional sales that
will be recorded for April. He points out the company is fundamentally in sound financial shape and he would hate to see its future jeopardized by a minor bookkeeping problem. He is asking for the cooperation of all of the regional sales managers. He argues the
stockholders, employees, and managers will all be better off if the sales are predated. He
wants Morgan's assurance she will cooperate.

Required   What effect will predating the sales have on Green-Grow's balance sheet,
income statement, and statement of cash flows? Be specific about which accounts will be
affected and why. How will this practice solve the company's problem with the banks?
What would be the appropriate behavior for B. Elzebulb under the circumstances the
company is facing? What would be the appropriate behavior for Morgan?

PROBLEM 5-8   Evaluating Financing Arrangements

Selected financial statement information is presented below for two companies, Debt
Co. and Equity Co. The companies are in the same industry, and both have fiscal years
ending September 30. All amounts are in millions.

	Debt Co.	Equity Co.
Current assets	$ 4.00	$ 4.00
Total assets	10.00	10.00
Total liabilities	8.00	2.00
Interest expense	1.20	.20
Operating expenses	1.60	1.60

Cost of goods sold is 40% of sales revenue for both companies. Income taxes are 30% of
pretax income for both companies. Debt Co. has 250,000 shares of stock outstanding.
Equity Co. has 1,000,000 shares outstanding.

Required   Prepare an income statement (including earnings per share) for each company assuming sales revenues are:

a. $6 million

b. $5 million

c. $4 million

Explain the changes in net income and earnings per share for the companies for the different amounts of sales revenues. If you had $100,000 to invest in either of these companies and this amount would purchase the same number of shares in either, in which would you buy stock? Why?

PROBLEM 5-9   Estimating Future Activities

Van Gogh is considering a business opportunity selling artificial flowers, especially irises and lilies. He needs $25,000 in financing to begin operations. He has $15,000 in savings he can invest. He has spoken with a local bank about borrowing the additional $10,000 he needs. The bank has indicated it will consider the loan but has asked for a set of financial statements that describes what Van believes the company's financial condition will look like at the end of the first three months of operations. Van has asked for your assistance in preparing the financial statements. He has provided you with the following expectations:

a.   Plant assets costing $22,500 will be needed.

b.   Inventory of $5,000 will be purchased for the first month. The inventory will be paid for in the month following purchase. The amount of inventory purchased each month will equal the amount sold in the prior month.

c.   Average monthly sales should be about $7,500. Two-thirds of the sales will be for cash each month, and one-third will be for credit. Credit sales will be collected in the month following sale.

d.   The cost of the inventory sold will be $4,000 each month.

e.   The interest on the loan will require a payment of $125 at the end of each month. An additional $100 will be paid to the bank each month to repay the loan.

f.   Operating expenses, other than depreciation, each month should be $1,000. These will be paid in cash. Depreciation should be $200 each month.

g.   Van expects to withdraw $1,000 from the business each month for living expenses.

In addition, he has provided the following work sheet, completed for the first month of operations:

	First Month	Second Month	Third Month
Sales revenues	$7,500		
Cost of goods sold	(4,000)		
Gross profit	3,500		
Depreciation	(200)		
Other operating expenses	(1,000)		
Income from operations	2,300		
Interest expense	(125)		
Net income	$2,175		
Cash	$5,275		
Accounts receivable	2,500		
Inventory	1,000		
Plant assets, net of depreciation	22,300		
Total assets	$31,075		
Accounts payable	5,000		
Notes payable	9,900		
Investment by owner	15,000		
Retained Earnings	1,175		
Total liabilities & owners' equity	$31,075		
Cash collected from customers	$5,000		
Cash paid to suppliers	0		
Cash paid for operating expenses	(1,000)		
Cash paid for interest	(125)		
Cash paid for plant assets	(22,500)		
Cash received from bank	10,000		
Cash received from owner	15,000		
Cash paid to repay loan	(100)		
Cash paid to owner	(1,000)		
Change in cash	$5,275		

Required   Complete the work sheet for the second and third months.

PROBLEM 5-10   Preparing Financial Statements

The following account balances are provided for Rustic Co. at December 31, 1996. Revenues and expense accounts cover the prior fiscal year. All numbers are dollars except shares outstanding.

Required   From these data, prepare a classified balance sheet and multi-step income statement in good form. Report total current assets, total assets, total current liabilities, total liabilities, total contributed capital, total stockholders' equity, total liabilities and stockholders' equity, total operating revenues, gross profit, operating income, income before taxes, net income, and earnings per share.

Account	Amount
Accounts Payable	$14,000
Accounts Receivable	18,000
Accumulated Depreciation	30,000
Cash	6,000
Common Stock, Par Value	20,000
Cost of Goods Sold	35,000
Current Portion of Long-Term Debt	2,000
Income Taxes	6,000
Interest Expense	4,000
Interest Payable	500
Inventory	34,000
Long-Term Debt	40,000
Net Income	12,000
Paid-In Capital in Excess of Par	30,000
Patents and Trademarks	4,000
Prepaid Insurance	2,500
Property, Plant, and Equipment, Cost	150,000
Retained Earnings	78,000
Sales Revenues	110,000
Selling, General, and Administrative Expenses	65,000
Service Revenues	12,000
Supplies	3,000
Wages Payable	3,000
Shares Outstanding	20,000

PROBLEM 5-11 Multiple Choice Overview of Chapter

1. Which of the following is not a statement you would expect to find in a corporate annual report?
   a. Statement of financial position
   b. Statement of earnings
   c. Statement of cash flows
   d. Statement of accounts receivable

2. The following assets appear on the balance sheet for Astroid Co.:

Accounts receivable	$ 50,000
Accumulated depreciation	160,000
Cash	20,000
Intangible assets	60,000
Inventory	100,000
Plant assets	400,000

   The amount of current assets reported by Astroid is:
   a. $170,000
   b. $150,000
   c. $230,000
   d. $470,000

3. The following information was reported on the income statement of Wagon Wheel Co.:

Sales revenues	$450,000
Cost of goods sold	200,000
Selling, general, and administrative expenses	150,000
Interest expense	30,000

Wagon Wheel's gross profit and operating income would be:

	Gross profit	Operating income
a.	$300,000	$70,000
b.	$250,000	$70,000
c.	$250,000	$100,000
d.	$100,000	$70,000

4. Which of the following is a *false* statement regarding the statement of stockholders' equity?
   a. It lists changes in contributed capital and retained earnings for a fiscal period.
   b. It contains information about net income and dividends for a fiscal period.
   c. It reports the net change in stockholders' equity for a fiscal period.
   d. It reports increases or decreases in stocks and bonds for a fiscal period.

5. A balance sheet that provides information for more than one fiscal period is:
   a. a classified balance sheet
   b. a comparative balance sheet
   c. a consolidated balance sheet
   d. a combined balance sheet

6. Working capital is the amount of:
   a. cash and cash equivalents available to a company at the end of a fiscal period.
   b. long-term investments available at the end of a fiscal period less long-term debt at the end of the period.
   c. current assets available at the end of a fiscal period less current liabilities at the end of the period.
   d. total assets available at the end of a period that can be converted to cash.

7. The statement of cash flows for the Fieldspar Exploration Co. reported:

Cash paid for equipment	$150,000
Cash paid to employees	200,000
Cash paid to owners	75,000
Cash paid to suppliers	280,000
Cash received from creditors	100,000
Cash received from customers	600,000

What were Fieldspar's net cash flows from operating, financing, and investing activities?

	Operating	Financing	Investing
a.	$120,000	$25,000	$(150,000)
b.	$250,000	$100,000	$(430,000)
c.	$320,000	$100,000	$(430,000)
d.	$120,000	$100,000	$(430,000)

8. A statement of cash flows, prepared using the indirect method, would report cash collected from customers as:
   a. an addition to cash flow from financing activities.
   b. a subtraction from cash flow from financing activities.

    c.   an addition to net income in computing cash flow from operating activities.
    d.   a subtraction from net income in computing cash flow from operating activities.

9. Flag Ship Co. reported depreciation and amortization expense of $300,000 for the latest fiscal year. The depreciation and amortization expense would:
    a.   increase cash flow for the year $300,000.
    b.   decrease cash flow for the year $300,000.
    c.   have no effect on cash flow for the year.
    d.   have an effect on cash flow if assets were purchased during the year.

10. Orange Bowl Co. reported plant assets for the latest fiscal year of $5 million, net of accumulated depreciation. From this information, which of the following is an accurate statement about the company?
    a.   The amount the company would receive if it sold its plant assets at the end of the fiscal year would be $5 million.
    b.   The company would have to pay $5 million to replace its assets if they were replaced at the end of the fiscal year.
    c.   The book value of the company's plant assets at the end of the fiscal year was $5 million.
    d.   The amount the company paid for the plant assets it controlled at the end of the fiscal year was $5 million.

C A S E S

CASE 5-1 Analysis of Corporate Financial Statements

Financial statements for McDonald's Corporation are provided below from a recent annual report. Examine these statements and answer the questions that follow the statements.

Consolidated Statement of Income
For the year ended December 31

(In millions of dollars, except per common share data)	1993
Revenues	
Sales by Company-operated restaurants	$5,157.2
Revenues from franchised restaurants	2,250.9
Total revenues	7,408.1
Operating costs and expenses	
Company-operated restaurants	
Food and packaging	1,735.1
Payroll and other employee benefits	1,291.2
Occupancy and other operating expenses	1,138.3
	4,164.6
Franchised restaurants-occupancy expenses	380.4
General, administrative, and selling expenses	941.1
Other operating income	(62.0)
Total operating costs and expenses	5,424.1

continued

Operating income	$1,984.0	
Interest expense	316.1	
Other nonoperating income	7.8	
Income before provision for income taxes	1,675.7	
Provision for income taxes	593.2	
Net income	$1,082.5	
Net income per common share	$2.91	
Dividends per common share	$.42	

Consolidated Balance Sheet

(In millions of dollars) December 31,	1993	1992
Assets		
Current assets		
Cash and equivalents	$185.8	$436.5
Accounts receivable	287.0	245.9
Notes receivable	27.6	33.7
Inventories	43.5	43.5
Prepaid expenses and other current assets	118.9	105.1
Total current assets	662.8	864.7
Other assets		
Notes receivable due after one year	90.0	99.0
Investments in and advances to affiliates	446.7	399.7
Miscellaneous	338.6	330.7
Total other assets	875.3	829.4
Property and equipment		
Property and equipment, at cost	13,459.0	12,658.0
Accumulated depreciation and amortization	(3,377.6)	(3,060.6)
Net property and equipment	10,081.4	9,597.4
Intangible assets, net (of amortization)	415.7	389.7
Total assets	$12,035.2	$11,681.2
Liabilities and shareholders' equity		
Current liabilities		
Notes payable	$193.3	$ 411.0
Accounts payable	395.7	343.3
Income taxes	56.0	109.7
Other taxes	90.2	74.8
Interest payable	132.9	133.3
Other liabilities	203.9	203.1
Current maturities of long-term debt	30.0	269.4
Total current liabilities	1,102.0	1,544.6
Long-term debt	3,489.4	3,176.4
Other long-term liabilities	334.4	319.2
Deferred income taxes	835.3	748.6
Shareholders' equity		
Capital stock	772.7	715.3
Retained earnings	7,612.6	6,727.3
Other adjustments	(2,111.2)	(1,550.2)
Total shareholders' equity	6,274.1	5,892.4
Total liabilities and shareholders' equity	$12,035.2	$11,681.2

Note: Slight modifications have been made to the format of the statements for purposes of simplifying the presentation.

Required   Use the financial statements to answer each of the following questions:

a.   What were the accrual basis operating results for McDonald's for 1993? What was its primary nonoperating expense? What were the major sources of income and major operating expenses for the company?

b.   What were the company's return on total assets and return on stockholders' equity for 1993? If you owned 10,000 of the company's shares of stock, what was your claim on the company's earnings for 1993? How much cash would you have received from the company?

c.   What have been McDonald's major sources of financing? What changes occurred in the company's finances during 1993?

d.   What were McDonald's most important assets? What changes occurred in its assets during 1993? What assets may be important to the company that are not reported on its balance sheet?

CASE 5-2   Comparing Financial Statement Information

Selected financial statement information for 1993 is provided below for The Coca-Cola Company and PepsiCo, Inc. The data are expressed in $millions.

	Coke	Pepsi
Sales revenue	$13,957	$25,021
Cost of goods sold	5,160	11,946
Operating expenses	5,695	10,168
Net income	2,176	1,588
Cash from operating activities	2,508	3,134
Cash from (for) investing activities	(885)	(2,771)
Cash from (for) financing activities	(1,540)	(303)
Current assets	4,434	5,164
Plant assets, net	3,729	8,856
Total assets	12,021	23,706
Current liabilities	5,171	6,575
Long-term liabilities	2,266	10,792
Stockholders' equity	4,584	6,339

Required   Compare the operating, investing, and financing activities of the two companies from the information provided. Comparisons can be made by converting income statement numbers to percentages by dividing by sales revenues. Divide balance sheet numbers by total assets. Divide cash flow numbers by cash from operating activities. Also, you may wish to compare income and cash flow numbers to balance sheet numbers (e. g., sales to total assets).

CASE 5-3   Interpreting Cash Flows

The statement of cash flows for Compaq Computer Corporation appears on page 236. This statement is prepared using the direct format.

Consolidated Statement of Cash Flows
Compaq Computer Corporation

Year ended December 31, In millions	1993	1992	1991
Cash flows from operating activities:			
Cash received from customers	$ 6,731	$ 3,595	$ 3,325
Cash paid to suppliers and employees	(6,331)	(3,642)	(2,823)
Interest and dividends received	20	32	32
Interest paid	(64)	(41)	(36)
Income taxes paid	(116)	(3)	(104)
Net cash provided by (used in) operating activities	240	(59)	394
Cash flows from investing activities:			
Purchases of property, plant, and equipment, net	(145)	(159)	(189)
Proceeds from sale of investment in Conner Peripherals, Inc.		241	
Investment in Silicon Graphics, Inc.		135	(135)
Other, net		13	(17)
Net cash provided by (used in) investing activities	(145)	230	(341)
Cash flows from financing activities:			
Purchases of treasury shares		(216)	(82)
Proceeds from sale of equity securities	142	57	23
Repayment of borrowings		(73)	(1)
Net cash provided by (used in) financing activities	142	(232)	(60)
Effect of exchange rate changes on cash	33	(34)	24
Net increase (decrease) in cash and cash equivalents	270	(95)	17
Cash and cash equivalents at beginning of year	357	452	435
Cash and cash equivalents at end of year	$ 627	$ 357	$ 452
Reconciliation of net income to net cash provided by (used in) operating activities:			
Net income	$ 462	$ 213	$ 131
Depreciation and amortization	156	160	166
Provision for bad debts	33	14	9
Equity in net income of affiliated company		(15)	(20)
Gain on sale of investment in affiliated company		(86)	
Deferred income taxes	(38)	34	(9)
Loss on disposal of assets	2	14	4
Exchange rate effect	15	11	(4)
Income tax refund		51	
Decrease (increase) in accounts receivable	(484)	(412)	138
Decrease (increase) in inventories	(289)	(396)	108
Decrease (increase) in prepaid expenses and other current assets	24	(53)	(132)
Increase (decrease) in accounts payable	125	325	(96)
Increase (decrease) in income taxes payable	78	38	(3)
Increase in other current liabilities	156	43	102
Net cash provided by (used in) operating activities	$ 240	$ (59)	$ 394

Required   Use the statement above to answer the following questions:

a.   What were Compaq's primary sources of cash in 1993? What were its primary uses of cash in 1993?

b. What was the primary cause of the increase in cash flow from operating activities from 1992 to 1993?

c. Was Compaq growing from 1991 to 1993? Explain.

d. Evaluate Compaq's cash flows. Did the company appear to be obtaining sufficient cash to meet its needs?

e. What primary explanations are provided for the difference between Compaq's cash flow from operating activities and net income?

PROJECTS

PROJECT 5-1   Comparing Financial Statements

Select three recent corporate annual reports from your library. Select firms from the same industry (e.g., automobile manufacturing, paper, chemicals, airlines, etc.). Prepare a comparative analysis for these companies using the following table as a guide:

	Company 1	Company 2	Company 3
Current assets/Total assets			
Plant assets, net of depreciation/Total assets			
Total liabilities/Total assets			
Current assets/Current liabilities			
Cost of goods sold/Sales revenues			
Operating expenses/Sales revenues			
Income from operations/Total assets			
Income from operations/Stockholders' Equity			
Net cash from operating activities/Net income			
Net cash from investing activities/Total assets			
Net cash from financing activities/Total assets			

Write a short report comparing the three companies. The report should address the questions: Which of the companies appears to be in the best financial condition? Which appears to be in the worst?

PROJECT 5-2   Comparing Financial Statements

Follow the format of Project 5-1. But, select three companies from different industries. Try to find a utility, a retail company, and a manufacturing company. Use the table in 5-1 as a format to compare the companies. Write a report describing similarities and differences in the financial information among the three companies.

PROJECT 5-3   Comparing Financial Statements

Locate recent annual reports for 10 different companies in your library. Prepare a table or list that identifies the following financial statement information: List the different titles you find for the balance sheet, income statement, statement of stockholders' equity, and statement of cash flows and indicate how many times each was used. List each of the major captions in each of the financial statements and indicate how many times each was used. List how many fiscal years were included in each of the financial statements. How many of the statements of cash flows were prepared using the direct method? How many using the indirect method? What conclusions can you draw about the formats and captions used by companies in their financial statements?

PROJECT 5-4   Answering Financial Reporting Questions

Find a recent issue of *Accounting Trends and Techniques* (published by the American Institute of Certified Public Accountants) in your library. Look for information in this publication to answer the following questions:

a.   In what month do most corporations end their fiscal years? What are the second and third most popular months?

b.   What are the most popular titles used for the balance sheet?

c.   What titles are used by corporations to refer to the stockholders' equity section of the balance sheet?

d.   What titles are used for the income statement?

e.   What proportion of companies use the multiple-step form of the income statement?

f.   What titles are used for cost of goods sold on the income statement?

g.   What proportion of companies use the indirect method of presenting the statement of cash flows?

PROJECT 5-5   Researching Financial Problems

Suppose you were interested in investing in the airlines industry. Develop an approach you might use to find out which airline companies have demonstrated strong financial health in the last 10 years and which have demonstrated poor financial health. What information would you want to examine to assist in your decision? How would you obtain this information? List the periodicals and other publications that would be relevant for your analysis.

PROJECT 5-6   Using Business Journals

Use a periodicals index, such as the *Accountants Index* or the *Business Periodicals Index*, to identify recent articles that discuss problems or limitations of financial statements. Use key words such as "financial statements" and "financial reporting." Select an article from a journal available in your library. Read the article and write a summary of the problem or limitation discussed in the article.

Chapter
6

Reporting Accruals and Cash Flows

This chapter considers relationships between accrual and cash measures of operating activities. These relationships have a major effect on information reported in financial statements. Understanding the relationships is essential to understanding accounting information. The chapter examines timing differences between when revenues and expenses occur and when cash is received or paid. These transactions affect the income statement through the recognition of revenues and expenses. They affect the balance sheet primarily through current asset and liability accounts. These accounts capture differences in timing between (1) recognition of revenues and expenses and (2) cash flows. These events also affect the statement of cash flows when the statement reconciles accrual and cash basis measures of operating activities.

This chapter examines relationships between measurement rules and accounting reports.

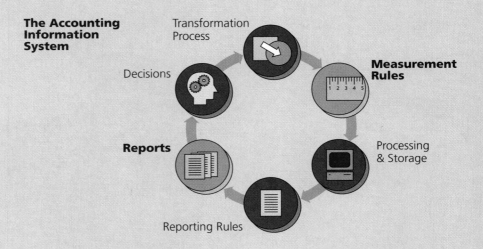

Major topics covered in this chapter include:

- Internal transaction adjustments for timing differences between accrual and cash measures.
- The effects of accrual and deferral adjustments on balance sheet and income statement accounts.
- The effects of timing differences on the reporting of cash flows.
- The importance of cash flow information for interpreting performance.

Once you have completed this chapter, you should be able to:

1. Differentiate external from internal transactions and explain the purpose of both.
2. Identify examples of internal transactions.
3. Define accrual and deferral accounts and transactions.
4. Identify accrued revenues.

5. Identify accrued expenses.
6. Identify deferred revenues.
7. Identify deferred expenses.
8. Compare the direct and indirect formats of the statement of cash flows.
9. Explain the relationship between the indirect format of the statement of cash flows and accruals and deferrals.
10. Interpret cash flow information as a basis for analyzing corporate financial performance.
11. Identify relationships between financial statements and components of the transformation process.

INTERNAL TRANSACTIONS

Objective 1
Differentiate external from internal transactions and explain the purpose of both.

In addition to **external transactions,** such as the exchange of goods for cash, organizations also account for **internal transactions.** External transactions occur when resources are exchanged between an organization and those with whom it contracts. Internal transactions identify economic consequences of these exchanges in the appropriate fiscal periods. For example, an organization pays $6,000 for an insurance policy on December 1, 1996. The policy provides insurance coverage for 1997 and 1998. An external transaction occurs when the policy is purchased in 1996. Internal transactions are recorded in 1997 and 1998 to recognize the consumption of the resource in the periods that benefit from its use. These transactions are necessary if the financial statements are to report the proper amount of assets and expenses for each of these years. **Recording internal transactions is necessary because of timing differences between (1) activities that produce and sell goods and services and (2) cash flows.** Recognition of internal transactions occurs through a process of adjusting account balances, normally at the end of a fiscal period. Adjustments result in the recognition of revenues or expenses in one fiscal period, though cash flows have occurred or will occur in a different period.

Adjustments occur when contracts extend beyond the current fiscal period. For instance, a contract may be initiated when goods are transferred from seller to buyer. The contract may be completed when cash is transferred from buyer to seller. If these events occur in the same fiscal period, accounting for the transactions is relatively simple. If these events occur in different periods, however, the accounting becomes more complex. Decisions must be made about when to recognize revenues or expenses and how much to recognize. Internal transactions are the results of these decisions.

To illustrate adjustments, consider the following example. Exhibit 6-1 provides the balance sheet for The Party Animal, Inc., a retailer of party goods, at the end of its 1997 fiscal year.

The following (12) summary transactions occurred during 1998:

1. Sold goods that cost $123,000 for $357,000. All sales were on credit.
2. Collected $370,000 in cash from customers.
3. Purchased $140,000 of merchandise on credit.

4. Paid $132,000 to suppliers for merchandise.
5. Paid $93,000 of wages to employees.
6. Paid $5,000 for utilities expenses.
7. Purchased $12,500 of supplies for cash.
8. Paid $14,000 for advertising.
9. Paid $18,000 in interest.
10. Paid $26,000 for principal on notes payable.
11. Paid $24,000 in income taxes.
12. Paid $20,000 in dividends.

Exhibit 6-1

The Party Animal, Inc.
Balance Sheet
December 31, 1997

Assets

Current assets:	
Cash	$ 20,600
Accounts receivable	50,400
Merchandise inventory	88,000
Supplies	13,500
Prepaid insurance	12,000
Total current assets	184,500
Property, plant, and equipment:	
Equipment	92,100
Buildings	180,000
	272,100
Less: accumulated depreciation	110,700
	161,400
Land	60,000
Total property, plant, and equipment	221,400
Total assets	$405,900

Liabilities

Current liabilities:	
Accounts payable	$ 46,800
Wages payable	17,900
Interest payable	18,000
Income taxes payable	5,000
Notes payable, current portion	26,000
Total current liabilities	113,700
Long-term liabilities:	
Notes payable, long-term	120,000
Total liabilities	233,700

Stockholders' Equity

Common stock, no par, 100,000 shares authorized and issued	100,000
Retained earnings	72,200
Total stockholders' equity	172,200
Total liabilities and stockholders' equity	$405,900

These are external transactions. They represent exchanges with customers, suppliers, creditors, and owners. They do not include all of the transactions that need to be reported on Party Animal's financial statements, however. For example, there is no transaction to recognize depreciation expense or insurance expense. The transactions missing from this list are internal transactions.

Once the effects of the external transactions are recorded, the balance sheet account balances would appear as follows (transaction numbers are in parentheses):

December 31,	1997	External Transaction Effects	1998
Assets			
Current assets:			
Cash		+370,000 (2)	
		−132,000 (4)	
		−93,000 (5)	
		−5,000 (6)	
		−12,500 (7)	
		−14,000 (8)	
		−18,000 (9)	
		−26,000 (10)	
		−24,000 (11)	
		−20,000 (12)	
	$ 20,600	25,500	$ 46,100
Accounts receivable		+357,000 (1)	
		−370,000 (2)	
	50,400	−13,000	37,400
Merchandise inventory		−123,000 (1)	
		+140,000 (3)	
	88,000	17,000	105,000
Supplies	13,500	+12,500 (7)	26,000
Prepaid insurance	12,000		12,000
Total current assets	**184,500**		
Property, plant, and equipment:			
Equipment	92,100		92,100
Buildings	180,000		180,000
	272,100		
Less: accumulated depreciation	110,700		110,700
	161,400		
Land	60,000		60,000
Total property, plant, and equipment	**221,400**		
Total assets	**$405,900**		

December 31,	1997	External Transaction Effects	1998
Liabilities			
Current liabilities:			
Accounts payable		+ 140,000 (3)	
		− 132,000 (4)	
	$ 46,800	8,000	$ 54,800
Wages payable	17,900	− 93,000 (5)	− 75,100
Interest payable	18,000	− 18,000 (9)	0
Income taxes payable	5,000	− 24,000 (11)	− 19,000
Notes payable, current portion	26,000	− 26,000 (10)	0
Total current liabilities	**113,700**		
Long-term liabilities:			
Notes payable, long-term	120,000		120,000
Total liabilities	**233,700**		
Stockholders' Equity			
Common stock	100,000		100,000
Retained earnings		64,190 (a)	
		20,000 (12)	
	72,200	44,190	116,390
Total stockholders' equity	**172,200**		
Total liabilities and stockholders' equity	**$405,900**		

(a)Adjustments for revenues and expenses. These accounts will be examined in detail later.

The following sections consider internal transactions.

Depreciation

Objective 2
Identify examples of internal transactions.

Assume management expected the equipment, costing $92,100, to have a useful life of 10 years when it was purchased. The equipment was purchased prior to 1998, but a portion of the cost of the equipment has been consumed during 1998, because the equipment wears out as it is used. To recognize the portion consumed, management might allocate one-tenth of the cost of the equipment to each year of its estimated useful life. Then, the company would record $9,210 ($92,100/10 years) of depreciation expense for the equipment in 1998.

Cost of Asset consumed in 1998 = $92,100/10 Years of Useful Life

Year 1	Year 2	Year 3	Years 4–9	Year 10
$9,210	$9,210	$9,210	$9,210 per year	$9,210

Assume management expected the buildings, costing $180,000, to have a useful life of 30 years when they were purchased. Management might allocate one-thirtieth of the cost of the buildings to each year. The depreciation expense for 1998 would be $6,000 ($180,000/30 years). Therefore, total depreciation for buildings and equipment would be $15,210 for the year. This internal transaction would be recorded as an increase in ACCUMULATED DEPRECIATION and as an increase in DEPRECIATION EXPENSE. Therefore, assets and income are reduced:

Assets =		Liabilities + Owners' Equity	+ (Revenues − Expenses)	
Accumulated Depreciation	− 15,210		Depreciation Expense	− 15,210

The 1998 balance for accumulated depreciation is the prior year balance plus the amount of depreciation recorded in 1998 ($125,910 = $110,700 + $15,210). Note that recognition of depreciation expense does not involve cash. The cash payment for the assets occurred when they were acquired. Also, note that no external exchanges occurred in recognizing depreciation.

Insurance

Assume prepaid insurance was purchased in 1997 and provides coverage for a three-year period, beginning in 1998. Since one-third of the cost of the insurance was consumed during 1998, the company should record INSURANCE EXPENSE of $4,000 ($12,000/3 years) for 1998:

Cost of Insurance consumed in 1998 = $12,000/3 Years

Year 1	Year 2	Year 3
$4,000	$4,000	$4,000

This internal transaction would be recorded as a decrease in PREPAID INSURANCE and as an increase in INSURANCE EXPENSE. Therefore, assets and income are reduced:

Assets =		Liabilities + Owners' Equity	+ (Revenues − Expenses)	
Prepaid Insurance	− 4,000		Insurance Expense	− 4,000

As in the depreciation example, recognition of insurance expense does not involve cash. Cash was paid when the asset was purchased in 1997. No external exchanges occurred for insurance during 1998.

Supplies

Another asset that has been consumed without any explicit recognition is supplies. Office and maintenance supplies are consumed throughout the year as part
of the company's operations. To determine how much of the asset has been consumed, the company must count or estimate the amount of asset left at the end
of the fiscal period. For example, if $16,000 of supplies remain at the end of
1998, management can assume the company has consumed $10,000 of supplies:

Supplies available at beginning of year	$13,500
Supplies purchased during 1998	12,500
Total supplies available during year	26,000
Less: supplies remaining at end of year	16,000
Supplies consumed in 1998	$10,000

This internal transaction would be recorded as a decrease in SUPPLIES and
as an increase in SUPPLIES EXPENSE. Therefore, assets and net income are
reduced:

Assets =	Liabilities + Owners' Equity	+ (Revenues − Expenses)
Supplies − 10,000		Supplies Expense − 10,000

As in the prior examples, recognition of supplies expense does not involve
cash. Cash was paid when the supplies were purchased.

Interest

An additional adjustment is needed for interest expense incurred during the year
on the debt owed to the bank. Interest accumulates on debt throughout a fiscal
period. Management recognizes these expenses during the period in which they
occur, rather than waiting until cash is paid.

Assume Party Animal pays interest and principal to the bank at the beginning of each fiscal year. The $18,000 of interest paid in transaction 9 was paid at
the beginning of 1998 for interest incurred during 1997. Assume the company
incurred 10% interest on notes payable during 1998. The balance of notes
payable is $120,000 after the payment of $26,000 at the beginning of 1998.
Thus, the company incurred $12,000 ($120,000 × .10) of interest expense for
1998. The company will pay this interest to the bank when it is due in January
1999.

Interest expense recognized in 1998 would be recorded as an increase in IN-
TEREST PAYABLE and as an increase in INTEREST EXPENSE. Therefore,
liabilities are increased and income is reduced:

Assets =	Liabilities + Owners' Equity	+ (Revenues − Expenses)
0	Interest Payable 12,000	Interest Expense − 12,000

*Remember that the equation Assets = Liabilities + Owners' Equity + (Revenues − Expenses)
must balance. Therefore, when no asset account is affected by a transaction, a zero is shown to
complete the equation.*

As in the prior examples, recognition of interest expense does not involve cash. Cash is paid when interest becomes due to creditors. For example, assume Party Animal pays the amount owed for interest incurred in 1998 at the beginning of 1999. The transaction would be recorded in 1999 by decreasing CASH and decreasing INTEREST PAYABLE:

Assets =	Liabilities + Owners' Equity	+ (Revenues − Expenses)
Cash − 12,000	Interest Payable − 12,000	

Note the cash payment for interest occurs in 1999. The expense associated with interest was recognized in 1998 when it was incurred.

Wages

A company incurs wages expense when employees earn the wages by providing services. Employees may not be paid at the time wages are earned. Therefore, the amount of wages expense may not equal the amount paid to employees during a fiscal period. Party Animal had $17,900 of wages payable at the end of 1997. This amount would have been paid to employees early in 1998 for services they provided in 1997. Assume employees earned $85,000 of wages during 1998. The company paid $93,000 in wages during the year (transaction 5). Therefore, the company owes $9,900 of wages at the end of 1998:

Wages payable at beginning of 1998	$ 17,900
Wages expense for 1998	85,000
Total wages to be paid	102,900
Less: wages paid during 1998	93,000
Wages payable at end of 1998	$ 9,900

This liability would be recognized as an increase in WAGES PAYABLE and an increase in WAGES EXPENSE for wages incurred during 1998:

Assets =	Liabilities + Owners' Equity	+ (Revenues − Expenses)
0	Wages Payable 9,900	Wages Expense − 9,900

The liability would be reduced during 1999 when the wages owed are paid to employees.

Income Taxes

Corporations pay taxes on income earned during a fiscal year. A portion of taxes incurred in one period may be paid in another period. Therefore, like wages, the amount of income tax expense and the amount paid for income taxes often differ for a fiscal period. (The use of different rules for computing taxable and fi-

nancial income also complicates the recognition of income taxes. We will consider these differences in a later chapter.) Assume Party Animal incurred $22,000
of income tax expense on income earned during 1998. It would recognize the
tax by increasing INCOME TAXES PAYABLE and increasing INCOME TAX
EXPENSE, which reduces net income:

Assets =	Liabilities + Owners' Equity		+ (Revenues − Expenses)
0	Income Taxes Payable	22,000	Income Tax Expense − 22,000

Notes Payable

A final internal transaction occurs when Party Animal recognizes the amount of
notes payable that will become due in 1998. This amount is transferred from
NOTES PAYABLE, LONG-TERM to NOTES PAYABLE, CURRENT
PORTION. The amount of the transfer depends on the repayment schedule
that is part of the loan agreement with the bank. Assume Party Animal is obligated to pay $20,000 of the note principal during 1999. The transaction reduces
the long-term liability and increases the current liability at the end of 1998:

Assets =	Liabilities + Owners' Equity		+ (Revenues − Expenses)
0	Notes Payable, Current Portion	20,000	
	Notes Payable, Long-Term	− 20,000	

Summary of Adjustments

Once the effects of the adjustments for internal transactions are added to the external transaction effects, Party Animal can prepare its income statement and balance sheet for 1998 as shown in Exhibits 6-2 and 6-3.

Recording and reporting adjustments for internal transactions are essential
parts of the accounting process. Most of these adjustments result from timing differences between the recognition of revenues and expenses and the payment or
receipt of cash. External transactions also may be associated with timing differences. The next section classifies by category internal and external transactions
associated with timing differences.

SELF-STUDY PROBLEM 6-1

Consider each of the following independent transactions.

Required

Identify the effect of each transaction by writing the account titles and amounts
in the table provided on page 251.

Exhibit 6-2

The Party Animal, Inc.
Income Statement
For the Year Ended December 31, 1998

Sales revenue		$357,000
Cost of goods sold		123,000
Gross profit		234,000
Operating expenses:		
Wages expense	$85,000	
Utilities expense	5,000	
Depreciation expense	15,210	
Insurance expense	4,000	
Supplies expense	10,000	
Advertising expense	14,000	
Total operating expenses		133,210
Income from operations		100,790
Other revenues and expenses:		
Interest expense		12,000
Pretax income		88,790
Income tax expense		22,000
Net income		$ 66,790
Earnings per share of common stock (100,000 shares outstanding)		$ 0.67

Exhibit 6-3

The Party Animal, Inc.
Balance Sheet

December 31,	1997	All Transaction Effects	1998
Assets			
Current assets:			
Cash		+370,000 (2)	
		−132,000 (4)	
		−93,000 (5)	
		−5,000 (6)	
		−12,500 (7)	
		−14,000 (8)	
		−18,000 (9)	
		−26,000 (10)	
		−24,000 (11)	
		−20,000 (12)	
	$ 20,600	25,500	$ 46,100
Accounts receivable		+357,000 (1)	
		−370,000 (2)	
	50,400	−13,000	37,400
Merchandise inventory		−123,000 (1)	
		+140,000 (3)	
	88,000	17,000	105,000

December 31,	1997	All Transaction Effects		1998
Supplies		+ 12,500	(7)	
		− 10,000	(i)	
	$ 13,500	2,500		$ 16,000
Prepaid insurance	12,000	− 4,000	(i)	8,000
Total current assets	**184,500**			**212,500**
Property, plant, and equipment:				
Equipment	92,100			92,100
Buildings	180,000			180,000
	272,100			272,100
Less: accumulated depreciation	110,700	+ 15,210	(i)	125,910
	161,400			146,190
Land	60,000			60,000
Total property, plant, and equipment	**221,400**			**206,190**
Total assets	**$405,900**			**$418,690**
Liabilities				
Current liabilities:				
Accounts payable		+ 140,000	(3)	
		− 132,000	(4)	
	$ 46,800	8,000		$ 54,800
Wages payable		− 93,000	(5)	
		85,000	(i)	
	17,900	− 8,000		9,900
Interest payable		− 18,000	(9)	
		+ 12,000	(i)	
	18,000	− 6,000		12,000
Income taxes payable		− 24,000	(11)	
		+ 22,000	(i)	
	5,000	− 2,000		3,000
Notes payable, current portion		− 26,000	(10)	
		+ 20,000	(i)	
	26,000	− 6,000		20,000
Total current liabilities	**113,700**			**99,700**
Long-term liabilities:				
Notes payable, long-term	120,000	− 20,000	(i)	100,000
Total liabilities	**233,700**			**199,700**
Stockholders' Equity				
Common stock	100,000			100,000
Retained earnings		+ 66,790	(a)	
		− 20,000	(12)	
	72,200	46,790		118,990
Total stockholders' equity	**172,200**			**218,990**
Total liabilities and stockholders' equity	**$405,900**			**$418,690**

(a) Adjustments for revenues and expenses. (i) Internal transactions.

a. A company recognizes $2,000 of unpaid wages earned by employees.
b. A company identifies $1,200 of supplies remaining at the end of the month. It had $1,800 of supplies on hand at the beginning of the month and purchased $5,000 of supplies during the month.
c. A company recognizes $2,400 of interest on notes payable incurred during the month. The interest will be paid next month.
d. A company recognizes $3,700 of income taxes owed on current period income. The taxes will be paid during the coming fiscal period.
e. A company recognizes $8,000 of depreciation for the current fiscal period.
f. A company transfers $10,000 of notes payable, long term, to notes payable, current portion.
g. A company recognizes the consumption of one-third of a prepaid insurance policy for which it paid $6,000 last period.

Assets =		Liabilities + Owners' Equity		+ (Revenues − Expenses)	
Account	Amount	Account	Amount	Account	Amount
a.					
b.					
c.					
d.					
e.					
f.					
g.					

The solution to Self-Study Problem 6-1 appears at the end of the chapter.

ACCRUALS AND DEFERRALS

Objective 3
Define accrual and deferral accounts and transactions.

Differences in timing between when (1) goods or services are produced or sold and (2) cash is received or paid often result in transactions in which revenues or expenses are recognized in one period and cash flows are recognized in another. This section classifies these types of transactions, which are common for most companies. The adjustments considered earlier in the chapter are examples of accruals and deferrals.

Accrued revenues **and** *accrued expenses* **occur when revenues and expenses are recognized before cash is received or paid.**

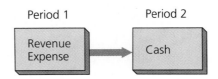

Period 1   Period 2

Revenue
Expense   →   Cash

Deferred revenues **and** *deferred expenses* **occur when revenues and expenses are recognized after cash is received or paid.**

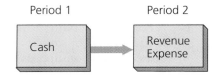

Internal transactions are examples of accruals and deferrals, but accruals and deferrals also may result from external transactions.

Accrued Revenues

Objective 4
Identify accrued revenues.

Assume that, beginning March 1, a company agrees to sell $1,200 of merchandise on the first of each month for three months to a customer. The customer agrees to pay $3,600 for the merchandise at the end of the three-month period.

The company has provided goods to the customer on March 1, April 1, and May 1, but cash is not received until May 31. Visualize the relationship between the revenues and cash flows as:

	March	**April**	**May**
Revenue	1,200	1,200	1,200
Cash Inflow	0	0	3,600

The company should recognize revenue of $1,200 on March 1, April 1, and May 1 when goods are provided to the customer. On each of these dates, it recognizes accounts receivable of $1,200 as well:

Assets =		**Liabilities + Owners' Equity**	**+ (Revenues – Expenses)**	
Accounts	March 1,200		Sales	March 1,200
Receivable	April 1,200		Revenues	April 1,200
	May 1,200			May 1,200

The asset, ACCOUNTS RECEIVABLE, represents the cash that will be received in the future. Once the cash is received in May, the balance of ACCOUNTS RECEIVABLE decreases and the balance of CASH increases:

Assets =		**Liabilities + Owners' Equity**	**+ (Revenues – Expenses)**
Cash	3,600		
Accounts			
Receivable	– 3,600		0

ACCOUNTS RECEIVABLE provides a record of the expected future cash flow until it is received. This account adjusts for the difference between the time revenue is recognized and cash is received. It is important to recognize the relationship among SALES REVENUE, ACCOUNTS RECEIVABLE, and CASH. As the following table shows, revenue is recognized at a different, earlier time than when cash is received.

Event	Revenue Recognition		Timing Adjustment		Cash Flow
1	Sales Revenue	3,600	Accounts Receivable	3,600	
2			Accounts Receivable	−3,600	Cash 3,600

The first transaction records revenue earned and a receivable for cash expected from the sale. The second transaction eliminates the receivable and records cash received. The net effect of these transactions is to increase cash and sales revenue by $3,600. Accounts receivable provides a means of adjusting for timing differences.

Accrued Expenses

Objective 5
Identify accrued expenses.

Timing differences can occur between expenses and cash flows. For example, assume a company borrows $10,000 from a bank on July 1 and pays $300 in interest each quarter. If the first interest payment is due September 30, the company would recognize $100 of interest expense at the end of July, August, and September, but it would not record a cash outflow until September 30. Visualize the relationship between the expense and the cash flow as:

	July	August	September
Expense	−100	−100	−100
Cash Outflow	0	0	−300

Just as ACCOUNTS RECEIVABLE represents an expected future cash inflow (until it is received) in the previous example, INTEREST PAYABLE represents an expected future cash outflow (until it is paid):

Assets =	Liabilities + Owners' Equity			+ (Revenues − Expenses)		
	Interest	July	100	Interest	July	−100
	Payable	August	100	Expense	August	−100
0		Sept.	100		Sept.	−100

The amount to be paid to the bank accumulates as INTEREST PAYABLE until it is paid. Once the cash is paid, the balance of INTEREST PAYABLE is reduced:

Assets =	Liabilities + Owners' Equity	+ (Revenues – Expenses)
Cash – 300	Interest Payable – 300	

The net effect of these transactions is to decrease net income by $300 and to decrease cash by $300:

Event	Revenue Recognition	Timing Adjustment	Cash Flow
1	Interest Expense – 300	Interest Payable 300	
2		Interest Payable – 300	Cash – 300

A similar relationship exists for other expenses, payables, and cash outflows. For some transactions, other assets also may be involved. For example, assume a company purchases $800 of inventory during February. The purchase is made on credit. $800 is paid to the supplier for the merchandise in March. $300 of the merchandise is sold in February and the remaining $500 is sold during March. The company should recognize the purchase as an asset when the purchase occurs in February. Cash is paid in March:

	February	March
Asset	800	0
Cash Outflow	0	– 800

A portion of the asset is consumed in February and the remainder in March. Therefore an expense is recognized in both months:

	February	March
Expense	– 300	– 500

When the inventory is purchased, INVENTORY increases along with ACCOUNTS PAYABLE:

Assets =	Liabilities + Owners' Equity	+ (Revenues – Expenses)
Inventory 800	Accounts Payable 800	

As the asset is consumed, an expense, COST OF GOODS SOLD, is recognized:

Assets =	Liabilities + Owners' Equity	+ (Revenues – Expenses)
Inventory Feb. – 300 March – 500		Cost of Feb. – 300 Goods Sold Mar. – 500

Finally, when the supplier is paid, CASH and ACCOUNTS PAYABLE are reduced:

Assets =	Liabilities + Owners' Equity	+ (Revenues − Expenses)
Cash − 800	Accounts Payable − 800	

Note the net effect of these transactions: The company has paid $800 in cash and has incurred a decrease in net income of $800 during the two months of February and March. The following table shows the recognition of expense at a different, earlier time than when cash is paid.

Event	Asset	Expense Recognition	Timing Adjustment	Cash Flow
1	Inventory 800		Accounts Payable 800	
2	Inventory − 800	Cost of Sales − 800		
3			Accounts Payable − 800	Cash − 800

The accounting process is complicated by the need to identify economic events with the fiscal periods that benefited from the events. The same adjustment process would be necessary if these transactions occurred in different fiscal years instead of different months. The timing of the expense and of the cash flow are different. Therefore, the accounting system provides a means for identifying the periods in which transactions should be recognized. Payables provide an accounting record for adjusting between the time when expenses (and sometimes assets) are recognized and when cash is paid.

Deferred Revenues

Objective 6
Identify deferred revenues.

Deferred revenue occurs when cash is received before revenue is earned. Assume that on October 1, a company rents equipment to a customer for three months for $250 per month. The customer pays the $750 rental fee in advance on October 1. While the company receives the cash on that day, the rent will not be earned until a portion of the rental period has passed. The customer receives services in October, November, and December. The cash flow occurs in October. As a result, the company defers the revenue on October 1 until it is earned in October, November, and December. Visualize the relationship between the revenue and the cash flow as:

	October	November	December
Revenue	250	250	250
Cash Inflow	750	0	0

When cash is received before revenue is earned, it is recorded in a liability account such as UNEARNED RENT. **Deferred revenues are liabilities.** They represent an obligation to provide goods and services to customers in the future. The obligation arises because customers have paid for goods and services they have not received yet:

Assets =	Liabilities + Owners' Equity	+ (Revenues − Expenses)
Cash 750	Unearned Rent 750	

As the rent is earned during the three months, revenue is recognized and the liability is reduced:

Assets =	Liabilities + Owners' Equity		+ (Revenues − Expenses)	
0	Unearned Rent	Oct. − 250 Nov. − 250 Dec. − 250	Rent Revenue	Oct. 250 Nov. 250 Dec. 250

Thus, unearned revenue accounts, such as UNEARNED RENT, provide a means of adjusting for the earlier time when cash is received and the later time when revenue is earned:

Event	Cash Flow	Timing Adjustment	Revenue Recognition
1	Cash 750	Unearned Rent 750	
2		Unearned Rent − 750	Rent Revenue 750

The net effect of the transactions is to increase cash and rent revenue by $750.

Deferred Expenses

Objective 7
Identify deferred expenses.

A deferred expense results when cash is paid out before an expense has been incurred. For example, assume a company purchases a three-month property insurance policy for $2,400 on January 1 and pays cash at that time. While the cash outflow occurs on January 1, the benefits associated with the policy are consumed over the months of January, February, and March. The company should recognize an expense for the insurance each month as the policy is consumed. Visualize the relationship between the expense and the cash flow as:

	January	February	March
Expense	− 800	− 800	− 800
Cash Outflow	− 2,400	0	0

An asset account, such as PREPAID INSURANCE, represents the amount of a short-term resource available until it is consumed. **A deferred or prepaid expense account is an asset,** a resource expected to be consumed in the future for which cash has been paid:

Assets =		Liabilities + Owners' Equity	+ (Revenues − Expenses)
Cash	− 2,400		
Prepaid Insurance	2,400	0	0

As the asset is consumed, PREPAID INSURANCE is reduced and IN-SURANCE EXPENSE is recognized:

Assets =			Liabilities + Owners' Equity	+ (Revenues − Expenses)		
Prepaid	Jan.	− 800		Insurance	Jan.	− 800
Insurance	Feb.	− 800		Expense	Feb.	− 800
	Mar.	− 800			Mar.	− 800

The net effect of these transactions is to reduce cash and income by $2,400. The cash outflow occurs at a different, earlier time than when the expense is recognized.

Event	Cash Flow	Timing Adjustment	Expense Recognition
1	Cash − 2,400	Prepaid Insurance 2,400	
2		Prepaid Insurance − 2,400	Insurance Expense − 2,400

Summary of Accruals and Deferrals

Many of the transactions organizations record in their accounting systems result from timing differences. Asset and liability accounts, such as ACCOUNTS RE-CEIVABLE, INTEREST PAYABLE, UNEARNED RENT, and PREPAID INSURANCE, result from accrual and deferral transactions. Note that **accruals and deferrals result in transactions that must be recorded on more than one date.** At least one entry is required to record revenues or expenses, and at least one additional entry is required to record cash received or paid.

A close relationship exists between (1) current asset and liability accounts and (2) revenue and expense accounts. Current asset and liability accounts provide a link between the time revenues and expenses are recognized and the time cash is received or paid:

Accrued Revenue or Expense:

Revenue or Expense Recognition	Timing Adjustments	Cash Flow
Revenue or Expense	Current Asset or Liability	
	Current Asset or Liability	Cash Received or Paid

Deferred Revenue or Expense:

Cash Flow	Timing Adjustments	Revenue or Expense Recognition
Cash Received or Paid	Current Asset or Liability	
	Current Asset or Liability	Revenue or Expense

SELF-STUDY PROBLEM 6-2

For each of the following independent situations, identify the effect on the balance sheet account. Use + and − to indicate an increase or decrease in the account. Complete each set of transactions using the format provided. The first one is done for you.

a. **Transaction**	**Effect on Accounts Receivable**
Sold $12,000 of goods on credit	+$12,000
Collected $10,000 from customers	−10,000
Net change	+2,000
b.	**Effect on Inventory**
Sold goods costing $8,000	
Purchased $9,500 of inventory on credit	
Net change	
c.	**Effect on Accounts Payable**
Purchased $9,500 of inventory on credit	
Paid $11,500 in cash to suppliers	
Net change	
d.	**Effect on Wages Payable**
Accrued $7,000 of unpaid wages	
Paid $6,300 in wages to employees	
Net change	
e.	**Effect on Prepaid Insurance**
Consumed 1 month of a 6-month insurance policy costing $6,000	
Paid $6,000 for a 6-month insurance policy	
Net change	
f.	**Effect on Unearned Rent**
Earned 1 month's rent from a 1-year lease of property for $12,000 per year	
Received $12,000 in cash advance for a 1-year lease	
Net change	
g.	**Effect on Plant Assets**
Recognized $4,000 of depreciation expense	
Net change	

The solution to Self-Study Problem 6-2 appears at the end of the chapter.

RECONCILIATION OF NET INCOME AND CASH FLOWS

The statement of cash flows reports the cash flow effects of transactions during a fiscal period. For example, the cash flow statement for The Party Animal, Inc. for 1998 would appear as in Exhibit 6-4. This statement is prepared using the direct format described in Chapter 5.

Exhibit 6-4

The Party Animal, Inc.
Statement of Cash Flows
For the Year Ended December 31, 1998
(Direct Format)

Cash flow from operating activities:

Receipts:		
Collections from customers		$370,000
Payments:		
To suppliers of inventory	$(132,000)	
To employees	(93,000)	
For utilities	(5,000)	
For supplies	(12,500)	
For advertising	(14,000)	
For interest	(18,000)	
For income taxes	(24,000)	
Total cash payments		298,500
Net cash flow from operating activities		71,500
Cash flow from financing activities:		
Payment of notes payable	(26,000)	
Payment of dividends	(20,000)	
Net cash flow from financing activities		(46,000)
Net increase in cash		25,500
Cash balance, December 31, 1997		20,600
Cash balance, December 31, 1998		$ 46,100

This statement provides a description of the events that resulted in the receipt or payment of cash during the fiscal year. Exhibit 6-3 showed these events as transactions affecting the cash balance during 1998. External decision makers do not have access to information about individual transactions. Therefore, the financial statements provide information summarizing the effects of the transactions.

The direct format does not explain the relationship between cash flows for the year and the results of operations reported on the income statement. Net income for Party Animal was $64,190, while net cash inflow from operating activities was $71,500. An explanation of this difference is provided by a separate schedule accompanying the statement of cash flows. This schedule is similar to information presented on the statement of cash flows when it is prepared following the indirect format. This section describes the reconciliation by examining the indirect format, which is used by most corporations.

Objective 8
Compare the direct and indirect formats of the statement of cash flows.

The indirect format of the statement of cash flows does not report cash flow effects of operating activities directly. Instead, this method converts net income on an accrual basis to cash flow from operating activities on a cash basis. Therefore, **the indirect format adjusts accrual basis information to a cash basis rather than reporting cash flow information directly.** Both the direct and indirect methods report the same amount of cash flow from operating activities. Exhibit 6-5 presents the indirect format of the statement for The Party Animal, Inc., which is explained in the following paragraphs.

Percentage of Major Corporations Reporting Cash Flows Using the Direct and Indirect Formats

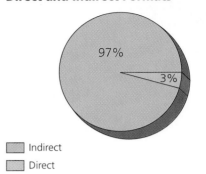

(Data source: Accounting Trends and Techniques, 1994)

Exhibit 6-5 does not present the sources and uses of cash associated with operating activities directly. Instead, it presents them as the indirect result of changes in working capital accounts and other adjustments. This presentation is more complex than the direct method. Nevertheless, it is commonly used in practice. **The cash flow from the operating activities section in the indirect format is designed to reconcile accrual and cash basis performance measures.**

The cash flow from investing and financing sections are identical between the direct and indirect formats. Therefore, the following discussion will focus only on the operating section.

Objective 9
Explain the relationship between the indirect format of the statement of cash flows and accruals and deferrals.

To understand the indirect format, you must understand accruals and deferrals. The difference between net income and cash flow from operating activities results from accruals and deferrals for a fiscal period. Recall that accruals and deferrals occur because of timing differences between cash flows and revenues or expenses. These timing differences affect the balances of current asset and current liability accounts:

Accrued Revenue or Expense:

Revenue or Expense Recognition	Timing Adjustment	Cash Flow
Revenue or Expense	Current Asset or Liability	
	Current Asset or Liability	Cash Received or Paid

Deferred Revenue or Expense:

Cash Flow	Timing Adjustment	Revenue or Expense Recognition
Cash Received or Paid	Current Liability or Asset	
	Current Liability or Asset	Revenue or Expense

The difference between cash and accrual measures is equal to the change in the relevant current asset or liability account. Consider the prepaid insurance example we examined earlier. A company purchases a three-month property insur-

Exhibit 6-5

The Party Animal, Inc.
Statement of Cash Flows
For the Year Ended December 31, 1998
(Indirect Format)

Cash flow from operating activities:

Net income		$66,790
Noncash adjustments to income:		
Depreciation expense	$15,210	
Decrease in accounts receivable	13,000	
Increase in inventory	(17,000)	
Increase in supplies	(2,500)	
Decrease in prepaid insurance	4,000	
Increase in accounts payable	8,000	
Decrease in wages payable	(8,000)	
Decrease in interest payable	(6,000)	
Decrease in income tax payable	(2,000)	
Net adjustments to income		4,710
Net cash flow from operating activities		71,500
Cash flow from financing activities:		
Payment of notes payable	(26,000)	
Payment of dividends	(20,000)	
Net cash flow from financing activities		(46,000)
Net increase in cash		25,500
Cash balance, December 31, 1997		20,600
Cash balance, December 31, 1998		$46,100

ance policy for $2,400 on January 1 and pays cash at that time. While the cash outflow occurs on January 1, the value associated with the policy is consumed over the months of January, February, and March. The company recognizes an expense for the insurance each month as the policy is consumed:

	January	February	March
Expense	-800	-800	-800
Cash Outflow	-2,400	0	0

The amount of expense recognized in January is $800. The amount of cash paid is $2,400. The link between insurance expense and cash paid for insurance is prepaid insurance.

Cash	-2,400	Prepaid Insurance	2,400	
		Prepaid Insurance	-800	Insurance Expense -800
		Change	1,600	

The effect of the expense is to reduce net income in January by $800. The transactions reduced cash in January by $2,400. The difference is the increase in prepaid insurance in January of $1,600:

Effect on net income	$ (800)
Less increase in prepaid insurance	(1,600)
Effect on cash flow from operating activities	$(2,400)

Therefore, under the indirect method, $1,600 would be subtracted from income as a noncash adjustment on the statement of cash flows.

The adjustments to net income on the statement of cash flows result from accruals and deferrals. The amount of the accruals and deferrals can be determined, in most cases, by the change in the appropriate current asset or current liability account. The following sections examine these changes.

Accounts Receivable

Consider the relationships among sales revenue, accounts receivable, and cash flow. Sales revenue results in an increase in net income, but it results in an increase in cash only when cash has been collected. Exhibit 6-3 (on page 249) indicates that Party Animal experienced a decrease in accounts receivable of $13,000 during 1998:

	1997	Transactions	1998
Sales on credit		+357,000(1)	
Cash collected from customers		−370,000(2)	
Accounts receivable	50,400	−13,000	37,400

Accounts receivable decreases when cash collected during a period ($370,000) is greater than sales made on credit ($357,000). The difference between the amount reported as an increase in income for the year ($357,000) was $13,000 less than the amount of cash flow from customers for 1998 ($370,000). Therefore, to determine the amount of cash flow from operating activities for the year, the $13,000 decrease in accounts receivable should be added to net income.

Net Income	Adjusted for Timing Differences	= Cash Flow from Operating Activities
Sales Revenue	+ Decrease in Accounts Receivable	= Cash Collected from Customers
$357,000	+ $13,000	= $370,000

Thus, the direct format (Exhibit 6-4) reports cash flow from sales directly by reporting cash collected from customers. The indirect format reports the same result but does so indirectly by adding the decrease in accounts receivable to net income (Exhibit 6-5). An increase in accounts receivable for a period would be subtracted from net income in calculating cash flow.

Inventory

The change in inventory during a period results from inventory sales and purchases. In Exhibit 6-3, Party Animal's inventory balance increased $17,000 in 1998:

	1997	Transactions	1998
Purchase of inventory		+140,000(3)	
Cost of goods sold		−123,000(1)	
Merchandise inventory	88,000	17,000	105,000

Therefore, $17,000 more of inventory was purchased during 1998 than was sold. The inventory sold was part of cost of goods sold for 1998 and reduced net income. But, inventory purchased was $17,000 more than the amount of expense recorded:

Net Income	Adjusted for Timing Differences	= Amount Purchased
Cost of Goods Sold	− Increase in Merchandise Inventory	= Purchase of Inventory
− $123,000	− $17,000	= − $140,000

Because expense was less than the purchase by $17,000, this amount is subtracted from net income in calculating cash flow from operating activities. If merchandise inventory had decreased during the period, the company would add the decrease to net income in computing cash flow from operating activities.

Cash flow associated with inventory also involves accounts payable. Remember that payment for inventory is a two-step process. Party Animal acquired inventory on credit in step 1. Then, it paid cash to the creditors in step 2. Step 2 involves an adjustment to the balance of accounts payable, considered next.

Accounts Payable

Exhibit 6-3 reveals accounts payable increased during 1998:

	1997	Transactions	1998
Purchase of inventory		+140,000(3)	
Payment to suppliers		−132,000(4)	
Accounts payable	$46,800	8,000	54,800

The increase in accounts payable indicates Party Animal purchased more inventory during 1998 than it paid for during the year. That is, the amount of inventory acquired was $8,000 more than the amount of cash paid for inventory:

Amount Purchased	Adjusted for Timing Differences	= Cash Flow from Operating Activities
Purchase of Inventory	+ Increase in Accounts Payable	= Cash Paid to Suppliers
− $140,000	+ $8,000	= − $132,000

Because the cash outflow was less than the amount purchased, the increase in accounts payable should be added back to net income in computing cash flow from operating activities (Exhibit 6-5). If accounts payable had decreased during the period, the company would subtract the decrease from net income.

The amount of cash paid to suppliers during 1998 can be determined by looking at the change in MERCHANDISE INVENTORY (step 1) and the change in ACCOUNTS PAYABLE (step 2) together. Changes in both of these accounts explain the difference between the cost of goods sold (inventory consumed during the period) and the cash paid to suppliers during 1998.

Net Income	Adjusted for Timing Differences	= Cash Flow from Operating Activities
Cost of Goods Sold	− Increase in Merchandise Inventory + Increase in Accounts Payable	= Cash Paid to Suppliers
− $123,000	− $17,000 + $8,000	= − $132,000

This amount agrees with the amount of cash paid to suppliers for inventory reported on the direct format of the statement of cash flows (Exhibit 6-4).

The statement of cash flows reports the two-step adjustment in two parts, the change in inventory and the change in accounts payable. Understanding the relationship between these accounts is important for interpreting the statement.

Interest Payable

Exhibit 6-3 indicates interest payable decreased $6,000 during 1998:

	1997	Transactions	1998
Payment of interest		− 18,000 (9)	
Interest expense		+ 12,000	
Interest payable	18,000	− 6,000	12,000

The decrease resulted from a payment of $18,000 for interest and recognition of interest expense of $12,600. Therefore, the effect on net income was $6,000 less than the cash outflow:

Net Income	Adjusted for Timing Differences	= Cash Flow from Operating Activities
Interest Expense	− Decrease in Interest Payable	= Cash Paid for Interest
− $12,000	− $6,000	= − $18,000

More cash was paid out than was recognized as expense in computing net income. Therefore, the decrease in interest payable is subtracted from net income in computing cash flow from operating activities (Exhibit 6-5).

Depreciation

Party Animal recognized $15,210 of depreciation expense in computing current period income (Exhibit 6-2). This expense also is represented on the balance sheet by the increase in accumulated depreciation. No cash flow was associated with the expense during the current period. The cash outflow occurred previously when fixed assets were purchased, not during the current period when they were used. The cash outflow appeared on the statement of cash flows as an investing activity in the period in which the assets were purchased. Therefore, no additional cash outflow is associated with depreciation expense during the current fiscal period. Because depreciation expense was subtracted from revenues on the income statement in calculating net income, it must be added back to net income in computing cash flow from operating activities:

Net Income	Adjusted for Timing Differences	= Cash Flow from Operating Activities
Depreciation Expense	+ Increase in Depreciation	= Cash Paid for Depreciation
− $15,210	+ $15,210	= $0

Depreciation does not affect current assets or liabilities. Accumulated depreciation plays much the same kind of role. The change in accumulated depreciation results from a timing difference between when depreciation expense is recognized and when cash is paid. Perhaps it is simpler to remember, however, that noncash expenses, like depreciation, are added to net income in computing cash flow from operating activities.

Other noncash expenses include amortization expense for patents and other intangible assets. These expenses also should be added back to net income in computing cash flow from operating activities. Cash outflow occurs when intangible assets are purchased or when costs are incurred in creating them, not when they are amortized. Like depreciation, amortization is an expense that reduces net income. But, it does not reduce cash. Therefore, expenses that do not affect cash, such as depreciation and amortization, must be added back to net income in computing cash flow from operating activities.

Summary of Adjustments for the Indirect Method

The reasoning behind other adjustments to net income using the indirect format is the same as that for accounts receivable, merchandise inventory, accounts payable, and interest payable. This reasoning leads to the observations that:

1. Increases in current asset balances are subtracted from net income in computing cash flow from operating activities. Decreases in current asset balances are added to net income.
2. Increases in current liability balances are added to net income in computing cash flow from operating activities. Decreases in current liability balances are subtracted from net income. (Note that this is the opposite of the current asset treatment.)
3. Noncash expenses, such as depreciation and amortization, are added to net income in computing cash flow from operating activities. Occasionally, a company will report a noncash revenue that is subtracted from net income. Gains and losses from sales of long-term assets (plant assets or investments) are subtracted (for gains) or added (for losses) because these gains and losses do not provide or use cash beyond the amount reported as cash from or for investing activities.

> Net Income
> \+ Depreciation and Amortization Expense
> − Increases in Current Asset Accounts
> \+ Decreases in Current Asset Accounts
> \+ Increases in Current Liability Accounts
> − Decreases in Current Liability Accounts
> = Cash Flow from Operating Activities

You should verify from Exhibit 6-5 that these relationships are followed consistently on the statement of cash flows using the indirect format.

Note that net income is not adjusted for the change in notes payable, current portion, though it is a current liability. This change is associated with the payment of long-term debt and is reported as a financing activity. Notes payable are not part of the operating activities of the company because they have no effect on net income or cash flow from operating activities. Interest associated with the notes does affect net income and cash flow, however, and is included as part of the adjustments.

The indirect format reconciles net income and cash flow. The reconciliation is made by examining changes in accounts that adjust for differences in timing between (1) revenues and expenses and (2) cash flows. Most of these timing differences are captured in working capital accounts. These accounts identify accruals and deferrals necessary to adjust for timing differences between the accrual basis and the cash basis. **You will find it difficult to understand accounting information without understanding these relationships.** They are central to accounting measurement and to reporting the transformation process.

INTERPRETATION OF CASH FLOWS

Objective 10
Interpret cash flow information as a basis for analyzing corporate financial performance.

Changes in current asset and current liability accounts can reveal strengths and weaknesses in a company's operating activities. For example, a significant increase in accounts receivable during a period may indicate a company is having difficulty collecting on its sales. Thus, while net income may appear favorable, cash flows may be unfavorable. Similarly, a significant increase in accounts payable may indicate a company is having difficulty meeting its current obligations. Profitability is not sufficient to ensure success in a business organization. Profits must be accompanied by favorable cash flows that signal the ability of a company to convert its revenues into cash on a timely basis.

For example, Exhibit 6-6 illustrates a major increase in cash flow for McDonald's in 1993, compared with 1992. The increase in cash flow was accompanied by an increase in net income. The difference between cash flow and net income can be explained by increases in accounts receivable, accounts payable, income taxes, and depreciation. McDonald's net income is associated with a strong cash flow from operating activities.

Exhibit 6-6   A Comparison of Net Cash Flow from Operating Activities and Net Income for McDonald's

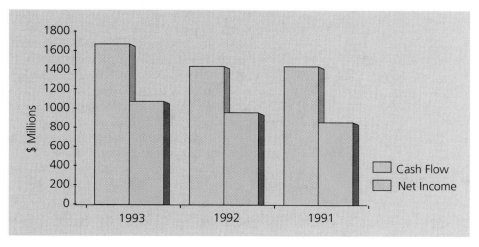

Data source: 1993 annual reports

Exhibit 6-7 compares cash flows and net income for McDonald's with Delta Airlines for 1993. The exhibit illustrates important differences in the financial activities of the two firms. McDonald's reported net income and operating cash flows that were positive. The company also reported major cash outflows for investing and financing activities that are consistent with a healthy financial condition. The statement of cash flows reveals that McDonald's investment in new plant assets was approximately twice the amount of depreciation recorded for the period. Plant expansion indicates growth and expected future profitability. The company also paid dividends to stockholders at amounts above prior years. It retired debt and repurchased common stock. These activities indicate the company was using its cash to strengthen its financial position.

Exhibit 6-7   A Comparison of Net Income and Cash Flows for McDonald's and Delta Airlines

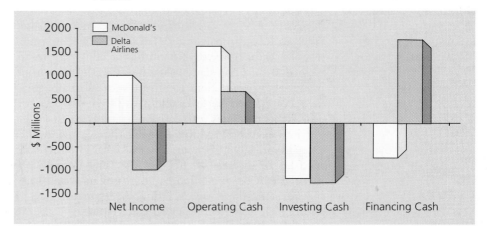

Data source: 1993 annual reports

Delta, on the other hand, provides a very different picture. Large losses were accompanied by a positive cash flow from operating activities. In addition to noncash expenses (depreciation and amortization), decreases in receivables and increases in payables explain most of the difference between income and cash flow. The cash flow statement reveals investment in plant assets for 1993. The investment was funded by a large increase in debt and stock. Thus, while McDonald's was investing about the same amount as Delta, it was funding the investment from operating activities rather than from new financing.

These comparisons illustrate the importance of evaluating a company's cash flows along with its net income. Future chapters will examine the use of the financial statements to analyze and interpret companies' economic activities in more depth.

FINANCIAL STATEMENTS AND THE TRANSFORMATION PROCESS

Objective 11

Identify relationships between financial statements and components of the transformation process.

A summary of the relationships between financial statements and the transformation process concludes this chapter. Exhibit 6-8 depicts these relationships. Components of the transformation process include operating, investing, and financing activities. The financial statements provide information about each of these activities and interrelationships among them. Later chapters of this book will examine this information and its use in decision making.

Exhibit 6-8   Financial Statement Reporting of Major Components of the Transformation Process

Statement of Cash Flows	Income Statement	Balance Sheet	Statement of Stockholders' Equity
Operating Activities	Income from Operations	Current Assets and Current Liabilities	
Investing Activities	Nonoperating Revenues and Expenses	Long-Term Assets	
Financing Activities	Nonoperating Revenues and Expenses	Long-Term Liabilities and Equity	Changes in Stockholders' Equity

The statement of cash flows, income statement, and balance sheet provide information associated with operating, investing, and financing activities. This information is clearly identified in three sections on the statement of cash flows. The income statement communicates information primarily about operating activities. Gains and losses associated with selling assets other than inventory represent results of investing activities. Interest revenue often results from investing activities, as well. Interest expense results from financing activities. Financing activities result in long-term liabilities and equity on the balance sheet. Long-term assets are the result of investing activities. Most current assets and liabilities result from operating activities, timing differences between revenues and cash inflows or expenses and cash outflows. The statement of changes in stockholders' equity provides detailed information about results of equity financing activities.

SELF-STUDY PROBLEM 6-3

Consider each of the following independent situations. Identify the adjustment that would be made to net income in computing cash flow from operating activities. Parentheses indicate a negative effect on net income. Use ( ) to indicate a cash outflow. Use the format provided:

a.	Amount
Sales revenues	$12,000
Increase in accounts receivable	2,000
Cash collected from customers	
b.	
Cost of goods sold	$ (8,000)
Increase in inventory	1,500
Decrease in accounts payable	2,000
Cash paid to suppliers	
c.	
Wages expense	$ (7,000)
Increase in wages payable	700
Cash paid to employees	

d.	Amount
Insurance expense	$ (1,000)
Increase in prepaid insurance	5,000
Cash paid for insurance	
e.	
Rent revenue	$ 1,000
Increase in unearned rent	11,000
Cash received in advance from customer	
f.	
Depreciation expense	$ (4,000)
Decrease in plant assets	4,000
Cash paid for depreciation	

Once you have completed the problem, compare it with Self-Study Problem 6-2.

The solution to Self-Study Problem 6-3 appears at the end of the chapter.

REVIEW   *Summary of Important Concepts*

1. Internal transactions:
   a. Internal transactions are important for complete recognition of revenues and expenses during a fiscal period.
   b. Internal transactions adjust account balances for revenues and expenses that should be recognized though external transactions have not occurred.
   c. Internal transactions often involve current asset or liability accounts in addition to revenues and expenses.

2. Adjustments and the balance sheet and income statement:
   a. Accruals and deferrals adjust for timing differences between when revenues or expenses are recognized and when cash is received or paid.
   b. Accrued revenues occur when revenues are recognized before cash is received.
   c. Accrued expenses occur when expenses are recognized before cash is paid.
   d. Deferred revenues occur when revenues are recognized after cash is received.
   e. Deferred expenses occur when expenses are recognized after cash is paid.

3. Timing differences and cash flow reporting:
   a. The indirect format of the statement of cash flows reconciles net income with cash flow from operating activities.
   b. The indirect format adjusts net income for changes in current asset and current liability account balances and for noncash expenses or revenues in computing cash flow from operating activities.
   c. Changes in working capital account balances identify differences between the amounts of revenues and expenses recognized during a fiscal period and the amounts of cash received or paid.

4. Cash flow information:
   a. Information about the sources and uses of cash provides a picture of a company's ability to meet its payment obligations now and in the future.
   b. Cash flow information, along with that on the income statement and balance sheet, provides insight into a company's operating, investing, and financing activities.

D E F I N E   *Terms and Concepts Defined in This Chapter*

accrued expenses   deferred expenses
accrued revenues   deferred revenues

S O L U T I O N S

SELF-STUDY PROBLEM 6-1

Assets =		Liabilities + Owners' Equity		+ (Revenues − Expenses)	
Account	**Amount**	**Account**	**Amount**	**Account**	**Amount**
a.	0	Wages Payable	2,000	Wages Expense	−2,000
b. Supplies	−5,600*			Supplies Expense	−5,600
c.	0	Interest Payable	2,400	Interest Expense	−2,400
d.	0	Income Taxes Payable	3,700	Income Tax Expense	−3,700
e. Accumulated Deprec.	−8,000			Depreciation Expense	−8,000
f.	0	Notes Payable, Current Portion	10,000		
		Notes Payable, Long-Term	−10,000		
g. Prepaid Insurance	−2,000			Insurance Expense	−2,000

$1,800 beginning supplies + $5,000 purchased − $1,200 remaining = $5,600 used during the month.

SELF-STUDY PROBLEM 6-2

a. **Transaction**	**Effect on Accounts Receivable**
Sold $12,000 of goods on credit	+$12,000
Collected $10,000 from customers	−10,000
Net change	+$2,000

b. **Transaction**	**Effect on Inventory**
Sold goods costing $8,000	− $8,000
Purchased $9,500 of inventory on credit	+9,500
Net change	+ $1,500

c. **Transaction**	**Effect on Accounts Payable**
Purchased $9,500 of inventory on credit	+ $9,500
Paid $11,500 in cash to suppliers	− 11,500
Net change	− $2,000

d. **Transaction**	**Effect on Wages Payable**
Accrued $7,000 of unpaid wages	+ $7,000
Paid $6,300 in wages to employees	− 6,300
Net change	+ $700

e. **Transaction**	**Effect on Prepaid Insurance**
Consumed 1 month of a 6-month insurance policy costing $6,000	− $1,000
Paid $6,000 for a 6-month insurance policy	+6,000
Net change	+ $5,000

f. **Transaction**	**Effect on Unearned Rent**
Earned 1 month's rent from a 1-year lease of property for $12,000 per year	− $1,000
Received $12,000 cash in advance for a 1-year lease	+ 12,000
Net change	+ $11,000

g. **Transaction**	**Effect on Plant Assets**
Recognized $4,000 of depreciation expense	− $4,000
Net change	− $4,000

SELF-STUDY PROBLEM 6-3

a.	**Amount**
Sales revenues	$12,000
Increase in accounts receivable	− 2,000
Cash collected from customers	**$10,000**
b.	
Cost of goods sold	$(8,000)
Increase in inventory	− 1,500
Decrease in accounts payable	− 2,000
Cash paid to suppliers	**$(11,500)**

c.	Amount
Wages expense	$(7,000)
Increase in wages payable	+700
Cash paid to employees	$(6,300)
d.	
Insurance expense	$(1,000)
Increase in prepaid insurance	−5,000
Cash paid for insurance	$(6,000)
e.	
Rent revenue	$1,000
Increase in unearned rent	+11,000
Cash received in advance from customer	$12,000
f.	
Depreciation expense	$(4,000)
Decrease in plant assets	+4,000
Cash paid for depreciation	$0

EXERCISES

6-1. Write a short definition for each of the terms listed in the *Terms and Concepts Defined in This Chapter* section.

6-2. Distinguish between external and internal transactions. Why are internal transactions necessary?

6-3. Identify each of the following as external or internal transactions. Also, identify the accounts that would be affected by each transaction:
   a. Sale of merchandise to customers for $1,500 on credit (ignore effect on inventory).
   b. Collected $1,250 in cash from customers for prior sales.
   c. Rented space in a building to a customer for $24,000. The rent covers one year and the customer paid in advance.
   d. Earned rent for the first month from transaction (c).
   e. Purchased property insurance for one year and paid $12,000.
   f. Incurred expense for first month from transaction (e).

6-4. Zung Tea Co. purchased property insurance on January 1, 1995, for $1,200. The insurance covers a three-month period. Insurance expense is recorded each month. Complete the following tables for transactions in January, February, and March 1995. Identify the net effect of the transactions for the three months on the company's financial statements by placing the correct dollar amounts in the following tables.

	January	February	March	Total
Expense				
Cash Outflow				

Effect for three months: Timing Adjustment

Cash	Prepaid Insurance	
	Prepaid Insurance	Insurance Expense

6-5. Pierre Tire Co. borrowed $15,000 from a bank on April 1, 1996. $450 of interest is paid on the loan each quarter, beginning June 30. Interest is accrued each month. Complete the following tables for July, August, and September, 1996. Identify the net effect of the transactions for the three months on the company's financial statements by placing the correct amounts in the following tables.

	July	August	September	Total
Expense				
Cash Outflow				

Effect for three months: Timing Adjustment

Interest Expense	Interest Payable	
	Interest Payable	Cash

6-6. Big Bang Chemical Co. signed a contract with Holes 'R' Us Construction, Inc., on April 1, 1995. Big Bang agreed to provide Holes 'R' Us with goods priced at $7,500 each month for three months, beginning April 1. Holes 'R' Us agreed to pay $22,500 for the goods on June 30. Complete the following tables for Big Bang for April, May, and June. Identify the net effect of the transactions for the three months on the company's financial statements by placing the correct amounts in the following tables.

	April	May	June	Total
Revenue				
Cash Inflow				

Effect for three months: Timing Adjustment

Sales Revenue	Accounts Receivable	
	Accounts Receivable	Cash

6-7. Wowee Press, Inc. publishes a weekly magazine. Subscriptions for three months are $45. Customers submit payment in December for issues beginning in January. By December 31, 1995, Wowee Press had received $900,000 in subscriptions. Revenues are recorded each month as earned. Complete the following tables for transactions in December 1995 and for January, February, and March, 1996. Identify the net effect of the transactions for the four months on the company's financial statements by placing the correct amounts in the following tables.

	December	January	February	March	Total
Revenue					
Cash Inflow					

Effect for four months: Timing Adjustment

Cash	Unearned Revenue	
	Unearned Revenue	Sales Revenue

6-8. Consider each of the following independent transactions. Identify the effect of each transaction by writing the account titles and amounts in the table provided below.
   a. A company recognizes $6,000 of unpaid wages earned by employees.
   b. A company identifies $4,000 of supplies remaining at the end of the month. It had $1,300 of supplies on hand at the beginning of the month and purchased $14,000 of supplies during the month.
   c. A company recognizes $3,600 of interest on notes payable incurred during the month that will be paid next month.
   d. A company recognizes $12,000 of income taxes owed on current period income. The taxes will be paid during the coming fiscal period.
   e. A company recognizes $10,000 of depreciation for the current fiscal period.
   f. A company transfers $40,000 of notes payable, long-term, to notes payable, current portion.
   g. A company recognizes the consumption of one-third of a prepaid insurance policy for which it paid $18,000.

Assets =		Liabilities + Owners' Equity		+ (Revenues − Expenses)	
Account	Amount	Account	Amount	Account	Amount
a.					
b.					
c.					
d.					
e.					
f.					
g.					
Total		Total		Total	

6-9. Complete the following table to distinguish between accruals and deferrals. Write *accrued revenue, accrued expense, deferred revenue,* or *deferred expense* in the appropriate box.

Cash is paid in June and a related expense is recognized in July.	
A revenue is recognized in June for which cash is received in July.	
Expense is recognized in June for which cash is paid in July.	
Cash is received in June and a related revenue is recognized in July.	

6-10. For each item listed below, identify whether it would appear on the statement of cash flows as part of the computation of cash flow from operating activities, cash flow from investing activities, or cash flow from financing activities. Also, indicate whether the item is added or subtracted in computing cash flow using the indirect method of preparing the statement of cash flows:
a. Purchase of plant assets
b. Increase in accounts payable
c. Decrease in accounts receivable
d. Payment of long-term debt
e. Net income
f. Depreciation expense
g. Payment of dividends
h. Issuing stock
i. Increase in inventory
j. Decrease in taxes payable
k. Disposal of plant assets

6-11. The following information is available for Hourglass Watch Co. for the first six months of 1995:

Revenues	$65,000
Expenses	37,500
Increase in accounts receivable	4,000
Decrease in inventory	6,000
Decrease in supplies	2,500
Increase in accounts payable	6,500
Decrease in wages payable	1,500
Depreciation expense	4,500
Patent expense	1,000

Determine the cash flow from operating activities for the six-month period.

6-12. Use the information provided in each of the following independent situations to answer the questions. Briefly explain your answer to each question.
a. Cash collected from customers for a fiscal period was $15,000. Accounts receivable increased during the period by $3,000. What was sales revenue for the period?
b. Cash paid to suppliers for merchandise during a period was $27,500. Accounts payable decreased during the period by $2,000. Inventory increased during the period by $3,500. What was cost of goods sold for the period?

c. Interest paid during a period was $3,000. Interest payable decreased during the period by $750. What was interest expense for the period?

d. Cash flow from operations for a period was $20,000. Current assets decreased during the period by $4,000. Current liabilities decreased by $2,500. What was net income for the period?

6-13. Use the information provided in each of the following independent situations to answer the questions. Briefly explain your answers.

a. Net cash flow from operations for a period was $39,000. Noncash revenues were $21,000. Noncash expenses were $25,500. What was net income for the period?

b. Wages expense for a period was $70,500. Wages payable increased during the period by $10,500. How much cash was paid to employees during the period?

c. Cash collected from customers for a fiscal period was $124,500. Sales revenue for the period was $141,000. Accounts receivable at the beginning of the period was $33,000. What was the balance in accounts receivable at the end of the period?

d. Net income for a period was $49,500. Current assets increased during the period by $7,500. Current liabilities increased by $12,000. How much was cash flow from operations for the period?

6-14. Listed below are changes in account balances. For each item where appropriate, indicate the adjustment that would be made to net income in the operating cash flow section of a cash flow statement using the indirect method and the reason for the adjustment. Item a. is provided as an example.

Account Balance	Adjustment and Reason
a. Accounts receivable increased $10,000	Subtract $10,000 from net income because cash collected from customers was $10,000 less than sales for the period.
b. Accounts payable increased $7,500	
c. Inventory decreased $50,000	
d. Notes payable increased $100,000	
e. Equipment decreased $80,000	
f. Prepaid insurance decreased $22,000	
g. Wages payable decreased $8,000	
h. Unearned revenue increased $13,000	

6-15. The following information was reported by The Boeing Company in a recent year (in millions):

Decrease in inventories	3,170
Decrease in unearned revenues	724
Depreciation and amortization	1,356
Increase in accounts payable	1,104
Increase in accounts receivable	466
Increase in income taxes payable	454
Increase in other receivables	602
Net earnings	2,770
Noncash revenues	394

What was Boeing's cash flow from operating activities for the fiscal year?

6-16.   Following is a statement of cash flows reported by Time–Warner for a recent fiscal year.

	Consolidated Statement of Cash Flows
	Year Ended December 31, 1993 (millions)
Operations:	
Net loss	$(221)
Adjustments for noncash and nonoperating items:	
Depreciation and amortization	424
Noncash interest expense	185
Noncash gains and losses (net)	(134)
Receivables	(71)
Inventories	20
Accounts payable and other liabilities	213
Other balance sheet changes	(159)
Cash provided by operations	257
Investing activities:	
Investments and acquisitions	(175)
Capital expenditures	(198)
Investment proceeds	103
Cash used by investing activities	(270)
Financing activities:	
Increase in debt	3,115
Repurchase of stock	(3,494)
Dividends paid	(299)
Other	(51)
Cash used by financing activities	(729)
Decrease in cash and equivalents	$ (742)

Note: Slight modifications have been made to the format of the statement for purposes of simplifying the presentation.

Use the statement to answer the following questions:
a.   What was the primary source of cash flow for the company?
b.   Why did the company receive a net cash inflow from operations when it incurred a net loss for the period?
c.   What were the primary uses of cash during the period?
d.   Did receivables, inventories, and accounts payable increase or decrease during the year?
e.   If revenues were $6,581 million for 1993, how much cash was collected from customers for the year?

6-17. Consider the following pattern in selected year-end data for Profit Co.:

Year	1	2	3	4	5	6
Cash flow from operating activities	$20,000	$25,000	$18,000	$12,000	$ 6,000	$ 2,000
Receivables	35,000	37,000	42,000	45,000	50,000	53,000
Inventory	70,000	76,000	80,000	84,000	86,000	90,000
Payables	24,000	28,000	32,000	46,000	57,000	66,000
Net income	50,000	53,000	55,000	59,000	63,000	55,000

Provide an explanation for the changes over the six-year period. What difficulties do you believe the company is facing?

6-18. Capital Co. has experienced the following results over the past three years: (in thousands)

Year	1	2	3
Net income (loss)	$ 2,000	$(10,000)	$ (8,000)
Depreciation and amortization	(9,000)	(11,000)	(14,000)
Net cash flow from operating activities	13,000	15,000	18,000
Net expenditures for plant assets	9,000	6,000	5,000

The price of Capital Co.'s common stock has declined steadily over the three-year period. At the end of year 3, it is trading at $10 per share. Early in year 4, Boone Icahn, who specializes in taking over poor performing businesses, has offered shareholders of Capital $18 per share for their stock. Why would Icahn be willing to pay such an amount? What does he see in the company that suggests value?

6-19. Martha Rosenbloom holds stock in several major corporations. Each year she receives a copy of the companies' annual reports. She looks at the pictures, reads the discussion by management, and examines some of the primary financial statement numbers. She has a pretty good understanding of some of the financial statement information. She tells her friends she doesn't know how to make heads or tails of the statement of cash flows, however. She doesn't understand how depreciation and changes in current assets and liabilities have anything to do with cash. A mutual friend, Arthur Doyle, has found out that you are taking accounting and asks you to help Martha. Write Martha a letter explaining the cash flow from operating activities section of the statement of cash flows found in most annual reports. Martha's address is 945 Oak Lane, Anytown, USA.

6-20. Explain how a company can have a net loss for a fiscal period but have a net increase in cash from operating activities.

6-21. Dollar Sign Corp. sold $15,000 of merchandise on credit during April. The merchandise cost the company $9,000. It purchased $12,500 of inventory on credit during April. Also, it collected $11,000 from customers and paid $8,000 to suppliers. What effect did these transactions have on cash, accounts receivable, inventory, accounts payable, revenues, and expenses?

6-22. Complete the following table describing the relationship between financial statements and components of the transformation process. Identify the portions of each statement that provide information about operating, investing, or financing activities.

Statement of Cash Flows	Income Statement	Balance Sheet	Statement of Stockholders' Equity
Operating Activities			
Investing Activities			
Financing Activities			

PROBLEMS

PROBLEM 6-1 Adjustments

Gorby Chef Restaurant reported the following balance sheet and income statement:

Gorby Chef Restaurant
Balance Sheet
March 31, 1996

Assets
Current assets:
Cash	$ 18,300
Supplies	20,850
Prepaid rent	13,500
Total current assets	52,650

Plant assets:
Building	150,000
Accumulated depreciation	(30,000)
Total plant assets	120,000
Total Assets	$172,650

Liabilities and Stockholders' Equity
Current liabilities:
Unearned revenue from gift certificates	$ 16,050
Total current liabilities	16,050
Notes payable	45,000
Total Liabilities	61,050

Stockholders' equity:
Common stock	60,000
Retained earnings	51,600
Total Stockholders' Equity	111,600
Total Liabilities and Stockholders' Equity	$172,650

Gorby Chef Restaurant
Income Statement
For the Three Months Ended March 31, 1996

Sales revenue	$144,000
Cost of dinners sold	49,500
Wages expense	44,100
Rent expense	9,000
Total expenses	102,600
Net income	$ 41,400

The company failed to record the following adjustments at the end of March:

a. The prepaid rent account represents three months rent paid at the beginning of March. Rent expense has not been recorded for March.

b. Wages owed but unpaid at the end of March total $6,150. The related expense has not been recorded.

c. In addition to the sales revenue shown, gift certificates totaling $13,800 were redeemed during the period.

d. The building is being depreciated over a 25-year estimated useful life. No depreciation has been recorded for the current quarter.

e. The amount of supplies available at the end of March was $4,500.

f. Interest accumulates on the note payable at 12% per year. No interest has been recorded for the quarter.

Required Make adjustments in the following tables to prepare a corrected balance sheet and income statement for Gorby Chef.

Gorby Chef Restaurant
Balance Sheet
March 31, 1996

	Uncorrected	Adjustments	Corrected
Assets			
Current assets:			
Cash	$ 18,300		
Supplies	20,850		
Prepaid rent	13,500		
Total current assets	52,650		
Plant assets:			
Building	150,000		
Accumulated depreciation	(30,000)		
Total plant assets	120,000		
Total Assets	$172,650		

	Uncorrected	Adjustments	Corrected
Liabilities and Stockholders' Equity			
Current liabilities:			
Unearned revenue from gift certificates	$ 16,050		
Total current liabilities	16,050		
Notes payable	45,000		
Total Liabilities	61,050		
Stockholders' equity:			
Common stock	60,000		
Retained earnings (a)	51,600		
Total Stockholders' Equity	111,600		
Total Liabilities and Stockholders' Equity	$172,650		

(a) Retained earnings must be adjusted for the change in net income resulting from the corrections.

Gorby Chef Restaurant
Income Statement
For the Three Months Ended March 31, 1996

	Uncorrected	Adjustments	Corrected
Sales revenue	$144,000		
Cost of dinners sold	(49,500)		
Wages expense	(44,100)		
Rent expense	(9,000)		
Total expenses	(102,600)		
Net income	$ 41,400		

PROBLEM 6-2 Accruals and Deferrals

Nifty Threads Clothing Store had the following information available at December 31, 1996.

a. A 12%, $4,000 note payable had been outstanding since August 1, 1996. Under the terms of the note, the amount of the note plus interest is to be paid on February 1, 1997. No interest has been recorded on the note.

b. In December 1996, a local high school band made a $3,000 deposit toward new uniforms. At December 31, 1996, one-third of the order had been delivered to the customer. Unearned revenue had been credited when cash was received.

c. Part of the store space is rented to Van Johnson, who operates an alteration shop. At year end, Van had not yet paid the $250 rent for December 1996 and no revenue had been recorded.

d. On August 1, 1996, Nifty Threads had purchased and paid for a one-year fire insurance policy costing $1,200. This amount had been recorded as prepaid insurance.

Required   Complete the following table for the transactions described on page 282.

Assets =	Liabilities + Owners' Equity	+ (Revenues − Expenses)

PROBLEM 6-3   Effects of Transactions on Current Assets and Liabilities

For each of the following independent situations, identify the effect on the balance sheet account. Use + and − to indicate an increase or decrease in the account. Complete each set of transactions using the format provided.

a.

Transaction	Effect on Accounts Receivable	Effect on Net Income	Effect on Cash Flow
Sold $6,000 of goods on credit			
Collected $8,250 from customers			
Net change			

b.

Transaction	Effect on Inventory	Effect on Net Income	Effect on Cash Flow
Sold goods costing $2,250			
Purchased $1,800 of inventory on credit			
Net change			

c.

Transaction	Effect on Wages Payable	Effect on Net Income	Effect on Cash Flow
Accrued $1,500 of unpaid wages			
Paid $1,275 in wages to employees			
Net change			

d.

Transaction	Effect on Prepaid Insurance	Effect on Net Income	Effect on Cash Flow
Consumed 1 month of a 3-month insurance policy costing $6,750			
Paid $6,750 for a 3-month insurance policy			
Net change			

e.

Transaction	Effect on Unearned Rent	Effect on Net Income	Effect on Cash Flow
Earned 1 month's rent from a 6-month lease of property for $13,500 per 6 months			
Received $13,500 cash in advance for a 6-month lease			
Net change			

f.

Transaction	Effect on Accumulated Depreciation	Effect on Net Income	Effect on Cash Flow
Recognized $10,500 of depreciation expense			
Net change			

PROBLEM 6-4   Ethical Issues in Accounting

Hides, Inc. manufactures leather goods: belts, purses, and specialty items. These goods are
sold to retailers throughout the country. The company's fiscal year ends December 31.
In December 1995, the company received orders for $12,000 of goods. Checks were re-
ceived with the orders. The goods will be manufactured and shipped in January. Hides
recorded the orders in December as:

Assets =	Liabilities + Owners' Equity	+ (Revenues − Expenses)
Cash $12,000		Sales Revenue 12,000

The company reported the following summary information in its financial statements for
1995:

Assets	$250,000
Liabilities	240,000
Owners' equity	10,000
Revenues	90,000
Expenses	83,000

Required   Discuss any concerns you would have with the way in which Hides recorded the December orders. How should the transaction have been reported? What effect
would the entry have on the company's summary financial information? What ethical
problems are posed by this situation?

PROBLEM 6-5   Adjustments

Flash-in-the-Pan Co. manufactures cooking products. On August 1, 1996, the company
borrowed $125,000 from creditors. Semiannual interest payments of $7,500 are to be
made to creditors beginning January 31, 1997. On July 1, 1996, the company purchased a
one-year insurance policy for $10,000 and recorded it as prepaid insurance. On January
1, 1996, the company purchased equipment for $50,000. The equipment has an expected
life of four years. On October 1, 1996, the company rented some of its unused warehouse space to another company. The other company agreed to pay $15,000 for the
space every six months, beginning April 1, 1997.
      Summary information reported by Flash for the fiscal year ended December 31,
1996, included:

Assets	$625,000
Liabilities	250,000
Owners' equity	375,000
Revenues	150,000
Expenses	112,500

Owners' equity ($375,000) has been adjusted for the effect of revenues and expens-
es. Flash failed to record any adjustments at the end of 1996 for interest, prepaid insurance, depreciation, and rent.

Required Complete the following table for the adjustments that Flash should make and describe the effect the transactions would have on the summary financial information:

Assets =	Liabilities + Owners' Equity	+ (Revenues – Expenses)

PROBLEM 6-6 Adjustments

The following account balances existed for Sounds, Inc., a recording studio, for three months ended August 31, 1997, prior to adjustments:

	Unadjusted	Adjustments	Adjusted
Cash	$ 52,500		
Accounts Receivable	35,250		
Supplies	19,200		
Prepaid Insurance	4,050		
Equipment	468,000		
Accumulated Depreciation–Equipment	(129,000)		
Buildings	649,500		
Accumulated Depreciation–Buildings	(85,500)		
Land	58,500		
Total Assets	**$1,072,500**		
Unearned Revenues	$ 36,000		
Accounts Payable	27,900		
Interest Payable	6,000		
Wages Payable	0		
Notes Payable	420,000		
Common Stock	300,000		
Retained Earnings (a)	224,100		
Total Liabilities & Stockholders' Equity	**$1,014,000**		
Rent Revenues	$ 100,500		
Wages Expense	(36,000)		
Supplies Expense	0		
Insurance Expense			
Interest Expense	(6,000)		
Depreciation Expense			
Net Income	**$ 58,500**		

(a) Net income has not been added for the current year.

The following additional information is available for transactions that have not been recorded for August:

a. Unearned revenues represent contracts for use of studio facilities. $12,000 of this amount had been earned by August 31.
b. $10,050 of supplies remained on hand on August 31.
c. Interest accumulates on the note in the amount of $3,000 per month. Interest has not been recorded for August.
d. $4,350 of wages earned in August that are unpaid.
e. The insurance provides coverage for one year. The cost was $5,400 for the year.
f. Depreciation on equipment is $1,500 per month. Depreciation on buildings is $600 per month. No depreciation has been recorded for the quarter.

Required   Record necessary adjustments in the table.

PROBLEM 6-7   Interpreting a Cash Flow Statement

A statement of cash flows is provided for Sara Lee Corporation for a recent fiscal year:

**Consolidated Statement
of Cash Flows**

(Dollars in millions)	July 3, 1993
Operating Activities	
Net income	$ 704
Adjustments for noncash charges included in net income:	
Depreciation and amortization of intangibles	522
Increase in deferred taxes	27
Other noncash credits, net	(117)
Decrease in accounts receivable	57
Increase in inventories	(124)
Increase in other current assets	(40)
Decrease in accounts payable	(10)
Decrease in accrued liabilities	(169)
Net cash from operating activities	850
Investing Activities	
Purchase of property and equipment	(728)
Acquisitions of businesses	(352)
Dispositions of businesses	31
Sales of property	51
Other	31
Net cash used in investment activities	(967)
Financing Activities	
Issuances of common stock	66
Purchases of common stock	(77)
Borrowing of long-term debt	256
Repayments of long-term debt	(300)
Short-term borrowings, net	609
Payments of dividends	(306)
Net cash from financing activities	248
Effects of changes in foreign exchange rates on cash	(4)
Increase in cash and equivalents	$ 127

Note: Slight modifications have been made to the format of the statement for purposes of simplifying the presentation.

Required Use the information from the statement of cash flows to answer the following questions:

a. What was the amount of change in Sara Lee's cash account for 1993?
b. What were the primary sources of cash for the company?
c. What were the primary uses of cash?
d. Why were depreciation and amortization added to net income in computing cash flow from operating activities?
e. Why were the decrease in receivables added, the increase in inventory subtracted, and the decrease in accounts payable subtracted from net income in computing cash flow from operating activities?
f. Why were purchase of property and equipment, sales of property, and acquisitions listed as investing activities?
g. Did short-term debt increase or decrease during the year?
h. How much new long-term debt was issued during the year? How much old long-term debt was paid off?
i. Does the company appear to be facing a cash flow problem? Explain your answer.

PROBLEM 6-8 Evaluating Income and Cash Flows

Selected financial statement information is reported below for High Rise Co., a real estate developer. All amounts are in thousands.

For the year ended December 31, 1997

Sales revenue	$11,200
Cost of goods sold	6,400
Operating expenses	2,800
Net income	2,000
Dividends paid	1,000

For December 31	1997	1996
Cash	$ 1,340	$1,940
Accounts receivable	4,600	2,200
Inventories	9,400	5,000
Accounts payable	3,800	2,600
Notes payable	10,000	6,000

Required Prepare a statement of cash flows for High Rise, assuming that all important cash flow activities are reflected in the information provided above. What financial problems do you see in examining the financial information presented for High Rise? What are some potential causes of these problems?

PROBLEM 6-9 Interpreting the Cash Flow Statement

Portions of the consolidated statement of cash flows and income statement for Marvel Entertainment Group, Inc., are provided on page 288.

	(Dollars in millions) Year ended December 31, 1993
Cash flows from operating activities:	
Net income	$ 56.0
Adjustments to reconcile net income to net cash:	
Depreciation and amortization	12.3
Provision for deferred income taxes	5.6
Increase in accounts receivable	(9.1)
Increase in inventories	(6.1)
Increase in other assets	(4.6)
Increase in accounts payable	3.9
Decrease in accrued expenses and other	(21.8)
Net cash provided by operating activities	$ 36.2

	Year ended December 31, 1993
Net revenues	$415.2
Cost of sales	215.3
Gross profit	199.9
Selling, general & administrative expenses	85.3
Interest expense, net	14.6
Amortization of goodwill, intangibles and deferred charges	10.1
Income before provision for income taxes	89.9
Provision for income taxes	38.4
Income before other adjustments	51.5
Other adjustments	4.5
Net income	$ 56.0

Required   Use the information from the financial statements to answer each of the following questions:

a.   How much cash did Marvel collect from customers in fiscal 1993?

b.   How much cash did Marvel pay for operating costs for 1993? Consider all adjust–ments related to operating expenses.

c.   How much cash did Marvel pay for income taxes in 1993? The increase in deferred taxes represents the amount of taxes not paid in 1993.

PROBLEM 6-10   Comparing Cash Flows

Portions of the statements of cash flows for two corporations are provided at the top of the next page for fiscal years ended in 1993:

(in millions)	Intel Corporation	Allied Products
Net income	$2,295	$15
Adjustments:		
Depreciation	717	7
(Increase) decrease in accounts receivable	(379)	30
(Increase) decrease in inventories	(303)	22
(Increase) decrease in other assets	(68)	2
Increase (decrease) in payables	146	(5)
Other adjustments	393	7
Net cash provided by operating activities	2,801	78
Net cash provided by (used in) investing activities	(3,337)	63
Net cash provided by (used in) financing activities	352	(92)
Net change in cash	(184)	49

Required Write a short report comparing the financial performances of the two companies.

PROBLEM 6-11   Interpreting Cash Flows

A portion of the statement of cash flows is provided below from the 1993 annual report of The Limited, Inc.

(thousands)	1993	1992	1991
Cash Flows from Operating Activities:			
Net Income	**$390,999**	$455,497	$403,302
Impact of Other Operating Activities on Cash Flows			
Depreciation and Amortization	**271,353**	246,977	222,695
Special and Nonrecurring Items	**(2,617)**	–	–
Changes in Assets and Liabilities			
Accounts Receivable	**(219,534)**	(101,545)	(65,536)
Inventories	**70,006**	(73,657)	(144,884)
Accounts Payable and Accrued Expenses	**14,943**	118,289	8,792
Income Taxes	**20,773**	82,369	30,371
Other Assets and Liabilities	**(97,784)**	26,198	20,897
Net Cash Provided by Operating Activities	**448,139**	754,128	475,637

Required Prepare a short report comparing the operating activities of The Limited for the three years.

PROBLEM 6-12   Interpreting Cash Flows

Required   Identify whether each of the following statements is "True" or "False." Explain your answers. Write in complete sentences. Computations may be used as part of your explanation.

a.   When a company prepares the cash flow statement using the indirect method, it adds depreciation expense to net income because depreciation is a source of cash during a fiscal period.

b.   Alpha Co. reported an increase in accounts receivable of $2 million during 1993. As a result, Alpha's cash flow from operating activities was $2 million less than its operating revenues.

c.   Beta Co. purchased $40 million of merchandise inventory during 1993. Beta's accounts payable increased from $5 million to $8 million during the year. Beta's cash flow statement (indirect method) would report an adjustment to net income of −$3 million.

d.   Delta Co. reported cost of goods sold of $27 million for 1993. Its merchandise inventory increased by $8 million during the year. If all inventory purchased was paid for in cash, Delta's cash payments to suppliers of inventory during the year were $35 million.

e.   Gamma Co. reported:

Net cash flow for operating activities	− $80
Net cash flow from investing activities	35
Net cash flow from financing activities	50
Net change in cash	$ 5

From this information it appears that Gamma is facing financial problems.

PROBLEM 6-13   Multiple-Choice Overview

1.   Which of the following is an internal transaction?
  a.   purchase of inventory on credit
  b.   recognition of depreciation on plant assets
  c.   payment of amount owed to creditors
  d.   receipt of cash for rent to be earned in the future

2.   April Shower Co. recognized $500 of interest on notes payable during September. The interest will be paid in December. Which of the following is the correct effect of the transaction?

	Interest payable	**Income from operations**
a.	+ $500	− $500
b.	+ $500	+ $500
c.	− $500	+ $500
d.	− $500	− $500

3. Finkle Stein Co. recognized $800 of rent earned during November. The rent was received in October. Which of the following is correct for this transaction?

	Cash	Income from operations
a.	+ $800	+ $800
b.	+ $800	− $800
c.	$0	− $800
d.	$0	+ $800

4. The primary purpose of adjustments is to:
   a. increase net income.
   b. minimize income taxes payable.
   c. correct errors that have been made during a period.
   d. obtain the proper account balances at the end of a period.

5. At December 31, Dinosaur Pest Control had not yet paid December's rent of $3,000. As of the same date, Dinosaur had collected $2,500 from customers for services that had not yet been performed. Which combination of the following items does the firm have at December 31?
   a. accrued revenue, accrued expense
   b. accrued revenue, deferred expense
   c. deferred revenue, accrued expense
   d. deferred revenue, deferred expense

6. A statement of cash flows, prepared using the indirect method, would report an increase in accounts receivable as:
   a. an addition to cash flow from financing activities.
   b. a subtraction from cash flow from financing activities.
   c. an addition to net income in computing cash flow from operating activities.
   d. a subtraction from net income in computing cash flow from operating activities.

7. Flag Ship Co. reported depreciation and amortization expense of $300,000 for the latest fiscal year. The depreciation and amortization expense would:
   a. increase cash flow for the year $300,000.
   b. decrease cash flow for the year $300,000.
   c. have no effect on cash flow for the year.
   d. have an effect on cash flow if assets were purchased during the year.

8. Rust Iron Co. purchased a three-month insurance policy on March 1, 1995. The company paid $3,000 for the policy. The amount of insurance expense and cash outflow the company should report for March would be:

	Insurance Expense	Cash Outflow
a.	$3,000	$3,000
b.	3,000	1,000
c.	1,000	3,000
d.	1,000	1,000

9. Micro Fish Co. recognized $10,000 of interest expense in 1996. The balance of the company's interest payable account decreased $2,000. The amount of cash paid by the company for interest in 1996 was:
   a. $10,000
   b. $12,000
   c. $2,000
   d. $8,000

10. Operating activities are reflected on a company's balance sheet primarily in:
    a. plant assets.
    b. current assets and liabilities.
    c. income from operations.
    d. cash flow from operating activities.

CASES

CASE 6-1 Analysis of Corporate Financial Statements

The 1994 financial statements for Nike, Inc. are provided in Appendix B near the end of this text. Examine these statements and answer the following questions.

Required   Use the financial statements to answer each of the following questions:

a. What were Nike's major operating activities during 1994? What were the major differences between the accrual and cash flow effects of these activities?

b. What were the company's return on total assets and return on stockholders' equity for 1994? If you owned 10,000 of the company's 73,200,000 shares of stock, what was your claim on the company's earnings for 1994? How much cash would you have received from the company?

c. What were the company's major sources of cash for 1994? What have been its major sources of financing? What major financing activities occurred in 1994?

d. What major investing activities occurred in 1994? What were the company's most important assets? What assets may be important to the company that are not reported on its balance sheet?

CASE 6-2 Interpreting Cash Flows

Review the financial report of Nike, Inc. in Appendix B.

Required   Prepare a short report analyzing each of the following issues:

a. What were the accrual and cash basis results of operating activities for 1994? Explain any major differences between the two results.

b.   Identify which current assets and liabilities increased and decreased during 1994. Which of these represent accruals and which represent deferrals?

c.   What has been the relationship between net income and cash flow from operating activities over the 1992–1994 period? What accounts for changes in the relationship over the three years?

d.   How would you assess the company's financial performance for 1994?

PROJECTS

PROJECT 6-1   Comparing Financial Statements

Locate recent annual reports for three different companies in your library. Prepare a table comparing the cash flow from operating activities of the companies. List each company, major adjustments to net income, and net cash flow from operating activities. Describe the major differences you observe among the companies.

PROJECT 6-2   Researching Cash Flow

Write a comparative analysis of three companies in a particular industry. Focus your analysis on cash flow from operating activities. Explain major differences among the companies and draw conclusions about the relative strengths of each company. Explain differences between the amount of net income and amount of cash flow from operating activities for each company.

PROJECT 6-3   Using Business Journals

Use a periodicals index, such as the *Accountants Index* or the *Business Periodicals Index,* to identify recent articles that discuss cash flow problems faced by specific companies. Select an article from a journal available in your library. Read the article and write a summary of the problem discussed in the article.

PROJECT 6-4   Accruals and Deferrals

Assume you are trying to explain to someone who has little knowledge of accounting the reason for accruals and deferrals. Write an explanation that defines these terms, describes why they are necessary, and gives examples. Show your explanation to a friend and ask whether the person understands your explanation. If necessary, revise your explanation to respond to your friend's understanding of these concepts.

PROJECT 6-5   Examining Changes in Cash Flow

Examine a recent corporate annual report. Write a memo to your instructor in which you compare the cash flow statements for the three most recent years. What major changes occurred during the period that affected cash flows from operating, investing, and financing activities? What conclusions can you draw about the financial performance of the company from these changes?

Chapter 7

The Accounting Profession

CHAPTER

Overview

The first six chapters of this book introduced the accounting information system. This chapter looks at the accounting profession. Accountants develop accounting systems, establish measurement and reporting rules, manage the processing of accounting information, and interpret accounting reports. The profession includes accountants in every segment of society and in every type of organization. Also, it includes rule-making, enforcement, and professional organizations that promote quality and integrity in the work performed by accountants.

This chapter examines the different types of work performed by accountants. It discusses the educational background and skills necessary for entry into the accounting profession. It provides a historical overview of the development of the profession and of the contemporary practice of accounting. And, it describes the process by which accounting measurement and reporting rules are developed in the U.S.

Major topics covered in this chapter include:

- The functions of the accounting profession.
- The historical development of accounting.
- The development of accounting standards.

CHAPTER

Objectives

Once you have completed this chapter, you should be able to:

1. Explain the term "accounting profession."
2. Identify responsibilities of accountants in business organizations.
3. Identify responsibilities of public accountants.
4. Identify the purpose of an audit report.
5. Identify responsibilities of accountants in governmental and nonprofit organizations.
6. Explain the role of accountants in education.
7. Discuss educational requirements for entry into the accounting profession.
8. List important events in the development of accounting and understand their effects on contemporary accounting.
9. Identify organizations responsible for setting accounting standards in the U.S.
10. Explain why accounting standards are important to our economy.
11. List steps in the process of establishing accounting standards.
12. Identify the primary components of the conceptual framework used in establishing accounting standards for businesses in the U.S.

ACCOUNTING AS A PROFESSION

Objective 1
Explain the term "accounting profession."

A profession is a group of individuals who share specific skills and training. This group is accepted by society as being qualified to engage in certain services or activities that serve the public need. Most professions require their members to meet licensing requirements and often are regulated by governmental authorities. The accounting profession includes those who have attained a high level of knowledge of accounting through education and experience. These individuals use their skills to develop accounting systems, to prepare and evaluate accounting information, and to assist decision makers with the analysis and interpretation of this information. Some of these responsibilities require accountants to be licensed to perform certain services. To acquire a license, an accountant generally must complete a college degree with a specified number of business and accounting courses, pass a qualifying examination administered by the profession, and obtain experience in accounting practice.

The accounting profession encompasses accountants who work in businesses, public accounting firms, governmental and nonprofit organizations, and educational institutions. One of the distinguishing features of a profession is self-regulation. The accounting profession includes several professional organizations that oversee the activities of accountants. These organizations establish standards that are designed to promote competency and ethical behavior on the part of accounting practitioners for entry and continuation in the accounting profession.

The following sections examine the qualifications and responsibilities of accountants in more depth.

Percentage of 1.2 Million U.S. Accountants in Various Organizations

- Management Accounting
- Public Accounting
- Governmental Accounting
- Education

(Data source: Institute of Management Accountants)

Management Accounting

Accountants play several roles in supporting the management of business organizations:

Management Accounting

Information Systems Development

Financial Accounting Management

Financial Reporting

Financial Planning and Analysis

Cost Accounting and Management

Internal Auditing

Management accounting includes all accounting functions within business organizations. Many accountants who work in business organizations belong to the Institute of Management Accountants (IMA). The IMA is a national professional organization of management accountants and the sponsor of the Certified Management Accountant (CMA) program for individuals who meet education requirements and pass the CMA Examination, which is offered twice each year. The CMA designation is intended to indicate the attainment of professional competency in managerial accounting. Becoming a CMA normally is not required for employment in accounting, though it may enhance professional career opportunities. The IMA promotes ethical standards, continuing education, and research that assists in the practice of management accounting. Accountants are expected to update their knowledge and skills on an ongoing basis. CMAs must meet continuing education requirements each year.

Information Systems Development. All organizations require information systems to collect, summarize, and report information needed by internal and external decision makers. Larger organizations often maintain an information systems department. This department is responsible for designing and implementing information systems for a variety of functions, such as accounting, production, purchasing, and customer orders. Typically, these systems are computerized. Therefore, employees of these departments include programmers and computer systems analysts who understand how computers process data. Accountants assist in the development of these systems, particularly those needed to process accounting information. These accountants normally have been educated in both accounting and computer information systems.

Financial Accounting Management. Accountants oversee the processing of accounting information. While entering transactions in the accounting system is primarily a clerical activity, accountants are responsible for managing this activity to ensure efficiency and accuracy. Accountants are responsible for adjusting and closing entries and other nonroutine bookkeeping activities for which a detailed understanding of accounting is required. Also, accountants are responsible for providing information from the accounting system to meet the needs of other managers. They work with the information systems department in designing reports and procedures to get the needed information to the appropriate users promptly and accurately.

Financial Reporting. Accountants prepare financial statements and other reports for distribution to owners, creditors, employees, and regulatory authorities. Most large corporations prepare these reports quarterly. Most of these reports must be prepared in accordance with generally accepted accounting principles (GAAP) if they are distributed to owners, creditors, and other external users. Reports filed with regulatory authorities, such as the Securities and Exchange Commission (SEC), also must conform with GAAP. Some organizations must report to other regulatory authorities. For example, businesses that contract with governmental agencies must report to a contracting authority such as the Department of Defense. Most financial institutions must report to federal and state banking authorities. These authorities establish reporting requirements for the organizations that report to them.

Various governmental authorities require reports to determine conformity with fair trade and labor regulations. Other reports collect data for governmental economic planning. These reports provide indicators of how well the economy is performing, such as the amount of sales and the number of employees during a period.

Most businesses are required to file a variety of reports with taxing authorities at the federal, state, and local levels. These reports are used to determine compliance with income, sales, payroll, and other tax regulations.

Financial Planning and Analysis. Accountants play a direct role in the management of organizations making decisions that require an understanding of accounting information. Accountants analyze and interpret financial statements and other accounting reports to determine how well a company is performing. This information is used by managers in planning future operations and in making strategic decisions about obtaining and using resources.

Accountants assist in decisions about obtaining new capital from owners and creditors, the purchase of new assets, mergers with and acquisitions of other companies, sale of divisions, development of new product lines, expansion into new locations, replacement of assets, and strategies for improving performance and profitability.

Cost Accounting and Management. *Cost accounting* **includes those functions necessary to accumulate and report a company's costs.** *Cost management* **includes strategies and methods to reduce costs and increase competitiveness.** Accountants monitor a company's operations to determine whether actual costs for developing, purchasing, producing, marketing, and servicing products are consistent with expectations. They develop and analyze information to determine whether a company is operating efficiently and effectively. If costs are out of line with expectations, they notify managers and employees and work with them to identify corrective actions. Accountants may work with managers and engineers in production and development to find ways to improve efficiency by reducing production costs.

Internal Auditing. Internal auditing is the process of evaluating a company's activities to assess whether appropriate procedures are being used and whether management policies are being implemented. Internal auditors identify ways for departments to improve their operations. Also, they consider whether departments and divisions are operating in the best interest of the company as a whole. Thus, they are concerned with how decisions are made and with how decisions made in one department affect other departments. Internal auditors also are concerned with the procedures a company uses to safeguard its resources to prevent theft, fraud, and mismanagement.

Internal control **is an organization's plan and the procedures it uses to safeguard its assets, ensure reliable information, promote efficiency, and encourage adherence to policies.** Federal law requires corporations that report to the SEC to have a system of internal controls. Internal control procedures include various techniques for promoting the control objectives. Procedures should be developed to identify, train, and retain competent employees. Employee responsibilities should be clearly defined so employees understand what is expected of them and how they will be evaluated. Company policies should establish how decisions are to be made and who has the authority to make them. Appropriate authorization for the use of resources is an important internal control procedure. Employee responsibilities should be divided so no single employee has control over acquisition, use, and record keeping associated with resources. Separation of duties reduces the likelihood an employee can steal or misuse resources without being discovered by someone else in the organization. The following illustration summarizes some major internal control procedures:

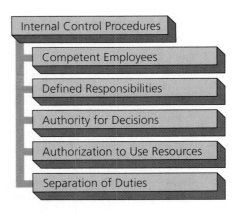

Internal auditors help in developing and evaluating a company's system of internal controls to ensure the system is operating effectively. They monitor the activities of employees to determine if procedures are being followed. They investigate areas in which internal controls may be deficient or may not be operating properly. From the investigation, they determine whether inefficiency or misuse of resources is a problem. Internal auditors normally report to top management or to a company's board of directors any problems that warrant attention.

Many internal auditors belong to the Institute of Internal Auditors (IIA). The IIA, a national professional organization, sponsors the Certified Internal Auditor (CIA) Examination, which is offered nationally each year. The CIA designation is intended to indicate the attainment of professional competency in internal auditing. Being a CIA is not a normal requirement for employment in accounting, though, like the CMA, it may enhance professional career opportunities. Also, like the IMA, the IIA develops standards of professional and ethical conduct for internal auditors. CIAs are expected to complete continuing education requirements each year. An individual may be both a CMA and a CIA.

Public Accounting

Accountants provide services to the public as auditors, compilers and reviewers of financial statements, tax advisers, and consultants, as illustrated on the next page.

Objective 3
Identify responsibilities of
public accountants.

Independent auditing services are provided in the U.S. by certified public accountants (CPAs). A CPA is an individual who has met education, examination, and experience requirements imposed by a state government. A State Board of Public Accountancy is responsible for establishing and overseeing certification requirements.

To become a CPA, an individual must pass the Uniform CPA Examination. This national examination, which is offered twice a year (May and November) in all states and territories, includes three sections (Practice and Theory, Business Law, and Auditing). Most states require applicants for the examination to have a college degree that includes a minimum number of hours in accounting and business administration courses. The number of hours varies from state to state. Many states have passed legislation requiring applicants to have completed a minimum of 150 semester (or equivalent quarter) hours of course work, including a bachelor's degree. This legislation generally requires at least 30 hours of accounting courses. Some states require experience in accounting, usually by working for a CPA, before licensing a person who has passed the CPA examination to practice as an independent accountant.

Many CPAs belong to the American Institute of Certified Public Accountants (AICPA) and to a state society of CPAs in the state where they practice. The AICPA is a national professional organization that, along with the state societies, oversees the practice of public accounting in the U.S. Members are required to complete an average of 40 hours of continuing professional education each year and to abide by a strict code of ethics and professional conduct. These requirements are intended to ensure that CPAs remain current in their knowledge and provide quality professional service to the public.

CPA firms may be large, with thousands of professionals, or may be small, perhaps with only one professional. The largest international accounting firms have offices throughout the world. The six largest firms, known as the "Big Six," are: Arthur Andersen, Coopers and Lybrand, Deloitte and Touche, Ernst and Young, KPMG Peat Marwick, and Price Waterhouse.

Learning Note — All CPAs are not in public practice. A CPA may work in business, in governmental and non-profit organizations, and in education. Anyone who passes certification requirements can be a CPA. A CPA also may be a CMA and a CIA.

Certification of accountants in public practice is common in most countries. The European equivalent of the CPA is the chartered accountant (CA). To become a chartered accountant, candidates must pass several exams and serve an apprenticeship with a chartered accounting firm.

Auditing. The public practice of auditing differs from internal auditing. Internal auditors are employees of the organizations they audit; therefore, they are not independent of those organizations. To provide auditing services, external auditors must be independent, in fact and appearance, of the organizations they audit. Therefore, they are referred to as independent auditors or independent accountants. An external financial audit provides assurance to owners, creditors, governmental authorities, and others who rely on a company's financial reports that they are faithful representations of the company's economic activities.

An audit involves a detailed, systematic investigation of a company's accounting records. The auditor attempts to verify that the numbers and disclosures made by management in its financial reports are consistent with the company's actual financial position and operating results. Records, operating procedures, contracts, resources, and management policies and decisions are examined to provide evidence of the fairness of financial report information. Auditors determine if internal control procedures exist and are being used. They compare the information in financial reports with information from prior years and other sources to confirm the fairness of the reports.

Objective 4
Identify the purpose of an audit report.

A primary purpose of public accounting is attestation. *Attestation* **occurs when an auditor affirms the fairness of financial statements by signing an audit report.** Auditors issue an audit report upon completion of their audit work. **The** *audit report*, **or** *audit opinion*, **provides public notice of the auditor's belief about the fairness of the accompanying financial information.** Only a licensed CPA may give a formal opinion about audited financial information. Exhibit 7-1 provides an example of an auditor's report.

Exhibit 7-1   Example of the Auditor's Report

Independent Accountants' Report

The Shareholders
H.J. Heinz Company:

We have audited the accompanying consolidated balance sheets of H.J. Heinz Company and subsidiaries as of April 27, 1994 and April 28, 1993, and the related consolidated statements of income, retained earnings and cash flows for each of the three years in the period ended April 27, 1994. These financial statements are the responsibility of the company's management. Our responsibility is to express an opinion on these financial statements based on our audits.

We conducted our audits in accordance with generally accepted auditing standards. Those standards require that we plan and perform the audit to obtain reasonable assurance about whether the financial statements are free of material misstatement. An audit includes examining, on a test basis, evidence supporting the amounts and disclosures in the financial statements. An audit also includes assessing the accounting principles used and significant estimates made by management, as well as evaluating the overall financial statement presentation. We believe that our audits provide a reasonable basis for our opinion.

In our opinion, the financial statements referred to above present fairly, in all material respects, the consolidated financial position of H.J. Heinz Company and subsidiaries as of April 27, 1994 and April 28, 1993, and the consolidated results of their operations and their cash flows for each of the three years in the period ended April 27, 1994 in conformity with generally accepted accounting principles.

As discussed in Note 11 to the Consolidated Financial Statements, the company adopted the provisions of Statement of Financial Accounting Standards No. 106, "Employers' Accounting for Postretirement Benefits Other Than Pensions" in Fiscal 1993.

Coopers & Lybrand

600 Grant Street
Pittsburgh, Pennsylvania
June 14, 1994

The audit report contains several important sections as described in Exhibit 7-2.

Exhibit 7-2 Sections of an Audit Report

Address

- **¶ 1 Coverage and responsibility**
- **¶ 2 Purpose of audit and work performed**
- **¶ 3 Opinion**
- **¶ 4 Special information**

Signature and Date

An audit report often is addressed to the shareholders of the company. Normally, an audit is performed on behalf of the shareholders and other external parties. Audits may be requested for special purposes, for example, to secure a bank loan or as part of merger negotiations. The audit report may be addressed to specific users who will receive the report, such as bank loan officers. Auditors are responsible for protecting the interests of those who will use audited financial statements.

Many corporations have formed audit committees. **An *audit committee* is composed of members of a corporation's board of directors who discuss the audit and its findings with the independent auditors.** The audit committee is informed by auditors of any important problems discovered during the audit. The committee keeps other members of the board informed of audit activities.

First Paragraph. The first paragraph of the audit report identifies the statements and fiscal periods covered by the audit. A typical audit will cover all the primary financial statements: income statement, balance sheet, and statement of cash flows. The most recent three years of operations normally are covered by the audit. For most large corporations, the audited financial statements are the consolidated statements of the parent and its subsidiaries.

The first paragraph also describes the responsibilities of auditors and management. Management is responsible for preparing the statements. By publishing the statements for external users, management asserts the statements are a fair and accurate description of a company's economic activities. Auditors are responsible for competently using the technology available to them to confirm (or disconfirm) the assertions of management. This technology includes procedures to obtain evidence to support the auditors' beliefs. For example, auditors inspect certain resources, such as inventory and fixed assets, to confirm their existence.

Second Paragraph. The second paragraph of the audit report summarizes the audit process. *Generally accepted auditing standards (GAAS)* **include procedures used in conducting an audit to help auditors form an opinion about the fairness of the audited statements.** GAAS are developed in the U.S. by the Auditing Standards Board (ASB). The ASB is a division of the AICPA. Auditing standards are published and updated periodically by the AICPA. Failure to conform with GAAS in an independent audit is a major violation of a CPA's responsibilities.

From evidence collected from using GAAS, auditors assert the financial statements are free of material misstatement. *Materiality* **is a criterion for establishing the importance of a potential misstatement in audited financial statements.** Financial statements contain estimates and allocations that depend on management judgment. In addition to finding errors in accounting records, auditors may disagree with managers about their estimates and allocations. Unless these errors and disagreements are material (important) to the overall amounts reported on the financial statements, however, auditors are not required to take action on these issues.

Auditors examine accounting records on a "test basis." Auditors do not examine 100% of a company's transactions. Instead, auditors use sampling techniques to select representative transactions. By verifying these transactions, auditors form an opinion about the financial statements as a whole. Sampling is necessary because the cost of auditing all a company's records generally is prohibitive.

Third Paragraph. The third paragraph of the audit report states the auditor's opinion. An opinion may be one of several types:

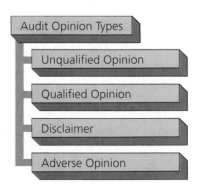

Audit Opinion Types

Unqualified Opinion

Qualified Opinion

Disclaimer

Adverse Opinion

Most audit reports provide an **unqualified opinion**. This opinion states that the auditor believes the financial statements fairly present the company's actual economic events for the period covered by the audited statements. Fair presentation means the financial statements are prepared in conformity with GAAP and are free from material omissions and misstatements.

A **qualified opinion** is issued when the auditor believes the statements are fairly presented except for the presentation of specific items. The exceptions are for accounting procedures the auditor does not believe conform with GAAP.

A **disclaimer** is issued when the auditor does not believe sufficient evidence is available or the auditor cannot perform sufficient audit work to form an opinion about the fairness of the financial statements. This problem may arise because of limitations placed on the audit by management or because of missing or incomplete records.

An **adverse opinion** is issued when the auditor believes the financial statements do not fairly represent a company's economic activities. Such an opinion is issued if the auditor believes the statements are potentially misleading. A company whose statements contain major departures from GAAP could receive an adverse opinion.

Almost all audit reports for major corporations contain unqualified opinions or opinions with minor qualifications. The SEC requires major corporations to file reports that do not contain qualifications (except for certain minor ones), disclaimers, or adverse opinions. Therefore, these corporations are required to conform with GAAP and to provide the information necessary to satisfy their auditors that their statements are fairly presented. When a major disagreement exists between an auditor and a client company, the auditor may withdraw from the audit without issuing an opinion or the company may seek a different auditor. SEC-regulated corporations must report major disagreements and auditor changes to the SEC.

Qualified opinions, disclaimers, and even adverse opinions are more common for businesses that are not regulated by the SEC and for governmental and nonprofit organizations. These organizations may not be required to conform with GAAP, and their audit reports may include departures from GAAP.

Fourth Paragraph. The first three paragraphs are standard for most corporate audit reports. A fourth paragraph is included only if the auditor believes additional information that is not contained in the earlier paragraphs should be noted in the opinion. In Exhibit 7-1, the auditor notes the company has changed accounting methods for a particular item. Companies are expected to be consistent in their application of accounting methods from year to year. When a company changes methods that may have an effect on the amounts reported in the financial statements, the auditor is required to note the change in the audit report to alert its readers.

Signature and Date. Audit reports must be signed by the public accounting firm that performed the audit, thus indicating its responsibility. The date of the audit report is the date all audit work was completed for the periods covered by the report. The auditor is responsible for disclosing any material information that might affect a decision maker's interpretation of the financial statements through the date of the audit report.

Other Audit Report Formats. The standard audit report described above is the most common report included in annual reports of U.S. corporations. Variations exist, however. Some public accounting firms prefer a modified format of the standard report. The audit report normally will convey the same information for most major corporations, regardless of variations in format.

Audit reports for foreign corporations differ from those of U.S. corporations. Different countries establish their own auditing and accounting standards. The format of the audit report depends on the auditing standards of the country in which a company has its principal operations. For example, the following report is typical of a British audit report:

> We have audited the accounts set out on pages xx to xx in accordance with Auditing Standards.
>
> In our opinion the accounts give a true and fair view of the state of affairs of the company and of the group at (date) and of the profit and source and application of funds of the group for the year then ended and have been properly prepared in accordance with the Companies Act of 1985.

Though shorter than U.S. audit reports, the British report includes similar information. Several terminology differences are apparent: "true and fair view" substitutes for "present fairly." "State of affairs" refers to financial position; "profit" refers to operating results, and "source and application of funds" to changes in cash and other working capital items. The term "group" is common in European reporting and refers to a parent and its consolidated subsidiaries. The Companies Act is legislation regulating accounting and financial reporting in the United Kingdom.

Management Responsibilities for Financial Statements. The audit report for U.S. corporations notes that financial statements are the responsibility of management. Most corporate annual reports include a statement by management identifying its responsibilities. For example, the following was included in the 1994 annual report of H.J. Heinz Company:

> Responsibility for Financial Statements
>
> Management of H.J. Heinz Company is responsible for the preparation of the financial statements and other information included in this annual report. The financial statements have been prepared in conformity with generally accepted accounting principles, incorporating management's best estimates and judgments, where applicable.
>
> Management believes that the company's internal control systems provide reasonable assurance that assets are safeguarded, transactions are recorded and reported appropriately, and policies are followed. The concept of reasonable assurance recognizes that the cost of a control procedure should not exceed the expected benefits. Management believes that its systems provide this appropriate balance. An important element of the company's control systems is the ongoing program to promote control consciousness throughout the organization. Management's commitment to this program is emphasized through written policies and procedures (including a code of conduct), an effective internal audit function and a qualified financial staff.
>
> The company engages independent public accountants who are responsible for performing an independent audit of the financial statements. Their report, which appears herein, is based on obtaining an understanding of the company's accounting systems and procedures and testing them as they deem necessary.
>
> The company's Audit Committee is composed entirely of outside directors. The Audit Committee meets regularly, and when appropriate separately,

with the independent public accountants, the internal auditors and financial management to review the work of each and to satisfy itself that each is discharging its responsibilities properly. Both the independent public accountants and the internal auditors have unrestricted access to the Audit Committee.

Through this report, management acknowledges its responsibility for the financial statements, for implementing a system of internal controls to ensure reliability of the statements, and to work with its external auditors. The report also describes the role of the corporation's audit committee. Most large U.S. corporations are required by law to maintain a system of internal controls and to provide a statement of management responsibility with their annual financial reports.

Limitations of the Audit. Auditors are responsible for being competent in audit technology and for using this technology to the best of their abilities. They are expected to use reasonable judgment and due diligence in performing the audit, and should demonstrate the highest integrity and remain unbiased in their judgments. But, no audit, however well performed, can provide complete assurance that a company's financial statements are totally accurate. While auditors should be alert to the possibility of management fraud, elaborate schemes have been perpetrated by some managers to prevent the auditor from detecting the fraud and its effect on the financial statements. Most cases in which auditors have failed to discover material misstatements have involved fraud on the part of a company's managers and/or employees.

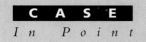
C A S E
I n   P o i n t

One of the most elaborate of recent management frauds was the ZZZZ Best case. The company was started by a young entrepreneur on a small budget to provide cleaning services for businesses and other clients. The business grew rapidly and became a major corporation. The top managers of the company colluded to defraud their investors by reporting exaggerated revenues. They reported cleaning contracts that did not exist. These nonexistent contracts and revenues were used to raise additional capital. Instead of investing the money in the company, managers used it for their own purposes.

The managers engaged in major deception to prevent the company's auditors from discovering their fraud. The auditors were shown several locations throughout the country where the company supposedly was working on contracts. In reality, these locations had been rented or borrowed temporarily and were made to look like work sites. Records and contracts were forged to make the auditors believe the work was legitimate.

Compilation and Review. In addition to audits, public accountants provide compilation and review services, especially for smaller businesses. *Compilation* **occurs when an independent accountant prepares financial statements for a client from the client's accounting records.** *Review* **occurs when an independent accountant examines a client's financial statements to provide assurance they appear to be in good order.** Compilation is a service requested by organizations that may not have the expertise to prepare their own financial statements. Review is a service requested by organizations that do not require an audit. Instead, they need an independent examination of their financial statements to provide some assurance the statements report the organization's economic activities. For example, as part of a loan arrangement, a bank may request a company provide financial statements that have been reviewed by an independent accountant. Financial statements that have been compiled or reviewed by a public accountant are unaudited. Therefore, they should not be relied on as being a faithful representation of a company's economic activities to the extent of audited statements.

Tax Advising. Another service performed by public accountants is tax advising. Public accountants work with individuals and businesses to prepare tax returns and to help with tax planning. Tax laws and regulations often are complex. Most people do not have the time or expertise to comply with reporting requirements and to avoid overpayment of taxes. Businesses may employ their own tax professionals to assist with reporting and planning requirements. Most companies, however, rely on public accountants for part or most of this work.

Tax regulations change frequently; therefore, tax professionals continuously update their knowledge to remain current. They use this expertise to advise clients on business and personal financial strategies that will minimize their tax obligations. Much of this advice focuses on income taxes, especially at the federal level. State, local, and international tax issues are important, as well, for many corporations. Estate and gift taxes are an important concern for many individuals.

Since many corporations pay taxes on their income, effective tax planning can save these companies large amounts of money. Taxes can have a major effect on the accounting methods used by businesses. Accounting methods determine how much revenue or expense will be reported during a fiscal period. By selecting methods that reduce revenues and increase expenses for a period, a company can reduce its required tax payments. Accounting and tax measurement rules limit the choices available to companies. Thus, considerable skill may be required to identify methods that will reduce taxes and not violate accounting or tax rules. The effect of taxes on accounting methods will be considered in future chapters.

Consulting. Another major service provided by public accountants is consulting. Consulting encompasses a wide variety of activities:

Accountants assist businesses in designing and implementing information systems. This assistance may involve selecting hardware and software, tailoring the system to the needs of the business, and training employees to use the system and understand the information it provides. Public accounting firms also may provide bookkeeping services for their clients, especially for those too small to have their own accounting departments. Accounting firms often use computers to maintain accounting records and prepare financial statements for clients.

Accountants assist managers in understanding financial information about their businesses. They may examine a company to identify ways it could operate more effectively or efficiently. They may examine other companies that are merger or acquisition prospects to estimate the value of these companies. They may help companies identify personnel for positions in a company, especially where specific managerial or financial skills are required for the positions.

Accountants also work with individuals and small business owners. They help them understand their finances and plan their personal or business financial activities. They advise them on investments, resource acquisitions, insurance needs, retirement plans, and many other issues. Accountants are multipurpose financial advisers.

Governmental and Nonprofit Organizations

Objective 5
Identify responsibilities of accountants in governmental and nonprofit organizations.

Accounting activities in federal, state, and local governments and in nonprofit organizations, such as nonprofit hospitals and universities, are similar to those of businesses. These nonbusiness organizations require accounting systems, prepare financial reports, analyze financial information for decision purposes, and develop internal control systems. Often they are audited by independent accountants. In these respects, the earlier discussion of business organization accounting applies to nonbusiness organizations as well. Management accountants work in governmental and nonprofit organizations as they do in businesses. Public accountants provide auditing and other services to governmental and nonprofit organizations.

Nonbusiness organizations are different from businesses in several respects. The production of goods is not a major activity for most nonbusiness organizations. Therefore, some of the cost accounting issues that are critical for many businesses are not as important for these organizations. Most nonbusiness organizations are tax exempt. Therefore, the tax issues that apply to businesses are not of concern. Tax-exempt organizations are required to file tax reports, however, and to establish that they have met requirements for tax-exempt status.

A major accounting issue for governments involves the receipt, rather than payment, of taxes. Taxes are a major source of revenues for governments. Accountants who work in government are concerned with tax assessment and compliance. Assessment involves determination of the amount of taxes owed by individuals and businesses. Compliance involves ensuring that amounts owed are collected. The best known of the organizations concerned with these issues is the Internal Revenue Service (IRS), which is a major employer of accountants. Similar organizations exist at the state government level.

Governments also are involved in audit activities. State governments have an audit division responsible for auditing the various departments and divisions of state government. In some states, these auditors have responsibility for local governments, as well. The General Accounting Office (GAO) is responsible for auditing the federal government. The GAO audits federal government departments and activities and reports its findings to Congress. Other governmental agencies are involved in audits of organizations that receive governmental funds and contracts. Governmental agencies also audit businesses regulated by federal agencies, such as certain banks, savings and loans, and other financial institutions.

Accountants also are employed by governmental organizations such as the Federal Bureau of Investigation (FBI). Criminal behavior often involves theft and fraud. Accountants investigate suspected cases of financial mismanagement to identify the existence, type, and amount of criminal behavior.

Education

Objective 6
Explain the role of accountants in education.

Accounting is taught in high schools, community colleges, four-year colleges and universities, and graduate schools. The number of accounting faculty has risen sharply in the past two decades as the demand for accounting courses and graduates has increased. Accounting faculty are educated as accountants, as educators, and as researchers. Many have been employed in the practice of accounting.

Accounting faculty typically have completed a master's degree in accounting or business administration. Many have completed a doctorate with a specialization in accounting. The doctorate is particularly important for those who want faculty positions in universities with research expectations. The task of these faculty is both to disseminate knowledge through teaching and to expand knowledge in the accounting discipline through research. Faculty in larger universities often specialize in a particular area of accounting, such as managerial, auditing, accounting systems, or taxation.

Preparation for an Accounting Career

Objective 7
Discuss educational requirements for entry into the accounting profession.

The previous section described employment opportunities available in accounting. The flexibility an accounting degree offers for employment in a wide variety of organizations has made accounting a popular college major. To take advantage of these opportunities, students must obtain both a high level of technical knowledge and a broad level of professional skills.

Accounting is a technical profession. Students typically take courses in the preparation and analysis of financial accounting information, in management and cost accounting, in governmental and nonprofit accounting, in accounting information systems, in taxation of individuals and corporations, and in auditing. Along with courses in business administration, these courses help develop the technical and business skills needed by accountants.

In addition to technical knowledge, skills in communication, group behavior, problem solving, and logical reasoning are required of accountants. Knowledge of accounting is not sufficient. An accountant must be able to communicate technical information to those who use accounting information. Clear and effective presentation and writing skills are essential. Accountants often work in teams with managers, engineers, and other accountants; they must be able to work effectively in these settings to achieve team objectives. They must be able to provide leadership and guidance in achieving group goals when the need arises.

Accountants are required to use judgment in solving problems. Often, problems do not have obvious answers. Choices have to be made among alternatives. An ability to grasp the relevant facts, identify alternatives, and propose workable solutions is critical to success. Accountants should enjoy working with people. Public accountants, in particular, must market their services to clients. A willingness to accept responsibility, without close supervision, is an important attribute.

Perhaps the most important requirement for success in accounting is integrity. Accountants must make difficult choices. They are under constant pressure to make choices that will affect the welfare of managers, stockholders, colleagues, and other individuals. These choices require accountants to be fair and unbiased in their decisions. The reputation of the accounting profession for fairness and ethical behavior is essential to the role it plays in society.

Students interested in accounting careers should take every opportunity to develop the skills required by the profession. For example, courses in writing, public speaking, and group behavior are highly desirable. Courses in business ethics and leadership can be valuable. Humanities and liberal arts courses that require exercising independent thought and judgment can be useful. Mathematics can help in developing reasoning skills.

Another skill increasingly useful for accountants is the ability to speak a foreign language. The globalization of business has led to increasing interrelationships between accountants and managers of multinational corporations. The ability to converse with foreign managers, along with an understanding of their cultures, can be extremely valuable. An understanding of international business and accounting is important in addition to developing these skills.

Accounting provides an excellent background for a variety of career opportunities. Corporate managers often find an accounting education prepares them for their decision-making responsibilities. Financial analysts and bank officers frequently have accounting backgrounds. An accounting education also is good preparation for those who plan to attend law school, especially if they are interested in corporate or tax law.

SELF-STUDY PROBLEM 7-1

Listed below are responsibilities of the accounting profession. For each item, identify whether the responsibility is provided by management accountants, public accountants, governmental and nonprofit accountants, or accounting educators. Some responsibilities may be provided by more than one type of accountant.

1. Development of accounting systems.
2. Evaluation of whether company policies are being implemented.
3. Preparation of tax returns.
4. Determination that taxpayers have complied with tax regulations.
5. Development of new accounting knowledge.
6. Independent evaluation of an organization's financial statements.
7. Advising managers about the interpretation of financial information.
8. Determination of the cost of producing goods and services.
9. Preparation of those who wish to enter the accounting profession.
10. Providing financial planning advice to individuals and business managers.

The solution to Self-Study Problem 7-1 appears at the end of the chapter.

THE HISTORICAL DEVELOPMENT OF ACCOUNTING

Accounting has evolved over a long period of time. It has changed in response to economic, social, and political events that have affected the need for accounting information. Exhibit 7-3 lists some of the important events in the development of accounting.

Exhibit 7-3   Important Events in Accounting History

Objective 8
List important events in the development of accounting and understand their effects on contemporary accounting.

Date	Event
2000 B.C.	Development of Record Keeping
1200–1400 A.D.	Development of Modern Bookkeeping
1494	Pacioli's Method of Venice
1750–1850	Industrial Revolution and Rise of the Corporation
1792	New York Stock Exchange Formed
1887	American Institute of Accountants Formed
1896	First CPA Examination
1913	Income Taxation Approved in the U.S.
1929	Collapse of Stock Market
1933	Securities Act of 1933
1934	Securities and Exchange Act of 1934 and Formation of Securities and Exchange Commission
1936	Committee on Accounting Procedure Formed
1959	Accounting Principles Board Formed
1973	Financial Accounting Standards Board and International Accounting Standards Committee Formed
1984	Governmental Accounting Standards Board Formed
1991	Federal Accounting Standards Advisory Board Formed

Historical Developments to the Early 1900s

Accounting is as old as recorded history; in fact, writing and math sprang from the need for record keeping. Ancient Babylonian cuneiform tablets recorded information about the quantity and types of agricultural goods produced. Modern forms of record keeping can be traced to the Middle Ages. Trade became important in Europe with the development of ships and navigation tools. Bookkeeping developed to document resources exchanged in commerce and debtor and creditor relationships. It was a common practice for an accountant to accompany commercial voyages. The accountant was responsible for keeping track of goods to be traded, recording amounts of exchanges, and reporting to investors on the outcomes of their ventures.

One of the first known descriptions of double-entry bookkeeping was published in 1494 by Luca Pacioli, an Italian monk. Italy was the center of commerce in the Western world at the beginning of the Renaissance. It lay on the major trade routes between Europe and Asia. Therefore, it is no surprise that accounting was practiced in Italy during this period. Pacioli referred to his method of bookkeeping as the Method of Venice. This method provided the foundation for modern accounting.

The Industrial Revolution. Accounting advanced during the Industrial Revolution (approximately 1750–1850). This was a period of rapid development of manufacturing technology. New products and production processes required greater investments of capital and better management skills than before. The corporation became an important form of business organization because of its ability to raise large amounts of capital. Corporate managers required more sophisticated accounting systems than their predecessors to provide information necessary for operating complex organizations. Managerial accounting techniques developed to assist managers in tracking manufacturing costs and in evaluating the performances of their companies.

The corporate form of organization has had an important effect on the use of accounting information by managers. A single manager cannot oversee the activities of a large, complex organization. Therefore, an organized hierarchy of managers performing specific tasks is needed in these corporations. Lower levels of managers report to higher levels. Managers in different divisions or locations must communicate with managers in other divisions or locations. Accounting information provides a means for managers to communicate with each other about many aspects of corporate activities. Many accounting procedures and reporting formats have been developed to meet these needs. This information is not regulated, as is information provided to stockholders, since managers are the providers and users of the information. Thus, each corporation develops its own internal reporting procedures to help managers make planning and control decisions.

Market and Professional Developments. The New York Stock Exchange (NYSE) was formed in 1792. The exchange was important for facilitating the growing trade in corporate stocks. Also, it was important because it required financial reporting by member corporations by the early 1900s. The NYSE's efforts were one of the first attempts in the U.S. to regulate reporting to stockholders.

Increasing operating complexity and demand for capital created a need for accounting information and for greater accounting skills. The earliest major professional accounting organization in the U.S. was created in 1887. The American Institute of Accountants later became the American Institute of Certified Public Accountants (AICPA). Since its formation, the AICPA has played a major role in determining the qualifications of public accountants and in regulating their activities.

Income Taxation. Adoption of the 16th amendment to the U.S. Constitution in 1913 permitted federal taxation of individual and corporate income. Taxation of income is not possible without rules and reporting requirements that determine how income will be computed. Therefore, taxation has had an important effect on accounting practice and the accounting profession. The Internal Revenue Service (IRS) was created as a governmental agency to oversee tax reporting and collection. The Internal Revenue Code legislates tax accounting and reporting rules. These tax rules were developed primarily from the accounting and financial reporting rules used by businesses.

Income taxes are important to business accounting for two reasons. First, they create an incentive for the federal government to monitor accounting practices. The government is concerned with full and fair reporting of income to ensure the proper payment of taxes. Second, most individuals and many small businesses rely on accounting rules used in computing their taxes when they report on their financial conditions. For example, if an individual wishes to obtain a mortgage to purchase a home, the lending financial institution may ask for a copy of the person's most recent federal tax return. Also, many proprietorships, partnerships, and some small corporations maintain their accounting records using accounting rules acceptable for tax reporting. When they wish to borrow money, they often provide financial reports developed from these accounting records to lending institutions.

Federal Regulation in the 1900s

The early 1900s was a period of intense corporate activity. Many corporations were created and many individuals invested in stock. The collapse of the stock market in 1929 resulted in the loss of much personal wealth and a demand for increased regulation of corporate financial reporting. Many people believed a cause of the collapse was a lack of sufficient information about corporate activities and a lack of governmental oversight of the stock markets.

In response to these concerns, the U.S. Congress passed the **Securities Act of 1933**. This legislation required most corporations to file registration statements before selling stock to investors. As a part of these statements, corporations were required to provide financial reports containing balance sheets and income statements. Additional legislation, the **Securities and Exchange Act of 1934**, required corporations to provide annual financial reports to stockholders. The legislation also required that these reports be audited by independent accountants. The 1934 act also created the Securities and Exchange Commission (SEC) as a federal agency reporting to Congress. The SEC was given responsibility for overseeing external financial reporting by publicly traded corporations.

Learning Note   Corporate stocks and bonds are referred to as securities. Stocks are equity securities. Bonds are debt securities. Publicly traded corporations are those whose securities are traded through security exchanges and brokers.

Currently, the SEC requires publicly traded corporations to publish annual and quarterly financial reports. These reports contain information about the corporations' business activities and their financial statements. Annual financial statements must be audited by independent CPAs.

In addition, annual and quarterly registration statements must be filed by corporations with the SEC. **Annual registration statements filed by corporations with the SEC are known as** *Form 10-K reports*. They are required by Section 10-K of the 1934 act. A 10-K describes a corporation's business and its management and financial activities. Much of the information referred to in a 10-K is provided in the annual report. Quarterly statements are known as 10-Q's. Other statements are required periodically if specific events occur. For example, if a corporation issues new shares of stock, it must file a registration statement. If it changes auditors, it must file a Form 8-K report.

Another document that corporations are required to provide to stockholders is a proxy statement. **A** *proxy statement* **provides information about matters that will be considered at a corporation's annual stockholders' meeting.** These matters frequently include election of members of the board of directors, adoption of management compensation plans, and selection of an independent auditor. The proxy statement provides information about the members of the board of directors and their compensation, major stockholders, stock owned by managers, compensation of managers, and management and employee compensation and retirement plans.

A *proxy* **is a document that authorizes management to cast votes for its stockholders at a stockholders' meeting.** If stockholders cannot attend the meeting and wish for management to vote for them, they can sign and return the proxy to the managers.

During the 1900s financial accounting has become a highly regulated and formalized process. Publicly traded corporations must provide audited financial reports to their stockholders. These statements should provide full disclosure of accounting information in accordance with GAAP. The managers and auditors of companies who fail to provide this information or who do so fraudulently are subject to civil and criminal prosecution.

SELF-STUDY PROBLEM 7-2

Several major events have been important for the development of modern accounting practice in the U.S. Explain the importance of each of the following events:

1. The Industrial Revolution
2. The income tax
3. The securities legislation of 1933 and 1934

The solution to Self-Study Problem 7-2 appears at the end of the chapter.

THE DEVELOPMENT OF ACCOUNTING STANDARDS

Objective 9
Identify organizations responsible for setting accounting standards in the U.S.

The SEC is responsible for enforcement of reporting and auditing requirements. Occasionally, the SEC also establishes accounting standards for corporations to use in providing financial reports to their investors. For the most part, accounting standards (GAAP) have been established in the U.S. by private, rather than governmental, organizations. Private standard setting is not common outside the U.S. Most other nations rely on laws enacted by government to establish accounting standards. These standards frequently serve the needs of the government for information about corporate activities.

The AICPA Committee on Accounting Procedure

In 1939, the AICPA Committee on Accounting Procedure (CAP) began to issue accounting and financial reporting standards. This organization and its replacements have been recognized by the SEC as the source of GAAP for U.S. corporations. GAAP consist of the pronouncements of the authoritative organizations that have been established to set accounting standards. Members of the CAP participated in the organization on a part-time basis. Most were practicing accountants who maintained their own firms.

The CAP was replaced in 1959. Nevertheless, the AICPA continues to play a role in setting accounting standards. Its committees are instrumental in identifying accounting issues and in recommending appropriate accounting procedures. In addition, the AICPA, through its Auditing Standards Board, remains the primary organization for establishing procedures used by independent auditors. The AICPA regulates the auditing profession by requiring auditors to comply with auditing standards and to meet continuing education requirements. Accounting firms that are AICPA members must be reviewed periodically by other accounting firms to assess the quality of their audit work.

The Accounting Principles Board

The CAP was criticized as being controlled by the AICPA and audit firms. In 1959, the Accounting Principles Board (APB) replaced the CAP. The APB was not controlled by the AICPA. Most members of the APB participated on a part-time basis and included representatives who were not practicing accountants. The APB was more independent of the accounting profession than was the CAP. Nevertheless, the APB also was criticized as being too much under the control of the accounting profession.

The Financial Accounting Standards Board

Perceived inadequacies in the operations of the APB led to its being replaced in 1973 by the Financial Accounting Standards Board (FASB). The FASB continues as the primary organization for setting GAAP for businesses in the U.S. The FASB has seven full-time members appointed by a supporting organization, the Financial Accounting Foundation (FAF). The FASB is privately funded through the efforts of the FAF. The FAF includes representatives from the accounting profession, industry, government, financial institutions, the securities industry, and the investing public. Thus, it is intended to be broadly representative of those who have an interest in accounting and financial reporting. The FASB issues standards that establish GAAP for corporations and other businesses.

The FASB also sets accounting and financial reporting standards for nonprofit organizations other than governmental units. These organizations are not subject to SEC regulation, however, and compliance with GAAP is largely voluntary. Many organizations that receive federal funding are required by the federal government to be audited for compliance with GAAP.

Governmental Accounting Standards

The Governmental Accounting Standards Board (GASB) was created in 1984 to establish GAAP for state and local governmental units. Like the FASB, the GASB reports to the FAF, which appoints its members and oversees its activities.

The federal government is not subject to FASB or GASB standards but establishes its own accounting rules. The federal government does not have a coherent set of GAAP for all of its agencies and departments. The Federal Accounting Standards Advisory Board (FASAB) was created in 1991 to assist with the establishment of accounting standards for agencies and departments of the federal government. The FASAB attempts to identify the needs of users of federal financial information and to develop financial reports to meet those needs.

International Accounting Standards

The regulation of financial accounting and reporting is an international activity. Considerable diversity exists in accounting standards among nations. The International Accounting Standards Committee (IASC) was created in 1973 as an international effort to study accounting issues and to reduce the diversity of standards. The IASC has issued accounting standards that identify preferred accounting methods for activities such as inventory estimation and consolidation but has no enforcement power. Nevertheless, it influences accounting practices in most developed and developing nations because of the growing globalization of trade and security markets. Some countries, especially developing ones, have adopted IASC standards as their GAAP.

THE PURPOSE OF ACCOUNTING STANDARDS

Objective 10
Explain why accounting standards are important to our economy.

Accounting standards prescribe financial accounting and reporting practices for most major corporations. The rules used by corporations to measure and report their transformation activities should conform to GAAP. An elaborate regulatory procedure exists for establishing accounting standards, and also serves to monitor compliance with the standards. This process serves several important functions in our society.

Providing a Basis for Contracting

Managers contract with stockholders to manage the operations of corporations for the stockholders' welfare. Stockholders contract with managers to compensate the managers for their services; this compensation depends on company performance. Without accounting information, these contracts would be unenforceable since stockholders could not judge company performance. Accounting information provides an important means of assessing manager performance and determining compensation.

Specific performance measures are needed in contracts to define the rules of the game. Accounting standards provide a basis for determining performance measures that can be verified by both managers and stockholders. For example, compensation contracts may provide for a bonus to be paid to certain managers if a corporation's earnings increase by 10% over the prior year. Standards are needed to determine how earnings will be measured so managers and stockholders can agree earnings increased by 10%.

Contracts also are important for creditors, employees, and other groups. For example, creditors are concerned about how much of a corporation's resources are transferred to stockholders as dividends. Limitations often are placed on these payments that depend on the amount of earnings or working capital. Accounting rules define how earnings and other amounts will be measured. Employees contract for compensation and benefits, including retirement and health care. Accounting information can assist them in determining whether benefits are being funded and whether an organization is likely to be able to continue to provide jobs, compensation, and benefits.

Assuring Reliability of Information

Managers need to assure investors that the information they report about the performance of their businesses is accurate and reliable. GAAP and audits by independent CPAs help meet this need. GAAP limit managers' abilities to select the methods they use to calculate accounting numbers. Since measurement rules are established by someone other than management, investors have some assurance accounting information is not being manipulated to serve the interests of managers.

Accounting standards provide a basis against which a corporation's accounting information can be audited. An auditor examines whether the procedures used by managers to develop and report accounting information to external users are in compliance with GAAP. If the procedures are not in compliance with GAAP, auditors should note the discrepancy in their audit reports. GAAP provide a standard of measurement for auditors, as well as for managers who report accounting information.

Controlling the Cost of Reporting and Maintaining Equity

Reporting to external users is expensive. Corporations must maintain information systems for financial reporting. Standards control the amount and type of information corporations are expected to provide. Individual users cannot force a corporation to provide information not mandated by regulation. All corporations in a particular industry are subject to the same reporting requirements. Therefore, no corporation or user has an unfair advantage over others.

The public reporting of information is important, so all users have equal access to important information. Standards require the reporting of information useful to those who make investment decisions. Federal laws prohibit the use of information for personal gain by those with unfair access to information. In particular, managers, directors, and others who have access to inside information are prohibited from using this information to earn profits by trading in corporate securities.

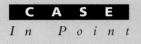

In March 1992, Sheldon M. Stone, a former Boston real estate developer, pleaded guilty to securities fraud. Stone assisted a law firm employee in securing a mortgage for a condominium she was buying by financing her down payment. In return, the employee provided Stone with confidential information regarding a pending takeover of Parisian, Inc. The law firm was assisting with the takeover. Stone, and a partner, purchased 22,000 shares of Parisian and later sold the stock for a profit of $273,375.

Determining Fair Business Practices and Economic Analysis

The federal and state governments use accounting information in regulating business practices and in setting economic policies. The government monitors corporate profits and trade activities. Policies are enacted to control business activities that lead to unreasonable profits or noncompetitive trade.

The government insures depositors in many financial institutions against loss of their deposits. Federal and state agencies are responsible for overseeing the activities of these institutions to protect the interests of depositors. The accounting practices of these institutions are important so their financial conditions can be monitored reliably.

Other organizations, such as public utilities, are under the direct supervision of regulatory agencies. These agencies set the rates these organizations can charge to earn a fair return for their investors. Accounting standards are important to ensure rates are determined fairly and similar organizations receive equitable treatment from regulators.

Also, the government sets policies to promote economic activity and to control inflation and unemployment. It uses accounting information from companies in setting these policies. Accounting standards ensure the availability of reliable information for these purposes.

Providing a Basis for Litigation

Investors and other users of accounting information can sue managers and auditors for issuing false or misleading information. Litigation protects users from unscrupulous managers and from gross negligence on the part of auditors. It is the responsibility of managers to provide accurate and timely accounting information. Auditors certify that financial statement information fairly presents a company's economic activities, while GAAP provide a benchmark against which reported information can be compared. Failure to comply with accounting and auditing standards is a basis for litigation.

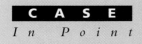

In 1992, a jury awarded $338 million to a British corporation for negligence by Price Waterhouse in its audits of an Arizona bank. The bank was purchased in 1987 by the British company. Price Waterhouse audited the bank in 1985 and 1986. After the purchase, the bank was forced to write down the reported value of some of its major assets.

Several other major CPA firms settled lawsuits in the early 1990s for audits of savings and loans and other companies. For example, Ernst & Young paid $63 million for investor claims from the collapse of Lincoln Savings & Loan Association. Coopers & Lybrand paid approximately $50 million to settle a suit over failure to discover misstatements in its audits of MiniScribe Corporation.

SETTING ACCOUNTING STANDARDS

Accounting standards are important to protect the interests of investors, managers, and the general public. Therefore, the standards must be perceived as being reasonable and responsive to the needs of different constituents. Arbitrary and unnecessary standards do not serve the needs of society. For these reasons, accounting standards are established through a political process. This process provides an opportunity for interested parties to express their opinions and to provide information that may have a bearing on prospective standards. The fact that accounting standards are referred to as *generally accepted* accounting principles is not accidental. To serve the needs of society, accounting standards must be accepted by those who are affected by them. Therefore, the process of establishing standards includes an opportunity for all interested parties to inform standard setters of their needs and concerns. This process increases the likelihood that standards will be accepted by those affected and that the benefits derived from the standards will exceed the costs of standard setting and reporting.

The Standard-Setting Process

Objective 11
List steps in the process of establishing accounting standards.

The process used by the FASB is typical of that used by other organizations, such as the GASB and the IASC. The process consists of the following steps:

1. Accounting issues are identified and evaluated for consideration.
2. A discussion memorandum is issued and responses are solicited.
3. Public hearings are held.
4. An exposure draft is issued and responses are solicited.
5. Additional public hearings are held as needed.
6. A standard is issued.
7. Existing standards are reviewed and modified as needed.

Accounting issues may be identified by the accounting profession, managers, investors, or by the FASB staff. The staff evaluates the issues, and the board determines those issues that appear to be important for it to address.

A *discussion memorandum* **is a document that identifies accounting issues and alternative approaches to resolving the issues.** All interested parties are encouraged to respond to a discussion memorandum. The FASB staff summarizes responses to a discussion memorandum for the board. Public hearings may be held to obtain additional information.

The board develops a proposed standard after reviewing responses. Alternatively, the board can decide to drop an issue or postpone further consideration. If a proposal is issued, it represents the views of the board, not necessarily the views of a majority of respondents. Nevertheless, the board must justify its views and demonstrate that its decisions are not arbitrary.

The board issues its proposal in the form of an exposure draft. **An** *exposure draft* **is a document that describes a proposed accounting standard.** It identifies requirements that may be contained in an actual standard. Responses again are solicited and public hearings sometimes are held.

Once the board reviews responses to an exposure draft, it may modify and reissue the exposure draft or issue a standard. **An** *accounting standard* **is an official pronouncement establishing acceptable accounting procedures or financial report content.** FASB standards are known as *Statements of Financial Accounting Standards*. To be issued, a standard must be agreed to by at least five of the seven members of the board. The views of board members who vote against a standard are issued as part of the standard.

Once a standard has been issued, it becomes part of GAAP. An effective date is part of each standard; as a result, financial reports issued after this date must comply with it. Standards can be reviewed at any time to determine if they are serving their intended purposes and can be modified or replaced if found to be ineffective.

The Conceptual Framework for Accounting Standards

The conceptual framework was developed by the FASB in the late 1970s and early 1980s to provide guidance in the development of accounting standards. **The** conceptual framework **is a set of objectives, principles, and definitions to guide the development of new accounting standards.**

Objective 12
Identify the primary components of the conceptual framework used in establishing accounting standards for businesses in the U.S.

The FASB conceptual framework includes four major components: (1) objectives of financial reporting, (2) qualitative characteristics of accounting information, (3) elements of financial statements, and (4) recognition and measurement in financial statements.

The objectives of financial reporting provide an overall purpose for financial reports. The purpose of financial reports is to provide information useful to current and potential investors, creditors, and other users in making decisions. Financial reports should help these decision makers assess the amounts, timing, and uncertainty of prospective cash flows to the decision makers and to business organizations. Financial reports should also provide information about resources, claims to resources, and changes in resources for business organizations.

Qualitative characteristics are attributes that make accounting information useful. The characteristics of information are described as a hierarchy, with understandability and usefulness for decision making being the most important, as depicted in Exhibit 7-4:

Exhibit 7-4   Qualitative Characteristics of Accounting Information

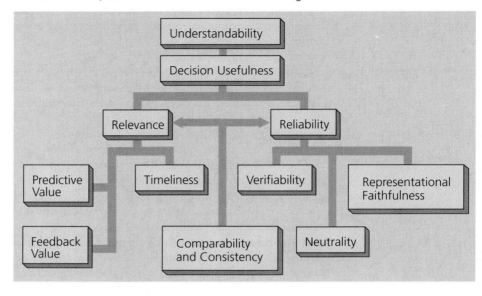

Adapted from Statement of Financial Accounting Concepts No. 2, Qualitative Characteristics of Accounting Information, FASB, May 1980.

Relevance and reliability are considered to be the two primary qualities that result in accounting information's being useful. Relevant information should be timely and have predictive or feedback value. Reliable information should faithfully represent economic events and should be verifiable and neutral. Information about an organization is more valuable when it can be compared with information from other organizations and when it is prepared using consistent methods over time.

Elements of financial statements provide definitions of the primary classes of items contained in financial statements. Elements include assets, liabilities, equity, investments by owners, distributions to owners, revenues, expenses, gains, and losses.

Recognition and measurement criteria identify information that should be contained in financial statements. The primary financial statements are described in the conceptual framework, along with the items that should be contained in each statement. To be included in the financial statements, an item should meet the definition of an element of a financial statement. Also, it should be relevant to decision makers and measurable with sufficient reliability to be useful. Revenues should be recognized when earned—that is, when an organization has substantially accomplished what it must do to be entitled to the benefits from the revenues. Expenses are recognized when an organization's resources are consumed in revenue-generating activities.

When the FASB is deciding on new accounting standards, it refers to the conceptual framework for guidance. The guidance helps the FASB resolve new and emerging accounting problems. If standards are consistent with the framework, they are likely to be consistent among themselves. Therefore, preparers and users of financial accounting information should find a logical pattern to the information. The framework should help them better understand the content and limitations of financial reports.

SELF-STUDY PROBLEM 7-3

Descriptions are provided below for organizations that have had an effect on the accounting profession. Identify the name of each organization.

1. Creates auditing standards in the U.S.
2. Creates accounting standards in the U.S. for businesses and certain other organizations.
3. Enforces compliance with accounting standards for most corporations.
4. Enhances professional behavior for internal auditors.
5. Enhances professional behavior for public accountants.
6. Creates local and state governmental accounting standards.
7. Advises the federal government on the creation of accounting standards for federal agencies.
8. Attempts to develop uniformity in accounting standards among different nations.
9. Enhances professional behavior for management accountants.

The solution to Self-Study Problem 7-3 appears at the end of the chapter.

REVIEW *Summary of Important Concepts*

1. The accounting profession:
   a. The accounting profession includes those who have developed a high level of knowledge of accounting through education and experience. The profession includes management accountants, public accountants, governmental and non-profit accountants, and accounting educators.
   b. Management accountants provide services as employees of businesses and other organizations, including information systems development, financial accounting management, financial reporting, financial planning and analysis, cost management and control, and internal auditing.
   c. Public accountants provide services to businesses, governmental and nonprofit organizations, and individuals. These services include auditing, compilation and review of financial statements, tax advice, and consulting.
   d. An audit report summarizes the audit process and expresses the auditor's opinion about an organization's financial statements.
   e. Governmental and nonprofit accountants provide management accounting services to these organizations. In addition, they are concerned with tax assessment and compliance.
   f. Accounting educators create and disseminate accounting knowledge.

2. The historical development of accounting:
   a. Contemporary accounting has developed from the needs of individuals and organizations to maintain systematic records of their resources and transactions. Accounting is as old as written history.
   b. Contemporary accounting can be traced to the accounting methods developed in Europe at the beginning of the Renaissance.

c. The Industrial Revolution increased the need for accountants to help manage corporations.

d. The growing trade in corporate stocks led to increased professionalism and regulation of corporate accounting and reporting in the early 1900s.

e. Income taxation led to increased federal involvement with accounting procedures, which were the basis for calculation of taxable income.

f. The collapse of the stock market in 1929 led to legislation that created the SEC and led to federal regulation of corporate financial accounting.

3. The development of accounting standards:

a. Accounting standards are set in the U.S. primarily by private organizations. Corporate and nonprofit organization (except for governmental) standards are established by the Financial Accounting Standards Board. State and local governmental standards are established by the Governmental Accounting Standards Board.

b. Accounting standards are important in our society as a basis for contracting, for assuring reliability of financial information, for controlling the cost of reporting and maintaining equity among investors, for determining fair business practices and economic analysis, and as a basis for litigation.

c. Accounting standards are established through a lengthy due process that provides opportunity for all concerned parties to express their opinions about an accounting issue. The process involves issuing a discussion memorandum, written responses and public hearings, issuing an exposure draft, further responses and hearings, and issuing a standard. Standards may be reviewed, revised, or replaced at any time.

d. A conceptual framework provides guidance for the FASB in establishing accounting standards.

DEFINE *Terms and Concepts Defined in This Chapter*

accounting standard	cost accounting	internal control
attestation	cost management	materiality
audit committee	discussion memorandum	proxy
audit opinion	exposure draft	proxy statement
audit report	Form 10-K reports	review
compilation	generally accepted auditing	
conceptual framework	standards (GAAS)	

SOLUTIONS

SELF-STUDY PROBLEM 7-1

1. Accounting systems may be developed by management accountants or by public accountants. Larger corporations generally employ their own staffs for this purpose. Public accountants may assist these staffs or may provide services for organizations that do not have their own staffs.

2. Internal auditors, who are management accountants, evaluate company policies to ensure they are being implemented.

3. Public accountants prepare tax returns, though one does not have to be a CPA to provide this service. Some companies employ their own tax staffs.

4. Governmental accountants are responsible for tax compliance.

5. Accounting educators are primarily responsible for the development of new accounting knowledge.

6. Public accountants provide independent audit services.

7. Management accountants and public accountants help managers interpret financial information.

8. Management accountants are primarily responsible for cost accounting. Public accountants may consult with managers about cost management.

9. Educators prepare students for entry into the accounting profession.

10. Public accountants provide financial planning advice.

SELF-STUDY PROBLEM 7-2

Three major events include:

1. The **Industrial Revolution** produced large organizations that required access to large amounts of capital. As a means of obtaining this capital, corporations were formed. Because corporations generally result in a separation of owners from managers, a need for reliable reporting of financial activities by managers to owners and other external parties arose. This information is necessary for enforcing contracts among the parties. In addition, the size and complexity of corporations create a need for accounting systems to assist managers in planning and control decisions.

2. **Income taxation** of corporations increased governmental involvement with corporate accounting practices. These practices became the basis for determining taxable income. Standard practices were needed to determine reliably the amount of taxable income and to maintain equity among corporations so each organization was taxed fairly.

3. The collapse of the stock market in 1929 created a demand for **governmental regulation of corporate securities markets**. Regulation of accounting practices was a major part of the resulting legislation of 1933 and 1934. The federal government formed the SEC to oversee corporate accounting and financial reporting procedures and to enforce compliance with accounting standards. The SEC relied on the accounting profession to form organizations for the establishment of accounting standards. The SEC also required corporations to issue audited annual financial reports. The securities laws made corporate managers and their auditors subject to litigation for providing false or misleading accounting information. Increased growth and complexity of the security markets and corporations have resulted in greater regulation of accounting information reported to external parties. Accounting standard-setting organizations, such as the FASB, have created GAAP to control

the reporting of accounting information and to help maintain user confidence in this information.

SELF-STUDY PROBLEM 7-3

1. Auditing Standards Board (ASB)

2. Financial Accounting Standards Board (FASB)

3. Securities and Exchange Commission (SEC)

4. Institute of Internal Auditors (IIA)

5. American Institute of Certified Public Accountants (AICPA)

6. Governmental Accounting Standards Board (GASB)

7. Federal Accounting Standards Advisory Board (FASAB)

8. International Accounting Standards Committee (IASC)

9. Institute of Management Accountants (IMA)

EXERCISES

7-1.   Write a short definition for each of the terms listed in the *Terms and Concepts Defined in This Chapter* section.

7-2.   Self-regulation is an important attribute of a profession like accounting. What is the purpose of self-regulation? Describe some of the self-regulation procedures of the accounting profession.

7-3.   Management accountants are responsible for those activities in an organization necessary for ensuring that accounting information is available to information users when it is needed. What are some activities of management accountants necessary for completing these responsibilities?

7-4.   Sigfreid Fromm is a recent graduate in accounting. She has taken a position with Hand Writer Co. The company has three divisions that manufacture three products: pencils, pens, and colored markers. Financial information for the most recent fiscal period for each division includes:

Division	Pencils	Pens	Markers
Divisional revenues	$200,000	$ 300,000	$100,000
Divisional expenses	140,000	260,000	60,000
Divisional assets	600,000	1,000,000	200,000

One of Sigfreid's regular duties is to prepare an analysis of the performance of each division. Prepare an analysis of divisional performance from the information provided that

Sigfreid might provide to her supervisor. Which of the divisions appears to be most profitable? How is this responsibility typical of the tasks often performed by management accountants?

7-5. What is the purpose of internal auditing? Why is it important to an organization? Why is internal auditing an accounting responsibility?

7-6. List and briefly describe the primary internal control procedures discussed in the chapter.

7-7. Identify each of the following and explain how it relates to the professional practice of accounting in the U.S.:
a. CPA
b. CMA
c. CIA
d. AICPA
e. IMA
f. IIA
g. State Board of Public Accountancy

7-8. How does the public practice of auditing differ from internal auditing? What services are provided by external auditors?

7-9. Identify each of the sections of an audit report and explain its purpose.

7-10. Meese, Neese, and Reese is a CPA firm. The following situations arose in the firm's audits of several clients:
a. Bagdad Co. was determined to have used an accounting procedure for recording inventory that was inconsistent with generally accepted accounting principles. The CPA firm determined the procedure did not result in a material misstatement but believed the procedure should be revealed to financial statement users.
b. Stockholm Co. prepared its financial statements using accounting procedures that were inconsistent with generally accepted accounting principles. The CPA firm determined the procedures resulted in a material misstatement of financial position and operating results.
c. Bejing Co. prepared financial statements in conformity with generally accepted accounting principles. These statements revealed a loss during the fiscal year.
d. Nairobi Co. prepared financial statements but did not have sufficient accounting records to verify the accuracy of the statements.
What type of audit opinion would the CPA firm issue for each of these situations? How should users interpret the financial statements in response to the opinions?

7-11. Occasionally, financial reports are issued that contain misstatements. Managers sometimes engage in fraudulent behavior that is not uncovered by the company's auditors. As a result, the auditors issue an unqualified opinion on the misstated financial statements. Auditors often are blamed in these circumstances for failing to discover the fraud and report it to stockholders. What are the responsibilities of auditors for disclosing misstatements and revealing fraud?

7-12. Bill Flamingo owns a small pet store. He has applied for a loan from a local bank to expand his business. The bank has asked Bill to provide financial statements for the business that have been reviewed by a CPA. Bill relies on a local CPA firm to maintain his accounting records and to prepare his financial statements. He is unsure about what the bank is requesting for the business. He asks his CPA for guidance. Does the bank want audited financial statements? He is concerned that an audit would be too expensive for

the size of his business and for the amount he wants to borrow. Assume you are Bill's
CPA. Write a short memo to Bill explaining the difference between an audit and a compilation and review.

7-13. Many of the responsibilities of accountants in businesses are similar to those in governmental and nonprofit organizations. What are some of the major responsibilities of accountants in governments that do not exist for accountants in businesses?

7-14. A close friend knows you are taking an accounting class. The friend tells you he has
thought about majoring in accounting but doesn't know what kind of preparation he
needs for an accounting career. He asks you to describe the preparation he will need.
What can you tell him?

7-15. Why can it be said that accounting is as old as recorded history? Why is it not surprising
that modern accounting developed in Italy during the early Renaissance?

7-16. Three major developments in the history of accounting involved the Industrial Revolution, the 16th amendment to the U.S. Constitution, and the events subsequent to the
stock market crash of 1929. Explain briefly the significance of each of these events for
contemporary accounting.

7-17. Identify the major reporting requirements associated with each of the following:
a.   Securities Act of 1933
b.   Securities and Exchange Act of 1934
c.   10-K report
d.   10-Q report
e.   Proxy statement

7-18. Identify each of the following:
a.   The private sector organization currently responsible for setting financial accounting standards in the U.S.
b.   The private sector organization currently responsible for setting state and local governmental accounting standards in the U.S.
c.   The organization currently responsible for setting auditing standards in the U.S.
d.   The organization that exists to influence the development of international accounting standards.
e.   The private sector organization responsible for setting financial accounting standards
in the U.S. from 1959 to 1973.
f.   The organization responsible for helping with the establishment of accounting standards for federal government agencies.
g.   The organization responsible for the enforcement of financial accounting standards
in the U.S.

7-19. How would you react to the following statement? "Accounting standards impose costs
on corporations and their managers to protect the interests of investors."

7-20. What is meant by the term "generally accepted accounting principles"? What is the significance of the phrase "generally accepted"?

7-21. What is the purpose of the qualitative characteristics of financial reports? What are the
primary qualitative characteristics as defined by the FASB?

7-22. What is the primary objective of financial reporting according to the FASB?

PROBLEMS

PROBLEM 7-1   Describing the Accounting Profession

The high school from which you graduated is sponsoring a career day to inform students about career opportunities in various disciplines. You have been asked to participate in a panel discussion on professional careers that will be part of the career day. Your task is to present a 10-minute overview of the accounting profession and career opportunities in accounting.

Required   Prepare a detailed topic outline for your presentation that includes the issues you believe would be most important for your discussion. Consider how you might make the topic interesting and informative for a high school audience.

PROBLEM 7-2   Evaluating Internal Control

The Spring Valley Church is a small congregation with about 50 members. The church is financed by member donations. Most of these donations are collected during the Sunday morning service. Many of the donations are in cash. Other donations are by checks made payable to the church. Harvey Plump has served as treasurer for the church since becoming a member a few years ago. The church accepted Harvey's offer to serve as treasurer as an indication of his interest in being active in the church. Harvey listed several previous experiences with financial matters on his resumé as qualifying him for the position.

Once donations are collected each week, Harvey takes the money to the church office, where he counts it. He makes out a deposit slip and deposits the money in the church's account at a local bank. He records the deposit in the church's check register. He writes checks to pay the church's expenses. In some cases, he writes small checks to himself as reimbursement for incidental expenses he pays for the church. He opens bank statements received by the church each month and reconciles them with the church's check register. Harvey prepares a monthly statement of cash received and disbursed that is distributed to members of the congregation.

The church always seems to be lacking sufficient financial resources. A recent meeting was held to discuss expansion of the church's building, but current finances seem to make expansion impossible. Some members don't understand why the church's financial condition appears to be so bleak, since they believe they are making large donations.

The church has asked you, as a local accountant, to help them evaluate their financial situation.

Required   Evaluate the internal control problems of the Spring Valley Church. What explanation can be provided for the church's financial problems? How might you confirm your explanation?

PROBLEM 7-3   Evaluating Internal Control Procedures

Consider each of the following situations:

a.   Sales clerks in a retail store are assigned to a specific cash register. They are given a cash drawer containing $100 in change at the beginning of their shifts. They are required to enter the amount of each purchase on the cash register. The cash register records an identification and price for each item purchased. Cash payments are collected from customers and placed in the cash drawer. A copy of the cash register sales slip is given to the customer. At the end of each shift, the employee takes the cash drawer and cash register tape to a supervisor who counts the cash, verifies the sales, and signs an approval form. The sales clerk also signs the form that identifies the amount of cash and amount of sales for the day.

b.   A ticket seller at a movie theater is issued a cash drawer with $100 in change and a roll of prenumbered tickets when the theater opens each day. The seller collects cash from customers and issues the tickets. Each customer hands a ticket to a ticket taker who tears the ticket in half and gives half back to the customer. At the end of the day, the ticket seller returns the cash drawer and tickets to a supervisor.

Required   For each situation, discuss why the procedures are used and how they provide effective internal control.

PROBLEM 7-4   Understanding the Audit Report

A standard audit report contains reference to each of the following:

a.   Responsibility

b.   Generally accepted auditing standards

c.   Material misstatement and material respects

d.   A test basis

e.   Present fairly . . . in conformity with generally accepted accounting principles

Required   Explain why each of these terms is important for understanding the audit report and audit process.

PROBLEM 7-5   Public Accounting Services

Mirna McKenzie owns and manages several apartment complexes near a local college. She has maintained her own accounting records, but her business has grown past the point she feels competent to do her own accounting. Your CPA firm is near her apartments. You received a letter the other day from Mirna asking for a description of the kinds of services you could provide her business.

Required   Write a letter to Mirna describing the services of your firm. Assume you provide a full range of public accounting services. Her address is: Mirna McKenzie, McKenzie Apartments, 2200 Placid Place, Your Town.

PROBLEM 7-6   Ethical Issues in Public Accounting

A series of independent situations involving accountants in public practice is described below:

a.   Martin Hooper, CPA, accepted an engagement to provide a financial audit of Bremer Co. Hooper owns 15% of the stock Bremer has issued.

b.   Andrea Doria, CPA, accepted an engagement to provide an audit for First State Bank. She has never audited a bank and has no specific training in bank audits.

c. Zeeman Kline, CPA, audited Klasp Co. and issued an unqualified opinion on its financial statements. During the audit, he discovered a major discrepancy between certain assets reported on the financial statements and those owned by the company. He discussed the matter with the company president and was assured the accounts would be corrected next year.

d. Florence Nightingale, CPA, audited Community Hospital. She did not have time to complete all of the audit work prior to the time an audit report was needed by the hospital's board of directors. She decided to issue an unqualified report to meet the board's deadline and then complete the audit work. She felt sure she would not find any audit problems.

Required For each situation, explain why the CPA's actions violated ethical standards for external audits.

PROBLEM 7-7 The Importance of Financial Accounting Standards

Accounting and financial reporting to external decision makers is highly regulated in the U.S. Standards specify the types of information to be reported and how accounting numbers are to be calculated. Listed below are groups who benefit from these standards:

a. managers

b. stockholders

c. creditors

d. governmental authorities

e. auditors

f. employees

Required Explain why financial accounting standards are important to each of these groups.

PROBLEM 7-8 Setting Accounting Standards

Accounting standards are set in the U.S. in the private sector. Public hearings and written comments provide feedback during development of the standards. Opportunity is provided to those affected by standards to contribute information to standard-setting organizations such as the FASB.

Required Draw a diagram describing the major steps in the standard-setting process. Explain the purpose of each of the primary documents that results from the process.

PROBLEM 7-9 Ethical Issues in Auditing

Larry Clint is the president of Hometown Bank. The bank has several thousand depositors and makes loans to many local businesses and homeowners. Blanche Granite is a partner with a CPA firm hired to audit Hometown Bank. The financial statements the bank proposes to issue for the 1996 fiscal year include the following information:

Loans receivable	$4,000,000
Total assets	5,000,000
Net income	1,000,000

During the audit, Blanche discovers that many of the loans were made for real estate development. Because of economic problems in the region, much of this real estate remains unsold or vacant. The current market value of the property is considerably less than its cost. Several of the developers are experiencing financial problems, and it appears unlikely that the bank will recover its loans if they default. Blanche described this problem to Larry and proposed a write-down of the receivables to $2,800,000. The $1,200,000 write-down would be written off against earnings for 1996.

Larry is extremely upset by the proposal. He notes the write-off would result in a reported loss for the bank for 1996. Also, the bank would be in jeopardy of falling below the equity requirements imposed by the bank regulatory board to which the bank is accountable. He fears the board would impose major constraints on the bank's operations. Also, he fears depositors would lose confidence in the bank and withdraw their money, further compounding the bank's financial problems. He cites several economic forecasts indicating an impending improvement in the region's economy. Further, he notes the bank's demise would be a major economic blow to the local economy and could precipitate the bankruptcy of some of the bank's major customers.

Blanche acknowledges that Larry is correct in his perceptions of the possible outcomes of the write-off. Larry proposes an alternative to Blanche. The bank will write down the receivables by $300,000 for 1996. The remaining losses will be recognized over the next three years, assuming property values have not improved. Larry also tells Blanche that if she is unwilling to accept his proposal, he will fire her firm and hire new auditors. The bank has been a long-time client for Blanche's firm and is one of its major revenue producers. Blanche also recognizes Larry's proposal is not consistent with accounting principles.

Required What are the ethical problems faced by Blanche? What action would you recommend she take?

PROBLEM 7-10 The Purpose of the Conceptual Framework

The Financial Accounting Standards Board developed a conceptual framework to provide guidance in the development of financial accounting standards.

Required Discuss the primary components of the conceptual framework for business organizations and explain the purpose of each component.

PROBLEM 7-11 Evaluating the Quality of Financial Reports

The following statements describe the annual report issued by Short Sheet Co. for the fiscal year ended December 31, 1997:

a.   The report was issued on October 1, 1998.

b.   Income included management's estimates of the increased value of certain fixed assets during 1997.

c.   Procedures used to calculate revenues and expenses were different for 1997 than for 1996 and earlier years.

d. Procedures used by Short to calculate its net income differ from those used by the rest of its industry.

e. Short's financial statements were audited by an accounting firm owned by the president's brother.

f. Some of the company's major liabilities were not included in the annual report.

Required For each statement, identify the qualitative characteristic that has been compromised and explain the effect on report users.

PROBLEM 7-12 Multiple-Choice Overview of the Chapter

1. Which of the following is not a characteristic of a profession?
    a. a high level of knowledge and skills
    b. self-regulation
    c. government regulation of fees
    d. acceptance by society of qualifications to provide services

2. Management accountants may provide all of the following services except:
    a. financial reporting.
    b. financial planning and analysis.
    c. financial accounting management.
    d. financial auditing.

3. An organization's plan and the procedures used to safeguard assets ensure accurate information, promote efficiency, and encourage adherence to policies is its:
    a. internal control system.
    b. cost accounting system.
    c. financial accounting system.
    d. management information system.

4. An audit report of an independent accountant:
    a. is addressed to a company's managers.
    b. must contain only three paragraphs.
    c. is dated at the balance sheet date of the audited financial statements.
    d. identifies the responsibilities of the auditor.

5. Members of a corporation's board of directors responsible for working with the independent auditor are:
    a. the internal control committee.
    b. the audit committee.
    c. the management compensation committee.
    d. the management supervision committee.

6. Procedures used by an auditor in conducting an audit that form a basis for the auditor's opinion are:
    a. generally accepted auditing standards.
    b. generally accepted auditing principles.
    c. generally accepted accounting principles.
    d. generally accepted accounting standards.

7. A major development in the history of accounting was:
    a.   the Method of Venice.
    b.   the 13th amendment to the U.S. Constitution.
    c.   the management revolution.
    d.   the Securities Act of 1932.

8. A 10-K report is:
    a.   a quarterly financial report for the SEC.
    b.   a registration for a new stock issue with the SEC.
    c.   an annual financial report for the SEC.
    d.   a report of change in auditors for the SEC.

9. Financial accounting standards for businesses currently are established in the U.S. primarily by the:
    a.   Federal Accounting Standards Board.
    b.   Financial Accounting Standards Board.
    c.   Securities and Exchange Commission.
    d.   Accounting Principles Board.

10. All of the following are qualitative characteristics of financial reporting except:
    a.   relevance.
    b.   reliability.
    c.   representational faithfulness.
    d.   conservatism.

C A S E S

CASE 7-1 Examining a Statement of Financial Accounting Standards

Locate a copy of the FASB's Statement of Financial Accounting Standards No. 107 in your library.

Required   Review the statement and write a short report in which you identify each of the following:

a.   the topic covered by and the purpose of the statement

b.   the date the statement was issued

c.   the effect of statement requirements on financial statements

d.   the effect of statement requirements on financial disclosures

e.   the effective date of the statement

f.   the vote of the FASB members

g.   topics covered by appendices to the statement

CASE 7-2 Examining an Audit Report

Examine the auditor's report and the report of the audit committee provided as part of the annual report of Nike, Inc. in Appendix B of this book and answer the following questions:

a. Who was Nike's external auditor? What date did the auditor complete its audit work?

b. What was the auditor's responsibility with respect to the company's financial statements? What was the responsibility of management?

c. What are generally accepted auditing standards? Why are they important in an audit?

d. What kind of opinion did Nike's auditors issue? Why is this opinion important to the company?

e. What is an audit committee? How does the company's audit committee benefit its stockholders?

PROJECTS

PROJECT 7-1 Audits and Audit Reports

Obtain the most recent annual report available for each of three corporations from your library. Find the auditor's report in each annual report, usually just before or just after the financial statements; make a photocopy of each one; and label it with the company's name. Read and compare the three audit reports. What similarities do you find? What differences? Write a memorandum to your instructor reporting your findings. Attach the photocopies of the audit reports to your memo.

PROJECT 7-2 Interviewing an Accountant

Make an appointment with an accountant at a CPA firm, a business organization, or a governmental or nonprofit organization. Ask the accountant to describe his or her primary responsibilities and what kinds of activities occur during a regular business day. Ask the accountant to identify the primary skills and training needed for his or her position. Write a memorandum to your instructor reporting the results of your interview. Identify the person interviewed and the date of the interview.

PROJECT 7-3 Requirements of an Accounting Major

Review the requirements for a major in accounting at your college or university or at a university where you may be planning to complete your undergraduate degree. Identify the prerequisites and admission requirements for the accounting program, the course requirements for the major (including accounting, business, and nonbusiness courses), and other degree requirements. Determine if the program offers a fifth year or graduate degree program and the requirements of the program. Write a short report in which you describe the degree requirements.

PROJECT 7-4   **The Development of an Accounting Standard**

Locate a copy of the FASB's *Statements of Financial Accounting Standards* in your library. Select one of these standards and review the appendix on "Background Information." Make a copy of this section. Draw a diagram that illustrates the steps that occurred prior to the issuance of the statement. For each step, identify the event and the date it occurred. Attach the copy of the statement section to the diagram.

PROJECT 7-5   **Examining an Audit Failure**

Use an index, such as the *Business Periodicals Index* or *Accounting and Tax Index*, to identify a recent article that describes an example of an actual or a suspected audit failure. Make a copy of the article. Write a memo to your instructor identifying the event and the reasons cited in the article for the audit failure. Attach the copy of the article to the memo.

Section
II

Analysis and Interpretation of Financial Accounting Information

Chapter
8

Determining Value

CHAPTER

Overview

The second section of this book examines specific accounting issues related to operating, investing, and financing activities. These issues are important for interpreting accounting information that can be used to analyze companies' activities that affect their values. Throughout this section, we will consider the association between accounting information and company value. Therefore, it is important to have a conceptual model of value.

This chapter presents a value model. The model provides a basis for identifying attributes of companies that are important to their values. Also, it helps to identify relationships among attributes. These relationships link various attributes together to demonstrate how they affect value.

Major topics covered in this chapter include:

- Factors about investments that affect their values.
- The relationships among these factors in the valuation model.
- Applying the valuation model to various types of investments.
- Problems with determining valuation factors.
- Computing interest expense and interest revenue using the valuation model.

CHAPTER

Objectives

Once you have completed this chapter, you should be able to:

1. Identify the types of investment attributes that affect investment values.
2. Explain the value model for single-period investments.
3. Explain the value model for multiple-period investments.
4. Calculate the value of a series of expected cash flows.
5. Explain how risk affects the value of expected cash flows.
6. Apply the value model to calculate bond prices.
7. Apply the value model to calculate loan amounts and payments.
8. Apply the value model to investments in plant assets.
9. Apply the value model to a company-purchase decision.
10. Apply the value model to stock prices.
11. Explain why the value model can be difficult to apply to some investment decisions.
12. Distinguish between expected and realized returns.
13. Calculate interest expense and interest revenue for loans involving equal payments.
14. Calculate interest expense and interest revenue for loans involving unequal payments.

FACTORS AFFECTING VALUE

Objective 1
Identify the types of investment attributes that affect investment values.

The price of Nike, Inc.'s stock was approximately $60 per share at the beginning of October 1994. At this time, the price of The Limited, Inc.'s stock was approximately $20 per share. The prices of both companies' stocks had declined over the past several days. Why do stocks of various companies sell for different amounts? Why do these prices change over time? Obviously, these are important questions to investors. The valuation process that investors use to establish prices in markets often is quite complex. Many factors are considered by investors in arriving at the amounts they are willing to pay for an investment. Nevertheless, the concept of value is extremely important. One of the fundamental reasons that companies provide financial accounting information is to assist investors in valuing the companies' securities. In addition, managers, creditors, suppliers, and other decision makers are constantly making decisions about the values of assets and/or investments. Therefore, it is important to understand the fundamental concept of value as it applies to all types of investments.

Learning Note   The term "investment" is generally a reference to an asset. Investments in stocks, bonds, or equipment are all assets of the investor. At the same time, bonds and other loans are liabilities of the borrower, and stocks are equities of the issuer. The same principles of value apply whether one is concerned with value from the asset side or from the liability or equity side. Value to the investor or buyer is also value to the issuer or seller.

What are the basic attributes of an asset that affect its value? Consider the following decisions. Suppose you could invest the same amount in either of two assets, A or B. Investment A promises to pay $100 at the end of one year. Investment B promises to pay $200 at the end of one year. Assuming both payments are equally probable, which investment is more valuable? Investment B is more valuable because the expected return to the investor is higher. Thus, it is apparent that a major factor that affects the value of an asset is the amount of expected return to the investor. **If other attributes of assets are the same, assets that pay higher returns are more valuable than those that pay lower returns.**

Now, suppose you could invest the same amount in either of two assets, C or D. Both investments promise to pay $100. However, investment C promises to pay $100 at the end of six months, while investment D promises to pay $100 at the end of one year. If both payments are equally probable, investment C is more valuable. As an investor, you should prefer to receive a return sooner rather than later. You could use the $100 from investment C to make purchases six months before you could make these purchases with the $100 from investment D. Alternatively, you could reinvest the $100 from investment C and earn an additional return for six months. This additional return would not be available if you invested in D. Thus, another factor that affects the value of an asset is the timing of returns to the investor. **If other attributes of assets are the same, assets that pay returns sooner are more valuable than those that pay later.**

Consider one other factor of major importance. Suppose you could invest the same amount in either of two assets, E or F. Both promise to pay $100 at the end of one year. Investment E guarantees the payment with certainty. Investment F will pay $100 if some event occurs (e.g., the issuer has sufficient cash to make the payment) but does not guarantee the payment with certainty. Investment E would be more valuable than investment F because it is less risky. You can count on receiving $100 from E, but you might not receive $100 from F. Thus, another factor that affects the value of an asset is its risk. **If other attributes of assets are the same, less risky assets are more valuable than riskier assets.**

In summary, three primary attributes of investments affect their values as illustrated in Exhibit 8-1. These three are the amounts investors expect to receive, the time the amounts are expected, and the risk (or uncertainty) associated with the amounts.

Exhibit 8-1   Attributes of Investments That Affect Their Values

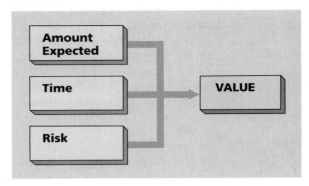

COMBINING AMOUNT, TIME, AND RISK TO DETERMINE VALUE

In reality, investments seldom can be compared in the way A and B, C and D, and E and F were compared in the preceding section. Instead, assets differ as to amount, timing, and risk. Thus, all three factors must be considered simultaneously in comparing asset values.

Value and Rate of Return for One Period

Objective 2
Explain the value model for single-period investments.

This task is not as complicated as it might seem at first. For example, assume that you invest $1,000 in a savings account with a bank. The bank pays 5% annual interest on the account. What will be the value of the investment at the end of one year? What will be the return on investment for one year? The total value of the investment will be the amount invested plus the return:

Value (end of year 1) = Value (beginning of year 1) + Return (for year 1)

The return for year 1 is the value of the investment at the beginning of the year times the rate of return on the investment:

Return (for year 1) = Value (beginning of year 1) × Rate of Return (for the year)

Learning Note   Rate of return for a period is the ratio of the amount of return for a period to the value of an investment at the beginning of the period. Thus, if the return for a year is $50 and the value at the beginning of the year is $1,000, the rate of return is 0.05 or 5% ($50/$1,000).

Thus, we can rewrite the equation of the value at the end of year 1:

Value (end) = Value (beginning) + [Value (beginning) × Rate of Return], or
Value (end) = Value (beginning) × [1 + Rate of Return]

To demonstrate, we can substitute the amounts from the savings account example into the equations:

Return (for year 1) = Value (beginning of year 1) × Rate of Return (for the year)
$50   = $1,000   ×   0.05

Value (end of year 1) = Value (beginning of year 1) + Return (for year 1)
$1,050   = $1,000   + $50

Value (end) = Value (beginning) + [Value (beginning) × Rate of Return], or
$1,050   = $1,000   +   [$1,000 × 0.05]

Value (end) = Value (beginning) × [1 + Rate of Return]
$1,050   = $1,000   ×   1.05

Thus, in general terms, we can express the value of an investment in terms of the amount of return expected from the investment and the time of the return:

Value (end) = Value (beginning) × [1 + Rate of Return]

If we abbreviate the terms by substituting FV for future value (value at end), PV for present value (value at beginning), and R (for rate of return), we can simplify the equation:

$FV = PV \times (1 + R)$

If we rearrange terms by dividing through by $(1 + R)$, we can state the present value of an investment in terms of its future value:

$PV = FV/(1 + R)$

To verify this present value computation, note that:

$1,000 = $1,050/(1.05)

Thus, we can state the value of an investment in terms of its expected future value and the rate of return expected from the investment.

The terms "present value" and "future value" are used frequently in reference to assets and liabilities. **The *present value* of an investment or liability is the amount it is worth or the amount owed at the beginning of a time period. The *future value* is the amount it is worth or the amount owed at some time in the future.**

Compounding Returns for More than One Period

Objective 3
Explain the value model for multiple-period investments.

Often investments extend beyond one period. For example, instead of receiving the return ($50) on the savings account at the end of the first year, suppose you reinvest the return in the account. How much will your investment be worth at the end of the second year if it continues to earn 5% interest? The amount of the investment at the beginning of the second year is the value of the investment at the end of the first year as calculated above: $1,050. Therefore, the value of the investment at the end of the second year is:

Value (end of year 2) = Value (end of year 1) × [1 + Rate of Return]
       $1,102.50   = $1,050   ×   1.05

The return for the second year is larger than for the first year because the return for year 2 was earned on the amount of the original investment plus the return earned in year 1 that was reinvested:

Amount invested	$1,000	⟶	$1,000.00
Earned in year 1	($1,000 × 0.05)	⟶	50.00
Earned in year 2	($1,050 × 0.05)	⟶	52.50
Value (end of year 2)		⟶	$1,102.50

This process of earning a return on a return from a prior period is known as **compounding**. The value of the investment at the end of year 2 is the value at the beginning of year 1 plus the return for years 1 and 2. We can express the investment value at the end of year 2 as:

$$FV = PV \times (1 + R)^t$$

where t represents the time over which an investment has been compounded. For example:

$$\$1,102.50 = \$1,000 \times (1.05)^2$$

And, we can express the present value of an investment as:

$$PV = FV/(1 + R)^t$$

This present value equation is important because it is a general statement about the value of any investment. **The value today of an investment (its present value or PV) is the amount the investor expects to receive in the future (the future value or FV of the investment) divided by 1 plus the rate of return (1 + R) raised to a power representing the time (t) until the return is received.**

The value of t can be any time period (e.g., a month, quarter, or year). The value of R must be for the same time period as t, however. Thus, if t is a year, R must be expressed as an annual rate. If t is a month, R must be expressed as a monthly rate. For example, if R is 12% when t is a year, R would be 1% when t is a month. R is sometimes referred to as the **discount rate** of the investment. The future value of the investment is discounted (reduced) back to its present value by dividing through by the discount rate.

Learning Note   Rates of return are normally expressed as annualized amounts. If the rate is for some period other than a year, the period always should be indicated.

Computing the Present Value of a Series of Expected Cash Flows

Objective 4
Calculate the value of a series of expected cash flows.

The present value formula is applicable to any type of investment. To illustrate, assume that you can purchase an investment that will pay you $100 per year at the end of each of the next three years. The rate of return for the investment is 8%. How much should you pay for the investment? This question asks you to determine the present value of the amounts you expect in the future. In this example and in many investments, the future value (FV) is a series of amounts that the investor expects to receive in the future. We can represent these amounts as future cash receipts (C) in the present value equation, and the answer can be calculated as follows:

$$PV = [C/(1 + R)^1] + [C/(1 + R)^2] + [C/(1 + R)^3]$$
$$PV = [\$100/(1.08)^1] + [\$100/(1.08)^2] + [\$100/(1.08)^3]$$

The amount you expect to receive in the future is $100 at the end of each of the next three years. Thus, the future value of the investment consists of three different amounts. The amount received at the end of year 1 is discounted for one year. The amount received at the end of year 2 is discounted for two years because it will not be received until the end of the second year. The amount received at the end of three years is discounted for three years. By computing each amount in brackets, we can determine that the investment value is:

$$PV = \$92.59 + \$85.73 + \$79.38 = \$257.70$$

If you pay $257.70 for the investment and receive a return of $100 each year for three years, you will earn an 8% rate of return on the investment. These calculations are illustrated in Exhibit 8-2. Each of the future expected amounts is discounted to its present value by the appropriate interest factor.

Exhibit 8-2   Discounting Expected Cash Flows to Their Present Value

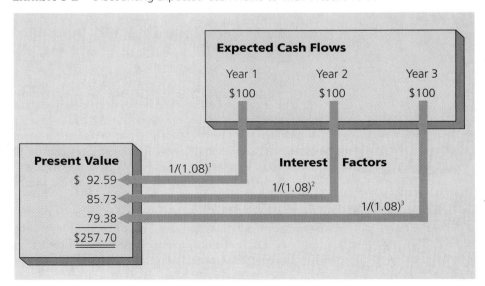

To include amounts received at different times, the present value equation can be written as:

$$PV = \Sigma\,[C/(1 + R)^t]$$

where Σ is a symbol representing summation. In words, the equation says: **The present value of an investment is the sum of the future amounts of cash expected from the investment, each divided by 1 plus the rate of return raised to a power denoting the time that the amount will be received.**

Risk in the Present Value Equation

Objective 5
Explain how risk affects the value of expected cash flows.

The present value equation considers the amount received from an investment and the time in which the amount is received. Recall that these are two of three primary factors that affect asset value. The third factor is risk. How does the present value factor incorporate risk?

Risk is represented by the rate of return. As the risk of an investment increases, the rate of return increases. Riskier investments must offer a higher rate of return to investors. Otherwise, investors will select low–risk investments. The higher rate of return is the price of risk. It is a premium the seller of the investment must pay to induce buyers to accept the risk. For example, assume that investors can purchase either of two investments, A or B. Both promise to pay $100 at the end of one year, but B is riskier than A. Investment A pays a 5% rate of return. To compensate investors for the higher risk, investment B must pay more than 5%. If B pays 7%, the price (present value) of the two investments would be:

PV (Investment A) = $100/1.05 = $95.24
PV (Investment B) = $100/1.07 = $93.46

Learning Note

The discount rate 1.05 for one period is the same as $(1.05)^1$. Therefore, the exponent (1 in this example) usually is left off the equation when only one period is involved. Recall from math that the rule of exponents is: $X^0 = 1$, $X^1 = X$, $X^2 = (X)(X)$, $X^3 = (X)(X)(X)$, and so forth, where X is any real number.

The exact relationship between risk and the rate of return is difficult to specify because it changes over time. The rate of return depends on the general level of interest rates at any time plus a premium for the amount of risk in an investment. The general level of interest rates can be thought of as the rate of return that an investment would pay if it were riskless. Thus, the rate of return (R) is the sum of the risk-free rate (R_f) and a risk premium (R_p) that is higher for riskier investments: $R = R_f + R_p$.

The general level of interest rates changes depending on investors' expectations about inflation and the level of interest set by the Federal Reserve Board, in the U. S. The Federal Reserve Board establishes the rate that banks pay for funds they borrow. This rate affects the rate banks charge to borrowers and thus affects interest rates throughout the economy. An approximation of the risk-free rate (R_f) can be obtained by observing the interest rate on short-term federal government securities, called treasury notes. The rate of return on these investments increases as the general level of interest rates increases. Treasury notes are almost riskless because the federal government is very unlikely to default on the payment of these notes. It can always print money to make payments if it does not have enough cash. Most other investments are riskier than treasury notes and pay higher rates of interest. (Some state and local government securities are tax exempt and pay lower rates of return than some U.S. government securities because of the tax advantage, not because of lower risk.) Savings accounts, short-term certificates of deposit (CDs), and similar investments are very low risk. Therefore, the rates of return for these investments are about the same as that of treasury notes. Corporate securities are riskier than government securities and savings accounts. Corporations must generate cash, normally from operating activities, to pay returns on their securities. Companies that do not generate sufficient cash may be unable to pay interest or principal on their debt or to pay returns to investors in their stocks.

Value Attributes and the Present Value Equation

The present value equation includes all three factors that affect the value of an asset: the amount of the return, the time that the return is received, and risk. These factors are illustrated in Exhibit 8-3. The arrows indicate the direction of change in each factor that would result in an increase in value. An increase in the amount of the return increases value. An increase in rate of return (risk) or of time decreases value.

Exhibit 8-3   Factors Affecting the Value of an Investment

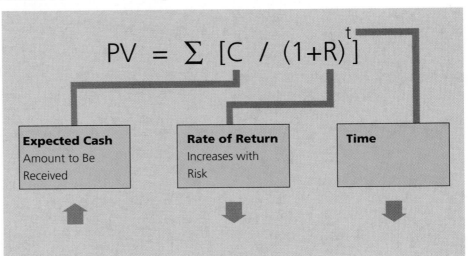

$$PV = \Sigma\ [C\ /\ (1+R)^t]$$

Expected Cash	Rate of Return	Time
Amount to Be Received	Increases with Risk	

The price of an asset does not necessarily increase (or decrease) just because the expected cash flow increases (or decreases). An increase (or decrease) in the rate of return accompanying the increase (or decrease) in cash flow can offset the cash flow effect. For example, earnings (and expected cash flows) for many companies decreased during the early 1990s during an economic recession. Stock prices increased, however, during this period. The increase was caused by a dramatic decrease in rates of return as the Federal Reserve reduced interest rates to stimulate the economy. The lower interest rates reduced the rate of return (R) at the same time that expected cash flows (C) were decreasing. The denominator (R) effect more than offset the numerator (C) effect and prices increased. After the recession, the Federal Reserve raised interest rates to reduce inflationary pressures. At the same time, earnings (and expected cash flows) for many companies were increasing. The rising interest rates offset the increases in cash flows, however, and stock prices remained relatively stable during late 1993 and 1994.

Varying the Amount of Cash Receipts

The amount of cash expected from an investment does not have to be the same each period in the present value equation. The value of C can vary from period to period. To illustrate, assume that you can acquire an investment that will pay you $300 at the end of the first year, $400 at the end of the second year, and $500 at the end of the third year. How much should you pay for this investment if you require a 10% rate of return? We can substitute values in the equation as follows:

$$PV = \$300/(1.10)^1 + \$400/(1.10)^2 + \$500/(1.10)^3 = \$978.97$$

Thus, you would pay $978.97 for an investment that would return $1,200 ($300 + $400 + $500) over three years. The amount you expect to earn on the investment, $221.03 ($1,200 − $978.97), provides you with a 10% annual return for the three years.

SELF-STUDY PROBLEM 8-1

Required
Determine the present value of each of the following:

a. An investment pays $1,000 to be received at the end of two years. The rate of return expected by investors is 8%.
b. An investment pays $500 per year at the end of each of the next two years. The rate of return expected by investors is 8%.
c. An investment pays $600 at the end of one year and another $400 at the end of two years. The rate of return expected by investors is 8%.

The solution to Self-Study Problem 8-1 appears at the end of the chapter.

APPLICATIONS OF THE PRESENT VALUE EQUATION

The present value equation applies to any investment. Various types of investments are described below to illustrate applications of the equation.

Bonds

Objective 6
Apply the value model to calculate bond prices.

A bond is a debt security issued by a government or corporation. The security is a contract that permits an organization to borrow money. In return, the organization promises to pay a return each period for a specified time. At the end of this time, the organization promises to repay the amount it borrowed. Bonds usually are issued in denominations of $1,000. Thus, at its maturity (repayment) date, each bond pays $1,000. This repayment is in addition to interest paid on the bonds over their lives. For example, assume that Debt Co. needs to borrow $3 million to purchase new equipment. It will issue $1,000 bonds that will pay a return of $70 in interest each year for three years. At the end of three years, each bond will pay $1,000. How much would investors pay for the bonds if they require a rate of return of 8% to compensate them for the risk of the investment?

To solve the problem, first consider the information provided by answering the questions: What amounts do investors expect to receive from the investment? When will the amounts be received? What is the rate of return required by investors?

The amounts investors expect to receive and the times received are:

Time	Amount
End of year 1	$ 70
End of year 2	70
End of year 3	70
End of year 3	1,000

The amount received in year 3 includes the interest payment of $70 plus the maturity value of the bond of $1,000. The rate of return is 8%. Therefore, we can substitute these values into the present value equation:

$$PV = \Sigma\, C/(1 + R)^t$$
$$PV = [\$70/1.08^1] + [\$70/1.08^2] + [\$70/1.08^3] + [\$1,000/1.08^3] = \$974.23$$

Thus, we should expect each bond to sell for $974.23. To obtain $3 million of financing, Debt Co. would need to issue approximately 3,080 bonds ($3,000,000/$974.23). The calculation of the bond price is illustrated in Exhibit 8–4.

Using Tables to Compute Present Values. The calculation of present values can be cumbersome if long periods are involved. Various computer programs and calculators include functions for calculating present values. For example, spreadsheet programs, such as Lotus and Excel, permit calculations of this type. Tables, such as those in the inside front and back covers of this book, also can be

Exhibit 8-4 Discounting Expected Cash Flows to Their Present Value

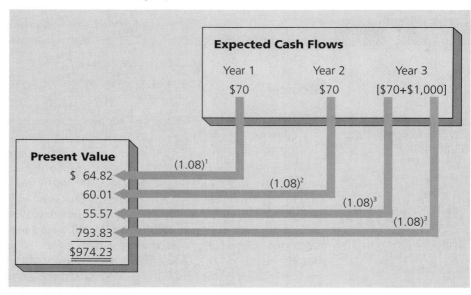

used for this purpose. These tables contain values that one would obtain from calculating interest factors used in the present value equation.

For example, to determine the value of $1/1.08^2$ from Table 1 (inside front cover), find the cell corresponding to the 8% column and the row for two periods. This value is 0.85734. To determine the present value of $70 to be received in two years at an 8% return, multiply $70 times 0.85734. This amount is the same as dividing $70 by 1.08^2:

$$PV = (\$70/1.08^2) = [\$70 \times (1/1.08^2)] = (\$70 \times 0.85734) = \$60.01$$

Values for years 1 and 3 can be obtained from Table 1 in the same manner. Thus, the present value of the bond could be calculated as:

$$PV = (\$70 \times 0.92593) + (\$70 \times 0.85734) + (\$70 \times 0.79383) + (\$1,000 \times 0.79383)$$
$$= \$974.23$$

This calculation is still rather cumbersome. A shorter method can be used for this equation because the interest payments each year are the same amounts. The next section describes this method.

Annuities. When a series of equal payments is made at regular intervals, the payments are known as an annuity. **An** *annuity* **is a series of equal payments over a specified number of equal time periods.** Thus, the $70 paid each year for three years is an annuity. Financial calculators and certain computer programs can calculate the values of annuities. Table 2 (inside back cover) provides annuity values. To calculate the present value of an annuity of three years at 8%, find the cell corresponding to the 8% column and the three–period row. The value is 2.57710. Thus, the present value of $70 per year for three years at 8% is:

PV = $70 × 2.57710 = $180.40

The present value of the bond, therefore, is the sum of the present value of the interest payments (using Table 2) and the present value of the maturity value of the bond (using Table 1):

PV = ($70 × 2.57710) + ($1,000 × 0.79383) = $974.23

These calculations are the same as those illustrated in Exhibit 8-4.

Observe that investors in Debt Co.'s bonds receive a return of $235.77 over the three years. They pay $974.23 for each bond and receive $210 ($70 × 3) in interest plus $1,000 of maturity value. Thus, their net return is $1,210 − $974.23 = $235.77. This net cash flow paid over the three years provides the investors with an 8% return.

The amount of return paid on the bonds each period ($70 in the Debt Co. example) identifies the coupon rate of the bond. **The** *coupon rate* **determines the amount of interest paid each period on a bond or other investment. Another name for coupon rate is** *stated rate*. For Debt Co., coupon rate was 7% ($70/$1,000). The interest paid was 7% of the maturity value of the bond and therefore was $70 per year. The coupon rate often differs from the market rate of return for bonds and other investments. **The** *market rate* **is the rate of return investors expect to earn from an investment. Other names for market rate are** *effective rate* **and** *yield to maturity*. Investors required a market rate of 8% on Debt Co.'s bonds. To obtain this market rate, they bought Debt Co.'s bonds at a **discount** (less than maturity value). They paid $974.23 for bonds that matured at a value of $1,000. This difference between what investors paid and what they received at maturity was part of their return and increased their total return from the 7% coupon rate on the bonds to the market rate of 8%.

Bonds and other investments also may sell at a **premium** (a price greater than maturity value). For example, assume Premium Co. issues bonds that mature in three years and pay a 10% coupon ($100 interest per year on a $1,000 bond). Because of risk that investors expect on the bonds and because of the current level of interest rates, investors require only an 8% return on Premium Co.'s bonds. How much will investors pay for the bonds?

The amounts investors expect to receive from the bonds would be:

Time	Amount
End of year 1	$ 100
End of year 2	100
End of year 3	100
End of year 3	1,000

Therefore, the price (or present value) of each bond would be:

$$PV = \$100/(1.08)^1 + \$100/(1.08)^2 + \$100/(1.08)^3 + \$1,000/(1.08)^3$$

The price is the sum of the future expected cash flows, discounted at the market rate of 8% over the three-year period. To calculate the price, we can use Table 1 and Table 2. The $100 interest payments are an annuity for three periods. From Table 2, the interest factor for an annuity discounted at 8% over three periods is 2.57710. The maturity value is a single amount received at the end of three periods. From Table 1, the interest factor for a single amount discounted at 8% and received at the end of three periods is 0.79383. Thus, the price of each bond would be:

$$PV = (\$100 \times 2.57710) + (\$1,000 \times 0.79383) = \$1,051.54$$

These calculations are illustrated in Exhibit 8–5.

Exhibit 8-5   Including Annuities in the Present Value Equation for Bonds

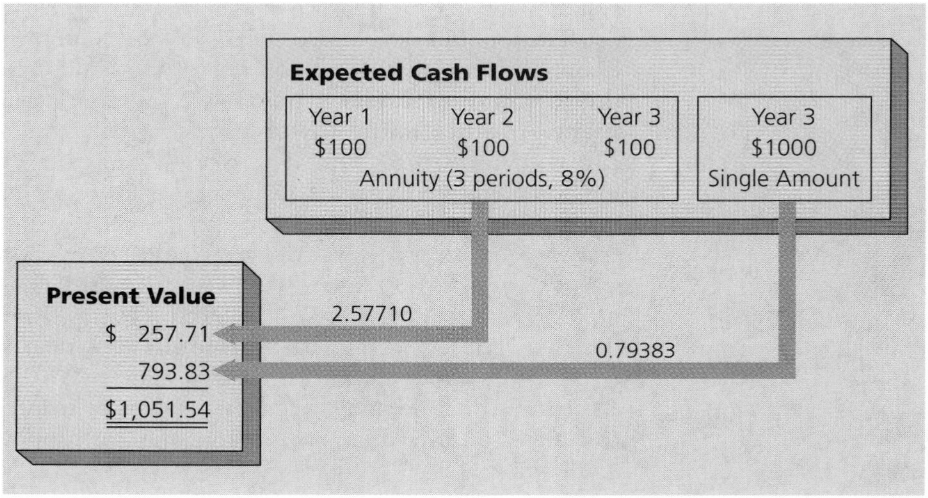

Expected Cash Flows

Year 1	Year 2	Year 3	Year 3
$100	$100	$100	$1000
	Annuity (3 periods, 8%)		Single Amount

Present Value

2.57710

0.79383

$ 257.71
793.83
$1,051.54

The bonds sell at a premium of $51.54 over maturity value. The net return to investors over the three-year investment is: $300 of interest + $1,000 maturity value − $1,051.54 paid for the bond = $248.46. This amount provides investors with an 8% annual return over the three years.

Bank Loans

Financing arrangements may work in a variety of ways. Bonds provide cash to the issuer of the bonds (the borrower), who then pays interest over the life of the bonds and repays the amount borrowed (the principal) at maturity. Other types of loans may provide for both interest and principal to be repaid at specific dates over the life of the loan. Arrangements with banks often are of this type.

For example, assume Debt Co. borrows an amount from a bank to be repaid in two years. The bank requires a return of 8% on the loan. Debt Co. will pay the bank $100,000 for principal and interest each quarter (every three months). How much money will Debt Co. receive from this loan?

The amounts the bank expects to receive from the loan would be:

Year	Quarter	Amount
Year 1	End of 1	$100,000
Year 1	End of 2	100,000
Year 1	End of 3	100,000
Year 1	End of 4	100,000
Year 2	End of 1	100,000
Year 2	End of 2	100,000
Year 2	End of 3	100,000
Year 2	End of 4	100,000

Therefore, the amount of the loan is the present value of an annuity of $100,000 over eight periods at 2% per period (8%/4 quarters per year):

$$PV = \$100,000/(1.02)^1 + \$100,000/(1.02)^2 + \ldots + \$100,000/(1.02)^8$$

We can solve the equation by using the interest factor for an annuity of eight periods at 2% per period from Table 2 = 7.32548. Thus,

$$PV = \$100,000 \times 7.32548 = \$732,548$$

Debt Co. would receive $732,548 from the loan. The bank would receive eight payments of $100,000. The interest earned over the eight quarters [$67,452 = ($800,000 − $732,548)] would provide the bank with an 8% rate of return.

Another, and perhaps more common, use of the present value equation for bank loans is to determine the amount of the payments to be made each period. For example, suppose that you want to purchase a new stereo that retails for $500. You can finance the purchase over 12 months at 12% (1% per month). In this example, you know how much money you need to invest in the stereo ($500). Also, you know the rate of return required by the lender (12%). The question to be decided is: How much will you pay each month on the loan? The amount of the payment is an annuity of 1% per period for 12 periods. We need to solve for the amount of C (cash payment) in the equation:

$$PV = \Sigma\, [C/(1 + R)^t]$$

Table 2 provides the interest factor for an annuity of 12 periods at 1% = 11.25508. Therefore,

$$\$500 = C \times 11.25508$$
$$C = \$500/11.25508 = \$44.42$$

Your monthly payments would be $44.42. The lender would receive $533 ($44.42 × 12 months). The $33 of interest would provide the lender with a return of 12% over the 12-month period.

Learning Note

$33 ÷ $500 does not equal 12% because the lender did not loan the full $500 for the 12 months. Each month a part of the payment received reduced the principal (the amount of the loan still outstanding). Therefore, over the 12 months the amount loaned gradually decreased from the initial $500 to $0.

Investments in Plant Assets

Objective 8
Apply the value model to investments in plant assets.

The present value equation can be applied to evaluating investment decisions for a variety of assets. For example, assume Jurassic Co. is considering whether to purchase some new equipment. If the purchase is made, the company expects to be able to produce 100,000 more units of its product each year than if the equipment is not purchased. It expects to be able to sell these units for a total of $1 million each year. The total annual costs associated with these additional units, excluding the cost of the equipment, is $750,000. The equipment is expected to last five years. Jurassic requires a 12% rate of return on its investment. What is the maximum amount the company should pay for the equipment? This question is another way of asking: what is the price (present value) of the company's investment? The net amount the company expects to receive each year is $250,000 ($1,000,000 − $750,000). It expects to receive this amount for five years. The interest factor for an annuity of five periods at 12% is 3.60478 from Table 2. Therefore, we can solve for the present value:

$$\text{PV} = \$250,000 \times 3.60478 = \$901,195$$

If Jurassic pays no more than $901,195 for the equipment, it can expect to earn at least a 12% return on its investment. Thus, if the cost of the equipment is $900,000, Jurassic should make the purchase. If the cost is $902,000, it should not, based on the information provided. (Other factors may be relevant to the decision that are not provided in this example.)

Purchasing a Company

Objective 9
Apply the value model to a company-purchase decision.

The present value equation can be used in decisions about whether to purchase a company. To illustrate, assume that you have a friend, Fresca, who is about to graduate from college. While in college, Fresca started a small snack shop near campus. She wants to sell the shop to you for $90,000, and you are considering purchasing it (with a loan from a local bank). You examine the financial statements for the company for the last four years and find that the store generated approximately $200,000 of cash inflow each year. Average total payments of $185,000 were made each year to cover the total costs of the shop. If you make the purchase, you plan to operate the shop for three years. At the end of this period you expect to be able to sell it for $60,000. You require a return of 11% on your investment. Should you purchase the shop? This question asks you to determine whether the present value of the expected cash flows is greater than the amount you would pay for the shop. To answer the question, you need to calculate the present value of the future amounts you expect to receive. Your net cash inflows each year would be:

Year	Amount
1	$15,000 ($200,000 − $185,000)
2	15,000
3	15,000
3	60,000

As in the bond example, we can separate these amounts into two parts. The $15,000 each year for three years is an annuity. From Table 2, the interest factor for an annuity for three periods at 11% is 2.44371. The interest factor for a single amount at the end of three periods at 11% is 0.73119 from Table 1. Therefore,

PV = ($15,000 × 2.44371) + ($60,000 × 0.73119) = $80,527

The maximum amount you should be willing to pay for the business is $80,527 if you are to earn a return of 11%. If you pay $90,000 for the shop, as Fresca has asked, you will earn less than 11%.

Stock Prices

Objective 10
Apply the value model to stock prices.

The present value equation also applies to investments in corporate stocks. To illustrate, suppose that Stable Corp. reported earnings per share of $3 for its most recent fiscal year. Assume that the earnings are a good estimate of the amounts investors will receive from their investments (either as dividends or higher stock prices) and that you require a return of 10% on your investment. What amount would you pay for Stable Corp.'s stock? This decision is similar to those we have examined earlier. We can estimate the amount to be received each period, and we know the discount rate. However, stocks do not have a fixed life. As long as the company continues to operate successfully, it could remain in business. Thus, the number of future amounts investors can receive is unlimited.

We could approach this problem in several ways. One approach would be to calculate the present value over a long period of time, say 25 years, and assume that we have accounted for most of the relevant amounts. From Table 2, we find that the interest factor for an annuity of 25 periods at 10% is 9.07704. Therefore,

PV = $3 × 9.07704 = $27.23

Consequently, you would expect to pay about $27.23 for each share of stock.

Another approach is to assume that the stock has an infinite life. Mathematically, the present value equation reaches a maximum value when an infinite life is assumed. This maximum value can be represented as:

$$PV = C/R$$

where C is the amount expected each period and R is the required rate of return. If we use this method:

PV = $3/0.10 = $30

Thus, the maximum price of the stock, if we assume an infinite life and a required return of 10%, is $30.

Exhibit 8-6 illustrates the price computation. As the number of periods included in the life of the stock increases, the price increases. A maximum value is reached, however, at the price represented by C/R.

Exhibit 8-6   Calculating Stock Price from the Present Value Equation

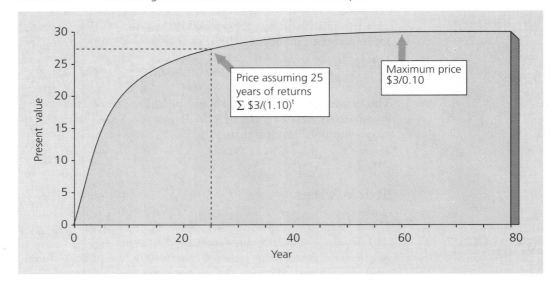

It is unlikely that a company's earnings will remain constant over time. In most cases, we should assume that earnings will grow. Suppose we expect the earnings of Growth Co. to grow at a rate of approximately 4% per year. What should the price of the stock be? Again, we could calculate the amounts we expect to receive for some long period and discount these values at 10%. This process would be quite tedious on a calculator. Using a spreadsheet, the task is not difficult, however. The amount we expect to receive each year is the amount from the previous year times 1.04. If we calculate this amount for each of 25 years, compute the present value for each year by dividing through by $(1 + R)^t$, and then sum the amounts, we obtain a price for the stock of $39.20. This price is sensitive to the number of periods included in the computation, however, because earnings are growing each year. If we make the same calculation for 50 years, the price is $48.85.

Another approach is to again assume an infinite life. The present value equation can be expressed as follows if we assume an infinite life and a constant growth rate:

PV = C / (R − G)

where G is the rate of growth. Thus, the price of the stock can be calculated as:

PV = $3/(0.10 − 0.04) = $50

This is the maximum price for the stock, assuming an infinite life, a constant growth rate of 4%, and a required return of 10%.

DETERMINING VALUE ATTRIBUTES

The present value equation provides an approach to estimating the values of investments. The approach is relatively straightforward. Financial calculators and

Objective 11
Explain why the value model
can be difficult to apply to
some investment decisions.

computers make the mathematical computations fairly simple. The real challenge in valuation is in determining the amounts that should be included in the equation. In some cases, these amounts are known. For example, if you purchase a corporate bond, you know how much interest you should receive each period (from the coupon rate) and the maturity value of the bond (usually $1,000). Once bonds are sold, you can determine the rate of return investors expect to earn (known as the yield to maturity). If you borrow money from a bank, you know the interest rate, the amount borrowed, and the amount of your payments.

In other situations, the amounts associated with the present value (or price) of an investment are not known. They must be estimated, and the estimation can be complex. Stock prices are an example. In the case described above, we assumed that earnings were a reliable measure of the amount investors expected to receive. In reality, earnings are only a general estimate of this amount. Investors must determine whether they believe that reported earnings are a reliable estimate. The growth rate also must be estimated. Finally, the rate of return must be estimated based on the amount of risk investors expect. Thus, the amount of risk must be estimated. There is no simple approach to determining these estimates.

Exhibit 8-7 demonstrates, however, that a relation exists between stock prices (per share of stock), earnings per share, and the variability of earnings (as a measure of risk). In this graph, stock price is measured on the horizontal (X) axis. Earnings per share (an accounting return measure) and variability of earnings (an accounting risk measure) are measured on the vertical (Y) axis. Data are shown for 1,520 major corporations for which information was available from 1983 to 1992. These companies were grouped into 20 portfolios after ranking the companies by their average stock prices. Values for each portfolio are represented in the exhibit by dots. Average earnings per share over the 10-year period are used for the return measure. The standard deviation of each company's returns over the 10-year period was used as a risk measure. The exhibit reports the average standard deviation for the companies in each portfolio. Standard deviation is a measure of the distribution of a variable. A higher standard deviation indicates a broader distribution and, therefore, more variability or risk. Appendix A of this chapter describes the calculation of standard deviation. You may wish to review the appendix if you are not familiar with this measure.

Observe from the company data that price increases as earnings increase and increases as the variability (standard deviation) of earnings decreases. These results are consistent with the present value formula: $PV = C/R$. We have substituted stock price for PV, earnings per share for C, and standard deviation of earnings for R.

Accounting information is provided to help investors make decisions about future returns and risk. Throughout the remainder of this book, we will examine how accounting information is used for these purposes. We will consider how accounting for operating, investing, and financing activities provides information for evaluating companies' risks and returns.

Expected and Realized Returns

The present value equation is based on investors' expectations about amounts they will receive in the future. Actual results often differ from expectations. If an investor purchases a corporation's common stock and the company's earnings

Exhibit 8-7   The Relation Between Stock Price, Earnings, and Earnings Variability

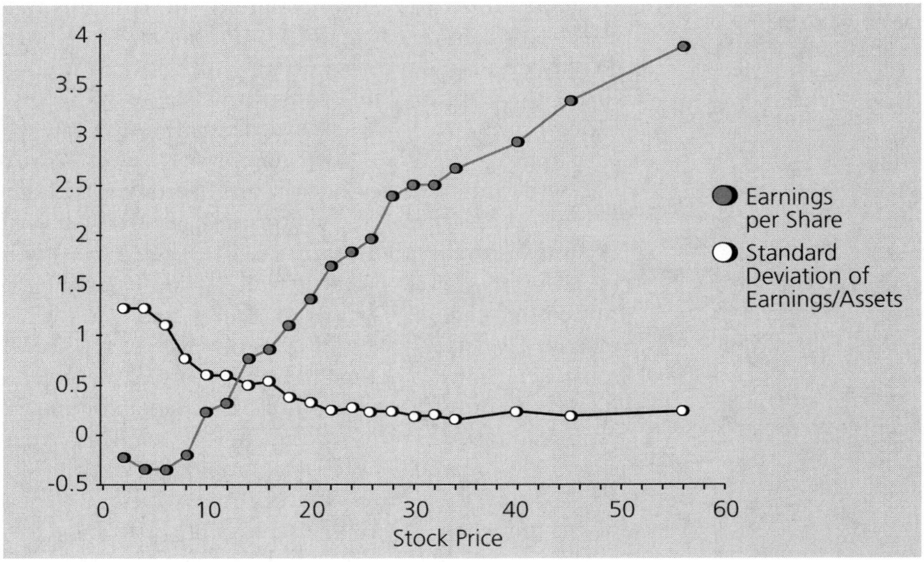

Source: 1993 COMPUSTAT Annual Industrial File. The standard deviation is multiplied by 10 to better fit the scale of the graph.

and cash generated from operations are below expectations, the stock's subsequent price and dividend payments may be less than expected. Consequently, the return to investors may be less than expected. Even investors in bonds may receive lower than expected returns. If a corporation's earnings and cash flows are very low, a company may be unable to make payments on its debt. Under these circumstances, investors in bonds and other creditors may receive lower than expected returns, or payments to creditors may be later than expected.

Present values are formed from expectations. Future performance determines whether or not expectations are met. As the risk of an investment becomes greater, the probability that actual results will differ from expectations increases. Risk can be thought of as representing a distribution of possible returns. As the distribution becomes larger, the probability of actual returns differing from expected returns increases as illustrated in Exhibit 8-8.

The exhibit illustrates returns for two types of investments, a low-risk investment and a high-risk investment. The probability distributions identify the range of possible returns. A low-risk investment has a relatively narrow range of returns, compared with a high-risk investment. Reasons for these differences in the range of returns will be discussed in remaining chapters of this book. The expected return for each investment can be approximated by the mean (average) return from the distribution. Observe that actual results may be better or worse than expectation for the investments illustrated in Exhibit 8-7.

Why Realized Returns Differ from Expectations

Realized results may differ from expectations either because investors did not properly consider all relevant information or because attributes of the investment

Exhibit 8-8   Risk as Measured by the Distribution of Returns

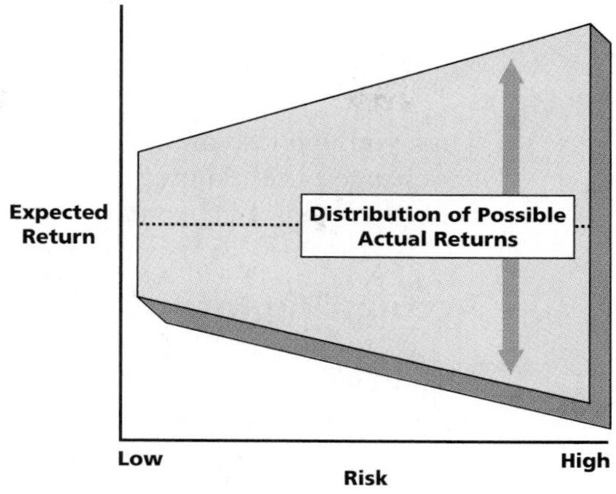

changed. Suppose you invest in the stock of Profit Co. You expect earnings of $4 per share to continue to grow at a rate of 5%, and you require a 12% return on your investment. Therefore, you estimate the value of the stock as follows:

$$PV = C/(R - G) = \$4/(0.12 - 0.05) = \$57.14$$

However, suppose that in your decision you failed to consider that Profit Co. recently lost a contract with a major supplier and competition from other companies has increased, reducing the company's sales. After investing, you discover that a more accurate measure of earnings would be about $3.50 per share and that growth will probably be only about 4%. Thus, the value of the stock is estimated as:

$$PV = \$3.50 / (0.12 - 0.04) = \$43.75$$

If you paid a higher price for the stock, you would lose money on your investment if the stock price dropped because of information about future earnings and earnings growth that you did not consider in your decision.

Also, consider how the value of an investment is affected by changes in attributes of the investment. Suppose you purchase the 20-year bonds of Debt Co. The bonds pay $100 interest each year. You purchased the bonds to yield a return of 8%. At the time of your purchase, the interest rate on treasury notes was 5%, indicating an expectation of low inflation. The amount you would expect to pay for each bond would be the sum of an annuity of 20 periods at 8% and a single payment at the end of 20 periods at 8%:

$$PV = (\$100 \times 9.81815) + (\$1,000 \times 0.21455) = \$1,196.37$$

Four years after you purchase the bonds, you want to sell them because you need money for a down payment on a house. At this time, the interest rate on treasury notes has increased to 8% because inflation is expected to be higher than it was four years earlier. Investors in Debt Co. bonds now require a return of 11% on the company's bonds. The amount you should expect to receive for each bond is the sum of an annuity of 16 periods at 11% plus a single amount at the end of 16 periods at 11%:

PV = ($100 × 7.37916) + ($1,000 × 0.18829) = $926.21

Thus, you will lose money on your investment, because the level of interest rates has changed the required return on the bonds. If the level of interest rates decreased instead of increasing, you would earn a profit from selling the bonds.

Accounting Information and Expectations

Keep in mind that expectations are not guarantees. Expectations may be wrong and frequently are. It is important for investors to form the best expectations they can. Investors should consider information about an investment in forming their expectations. Also, investors should expect to have access to as much information as other investors. If all investors have access to the same amount of reliable information, the investment process should be fair. Everyone should have the same opportunity to earn profits from their investments.

A major purpose of financial accounting information is to ensure that investors have sufficient, reliable information to make informed decisions. Another major purpose is to make sure that investors have access to the same information so that those with better or more information cannot take advantage of those with poorer or less information. It is up to investors, then, to make the best decisions they can with this information.

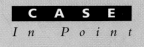

Investor response to information depends on their expectations. For example, General Motors' stock lost almost 15% of its value in October of 1994 even though the company announced an increase in quarterly earnings. The amount of the increase was less than expected by investors at a time when other companies were reporting earnings greater than expected. Therefore, investors revised downward their expectations about General Motors' future performance, leading to a decrease in the company's stock price. Investors also were concerned about the future performance of the company because of continued negative publicity about the safety of light trucks built by GM during the 1980s.

SELF-STUDY PROBLEM 8-2

Required

Determine the price of each of the following assuming a required rate of return of 10%:

a. A 10-year bond paying $1,000 at maturity and $80 per year interest.
b. A 10-year bond paying $1,000 at maturity and $120 per year interest.
c. The stock of a company that reported earnings per share of $2 and whose earnings are expected to grow at a rate of 3% per year. Assume that earnings are a good estimate of expected cash flows to investors.

The solution to Self-Study Problem 8-2 appears at the end of the chapter.

INTEREST EXPENSE AND REVENUE

The amount of interest expense (from the borrower's or issuer's perspective) or interest revenue (from the investor's perspective) associated with an investment is determined from the present value formula. How the formula is applied depends on the type of payments. Many loans require that principal and interest be repaid over the life of the loan in equal installments. If you purchase a car or house, you make monthly payments that include both interest and principal. Other types of loans, particularly many bonds, pay only interest over the life of the loan. Principal is repaid only at maturity. We consider each of these situations in the sections that follow.

Equal Installments

Objective 13
Calculate interest expense and interest revenue for loans involving equal payments.

Assume that Debt Co. borrows $1 million from a bank at 9% at the beginning of 1997. Principal and interest will be repaid in three equal annual installments beginning December 31, 1997. How much interest expense should Debt Co. report each year? How much interest revenue should the bank report each year?

To answer these questions, we first must determine the amount of the payments on the debt by solving for C (cash amount) in the present value equation:

$$PV = \Sigma \, C / (1 + R)^t$$
$$\$1,000,000 = \Sigma \, C / (1.09)^3$$

The interest factor for an annuity of three periods at 9% (from Table 2) is 2.53129. Therefore:

$$\$1,000,000 = C \times 2.53129$$
$$C = \$1,000,000 / 2.53129 = \$395,055$$

Thus, the amount of payment, including principal and interest, will be $395,055 each year. The amount of interest for the first year is the interest rate (discount rate) times the amount (present value) of the loan at the beginning of the first year: $1,000,000 × 0.09 = $90,000. Therefore, the amount of principal repaid at the end of the first year will be $305,055 ($395,055 − $90,000). Of the total payment of $395,055, $90,000 is for interest and $305,055 is for principal (repayment of the amount borrowed).

At the beginning of the second year, Debt Co. will owe the bank $694,945 ($1,000,000 − $305,055). **The present value of a loan is the amount of liability a borrower has for the loan.** For Debt Co. at the beginning of year 2, this liability is the amount borrowed less the amount of principal repaid in the first year. Interest for year 2 will be the amount still owed times 9%: $694,945 × 0.09 = $62,545. The amount of principal repaid at the end of the second year will be $332,510 ($395,055 − $62,545). This is the amount of total payment made in year 2 ($395,055) less the amount of interest ($62,545).

At the beginning of the third year, Debt Co. will owe the bank $362,435 ($1,000,000 − $305,055 − $332,510). This is the amount borrowed less the amount of principal repaid in the first and second years. Interest for year 3 will be the amount still owed times 9%: $362,435 × 0.09 = $32,620. The amount of principal repaid at the end of the third year will be $362,435 ($395,055 − $32,620). This is the amount of total payment made in year 3 ($395,055) less the amount of interest ($32,620).

As a result, the total principal repaid over the three years is $1,000,000 ($305,055 + $332,510 + $362,435). The total amount of interest over the three years is $185,165 ($90,000 + $62,545 + $32,620). These amounts can be summarized in a table as shown in Exhibit 8-9. This type of table is known as an **amortization table**. It indicates the amount owed each year, the amount paid, the amount of interest, and the amount of principal repaid.

Exhibit 8-9 Amortization Table for Repayment of Note and Interest

A	B	C	D	E	F
			(B × 0.09)	(C − D)	(B − E)
	Beginning	Total	Interest	Principal	Ending
Time	Present Value	Payment	Expense	Repaid	Present Value
Year 1	$1,000,000	$395,055	$ 90,000	$ 305,055	$694,945
Year 2	694,945	395,055	62,545	332,510	362,435
Year 3	362,435	395,055	32,620	362,435	0
Total			$185,165	$1,000,000	

To answer the questions about interest expense and revenue, we simply read from the table. The amount of interest expense reported by Debt Co. for the first year would be $90,000. This also would be the amount of interest revenue reported by the bank. The table also indicates the amount of liability reported by the company at the end of each year, the present value at the end of the year (column F).

Unequal Installments (Bonds)

Objective 14
Calculate interest expense and interest revenue for loans involving unequal payments.

Suppose that Debt Co. issued bonds rather than borrowing from the bank. Assume the three-year bonds had a coupon rate of 7% but investors required a 9% return, as with the note to the bank. How much interest expense would Debt Co. record each year?

In this example, the first step is to determine the present value of the bonds because this information is not provided in the description. The amount investors would receive each year would be the coupon rate (7%) times the maturity value of the bonds ($1,000 for each bond). Therefore, for each bond, the amounts received would be:

Time	Amount
End of year 1	$ 70
End of year 2	70
End of year 3	70
End of year 3	1,000

The repayment is not in equal installments. Interest is paid in three equal amounts, but principal is repaid as a single amount at the end of year 3. The present value of each bond would be the sum of an annuity of three periods at 9% plus a single amount at the end of three years at 9%:

$$PV = (\$70 \times 2.53129) + (\$1,000 \times 0.77218) = \$949.37$$

Observe that the required rate of return (also called the market rate of return) is used as the discount rate. The coupon rate determines the amount of interest paid each period.

Assume Debt Co. issues 1,000 bonds at $949.37 per bond. The present value of the bonds at the beginning of year 1 will be $949,370 (1,000 × $949.37). This present value is the amount of liability associated with the bonds. Thus, at the beginning of year 1, Debt Co. would report a liability for its bonds of $949,370. The amount of interest paid in year 1 will be $70,000 ($70 × 1,000). The amount of interest expense on the bonds in the first year will be $85,443 ($949,370 × 0.09). This is the present value of the bonds at the beginning of year 1 times the discount rate of 9%. Exhibit 8-10 illustrates the payments in an amortization table.

Exhibit 8-10   Amortization Table for Bond Payments

A	B	C	D	E	F
			(B × 0.09)	(C − D)	(B − E)
	Beginning	Total	Interest	Principal	Ending
Time	Present Value	Payment	Expense	(Accumulation)	Present Value
Year 1	$949,370	$ 70,000	$85,443	− $15,443	$ 964,813
Year 2	964,813	70,000	86,833	− 16,833	981,646
Year 3	981,646	70,000	88,354*	− 18,354	1,000,000
Year 3		1,000,000			0

The $6 difference between $88,354 and $88,348 ($981,646 x 0.09) is due to rounding.

The payment of bonds differs from the payment of the note in several respects. First, the bonds are not repaid in equal installments. Instead, the principal (maturity value of $1,000,000) is all repaid at the end of the third year. When bonds are sold at a discount, the amount of interest expense (column D) is greater than the amount of interest paid (column C) each year. The difference between the amount of expense and the amount paid increases the principal of the bonds each year (column E). In year 1, for example, $964,813 = $949,370 − (−$15,443). Thus, the principal is accumulating (increasing) each period until it reaches the maturity value of the bonds ($1,000,000) that will be repaid at the end of year 3. The present value at the end of each year is the amount of Debt Co.'s liability at that date. Thus, the amortization table provides calculations of both the interest expense and liability a company would report on its financial statements.

If the coupon rate on Debt Co.'s bonds had been greater than the market return, the bonds would have sold for more than $1,000 each. When bonds are sold at a premium, the amount of interest expense recognized each period is less than the amount of interest paid, and the amount of principal decreases each period. This process is illustrated in Self-Study Problem 3.

SELF-STUDY PROBLEM 8-3

Debt Co. issued 1,000, $1,000 bonds at the beginning of 1996. The bonds pay 11% interest annually and mature at the end of 1998. Investors require a 9% return.

Required

Determine the amount of interest expense Debt Co. would report each year.

The solution to Self-Study Problem 8-3 appears at the end of the chapter.

R E V I E W   *Summary of Important Concepts*

1. Three primary factors affect the value of an asset or investment:
    a.   The amount investors expect to receive from the investment.
    b.   The time the amount is to be received.
    c.   The rate of return used to discount the investment; the rate reflects the investment's risk.
    d.   These factors are combined in the present value formula. This formula computes the present value (PV) of an investment as the sum (Σ) of the cash flows (C) expected from the investment after each cash flow has been discounted by 1 plus the rate of return (1 + R) adjusted for the time (t) in which the cash flow is expected:

    $$PV = \Sigma\, C / (1 + R)^t$$

2. The present value formula can be applied to many types of investments:
    a.   Bond prices are the present value of expected future interest payments plus the present value of the maturity payment of the bond.
    b.   The amounts of bank loans are the present values of expected future payments of interest and principal. Usually both principal and interest are repaid in equal installments. The present value formula can be used to determine the amount of these installments.
    c.   The values of plant assets are the present values of the net cash flows a company expects from using the assets. These values can be compared with the cost of the assets to decide whether assets should be purchased.
    d.   The value of a company is the present value of future cash flows expected by owners.
    e.   Stock prices are the present values of future cash flows expected by investors. Earnings provide an estimate of these future cash flows. Most stocks have unlimited lives. Therefore, the present value formula can be modified to compute present value as the expected cash flows divided by the rate of return: PV = C / R.

3. The amounts, timing, and risk associated with investments may be difficult to determine. Accounting information is used to estimate these amounts.
    a.   Expected returns (cash flows) often differ from actual returns.
    b.   Investors may not interpret information correctly or may not use all relevant information in making their decisions. Also, conditions change that affect the amounts, timing, and risks of investments.

4. Interest expense and revenue can be determined from the present value formula.
   a. The interest expense (or revenue) for a period is the present value of a liability (or investment) at the beginning of the period times the rate of return on the liability (or investment).
   b. Amortization tables are useful for computing and reporting interest and principal amounts for loans and bonds (as liabilities or as investments).

D E F I N E   *Terms and Concepts Defined in This Chapter*

annuity   future value   stated rate
coupon rate   market rate   yield to maturity
effective rate   present value

S O L U T I O N S

SELF-STUDY PROBLEM 8-1

a.   PV = $1,000/(1.08)^2 = $857.34

b.   PV = [$500/(1.08)^1] + [$500/(1.08)^2] = [$462.96 + $428.67] = $891.63

c.   PV = [$600/(1.08)^1] + [$400/(1.08)^2] = [$555.56 + $342.94] = $898.50

SELF-STUDY PROBLEM 8-2

a.   The interest factor for a single payment at the end of 10 years discounted at 10% is 0.38554 from Table 1. The interest factor for an annuity for 10 years discounted at 10% is 6.14457 from Table 2. Therefore:

PV = ($80 × 6.14457) + ($1,000 × 0.38554) = ($491.57 + $385.54) = $877.11

b.   Using the same interest factors as in (a):

PV = ($120 × 6.14457) + ($1,000 × 0.38554) = ($737.35 + $385.54) = $1,122.89

c.   The maximum price would be:

PV = $2/(0.10 − 0.03) = $28.57

SELF-STUDY PROBLEM 8-3

Step 1: Determine the price of the bonds. The company pays $110 interest each year ($1,000 × 0.11). The interest factor for an annuity over three years at 9% is 2.53129 from Table 2. The interest factor for a single payment at the end of 3 years, discounted at 9%, is 0.77218 from Table 1. Therefore:

$$PV = (\$110 \times 2.53129) + (\$1,000 \times 0.77218) = (\$278.44 + \$772.18) = \$1,050.62$$

Step 2: Determine the interest for year 1 for the bonds. The present value of the bonds would be $1,050,620 ($1,050.62 × 1,000 bonds). Therefore, the interest on the bonds would be $94,556 ($1,050,620 × 0.09, rounded to the nearest dollar).

Step 3: Prepare an amortization table:

A	B	C	D	E	F
			(B × 0.09)	(C − D)	(B − E)
	Beginning	**Total**	**Interest**	**Principal**	**Ending**
Time	**Present Value**	**Payment**	**Expense**	**(Repaid)**	**Present Value**
Year 1	$1,050,620	$ 110,000	$94,556	$15,444	$1,035,176
Year 2	1,035,176	110,000	93,166	16,834	1,018,342
Year 3	1,018,342	110,000	91,658	18,342	1,000,000
Year 3		1,000,000			0

The amount of interest Debt Co. would report each year is listed in column D. Note that the amount of interest in year 3 has been adjusted because of rounding error. Also, observe that the payments (column C) are greater than the expense (column D). Therefore, a portion of principal is repaid each year (column E), and the present value is reduced each year so that it equals the maturity value of the bonds ($1,000,000) at the end of year 3.

APPENDIX: THE CALCULATION OF STANDARD DEVIATION

The standard deviation is calculated from the difference between each number in a set of numbers and the mean (average) of the set. To illustrate, consider the following two sets of numbers:

	Set A	Set B
X1:	2	1
X2:	3	3
X3:	4	5
Sum:	9	9

Each set consists of three values (X1, X2, and X3). The sum of these values (X1 + X2 + X3) for set A is 9, and the sum for set B also is 9. Therefore, the mean for set A and for set B is 3, the sum divided by the number of values in the set: (X1 + X2 + X3)/3 = 9/3.

Next, the mean (M) is subtracted from each value, and the difference is squared to eliminate any negative amounts:

	Set A				Set B			
X1 − M:	(2 − 3) =	−1;	−1 × −1 = 1		(1 − 3) =	−2;	−2 × −2 = 4	
X2 − M:	(3 − 3) =	0;	0 × 0 = 0		(3 − 3) =	0;	0 × 0 = 0	
X3 − M:	(4 − 3) =	1;	1 × 1 = 1		(5 − 3) =	2;	2 × 2 = 4	

The squared differences are then summed:

Set A: $1 + 0 + 1 = 2$
Set B: $4 + 0 + 4 = 8$

For each sum of the differences, the mean is calculated:

Set A: $2/3 = 0.6667$
Set B: $8/3 = 2.6667$

Finally, the square roots of the means of the differences are calculated:

Set A: $\sqrt{0.6667} = 0.8165$
Set B: $\sqrt{2.6667} = 1.6330$

Thus, the standard deviation for set B is twice that for set A. This is a logical result because the width of the distribution of values is twice as large for set B as for set A:

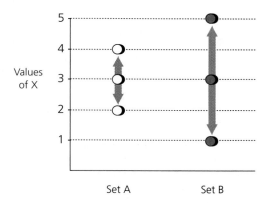

The distribution of set A is from a value of 2 to a value of 4. The distribution of set B is from 1 to 5, twice as large. In this example, the standard deviation is determined by the range of the three values included in each set. If more values were included, the standard deviation would depend on the average of the squared difference of each value from its mean. Nevertheless, the standard deviation is a measure of the distribution of values in a set of numbers. A larger standard deviation indicates a larger distribution.

EXERCISES

8-1. Write a short definition of each of the terms listed in the *Terms and Concepts Defined in This Chapter* section.

8-2. How much is an asset worth if it pays $1,000 at the end of one year and if it provides a return of 8%? How much is it worth if it pays a return of 9%? 10%? What can you conclude about the effect of the rate of return on the value of an asset?

8-3. How much is an asset worth if it pays $800 at the end of one year and if it provides a return of 8%? How much is it worth if it pays $900? $1,000? What can you conclude about the effect of the amount received from an asset on the value of the asset?

8-4. How much is an asset worth if it pays $1,000 at the end of one year and if it provides a return of 5%? How much is the asset worth if it pays $1,000 at the end of two years? Three years? What can you conclude about the effect of the time until an asset pays a return on the value of the asset?

8-5. A wealthy uncle has offered to give you either of two assets: (a) an asset that pays $500 at the end of three years or (b) an asset that pays $100 at the end of each year for five years. Assume that either asset earns a 7% annual rate of return. Which asset should you choose?

8-6. Assume you borrow $10,000 on April 1, 1996, at an annual rate of 7%. How much will you owe on March 31, 1997, if you make no payments until that date? How much will you owe on March 31, 1998, if you make no payments until that date? If you pay the interest incurred for the first year on March 31, 1997, how much will you owe on March 31, 1998, if you make no other payments until that date?

8-7. Assume you received a loan on July 1, 1992. The lender charges annual interest at 5%. On June 30, 1997, you owe the lender $510.52. Assuming you made no payments for principal or interest on the loan during the five years, how much did you borrow?

8-8. What is the present value of an annuity of $200 per year for five years if the required rate of return is 8%? What is the present value of the annuity if the required rate of return is 10%?

8-9. What is the present value of an investment that pays $80 at the end of each year for 10 years and pays an additional $1,000 at the end of the tenth year if the required rate of return is 7%? 8%? 9%?

8-10. Edgar Poe owns Raven Co. On January 1, 1994, the beginning of the company's fiscal year, Poe borrowed $600,000 at 10% annual interest to purchase equipment. The loan is to be repaid over five years in equal annual installments. How much will Poe pay each year? What will be the amount of interest expense reported by Raven Co. for the loan in 1994? In 1995?

8-11. Waldo Co. issued $1 million of 5-year, 8% bonds on January 1, 1996. The bonds pay interest semiannually. How much did the bonds sell for under each of the following situations?
  a.   The bonds sold to yield 8%.
  b.   The bonds sold to yield 6%
  c.   The bonds sold to yield 10%.

8-12. For each of the following independent situations determine (a) whether the bonds sold at face (maturity) value, at a premium (more than face value), or at a discount (less than face value), and (b) whether interest expense recognized each year for the bonds was less than, equal to, or greater than the amount of interest paid on the bonds:
  a.   Bonds with a coupon rate of 8% were sold to yield a market rate of 10%.
  b.   Bonds with a coupon rate of 10% were sold to yield a market rate of 8%.
  c.   Bonds with a coupon rate of 8% were sold to yield a market rate of 8%.

8-13. Gen Sing Co. issued 10-year bonds with a face value of $10 million on October 1, 1996. The bonds pay interest at 7% annually. The bonds sold at 93.29% of face value to yield an effective rate of 8%. How much interest expense should Gen Sing recognize on the bonds for the fiscal year ended September 30, 1997? What amount of net liability would the company report for the bonds on its 1997 balance sheet? How much total expense would the company recognize for the bonds over the 10 years they are outstanding?

8-14. Turn Buckle Co. financed new equipment costing $50,000 with a five-year loan from a local bank. The bank charged 11% interest on the note. What would Turn Buckle's annual payments be to the bank each year, assuming the note and interest are paid in equal annual installments? How much interest expense would the company record for the first year of the note? For the second year?

8-15. An investment is expected to pay a return of $100 per year. The discount rate for the investment is 6%. What will the price of the security be if it has a life of 5 years? 10 years? 20 years? The life is infinite?

8-16. An investment has a life of 10 years. The discount rate for the investment is 6%. What will the price of the investment be if it is expected to pay a return of $10 per year? $100 per year? What will be the price of the investment if it has an infinite life and is expected to pay a return of $10 per year? $100 per year?

8-17. Alicia Smith is considering an investment in securities. She has heard that stocks have provided higher returns than bonds or certificates of deposit (CDs) in recent years. Why should Alicia expect stocks to perform better than other investments, on average? What types of risks should Alicia consider when evaluating alternate investments? How are investments in stocks, bonds, and CDs affected by these types of risk?

8-18. What is the maximum amount a company should pay for equipment that it expects will increase its net income by $250,000 per year for five years if the company requires a 12% return on its investment?

8-19. Big Buy Co. is considering a purchase of Hidden Assets Co. Hidden Assets Co. earned net income of $4 million in 1995. Its net income is expected to grow at the rate of 3% for the foreseeable future. If Big Buy Co. requires a return of 11% on its investments, how much should it pay for Hidden Assets?

8-20. Old Money Co. borrowed $1 million from a bank on January 1, 1995. The loan is repaid in annual installments over a three-year period. The bank required a 9% return. How much did Old Money pay the bank each year? How much interest expense did it incur each year?

PROBLEMS

PROBLEM 8-1 Attributes Affecting Asset Value

Jackson Smythe has accumulated about $10,000 of savings. He has kept his money in a savings account at a local bank. The bank pays him about 4% interest annually. Jackson has little understanding of investments and has asked you to help him evaluate alternatives. He has considered investing his money in corporate bonds that pay a return of 8%. Also, he has considered investing in stocks that have paid an average return of about 14%.

Required   Write a memo to Jackson explaining investment attributes that affect the investment's value and explaining why different investments pay different rates of return.

PROBLEM 8-2   Computing Present Value

Tyrone Flower plans to choose one of three alternative investments. Investment A pays $500 at the end of each year for four years. Investment B pays $2,250 at the end of four years. Investment C pays $300 at the end of each year for three years and pays $1,200 at the end of the fourth year. Tyrone requires a return of 8% on each of these investments.

Required   Provide information to help Tyrone decide how much he should pay for each of these investments.

PROBLEM 8-3   Repaying a Note

Platitude Co. borrowed $400,000 from a bank on May 1, 1996. The bank required a return of 12% on the loan. The loan is to be repaid over 12 months in equal installments. Platitude's fiscal year ends on December 31.

Required   Prepare an amortization table for the loan for the 12-month period. How much interest expense would Platitude report on the loan for its 1996 fiscal year? How much interest expense would it report for 1997? What amount of liability would Platitude report for the loan at the end of 1996? At the end of 1997?

PROBLEM 8-4   Issuance and Amortization of Bonds

Icabod Crane Co. sold $10 million of 4-year, 9% debentures on July 1, 1995. The bonds sold to yield 8%. Interest is paid annually on June 30.

Required

a.   Determine the price of the bonds.

b.   Prepare an amortization schedule for the bonds.

c.   Use the following format to identify the transaction that Icabod Crane would use to record interest on the bonds on June 30, 1996:

Assets =	Liabilities + Equity	+ (Revenues − Expenses)

PROBLEM 8-5   Issuance and Amortization of Bonds

Plum Grove Co. sold $10 million of 4-year, 9% debentures on July 1, 1995. The bonds sold to yield 10%. Interest is paid annually on June 30.

Required

a.   Determine the price of the bonds.

b.   Prepare an amortization schedule for the bonds.

c.   Use the following format to identify the transaction that Plum Grove would use to record interest on the bonds on June 30, 1996:

Assets =	Liabilities + Equity	+ (Revenues − Expenses)

PROBLEM 8-6   Ethical Issues Related to Debt

Hiram Snerdly is an investment broker. Recently he contacted potential investors and offered to sell them bonds that were paying a 10% annual rate of interest. He noted that the bonds were paying a return much higher than other investments and that similar bonds were selling at a market rate of 6% interest. The bonds had a 10-year maturity and paid interest semiannually. Several investors purchased the bonds because of the high rate of interest but later were concerned to learn that the maturity value of $1,000 per bond was considerably less than the $1,350 they had paid for each bond.

Required   Compare the price of the bonds sold by Snerdly to bonds yielding a market rate of 6%? What was the approximate real rate of return earned by the investors? Did they have a right to be concerned about their investments? Do you see any ethical problems with Snerdly's sales pitch?

PROBLEM 8-7   Bond Interest and Cash Flows

Tazaki Co. is planning to issue $10 million of four-year bonds that will pay interest annually. The company needs $10 million to finance the acquisition of new facilities. The market rate of interest for the company's bonds is 8%. As an employee of the company's finance department, you have been asked to evaluate different coupon rates the company might use for the bonds.

Required   Answer each of the following questions:

a.   What determines the market rate of interest for a company's bonds?

b.   What amount of interest expense and interest payment would the company incur each year over the life of the bonds if they were issued at a coupon rate of 6%, 8%, or 10%?

c.   What total amount of expense and cash outflow would be incurred over the four-year period for each of the alternatives in b? What recommendation would you make to the company's top management about which coupon rate to use?

PROBLEM 8-8 Calculation of Notes Payable

You have decided to purchase a car. You have found a clean used car that will cost you $7,500. You can finance your purchase with a note at a local credit union at an annual rate of 12% for 24 months. The credit union will require a down payment of $500.

Required How much will your monthly payments be to the credit union? How much will you pay the credit union over the life of the note? How much of this amount will be interest? If you decide to pay off the note at the end of the first year, how much will you owe the credit union?

PROBLEM 8-9 Computing Bond and Stock Prices

A security's price is a function of expected cash flows from owning the security and the rate used to discount the expected cash flows. Listed below are attributes of several securities:

a. A bond with a maturity value of $1,000, a 10-year maturity, paying 8% interest, with semiannual payments.

b. A share of preferred stock with a par value of $100, paying an 8% annual dividend.

c. A share of common stock with a par value of $10, expected cash flows for the current year are $2 per share and are expected to grow at a rate of 5% per year.

Required Calculate the price of each security, assuming a discount rate of (a) 6%, (b) 8%, and (c) 10%. What conclusions can you draw about the effects of discount rates on the prices of bonds and stocks?

PROBLEM 8-10 Evaluating the Effect of Earnings on Stock Prices

Information is provided below for Vulcan Materials Company:

Year	1984	1985	1986	1987	1988	1989	1990	1991	1992	1993
Earnings per Share	1.86	1.74	2.06	2.69	3.30	3.30	3.10	1.38	2.41	2.39
Stock Price	17.375	22.75	31.125	32.75	41.50	44.50	34.00	36.00	48.25	46.875

Required Evaluate the relationship between Vulcan's stock price and earnings per share. Does earnings per share appear to be a good signal of the expected cash flows to stockholders? What factors other than expected cash flows might affect Vulcan's stock price?

PROBLEM 8-11 Risk and Return of Corporate Securities

Investors typically expect higher returns from common stocks than from preferred stocks and higher returns from preferred stocks than from bonds.

Required (a) Explain the effect of a corporation's earnings on the returns to owners of its bonds, preferred stock, and common stock. (b) Explain the effect of a corporation's earnings on the risks of its securities. (c) Use your explanations in (a) and (b) to demonstrate why investors expect higher returns from common stock than from preferred stock, and from preferred stock than from bonds. Use a diagram or graph to illustrate the relationships among risk and return for the three types of securities.

PROBLEM 8-12 Multiple-Choice Overview of the Chapter

1. The present value of an investment is $600. The investment earns a 7% annual rate of return. The investment consists of one payment made at the end of two years. The amount an investor should receive from the investment at the end of the second year would be:
   a. $600/(1.07)^2$.
   b. $600 \times (1.07)^2$.
   c. 600×1.07.
   d. $600/1.07$.

2. The present value of an investment that paid $500 at the end of three years and earned a 6% return would be:
   a. $419.81.
   b. $471.70.
   c. $30.00.
   d. $470.00.

3. The present value of an investment that paid $100 at the end of each year for five years and earned a 6% return would be:
   a. $470.00.
   b. $471.70.
   c. $373.63.
   d. $421.24.

4. A company borrowed $100,000 from a bank on July 1, 1996. The company made monthly payments of $5,235 on the note at the end of each month from July through December. Total interest expense on the note for this six-month period was $4,410. The total amount the company would report on its December 31, 1996 balance sheet for notes payable for this note would be:
   a. $100,000.
   b. $95,590.
   c. $73,000.
   d. $68,590.

5. Kibuki Co. issued $5 million of bonds at a market rate of 7%. The bonds have a coupon rate of 8%. Which of the following is correct:

	The bonds sold at a	The annual rate of interest paid on the bonds is
a.	Discount	7%
b.	Discount	8%
c.	Premium	7%
d.	Premium	8%

6. Rubble Co. sold 10-year bonds at a discount. Net cash flow on the bonds includes the effects of issue price, interest payments, and principal payment. Over the total life of the bonds, the amount of interest expense on the bonds:
   a. would be greater than net cash flow.
   b. would be equal to net cash flow.
   c. would be less than net cash flow.
   d. would not be determinable from available information.

7. Oshima Co. issued $10 million of 6% bonds on November 1, 1996. The bonds pay interest semiannually on May 1 and November 1 each year. The amount of interest payable the company should report on its December 31, 1996 balance sheet would be:
   a. $0.
   b. $100,000.
   c. $300,000.
   d. $600,000.

8. The price of common stock can be calculated as:
   a. expected cash flows to investors times its discount rate.
   b. expected cash flows divided by its discount rate.
   c. its discount rate divided by expected cash flows.
   d. the sum of expected future cash flows.

9. The price of a share of common stock with expected annual cash flow of $4 per share, a required rate of return of 10%, and an expected growth rate of 4% would be:
   a. $40.
   b. $41.60.
   c. $100.
   d. $66.67.

10. Assume that you borrowed $1,000 from a bank. The bank charges 12% interest and requires that the loan be repaid in 24 monthly installments. The interest expense you would incur for the first year would be:
    a. $120.
    b. more than $120.
    c. less than $120.
    d. less than interest expense for the second year.

CASES

CASE 8-1   Borrowing Costs

Darren Driver is in the market for a new car. He has found a model he likes and has received prices from two dealers. The first dealer will charge $20,000 for the car. Darren will receive a rebate of $1,000 from the manufacturer, for a net price of $19,000. The dealer also will allow Darren $3,500 for his old car as a trade-in. The dealer will finance the purchase for four years at 12% per year. Interest and principal will be paid in four annual installments. The second dealer will charge $19,000 for the car after the $1,000 rebate. This dealer will allow $3,000 for the old car and will finance the purchase for four years at 10% per year, also payable in four annual installments.

Required   Which is the better deal? Provide evidence to support your answer. (You do not have to prepare an amortization table.)

CASE 8-2   Principal and Interest Payments

Homer Body has decided to purchase a house. The price of the house is $80,000 after a down payment of $20,000. The bank will finance the purchase for 25 years at 9%. Alternatively, they will finance the house for 15 years at 8%. Either option will require equal annual payments.

Required   Evaluate the options for Homer. Provide a memo that explains how much total interest Homer will pay in each option and how much his total payments will be each year and over the life of the loan. Advise Homer about which choice he should take and the factors that are important in making the decision. (You do not have to prepare an amortization table.)

PROJECTS

PROJECT 8-1   Comparing Investment Risk and Return

Obtain information about average rates of return on U.S. treasury bonds, on corporate bonds, and on corporate stocks. *Economic Indicators*, the *Federal Reserve Bulletin*, publications of investment companies, such as Moody's Investor Services, and *The Wall Street Journal* provide this type of information. Prepare a table that reports annual data for each type of investment over the past 10 years. What conclusions can you draw about the risk and return of each type of investment?

PROJECT 8-2   Comparing Stock Price Behavior

Obtain stock price information for five companies for the last 10 years. Use closing prices at the end of the companies' fiscal years. Prepare a chart illustrating the relationship between each company's stock price and its earnings per share over the 10-year period. What conclusions can you draw about the relationship between earnings and stock price for each company?

PROJECT 8-3   Interest Rates and Present Values

Use a spreadsheet to prepare a table and chart that demonstrate what happens to the present value of an investment as the number of periods in which payments are made to investors increases from 10 to 80 (in increments of 10) and as the required rate of return increases from 8% to 10% to 12%. Assume that the amount of the payments is $100 per period (an increase of $1,000 for each 10-period increment). What conclusions can you draw from these data?

PROJECT 8-4   Effects of Interest Rate Changes

Use an index of business periodicals to identify articles that describe a recent change in interest rates and the effect of the change on bonds and stocks. Summarize the effects of the interest rate change as described in the article. In particular, note whether the change increased or decreased interest rates and whether the effect on bond and stock prices (or rates of return) was positive or negative. Include a copy of the article with your summary.

Chapter
9

Financing Activities

Chapter 8 considered how value is determined for assets, including investments in companies, stocks, bonds, and other securities. The value of a company and the value of securities it issues are affected by the company's operating, investing, and financing activities. This chapter describes the primary financing activities of a corporation. Chapter 10 examines the use of this information in decisions managers, investors, and others make about a company. It examines the use of this information in valuing companies and their securities.

This chapter examines debt and equity as sources of financing. An organization incurs debt when it borrows from other organizations or individuals. Debt consists of short-term and long-term obligations. These obligations are contractual relationships in which an organization receives cash, other resources, or services. In exchange, an organization agrees to repay creditors or provide future services or benefits. Debt is a major source of financing for many organizations. Financial resources obtained from debt are used to acquire other resources.

Every organization has owners who have invested in that business to receive a return on their investments. Equity financing activities occur when owners provide financial resources to a business by investing in it and when a business distributes a return to its owners. Organizations report information about their debt and equity transactions on their balance sheets, statements of cash flows, and statements of stockholders' equity:

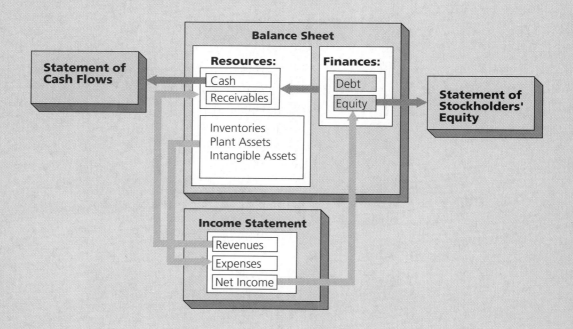

Other information accompanying these statements describes terms of debt contracts and constraints imposed on an organization because of its obligations. This chapter describes this information and accounting rules (GAAP) organizations use to measure and report their debt and equity.

Major topics covered in this chapter include:

- Characteristics and measurement of obligations.
- Obligations to lenders.
- Obligations to suppliers and customers.
- Obligations to employees.
- Taxes and other obligations.
- Stockholder investment and retained earnings.
- Transactions affecting stockholders' equity.
- Classes of stock.

C H A P T E R

O b j e c t i v e s

Once you have completed this chapter, you should be able to:

1. Identify primary types of debt transactions.
2. Identify information companies report about obligations to lenders.
3. Identify obligations to suppliers and creditors.
4. Explain major accounting issues associated with employee obligations.
5. Distinguish between current and deferred income tax liabilities.
6. Identify other types of obligations reported by corporations.
7. Identify the primary information reported in the stockholders' equity section of a corporate balance sheet.
8. List the primary components of contributed capital and explain how the components are measured.
9. Summarize balance sheet information about stock shares authorized, issued, and outstanding.
10. Explain what retained earnings reveals about a corporation.
11. Identify the types of events that change stockholders' equity during a fiscal period.
12. Distinguish stock dividends from cash dividends and explain the effect of dividends on equity.
13. Discuss the effect a corporation's foreign operations may have on stockholders' equity.
14. Distinguish preferred stock from common stock and discuss why corporations may issue more than one type of stock.
15. Summarize the effects stockholders' equity transactions have on net income and cash flow.

TYPES OF OBLIGATIONS

Objective 1
Identify primary types of debt transactions.

Organizations engage in a variety of debt transactions that obligate them to make future payments of cash or to provide goods or services. Most of these obligations are reported by organizations as liabilities on their balance sheets. Liabilities represent contractual relationships with creditors, suppliers, customers, employees, and others.

An organization incurs debt when it borrows from creditors. A debt transaction occurs when a company borrows from a financial institution (such as a bank), another company, or an individual. The company signs a note (a contract) in which a lender agrees to provide financial resources to a borrower in exchange for a legally enforceable promise by the borrower to repay the amount borrowed (the principal) plus interest.

In addition to contracts with creditors, organizations contract with suppliers, employees, and other providers of goods and services. For example, a department store acquires merchandise on credit from a manufacturer and agrees to pay for the goods in the near future. Companies contract with employees for their services in exchange for compensation, of which a portion (such as retirement benefits) may be deferred to the future. Thus, obligations to creditors, suppliers, and employees are part of an organization's liabilities.

The term "liability" encompasses an organization's obligations to provide future payments, goods, or services. **Three attributes define a liability: (1) a present responsibility exists for an organization to transfer resources to some other entity at some future time, (2) the organization cannot choose to avoid the transfer, and (3) the event causing the responsibility already has occurred.**[1] A liability links a past event (receiving something of value) and a future event (giving something of value in exchange for what was received).

Exhibit 9-1 provides an excerpt showing company liabilities reported on a recent PepsiCo, Inc. balance sheet. PepsiCo's liabilities are similar to those of many large corporations. They represent obligations to lenders (short-term and long-term debt), suppliers (accounts payable), employees (compensation and benefits), and governments (income taxes). Future sections of this chapter examine each of these types of obligations.

Exhibit 9-1

Liabilities from Balance Sheet of PepsiCo, Inc.

(in millions) December 25, 1993, and December 26, 1992	1993	1992
Liabilities		
Current Liabilities:		
Short-term borrowings	$2,191.2	$ 706.8
Accounts payable	1,390.0	1,164.8
Income taxes payable	823.7	621.1
Accrued compensation and benefits	726.0	638.9
Accrued marketing	400.9	327.0
Other current liabilities	1,043.1	1,099.0
Total Current Liabilities	6,574.9	4,557.6
Long-Term Debt	7,442.6	7,964.8
Other Liabilities	1,342.0	1,390.8
Deferred Income Taxes	2,007.6	1,682.3

---

[1] "Elements of Financial Statements," *FASB Statement of Financial Accounting Concepts No. 6* (Norwalk, CT: FASB, 1985), par. 36.

OBLIGATIONS TO LENDERS

Objective 2
Identify information
companies report about
obligations to lenders.

An organization's short-term and long-term borrowings are obligations to lenders. Typically, these obligations are a major portion of an organization's liabilities. They usually are reported on the balance sheet as short-term, or current, and long-term debt (see Exhibit 9-1). An organization has an obligation to repay short-term debt during the coming fiscal period. Short-term debt includes obligations that mature in the coming fiscal year, including installments of long-term debt that will become due in the coming year. For example, notes issued in 1996 that will become due in 1997 are classified as short-term debt on the December 31, 1996 balance sheet. In addition, any portion of long-term debt that will become due in 1997 is classified as short term on the December 31, 1996 balance sheet.

Several types of obligations to lenders are reported by corporations. The following sections examine accounting and reporting issues for various types of debt.

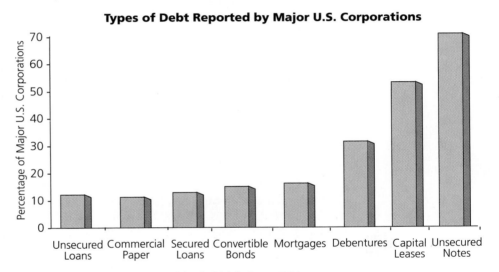

Data source: AICPA, Accounting Trends & Techniques, 1994.

Long-Term Debt

Long-term debt consists of notes and bonds payable. **Notes and bonds payable are contracts between a borrower and a creditor. They certify that the borrower will repay the amount borrowed at specified dates and will pay specified amounts of interest.** Some companies issue debt that is secured by specific assets, such as real estate. *Debentures*, **which are unsecured bonds,** frequently are issued by major corporations. If a company is forced to liquidate to repay its creditors, secured debt is repaid from the sale of the assets provided as collateral for the debt. Unsecured debt is paid from the sale of other assets. Secured debt typically is less risky than unsecured debt.

Debt can be issued with any maturity date. Most bonds are issued for 10, 20, or 30 years. Companies must disclose information in their financial reports describing the maturity dates for their long-term debt. For example, PepsiCo reported in a note to its 1993 financial statements that its long-term debt included $3,873.8 million of long-term notes that would become due from 1994 to 2008. The average interest rate on these notes was 6.5%.

A wide variety of attributes can be found among notes. They vary with respect to how cash flows are arranged: Some may require interest and principal payments over the life of the note; some may require principal repayments at the end of the note's life; others may require interest *and* principal payments at the end.

Bond attributes also vary. Most bond issues are repaid at the end of a fixed period, such as 10 years. Others are issued so a portion of the bonds are repaid each year over the life of the bonds. For example, an organization might issue $10 million of 10-year bonds. Each year, one-tenth of the bonds are repaid. Such bonds are known as **serial bonds** and are commonly issued by governments.

In addition to issuing debt, a company can repurchase its debt if it has sufficient cash and wishes to reduce its future interest and principal payments. Or, a company may repurchase existing debt and replace (refinance) this debt with new debt. Refinancing often occurs when interest rates in the economy move downward so that a company can issue new debt at a lower interest rate than its existing debt. Some bonds require bondholders to resell bonds to the issuer at specific dates and amounts if the issuer chooses to repurchase the bonds. **Callable bonds** are bonds that a company can reacquire from bondholders after the bonds have been outstanding for a specific period. For example, a company may issue 30-year bonds that are callable after 5 years at 102% of maturity value. After this 5-year period, the company may choose to require bondholders to sell their bonds back to the company, at a 2% premium over the maturity value.

A gain or loss may result when a company repurchases its debt. For example, if debt is recorded on a company's books at $2 million and the company repurchases the debt for $2,050,000, it would record a loss of $50,000. The loss is the excess of the repurchase price over the amount recorded for the debt on the books of the issuer (book value). If the repurchase price is less than the book value of the debt, the issuer would record a gain.

Learning Note

Gains increase net income and losses decrease net income. These terms usually are used in place of revenues and expenses for items that are not a primary part of a company's operating activities.

A corporation's financial statements and accompanying notes provide information to help users determine the amount of debt the company has outstanding, changes in the amount during a fiscal period, interest rates on its debt, interest expense recorded during a period, and current and future cash flows associated with existing debt and interest payments.

OBLIGATIONS TO SUPPLIERS AND CUSTOMERS

Objective 3
Identify obligations to
suppliers and creditors.

Most corporations purchase goods or services from suppliers on credit. These transactions produce accounts payable, sometimes referred to as trade payables. PepsiCo reported accounts payable of $1,390 million in 1993 (Exhibit 9-1). These liabilities result from the purchase of merchandise, materials, and supplies from suppliers. Typically, they are short-term obligations that will be repaid within 60 days. Though accounts payable are a source of short-term financing, they result from operating activities. They facilitate the acquisition of resources used frequently in operating activities. Once credit has been established, a company can order merchandise or materials from suppliers without having to arrange prepayment.

Suppliers frequently offer discounts to purchasers if they pay their accounts within a specified period. The discounts are offered to speed the payment of accounts and, therefore, to speed cash inflow for the supplier. For example, assume Ball Bearing Co. orders a supply of steel ingots from Steel Ingot Co. The cost of the order is $300,000. The company placed the order on June 1, 1996, and received the order on June 20 with a billing statement. The bill is for $300,000 payable within 30 days after June 20. In addition, Steel Ingot offers a 2% discount if the payment is received within 10 days (by June 30). Credit terms of this type often are reported in a form such as 2/10, n/30 (2% discount if paid in 10 days; otherwise, net amount due in 30 days). Thus, if Ball Bearing takes advantage of the discount, it will save $6,000 (2% × $300,000) on its purchase. The 2% discount results from paying the account 20 days earlier than it otherwise would be due. On an annualized basis, this discount amounts to about a 36% interest rate.[2] Therefore, companies should take advantage of these savings. The purchase may be recorded at the amount the company expects to pay for the order, which should be $294,000. The following transactions are likely:

> June 1, 1996: No transaction is recorded because no exchange or contractual relationship has occurred.
> June 20, 1996: The order is received.

Assets =		Liabilities + Equity		+ (Revenues − Expenses)
Materials Inventory	294,000	Accounts Payable	294,000	

June 28, 1996: Payment is made.

Assets =		Liabilities + Equity		+ (Revenues − Expenses)
Cash	− 294,000	Accounts Payable	− 294,000	

---

[2] To determine the annualized rate, divide 365 days by 20 days to determine the number of 20-day periods in a year: 365/20 = 18.25. Then multiply the number of 20-day periods by the discount rate permitted for payment within 20 days: 18.25 × .02 = .365 or 36.5%.

If the account is not paid within the discount period, the additional $6,000 of payment should be recorded as an expense. Managing credit is an important function in most organizations. Accounting information can help managers understand the importance of these decisions.

Corporations also may incur obligations to customers. These liabilities, referred to as **unearned revenues**, result when customers pay for goods and services they will receive in a future fiscal period.

For example, suppose you purchase a round-trip ticket from Delta Airlines for $500 on October 1. The ticket is good for a trip you will take during Christmas vacation. The airline incurs an obligation for the $500 when you purchase the ticket. The obligation is fulfilled and revenue is earned when you use the ticket. Thus, the airline would record the following information, assuming you fly on December 20 and return on January 3.

Assets =			Liabilities + Equity		+ (Revenues − Expenses)	
Oct. 1	Cash	500	Unearned Revenue	500		
Dec. 20			Unearned Revenue	− 250	Revenues	250
Jan. 3			Unearned Revenue	− 250	Revenues	250

Warranties are another important customer obligation for many companies. **A** *warranty* **is a promise by a seller to repair or replace defective products or to service products over a period of time.** Typically, products are warrantied for a limited period, such as 90 days or one year. Estimated warranty costs should be recognized at the time goods and services are sold. For example, if Ford Motor Company sells $5 billion of automobiles in September, it would recognize a liability and expense for the estimated warranty costs associated with the automobiles sold. If this amount were $100 million, it would record:

Assets =		Liabilities + Equity		+ (Revenues − Expenses)	
	0	Obligation for Warranties	100,000,000	Warranty Expense	− 100,000,000

Warranty expenses are accrued to match them with revenues earned from the sale of warrantied products. When warranty costs are incurred on products that have been sold, warranty obligations are reduced. For example, assume Ford incurred a cost of $3 million during December to replace defective parts. The costs would affect the company's accounts as follows:

Assets =		Liabilities + Equity		+ (Revenues − Expenses)	
Parts Inventory	− 3,000,000	Obligation for Warranties	− 3,000,000		

Most corporations do not report separately the amount of accrued or actual warranty costs in their financial statements. These amounts are included with other liability and expense items. For competitive reasons, some companies are not anxious to disclose their warranty costs.

OBLIGATIONS TO EMPLOYEES

Many companies provide both current and deferred compensation for their employees. Current compensation consists of wages, medical benefits, vacation and sick leave, and disability income. Deferred compensation includes retirement benefits, such as retirement income and medical benefits. Companies recognize current compensation as expense when it is incurred. Wages expense is recognized at the time employees earn the wages. The same is true of other current benefits. Unpaid wages and benefits are accrued as expense at the end of a fiscal year and are reported as current liabilities. PepsiCo reported a current liability for compensation and benefits of $726 million in 1993 (Exhibit 9-1).

Deferred compensation (long-term liabilities) poses more complex accounting issues. Until recently, many companies did not record liabilities for deferred compensation. Retirement benefits were expensed in the period in which benefits were paid or at the time employees retired. At the same time, sufficient resources were not being invested by some companies to provide for retirement benefits. These unfunded obligations were not reported, and, in some cases, the amounts were not even known by management. The FASB now requires corporations to report information about deferred compensation in their annual reports.

Reporting of deferred compensation can be very complex. We will consider only the primary reporting issues for deferred compensation. **The primary accounting issues for employee obligations are (1) determining the amount of benefits earned by employees and owed by a company, and (2) determining the amount invested by a company to meet these obligations and the amount earned on these investments.**

Objective 4
Explain major accounting issues associated with employee obligations.

Pension Plans

A pension plan is a contract between a company and its employees. The company agrees to provide future retirement benefits in exchange for current services provided by employees. Two types of pension plans are common. A **defined contribution plan** invests contributions by an employer and/or its employees during the period of employment. These investments and their earnings are then used to provide retirement benefits. The amount employees receive is determined by the value of the investments. A **defined benefit plan** promises employees retirement income that is a percentage of their preretirement earnings. Typically, a formula is used to determine the amount of income a retired employee receives each month. The formula generally includes the number of years the employee worked and the wages the employee earned prior to retirement.

Pension plans provide a trade-off between current and future compensation for employees. They are beneficial to employees because they provide for retirement with "before-tax dollars." That is, employees normally do not pay income taxes on amounts contributed to pension plans until retirement benefits are received. Thus, they can accumulate much higher investments to provide retirement incomes than if contributions were taxed.

Employers benefit from pension plans because the plans encourage workers to be productive. Employees have a stake in the future welfare of the company because they are relying on it to pay retirement benefits. Often, employers also receive tax benefits for contributions made to employee pension plans. Further, pension plans may permit a company to reduce its current cash outflow by deferring employee compensation to future periods.

Defined contribution plans transfer the risk associated with plan earnings to employees. Employee retirement benefits are determined by plan earnings and accumulations. The employer does not guarantee the level of benefits employees will receive.

Accounting for a defined contribution plan is relatively simple. Periodic contributions are made to an investment fund. The fund manager invests the contributions in stocks, bonds, real estate, and other investments. An account is maintained for each employee until the employee retires. Then, the employee is paid retirement benefits from his or her account. Unpaid benefits may become part of the employee's estate, upon death. Contributions made by a company to a defined contribution plan are recorded as an expense when contributions are made to the plan investment account.

Accounting for defined benefit plans is much more complex. Defined benefit plan risk remains primarily with the employer, and plan terms stipulate the level of benefits employees will receive when they retire. The employer is obligated to provide these benefits whether or not plan assets have accumulated a sufficient amount to pay the costs. A company, or its pension plan administrators, must estimate (1) how long individual employees will work for the company, (2) how much their wages will increase until they retire, (3) how long employees will live after they retire, and (4) how much plan assets will earn to provide for retirement benefits. From this information, an estimate is made of the present value of expected future benefits earned by employees and the present value of expected earnings from pension plan assets each fiscal period.

Corporations are required by GAAP to report information about their pension plans. This information describes the obligation to employees and the assets available in the company's pension plan to meet these obligations. For example, PepsiCo reported in a note to its financial statements in 1993 that its obligation to employees was $956.6 million. This pension obligation is referred to as the **projected benefit obligation**. Also, PepsiCo reported that plan assets were valued at $1,018.7 million in 1993. After adjustments for obligations from prior years, PepsiCo's net pension assets were $800,000 greater than its pension liabilities. This net asset was included on PepsiCo's balance sheet. If liabilities had been greater than assets, a net liability would have been reported. The amount usually is included along with other assets or liabilities, rather than being reported separately on the balance sheet. Financial report users must examine the notes accompanying the financial statements to determine the amount of the asset or liability.

PepsiCo also reported (in notes) that its pension expense for 1993 was $31.9 million. This was the amount earned by employees during 1993 in excess of earnings from pension plan assets. This expense was included among other expenses on PepsiCo's income statement.

Thus, to summarize a complex topic, two calculations are made by a company in notes to its financial statements. These are illustrated below:

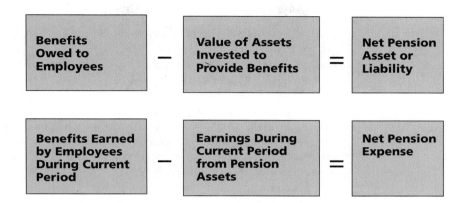

The net pension asset or liability is reported on a company's balance sheet. The net pension expense is reported on its income statement.

The funding of pension plans is an important consideration when examining a company's financial position. Substantial unfunded obligations will require future cash payments just as though the company had borrowed from creditors. Failure to provide for these obligations can increase the risk to investors that a company will not be able to generate cash flows to pay interest or dividends.

Though accounting for pension obligations for defined benefit plans is very complex, two amounts are of primary importance: (a) the net asset or liability which indicates whether a company is investing sufficiently in its pension plans to meet expected future obligations and (b) the net periodic pension cost which indicates whether a company's pension plan assets are earning a sufficient amount to cover benefits earned by employees during the current period.

Other Postemployment Benefits

Many companies provide retired employees with health care, life insurance, and other benefits. Accounting for these benefits is similar to accounting for pensions. The FASB adopted a new standard in 1990 requiring publicly-traded corporations to report information about their obligations for these postemployment benefits.

Like pension obligations, corporations report the net amount of liability (or asset) associated with other postemployment benefits. PepsiCo reported in 1993 that its liability was $650.9 million. This liability was a portion of Other Liabilities reported on PepsiCo's balance sheet (Exhibit 9-1). The expense PepsiCo incurred in 1993 for these benefits earned by employees was $36.2 million.

Like pension benefits, other postemployment benefits can result in obligations that affect a company's future cash flows and profitability. Many U.S. corporations have underfunded their obligations for employee benefits. Recognition of these obligations has had a major effect on the balance sheets and income statements of some of these organizations.

OBLIGATIONS TO GOVERNMENTS

Objective 5
Distinguish between current and deferred income tax liabilities.

Most companies pay taxes, including local, state, federal, and foreign income taxes, property taxes, sales taxes, and social security taxes. Many of these are recognized in the period in which the obligation for the taxes arises. For example, assume a company receives a statement for property taxes of $500,000. The taxes are for July 1, 1995, to June 30, 1996. The amount of the tax is an expense for this period. If the company's fiscal year ends December 31, half of the tax is an expense for 1995 and half for 1996.

Income taxes pose a special accounting problem for many corporations. Most large corporations are required to pay income taxes on their earnings. These companies report an income tax expense (sometimes labeled "provision for income taxes") on their income statements. For example, PepsiCo reported a provision for income taxes of $834.6 million in 1993, which is based on the income reported for the current year.

The amount of income tax obligation a company incurs for a fiscal period generally is not the same as the amount reported on its income statement. Income tax expense is the amount of tax associated with the income recognized on its income statement. The amount of income recognized for tax purposes (on a company's tax return) often differs from the income statement amount. Tax rules permit some revenues to be deferred. The amount of expenses a company recognizes for tax purposes also may differ from the amount reported on its income statement. Thus, taxes owed for a fiscal year often differ from income tax expense. If the amount of income tax expense for a period is greater than the amount of income taxes payable for the period, deferred taxes are increased. If the amount of income tax expense for a period is less than the amount of income taxes payable for the period, deferred taxes are decreased. When a company reports a *deferred tax liability* on its balance sheet, the liability represents **an estimate of income taxes that the company will pay in the future related to income it already has earned.**

PepsiCo reported deferred income taxes of $2,007.6 million in 1993 (Exhibit 9-1). Deferred taxes increased from $1,682.3 million in 1992. The transaction that accounted for the increase of $325.3 million was:

Assets =		Liabilities + Equity		+ (Revenues − Expenses)	
		Income Taxes Payable	509,300,000	Income Tax Expense	−834,600,000
	0	Deferred Income Taxes	325,300,000		

PepsiCo's income tax expense on its income statement was $325.3 million greater than the amount of taxes it owed, based on its income tax returns.

INCOME TAXES PAYABLE is a current liability that will be paid when current period taxes are due. DEFERRED INCOME TAXES typically are reported as part of long-term liabilities. They represent future taxes that may be owed to the government when income that was deferred for tax purposes is recognized in a future period.

OTHER OBLIGATIONS

Objective 6
Identify other types of obligations reported by corporations.

A variety of other obligations may be reported by organizations. Some of these appear on the balance sheet, while others are reported only in notes. Examples include lease commitments and other commitments and contingencies.

GAAP require companies to report contingencies and commitments that may result in future obligations. **A** *contingency* **is an existing condition that may result in an economic effect if a future event occurs.** For example, PepsiCo reported in its 1993 annual report:

> PepsiCo is subject to various claims and contingencies related to lawsuits, taxes, environmental and other matters arising out of the normal course of business. Management believes that the ultimate liability, if any, in excess of amounts already provided arising from such claims or contingencies is not likely to have a material adverse effect on PepsiCo's annual results of operations or financial condition. At year-end 1993 and 1992, PepsiCo was contingently liable under guarantees aggregating $276 million and $200 million, respectively. The guarantees are primarily issued to support financial arrangements of certain bottling and restaurant franchisees and PepsiCo joint ventures. PepsiCo manages the risk associated with these guarantees by performing appropriate credit reviews in addition to retaining certain rights as a franchisor or joint venture partner.

A current obligation does not exist for most contingencies. If some future event occurs, however, an obligation might result. For example, if another entity defaults on a loan guaranteed by PepsiCo, the company could become liable for repayment of the loan.

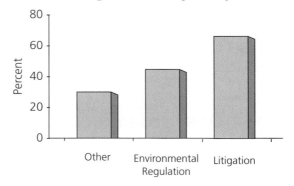

Loss Contingencies of Major Corporations

Data source: AICPA, Accounting Trends & Techniques, 1994.

If a probable loss will result from a contingency and the amount of the loss can be estimated reasonably, it should be included as a liability on a company's balance sheet. Also, the amount of expected loss is recognized as a deduction in computing net income.

A *commitment* **is a promise to engage in some future activity that will have an economic effect.** Commitments often involve future sales or purchases. For example, Delta Airlines reported in 1993 that it had committed to purchase aircraft expected to cost $3.84 billion. This amount was not a liability on Delta's balance sheet. A liability does not result until the company purchases the aircraft, usually after they have been manufactured.

A common form of commitment is for leased assets. Certain leases, known as **capital leases**, are treated as purchase arrangements. The present value of future lease payments are treated as liabilities and are reported on the balance sheet. For example, PepsiCo reported a liability for capital leases of $291 million in 1993. (Capital leases will be examined in Chapter 11.)

In addition to capital leases, companies use **operating leases** to acquire access to resources. The cost of operating leases is recorded as an expense in the period in which the leased assets are used. Liabilities are not recorded for these activities. Some of these leases are noncancellable, however, resulting in a commitment for future payments. The minimum amount of these future payments is reported in notes to the financial statements. For example, PepsiCo disclosed the following operating lease commitments in its 1993 annual report (in millions):

1994	1995	1996	1997	1998	After 1998	Total
$247.2	$219.7	$197.7	$171.6	$155.5	$894.9	$1,886.6

These disclosures are intended to assist investors and other decision makers in evaluating the effect existing conditions are likely to have on future cash flows and profits.

A variety of other obligations may be reported by corporations. For example, dividends declared but unpaid at the end of a fiscal year are reported as a current liability, DIVIDENDS PAYABLE. The types of liabilities reported by companies vary for different industries. Customer deposits are common for utility companies. Air traffic liability for unused tickets is reported by airlines. Terminology varies considerably among corporations. Careful reading of explanations provided in notes to the financial statements often will clarify the items listed on the balance sheet.

LIABILITIES REPORTED BY FOREIGN CORPORATIONS

Foreign corporations report most of the same types of liabilities as U.S. corporations. The liability sections of the balance sheets of foreign corporations often appear very similar to those of U.S. corporations. Accounting rules for measuring these liabilities may differ, however. Many countries do not require corporations to accrue employee pension benefits during the periods in which they are earned. Postemployment health care benefits are not a responsibility of many foreign corporations. These benefits are provided by the government rather than by corporations. Practices concerning deferred income taxes also vary considerably among countries. Many Japanese and European corporations do not recognize deferred taxes. Measurement of lease obligations also varies across nations. Considerable care must be used in comparing liabilities of foreign and U.S. corporations.

SELF-STUDY PROBLEM 9-1

The following information is excerpted from the liabilities section of the 1993 balance sheet of Xerox Corporation (in millions):

Short-term debt and current portion of long-term debt	$2,698
Accounts payable	541
Accrued compensation and benefits	511
Unearned income	335
Other current liabilities	1,926
Long-term debt	5,157
Deferred income taxes	2,608
Liability for postretirement benefits	997

Required

From this list, identify the amount of obligations Xerox had to each of the following at the end of 1993: suppliers of goods and services, customers, lenders, governments, and employees.

The solution to Self-Study Problem 9-1 appears at the end of the chapter.

STOCKHOLDER INVESTMENT AND RETAINED EARNINGS

Objective 7
Identify the primary information reported in the stockholders' equity section of a corporate balance sheet.

Liabilities are obligations of a company to make payments or to provide goods or services. A company has a legal responsibility to meet its obligations. Creditors' claims against a company are legally enforceable. Stockholders' equity also represents a claim against a company, a claim by investors who own stock in the company. These claims are to the company's earnings, however, and as a rule, are met only when a company is successful in earning profits. Profits represent value created by a company during a period in excess of the costs incurred during that period. This excess value increases the value of the stockholders' claims. These claims are reduced when a company pays dividends to its stockholders. If a company fails to earn profits, stockholder value generally decreases, even when dividends are not paid. Stockholder value is lost when a company incurs losses from its operating activities. Furthermore, claims of creditors take precedence over claims of owners. Creditor claims should be met before cash or other assets are distributed to owners. Thus, an important distinction exists between liabilities and equity.

Exhibit 9-2 reproduces the owners' equity section of a recent balance sheet for PepsiCo, Inc.

This exhibit illustrates information corporations report in their balance sheets about their owners' equity. Corporate owners' equity is referred to as **stockholders'** or **shareholders' equity**, because owners hold shares of stock as an indication of their ownership.

Exhibit 9-2 Stockholders' Equity Section of Balance Sheet for PepsiCo, Inc.

(in millions) December 25, 1993, and December 26, 1992	1993	1992
Shareholders' Equity		
Capital stock, par value 1⅔¢ per share: authorized		
1,800.0 shares, issued 863.1 shares	$ 14.4	$ 14.4
Capital in excess of par value	879.5	667.6
Retained earnings	6,541.9	5,439.7
Currency translation adjustment and other	(183.9)	(99.0)
	7,251.9	6,022.7
Less: Treasury stock, at cost: 64.3 shares in		
1993 and 1992	(913.2)	(667.0)
Total Shareholders' Equity	$6,338.7	$5,355.7

Two primary categories of information about stockholders' equity are presented in Exhibit 9-2. The first category is contributed capital. *Contributed capital* **is the direct investment made by stockholders in a corporation.** Contributed capital for PepsiCo consists of **capital stock** and **capital in excess of par value**. The second category is retained earnings, profits reinvested in a corporation. (Currency translation and treasury stock are explained later in this chapter.)

Contributed Capital

Objective 8
List the primary components of contributed capital and explain how the components are measured.

Corporations issue shares of stock to their owners in exchange for cash (and occasionally other resources such as property). *Common stock* **represents the ownership rights of investors in a corporation.** The term *capital stock* sometimes is used instead of common stock. Each share of common stock represents an equal share in the ownership of a corporation. Owners of these shares have a right to vote on the activities of a corporation and to share in its earnings. An owner of 10,000 shares of common stock of a corporation that has 100,000 shares of stock outstanding has a right to 10% of the dividends paid to owners. Also, this owner controls 10% of the votes that can be cast on issues voted on by the stockholders.

Par Value. U.S. corporations must be chartered by a specific state. **A** *charter* **is the legal right granted by a state that permits a corporation to exist.** The charter establishes a corporation as a legal entity and sets limits on its activities to protect its owners and others who contract with it. Among other things, a corporation's charter specifies the maximum number of shares the corporation is authorized to issue.

Some states require corporate stock to have a par value. **The** *par value* **of stock is the value assigned to each share by a corporation in its corporate charter.** A state may require a corporation to maintain an amount of equity equal to or greater than the par value of its stock. This amount cannot be transferred back to the owners unless the corporation liquidates its assets and goes out of business. Originally, par value was intended to protect a corporation's creditors by requiring owners to maintain a certain level of investment in a corporation. Such protection was important in the late 1800s and early 1900s because, at that time, corporations were not required to provide financial reports to their creditors or investors. Managers argued that public reporting of financial information could jeopardize a company's competitive position by allowing competitors to learn about the company's operations.

With the increased requirements for financial reporting that have developed during the 1900s, par value has lost much of its significance. For corporations chartered in states that do not require a par value, stock is issued without a par value and is known as no-par stock. When a par value exists, it often is set at a low amount, as in Exhibit 9-2 ($1^{2}/_{3}$¢ per share).

Capital in Excess of Par Value. Normally, stock is sold by a corporation at a price greater than its par value. For example, if 10,000 shares of $1 par value stock are sold by a corporation for $5 per share, stockholders' equity would include:

Common stock, par value	$10,000
Paid-in capital in excess of par	40,000
Total contributed capital	$50,000

Paid-in capital in excess of par value **is the amount received by a corporation from sale of its stock in addition to the stock's par value.** Corporate financial reports refer to paid-in capital in excess of par as paid-in capital, contributed capital in excess of par, proceeds in excess of par value, additional paid-in capital, surplus, premium on capital stock, and a variety of other names.

The total contributed capital from par value stock is the sum of capital stock (at par value) and paid-in capital in excess of par value. Total contributed capital for PepsiCo at the end of 1993 was $893.9 million ($14.4 + $879.5) as shown in Exhibit 9-2.

Occasionally, a corporation will establish its own **nominal**, or **stated**, **value** for its no-par stock. That value will appear on the balance sheet in place of par value. In such cases, contributed capital will equal the sum of the stated value of the capital stock and the paid-in capital in excess of stated value.

While the various terms associated with capital stock can be confusing, take care to understand the basic concept. **Contributed capital is the amount paid in to a corporation directly by its stockholders.**

Percentage of Major Corporations with Par, No Par, and Stated Value Stock

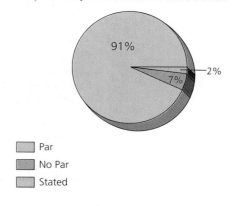

- Par
- No Par
- Stated

(Data source: Accounting Trends & Techniques, 1994)

Shares of Stock and Treasury Stock

Objective 9
Summarize balance sheet information about stock shares authorized, issued, and outstanding.

A corporation discloses in its annual report the number of shares of stock authorized by its charter. PepsiCo reported 1,800 million shares authorized (see Exhibit 9-2). *Authorized shares* **are the maximum number of shares a corporation can issue without receiving approval from stockholders and the state to amend its charter.** Also, a corporation reports the number of shares of stock that have been issued (sold) to investors and the number of shares currently held by investors. *Issued shares* **are the number of shares that have been sold by a corporation to investors.** *Outstanding shares* **are the number of shares currently held by investors.** The difference (if any) between the number of shares issued and the number of shares outstanding is held by a company as treasury stock, shares a corporation has repurchased from its investors. PepsiCo reported 64.3 million shares of treasury stock at the end of 1993 (see Exhibit 9-2). At the end of 1993, the number of shares of PepsiCo stock issued was 863.1 million. Therefore, 798.8 million shares were outstanding at the end of 1993 (863.1 − 64.3).

Treasury stock **is stock a corporation sold to its investors and then repurchased from them.** Because it is held by the corporation, it is not outstanding. TREASURY STOCK is a contra-stockholders' equity account. The cost of treasury stock is subtracted from other equity accounts to compute total stockholders' equity. The cost of treasury stock is the amount a corporation paid to investors to repurchase the stock.

PepsiCo notes (Exhibit 9-2) that the cost of treasury stock held at the end of 1993 was $913.2 million. The average price it paid for this stock was about $14.20 per share ($913.2/64.3). It may have repurchased the stock at several different times at different prices.

Once a corporation repurchases shares of its stock, it may choose to retire those shares rather than hold them in treasury. Shares that have been retired are not included in the number of shares issued.

Percentage of Major Corporations Reporting Treasury Stock

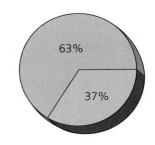

63%

37%

▢ Treasury Stock
▢ No Treasury Stock

(Data source: Accounting Trends & Techniques, 1994)

Learning Note   Amounts shown on the balance sheet are totals accumulated over the life of a company. They are not the result of current year activities only. Therefore, the 64.3 million shares of treasury stock PepsiCo reported for 1993 was the total stock it held in treasury at the end of 1993.

Retained Earnings

Recall from Chapter 2 that **retained earnings is profit reinvested in a corporation**. Other titles appearing in annual reports for retained earnings include

Objective 10
Explain what retained earnings reveals about a corporation.

reinvested earnings; net income, earnings, or profit retained in the business; or net income, earnings, or profit reinvested in the business. The amount of retained earnings indicates the accumulated net income invested in corporate resources. For example, assume that Harbor Co. began business on January 1, 1993. Its net income and dividends for 1993 through 1997 were:

Year	Net Income	Dividends	Increase in Retained Earnings	Balance of Retained Earnings
1993	$250,000	$100,000	$150,000	$ 150,000
1994	340,000	100,000	240,000	390,000
1995	416,000	200,000	216,000	606,000
1996	434,000	200,000	234,000	840,000
1997	500,000	300,000	200,000	1,040,000

Retained earnings is the accumulation of net income earned by a corporation over its life less the amount of dividends it has paid to investors.[3]

PepsiCo had accumulated $6,541.9 million of retained earnings by December 25, 1993 (Exhibit 9-2). Thus, in addition to over $890 million of financing provided directly by owners as contributed capital, PepsiCo generated over $6,500 million of financing from profitable operations.

Summary of Measuring and Reporting Stockholders' Equity

In addition to reporting the amount of par value and paid-in capital in excess of par, corporations are required by GAAP to report the number of shares of stock authorized, issued, and outstanding. This information may be reported either on the balance sheet or as a part of accompanying notes. The cost of stock a corporation has repurchased from its stockholders is deducted on the balance sheet as treasury stock in reporting total stockholders' equity (see Exhibit 9-2).

The primary events in the transformation process that affect stockholders' equity are the issuance of stock (contributed capital) and the reinvestment of net income (retained earnings). The accounting system measures these events by the amount of cash received from the sale of stock by a corporation and by the amount of net income reinvested in the corporation.

SELF-STUDY PROBLEM 9-2

Bovine Co. began operations in January 1995. At that time, it issued 100,000 shares of $1 par value common stock. The stock sold for $5 per share. The company's charter permits it to issue 250,000 shares of stock. In 1997, the company

---

[3]   Other transfers can be made from retained earnings for special purposes. Some of these transfers are examined later.

Percentage of Total Stockholders' Equity Composed of Contributed Capital and Retained Earnings for Selected Corporations

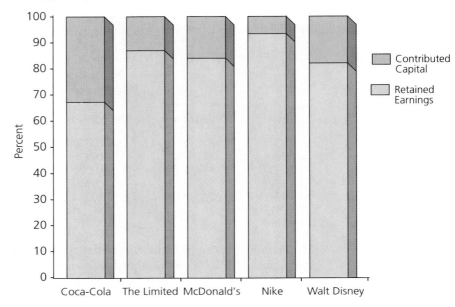

Data source: 1993 annual reports.

repurchased 8,000 shares of stock at a cost of $7 per share. Bovine's net income and cash dividend payments have been:

Year	Net Income	Dividends
1995	$ (60,000)	$ 0
1996	140,000	50,000
1997	220,000	100,000

Required

Draft the stockholders' equity section of Bovine's balance sheet for the years ended December 31, 1997 and 1996.

The solution to Self-Study Problem 9-2 appears at the end of the chapter.

CHANGES IN STOCKHOLDERS' EQUITY

Objective 11
Identify the types of events that change stockholders' equity during a fiscal period.

The statement of stockholders' (or shareholders') equity describes events that have changed the amount of stockholders' equity during the fiscal periods covered by the statement. Exhibit 9-3 provides the statement of stockholders' equity for PepsiCo, Inc. for 1993. The following sections describe each of the items listed in the exhibit.

Exhibit 9-3   Statement of Stockholders' Equity for PepsiCo, Inc.

(shares in thousands, dollars in millions)

	Capital Stock Shares	Capital Stock Amount	Capital in Excess of Par Value	Retained Earnings	Translation Adjustment and Other	Total
Shareholders' Equity, December 26, 1992	798,806	$(652.6)	$667.7	$5,439.7	$ (99.0)	$5,355.8
1993 Net income	—	—	—	1,587.9	—	1,587.9
Cash dividends declared	—	—	—	(485.7)	—	(485.7)
Currency translation adjustment	—	—	—	—	(77.0)	(77.0)
Purchase of treasury stock	(12,371)	(463.5)	—	—	—	(463.5)
Shares issued for acquisitions	8,896	170.2	164.6	—	—	334.8
Stock options exercised	3,415	46.6	47.1	—	—	93.7
Conversion of bonds and other	35	0.5	0.2	—	(7.9)	(7.2)
Shareholders' Equity, December 25, 1993	798,781	$(898.8)	$879.6	$6,541.9	$(183.9)	$6,338.7

Minor adjustments have been made to the format to simplify the presentation.

The format of the statement of stockholders' equity varies from corporation to corporation. Nevertheless, the statement lists the events that have resulted in changes in stockholders' equity during the past fiscal year. Though Exhibit 9-3 provides information for 1993, the complete statement in PepsiCo's annual report includes information for 1992 and 1991 as well.

Net Income

Exhibit 9-3 identifies transactions typical of those considered in prior chapters. For example, PepsiCo's 1993 net income of $1,587.9 million was added to retained earnings:

	Capital Stock Shares	Capital Stock Amount	Paid-In Capital	Retained Earnings
Net income				1,587.9

In total, revenues were $25,109.4 million and expenses were $23,521.5 million (from PepsiCo's income statement). The balances of these accounts are transferred to retained earnings, increasing it by the amount of net income. This transaction preserves the relationship: assets = liabilities + owners' equity + (revenues − expenses).

The transfer was made by closing the revenue and expense accounts:

Assets =	Liabilities + Equity		+ (Revenues − Expenses)	
0	Retained Earnings	1,587.9	Revenues	− 25,109.4
			Expenses	23,521.5

Cash Dividends

During 1993, PepsiCo declared cash dividends totaling $485.7 million to stockholders (from Exhibit 9-3):

	Capital Stock		Paid-In Capital	Retained Earnings
	Shares	Amount		
Cash dividends				(485.7)

This transaction resulted in the payment of cash to stockholders, reducing the amount of cash held by the company and reducing its retained earnings:

Assets =	Liabilities + Equity		+ (Revenues − Expenses)
Cash − 485.7	Retained Earnings	− 485.7	

Cash dividends are paid only on shares outstanding. They are not paid on shares held in treasury, because a company would be paying dividends to itself.

Several dates are important for dividend transactions. **The** *date of declaration* **for dividends is the date a corporation's board of directors announces that a dividend will be paid. The** *date of record* **for a dividend is the date used to determine the recipients of the dividend.** All registered owners on the date of record receive the dividend. Anyone purchasing shares too late to be registered by the date of record will not receive dividends. **The** *date of payment* **for a dividend is the date the dividends are mailed to recipients.**

Dividends **declared** during a fiscal period are reported on a corporation's statement of stockholders' equity as a reduction in retained earnings. Dividends paid during a fiscal period are reported on the corporation's statement of cash flows. These amounts will not always be the same. For example, a company may declare a dividend near the end of its fiscal year but not pay the dividend until the following fiscal year. Dividends that have been declared but that have not been paid are reported as a current liability, DIVIDENDS PAYABLE.

Issuance of Stock

PepsiCo issued 12,346 (8,896 + 3,415 + 35) thousand shares of stock during 1993 (from Exhibit 9-3):

	Capital Stock		Paid-In Capital	Retained Earnings
	Shares	**Amount**	**Paid-In Capital**	**Retained Earnings**
Shares issued for acquisitions	8,896	170.2	164.6	
Stock options exercised	3,415	46.6	47.1	
Other	35	0.5	0.2	

These shares were issued for specific purposes: acquisitions of other companies and stock options.

In addition, companies may sell shares directly to investors. When a company issues new shares of stock, each current stockholder normally has a right to purchase a portion of these shares equal to the percentage of shares owned prior to the sale. **The right to maintain the same percentage of ownership when new shares are issued is known as the** *preemptive right* **of stockholders.** This right prevents management from diluting the control (and wealth) of current owners by selling new shares to someone other than the current owners. When a company is preparing to issue new shares, it normally issues stock rights to existing owners. These certificates authorize the recipient to purchase new shares. The number of rights a stockholder receives depends on the number of shares owned. Stock rights may be sold to others interested in purchasing the company's stock if the original recipient does not wish to purchase the new shares.

Acquisition of Other Companies. PepsiCo issued 8,896 thousand shares of stock to acquire another company (from Exhibit 9-3). The stock was issued to the previous owners of other companies in exchange for their stock holdings in those companies. The acquisition increases the assets of PepsiCo:

Assets =		Liabilities + Equity		+ (Revenues − Expenses)
Long-Term Investment in Other Companies	334.8	Capital Stock	170.2	
		Capital in Excess of Par Value	164.6	

The new assets acquired by PepsiCo are valued by the market value of stock given in exchange for the assets. Shares of stock may be only part of the total price paid for an acquisition. Cash or other assets also may be included in the exchange. New assets would be valued at the fair market value of the assets given up in the exchange.

Stock Options. PepsiCo issued 3,415 thousand shares of stock as part of a stock option plan (from Exhibit 9-3). Stock options are rights to purchase shares of stock at a specified price. Options frequently are granted to employees and managers of a company as part of incentive compensation arrangements. A note to PepsiCo's statements describes the option arrangement, as shown below.

> PepsiCo has established certain employee incentive plans under which stock options are granted. A stock option allows an employee to purchase a share of PepsiCo Capital Stock (Stock) in the future at the fair market value on the date of the grant.
>
> Under the PepsiCo SharePower Stock Option Plan (SharePower), approved by the Board of Directors and effective in 1989, essentially all employees other than executive officers, part-time and short-service employees may be granted stock options annually. The number of options granted is based on each employee's annual earnings. The options generally become exercisable ratably over five years from the grant date and must be exercised within 10 years of the grant date. SharePower options were granted to approximately 118,000 employees in 1993 and 114,000 employees in 1992.

This note describes options issued to employees as part of their compensation arrangements. *Stock options* **permit those to whom the options have been granted to purchase a specified number of shares of a company's stock at a predetermined price.** For example, assume that employees receive options to purchase 10,000 shares of Option Co.'s stock on January 2, 1996. The options permit the employees to purchase the shares at $50 per share on January 2, 1997. If the company does well in 1996, so that the stock price increases above $50 per share by the end of the year, the employees will profit from exercising their options. The options provide an incentive for employees to be productive and help their company's stock price to increase.

When a company sponsors an Employee Stock Ownership Plan (ESOP), it may provide for loans to the plan to acquire shares of stock or may provide shares to the plan for future distribution. The shares are not distributed until employees provide services to earn the shares, however. These shares are like treasury stock until they are earned by employees. Therefore, a company's stockholders' equity may include an item for employee compensation related to an ESOP that reduces its stockholders' equity.

Stock option plans can be complex. Many types of plans exist and accounting recognition varies according to plan type and terms. Stock option plans often result in tax benefits to corporations. Therefore, tax regulations often determine the terms of stock option plans so corporations can benefit from tax deductions associated with their options.

Conversion of Bonds. PepsiCo issued 35,000 shares of common stock in exchange for the conversion of bonds (from Exhibit 9-3):

| | Capital Stock | | Paid-In Capital | Retained Earnings |
	Shares	Amount		
Conversion of bonds	35	0.5	0.2	

Convertible bonds **are bonds that can be converted into shares of stock.** When bonds are converted, they are exchanged by bondholders for shares of common stock. The contract that permits this exchange was established when the bonds were first sold. For PepsiCo, the transaction reduced the amount of debt the company had outstanding and increased its contributed capital by $700,000 ($500,000 of par value and $200,000 of paid-in capital):

Assets =	Liabilities + Equity		+ (Revenues − Expenses)
	Bonds Payable	− .7	
	Capital Stock	.5	
0	Paid-In Capital	.2	

Convertible bonds attract investors who want protection in case a company is not successful in its operations but who also want an opportunity to share in a company's earnings if it is successful. Bondholders are promised an annual interest payment and are provided more protection than stockholders if a company liquidates. But, if a company is successful, convertible bondholders can convert their bonds into stock to take advantage of higher returns. Because of the conversion feature, convertible bonds often pay a lower interest rate than comparable nonconvertible bonds.

Stock Dividends

Objective 12
Distinguish stock dividends from cash dividends and explain the effect of dividends on equity.

Corporations sometimes issue stock dividends. *Stock dividends* **are shares of stock distributed by a company to its current stockholders without charge to the stockholders.** The effect of a stock dividend is to increase the number of shares of stock a company has outstanding and the number held by each stockholder. The increase in shares for each stockholder is proportional to the number owned before the distribution. For example, assume you owned 1,000 shares of Dividend Co.'s stock on June 1, 1996, the date the company distributed a 5% stock dividend. You would have received 50 additional shares of stock on July 1 (1,000 shares × 5%). The total number of shares of common stock outstanding increased by 5% as a result of this distribution.

Unlike cash dividends, stock dividends do not decrease a corporation's cash, since no cash is paid out. Stock dividends are subtracted from retained earnings and do not change the total amount of stockholders' equity. They simply transfer an amount from retained earnings to contributed capital. The amount of the transfer is determined by the market price of the stock at the time the dividend is declared.

Occasionally, corporations issue large stock dividends known as stock splits. **When a corporation declares a** *stock split*, **it issues a multiple of the number of shares of stock outstanding prior to the split.**

A split does not change a company's total stockholders' equity. In some cases, a company will reduce the par value of its common stock in proportion to the magnitude of a stock split. Thus, if the par value is $10 per share prior to a 2-for-1 split, the par value will be $5 per share after the split. By changing the par value, the company maintains the same amount of contributed capital on its books after the split as before, and no account balances are altered. If a company does not reduce its par value, an amount is transferred from retained earnings to contributed capital equal to the par value of the additional stock issued.

Foreign Currency Adjustments. A common adjustment to stockholders' equity for multinational corporations is a foreign currency adjustment. Multinational corporations are companies that operate in foreign and domestic markets. Therefore, a portion of their operations is conducted in foreign currency, such as British pounds or Japanese yen. When preparing financial statements in the U.S., these companies translate their foreign operations into U.S. dollars. *Foreign currency translation* **is the process of converting the financial results of operations that occur in a foreign currency into U.S. dollars for financial reporting purposes.**

Objective 13
Discuss the effect a corporation's foreign operations may have on stockholders' equity.

A *translation adjustment* **is the gain or loss from translating the operations of a company's foreign subsidiaries into U.S. dollars for purposes of reporting consolidated financial statements.** These adjustments may result in gains or losses depending on whether the dollar has gained or lost value relative to other currencies during a period. Translation adjustments often are reported in the stockholders' equity section of the balance sheet. Reporting on the balance sheet, rather than the income statement, is permitted when a company's foreign investment is permanent so that gains and losses are not actually converted into dollars.

OTHER STOCKHOLDERS' EQUITY ITEMS

In addition to those considered for PepsiCo, several other types of transactions may be reported by corporations. These include transactions related to preferred stock, minority interests of subsidiaries owned by a corporation, and appropriations of retained earnings. The following sections describe these transactions.

Preferred Stock

Objective 14
Distinguish preferred stock from common stock and discuss why corporations may issue more than one type of stock.

Some corporations issue more than one type or class of stock. The classes may differ with respect to voting and dividend rights. A corporation's annual report will describe the different classes of stock issued by a company. One type of stock issued by many companies, in addition to common stock, is preferred stock.

Preferred stock **is stock that has a higher claim on dividends and assets than common stock.** Cash dividends must be paid to preferred stockholders before they can be paid to common stockholders. Preferred stock-

Percentage of Major Corporations Issuing Preferred Stock

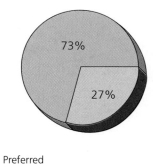

73%

27%

☐ No Preferred
☐ Preferred

(Data source: Accounting Trends & Techniques, 1994)

holders also often have a liquidation preference over common stockholders. If a corporation becomes unable to meet its obligations and must liquidate its assets, preferred stockholders will be paid before common stockholders. Therefore, preferred stock is a less risky investment than common stock. Preferred stockholders normally do not have voting rights in a corporation. Thus, preferred stockholders participate in the profits of a corporation but not in decisions about its operations. Like bonds, some preferred stock is convertible. Convertible preferred stock can be exchanged for shares of common stock under the provisions of the preferred stock agreement. In rare cases, preferred stock may be exchanged for bonds rather than common stock.

Corporations issue preferred stock to attract investors who do not want to take as much risk as common stockholders. If a company does well, preferred stockholders will receive a reasonable return on their investments and may be able to convert their shares to common stock. If a company does poorly, preferred stockholders are likely to receive higher returns than common stockholders and are more protected against loss in case of liquidation.

Exhibit 9-4 provides an example of the stockholders' equity presentation from a recent annual report of McDonald's. Preferred stock is presented on the balance sheet before common stock. The numbers of shares authorized, issued, and outstanding also are reported on the statement or in the notes. Thus, the reporting of preferred stock is similar to that of common stock. The issuance of preferred stock results in cash inflow to a corporation, just as does the issuance of common stock.

Exhibit 9-4   Stockholders' Equity Section of Balance Sheet for McDonald's Corporation

(in millions of dollars)	December 31, 1993	1992
Shareholders' equity		
Preferred stock, no par value; authorized—165.0 million shares; issued—5.7 and 5.8 million	$ 677.3	$ 680.2
Common stock, no par value; authorized—1.25 billion shares; issued—415.2 million	46.2	46.2
Additional paid-in capital	302.8	260.2
ESOP notes	(253.6)	(271.3)
Retained earnings	7,612.6	6,727.3
Foreign currency translation adjustment	(192.2)	(127.4)
	8,193.1	7,315.2
Common stock in treasury, at cost; 61.5 and 51.6 million shares	(1,919.0)	(1,422.8)
Total shareholders' equity	$6,274.1	$5,892.4

Preferred stock often is cumulative. When stock is cumulative, any dividends that were not paid in prior years must be paid in the current year before a dividend can be paid to common stockholders.

Payments of cash dividends are made to preferred stockholders in the same manner as to common stockholders. The amount of dividend payment, however, often differs between the two types of stock. Usually, preferred stockholders receive the stated dividend rate. Dividends to common stockholders usually depend on the profitability of a company. When a company is highly profitable, it normally pays larger dividends to common stockholders than when it is less profitable. If it is unprofitable, it may skip dividends for the current year. If preferred stock is cumulative, any skipped dividends must be paid in a future year. Most often, cash dividends are paid quarterly on both common and preferred stock, resulting in a cash outflow and reduction of retained earnings.

Participating preferred stock permits stockholders to participate in the earnings of the issuer in an amount greater than the stated rate. For example, assume the stated rate on preferred stock is 5%, but a cash dividend is paid to common stockholders that is 10% of par. If the preferred stock is participating, the preferred stockholders may receive a dividend of up to 10%.

Accountants disagree about whether preferred stock and similar securities are properly classified as equity. These securities have some of the characteristics of equity and some of debt. The fact that preferred stock pays a fixed rate and does not provide voting rights makes it similar to debt. The fact that a legal obligation to pay dividends does not exist unless sufficient profits are earned to make the payment makes it similar to equity. The classification of some securities as debt or equity is arbitrary because the securities have some attributes of each.

Redeemable preferred stock, in particular, is controversial because a company has the right to repurchase the stock just as it would if it were repaying creditors. In some cases, a redemption is required at a specific date. Therefore, redeemable preferred stock often is reported as a separate item on the balance sheet between liabilities and equity.

Care should be used in examining a corporation's financial statements to distinguish common stock from other types of stock. Though not an expense, preferred dividends reduce the amount of net income available for distribution to common stockholders. Normally, these dividends must be paid before dividends can be paid to common stockholders.

Minority Interest

Minority interest **is the portion of a subsidiary's stockholders' equity owned by shareholders other than the parent corporation.** For example, assume that Parent Co. owns 80% of Subsidiary Co.'s stock. Subsidiary reports total stockholders' equity of $2,000,000 for fiscal 1995. The minority interest associated with the 20% of the stock that Parent does not own would be $400,000. Parent would report this amount as minority interest on its balance sheet.

Corporations differ in their reporting of minority interest. Some report it as part of stockholders' equity—a portion of the consolidated company's total equity held by outside interests. Some corporations report minority interest as a liability—a claim by outside interests against a portion of the consolidated company's resources. Other companies include minority interest as a separate category between liabilities and equity.

Appropriation of Retained Earnings

An *appropriation of retained earnings* **transfers part of the retained earnings balance to a restricted retained earnings account.** It is used to signal management's intent to conserve cash for a specific purpose by restricting it from being distributed as dividends. The new account title might be RETAINED EARNINGS—APPROPRIATION FOR PLANT EXPANSION or something similar. Appropriations are rare among U.S. companies but sometimes are found in financial statements of foreign companies.

Stockholders' equity can be complex for some corporations because of the many types of transactions that can occur as part of a company's financing activities. Transactions such as the issuance or repurchase of stock for cash, the issuance of stock to acquire other businesses, the issuance of stock to employees, the conversion of bonds and preferred stock to common stock, and the payment of cash dividends and stock dividends are typical.

SELF-STUDY PROBLEM 9-3

Excerpts from financial statements for Vulcan Materials Company are provided below. From this information, answer the following questions:

1. What was Vulcan's total contributed capital for 1993?
2. How many shares of common stock were outstanding at the end of 1993?
3. What dollar amount of treasury stock did Vulcan hold at the end of 1993?
4. What was the net change in the number of treasury shares held by Vulcan during 1993?
5. What was the amount of dividend per share paid by Vulcan during 1993, assuming that 45 million shares were outstanding when dividends were paid?
6. What was the dividend payout ratio for 1993 for Vulcan?
7. How much net cash flow was generated from financing activities associated with stockholders' equity during the current year? What were the sources of this cash flow?
8. How much net income was generated from financing activities associated with stockholders' equity during the current year?

Vulcan Materials Company
(Excerpt from the Consolidated Balance Sheet)

(Amounts in thousands)	1993	1992
Shareholders' equity		
Common stock, $1 par value	$ 46,573	$ 46,573
Capital in excess of par value	4,587	3,962
Retained earnings	1,009,912	967,979
Total	1,061,072	1,018,514
Less cost of stock in treasury	358,109	318,402
Total stockholders' equity	$ 702,963	$ 700,112

Statement of Shareholders' Equity
for 1993

(Amounts and shares in thousands)	Shares	Amount
Common stock, $1 par value		
Authorized: 160,000 shares		
Issued at beginning of year	46,573	$ 46,573
Issued at end of year	46,573	46,573
Capital in excess of par value		
Balance at beginning of year		$ 3,962
Distributions under Performance Share Plan		625
Balance at end of year		4,587
Retained earnings		
Balance at beginning of year		967,979
Net earnings		88,229
Cash dividends on common stock		(46,296)
Balance at end of year		1,009,912
Common stock held in treasury		
Balance at beginning of year	(9,350)	(318,402)
Purchase of common shares	(895)	(39,985)
Distributions under Performance Share Plan	21	278
Balance at end of year	(10,224)	(358,109)
Total		$ 702,963

The solution to Self-Study Problem 9-3 appears at the end of the chapter.

INTERNATIONAL REPORTING OF EQUITY

The reporting of stockholders' equity by foreign corporations is similar to that by U.S. corporations. Most industrialized nations use similar reporting rules, though some major differences exist. It is not safe to assume that amounts reported in the financial statements of foreign corporations are measured using the same rules as those reported by U.S. corporations. Each nation sets its own accounting and reporting rules.

Learning Note — Foreign corporations whose stock is listed on U.S. stock exchanges issue annual financial reports that conform with U.S. GAAP. These companies may issue a different annual report to stockholders in their own countries, using different accounting rules.

Major differences in terminology can be found among financial statements in various countries. Terms such as "share capital" are used to refer to common stock. "Share premium" refers to paid-in capital in excess of par value. "Earned surplus" or "profit and loss" may be used instead of retained earnings. Reserve accounts also are common in many countries. These accounts identify portions of stockholders' equity that are restricted and usually cannot be used to pay dividends. Therefore, care must be used in reading foreign statements to make sure the items are understood.

In addition, measurement rules may differ among countries. For example, British companies and those in certain other countries are permitted to recognize increases in the market values of assets if the increases are expected to be permanent. These increases also result in increases in stockholders' equity. Recognition of these increases is permitted in the U.S. only for investments in certain types of securities. As a rule, assets are reported at their historical cost and equity is not adjusted for increases in market value until assets are sold.

SUMMARY OF FINANCIAL STATEMENT REPORTING OF EQUITY

Objective 15
Summarize the effects stockholders' equity transactions have on net income and cash flow.

The effects of most stock–related transactions are observed on the balance sheet and on the statement of stockholders' equity—these transactions are financing activities. Because they do not involve the operating activities of a business, revenues and expenses are not affected. Therefore, the income statement is not affected by stock-related transactions. In fact, **a corporation cannot create income through transactions involving its own stock**.

When a corporation issues stock, it receives cash, but it does not earn revenue since it has not provided goods or services to customers. Even if a corporation repurchases some of its stock (as treasury stock) and resells the stock at a higher price, it does not earn revenue, though it creates additional cash inflow. The link between stockholders' equity and the income statement is in the transfer of net income to retained earnings. The results of a company's operating activities (net income) increase (or decrease in the case of a loss) stockholders' equity. But, stock-related transactions do not increase (or decrease) net income.

Two stock-related cash flow items are prominent on the statement of cash flows. Both appear in the financing activities section. One is the payment of cash dividends to stockholders, a cash outflow; the other is the issuance or repurchase of stock. Generally when stock is issued, a corporation receives cash, and when stock is repurchased, cash is paid out. For example, the 1993 statement of cash flows for PepsiCo reported:

(in millions)	
Cash Flow from Financing Activities:	
Cash dividends paid	$(461.6)
Purchase of treasury stock	(463.5)
Proceeds from exercise of options	68.6

Parentheses denote cash outflows.

Exhibit 9-5 summarizes the stockholders' equity transactions considered in this chapter.

Exhibit 9-5   Summary of Financial Statement Effects of Stockholders' Equity Transactions

Transaction	Cash	Other Assets	Liabilities	Contributed Capital	Retained Earnings	Net Income
Issue stock	I			I		
Repurchase stock	D				D(a)	
Transfer net income					I	D(b)
Acquire companies		I		I		
Conversion of bonds			D	I		
Exercise options	I			I		
Pay cash dividends	D				D	
Issue stock dividends				I	D	
Translation adjustments		I/D(c)			I/D(c)	

I = Increase, D = Decrease

(a) Reported as Treasury Stock that is deducted as part of stockholders' equity.
(b) Net effect of transferring net income to retained earnings.
(c) Translation adjustments may either increase or decrease the reported amount of assets, liabilities, and stockholders' equity depending on whether the dollar increases or decreases in value relative to other currencies.

REVIEW   *Summary of Important Concepts*

1. The characteristics and measurement of obligations:
   a. Liabilities result from contractual relationships with lenders, suppliers, customers, employees, governments, and other parties.
   b. Three attributes of a liability are (1) a present responsibility exists for an organization to transfer resources to some other entity at some future time, (2) the organization cannot choose to avoid the transfer, and (3) the event causing the responsibility has already occurred.

2. Obligations to lenders include notes and bonds payable.

3. Obligations to suppliers and customers include accounts payable, deferred income (unearned revenues), and warranties.

4. Obligations to employees:
   a. Obligations to employees result from deferred compensation for pensions and other postemployment benefits.
   b. The primary accounting issues for employee obligations are (1) determining the amount of benefits earned by employees and owed by a company, and (2) determining the amount invested by a company to meet these obligations and the amount earned on these investments.

5. Taxes and other obligations:
   a. Deferred income taxes result from differences between income tax expense and the amount of current tax obligation for income taxes as reported on a company's tax return.

     b.   Contingencies and commitments are potential future liabilities. The existence and amount of the liabilities depend on future events. If a probable loss will result from a contingency and the amount of the loss can be estimated reasonably, it should be included as a liability on a company's balance sheet.

6.   Stockholder investment and retained earnings:
    a.   The balance sheet reports the amount of a corporation's contributed capital and retained earnings.
    b.   Contributed capital includes the par or stated value of stock and paid-in capital in excess of par or stated value. If stock has no par or stated value, the entire amount of contributed capital is reported as common or capital stock.
    c.   Stock repurchased by a corporation from its stockholders is reported on the balance sheet as treasury stock.

7.   Transactions affecting stockholders' equity:
    a.   The statement of stockholders' equity reports events that affected the amount of stockholders' equity during a fiscal period. Common events include net income, cash dividends, issuing stock, repurchasing stock, stock dividends, exercise of stock options or warrants, and conversion of preferred stock or bonds.
    b.   Foreign currency adjustments are reported on the balance sheet as additions or subtractions in computing stockholders' equity.
    c.   A company cannot create income through transactions involving its own stock.
    d.   The primary stockholders' equity transactions that affect cash flow are the issuance or repurchase of stock and the payment of cash dividends.

8.   Corporations may issue preferred stock in addition to common stock. Preferred stock has a higher claim to dividends and assets than common stock.

9.   Amounts reported in the financial statements of foreign corporations often are measured using rules that differ from those in the U.S. Terminology used in these reports also may differ from that used in the U.S.

DEFINE   *Terms   and   Concepts   Defined   in   This   Chapter*

appropriation of retained earnings	date of payment	par value
authorized shares	date of record	preemptive right
charter	debentures	preferred stock
commitment	deferred tax liability	stock dividends
common stock	foreign currency translation	stock options
contingency	issued shares	stock split
contributed capital	minority interest	translation adjustment
convertible bonds	outstanding shares	treasury stock
date of declaration	paid-in capital in excess of par	warranty

SOLUTIONS

SELF-STUDY PROBLEM 9-1

Obligations in millions

Suppliers: Accounts payable	$ 541
Customers: Unearned income	$ 335
Lenders:	
Short-term debt and current portion	
of long-term debt	$2,698
Long-term debt	5,157
Total	$7,855
Governments: Deferred income taxes	$2,608
Employees:	
Accrued compensation and benefits	$ 511
Liability for postretirement benefits	997
Total	$1,508

Other current liabilities cannot be assigned.

SELF-STUDY PROBLEM 9-2

Bovine Co.
Stockholders' Equity

December 31,	1997	1996
Contributed capital:		
Common stock: $1 par, 250,000 shares		
authorized, 100,000 shares issued	$100,000	$100,000
Paid-in capital in excess of par	400,000	400,000
Retained earnings	150,000	30,000
Less treasury stock, 8,000 shares at cost	(56,000)	0
Total stockholders' equity	$594,000	$530,000

SELF-STUDY PROBLEM 9-3

1. Total contributed capital: $46,573,000 + 4,587,000 = $51,160,000.

2. Common shares outstanding: 46,573,000 issued − 10,224,000 in treasury = 36,349,000.

3. Treasury stock: $358,109.

4. Net change in treasury stock: 895,000 shares purchased − 25,000 shares reissued = 870,000 net increase in shares held in treasury.

5. Dividend per share: $46,296,000 paid/45,000,000 shares outstanding = $1.03.

6. Dividend payout ratio: $46,296,000 dividends/$88,229,000 net earnings = 52.5%.

7. Net cash outflow: $46,296,000 dividends + $39,985,000 purchase of stock = $86,281,000.

8. Net income is not generated by financing activities.

EXERCISES

9-1. Write a short definition for each of the terms listed in the "Terms and Concepts Defined in This Chapter" section.

9-2. On May 12, 1996, High Tech Co. contracted with Zermatt Labs to construct robotic equipment according to specifications provided by Zermatt. In exchange, Zermatt agreed to pay $300,000 to High Tech on June 1, 1996, and an additional $300,000 to High Tech when construction is completed and the equipment is installed. High Tech has agreed to complete the construction and installation by August 1, 1997. Should Zermatt report a liability on its financial statements for the fiscal year ended June 30, 1996, as a result of this contract? Should High Tech report a liability on its financial statements for the same period? Explain.

9-3. On November 22, 1996, Dairy Farms, Inc. signed an agreement with First Farmer's Bank. The agreement permits Dairy Farms to obtain up to $500,000 of cash from the bank anytime during the coming year. Any amount obtained is to be repaid in monthly installments of 5% of the amount borrowed plus interest at an annual rate of 10% of the amount borrowed. At the end of its fiscal year, on December 31, 1996, Dairy Farms had not obtained any money from the bank. Should Dairy Farms report a liability on its 1996 financial statements? Explain.

9-4. Long Fellow Co. ordered $100,000 of materials from Wads Worth Co. on March 23, 1996. Long Fellow received the materials on April 5, with terms 3/10, n/30. On April 12, Long Fellow paid for the materials. What transactions should Long Fellow record on March 23, April 5, and April 12? Use the following format:

Assets =	Liabilities + Equity	+ (Revenues − Expenses)

If Long Fellow made the payment on April 22, instead of April 12, what transaction would it record?

9-5. Natty Bumpo Co. sold $3 million of merchandise to customers in fiscal 1995. The merchandise was sold with a one-year warranty. Bumpo agreed to repair or replace defective merchandise that was returned to the company within one year of the purchase date. At the end of the 1995 fiscal year, Bumpo estimated that outstanding warranties would cost the company $200,000 during 1996. Actual warranty costs during fiscal 1996 amounted to: parts—$80,000, labor—$118,000, shipping—$9,000. What transactions should Bumpo record in 1995 and 1996 for the warranties? Use the following format:

Assets =	Liabilities + Equity	+ (Revenues − Expenses)

9-6. H.J. Heinz Company reported net pension costs (expenses) of $8,276,000 for its 1994 fiscal year. The company also reported prepaid pension costs of $160,460,000 at the end of the year. What effect did these amounts have on the company's 1994 balance sheet and income statement? What information do these disclosures provide about the funding status of the company's pension plan?

9-7. While auditing the 1995 financial statement of Monte Zuma Co., you discover that no provision has been made for postemployment benefit obligations associated with the company's provision of health care benefits to retired employees. When asked about the matter, Mr. Zuma, the president of the company, responded that the company paid for health care costs of retired employees each year as the costs were incurred. Therefore, no obligation existed. Write a short memo to the president explaining why postemployment benefits result in an obligation for the company that should be reported on its balance sheet.

9-8. Archer Daniels Midland Company reported income taxes of $211,500,000 in 1993. Of this amount, $19,646,000 was deferred and $191,854,000 was for the current period. What transaction would the company have recorded for its taxes in 1993? Use the following format:

Assets =	Liabilities + Owners' Equity	+ (Revenues − Expenses)

Explain why corporations recognize deferred taxes. What effect do these have on the income statement?

9-9. Pork Barrel Corp. reported the following information at the end of its 1996 fiscal year:

Accounts payable to suppliers	$ 800,000
Notes payable	3,500,000
Unfunded pension obligations	4,200,000
Loan guarantees for subsidiaries	2,000,000
Pending lawsuit against the company	5,000,000
Commitment to purchase materials in 1995	1,500,000
Capital leases (present value of future payments)	4,000,000
Noncancellable operating leases for 1995	1,800,000

All required principal and interest payments on the loans guaranteed by the company were paid by subsidiaries during the current year. The company's legal counsel believed the company would not have to pay any claims from the lawsuit. How much total liability did the company report for these items on its 1996 balance sheet? Explain your answer.

9-10. Organizations often lease resources rather than purchasing them. What two types of leases are commonly used to acquire access to resources? How do they differ? How does the type of lease affect a company's reported liabilities?

9-11. Jewels Vern Co. ordered $200,000 of merchandise for resale during December 1995. Title to the goods is transferred to the company at the time the merchandise is received. By the end of December, the company had received billing invoices for $100,000 of the merchandise, it had received $125,000 of the merchandise, it had paid $50,000 of the bills for merchandise received, and it had sold merchandise received during December that cost it $30,000. How would these events affect the company's assets, liabilities, and expenses for the year ended December 31, 1995? Explain your answer.

9-12. The stockholders' equity section of the balance sheet of The Coca-Cola Company is presented below:

December 31,	1993
(In millions except share data)	
Share-Owners' Equity	
Common stock of $.25 par value—	
Authorized: 2,800,000,000	
Issued: 1,703,526,299 shares	$ 426
Capital surplus	1,086
Reinvested earnings	9,458
Foreign currency translation adjustment and other	(505)
	10,465
Less treasury stock, at cost (406,072,817 shares)	5,881
Total	$ 4,584

How much contributed capital did Coca-Cola report for 1993? What was the total par value of Coke's outstanding stock? What was the amount of paid-in capital in excess of par? How much retained earnings did Coke report?

9-13. Diamond Jim Corp. issued 200,000 shares of common stock in March 1995. It was authorized to issue up to 1 million shares. The stock had a par value of $1 per share and sold at $10 per share. In December 1995, the company reported net income for 1995 of $150,000. It paid dividends of $50,000 during 1995. In May 1996, the company repurchased 20,000 shares of its stock at $20 per share. It reported net income of $200,000 in 1996, and paid dividends of $75,000 during the year. Prepare the stockholders' equity section of the company's balance sheet for 1995 and 1996.

9-14. What is the purpose of the statement of stockholders' equity? What does this statement report that is not reported on the balance sheet?

9-15. Rubbermaid, Inc. reported the following information for the fiscal year ended December 31, 1993: net earnings: $211,413,000; cash dividends: $64,938,000; stock issued for employee stock plans: par value $118,000; paid-in capital in excess of par $2,807,000; increase in foreign currency translation adjustment: $6,567,000. Complete the following statement of stockholders' equity for Rubbermaid.

(Dollars in thousands)	Par Value of Common Shares	Paid-In Capital in Excess of Par	Retained Earnings	Foreign Currency Translation Adjustment	Total Shareholders' Equity
Balance at December 31, 1992	$160,239	$5,003	$820,453	$1,954	$987,649
Net earnings					
Cash dividends					
Employee stock plans					
Foreign currency adjustment					
Balance at December 31, 1993					

9-16. During its 1995 fiscal year, Colridge Co. had the following transactions:
  a. Issued 100,000 shares of stock with a market value of $3.4 million to acquire Tennyson Co.
  b. Sold 200,000 shares to investors for $6.6 million.
  c. Repurchased 30,000 shares of its stock at a cost of $980,000.
  d. Transferred $4.7 million of net income to retained earnings.
  e. Paid cash dividends of $2 million.
  f. Issued a stock dividend, totaling 250,000 shares. The market value of the stock was $860,000.
  g. Issued stock worth $500,000 in exchange for convertible bonds with the same value.

Complete the following table by indicating the effect each transaction would have on each account or account type:

	Cash	Other Assets	Liabilities	Contributed Capital	Retained Earnings	Net Income
a.						
b.						
c.						
d.						
e.						
f.						
g.						

9-17. Micro Nesia Co. issued 600,000 shares of common stock in 1996. The stock sold for $10 per share. What amount would the company report for common stock, paid-in capital in excess of par, and total contributed capital for this transaction? Complete the following table based on these assumptions:
  a. The stock had a par value of $1 per share.
  b. The stock was no-par.
  c. The stock had a stated value of $2 per share.

	Common Stock	Paid-In Capital in Excess of Par	Total Contributed Capital
a.			
b.			
c.			

9-18. Creole Pepper Co. had 100,000 shares of no-par common stock and 20,000 shares of 7%, $10 par preferred stock outstanding at the end of its 1995 fiscal year. The company paid a 50¢ a share dividend to common stockholders and the required dividend to preferred stockholders. Net income for the year was $300,000. How much total dividend did Creole pay? What was the amount of net income available for common stock in 1995?

9-19. Cardboard Box Co. issued 100,000 shares of $1 par value stock during 1996 at a price of $18 per share. The company earned net income of $500,000 for the year and paid dividends of $200,000. It had a translation gain of $60,000 on foreign subsidiaries for which the functional currency was the foreign currency. It sold 10,000 shares of treasury stock for $17 per share. The market price was $12 per share when the treasury stock was purchased. The company reported the following information at the end of its 1995 fiscal year:

Common stock	$ 400,000
Paid-in capital	3,000,000
Retained earnings	5,200,000
Translation adjustments	(460,000)
Treasury stock	(350,000)
Total stockholders' equity	$7,790,000

Determine the amounts that would be reported for stockholders' equity at the end of the 1996 fiscal year. (Hint: The difference between the sales and purchase price of treasury stock should be included in paid-in capital.)

9-20. Mack-a-Roni Co. issued 200,000 shares of $1 par value stock during 1996 at a price of $8 per share. The company earned net income of $340,000 for the year and paid dividends of $250,000. Cash flow from operating activities was $355,000. It had a translation loss of $50,000 on foreign subsidiaries for which the functional currency was the foreign currency. It sold 20,000 shares of treasury stock for $8 per share. The market price was $6 per share when the treasury stock was purchased. Calculate the effect of these transactions on the company's net income and cash flows for the year. (Hint: The difference between the sales and purchase price of treasury stock is included in paid-in capital.)

PROBLEMS

PROBLEM 9-1   Identifying Liabilities

A business may contract with banks, individuals, and other companies to borrow money. Also, it may contract with suppliers, employees, and customers.

Required   Identify the types of obligations that a business may incur in these contractual relationships. How are these obligations reported by a business on its balance sheet? What are the purposes of the obligations?

PROBLEM 9-2   Interpreting Long-Term Debt

BellSouth Telecommunications reported the following information in its 1993 annual report:

Long-term debt consists primarily of debentures and notes issued by Bell-South Telecommunications. Interest rates and maturities of the amounts outstanding are summarized as follows at December 31:

Description	Interest Rates	Maturities	1993	1992
Debentures	3¼%–6⅞%	1995–2033	$1,270.0	$ 605.0
	7⅜%–8¼%	1999–2033	1,935.0	3,335.0
	8½%–10¾%	2001–2029	1,400.0	2,375.0
			4,605.0	6,315.0
Other long-term debt			. . .	. . .
Unamortized discount, net			(62.6)	(53.0)
Total			$7,380.7	$7,359.7

Maturities of long-term debt outstanding at December 31, 1993, are summarized below:

	1994	1995	1996	1997	1998	Thereafter	Total
Maturities	$213.8	$127.8	$66.1	$141.1	$764.2	$6,344.1	$7,657.1

Required Answer each of the following questions:

a. What are debentures? How do they differ from other forms of long-term debt?

b. What is unamortized discount? Why is it subtracted in calculating total long-term debt?

c. What is the purpose of the schedule reported by BellSouth? What information does it provide for external decision makers?

PROBLEM 9-3 Interpreting Pension Costs

Westinghouse reported the following information in its 1993 annual report:

Net Periodic Pension Costs (in millions)	1993
Cost of benefits earned	585
Recognized return on plan assets	(454)
Net periodic pension cost	$ 131

Funding Status (in millions) At December 31	1993
Projected benefit obligation for service to date	(5,841)
Plan assets at fair value	4,226
Projected benefit obligations in excess of plan assets	(1,615)
Net adjustments	2,476
Prepaid pension contribution	$ 861

Required Answer each of the following questions:

a. How much pension expense or revenue did Westinghouse recognize during 1993?

b. What was the return on plan assets in 1993? How did the return affect the amount of pension expense or revenue reported by Westinghouse?

c. What amount of retirement benefits was earned by employees in 1993?

d. What amount of asset or liability did Westinghouse recognize for its pension obligations in 1993?

e. What amount of obligation is owed to employees for services performed to date?

PROBLEM 9-4 Defining Liabilities

Reichman Co. reported income taxes payable and compensation and benefits payable among its current liabilities on its 1996 balance sheet. Also, the company reported deferred income taxes and deferred benefits and compensation among its long-term liabilities.

Required What criteria should be met for an item to be reported as a liability? Differentiate between current and long-term liabilities. What arguments can you provide for reporting these items as liabilities? What arguments can you provide for not reporting these items?

PROBLEM 9-5 Explaining Changes in Debt

Warner-Lambert Company reported the following information on its 1993 balance sheet:

(in millions)	1993	1992
Current liabilities:		
Notes payable—banks and other	$145.3	$171.5
Other short-term debt	507.5	0.0
Current portion of long-term debt	21.8	126.5
Long-term debt	546.2	564.6

The following information was reported on the company's cash flow statement:

(in millions)	1993
FINANCING ACTIVITIES:	
Proceeds from borrowings	$627.6
Principal payments on borrowings	(192.1)

The proceeds were used for notes payable and other short-term debt. The payments were for notes payable and current portion of long-term debt.

Required Explain the change in short-term (notes payable, other short-term debt, and current portion of long-term debt) and long-term debt balances to the extent possible from the information provided above.

PROBLEM 9-6   **Analysis of Other Postemployment Benefits**

The Coca-Cola Company reported the following information on its 1993 annual report (in millions):

Year ended December 31,	1993	1992
Accrued postemployment benefit liability	$233	$234
Net periodic postemployment benefit expense	30	29

Required   Why do accounting standards require companies to report postemployment benefit obligations? What effect did the obligation have on Coca-Cola's balance sheet and income statement in 1993? What steps can a company take to reduce its liability and expense for postemployment benefits?

PROBLEM 9-7   **Reporting Income Taxes**

McDonald's Corporation reported income taxes on its 1993 income statement of $593.2 million. Its statement of cash flows indicated the company paid income taxes of $521.7 million in 1993. The company's deferred tax liability increased by $52.4 million in 1993.

Required   Use the following format to identify the transactions McDonald's recorded during 1993 to account for these events:

Assets =	Liabilities + Equity	+ (Revenues − Expenses)

What information do deferred taxes provide external users about a company's future cash flows? Is the amount of deferred taxes reported by a company a reliable estimate of the company's current obligation for future tax payments? Explain your answer.

PROBLEM 9-8   **Interpreting Stockholder's Equity on the Balance Sheet**

The following information was reported by Marvel Entertainment, Inc. on its 1993 balance sheet:

(In millions)	December 31,	1993
Shareholders'	Common stock—$.01 par value	
Equity	Authorized 250,000,000 shares	
	Issued 97,642,992 shares	$ 1.0
	Additional paid-in capital	47.0
	Retained earnings	100.7
	Cumulative translation adjustment	(1.4)
	Total stockholder's equity	147.3

Required   Answer the following questions:

a. What is the purpose of each of the stockholders' equity items on the balance sheet?

b. What is the difference between authorized and issued shares? How many shares of stock did Marvel have outstanding at the end of 1993?

c. What average price did Marvel receive for the shares it sold to investors?

PROBLEM 9-9 Determining Stockholders' Equity

Ricardo Ball Co. began operations in October 1992. It issued 300,000 shares of $1 par value common stock and 10,000 shares of 8%, $100 par value preferred stock. The preferred stock is cumulative, nonvoting, and nonparticipating. The common stock sold for $10 per share and the preferred sold at par. The company is authorized to issue 1 million shares of common and 50,000 shares of preferred stock. In June 1994, the company repurchased 20,000 shares of common stock at a cost of $20 per share. The company's net income and cash dividend payments to common stockholders were:

Year	Net Income	Common Dividends
1993	$100,000	$ 0
1994	$400,000	$100,000
1995	$600,000	$200,000

The required cash dividends were paid to preferred stockholders each year.

Required Draft the stockholders' equity section of Ricardo Ball Co.'s balance sheet for the 1994 and 1995 fiscal years.

PROBLEM 9-10 Interpreting a Statement of Stockholders' Equity

A statement of stockholder's equity for Georgia-Pacific Corporation is provided below:

Statement of Shareholders' Equity — **Georgia-Pacific Corporation and Subsidiaries**

(Millions Except Shares)

Common Stock Shares		Total	Common Stock	Additional Paid-In Capital	Retained Earnings	Long-term Incentive Plan Deferred Compensation	Other
88,111,000	Balance at December 31, 1992	2,508	70	1,094	1,393	(39)	(10)
	Net loss	(34)	—	—	(34)	—	—
	Cash dividends declared	(142)	—	—	(142)	—	—
	Common stock issued:						
107,000	Stock option plan	7	—	7	—	—	—
1,575,000	Employee stock purchase plans	55	1	54	—	—	—
476,000	Long-term incentive plan	26	—	43	—	(17)	—
	Other	(18)	—	4	—	—	(22)
90,269,000	Balance at December 31, 1993	$2,402	$71	$1,202	$1,217	$(56)	$(32)

Required   Answer each of the following questions:

a.   What primary events affected owners' equity for the company during 1993?

b.   How many shares of common stock were issued during 1993? For what purposes were they issued? Who received these shares?

c.   What was the par value of the company's stock? What was the average per-share issue price of the company's stock?

d.   How much treasury stock did the company have outstanding at the end of 1993?

e.   Did the company maintain its capital during 1993? Explain your answer.

PROBLEM 9-11   Interpreting Stockholders' Equity Transactions

Portions of the statement of stockholders' equity and statement of cash flows for Genuine Parts Co. are provided below:

Consolidated Statement of Shareholders' Equity
Genuine Parts Co. and Subsidiaries

(dollars in thousands)	Common Stock	Additional Paid-In Capital	Retained Earnings	Treasury Stock	Total Shareholders' Equity
Balance at December 31, 1992	$124,163	0	$1,192,209	0	$1,316,372
Net income	0	0	257,813	0	257,813
Cash dividends declared	0	0	(131,681)	0	(131,681)
Stock options exercised	119	$2,566	74	0	2,759
Balance at December 31, 1993	**$124,282**	**$2,566**	**$1,318,415**	**0**	**$1,445,263**

Consolidated Statement of Cash Flows
Genuine Parts Co. and Subsidiaries

(dollars in thousands)	Year Ended December 31 1993
Net Cash Provided by Operating Activities	$200,571
Net Cash Used in Investing Activities	(118,233)
Financing Activities:	
Stock options exercised	2,759
Dividends paid	(129,846)
. . .	. . .
Net Cash Used in Financing Activities	(127,126)
Net Decrease in Cash and Cash Equivalents	$ (44,788)

. . . *indicates items omitted.*

Required   Explain the relationship between items reported on the statement of stockholders' equity and the statement of cash flows. Also, explain the relationship between items reported on the statement of cash flows and the income statement for Genuine Parts.

PROBLEM 9-12   **Interpreting Stock Transactions**

Peggy Sue owned 1,000 shares of Holly Co.'s 1 million shares of common stock at the beginning of 1996. She paid $10,000 for her shares of stock in 1992. On January 1, 1996, the company's stock had a total par value of $1 million and a total paid-in capital value of $9 million. The stock had a total market value of $50 million. The company sold 200,000 shares of stock during the year at a price of $60 per share. Peggy Sue purchased 200 shares of the new issue. After the sale of stock, the company issued a 4-for-1 stock split, reducing the par value of the stock to $0.25 per share. During 1996, the company earned net income of $4 million and paid a cash dividend of $1.5 million.

Required   Answer each of the following questions:

a.   What percentage of the company's stock did Peggy Sue own at the beginning of 1996? At the end of 1996?

b.   What was the total par value and total contributed capital for Holly Co. stock at the end of 1996?

c.   What amount of dividend did Peggy Sue receive in 1996? What was the dividend payout ratio for the company? What was the cash dividend yield for Peggy Sue?

PROBLEM 9-13   **Ethical Problems in Stock Transactions**

Perka Wits is an operations manager for Tall Timber Co. Through the company's stock option plan and other purchases, Perka has obtained 20,000 shares of the company's stock, less than 1% of the total shares of the company. The stock is currently trading at about $25 per share. The price has risen steadily over the last couple of years as the company has taken advantage of favorable industry conditions. Perka has advised a number of friends and relatives to buy the company's stock because she believes the company will continue to do well.

Perka is in charge of most of the company's timber holdings. One of Perka's field supervisors has informed her that employees have discovered a new disease in a portion of the company's trees. The trees are dying at an alarming rate, and the disease is spreading rapidly. Though the supervisor believes a treatment can be developed and hopes to minimize the effects, he believes the disease will create a major financial problem for the company in the near future. Perka realizes she will have to inform the company president of the problem and is preparing the necessary information. She wonders if she should sell her stock in the company before the information becomes public. Also, she is considering informing her friends and relatives that they should sell the stock, though she would not tell them the reason for her advice.

Required   What should Perka do?

PROBLEM 9-14   **Understanding Preferred Stock**

Sprint Corporation reported it had 208,000 shares of redeemable preferred stock outstanding at December 31, 1993. The stock had a stated value of $100 per share for a total stated value of $20.8 million. The stock was nonparticipating, nonvoting, cumulative, with a $7\frac{3}{4}$% annual dividend rate. The company reported the stock is "redeemed through a sinking fund at the rate of 12,000 shares, or $1.2 million per year, until 2008, at which time all remaining shares are to be redeemed. . . . In the event of default, the holders of the company's redeemable preferred stock are entitled to elect a certain number of directors until all arrears in dividend and sinking fund payments have been paid." (From Sprint Corporation Annual Report, 1993.)

Required   Answer each of the following questions:

a.   What is preferred stock? What preferences do preferred stockholders normally obtain? What preferences did Sprint's preferred stockholders obtain?

b.   What do the terms "nonparticipating," "nonvoting," and "cumulative" mean in terms of the rights of the stockholders?

c.   How much total dividends was the company expected to pay each year on the preferred stock? What effect did these payments have on common stockholders?

d.   What is redeemable stock? Why would Sprint issue redeemable stock? What is the purpose of a sinking fund? How much stock will the company need to redeem in 2008 if it follows its stated redemption policy?

PROBLEM 9-15   Interpreting Financial Statements

Excerpts from financial statements for Dresser Industries, Inc. are provided below.

Dresser Industries, Inc.
Excerpt from Balance Sheet

In Millions—October 31,	1993	1992
Shareholders' Investment		
Common shares, $0.25 par value	$ 41.6	$ 41.6
Capital in excess of par value	434.7	439.0
Retained earnings	954.6	911.7
Cumulative translation adjustments	(87.9)	(41.1)
Other adjustments	(13.8)	(4.0)
	1,329.2	1,347.2
Less treasury shares, at cost	385.6	397.8
Total shareholders' investment	$ 943.6	$ 949.4

Statement of Shareholders' Investment

In Millions—Year Ended October 31,	1993
Common Shares, Par Value	
Beginning of year	$ 41.6
End of Year	$ 41.6
Capital in Excess of Par Value	
Beginning of year	$ 439.0
Shares issued under employee benefit and dividend plans	(4.3)
End of year	$ 434.7
Retained Earnings	
Beginning of year	$ 911.7
Net earnings	126.7
Dividends on common shares	(82.4)
Other	(1.4)
End of year	$ 954.6

In Millions—Year Ended October 31,	1993
Cumulative Translation Adjustments	
Beginning of year	$ (41.1)
Adjustments due to translation rate changes	(46.8)
End of year	$ (87.9)
Other adjustments, end of year	$ (13.8)
Treasury Shares, at Cost	
Beginning of year	$(397.8)
Shares acquired	0
Shares issued under employee and director	
benefit plans	12.2
End of year	$(385.6)
Total Shareholders' Investment, End of Year	$ 943.6

Required   Answer the following questions:

a.   What was Dresser's total contributed capital for 1993?

b.   Did Dresser report a gain or loss from foreign currency translation adjustments during 1993 as reported on the balance sheet?

c.   What dollar amount of treasury stock did Dresser hold at the end of 1993?

d.   What was the amount of divided per share paid by Dresser during 1993, assuming that 135 million shares were outstanding when dividends were paid?

e.   What was the divided payout ratio for 1993 for Dresser?

f.   How much net cash flow was generated from financing activities associated with stockholders' equity during the current year? What were the sources of this cash flow?

g.   How much net income was generated from financing activities associated with stockholders' equity during the current year?

PROBLEM 9-16   Multiple-Choice Overview of the Chapter

1. On May 1, Ishida Co. purchased $10,000 of merchandise on credit with terms 2/10, n/30. The amount the company would pay for the merchandise on each of the following dates would be:

	May 8	**May 12**	**June 2**
a.	$9,800	$10,000	$10,000
b.	$9,800	$9,800	$10,000
c.	$9,800	$9,800	$9,800
d.	$10,000	$10,000	$10,000

2. A company's pension plan assets are estimated to have a market value of $8 million at the end of the 1996 fiscal year. The company's estimated obligation to employees

for pension benefits at the end of 1996 is $14 million. As a result of these events, the company would probably report which of the following on its 1996 balance sheet?
   a.   An asset
   b.   A liability
   c.   An asset and a liability
   d.   Neither an asset or a liability

3. Axel Corp. reported income taxes on its 1995 income statement of $300,000. It reported taxes payable for 1995 of $250,000 based on its taxable income. As a result of these events, the company's deferred income taxes account:
   a.   increased by $50,000.
   b.   decreased by $50,000.
   c.   decreased income tax expense by $50,000.
   d.   increased income tax expense by $50,000.

4. Weimar Co. reported an unused line of credit of $2 million and a contingency for loan guarantees of $1.3 million at the end of 1997. The amount of liability the company would report on its 1997 balance sheet associated with these items would be:
   a. $0.
   b.   1.3 million.
   c. $2 million.
   d. $3.3 million.

5. Echo Co. reported the following operating lease commitments in its 1995 annual report (in millions): 1996—$12, 1997—$10, 1998—$9, 1999—$5, 2000—$3, after 2000—$8. The amount of liability the company would report on its 1995 annual report for these leases would be:
   a. $47 million.
   b.   the present value of $47 million.
   c. $12 million.
   d. $0.

6. A stockholder who owns 5% of the common stock of a corporation has a right to each of the following except:
   a.   to 5% of any dividends paid to common stockholders.
   b.   to cast votes on matters brought to stockholders for a vote.
   c.   to receive a dividend of 5% of net income for the current period.
   d.   to purchase 5% of any additional common stock issued by the company.

7. If a company sells 100,000 shares of $1 par value stock for $8 per share, the amount of paid-in capital in excess of par from the sale would be:
   a. $700,000.
   b. $800,000.
   c. $100,000.
   d. $900,000.

8. A corporation had retained earnings of $400,000 at December 31, 1995. Net income for 1996 was $175,000, and the company paid a cash dividend of $75,000. Also, the company repurchased shares of its stock during the year at a total cost of $50,000. The balance of retained earnings at December 31, 1996, would be:
   a. $450,000.
   b. $550,000.
   c. $575,000.
   d. $500,000.

9. A corporation issued a 10% stock dividend during its 1996 fiscal year. The market value of the stock was $20 per share at the time the dividend was issued. One million shares of stock were outstanding. The par value of the stock was $1 per share. Which of the following correctly identifies the effect on the financial statements of this transaction?

	Assets	Equity	Net Income
a.	increase	decrease	no effect
b.	no effect	decrease	no effect
c.	no effect	no effect	no effect
d.	no effect	decrease	decrease

10. All of the following are typically true of preferred stock except:
   a. it has a fixed dividend rate.
   b. it has a higher claim to dividends than common stock.
   c. it has a higher liquidation claim than common stock.
   d. it has a higher claim to voting rights than common stock.

C A S E S

CASE 9-1 Making Credit Decisions

As an employee of the loan department of Metropolitan Bank, one of your primary tasks is analyzing information provided by organizations applying for commercial loans. Most applicants are small businesses seeking additional capital to acquire long-term assets. Other applicants are seeking financing to acquire existing businesses. A typical applicant is Cleopatra Jones, who owns Cleopatra's, a women's clothing store. Ms. Jones has applied for a loan of $30,000 to finance an expansion of her business.

Required   Identify the types of information you would need from Ms. Jones to help you make a loan decision. Explain why each type of information would be useful.

CASE 9-2 Interpreting Stockholders' Equity

A portion of the consolidated balance sheet of Unisys Corporation follows:

December 31 (Millions)	1993	1992
Total assets	$7,519.2	$7,548.7
Total liabilities	4,823.7	5,304.6
Stockholders' equity		
Preferred stock	1,570.2	1,578.0
Common stock, shares issued: 1993—171.2; 1992—162.6	1.7	1.6
Retained earnings (accumulated deficit)	159.8	(228.0)
Other capital	963.8	892.5
Stockholders' equity	2,695.5	2,244.1
Total liabilities and stockholders' equity	$7,519.2	$7,548.7

A note to the statement reveals:

> The Company has 360,000,000 authorized shares of common stock. In April of 1991, the Certificate of Incorporation of the Company was amended to change the par value of the common stock from $5 per share to $.01 per share. . . .
>
> In 1992, the Company resumed payment of dividends on preferred stock which had been suspended in February 1991. At December 31, 1993, preferred dividends of $107.8 million were in arrears, ...

Required   Prepare a report that explains the following:

a.   Of what economic significance is the par value of a company's stock? What is the significance of the decision by Unisys to restate the par value of its stock? What advantage exists for the company?

b.   What are the primary attributes of preferred stock? In what ways is preferred stock equity? In what ways is it debt? Why do companies issue preferred stock?

c.   What effect does the suspension of dividends on the preferred stock have on Unisys' financial statements? What economic effect does it have on the company? If the preferred stock and dividends in arrears were reported by Unisys as liabilities, what would the effect be on its balance sheet?

d.   Assess the financial condition of Unisys' common stockholders at the end of 1993.

CASE 9-3   Analyzing Liabilities and Stockholders' Equity

Review the financial statements of Nike, Incorporated provided in Appendix B of this book.

Required   Write a report that covers the following:

a.   What were the company's most important liabilities in 1994? How did the relative importance of the liabilities change from the prior year?

b.   How did changes in the company's liabilities affect cash flows associated with financing activities for 1994? How did the company's liabilities affect its net income in 1994?

c.   Describe major changes in the company's long-term debt during 1994.

d.   Explain the meaning and importance of each of the major items reported as part of the company's stockholders' equity.

e.   Describe each of the major stockholders' equity transactions that occurred during the 1994 fiscal year. Identify the cash flow and income effect of each transaction.

PROJECTS

PROJECT 9-1   Analysis of Liabilities

Locate recent annual reports for corporations in three different industries. Identify the primary similarities and differences in the companies' liabilities. Write a short report comparing the captions and relative amounts of different items in the liabilities section of the balance sheets.

PROJECT 9-2 Identifying Debt Transactions

Use a journal index (for example, the *Business Periodicals Index* or the *Accountant's Index*) or *The Wall Street Journal Index* to locate recent articles that discuss debt transactions of major corporations, such as the issuance of new debt. Summarize two articles that discuss reasons for the transactions. Include complete references to the articles.

PROJECT 9-3 Comparing Financial Statement Numbers

Locate recent annual reports of five corporations. Alternatively, use *Moody's Industrial Manual* or another source of financial statement information. Select companies from different industries. Include at least one utility, one financial institution, and one retail company. Complete the following table by identifying the ratio of the amount of debt to the company's total assets. For example, if a company has $1 million long-term debt and $5 million in total assets, the ratio for long-term debt would be .20. Short-term debt should include notes payable, current portions of long-term debt, and other similar items.

Name of Company	Industry	Short-Term Debt	Current Liabilities	Long-Term Debt	Total Liabilities

Write a short report to accompany the table comparing the relative amount of liabilities for the corporations. Indicate the source of your data.

PROJECT 9-4 Analysis of Stockholders' Equity

Locate recent annual reports for corporations in three different industries. Identify the primary similarities and differences in the companies' stockholders' equities. Write a short report comparing the captions, primary transactions, and relative amounts of different items in the stockholders' equity section of the balance sheets and in the statements of stockholders' equity.

PROJECT 9-5 Unethical Behavior

Use a journal index (for example, the *Business Periodicals Index* or the *Accountant's Index*) or *The Wall Street Journal Index* to locate a recent article that discusses a case involving insider trading or fraudulent trading activities of corporate stock. Summarize the article by explaining key activities associated with the insider trading or fraud. If the case resulted in penalties, identify them. Make sure you include a complete reference to the article.

PROJECT 9-6   Comparing Financial Statement Numbers

Locate recent annual reports of five corporations. Alternatively, use *Moody's Industrial Manual* or another source of financial statement information. Select companies from different industries. Include at least one utility, one financial institution, and one retail company. Complete the following table by identifying the ratio of the amount of each component of stockholders' equity to the company's total assets. For example, if a company has $1 million in preferred stock and $5 million in total assets, the amount of preferred stock would be .20. Preferred stock and common stock should include both par and paid-in capital in excess of par amounts for each class of stock.

Name of Company	Industry	Preferred Stock	Common Stock	Retained Earnings	Total Stockholders' Equity

Write a short report to accompany the table comparing the components of stockholders' equity for the corporations. Indicate the source of your data.

Chapter
10

Analysis of Financing Activities

Chapter 9 described accounting for equity and debt and identified various financial instruments and obligations corporations use to finance their assets and operating activities. Among these were common and preferred stock, bonds, notes, accounts payable, and leases. This chapter examines the use of accounting information by those who analyze financing activities. This analysis affects contractual relationships among managers, providers of capital, and providers of goods and services. Managers have a responsibility to make decisions that are in the interest of a company's owners. At the same time, they should operate within the constraints imposed by contracts with creditors, employees, and other resource providers, which are designed to protect the interests of these contracting parties. Thus, managers should make decisions that increase the value of a corporation to its stockholders and meet the company's obligations to creditors and other parties.

Managers use accounting information to make financing decisions. Investors use accounting information to evaluate whether management decisions are consistent with maximizing stockholder value. Creditors and other contracting parties use accounting information to evaluate whether management decisions are consistent with their interests.

The first part of this chapter examines the relationship between risk and return attributes of financial instruments. Risk and return associated with securities, such as stocks and bonds, affect their prices, as discussed in Chapter 8. Financing activities, in turn, affect security risk and return, as examined in this chapter. The latter part of the chapter considers how financing activities can be analyzed to assess their effect on risk and return.

Major topics covered in this chapter include:

- The effect of financing decisions on risk and return.
- Risk, return, and pricing of financial instruments.
- Using accounting information to evaluate financing activities.

After completing this chapter, you should be able to:

1. Explain the concept of capital structure.
2. Identify the effects of financing activities on financial statements.
3. Determine the effect of financial leverage on a company's earnings.
4. Determine the effect of financial leverage on a company's risk.
5. Explain the effect of financial leverage on common stock prices.
6. Determine the effect of preferred stock on risk and return.
7. Explain the effect of default and interest rate risk on bond prices.
8. Explain the effect of financial and interest rate risk on preferred stock prices.
9. Identify economic and company attributes that affect financial leverage.
10. Explain how accounting information is useful for evaluating financing activities.
11. Analyze a company's financing decisions.

RISK AND RETURN

Financing activities involve choices about how a company obtains cash to acquire other resources and to pay for services. Managers have several types of financial instruments from which to choose, including common stock, preferred stock, short-term debt, long-term debt, and leases. The risk and return attributes of these instruments vary. Managers have some discretion over these attributes, such as coupon rates, repayment schedules, conversion rights, call and redemption provisions, voting rights, and dividend payments. Exhibit 10-1 reports financing arrangements of several major corporations. The exhibit indicates the proportion of each company's finances composed of different types of liabilities and equities.

Exhibit 10-1   Financing Arrangements for Selected Corporations as a Percentage of Total Assets

	Coca-Cola	The Limited	McDonald's	Nike	Walt Disney
Current liabilities	43.0%	17.1%	9.2%	20.7%	24.0%
Long-term liabilities	18.9	23.9	38.7	4.0	33.2
Preferred stock	0.0	0.0	5.6	13.7	0.0
Common stock	12.6	7.7	2.9	5.1	7.5
Retained earnings	25.6	51.3	43.6	56.5	35.4

Data source: 1993 annual reports.

Objective 1
Explain the concept of capital structure.

Financing arrangements vary depending on a company's operating activities and performance. **The way in which a company chooses to finance its assets and operating activities is its** *capital structure*. For example, McDonald's capital structure includes a large proportion of long-term debt. McDonald's is in an industry that requires a large amount of investment in plant assets. Long-term debt is used to finance these assets. In contrast, Nike's capital structure contains little long-term debt. Instead, it has used a larger proportion of preferred stock.

Companies in the same industry may have different capital structures. For example, Coca-Cola and McDonald's are in the food industry. The Limited and Nike are in the apparel industry. The capital structures of these companies differ, however. Capital structures also vary for companies in different countries. High proportions of debt financing are common in some countries, Japan for example, because of economic and political conditions in those countries.

Accounting information about a company's capital structure is used by decision makers in assessing the risk and return they expect from contractual relationships with the company. The next section explains these concepts.

Financial Leverage

Objective 2
Identify the effects of financing activities on financial statements.

To understand how financing decisions affect a company's performance and value, consider the effect of financing decisions on a company's financial statements. Exhibit 10-2 illustrates this effect.

Exhibit 10-2   The Effects of Financing Decisions on Financial Statements

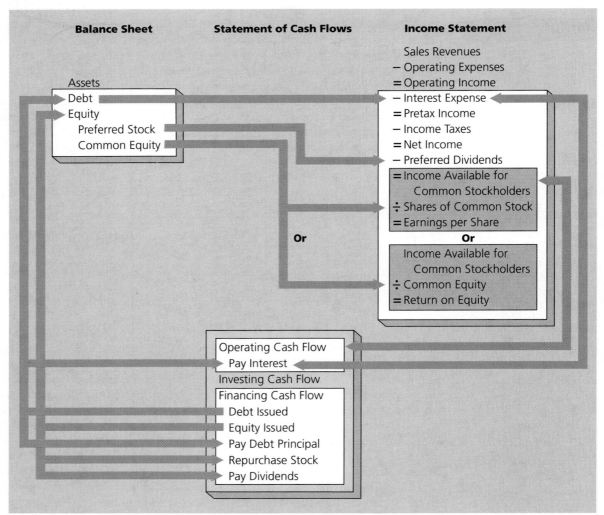

Sales revenues and operating expenses result from operating activities, primarily. Items appearing on a company's income statement from sales revenues through operating income are not affected by financing decisions. Those items below operating income are affected, however, as illustrated in Exhibit 10-2.

When a company borrows money, it incurs interest as the cost of using someone else's money. This cost reduces income. Therefore, net income is lower by the amount of interest expense incurred during a period. Borrowing money also reduces the amount of equity a company has to issue to finance its operations. If a company needs $10 million to acquire assets and it borrows $4 million, it will have to issue only $6 million of equity. If it sells its stock for $10 per share, it will need to sell 600,000 shares of stock. If it does not borrow any money, this company will need to issue 1 million shares of stock at $10 per share to obtain the $10 million of financing it needs. Therefore, earnings per share often is higher when a company borrows money than if it issues more shares of stock. This effect of debt on earnings per share is referred to as financial leverage. *Financial leverage* **is the use of debt to increase a company's earnings performance and commonly is measured by the ratio of debt to equity in a company's capital structure.** A highly financially levered company has a high proportion of debt to equity.

If we assume that earnings provide a measure of return used by investors to value a company's stock, higher earnings per share (resulting from using debt) will increase a company's stock price. This higher price occurs if the risk (discount rate) of the stock does not change. We will examine the effect of financing activities on risk later in this chapter. Observe, however, that the existence of debt in a company's capital structure can improve the company's earnings on a per share basis.

Another measure that provides similar information is return on equity. *Return on equity* **is income available for common stockholders divided by common stockholders' equity:**

Return on Equity = (Net Income − Preferred Dividends)/Common Equity

Return on equity (ROE), like earnings per share (EPS), is a measure of a company's relative performance after considering the effect of financing decisions. An advantage of ROE over EPS is that ROE can be compared across companies. EPS can be compared to other measures that are expressed on a per share basis, such as stock price, and it can be compared over time if the number of shares does not change. It is difficult to compare across companies, however, because companies have different numbers of shares outstanding. Therefore, if Company A reports earnings per share of $2 and Company B reports earnings per share of $3, we cannot determine that Company B has performed better than Company A. If Company B's return on equity is 25% and Company A's is 15%, however, we can be reasonably certain that Company B has performed better than Company A.

The issuance of debt and equity also affects a company's cash flows. It receives cash when debt and equity are issued, but pays out cash when principal, interest, and dividends are paid. Also, it pays out cash if it repurchases stock. Thus, in addition to evaluating the effect of financing decisions on a company's earnings, it is important to evaluate the effect on cash flows. In particular, it is important to determine whether a company can generate enough cash to meet its debt requirements in addition to its other needs. We will return to cash flow issues later. First, consider how financing activities affect stockholder returns.

The Return Effect of Financial Leverage

Objective 3
Determine the effect of financial leverage on a company's earnings.

To illustrate the effect of financing decisions on performance, consider the outcomes for two companies in Exhibit 10-3.

Both Equity Co. and Debt Co. have assets of $1,000 and both companies earn $250 of operating income. Thus, the companies are the same except for financing. Equity Co. uses 70% equity in its capital structure, while Debt Co. uses 70% debt. The result of this difference is that Equity Co. incurs less interest expense ($30 relative to $70 for Debt Co.). Tax rates for both companies are 30%. Therefore, Equity Co.'s net income and income available for common are higher than Debt Co.'s ($154 relative to $126). However, Equity Co. has to use more

Exhibit 10-3   The Effect of Financial Leverage on Return on Equity

	Equity Co.	Debt Co.
Assets	$1,000	$1,000
Debt	300	700
Equity	700	300
Shares	100	50
Operating income	250	250
Interest expense	30	70
Pretax income	220	180
Income taxes	66	54
Net income	154	126
Preferred dividends	0	0
Income available for common	154	126
Earnings per share	1.54	2.52
Return on equity	22%	42%

stock to finance its operations than Debt Co. Therefore, relative to the amount of equity investment in the company, Equity Co. earns a lower return (22%) than Debt Co. (42%).

Two major factors are important in this analysis. First, debt results in interest expense that reduces earnings. Second, debt also reduces the amount of equity that a company must issue. Therefore, return on equity (or earnings per share) often is higher when debt is included in a company's capital structure. **Debt can be beneficial to a company's stockholders.**

The Risk Effect of Financial Leverage

Objective 4
Determine the effect of financial leverage on a company's risk.

The use of debt can increase a company's return on equity, as discussed in the previous section. The use of debt is not without its cost, however. Consider the effect of financial leverage on the variability of earnings and return on equity described in Exhibit 10-4.

The exhibit illustrates three types of conditions for Equity Co. and for Debt Co. These three conditions correspond to a bad year, a normal year, and a good year. In a bad year, operating income for both companies is $50. In a normal year, operating income is $250, and in a good year, operating income is $450. Observe, however, that earnings and return on equity are not the same for each company. Equity Co. incurs a lower amount of interest than Debt Co. This expense is incurred whether the company has a bad, normal, or good year. If the year is bad, both companies report low incomes and returns on equity. Debt Co. reports a lower income than Equity Co. It reports a loss (and a negative ROE) because its interest expense is higher than its operating income. If the year is

Exhibit 10-4   The Effect of Financial Leverage on Risk

	Equity Co.			Debt Co.		
	Bad Year	**Normal Year**	**Good Year**	**Bad Year**	**Normal Year**	**Good Year**
Assets	$1,000	$1,000	$1,000	$1,000	$1,000	$1,000
Debt	300	300	300	700	700	700
Equity	700	700	700	300	300	300
Operating income	50	250	450	50	250	450
Interest expense	30	30	30	70	70	70
Pretax income	20	220	420	−20	180	380
Income taxes	6	66	126	−6	54	114
Net income	14	154	294	−14	126	266
Return on equity	2.0%	22.0%	42.0%	−4.7%	42.0%	88.7%

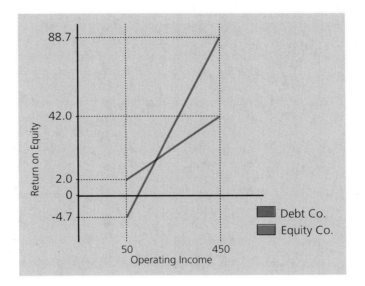

Objective 5
Explain the effect of financial leverage on common stock prices.

good, both companies report high incomes. Debt Co. reports a higher return on equity than Equity Co. because of its lower amount of equity.

Thus, in good years (and normal years), Debt Co. performs better than Equity Co. But, in bad years, Equity Co. performs better than Debt Co. The graph in Exhibit 10-4 depicts the relationship between operating income and return on equity for the two companies. As operating income increases, return on equity increases for both companies. It increases more rapidly for Debt Co. than for Equity Co., however. The slope of the line indicating the relationship is steeper for Debt Co. This relationship means that Debt Co. is riskier than Equity Co.

Debt Co.'s earnings and return on equity are more volatile than Equity Co.'s. This higher volatility means that earnings and return on equity are less certain. Therefore, we should assume that investors will require a higher rate of return

Exhibit 10-6   Effect of Preferred Stock on Return

	Issue Preferred Stock	Issue Common Stock
Existing assets	1,000	1,000
New assets	400	400
Existing equity	1,000	1,000
New preferred stock	400	0
New common stock	0	400
Operating income	300	300
Interest expense	0	0
Pretax income	300	300
Income taxes	90	90
Net income	210	210
Preferred dividends	32	0
Income available for common	178	210
Common equity	1,000	1,400
Return on equity	17.8%	15%

Prior to the new financing, Equity Co. had $1,000 of assets financed completely by common stock. The new financing will require either $400 of preferred stock or $400 of additional common stock. We will assume that the company expects operating income of $300 after its plant expansion. This amount would occur whether the company issues preferred or common stock. No interest will be incurred because the company has no debt. The tax rate is assumed to be 30%. Thus, the company will earn $210 of net income, regardless of which alternative it uses. If preferred stock is issued, however, the company will pay dividends of $32 (8% × $400) to preferred stockholders. This payment leaves $178 available for common stockholders (for dividends or reinvestment). Also, issuing preferred stock reduces the amount of common stock outstanding from the amount that would be necessary if common stock is issued. Therefore, return on common equity is higher if preferred stock is issued than if common stock is issued. Preferred stock produces a financial leverage effect similar to that of debt.

Issuing preferred stock also increases a company's risk, similar to the effect of debt. The preferred dividends usually must be paid, either in the current year or in some future year. If a company's net income is low, preferred stock will reduce return on equity because the dividends further reduce income available for common. If net income is high, preferred stock will increase return on equity because the amount of common equity will be less than if common stock were used to finance the company. Thus, preferred stock magnifies the effect of variations in net income on return on equity.

A disadvantage of preferred stock over debt financing is that dividends are not deductible for tax purposes. Therefore, a company does not reduce its tax payments as it does when it pays interest. If a company pays $1 million in dividends (preferred or common), its cash outflow is $1 million. If, however, it pays $1 million in interest and its tax rate is 30%, its actual cash outflow is only $700,000 because of the tax savings. On the other hand, preferred stockholders cannot force a company into bankruptcy as can debtholders. Preferred stock has some features of debt and some of equity. It is an alternative source of financing that appeals to some investors and to some companies.

SELF-STUDY PROBLEM 10-1

Andromeda Corp. began operations in October 1996. Common stock was issued at that time for a total of $80 million (10 million shares). During the fiscal year ended September 30, 1997, Andromeda's net income was $16 million after taxes of $8 million and its stock increased in value to $10 per share, its current price.

The company has an opportunity to expand its operations into a new product line, but the expansion will require new investment of $30 million. Management is considering how it might raise the new capital for this investment. Three alternatives are being considered. Option A provides for issuing new shares of common stock to raise the amount. Management believes the stock will sell at its current price. Option B provides for issuing 300,000 shares of $100 par value preferred stock with a $10 dividend rate. Management believes the shares would sell at their par value. Option C provides for issuing $30 million of 20-year, 8% bonds. Management believes the bonds would sell at face (maturity) value.

Assume the new investment will provide additional annual operating income to Andromeda of $9 million for the foreseeable future. Without the investment, Andromeda expects an annual net income of $16 million for the foreseeable future.

Required

What would be the effect of each option on Andromeda's common stockholders? What recommendations would you make to Andromeda's managers concerning this investment?

The solution to Self-Study Problem 10-1 appears at the end of the chapter.

RISK AND PRICES OF OTHER FINANCIAL INSTRUMENTS

Risk affects the prices of bonds, preferred stock, and other financial instruments. The following sections examine these effects.

Bond Prices

Objective 7
Explain the effect of default and interest rate risk on bond prices.

A primary concern of bond investors is the risk that an issuer might default on the payment of interest or principal. This financial risk often is referred to as **default risk**. The default risks of bonds are signaled by bond ratings. Rating agencies, such as Moody's and Standard and Poor's, evaluate default risk and assign a rating to many bonds, especially those that are widely traded. Exhibit 10-7 describes commonly used ratings.

Bonds rated Baa/BBB and above are **investment grade bonds**. Banks, insurance companies, and certain other organizations are permitted to invest only in investment grade bonds. Bonds rated Ba/BB and below are **speculative grade bonds**, also known as **junk bonds**. Deregulation of savings and loan institutions in the 1980s permitted these organizations to invest in junk bonds. Defaults on these bonds were associated with failures of many savings and loans.

In addition to letters to denote quality ratings, bonds are separated into groups within each rating class. For example, Moody's designates bonds in the

Exhibit 10-7   Bond Ratings

Grade	Rating Moody/S&P	Explanation
Investment Grade	Aaa/AAA Aa/AA A/A Baa/BBB	Best quality, lowest risk High quality Upper medium quality Medium quality
Speculative Grade	Ba/BB B/B Below B	Speculative quality Low quality Very low quality

highest group in each class with a 1, those in the middle group with a 2, and those in the lowest group with a 3. Bond ratings for some major corporations are listed below:

Corporation	Moody's Bond Rating
Coca-Cola	Aa3
The Limited	A1
McDonald's	Aa2
Delta Airlines	Ba1
Digital Equipment	Ba1
Unisys	Ba3
Macy's	Ca
Trans World Airlines	Ca

Data source: Moody's Investors Service, Moody's Bond Record, October 1994.

Corporations that have performed well, Coca-Cola, The Limited, and Mc-Donald's, have high ratings. Delta Airlines, Digital Equipment Company, and Unisys are rated below investment grade because of their poor performances. Companies that are in bankruptcy, Macy and TWA, are rated Ca.

Bonds with high ratings typically pay lower market returns (or yields) than those with low ratings. For example, Exhibit 10-8 describes average market returns for Baa- and Aaa-rated bonds from 1990 to 1994.

Yields were lower for higher rated bonds from 1990 to 1994. Yields were higher, however, for all ratings in 1990 than in other years. The higher yields resulted from higher interest rates throughout the economy in 1990. The Federal Reserve reduced interest rates from 1990 to 1993 to stimulate a recovery from the recession of this period. Interest rates went back up in 1994 as the economy began to prosper.

To illustrate the effect of changes in risk on bond prices, assume Capital Co. issued $10 million of 10-year bonds in April of 1995 at a nominal rate of 8%. The bonds were rated Aa, were sold to yield an 8% market rate, and paid interest semiannually. The price of each bond at the time it was issued would have been:

$$PV = \sum_{t=1}^{20} \frac{\$40}{(1.04)^t} + \frac{\$1,000}{(1.04)^{20}}$$

From Table 2, the interest factor for an annuity of 20 periods at 4% is 13.59033. From Table 1, the interest factor for a single payment at the end of 20 periods at 4% is 0.45639. Therefore, the price of each bond was $1,000 = [($40 × 13.59033) + ($1,000 × 0.45639)]. The bonds sold at maturity value because the nominal and market rates were equal.

The *primary market* **is the market in which new (or original) issues of stocks and bonds are sold.** This market determines the amount of cash a company will receive for its securities. Ignoring sales fees, Capital Co. would have received $10 million for its bonds issued in April 1995.

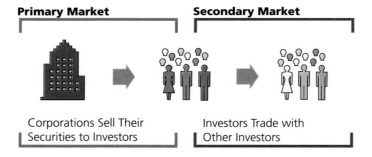

Once these bonds have been sold to investors, they may be resold in the *secondary market*, **a market in which investors sell to each other**. Thus, if you had purchased 10 of Capital's bonds for $10,000 in April 1995, you could sell them at a later date to other investors. The secondary market does not have a direct effect on the amount received by Capital or on amounts it reports on its fi-

Exhibit 10-8   Yield and Risk for Corporate Bonds

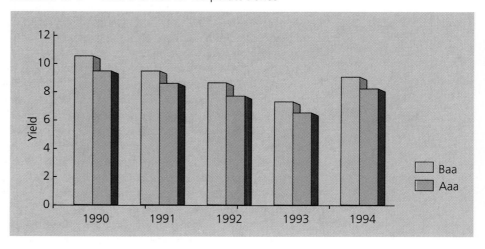

Data source: Moody's Investors Service, Moody's Bond Record, October 1994. Data are for September of each year.

nancial statements. Capital's operating performance and financial condition affect its bond prices in the secondary market, however.

For example, suppose you wished to sell your bonds in April 1997. Assume the general level of interest rates had not changed from April 1995. But, assume Capital's financial condition had worsened so its bonds had been downgraded to an A rating. As a result, the current market yield on the bonds had increased to 10% because of increased default risk. What effect did the increase in default risk have on the price of the bonds? The price of the bonds would be computed using an effective yield of 5% per semiannual period for a remaining life of 16 periods. Using values from Tables 1 and 2, the price per bond would be $891.62 = [($40 × 10.83777) + ($1,000 × 0.45811)]. Your investment of $10,000 has decreased in value to $8,916.20. If Capital's financial condition had improved, the value of your investment would have increased.

Changes in the rate used to discount the cash flows received from a bond affect the price of the bond. In addition to changes in the default risk of a bond, changes in the level of interest rates also affect a bond's or stock's price. As interest rates increase, the prices of existing stocks and bonds decrease. Interest rates affect the rate of return expected by investors in the price equation:

Price = Expected Cash Flow/Required Rate of Return

Thus, price decreases as the required rate of return increases. If the level of interest rates in the economy had increased between April 1995 and April 1997, the price you would receive for your bonds in 1997 would be lower than the amount you paid, even if their default risk remained unchanged. Most bonds pay a cash flow that is fixed at the time they are issued. For example, Capital Co. promised to pay $40 each six months plus $1,000 at maturity. This amount does not change even if market conditions, interest rates, or company attributes change, unless the company defaults. Therefore, the expected cash flows from a bond remain constant each period. Along with the level of interest rates in the economy, default risk does change, however, and accounting information is useful for bondholders and other creditors in assessing that default risk.

Preferred Stock Prices

Risk affects the prices of preferred stock as well. Preferred stock is an alternative financial instrument to either long-term debt or common stock. Preferred stock is less risky than common stock. Therefore, a company expects to pay a lower return on preferred than on common stock. In contrast to common stock, preferred stock may provide a source of cash without diluting control of a company, because preferred stock normally does not have voting rights.

Objective 8
Explain the effect of financial and interest rate risk on preferred stock prices.

Because preferred stocks generally do not have maturity dates, they have an indefinite life. Therefore, the price (P) of a share of preferred stock can be calculated from the expected cash flow to owners (C) and the required rate of return (R): P = C / R. For example, assume Capital Co. issued preferred stock with a par value of $100 and an annual dividend rate of $5. If the stock sold at a market return of 5%, the price of the stock should be $100 = ($5 / 0.05). A change in the rate of return after the sale would affect the price of the stock in the secondary market. If the rate decreased to 4.5% because of improvements in Capital's financial condition or a decrease in interest rates, the price should increase to approximately $111 = ($5 / 0.045).

Other Financing Instruments

In addition to stocks and bonds, corporations issue promissory notes, generally with a maturity of one to seven years, and short-term notes, often referred to as **commercial paper**. These notes normally are issued to financial institutions and to other corporations. They generally are marketable, and their prices are affected by changes in risk much the way bond prices are affected. Most other obligations, such as accounts payable and deferred compensation, are not marketable. A company's risk affects the uncertainty of cash flows to these creditors, suppliers, and employees, however. They may assess risk in much the same way as bond- and stockholders, though their investments are not priced in a securities market.

This section has examined the relationships between the prices of a company's financial instruments and their expected cash flows and risks. Financing activities affect expected cash flows and risks. The following sections examine capital structure decisions that affect security prices, cash flows, and risks.

SELF-STUDY PROBLEM 10-2

The El Roncho Salsa Co. issued $10 million of 8%, 10-year bonds on April 1, 1995. The bonds sold at their maturity value of $1,000 per bond. They pay interest semiannually on April 1 and September 1. Because of changes in the level of interest rates and changes in El Roncho's default risk, the market rate on the bonds increased to 10% by September 1, 1998.

El Roncho's net income for 1997 was $14 million. The company's 10 million shares of common stock were selling at $8 per share. In August 1998, the company projected that its net income for that year would decrease to $10 million.

Required

(a) Compute the price you would expect to pay for El Roncho's bonds in September 1998. (b) Explain the effect you would expect the information reported in August 1998 to have on the price of El Roncho's stock.

The solution to Self-Study Problem 10-2 appears at the end of the chapter.

ATTRIBUTES AFFECTING FINANCIAL LEVERAGE

Objective 9
Identify economic and company attributes that affect financial leverage.

The amount of financial leverage a company uses depends on economic conditions, such as the level of interest rates. Also, it depends on attributes of a company, such as the types of assets it uses and the stability of its earnings.

The level of interest rates in the economy is affected by federal government policies. Rates increase and decrease as the Federal Reserve Board increases and decreases the rate banks pay for funds. During the recession of the early 1990s, the Federal Reserve decreased rates sharply to stimulate the economy. Lower interest rates increase the amount of money companies and individuals borrow. More money means more buying, and more buying means more production, more profits, more jobs, and more taxes. As interest rates decline, the prices of existing stocks and bonds increase. Interest rates affect the discount rate (required rate of return) in the price equation:

Price = Expected Cash Flow/Required Rate of Return

Thus, price increases as the required rate of return decreases.

The level of interest rates has several effects on capital structure. Companies may choose to borrow more, thereby increasing their financial leverage. Lower interest rates also may stimulate companies to refinance existing debt. For example, assume a company's liabilities in 1992 included $30 million of long-term debt, paying 10% interest. If interest rates decreased in 1992 so the company could issue the same debt at 8%, the company could save $600,000 ($30 million × 2%) a year, before taxes, by refinancing its outstanding debt. The company might issue new debt at the lower rate and use the proceeds to repay its existing debt.

If the debt consisted of bonds, the price of the bonds in the secondary market would increase as interest rates decreased. Therefore, the current market price of the company's 10% bonds would be high relative to the price it would receive from issuing 8% bonds. Many bonds contain call provisions so a company can repurchase its bonds if interest rates decrease. The call price for most bonds is slightly higher than their face value. By selling $30 million of 8% bonds, the company could call its 10% bonds and repay them at only slightly more than $30 million, making call provisions useful for that company. Similarly, preferred stock may have a redemption provision that serves the same purpose.

Another way companies take advantage of lower interest rates is to reduce their financial leverage by issuing additional stock. At the beginning of the 1990s, many companies were highly levered. The amount of leverage was a cause of the recession, as many companies struggled to repay principal and interest on their debt. Bankruptcies were frequent. As stock prices increased because of lower interest rates, many companies took the opportunity to issue new shares of stock at higher market prices. Proceeds from these shares were used to repay debt.

Company attributes also affect capital structure decisions. Some companies rely on a large amount of plant assets. Large amounts of equipment and other facilities are needed to produce goods such as petroleum products, automobiles, or airplanes. Companies in these industries often use long-term debt to finance the acquisition of these assets. These companies generally are more highly levered than companies that do not need large amounts of plant assets. For example, service companies usually have small amounts of long-term debt.

Some companies' earnings are more volatile than others. Demand for some products remains relatively unchanged if the economy hits a downturn; examples include pharmaceutical and food products. Demand for other products decreases in an economic slump: automobiles, major appliances, and housing. Demand for some products actually increases in a downturn: fast foods and discount merchandise. A company with a stable demand, and therefore relatively stable earnings, can afford to be more highly levered than other companies. Companies with stable earnings face less likelihood that their earnings will decrease to a level at which they are unable to repay principal and interest on their debt.

This section has explained how financing activities can affect the risk and return of a company's financial securities. The next section examines specific uses of accounting information in analyzing financing activities.

THE IMPORTANCE OF ACCOUNTING INFORMATION

Objective 10
Explain how accounting information is useful for evaluating financing activities.

A primary use of accounting information is to help managers make capital structure decisions. This information also helps investors and other external users evaluate these decisions, which affect their own decisions to invest and extend credit. Financial statements and related disclosures provide information to evaluate financing activities. In addition to the amount of liabilities, preferred stock, and common stock, these reports provide information about dividend payments, the use of short-term and long-term debt, obligations to employees, and other commitments. Managers decide on the amount of debt and equity in a company's capital structure. These decisions depend on the financial needs of the company and expectations about future economic opportunities.

If managers expect an economic expansion, they may need more cash than will be available from operating activities in the short run. If they believe a company has good growth opportunities and can generate sufficient cash to meet principal and interest payments, they may be willing to increase financial leverage. If the company prospers during an economic expansion, higher financial leverage increases stockholder return and value. At the same time, managers must protect the company from a shortage of cash in an economic contraction. Declining sales can place a strain on cash flows and reduce stockholder returns and value.

In general, financing decisions reflect what management believes it can do with cash and the cash it expects to have available. A company can use cash to expand its operations. Or, it can pay cash to stockholders in the form of dividends or to repurchase shares of stock. Also, it can use cash to reduce debt.

Dividend Payments

Net income is a source of financing, increasing a company's equity. Cash flows from operating activities can be used to finance acquisition of additional assets. How much of a company's cash flow is available to finance assets depends on how much cash dividends it pays. Decisions about dividend payments during a fiscal period depend on a company's financial performance and on its dividend policy. The amount of dividends companies pay varies considerably. Some companies pay out most of their net income as dividends while other companies pay no dividends. Commonly used measures of dividend decisions are **dividends per share** and the *dividend payout ratio*, **the ratio of dividends per share to earnings per share**. Exhibit 10-9 describes 1993 dividend payout ratios for several major corporations.

Exhibit 10-9   Dividend Payout Ratios of Selected Corporations

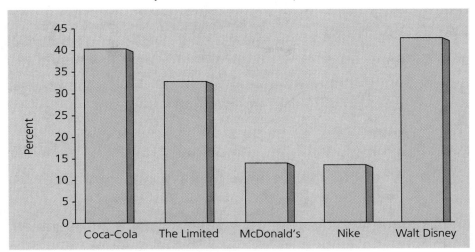

Data source: 1993 annual reports.

The dividend payout ratios for the companies in the exhibit vary from less than 15% for Nike and McDonald's to over 40% for Coca-Cola and Walt Disney. Companies with high growth potential, such as Nike and McDonald's, reinvest most of their profits. Companies in mature, stable industries, pay out more of their income to stockholders.

Investors often select stocks because of a particular investment strategy. Some investors want to own stocks that pay a stable dividend so they can use the cash receipts. Other investors want to own stocks that will grow in value because the issuing companies reinvest profits in new technology, products, and product markets. Therefore, different dividend policies appeal to different investors.

Corporations that pay dividends often attempt to maintain a stable dividend policy so investors can anticipate the amount of cash they will receive. These companies increase dividend payments only when they believe they will be able to sustain higher payments. They are reluctant to reduce dividend payments unless they expect a long-term decline in earnings. Therefore, a change in the amount of dividend per share paid by a company often is an important signal about a company's expected financial performance.

Remember that dividends paid out of earnings are a return *on* investment. Dividends paid in excess of earnings are a return *of* investment. A company that consistently pays dividends in excess of its earnings usually is not maintaining its capital. It is jeopardizing its ability to sustain its current level of earnings or to take advantage of growth opportunities.

The amount of dividends a company pays depends largely on the alternatives it has for investing its cash. If sufficient investment alternatives exist for a company to use cash from operating activities to create higher profits and cash flows, it should take advantage of these alternatives. For example, assume a company can reinvest its profits at a return of 15%, after taxes, while individual stockholders can earn only 10% on investments of similar risk, after taxes. Stockholders should prefer that the company retain the cash rather than pay dividends. Therefore, a company's dividend payments reveal information about its growth potential and dividend policies.

Taxation of dividends is another reason stockholders might want a company to reinvest profits rather than pay dividends. Dividends received are taxable income to the stockholders. Retained earnings are not taxed to stockholders until stock is sold. Profits earned by investors who sell their stock are taxed at a somewhat more favorable rate than dividends. Stockholders can defer the taxes on stock by holding the stock, rather than selling it. Most stockholders cannot control the timing of taxes on dividends, however.

Short-Term and Long-Term Debt

Many current liabilities are created from the ongoing operating activities of a business. These items include accounts payable and accrued liabilities, such as wages, interest, and taxes payable. A company also may borrow on a short-term basis to meet current cash flow needs. As a general rule, long-term debt should be used only to finance long-term assets. Revenues earned by a company from use of additional assets can be used to pay interest and principal on debt used to finance the assets. Current operating activities should be financed by cash generated by operating activities. A company that cannot generate sufficient cash from operating activities to meet its operating cash needs typically is facing major financial problems.

The analysis of short-term cash flows and obligations is important for managers and external decision makers. Creditors should have a particular interest in whether a company is generating sufficient cash flows to meet its current obligations.

As an example, Delta Airlines experienced cash flow problems that were reported in its 1994 annual report. Delta sold $489 million of accounts receivable to provide cash to meet some of its debt requirements. Delta's cash flow from operating activities was $1,324 million in 1994, up from $677 million in 1993. However, its cash outflows for investing activities were $1,510 million in 1994 and $1,327 million in 1993. To provide for its cash needs, the company issued preferred stock in 1993 and long-term debt in 1993 and 1994. These financing activities led Moody's to reduce Delta's bond rating to below investment grade, indicating a high default risk. As a result of the rating change, Delta was forced to repurchase some of its outstanding debt because of terms of its loan agreements.

Loan agreements **and** *debt covenants* **are restrictions placed on a company's economic activities by its creditors.** These contract terms protect creditors from management decisions that might reduce the value of their loans. These terms often restrict the amount of debt a company can issue, restrict dividends when profits are low, and require a company to maintain a certain level of working capital, equity, or profits. Accounting information is used by creditors to determine whether contract terms are being met. If the terms are not met, creditors can require early payment of their loans, require renegotiation of credit terms, take control of a company, or force a company into bankruptcy.

Loan agreements and debt covenants often are expressed in terms of accounting ratios. Ratios such as debt to equity, current, dividend payout, cash flow to current maturities of long-term debt, times interest earned, and quick (or acid–test) are common in loan agreements.[1] For example, an agreement might specify that a company should not exceed a debt to equity ratio of 1.2 to 1.

These ratios, other than those defined earlier, are calculated as follows:

Cash Flow to Current Maturities of Long–Term Debt Ratio = Net Cash Flow from Operating Activities ÷ Current Maturities of Long–Term Debt. This ratio measures the sufficiency of cash to meet current debt payments.

Times Interest Earned Ratio = Income Before Interest and Taxes ÷ Interest Expense. This ratio measures the sufficiency of current income to cover interest requirements.

Quick (or Acid–Test) Ratio = (Cash + Marketable Securities + Receivables) ÷ Current Liabilities. This ratio measures the sufficiency of current cash–generating assets to meet current obligations. It is a more conservative form of the current ratio.

Exhibit 10-10 illustrates the ratios with accounting information from recent annual reports of three companies.

Exhibit 10-10   Accounting Ratios for Selected Companies

	Delta	Coca-Cola	Nike
Financial Statement Information (in millions)			
Total debt	$10,327	$7,437	$ 633
Preferred stock	102	0.0	0.0
Total common equity	1,467	4,584	1,741
Current assets	3,223	4,434	1,770
Current liabilities	3,536	5,171	562
Cash flow from operating activities	1,324	2,508	575
Current maturities of long-term debt	227	19	4
Operating income	− 447	3,102	514
Interest expense	304	168	15
Cash, securities, receivables	2,596	2,288	1,223
Ratios			
Debt to Equity	7.04	1.62	0.36
Debt + Preferred Stock/Common Equity	2.11	1.62	0.36
Current Ratio	0.91	0.86	3.15
Cash Flow to Current Maturities of Long-Term Debt	5.83	132.00	143.75
Times Interest Earned	− 1.47	18.46	34.27
Quick Ratio	0.73	0.44	2.18

Data source: 1993/94 annual reports.

Delta's problems can be observed from the debt to equity, cash flow to current maturities of long-term debt, and times interest earned ratios. Times interest

[1]   Charles H. Gibson, *Financial Statement Analysis*, South–Western Publishing Co., 1992, p. 551.

earned is negative because the company reported an operating loss in 1993. From this analysis, it is apparent that Delta faced a problem because of the high proportion of debt in its capital structure.

Information about cash flows, current assets, and current liabilities is especially important for evaluating a company's ability to meet its current obligations. This analysis often is referred to as an analysis of liquidity. Current, cash flow, and quick ratios are called **liquidity ratios**. Information about profits and long-term or total assets, liabilities, and stockholders' equity is important for evaluating a company's ability to meet its long-term obligations. Ratios involving long-term obligations, such as the debt to equity ratio, sometimes are referred to as **debt** or **leverage ratios**. Profits generally are a good measure of long-run cash flow–generating ability. In the short run, however, they may not provide an accurate description of cash flow. Cash flow from operating activities often is a better measure of the ability of a company to meet its current cash requirements.

Ratios are useful for revealing relationships and patterns in accounting information. Many types of ratios can be computed. Memorizing ratios is much less important than understanding concepts that make ratios useful, however.

Learning Note — Considerable care must be used in comparing ratios for companies from different countries. Numbers used in ratios are affected by GAAP used in creating the numbers. Because GAAP vary among countries, accounting numbers, and therefore ratios, are not always comparable for companies from various countries.

Employee Benefits and Other Commitments

Long-term obligations such as deferred benefits, deferred taxes, leases and other commitments, contingencies, and minority interest require special consideration in assessing a company's capital structure. With the exception of leases and certain other commitments, the measurement of these items often is imprecise. Contingencies often are not included on the balance sheet at all. The amount of a contingency, such as the outcome of a lawsuit, is difficult to determine. Also, the probability of the contingency becoming an actual liability frequently is difficult to determine.

The amounts of deferred pension and other postemployment benefits also are "soft" numbers. They depend on management assumptions that vary considerably across companies. Assumptions about the rate at which wages and health care costs will increase are educated guesses. Managers have considerable latitude over the accrual of certain expenses associated with these plans. Though these amounts may provide some idea of future commitments for employee benefits, they should be viewed as only rough approximations. Trends in cash flows associated with these benefits may provide a better measure of the effect of the plans on a company's financial condition.

Financial decisions affect the risk associated with pension and other benefit plans. Employees contract with a company to provide services in exchange for current and future compensation. As a company's financial condition deteriorates, the potential for default on employee compensation increases. Companies that become bankrupt may default on their benefit plans. Certain plans, especially pension plans, often are insured by the federal government. Other types of benefit plans are not insured. Also, if a company's financial condition deteriorates, it may modify plan terms to reduce costs and cash outflows.

Deferred taxes are not legally owed to the government. An examination of trends in cash payments for income taxes may be a better measure of future cash requirements for taxes.

Minority interest results when a parent company owns less than 100% of a consolidated subsidiary. The equity represented by other owners (minority owners) is reported on the balance sheet, generally between liabilities and stockholders' equity. This item does not represent an existing obligation to make payments or to transfer other resources. Therefore, some analysts ignore this amount in evaluating a company's obligations and capital structure. It is not clear that minority interest, deferred taxes, and deferred benefit obligations increase the risk of a company in the same way as other liabilities. Comparing these liabilities among companies is difficult because of the variation in assumptions used in computing the amounts. Comparison is especially difficult for foreign corporations because they frequently do not report deferred benefits, taxes, and other commitments.

Lease commitments are contractual obligations to make future payments. Capitalized lease obligations are reported as a part of liabilities. Minimum future rental or lease payments for operating leases are disclosed in notes to financial statements. These commitments will affect a company's future cash requirements; therefore, they should be considered in evaluating its ability to meet maturing obligations. For example, Delta Airlines disclosed in 1994 that it had minimum lease commitments of $952 million in 1995. These should be considered in evaluating the company's ability to meet its current obligations in 1995. Some analysts include these amounts as part of liabilities when calculating liquidity and debt ratios.

Preferred stock is normally part of a company's equity. As noted earlier, preferred dividends usually are fixed payments that reduce cash flow available to common stockholders. They should be deducted from net income or cash flow in calculating accounting ratios such as return on equity. Some analysts consider material amounts of preferred stock as part of a company's obligations rather than as part of its equity. They include preferred stock in the numerator rather than the denominator of the debt to equity ratio.

This section has described how accounting information is helpful in evaluating financial decisions. The final section of this chapter examines financing decisions of Vulcan Materials Company using information from the company's financial statements and related disclosures.

AN ILLUSTRATION OF FINANCIAL DECISION ANALYSIS

Exhibit 10-11 provides information reported by Vulcan Materials Company in its 1993 annual report.

The type of analysis performed on accounting information depends on the purpose of the analysis. Different decision makers may have somewhat different reasons for analyzing this information. For example, the concerns of short-term creditors are different from those of long-term creditors. The concerns of creditors are different from those of owners. The general analysis that follows focuses

Exhibit 10-11   Vulcan Materials Company Selected Annual Report Information

(in thousands except per share amounts) December 31	1993	1992	1991
Income Statement:			
1. Operating income	$ 134,393	$ 140,494	$ 84,652
2. Interest expense	(9,171)	(9,768)	(11,205)
3. Provision for income taxes	(36,993)	(39,746)	(20,867)
4. Net income*	$ 88,229	$ 90,980	$ 52,580
5. Earnings per share	$2.39	$2.49	$1.38
6. Dividends per share	$1.26	$1.20	$1.20
7. Average common shares outstanding	36,975	37,780	38,216
Cash Flow Statement:			
8. Net cash from operating activities	$ 193,018	$ 201,100	$ 184,858
9. Payment of debt principal	(4,598)	(16,213)	(16,942)
10. Purchase of plant assets	(95,977)	(75,191)	(63,645)
11. Cash dividends paid	(46,296)	(45,095)	(45,664)
12. Cash available for other purposes	$ 46,147	$64,601	$58,607
Balance Sheet:			
13. Current assets	$ 302,613	$ 304,829	$ 285,147
14. Plant assets, net of depreciation	657,785	663,721	675,440
15. Other assets	118,153	115,365	112,524
16. Total assets	$1,078,551	$1,083,915	$1,073,111
17. Current liabilities	$ 140,815	$ 135,036	$ 135,388
18. Long-term debt	102,035	107,275	111,106
19. Other noncurrent liabilities	13,283	25,611	35,666
20. Deferred compensation and benefits	45,262	43,498	38,397
21. Deferred income taxes	74,193	72,383	69,626
22. Total liabilities	$ 375,588	$ 383,803	$ 390,183
23. Contributed capital	$ 51,160	$ 50,535	$ 50,036
24. Retained earnings	1,009,912	967,979	919,089
25. Treasury stock	(358,109)	(318,402)	(286,197)
26. Total stockholders' equity	702,963	700,112	682,928
27. Total liabilities and stockholders' equity	$1,078,551	$1,083,915	$1,073,111
28. Market value of stock	$1,701,563	$1,794,900	$1,368,000
29. Price per share	$46⅞	$48¼	$36
30. Shares outstanding	36,300	37,200	38,000
31. Debt to equity ratio	53.4%	54.8%	57.1%
32. Dividend payout	52.7%	48.2%	87.0%

Data source: 1993 annual report.
*Net income is before the effect of special adjustments in 1992.

Objective 11
Analyze a company's
financing decisions.

on the issues that can be useful to a variety of users. Modifications would need to be made to meet the needs of specific decision makers.

As a first step in the analysis, observe the company's overall financial condition and changes in the condition for the years reported. Net income (item 4) and earnings per share (item 5) increased in 1992 and decreased slightly in 1993.

The company's dividends per share (item 6) increased in 1993, suggesting the company was not facing a major financial problem. Also, the company's cash flow from operating activities remained strong. Though cash flow from operating activities declined slightly in 1993, it remained high relative to cash requirements. Cash flow from operating activities includes the effect of cash payments for interest and taxes. This cash flow was considerably higher than the amount needed by Vulcan to pay principal on debt (item 9). Thus, the company did not face a major risk of default or bankruptcy.

Vulcan used a portion of its cash flow from operating activities to acquire additional plant assets (item 10). After using its cash flow from operating activities to purchase assets, the company had a surplus of cash (item 12) after payment of dividends. The company was not facing a cash flow problem.

As a second step in the analysis, observe the financing activities made by the company's management. At the end of 1991, Vulcan's capital structure consisted of approximately 35% debt and 65% equity. Debt decreased from 1991 to 1993, while equity increased slightly. Therefore, the debt to equity ratio has decreased each year. Vulcan's financial risk has remained relatively constant. The company is not expanding, so it is not issuing additional debt or equity. It has reduced its debt ratio slightly. Other financial statement amounts remained relatively unchanged from 1991 to 1993.

As a third step, consider the effect of Vulcan's financing decisions on the return and risk of its stockholders and creditors. In addition, to the relative stability of debt and equity, two other financing decisions are important to observe. One is the relatively high dividend payout. Vulcan's dividend payout was approximately 50% of earnings in 1993 and 1992. It was higher in 1991 because earnings were much lower. Vulcan had higher cash flow from operating activities than it needed for investment purposes or to meet its debt requirements.

The company was not expanding. Total assets remained relatively unchanged from 1991 to 1993. The investment in new plant assets did not result in growth. Instead, they replaced other assets that were being depreciated and consumed. The company lacked good investment opportunities. Therefore, it used its cash to pay dividends to its stockholders and to repurchase shares of its own stock. By repurchasing shares, the company was reducing the number of shares outstanding. Thus, each share has the potential to become more valuable.

Vulcan was a stable company with few growth opportunities (at least during the 1990 to 1993 period). Changing its capital structure was not useful because it did not need additional capital and could comfortably cover its debt payments. As a result, it was a relatively low-risk company that paid a relatively high and stable cash return (dividend) to its stockholders. Its creditors were well protected by the levels of cash flow created from operating activities. Current liabilities remained relatively low compared with current assets and compared with operating cash flows. The company was very capable of meeting its operating needs and covering its debt requirements. The lack of growth opportunities and its stable asset base indicate that the company was not likely to create much additional value for its stockholders, however. We will examine the importance of investment and growth opportunities in the next two chapters.

SELF-STUDY PROBLEM 10-3

The following information is excerpted from the 1993 annual report of Wal-Mart Stores, Inc.:

(Amounts in millions except per share data)	1993	1992
Operating income	$ 2,819	$ 2,212
Interest expense	266	169
Pretax income	2,553	2,043
Income taxes	945	752
Net income	1,608	1,291
Earnings per share	1.40	1.14
Total current assets	8,575	6,415
Inventories and prepaid expenses	7,445	5,857
Plant assets, net of depreciation	5,079	3,724
Total assets	15,443	11,389
Current liabilities:		
Commercial paper	454	395
Accounts payable	3,454	2,651
Other accrued liabilities	1,056	914
Long-term debt due within one year	5	6
Capital lease obligations due within one year	35	24
Total current liabilities	5,004	3,990
Long-term debt	1,722	740
Long-term capital lease obligations	1,556	1,159
Deferred taxes	172	134
Total liabilities	8,454	6,023
Retained earnings	6,249	4,836
Total shareholders' equity	6,990	5,366
Net cash provided by operating activities	1,357	1,296
Net cash used in investing activities	(2,150)	(1,526)
Net cash provided by financing activities	811	230

Wal–Mart had no preferred stock.

Required

Answer each of the following questions:

a. What was the amount of each of the following ratios for Wal–Mart?
   1. Current ratio for 1993 and 1992
   2. Quick ratio for 1993 and 1992
   3. Debt to equity ratio for 1993 and 1992
   4. Times interest earned for 1993
   5. Return on equity for 1993
b. What were the primary financing decisions made by Wal–Mart's management in 1993?
c. Evaluate Wal–Mart's financing decisions based on its financial position, profitability, and cash flows.

R E V I E W *Summary of Important Concepts*

1. Capital structure:
   a. A company's capital structure is determined by the way it finances its assets and operating activities.

      b.   Higher proportions of debt increase the return to common stockholders when a company performs well but reduce returns when it performs poorly. Therefore, risk increases as the proportion of debt in capital structure increases.

2.   Financial leverage and company earnings:
      a.   The proportion of debt to equity in a company's capital structure is financial leverage. Financial leverage affects the risk and return of its debt and equity securities. It affects earnings per share and return on equity.
      b.   Financial leverage increases earnings per share when sales are high but decreases earnings per share when sales are low.

3.   Primary and secondary markets:
      a.   Securities are sold in primary (original issue) and secondary (resale) markets.
      b.   Prices in secondary markets change as expected cash flows, interest rate, and financial risk change.

4.   Economic and company attributes and financial leverage:
      a.   Analysis of financial decisions involves consideration of whether cash flows are sufficient to pay for current obligations and are likely to be sufficient in the future to pay for long-term obligations.
      b.   The proportion of debt in a company's capital structure often is higher for companies whose earnings are relatively stable over time. If earnings remain stable though the economy worsens, the company is able to pay higher amounts of principal and interest.

5.   Evaluation of financing activities:
      a.   Loan agreements and debt covenants protect the rights of creditors. If a company violates these agreements, creditors may require immediate repayment of debt or force a company into bankruptcy. These agreements often are expressed in terms of accounting ratios. Therefore, an analysis of accounting information is useful for determining whether agreements and covenants have been violated.
      b.   The analysis of accounting information may require special consideration of deferred compensation, deferred taxes, minority interest, operating lease commitments, and preferred stock.

Ratios discussed in this chapter:

$$\text{Return on Equity} = \frac{\text{Net Income} - \text{Dividends on Preferred Stock}}{\text{Average Common Stockholders' Equity}}$$

Return on equity (sometimes called return on common equity) is a measure of return on investment by common stockholders.

$$\text{Debt to Equity Ratio} = \frac{\text{Total Debt}}{\text{Total Stockholders' Equity}}$$

The debt to equity ratio is a measure of capital structure and is sometimes called debt to net worth. Net worth is total assets minus total liabilities.

$$\text{Debt to Total Assets Ratio} = \frac{\text{Total Debt}}{\text{Total Assets}}$$

The debt to total assets ratio is another common measure of capital structure. It also is known as debt to total capitalization (liabilities plus stockholders' equity) and as simply the debt ratio. Analysts sometimes include only long-term debt in these ratios. They may exclude unfunded pension obligations and deferred taxes from the debt category and may include the present value of future operating lease payments. They may include preferred stock as part of debt rather than equity.

$$\text{Dividends per Share} = \frac{\text{Dividends on Common Stock}}{\text{Average Number of Shares of Common Stock Outstanding}}$$

Dividends per share is a commonly used measure of dividend payment decisions.

$$\text{Dividend Payout Ratio} = \frac{\text{Dividends per Share}}{\text{Earnings per Share}}$$

The dividend payout ratio is another common measure of the relative amount of dividends paid by a corporation during a fiscal period.

$$\text{Cash Flow to Current Maturities of Long-Term Debt Ratio} = \frac{\text{Net Cash Flow from Operating Activities}}{\text{Current Maturities of Long-Term Debt}}$$

This ratio measures the sufficiency of cash to meet current debt payments.

$$\text{Times Interest Earned Ratio} = \frac{\text{Income Before Interest and Taxes}}{\text{Interest Expense}}$$

This ratio measures the sufficiency of current income to cover interest requirements.

$$\text{Current Ratio} = \frac{\text{Total Current Assets}}{\text{Total Current Liabilities}}$$

The current ratio is a measure of the ability of a company to meet its current obligations.

$$\text{Quick (or Acid-Test) Ratio} = \frac{\text{Cash + Marketable Securities + Receivables}}{\text{Total Current Liabilities}}$$

The quick ratio measures the sufficiency of current cash-generating assets to meet current obligations. This ratio is a more conservative form of the current ratio.

DEFINE *Terms and Concepts Defined in This Chapter*

capital structure
debt covenants
dividend payout ratio

financial leverage
loan agreements
primary market

return on equity
secondary market

SOLUTIONS

SELF-STUDY PROBLEM 10-1

	Current	Option A	Option B	Option C
Operating income	$24,000,000	$33,000,000	$33,000,000	$33,000,000
Interest expense	0	0	0	−2,400,000
Pretax income	24,000,000	33,000,000	33,000,000	30,600,000
Income tax (33⅓%)	−8,000,000	−11,000,000	−11,000,000	−10,200,000
Net income	16,000,000	22,000,000	22,000,000	20,400,000
Preferred dividends	0	0	−3,000,000	0
Net income available for common stockholders	$16,000,000	$22,000,000	$19,000,000	$20,400,000
Common shares	÷ 10,000,000	÷ 13,000,000	÷ 10,000,000	÷ 10,000,000
Earnings per share	$1.60	$1.69	$1.90	$2.04

The new project would increase income before interest and taxes by $9 million. If Option A is adopted, 3 million new shares of common stock must be issued at the current price to raise $30 million, and earnings per share would be $1.69. If Option B is adopted, dividends will be paid on preferred stock. After this payment, earnings per share would be $1.90 per share. If Option C is adopted, interest will be paid on the bonds. Earnings per share would be $2.04. Therefore, Option C provides the highest earnings per share from the assumptions provided.

Management should consider other factors in making a decision. Potential dilution of ownership will result if additional common stock is issued. If the company does not do as well as expected, preferred stock or bonds may have a negative effect on income available for common shareholders. Bonds increase the risk of bankruptcy and loss of control by stockholders.

SELF-STUDY PROBLEM 10-2

a. The price of El Roncho's bonds would be computed as follows:

Present value of interest payments of $40 per period for 13 remaining periods, discounted at 5%:

$$PV = \$40 \times 9.39357 = \$375.74$$

Present value of a single payment of $1,000 at the end of 13 periods, discounted at 5%.

$$PV = \$1,000 \times 0.53032 = \$530.32$$

The price of each bond would be $906.06 ($375.74 + $530.32).

b. El Roncho's common stock had been selling for $8 per share and its earnings per share was $1.40 ($14 million / 10 million shares). Its earnings per share would drop to $1 ($10 million / 10 million shares), based on the projection. Therefore, the price would be expected to drop. Much would depend on investors' expectations about the long-run profitability of the company. If they viewed the decline in profits as a permanent decrease, the price of the company's stock should decrease.

SELF-STUDY PROBLEM 10-3

a.	1993	1992
1. Current ratio = current assets ÷ current liabilities	8,575/5,004 = 1.71	6,415/3,990 = 1.61
2. Quick ratio = current assets − inventories and prepaid expenses ÷ current liabilities	8,575 − 7,445 = 1,130 1,130/5,004 = 0.23	6,415 − 5,857 = 558 558/3,990 = 0.14
3. Debt to equity ratio	8,454/6,990 = 1.21	6,023/5,366 = 1.12
4. Times interest earned: Income before interest and taxes ÷ interest expense	134,393/9,171 = 14.65	
5. Return on equity: average equity net income − preferred dividends return on equity	(5,366 + 6,990)/2 = 6,178 1,608 1,608/6,178 = 0.26	

b.   The primary financing decision was to increase liabilities. Accounts payable, long-term debt, and long-term capital lease obligations increased. An increase in accounts payable can indicate increased operating activity or difficulty in meeting current obligations. Long-term debt and lease obligations have the greatest impact in future years as they become current liabilities.

c.   Wal–Mart's financing decisions appear to be justified by its financial position, profitability, and cash flows. The amount of current liabilities is consistent with the amount of current assets. Accounts payable and short-term debt appear to be used primarily to finance inventories, which are a large portion of the assets of a retail company. Long-term debt is small relative to plant and long-term assets. These assets are financed primarily by operating activities. Observe that long-term liabilities are small relative to stockholders' equity, especially retained earnings, and that a significant portion of the cash flow used for investing activities comes from cash flow from operating activities. The company's profits and cash flows both appear to be quite strong, net income and net cash from operating activities increasing in 1993 relative to 1992.

EXERCISES

10-1.   Write a short definition for each of the terms listed in the "Terms and Concepts Defined in This Chapter" section.

10-2.   What is capital structure? Why do the capital structures of companies vary?

10-3.   During the summer of 1993, Delta Airline's stock was selling for approximately $55 per share. One year later, the price was approximately $40. What factors could account for the decrease in price? How can accounting information be useful in evaluating a company's stock price?

10-4.   Hester Prinn Co. had stockholders' equity of $18 million at the end of 1996. At the end of 1995, stockholders' equity was $16.3 million. Stockholders' equity in 1996 consisted of 1 million shares of common stock with a book value of $15 million and 30,000 shares of preferred stock with a book value of $3 million. No changes were made in the amount of preferred stock during 1996. During 1996, the company reported net income of $4 million. Interest expense was $500,000 for the year. The company paid preferred dividends of $10 per share and common dividends of $2 per share in 1996. Compute Hester Prinn's return on equity for 1996. What would this amount have been if the company had issued $5 million of bonds at the beginning of 1996 and had used the proceeds to repurchase 250,000 shares of its common stock at $20 per share, reducing common stockholders' equity at the end of 1996 to $11,450,000? Assume interest expense increased to $800,000, net income decreased to $3.79 million, and dividends per share remained at $2 per share for common stock.

10-5.   Why is return on equity commonly used to evaluate a company's performance in addition to its net income? Assume a company issued long-term bonds during a fiscal period, increasing its interest expense. The bonds were used to finance new plant assets. What effect would the financing and asset acquisition have on the company's financial leverage? What effect should the additional financing have on the company's risk and return?

10-6.   Words Worth Co. expects net income of $5 million for 1995. Pretax earnings were $7 million. The company's average total assets during 1995 were $25 million. It had no liabilities or preferred stock. It had 1 million shares of common stock outstanding. It is considering issuing $10 million of debentures to repurchase 300,000 shares of its common stock. If the debt had been outstanding in 1995, the company would have paid $900,000 in interest expense. Calculate the company's earnings per share and return on equity for 1995 as reported and as it would have been if the debt had been issued. Assume average stockholders' equity of $15 million for computing return on equity with debt financing.

10-7.   Kip Ling Co. had stockholders' equity of $100 million in 1996 and long-term debt of $10 million. It had 10 million shares of common stock outstanding. Its interest expense was $800,000, and its income tax rate was 30%. The company believes its annual income before interest and taxes will vary between $5 million and $15 million for the foreseeable future. The average is expected to be about $8 million. The company is considering issuing $25 million of additional debt to replace 3 million shares of its common stock. The additional debt would cost the company $3 million a year in interest. If you were asked by the company for advice on whether to issue the debt, what advice would you provide?

10-8.   Carlyle Co. has assets of $200 million and long-term debt of $110 million. The debt consists primarily of callable debentures with interest rates of 10% to 12%. Over the last couple of years, the general level of interest rates has decreased by about 2.5%. Carlyle could issue its debt at current rates of approximately 8%. Also, over the two-year period, Carlyle's stock price has increased approximately 30%. What effect might these changes have on Carlyle's financing decisions?

10-9.   Selected information is provided below for Georgia-Pacific Corporation from its 1993 annual report:

(in millions)	1993	1992	1991	1990	1989
Interest expense	$ 513	$ 565	$ 656	$ 606	$ 260
Income tax expense	41	(14)	266	354	426
Net income (loss)	(34)	(124)	(142)	365	661
Cash from operations	389	868	630	1,223	1,358
Total assets	10,545	10,912	10,622	12,060	7,056
Shareholders' equity	2,402	2,508	2,736	2,975	2,717

Evaluate the effect of the company's capital structure on its profitability, cash flow from operations, and risk for the five years presented.

10-10. Information for two companies is provided below from their annual reports:

(in millions)	1993	1992	1991	1990
General Mills				
Net income	$ 506.1	$ 495.6	$ 472.7	$ 381.4
Dividends	274.8	245.0	210.6	180.8
Wal-Mart				
Net income	$1,994.8	$1,608.5	$1,291.0	$1,076.9
Dividends	241.0	195.0	159.0	125.0

What do the dividend policies indicate about future prospects for the two companies?

10-11. Selected information from the 1993 annual report of Allied Products Corporation is provided below:

(in thousands)	
Net income	$ 15,284
Interest expense	6,376
Income tax expense	436
Net cash from operating activities	67,754
Cash flow from financing activities:	
Proceeds from issuance of long-term debt	33,348
Payments of short- and long-term debt	(139,769)
Preferred dividends paid	(1,782)
Current assets:	
Cash and marketable securities	44,416
Notes and accounts receivable, net	44,415
Inventories	44,724
Prepaid expenses	1,915
Current liabilities:	
Revolver loan	4,382
Current portion of long-term debt	39,343
Accounts payable	13,957
Other accrued liabilities	46,124
Total current liabilities	103,806

If you were a creditor, what concerns would you have about Allied Product's ability to pay its current obligations in 1993?

10-12.   The following information was reported in the 1993 annual report of Westinghouse Electric Corporation:

> In December 1991, the Corporation entered into a three-year $6 billion revolving credit agreement with a syndicate of domestic and international banks. . . . The facility is available for use by the Corporation . . . subject to the maintenance of certain financial ratios and compliance with other covenants. . . . Among other things, the covenants place restrictions on the incurrence of liens, the amount of debt on a consolidated basis and at the subsidiary level, and the amount of contingent liabilities. The covenants also require the maintenance of a maximum leverage ratio, minimum interest coverage ratios, and a minimum consolidated net worth. At December 31, 1993, the Corporation was in compliance with these covenants.

The revolving credit agreement permitted Westinghouse to borrow up to $6 billion over a three-year period, as needed. What are debt or loan covenants? Why are they required in conjunction with many loan agreements? What restraints are placed on Westinghouse by the loan agreements discussed above? What are contingent liabilities, leverage ratios, coverage ratios, and net worth? What incentives do these covenants provide for Westinghouse's management that might affect the company's reported accounting information?

10-13.   On August 1, 1995, Feinman Co. issued $4 million of 8%, 20-year bonds. The bonds were rated Aa and sold to yield a return of 8%. Sue Lin Tang purchased $20,000 of the bonds when they were issued. At the end of 1997, Tang decided to sell the bonds. The bond rating had been lowered to A early in 1997. What price did Sue pay for the bonds when she purchased them? Would the price of the bonds in the secondary market at the end of 1997 be lower or higher than the price Sue paid for the bonds? What factors, other than those associated with the bond rating, would affect the price? What factors might account for the lower rating?

10-14.   Ali Baba Co.'s capital structure includes $8 million of long-term debt that pays 10% annual interest. It also includes $2 million of preferred stock and $7 million of common stock and retained earnings. The preferred stock is cumulative and pays a 6% annual dividend. What effect does the preferred stock have on the risk and return of the long-term debt and common stock? Should the preferred stock be considered debt or equity?

10-15.   Intel Corporation reported the following information in its 1993 annual report:

(in millions)	1993
Current Liabilities:	
Short-term debt	$ 399
Long-term debt, current portion	98
Total current liabilities	2,433
Long-Term Liabilities:	
Long-term debt	426
Deferred income taxes	297
Other	688
Stockholders' Equity:	
Common stock	2,194
Retained earnings	5,306
Total stockholders' equity	7,500

Evaluate Intel's capital structure. Explain which amounts you would include in a computation of the company's debt to equity ratio and why.

10-16.   Merriweather Co. reported net income of $8 million in 1996. Its average stockholders' equity of $22 million included preferred stock of $5 million that was outstanding throughout the year. The company paid dividends of $2 million on common stock and $400,000 on preferred stock. Calculate the company's return on equity for 1996. How much would return on equity change if the company issued $5 million of common stock to repurchase all of its preferred stock?

10-17.   Lewis Thompson wants some advice. He has heard that some companies pay out a large portion of their earnings as dividends to stockholders. Other companies pay few or no dividends. A friend told him that dividends affect the value of stock and that he should invest in stocks that pay high dividend rates. What advice would you give him about this matter?

10-18.   When a company issues long-term debt, creditors often require the company to agree to certain restrictions on future activities. For example, a restriction may limit the amount of a company's debt to assets ratio and its dividend payout ratio. What is the purpose of these restrictions? How do they benefit creditors?

10-19.   Evaluate the following statement: Companies that issue a lot of new debt and equity to create cash are usually in bad financial condition.

10-20.   Harpoon Co. issued $10 million of 8% preferred stock at the beginning of 1995 at par value. Also at the same time, the company issued $20 million of 10%, 5-year bonds at face value. Interest is paid annually. At the beginning of 1996, the general level of interest rates increased by 2%. Evaluate the effect of the change in interest rates on the prices of the preferred stock and bonds.

PROBLEMS

PROBLEM 10-1   Identifying Capital Structure Choices

You are a financial manager with a medium-sized company, Kangaroo Express. The company is owned and managed by the Marsupial family. Currently, 60% of the company's total liabilities and stockholders' equity is composed of long-term notes. Current liabilities account for 20%, and the remainder consists of stock held by members of the Marsupial family. You have been asked to meet with the company's top management to discuss the company's capital structure and plans to raise capital for expansion.

Required   Write a short report describing alternative types of financing Kangaroo Express might consider. Explain the risk and return implications of each alternative for the Marsupials.

PROBLEM 10-2   Analyzing Credit-Paying Ability

Digital Equipment Corporation disclosed the following information in its 1993 annual report:

(in millions)	1993	1992
Net income (loss)	$(251.3)	$(2,795.5)
Net cash flow from operating activities	46.9	430.7
Net cash flow from financing activities	1,143.2	(36.4)
Interest payments	50.8	38.5
Bank loans and current portion of long-term debt	21.3	49.1
Total current liabilities	3,918.7	5,106.1
Total liabilities	6,064.9	6,353.4
Total current assets	6,882.5	7,120.8
Total assets	10,950.3	11,284.3

You are a financial analyst with a large investment company. Several clients are creditors and stockholders of Digital. One client in particular, Magnolia Smythe, has expressed concern about the company's recent net loss. She is concerned about the company's ability to meet its principal and interest payments and the effect of this on the company's stockholders.

Required   Write a memo to Magnolia explaining whether you think she should be concerned about the company's ability to meet its obligations and whether stockholders should be concerned about the company's performance. Use relevant information from the data presented above to support your explanations.

PROBLEM 10-3   Comparing Capital Structures

Financial statement information is provided below from the 1993 annual reports of two companies. Intel Corporation is a manufacturer of computer microprocessors. Pacific Gas & Electric is a privately owned utility.

(in millions) Intel Corporation	1993	(in millions) Pacific Gas & Electric	1993
Current assets	$ 5,802	Plant assets	$19,063
Plant assets, net	3,996	Other noncurrent assets	1,608
Other noncurrent assets	1,546	Current assets	3,128
Total assets	11,344	Total assets	27,163
Current liabilities	2,433	Common stock equity	8,446
Long-term debt	426	Preferred stock	883
Other noncurrent liabilities	985	Long-term debt	9,292
Preferred stock	0	Other noncurrent liabilities	557
Stockholders' equity	7,500	Current liabilities	3,241

Required   Compare the capital structures of the two companies. Explain why differences are likely to exist between the companies, considering their risk and return attributes.

PROBLEM 10-4   Assessing Default Risk

Information is provided below for Sears, Roebuck and Co. from its 1993 annual report:

(in millions)	1993	1992	1991	1990	1989
Net income	$ 2,374	$ (3,932)	$ 1,279	$ 902	$ 1,509
Interest expense	1,498	1,510	3,252	3,370	3,224
Total assets	90,807	85,490	106,435	96,253	86,972
Short-term debt	4,928	4,607	9,788	15,314	12,714
Long-term debt	12,926	13,735	19,170	12,636	10,036
Shareholders' equity	11,664	10,773	14,188	12,824	13,622

The company's income tax rate was approximately 20%. In September 1990, Moody's Investors Service lowered its rating on Sears's debt.

Required   Why do you think Moody's lowered its rating? Prepare an analysis of the accounting information provided above to justify your answer. Specific references should be made to amounts or ratios that substantiate your conclusions. For 1989, average total assets was $82,462 million and average shareholders' equity was $13,839 million.

PROBLEM 10-5   Analyzing Capital Structure Decisions

Late in 1988, RJR Nabisco was acquired by a group of investors in a leveraged buyout (LBO). Accounting information for the company before and after the buyout is presented below. The information is from the company's 1993 and 1987 annual reports.

(in millions)	1990	1989	1987
Net income (loss)	$ (429)	$ (1,149)	$1,209
Operating income	2,818	2,053	2,304
Interest expense	(3,000)	(2,937)	(489)
Current maturities of long-term debt	1,425	2,632	162
Total current liabilities	5,205	6,568	4,123
Long-term debt	16,955	21,948	3,884
Other noncurrent liabilities	2,653	2,873	1,797
Deferred income taxes	3,813	3,786	846
Redeemable preferred stock	1,795	0	173
Common stockholders' equity	2,494	1,237	6,038

Required   Answer each of the following questions:
a.   From the information before and after the LBO, how would you define an LBO?
b.   What explanation can you provide for why interest expense in 1990 and 1989 was considerably higher than interest paid?
c.   At the time of the LBO, RJR Nabisco's debt was rated below investment grade (to junk bond status). In late 1991, the debt was upgraded to investment grade by both Moody's and Standard & Poor's. What reasons can you provide for why these events might have occurred?
d.   If you were analyzing the company's performance after the LBO, what information would you consider to be most important? Why?

PROBLEM 10-6   Ethical Issues in Financing Decisions

Until late 1991, when he died, Robert Maxwell was chief executive officer and a major stockholder of Maxwell Communications Corporation. The company's performance declined in 1990 and 1991. To prevent a major decrease in the value of the company's stock, Maxwell secretly diverted £200 million from other companies he owned to purchase shares of Maxwell Communications' stock. The purchased shares were used by other companies owned by Maxwell as collateral for bank loans. Cash from the loans was used to finance interest payments and losses on operations. After Maxwell's death and discovery of the stock transactions, the stock lost most of its value.

Required   Were these transactions unethical? Why or why not?

PROBLEM 10-7   Analysis of Capital Structure

Information is provided below for Citicorp from its 1993 annual report:

(in millions)	1993	1992	1991
Income before taxes	$ 2,860	$ 1,418	$ (237)
Net cash provided by (used in) operating activities	2,984	(941)	(3,929)
Net cash provided by (used in) investing activities	(5,110)	3,191	(1,755)
Net cash provided by (used in) financing activities	2,179	(2,147)	4,306
Total loans (receivable), net of allowance for credit losses	134,588	135,851	147,636
Total assets (including loans)	216,574	213,701	216,986
Total deposits	145,089	144,175	146,475
Total liabilities (including deposits)	202,621	202,520	207,433
Preferred stock	3,887	3,212	2,140
Total stockholders' equity (including preferred stock)	13,953	11,181	9,489

Citicorp is one of the nation's largest banks. U.S. banking regulations require banks to maintain an equity to total assets ratio of 4%. In March 1992, Citicorp sold $150 million of additional preferred stock. The stock carried a dividend rate of 9.05%. The bank's common stock was not paying a dividend. The sale prompted Standard & Poor's to lower Citicorp's credit rating to BBB–, the lowest investment grade.

Required   Answer each of the following questions:
a.   What are Citicorp's primary revenues, expenses, assets, and liabilities?
b.   What was Citicorp's equity to asset ratio at the end of 1992? 1993?
c.   What effect did issuing additional preferred stock have on the bank's equity to asset ratio?
d.   What other activities could the bank use to increase this ratio? What are the advantages and disadvantages of using preferred stock?
e.   Why did Standard & Poor's lower Citicorp's credit rating as a result of its issuing additional preferred stock?

PROBLEM 10-8   Evaluating Financial Leverage

Information is provided below for Baker Hughes Incorporated:

(in thousands, except per share amounts)	1993
Operating income	$ 164,754
Interest expense	64,703
Income taxes (40%)	41,195
Net income	58,856
Earnings per share (173.1 million shares)	0.34
Total assets	3,143,340
Short-term borrowing	5,381
Current portion of long-term debt	3,067
Total current liabilities	495,837
Long-term debt	935,846
Deferred income taxes	78,306
Other long-term liabilities	19,021
Minority interest	3,682
Total stockholders' equity	1,610,648

Assume that during 1993, Baker Hughes had the opportunity to acquire additional assets at a price of $500 million. At the time, the company's stock was selling at $30 per share. The additional assets were expected to increase the company's operating income by $80 million annually (to $244,754,000) for the foreseeable future.

Required   Prepare a pro forma income statement, beginning with operating income, to explain whether Baker Hughes should finance the acquisition with debt or stock. Assume stock could be sold at $30 per share and debt could be issued at a 7% interest rate.

PROBLEM 10-9   Evaluating the Effect of Financial Leverage on Risk

Information is provided below for two companies, describing likely outcomes for the companies in various economic circumstances:

	Equity Co.			Debt Co.		
	Bad Year	Normal Year	Good Year	Bad Year	Normal Year	Good Year
Assets	800	800	800	800	800	800
Debt	200	200	200	600	600	600
Equity	600	600	600	200	200	200
Operating income	50	150	350	50	150	350

Assume that interest expense is 10% of total debt for both companies and that the income tax rate is 35% of pretax income for both companies.

Required   Calculate return on equity for each company for each outcome. Evaluate the effect of financial leverage on the risks of the two companies.

PROBLEM 10-10   Evaluating the Effects of Financial Leverage

Information is provided below from the 1993 annual report of The Walt Disney Company:

(in millions)	1993	1992
Operating income	$ 1,231.7	$ 1,428.6
Interest expense	157.7	126.8
Pretax income	1,074.0	1,301.8
Income taxes	402.7	485.1
Net income (before special adjustments)	671.3	816.7
Total assets	11,751.1	10,861.7
Total stockholders' equity	5,030.5	4,704.6
Long-term debt	2,385.8	2,222.4

The interest expense related primarily to the long-term debt.

Required   Calculate Walt Disney's return on equity for 1993. Did the company's financial leverage help or hurt the stockholders? (Hint: Consider what would have happened to return if equity had been used to replace the debt.)

PROBLEM 10-11   Evaluating Financing Cash Flows

Information is provided below from the 1993 annual report of Johnson & Johnson:

(in millions)	1993	1992
Cash flows from financing activities:		
Dividends to stockholders	$ (659)	$(587)
Repurchase of common stock	(632)	(740)
Proceeds from short-term debt	297	409
Retirement of short-term debt	(336)	(237)
Proceeds from long-term debt	511	560
Retirement of long-term debt	(468)	(264)
Proceeds from the exercise of stock options	43	74
Net cash used by financing activities	$(1,244)	$(785)

Required   Evaluate Johnson & Johnson's financial condition from the information provided. Does the company appear to be facing financial problems? What effect have these activities had on the company's capital structure?

PROBLEM 10-12   Multiple-Choice Overview of the Chapter

1. The way a company finances its assets and operating activities is its:
   a.   capital structure.
   b.   financial leverage.
   c.   return on equity.
   d.   present value.

2. The use of debt in a company's capital structure affects return on equity in which of the following ways?
   a.   It affects only the numerator of the ratio.
   b.   It affects only the denominator of the ratio.
   c.   It affects both the numerator and denominator of the ratio.
   d.   It affects neither the numerator nor the denominator of the ratio.

3. The effect of financial leverage on risk is to:
   a. increase risk.
   b. decrease risk.
   c. have no effect on risk.
   d. have an effect on risk only if a company reports a net loss.

4. Junk bonds are another name for:
   a. debentures.
   b. speculative grade bonds.
   c. investment grade bonds.
   d. bonds in default.

5. The market in which investors sell securities to each other is the:
   a. primary market.
   b. commodities market.
   c. secondary market.
   d. over-the-counter market.

6. Audabon Co. had net income of $2 million in 1996. Its interest expense was $1 million for the year. It had no preferred stock. Its average total assets were $15 million, and its average total equity was $5 million. Audabon's return on equity was:
   a. greater than 40%.
   b. less than 20%.
   c. 40%.
   d. 20%.

7. Baker Co. expects net income of $10 million in 1996 after taxes of $5 million. The company has 1 million shares of common stock outstanding. To raise $20 million of additional capital, Baker can either issue debt with an interest rate of 10% or issue 600,000 shares of additional common stock. Investment of the additional capital is expected to increase income, before the effect of additional interest and taxes, by $8 million. To maximize earnings per share, Baker should:
   a. increase its financial leverage.
   b. reduce its financial leverage.
   c. not alter its financial leverage.
   d. issue only common stock.

8. High amounts of financial leverage are most common for companies with:
   a. small proportions of plant assets and stable earnings.
   b. large proportions of plant assets and stable earnings.
   c. small proportions of plant assets and unstable earnings.
   d. large proportions of plant assets and unstable earnings.

9. Low dividend payout ratios are common for companies
   a. with low growth potential.
   b. in stable industries.
   c. with high growth potential.
   d. with stable earnings.

10. If a company is having difficulty paying interest and principal on its debt, creditors should be particularly concerned with:
    a. its return on assets.
    b. its return on equity.
    c. its debt to equity ratio.
    d. its cash flows.

C A S E S

CASE 10-1   Evaluating Capital Structure

Selected information for Hard Drive Inc. is provided below:

(in millions except per share amounts)	1996	1995
Earnings before interest and taxes	$ 742	$ 799
Interest expense	129	133
Earnings before income taxes	613	666
Income taxes	159	167
Net earnings	454	499
Net earnings per share	$3.44	$3.80
Average shares outstanding	131.9	131.3
Total current assets	4,487	4,452
Total assets	9,375	8,742
Total current liabilities	3,063	3,048
Long-term debt	954	792
Deferred income taxes	196	203
Other liabilities	532	442
Total stockholders' equity	4,630	4,257
Net cash provided by operations	1,358	1,307
Net cash used for investing activities	(1,232)	(1,443)
Net cash provided by financing activities:		
Increase (decrease) in notes payable and current portion of long-term debt	(143)	208
Increase in long-term debt	135	7
Issuance of common stock	19	55
Payment of dividends	(100)	(100)
Net cash provided by (used for) financing activities	(89)	170

Required   Write a short report describing Hard Drive's capital structure. Consider changes in the company's capital structure in 1996, and identify the causes of these changes. Identify Hard Drive's primary source of financing in 1996, and evaluate the company's financial condition at the end of 1996.

CASE 10-2   Evaluating Capital Structure Decisions

Water Bed Co.'s capital structure at the end of 1996 included $10 million of 9% bonds, $2 million of 7%, $100 par preferred stocks, and $20 million of common stock. The company's 10 million shares of common stock are selling at $5 per share. During 1996, the company earned $4 million of net income after tax expense of $1.5 million. It paid preferred dividends of $140,000 and dividends to common stockholders of $1 million.

Required   For each of the following independent events, explain the effect the event would have on the company's earnings per share, return on assets, and return on equity. What effect would you expect the event to have on the price of each type of security?

a. The company issued $15 million of new bonds to finance the purchase of additional plant assets. The bonds were issued at a market rate of 12%. The new assets are expected to produce additional pretax profits of $2 million.

b. The company issued $10 million of new common stock to repurchase its bonds. The stock sold at $5 per share.

c. The company issued $4 million of new 7% preferred stock to repurchase shares of the company's common stock. The preferred stock sold at its par value of $100. The common stock was repurchased at $6 per share.

d. Because of new competition, the company's profits are expected to decline to $3 million for the foreseeable future.

PROJECTS

PROJECT 10-1   Comparing Capital Structures

Obtain the most recent annual report available for each of three corporations from your library. Look for companies in different industries. Identify the primary components of the capital structure of each company. In particular, determine the relative proportion of short-term debt, other current liabilities, long-term debt, other long-term liabilities, preferred stock, and common stock in each company's capital structure. Provide a graph or diagram to illustrate the comparisons. Write a brief analysis of differences in the capital structures. What explanations can you provide for why the capital structures are different or are similar?

PROJECT 10-2   Comparing Bond Ratings

Use Standard & Poor's or Moody's bond surveys to identify corporate bond ratings for five companies. Make sure all the companies you identify do not have the same ratings. Examine the companies' accounting information to evaluate their debt and liquidity ratios. Write a short report explaining why you believe the companies have different ratings.

PROJECT 10-3   Evaluating Capital Structure

Identify a recent article in *The Wall Street Journal* or in a business periodical describing a company that has made a significant change in its capital structure, by issuing stock or debt, for example. Make a copy of the article. Write a memo to your instructor identifying the event and the reasons cited in the article for the change in capital structure. Attach the copy of the article to the memo.

PROJECT 10-4   Evaluating Credit Risk

Identify a recent article in *The Wall Street Journal* or in a business periodical describing a company that has had its bond rating changed. Make a copy of the article. Write a memo to your instructor identifying the event and the reasons cited in the article for the change in rating. Attach the copy of the article to the memo.

Chapter 11

Investing Activities

The primary purpose of financing activities is to obtain financial resources for organizations, as we have seen in Chapters 9 and 10. Investing activities determine how financial resources will be used. In particular, they involve choices about which assets an organization will obtain for use in its operating activities. Organizations invest their financial resources in assets, such as merchandise, materials, buildings, and equipment, that are required for use in their operating activities. Some of these assets, such as merchandise and materials, are associated directly with operating activities and will be considered when those activities are discussed in Chapters 13 and 14. Investing activities considered in this chapter include investments in such assets as cash, securities, other companies, buildings, equipment, and patents. Accounting for these investments includes accounting for their acquisition and disposal, accounting for expenses associated with use of the assets, identification of amounts reported for these assets on the balance sheet, and disclosure of information about the investing activities in notes to the financial statements. Protection and control of assets also is an important issue affecting accounting information. The measurement and reporting of investing activities affect the income statement and statement of cash flows in addition to the balance sheet, as illustrated below:

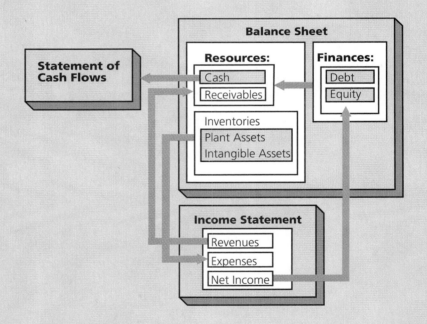

Major topics covered in this chapter include:

- Investments in cash and securities.
- Investments in plant and other long-term assets.
- Cash flow and accrual measures of investing activities.
- Control of assets.

Once you have completed this chapter, you should be able to:

1. Identify the purpose of investing activities.
2. Identify types of securities and explain why companies invest in them.

3. Explain accounting rules for investments in equity securities.
4. Identify methods used to account for acquisitions and mergers.
5. Explain accounting rules for investments in debt securities.
6. Distinguish between straight-line and accelerated depreciation methods.
7. Determine the accounting effects of disposing of plant assets.
8. Explain accounting rules for investments in natural resources.
9. Distinguish between operating and capital leases.
10. Explain accounting issues associated with intangible assets, deferred charges, and other assets.
11. Compare cash and accrual measurement of investing activities.
12. Identify asset control procedures.

TYPES OF ASSETS

Objective 1
Identify the purpose of investing activities.

Investing activities provide the resources an organization needs to operate. These resources are reported primarily as assets. Not all resources are included among assets, however. For example, the value of management and employee skills is not included. A company's balance sheet reports those assets for which identifiable costs can be reasonably determined. Exhibit 11-1 contains the asset section of the balance sheet reported by The Coca-Cola Company in its 1993 annual report. This exhibit will be used as a basis for discussing the types of assets reported by most corporations.

Most companies divide their assets into two primary categories: current and long term. **Current assets are those management expects to convert to cash or consume during the coming fiscal year.**[1] Some current assets are associated closely with a company's operating activities, which involve the use of those assets in producing and selling goods and services. Those assets (accounts receivable, inventories, and prepaid expenses) are examined in Chapter 13. Other current assets result from investment decisions concerning the amount of cash and short-term securities an organization needs to support its operating activities. Long-term assets include investments in securities, plant assets, and intangible assets.

INVESTMENTS IN LIQUID ASSETS

Liquid assets include cash and other resources that are readily exchanged for cash. In this section, we will examine cash and cash equivalents and securities.

---

[1]   In rare cases, a company's cycle of conversion, or operating cycle, is longer than a year. An operating cycle is the period from the time cash is paid for inventory until the inventory is sold and converted back to cash. In such cases, the longer operating cycle, rather than the fiscal year, is used as a basis for determining current assets.

Exhibit 11-1   Asset Section of Coca-Cola Balance Sheet

December 31, (in millions)	**1993**
Assets	
Current	
Cash and cash equivalents	$ 998
Marketable securities, at cost	80
	1,078
Trade accounts receivable	1,210
Finance subsidiary receivables	33
Inventories	1,049
Prepaid expenses and other assets	1,064
Total Current Assets	4,434
Investments and Other Assets	
Investments	
Coca-Cola Enterprises Inc.	498
Coca-Cola Amatil Limited	592
Other, principally bottling companies	1,125
Finance subsidiary receivables	226
Marketable securities and other assets	868
	3,309
Property, Plant, and Equipment	
Land	197
Buildings and improvements	1,616
Machinery and equipment	3,380
Containers	403
	5,596
Less allowances for depreciation	1,867
	3,729
Goodwill and Other Intangible Assets	549
	$12,021

Data source: 1993 annual report.

Cash and Cash Equivalents

Cash is central to an organization's operating, investing, and financing activities. These activities affect the amount of cash available to a company. Few measurement or reporting problems arise with cash. An organization increases its cash account when cash is received. It decreases the account when cash is paid. The primary accounting issues related to cash are cash management and control. Control is considered later in this chapter. Chapter 12 examines cash management.

     The amount of cash reported on a company's balance sheet normally includes cash and cash equivalents. **Cash and equivalents** encompass bank accounts, currency, checks, certain short-term investments, and other instruments that represent ready sources of money. The definition of cash equivalents usually includes marketable securities with maturities of three months or less. These investments are easily converted into cash and can be converted in a relatively short period. Therefore, they can be used to meet the company's cash needs. A company's statement of cash flows explains changes in cash *and equivalents* during a fiscal year.

Learning Note	A variety of noncash assets are used in a company's operating activities. These include accounts receivable, inventories, and prepaid expenses, such as supplies, rent, and insurance. These assets, considered in detail in Chapters 13 and 14, are associated with goods and services a company sells as part of its operating activities.

Securities

Securities that are part of an organization's assets include financial instruments such as stocks, bonds, certificates of deposit, and notes in which it has invested. These securities do not include a company's issuance or repurchase of its own financial instruments, such as bonds or stock. A company's own bonds and stocks are reported as part of the company's debt and equity. The repurchase of these securities is shown as a reduction of a company's liabilities or equity. A company's investments in another company's debt or equity securities are reported as assets, however. Debt securities include bonds, notes, and other debt instruments. Equity securities include preferred and common stock. For certain accounting rules (GAAP), only common stock is included in the equity category. This chapter examines some of these rules.

Companies report investments in securities in a variety of ways. Typically, these investments are classified as current or noncurrent. Short-term **marketable securities** are reported as current assets because the company expects to convert them to cash during the coming year. Other investments in securities are classified as long term or noncurrent. Securities are marketable if they are readily exchangeable for cash. Examples include stocks, bonds, and commercial paper of major corporations and government securities. It is the intent of management to convert securities to cash, not the type of security, that determines their classification as current or long term. For example, if General Motors invests in 10,000 shares of IBM stock, that investment may be classified as current or noncurrent, depending on whether GM management expects to sell the stock in the coming year. Investments in securities that are not readily marketable should not be classified as current assets, even if management plans to sell them during the coming year. If a market does not exist for the securities, management may have difficulty selling them.

Objective 2
Identify types of securities and explain why companies invest in them.

For most companies, short-term marketable securities result from a temporary excess of cash. The cash is invested to earn a return until the cash is needed. Long-term investments represent several different investment needs. For example, companies often create investments to fund the repurchase or repayment of their own debt. Investment funds are created to pay for retirement and other employee benefits. Investments are made in other companies to gain access to markets, resources, and technology. Thus, investments in securities serve a variety of purposes.

How a company accounts for its investments in securities depends on three attributes of the securities: type, length of investment, and (for long-term equity securities) amount of control. The type of investment is determined by whether a security is an equity, particularly common stock, or debt security. Length of investment is determined by whether management expects to sell an investment during the coming year. Amount of control applies only to long–term investments in equity securities. Control is determined by the extent of ownership a company has in other companies in which it invests. Exhibit 11-2 categorizes investments by type, length of investment, and control. Accounting measurement and reporting rules are associated with these categories.

Exhibit 11-2   Accounting for Investments in Securities

LENGTH OF INVESTMENT	TYPE OF INVESTMENT	
	Equity Securities	Debt Securities
Short-Term:	Market Value	Market Value or Amortized Cost
Long-Term:	**Amount of Control** Little Influence → Market Value; Significant Influence → Equity Method; Control → Consolidated Subsidiaries	Market Value or Amortized Cost

Except for investments in equity securities for which the equity method or consolidation is used (discussed later in this chapter), most investments in securities are accounted for using similar rules. Investments in securities are recorded at cost. Cost includes the price of the securities, brokerage fees, and similar transaction costs necessary to acquire the securities. Dividends or interest received from holding the investments are recognized as revenues when earned and are reported as nonoperating income on the income statement.

Learning Note

Financial institutions, such as banks and brokerage companies, are in the business of investing in securities. These organizations report the results of their securities-investing activities as part of their operating revenues and expenses rather than as nonoperating (other) revenues and expenses.

Differences exist in the values reported for different types of securities on a company's balance sheet. Also, the valuation of securities may affect a company's income statement. These differences are determined by (1) whether equity securities are marketable or not and (2) the intent of management when acquiring the investments.

Nonmarketable securities are reported on the financial statements at cost. Nonmarketable securities are those that are not readily tradeable because an established market does not exist. Marketable equity and debt securities are classified into one of three categories:

Trading Securities	Securities that a company actively trades by buying and selling on a regular basis. These securities are current assets.
Available-for-Sale Securities	Securities that a company plans to sell but does not actively trade. These securities are current or long-term assets depending on when a company plans to sell them.
Held-to-Maturity Securities	Debt securities that a company has the intention and ability to hold until maturity. These securities are long-term assets unless they mature during the next fiscal period. Equity securities cannot be held to maturity because this type of security has no maturity date.

All investments in trading or available-for-sale securities must be reported on a company's balance sheet at their fair market values. This rule sometimes is referred to as mark-to-market accounting. Fair market value is the amount for which a security could be sold at the balance sheet date in an established market. This rule applies to debt and equity securities that are marketable.

Debt securities are reported at cost if the investor has the intention and capability of holding the securities to maturity. In such cases, the amount an investor will receive for the investment is its maturity value. Therefore, these held-to-maturity investments are not affected by changes in market values prior to maturity.

INVESTMENT IN EQUITY SECURITIES

Objective 3
Explain accounting rules for investments in equity securities.

Several types of investment transactions are common for equity securities. These include purchase and sale of securities, recording dividends or other investment income, and valuation of securities at the end of a fiscal period. The effect of these transactions on a company's financial statements depends on the length of the investment and, for long-term investments, the extent of control the investor has on the issuer of stock.

Investment in Equity Securities—No Significant Influence

Companies often invest in the stocks of other companies. These stocks frequently are held for a limited time, until cash is needed. The investing company earns revenue on the investment while it is held, either in the form of dividends or increases in stock value. Of course, a loss occurs if the value of the stock decreases while it is held.

Equity investments are recorded at cost, including brokerage fees, when they are purchased. For example, if on November 1, 1996, Silicon Co. purchased 10,000 shares of Alfonso Co. stock at a cost of $100,000 as a short-term investment, the transaction would affect Silicon's accounts as follows:

Assets =		Liabilities + Equity	+ (Revenues − Expenses)
Cash	− 100,000		
Marketable Securities	100,000	0	0

At the end of the investor's fiscal year, the investment should be reported at its fair market value at the balance sheet date. The method used to report the adjustment to fair market value depends on Silicon's intention for holding the investment. Silicon may classify its investment as either (1) **trading securities** or (2) **available-for-sale securities**. If Silicon is actively involved in buying and selling Alfonso (and similar) stock, it would classify the stock as a trading security. If Silicon plans to sell its investment at some point but is not an active trader in the stock, it would classify the stock as available for sale.

For example, if the market value of Alfonso stock owned by Silicon is $105,000 on December 31, 1996, Silicon's year end, Silicon would record an increase in investment value. The increase would be reported as income of the current fiscal period if the stock is classified as a trading security:

Assets =		Liabilities + Equity	+ (Revenues − Expenses)	
Marketable Securities	5,000		Holding Gain	5,000

Silicon would report the market value of $105,000 ($100,000 cost + $5,000 adjustment) as an asset on its 1996 balance sheet. Because the stock is a trading security, it must be classified as a current asset. The HOLDING GAIN would be reported as nonoperating income on Silicon's income statement. The word "holding" indicates that the gain (or loss) resulted from a change in the market value of the investment while it was held (owned), not from selling the investment at an amount greater (or less) than its cost.

If Silicon reports its investment as an available-for-sale security, it would record the increase in investment value as:

Assets =		Liabilities + Equity		+ (Revenues − Expenses)
Allowance for Holding Gain	5,000	Unrealized Holding Gain	5,000	

The ALLOWANCE FOR HOLDING GAIN is an addition to Marketable Securities on the balance sheet. The investment would be classified as a current asset if Silicon's management expects to sell the investment during the 1997 fiscal year. Otherwise, it would be classified as long term.

The UNREALIZED HOLDING GAIN would be reported as an addition to Silicon's stockholders' equity rather than as part of the company's income. If this method is used, Silicon's balance sheet would reveal:

Silicon Co.
Balance Sheet
For the Year Ended December 31, 1996

Assets
Current assets
   Cash $ . . .
   Marketable securities, at market value (cost $100,000)   105,000
Stockholders' Equity
Common stock $ . . .
Retained earnings   . . .
Net unrealized holding gain   5,000

A company reports the net amount of holding gains and losses at the end of its fiscal year for its investments that are available for sale. For example, assume Silicon owned shares of Brandon Co. stock, in addition to Alfonso stock, at the end of 1996, and both investments were classified as short term:

	Cost	Market Value
Alfonso	$100,000	$105,000
Brandon	80,000	72,000
Total	$180,000	$177,000

Silicon would report the net market value of its investments of $177,000 as a current asset and would report a net unrealized holding loss of $3,000 ($180,000 − $177,000) for 1996 as an adjustment to its stockholders' equity. Note that this net effect is composed of the $5,000 increase to market for the Alfonso stock and the $8,000 decrease to market for the Brandon stock.

Short-term and long-term investments are reported separately. Thus, if Silicon owned long-term investments that cost $400,000 and had a market value of $420,000 at the end of 1996, it would report long-term investments of $420,000 and an unrealized holding gain of $20,000, in addition to its short-term investments.

Learning Note

Certain companies, particularly brokerage firms and banks, buy and sell securities on a continuous basis. These companies would classify most of their investments as **trading securities**. Therefore, increases or decreases in the market values of these companies' investments typically would be included on their income statements. Most other companies are likely to report their investments as **available-for-sale securities** rather than as trading securities.

When available-for-sale securities are sold, a gain or loss is recognized for the difference between the sales price and the cost of the investment. Assume Silicon sold the Alfonso shares for $112,000, including brokerage fees, on August 12, 1997. The sale would affect the company's accounts as follows:

Assets =		Liabilities + Equity		+ (Revenues − Expenses)	
Cash	112,000			Gain on Sale of	
Marketable Securities	− 100,000			Investments	12,000

The realized gain of $12,000 is reported on the income statement. Most companies report gains or losses from sale of securities as part of other revenues and expenses on their income statements. The unrealized holding gain for Alfonso stock recorded at the end of 1996 of $5,000 would be eliminated in calculating adjustments at the end of 1997, because the securities are no longer owned:

Assets =		Liabilities + Equity		+ (Revenues − Expenses)
Allowance for		Unrealized Holding		
Holding Gain	− 5,000	Gain	− 5,000	

In addition to market value adjustments, an investor should recognize revenue when dividends are received from investing in equity securities. Dividends received from equity investments should be recognized at the time they are earned. For example, assume Alfonso paid a dividend of $1,000 to Silicon on December 15, 1996. Silicon should record the transaction as investment income for its 1996 fiscal year:

Assets =		Liabilities + Equity	+ (Revenues − Expenses)	
Cash	1,000		Investment Income	1,000

Market value accounting is required for short-term equity investments and for long-term investments *when the investor does not have significant influence or control over the investee.* Influence or control is determined by the percentage of an issuer's common stock owned by an investor. The greater the ownership, the greater the control that is presumed. Three types of accounting rules (GAAP) are used:

Extent of Control	Accounting Rule
Little influence	Market value
Significant influence	Equity method
Control	Consolidation

The market value rule applies only when an investor cannot exert significant influence or control over an investee. GAAP presume significant influence exists when a company owns at least 20%, but no more than 50%, of another company's common stock. Control is presumed when more than 50% is owned. The current section has covered market value procedures. The following sections describe equity method and consolidation procedures.

Investment in Equity Securities—Significant Influence

If an investor has significant influence over another company, the fair market value method may not present an accurate description of transactions between the companies. For example, assume Big Co. owns 30% of the common stock of Little Co. It purchased the stock for $30 million on January 1, 1997. The purchase affected Big Co.'s accounts as follows:

Assets =		Liabilities + Equity	+ (Revenues − Expenses)
Cash	− 30,000,000		
Long-Term Investments	30,000,000	0	0

During 1997, Little Co. earned net income of $6 million. Big Co. had a poor year and generated a smaller-than-expected net income of $10 million. To bolster its profits, it used its influence over Little Co. to have its management pay an $8 million dividend in December 1997. Because Big Co. owned 30% of Little's stock, it received $2.4 million of the dividend. If the market measurement rule were used, the dividend would increase Big Co.'s revenues for 1997.

Because of the influence problem, GAAP require companies with significant influence to use the equity method of accounting for these investments. **The *equity method* requires an investor company to recognize revenue from an investee company's net income in proportion to the investor's ownership.** For example, if Little Co. reported net income of $6 million in 1997, Big Co. would record 30% of the net income as an increase in its investment and as revenue:

Assets =		Liabilities + Equity	+ (Revenues − Expenses)	
Long-Term Investments	1,800,000		Investment Revenue	1,800,000

This investment revenue sometimes is reported on the income statement as **equity in earnings of affiliated companies**.

Dividends received from Little Co. reduce Big Co.'s investment because they are considered to be a return of part of the $1,800,000 investment recognized by Big Co. For example, if Little Co. paid $4 million in dividends, Big Co. would record its 30% share as:

Assets =		Liabilities + Equity	+ (Revenues − Expenses)
Cash	1,200,000		
Long-Term Investments	− 1,200,000	0	0

Thus, while Little Co.'s retained earnings increased by $2 million in 1995 ($6 million of net income − $4 million of dividends), Big Co.'s investment increased proportionately by $600,000 ($2 million × .30):

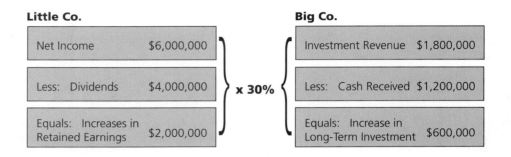

The book value of Big Co.'s investment in Little Co. would be $30.6 million after these transactions have been recorded ($30,000,000 + $1,800,000 − $1,200,000).

If, during 1998, Big Co. decided to sell its investment in Little Co. at a price of $30.3 million, the sale would affect its accounts as follows:

Assets =		Liabilities + Equity	+ (Revenues − Expenses)	
Cash	30,300,000		Loss on Sale of	
Long-Term			Investments	− 300,000
Investments	− 30,600,000			

The balance of LONG-TERM INVESTMENTS is reduced by the book value of Big Co.'s investment in Little Co. The difference between the cash received and the book value of the investment is a gain or loss on sale.

If the amount is material, the total amount of investments using the equity method often is reported as a separate asset. For example, Coca-Cola reported investments in Coca-Cola Enterprises, Coca-Cola Amatil, and other bottling companies (see Exhibit 11-1).

Investments in Equity Securities—Control

If a company owns over 50% of another company's voting stock, it controls the other company. The controlled company is a **subsidiary** of the controlling, or **parent**, company. The subsidiary's financial statements normally are consolidated as part of the parent corporation's consolidated financial statements. The consolidated statements report the parent and its subsidiaries as though they were one company.

For example, assume Parent Corp. owns 90% of Sub Corp.'s common stock at the end of 1997. Parent paid $45 million for Sub's stock at the beginning of the year. The acquisition affected Parent's accounts as follows:

Assets =		Liabilities + Equity	+ (Revenues − Expenses)
Cash	− 45,000,000		
Long-Term Investment	45,000,000	0	0

A part of Parent's assets and Sub's liabilities is a loan from Parent to Sub for $12 million. In addition, Sub sold goods priced at $5 million to Parent during the current fiscal year. Sub's cost for these goods was $3 million. Exhibit 11-3 describes the consolidation of the companies' financial statements at the end of 1997.

The consolidated balance sheet includes the assets and liabilities of both companies as shown in the right-hand column of Exhibit 11-3. For example, the consolidated assets of $235 million equal Parent's assets of $212 million plus Sub's assets of $80 million minus the adjustments for intercompany notes receivable (item a) and the long-term investment in Sub (item b). The intercompany receivable (item a) and payable (item c) are eliminated. In addition, the long-term investment account on the books of Parent (item b) and 90% (the parent's share) of Sub's stockholders' equity (item d) are eliminated. The remaining 10% ($5 million) of Sub's stockholders' equity is reported as minority interest. *Minority interest* **is the percentage of a subsidiary not owned by the parent.**

The consolidated income statement includes revenues and expenses as shown in the right-hand column. The intercompany revenue (item e) and cost of goods sold (item f) are eliminated. 10% (item g) of Sub's net income ($10 million) is reported as **minority interest in earnings** on the consolidated income statement.

Exhibit 11-3 Preparation of Consolidated Financial Statements

(in millions)	Parent Corp. Balances	Sub Corp. Balances	Adjustments Necessary for Consolidation			Parent Corp. Consolidated Statements
Total assets	$212	$80	a	Note receivable	(12)	
			b	Long-term investment	(45)	$235
Total liabilities	$ 96	$30	c	Note payable	(12)	$114
Stockholders' equity—sub		50	d		(45)	Minority Interest 5
Stockholders' equity—parent	116					116
Liabilities and stockholders' equity	$212	$80			(57)	$235
Revenues	$160	$70	e		(5)	$225
Expenses	(140)	(60)	f		3	(197)
Minority interest			g		(1)	(1)
Net income	$ 20	$10			(3)	$ 27

Learning Note

Not all countries require corporations to issue consolidated financial statements. Parent corporations may issue statements that do not include their subsidiaries. Also, rules about which companies must be included as part of consolidated reports vary among countries. Therefore, caution should be used in examining reports to determine which subsidiary companies have been included and which have been excluded.

Mergers and Acquisitions

Business combinations involve the merger of two companies or the acquisition of one company by another. **An** *acquisition* **occurs when one company acquires a controlling interest in another company, which continues to exist as a separate legal entity.** In the previous example, Parent Corp. acquired a majority of Sub Corp.'s common stock. Parent could accomplish this transaction in two ways. It could purchase Sub's shares. Sub's former stockholders would receive cash but would no longer be owners in Sub or Parent. Alternatively, Parent could have issued shares of its own stock in exchange for the stock of Sub. Sub's former stockholders would now be stockholders of Parent and its subsidiary. Under either of these arrangements, if Sub continued as a separate legal entity, Parent would issue consolidated financial statements.

On the other hand, if Parent owned all of Sub's common stock, it could retire Sub's stock and eliminate Sub as a separate legal entity. Sub's assets and liabilities would be combined with Parent's as part of a merger. **A** *merger* **occurs when companies combine their resources and operations so only one legal entity continues to exist.**

Objective 4
Identify methods used to account for acquisitions and mergers.

Two methods are used to account for mergers and acquisitions: the purchase method and the pooling of interests method. The **pooling of interests method** is used only when an acquisition or merger is accomplished primarily through the issuance of common stock. At least 90% of the common stock of one company in an acquisition or merger must be acquired through an exchange of the other company's common stock.[2] The **purchase method** is used when stock is acquired primarily through the exchange of cash, debt, or arrangements other than issuance of common stock. Most mergers and acquisitions are accounted for as purchases.

Purchase Method. In a purchase, the assets and liabilities of an acquired company are reported in consolidated financial statements at their **fair market value** at the date of acquisition. If a merger occurs, the assets and liabilities of the acquired company are combined in the new entity's accounting records at their fair market value. Therefore, the transaction is treated similarly to the company's purchase of new equipment or other assets. The purchase price determines the amount reported for the new assets and liabilities.

As an example, assume Parent Corp. purchased all of Sub Corp.'s common stock, paying $65 million in cash. At the time of the purchase, Sub's balance sheet reported assets with a book value of $80 million, liabilities of $30 million, and stockholders' equity of $50 million. Therefore, Parent paid $65 million for Sub's net assets (assets − liabilities) with a book value of $50 million. Parent paid the additional $15 million because it considered the value of Sub as a going concern to be greater than its book value. Book value does not consider the fair market value of assets and liabilities or the value of trained employees and established markets.

Sub's assets and liabilities would be valued by Parent at their fair market value, to the extent determinable. Assume Sub is merged with Parent. An ap-

---

[2] Other conditions also must be met for the pooling of interests method to be used. These conditions restrict the use of the method to situations in which stock-for-stock exchanges occur.

praisal of the value of Sub's identifiable assets and liabilities reveals assets with a market value of $93 million and liabilities with a market value of $34 million. Therefore, Parent has paid $65 million for net assets with an identifiable market value of $59 million ($93 − $34). Parent records the remaining $6 million it paid for Sub as goodwill. *Goodwill* **is the excess of cost over the market value of identifiable net assets resulting from the purchase of one company by another.** Goodwill represents the value of trained employees, established markets, and other resources that are not identified on Sub's balance sheet. It is an intangible asset.

The purchase of Sub would affect Parent's accounts as follows:

Assets =		Liabilities + Equity		+ (Revenues − Expenses)
Cash	− 65,000,000	Liabilities	34,000,000	
Assets	93,000,000			
Goodwill	6,000,000			

Parent would record Sub's individual assets and liabilities at their estimated market values. GAAP require goodwill to be amortized over a period not to exceed 40 years. If Parent amortized its goodwill over 10 years, it would recognize $600,000 of amortization expense each year.

Learning Note   Some countries, such as Great Britain, permit corporations to write off goodwill against stockholders' equity in the period in which goodwill is acquired. By writing off the goodwill, the corporation eliminates the amortization expense that would reduce its net income in future periods. Therefore, a company's reported net income will be higher than if goodwill had been amortized. Thus, a British company might report higher net income than an identical U.S. company because of the difference between U.S. and British GAAP concerning the amortization of goodwill.

Pooling of Interests. If the merger were a pooling of interests, Parent would have exchanged shares of its stock for Sub's shares. The new shares would be recorded at an amount equal to the *book value* of Sub's stockholders' equity. The assets and liabilities of Sub would be recorded by Parent at their book values as determined by Sub's accounting records:

Assets =		Liabilities + Equity		+ (Revenues − Expenses)
Assets	80,000,000	Liabilities	30,000,000	
		Common-Stock	50,000,000	

Parent would have recorded Sub's individual assets and liabilities. Assets and liabilities have been pooled rather than purchased. Goodwill does not result from a pooling of interests.

For tax purposes, corporations normally report mergers and acquisitions using the pooling of interests method. Assets and liabilities are reported at the same amount after the merger or acquisition as before. Therefore, the amount of depreciation that can be taken for tax purposes is determined by the book value of the assets acquired, not by their market value, even if the purchase method was used for financial reporting purposes.

SELF-STUDY PROBLEM 11-1

Consider each of the following independent long-term investment transactions that occurred on July 1, 1996:

a. Adam Co. acquired 35% of Smith Co.'s common stock for $20 million cash.
b. Adam acquired 100% of Smith Co.'s common stock in exchange for shares of Adam Co.'s own common stock. Smith was merged with Adam and no longer continued as a separate legal entity.
c. Adam purchased 10% of Smith Co.'s common stock for $8 million cash ($8 per share).
d. Adam acquired 95% of Smith Co.'s common stock in exchange for $84 million cash. Smith continued as a separate legal entity.

For each transaction in which Smith continued as a separate legal entity, assume Smith's net income for the fiscal year ended June 30, 1997, was $5 million. Also, assume Smith paid $2 million in dividends for the year ended June 30, 1997. No other intercompany transactions occurred during the year. The price of Smith's stock was $7 per share on June 30, 1997. Adam Co. owned no other long-term equity securities on this date.

Required

For each transaction, explain the accounting measurement and reporting rules Adam would use to account for the investment. Also, explain how, if at all, Smith's net income and dividends would affect Adam's accounts for the fiscal year ended June 30, 1997.

The solution to Self-Study Problem 11-1 appears at the end of the chapter.

INVESTMENT IN DEBT SECURITIES

Objective 5
Explain accounting rules for investments in debt securities.

When a company invests in debt securities, it is making loans to the issuer of the securities. These investments may be in the form of bonds, notes, or commercial paper issued by other organizations. Banks issue debt instruments in the form of certificates of deposit. The issuer of debt securities has an obligation to repay the principal borrowed from investors and to pay interest.

Debt securities may be marketable or nonmarketable. Marketable debt securities are those for which a market price is readily determinable. Some debt securities, such as bonds of major corporations or governments, trade on exchanges and in over-the-counter markets. Other debt securities, such as notes from customers, often are not marketable.

A company may purchase marketable debt securities for the purpose of reselling them when cash is needed, or it may intend to hold the securities until they mature. Securities that are expected to be resold are reported at their fair market value. Holding gains or losses normally are reported as an adjustment to stockholders' equity.

Held–to–maturity debt securities **are those for which an investor has the intent and ability to hold the securities until they mature.** Intent is determined by the purpose for which the debt was acquired. Ability is determined by whether an investor will need cash from the investment prior to maturity or whether other demands will require the investor to sell the investment before it matures. (Common stock does not have a maturity date and, therefore, cannot be classified as held to maturity.) Held-to-maturity debt securities should be classified as current assets if they mature during the coming fiscal year or as long-term assets if they do not mature during the coming fiscal year. Held-to-maturity securities are reported at amortized cost, as discussed later. Holding gains and losses are not reported for these securities in the income statement or balance sheet. The sections that follow consider accounting and reporting issues for debt securities.

Notes and Other Debt Securities

Accounting for investments in debt securities involves transactions associated with their purchase, interest earned, interest received, and their sale. For example, assume Silicon purchased $60,000 of short-term government notes on September 1, 1996. The notes pay interest at an annual rate of 5%. On September 1, the transaction to purchase the securities would affect Silicon's accounts as follows:

Assets =		Liabilities + Equity		+ (Revenues − Expenses)	
Cash	− 60,000				
Marketable Securities	60,000		0		0

At the end of its fiscal year, on December 31, Silicon would recognize $1,000 interest earned on the note for four months ($60,000 × .05 × 4/12):

Assets =		Liabilities + Equity		+ (Revenues − Expenses)	
Interest Receivable	1,000			Interest Revenue	1,000

At the end of 1996, Silicon would include the investment and receivable in its current assets. This investment would not be adjusted to its market value at the end of Silicon's fiscal year if Silicon expects to hold it to maturity or if the investment is not marketable.

If the notes mature on February 28, 1997, Silicon would record cash for the principal ($60,000) and interest received ($1,500 = $60,000 × .05 × 6/12). The company records the additional interest earned for two months during 1997 ($500 = $60,000 × .05 × 2/12) as interest revenue. These transactions would affect the company's accounts as follows:

Assets =		Liabilities + Equity	+ (Revenues − Expenses)	
Cash	61,500		Interest Revenue	500
Marketable Securities	−60,000			
Interest Receivable	−1,000			

Amortization schedules may be used for notes receivable to identify the amount of revenue recognized during a fiscal period. These schedules are common for long-term investments that pay principal and interest in installments over several fiscal periods. They serve the same purpose as those for notes payable, as discussed in Chapter 9.

Long-term receivables are common for financial services companies and for financial divisions of other companies. For example, automobile companies include divisions that finance the sale of automobiles to customers. Coca-Cola has a financing division to provide loans to bottling companies and customers that lease drink machines and other facilities from Coke. It reported receivables of $226 million in 1993 associated with its financing division (see Exhibit 11-1).

Long-Term Investments in Bonds

Bonds Held-to-Maturity. Accounting rules for long-term investments in bonds classified as held-to-maturity securities parallel those used to account for bonds payable. A company records the investment at cost, including brokerage fees. For example, assume Silicon purchased 100 Alfonso Co. bonds on July 1, 1996. The bonds pay interest semiannually on June 30 and December 31 at an annual coupon rate of 8%. The bonds sold at an effective yield of 10%. The effect of brokerage fees are included in computing the effective yield. The bonds mature on December 31, 1998, at a value of $1,000 per bond.

The price Silicon paid for each bond would be the present value of $40 each six months for five semiannual periods (July 1996 through December 1998), plus the present value of $1,000 at the end of five periods. The discount factor is 5% for each six-month period.

The interest factor for an annuity of five periods at 5% is 4.32948 (Table 2). The interest factor for a single payment at the end of five periods at 5% is 0.78353 (Table 1). Therefore, the price of each bond would be:

$$\$956.71 = (\$40 \times 4.32948) + (\$1,000 \times 0.78353)$$

The effect of the purchase transaction on Silicon's accounts would be:

Assets =		Liabilities + Equity	+ (Revenues − Expenses)
Cash	−95,671		
Long-Term Investments	95,671	0	0

The bonds sold at a discount (less than maturity value). The discount was $4,329 ($100,000 − $95,671). At each interest payment date, Silicon would record interest revenue and amortize the discount. Exhibit 11-4 provides an amortization schedule for the bonds.

Exhibit 11-4 Amortization Schedule for Bond Investment

a	b	c	d	e	f	g
Period	Present Value at Beginning of Period	Unamortized Discount	Interest Revenue (b × .05)	Interest Received	Amortization (d − e)	Present Value at End of Period (b + f)
1	$95,671	$4,329	$4,784	$4,000	$784	$ 96,455
2	96,455	3,545	4,823	4,000	823	97,278
3	97,278	2,722	4,864	4,000	864	98,142
4	98,142	1,858	4,907	4,000	907	99,049
5	99,049	951	4,951*	4,000	951	100,000

Adjustment made for rounding error

Therefore, on December 31, 1996, Silicon would record interest on the bonds:

Assets =		Liabilities + Equity	+ (Revenues − Expenses)	
Cash	4,000		Interest Revenue	4,784
Long-Term Investments	784			

The addition of $784 to long-term investments is the amount of discount amortized in 1996. Because Silicon purchased the bonds at less than maturity value, the discount is recognized over the life of the bonds as an increase in the asset and results in an increase in interest revenue. Over the life of the bonds, Silicon will earn $4,329 (the total discount amount) more than it paid for the bonds, in addition to the interest it receives in cash.

Silicon would report the bonds as long-term investments on its balance sheet at the end of 1996 at their book value of $96,455. The book value is the cost of the bonds, adjusted for amortization of the discount.

On June 30, 1997, Silicon would record:

Assets =		Liabilities + Equity	+ (Revenues − Expenses)	
Cash	4,000		Interest Revenue	4,823
Long-Term Investments	823			

Amortization of the discount increases LONG-TERM INVESTMENTS and INTEREST REVENUE. The company would continue to record interest until the bonds mature. On December 31, 1998, it would record the final interest payment:

Assets =		Liabilities + Equity	+ (Revenues − Expenses)	
Cash	4,000		Interest Revenue	4,951
Long-Term Investments	951			

Also, it would record receipt of principal:

Assets =		Liabilities + Equity		+ (Revenues − Expenses)	
Cash	100,000				
Long-Term Investments	− 100,000		0		0

Amortization of the discount has increased the long-term investment account to $100,000 on December 31, 1998. This is the amount of principal repaid on this date.

Available-for-Sale Securities. The prior discussion of bonds assumes that the bonds are classified as held-to-maturity securities. If a company purchases bonds or other marketable debt with the anticipation of selling the investment prior to maturity, the securities should be reported at their fair market value on balance sheet dates. Unrealized holding gains or losses would be reported as an adjustment to stockholders' equity. Interest revenue, adjusted for amortization of premium or discount, would be reported as shown above.

For example, assume Silicon invested in Alfonso bonds with the intent of selling them prior to maturity. Silicon would record its purchase at cost, as described above:

Assets =		Liabilities + Equity		+ (Revenues − Expenses)	
Cash	− 95,671	'			
Long-Term Investments	95,671		0		0

On December 31, 1996, Silicon would record interest on the bonds as in the earlier example:

Assets =		Liabilities + Equity		+ (Revenues − Expenses)	
Cash	4,000			Interest Revenue	4,784
Long-Term Investments	784				

A further adjustment would be needed for any difference between book value and market value at the balance sheet date. Assume the market value of the bonds was $98,000 on December 31, 1996. The book value on this date was $96,455 ($95,671 + $784). Therefore, an adjustment of $1,545 ($98,000 − $96,455) would be needed to bring the value of the bonds up to their market value:

Assets =		Liabilities + Equity		+ (Revenues − Expenses)	
Allowance for Holding Gain	1,545	Unrealized Holding Gain	1,545		

The unrealized holding gain would be reported as an addition to stockholders' equity. If the investment had been classified by Silicon as part of its trading securities, implying an intent to sell the securities in the near future, the gain would have been included in income rather than as an adjustment to stockholders' equity. Also, the bonds would be classified as a short-term, rather than long-term, investment.

If Silicon decided to sell the bonds prior to their maturity, it would receive an amount determined by the market value of the bonds at the date of sale. For example, assume Silicon sold the bonds on January 3, 1997, at a price of $98,100. The book value of Silicon's investment on this date was $96,455, not including the adjustment to fair market value on December 31, 1996. The sale of the bonds would result in a realized gain of $1,645:

Assets =		Liabilities + Equity		+ (Revenues − Expenses)	
Cash	98,100			Gain on Sale of	
Long-Term				Investments	1,645
Investments	− 96,455				

The gain on sale of investments would be reported by Silicon on its income statement for 1997. Also, the unrealized holding gain would be eliminated because the investment has been sold and the gain has been realized:

Assets =		Liabilities + Equity		+ (Revenues − Expenses)	
Allowance for		Unrealized			
Holding Gain	− 1,545	Holding Gain	− 1,545		

When bonds are bought or sold between interest payment dates, interest must be accrued on the bonds. For example, assume the sale in the previous example occurred on February 28, 1997, instead of on January 3, 1997. Silicon would have earned $1,333 ($100,000 × .08 × 2/12) of interest on the bonds for two months. Therefore, if the bonds are sold for $98,100 plus accrued interest, Silicon would record the sale as:

Assets =		Liabilities + Equity		+ (Revenues − Expenses)	
Cash	99,433			Interest Revenue	1,333
Long-Term				Gain on Sale of	
Investments	− 96,455			Investments	1,645

Two transactions have been recorded. Silicon received the interest it had earned since the last payment of interest ($1,333), in addition to the price of the bonds ($98,100). Silicon must collect the interest it has earned from the buyer because the buyer will receive the next interest payment for a full six months.

INVESTMENT IN PLANT ASSETS

Plant assets include land, buildings, and equipment used in a company's operating activities. Coca-Cola reported plant assets of $3,729 million in 1993 (Exhibit 11-1). This amount was net (after subtraction) of accumulated depreciation.

Transactions associated with plant assets include their purchase and disposal and their valuation on the balance sheet at the end of a fiscal period. Plant assets are recorded at cost, which includes the amount paid for them plus the cost of transportation, site preparation, installation, and construction necessary to make the assets usable. Plant assets are reported on the balance sheet at cost less accumulated depreciation.

Land is not subject to depreciation because it is not consumed. The cost of land associated with natural resources, such as oil or timber, that are consumed is allocated to expense through depletion (explained later in this chapter). Land generally is acquired as a site for office, manufacturing, and other facilities. The cost of land includes site preparation necessary for construction. Land improvements, such as paving and lighting, are treated as separate assets that are depreciated.

The next section considers depreciation for plant assets other than land.

Depreciation

Objective 6
Distinguish between straight-line and accelerated depreciation methods.

Plant assets that are consumed, such as buildings and equipment, are depreciated over their estimated useful lives. **Depreciation is the process of allocating the cost of plant assets to expense over the fiscal periods that benefit from their use.** Companies use a variety of depreciation methods. These methods fall into two general types: straight-line and accelerated. A third type, units-of-production, is used for certain assets described later. *Straight-line depreciation* **allocates an equal amount of the cost of a plant asset to expense during each fiscal period of the asset's expected useful life.** *Accelerated depreciation* **allocates a larger portion of plant asset cost to expense early in the asset's life.**

To illustrate, assume Silicon Co. purchased equipment on January 1, 1995, at a cost of $100,000. Management expects the equipment to have a useful life of five years. At the end of five years, management expects to sell the equipment as scrap metal with negligible value. Therefore, the depreciable cost of the asset is $100,000.

Straight-Line Depreciation.
Straight-line depreciation would allocate $20,000 ($100,000/5) of cost to depreciation expense each year over the life of the asset:

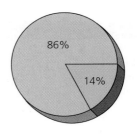

Depreciation Methods Used by Major U.S. Corporations for Financial Reporting

86%

14%

Straight-Line
Accelerated

(Data source: AICPA, Accounting Trends and Techniques, 1994.)

Depreciation Expense = Depreciable Cost ÷ Expected Life of Asset

Therefore, in 1995, depreciation would affect the company's accounts as follows:

Assets =		Liabilities + Equity	+ (Revenues − Expenses)	
Accumulated Depreciation	−20,000		Depreciation Expense	−20,000

ACCUMULATED DEPRECIATION is a contra-asset account offsetting EQUIPMENT. The net, or book value, of plant assets is the cost of assets minus accumulated depreciation. The book value of the equipment purchased on January 1 would be $80,000 at the end of 1995, $60,000 at the end of 1996, and so forth.

If the asset is expected to have a material sale or trade-in value at the end of its useful life, this value should be deducted from the cost in calculating depreciation. For example, if the equipment is expected to have a sale value of $5,000 at the end of its useful life, annual depreciation expense would be $19,000 = [($100,000 − $5,000)/5 years]. The amount an organization expects to receive for a plant asset at the end of its useful life is the asset's **residual**, or **salvage**, **value**. The residual value for many assets is negligible and often is omitted in calculating depreciation expense.

Accelerated Depreciation. Two methods of accelerated depreciation are common: the declining balance method and the sum-of-the-years'-digits method. *Declining balance depreciation* **allocates a multiple of the straight-line rate times the book value of an asset to depreciation expense.** A common multiple is 2, known as double–declining balance. An asset with a five-year life would be depreciated at a straight-line rate of 20% ($\frac{1}{5}$) if the straight-line method is used. Thus, double the straight-line rate would be 40% ($\frac{1}{5} \times 2$). If Silicon used the double–declining balance method for its asset, depreciation for 1995 would be calculated as:

Depreciation Expense = Book Value × (2 ÷ Expected Useful Life)

$$\$40,000 = \$100,000 \times \frac{2}{5}$$

The company would record accumulated depreciation and depreciation expense of $40,000 in 1995. Depreciation expense for 1996 would be calculated as:

$$\$24,000 = \$60,000 \times \frac{2}{5}$$

Observe that the book value, not the cost, is used in the calculation. The book value at the beginning of 1996 ($60,000) was multiplied times twice the straight-line rate.

Sum-of-the-years'-digits depreciation **allocates depreciation according to a fraction, n/N, in which n is remaining life of the asset at the beginning of the period and N is the sum of the years of the expected useful life of the asset.** For an asset with a five-year useful life, the sum would be 15 (1 + 2 + 3 + 4 + 5). Depreciation expense in the first year of the asset's life would be computed as:

$$\text{Depreciation Expense} = \text{Cost} \times \frac{5}{15}$$

$$\$33,333 = \$100,000 \times \frac{5}{15}$$

The remaining life of the asset at the beginning of the second year is four years. Therefore, depreciation expense in the second year would be:

$$\$26,667 = \$100,000 \times \frac{4}{15}$$

Observe that cost, not book value, is used in this calculation. If the asset had a residual value of $5,000, the depreciation expense would be computed as ($100,000 − $5,000) × 5/15 in year one and as ($100,000 − $5,000) × 4/15 in year two.

Units-of-Production Depreciation. In addition to the straight-line and accelerated methods, the units–of-production method is used by some companies for production equipment and facilities. **The** *units–of-production depreciation* **method produces a level amount of depreciation expense per unit of output, rather than per fiscal period.** For example, assume Silicon purchased for $30,000 a machine used to cut metal parts. Management expects the machine to produce 3 million components over its useful life. Depreciation could be computed based on the number of units produced during a fiscal period. The depreciation rate on the equipment would be $.01 per unit ($30,000/3,000,000). If 600,000 units were produced in 1996, $6,000 (600,000 × $.01) of depreciation expense would be recorded on the asset. If approximately the same number of units are produced each period, results of this method will be similar to those of straight-line depreciation. Other methods of allocating depreciation costs also are possible. For example, a company might allocate the cost of trucks on the basis of miles traveled or the cost of equipment based on the number of hours used.

Comparison of Depreciation Methods. A depreciation schedule reports the depreciation expense and book value of an asset over its useful life. Exhibit 11-5 provides a depreciation schedule for Silicon's asset for each of the methods previously considered.

Exhibit 11-5   Depreciation Schedule

Year	Straight-Line Book Value	Straight-Line Depreciation	Declining Balance Book Value	Declining Balance Depreciation	Sum-of-the-Years'-Digits Book Value	Sum-of-the-Years'-Digits Depreciation
0	$100,000		$100,000		$100,000	
1	80,000	$ 20,000	60,000	$ 40,000	66,667	$ 33,333
2	60,000	20,000	36,000	24,000	40,000	26,667
3	40,000	20,000	21,600	14,400	20,000	20,000
4	20,000	20,000	12,960	8,640	6,667	13,333
5	0	20,000	0	12,960	0	6,667
Total		$100,000		$100,000		$100,000

Year 0 is the purchase date at the beginning of the five-year period. As depreciation expense is recorded each year, accumulated depreciation increases and the book value of the asset decreases. Observe that the amount of depreciation recorded in years 1 and 2 is higher using the accelerated method than using the straight-line method. Each method allocates the cost of the asset to depreciation over the asset's life. Observe that the declining balance method requires the remaining book value of an asset to be expensed in the last year of its life, regardless of the amount. The $12,960 of depreciation expense computed using this method in Exhibit 11-5 was the amount necessary to write off the cost of the machine. It was not 40% of the book value at the beginning of the year.

Depreciation expense is prorated for plant assets acquired during a fiscal period. If a company acquired assets in April 1996, and its fiscal year end was December 31, it would record 9/12 of the full-year depreciation expense for these assets in 1996.

When a company continuously purchases and replaces plant assets, accelerated depreciation will result in lower net income than will straight-line depreciation. Most companies use straight-line depreciation for the majority of their assets, thereby reporting higher net incomes. Companies may use different depreciation methods for financial reporting and tax purposes. Accelerated depreciation is permitted for tax purposes for most plant assets. Accelerated depreciation reduces the amount of taxable income and the cash outflow for taxes. Tax rules specify the type of depreciation method and useful life that can be used for computing depreciation for tax purposes. For example, most office furniture and factory equipment can be depreciated for tax purposes over seven years using the double–declining balance method.

As an example of accounting and tax reporting differences, assume Silicon purchased equipment at a cost of $100,000. The equipment has no residual value and an expected useful life of ten years. Silicon depreciates the equipment for financial reporting purposes using the straight-line method and a ten-year life. Depreciation expense would be $10,000 for the first year. For tax purposes, it uses the double–declining balance method and a seven-year life. Depreciation expense would be $28,571 ($100,000 × ⅔) for the first year for tax purposes. The higher amount of expense for tax purposes would result in lower income for tax purposes than for financial reporting purposes. The difference would result in deferred income taxes as discussed in Chapter 9.

GAAP require corporations to report the depreciation methods they use. A note to Coca-Cola's financial statements disclosed:

> Property, plant, and equipment are depreciated principally by the straight-line method over the estimated useful lives of the assets.

Foreign corporations may use accounting methods for depreciation that differ from those used in the U.S. For example, Swiss companies may expense plant assets in the year in which they are acquired. These assets are reported on the companies' balance sheets at a book value of 1 Swiss franc. This practice results in lower reported net income and lower asset values for these companies relative to those of most nations. This extremely conservative practice helps protect creditors, such as banks, that provide most of the financing for Swiss companies.

Disposal of Plant Assets

Objective 7
Determine the accounting effects of disposing of plant assets.

Disposal of plant assets occurs when the assets are retired or sold. Each of these transactions involves elimination of an asset's cost and accumulated depreciation from the accounting records. For example, assume Silicon retired the equipment described in Exhibit 11-5 at the end of year 4 because it had become obsolete and had no sales value. If Silicon used straight-line depreciation, it would record the retirement by eliminating the asset and related accumulated depreciation from its accounts:

Assets =		Liabilities + Equity	+ (Revenues − Expenses)	
Equipment	− 100,000		Loss on Disposal of	
Accumulated			Plant Assets	− 20,000
Depreciation	80,000			

Through the end of year 4, $80,000 of accumulated depreciation had been recorded on the asset. The book value of the asset is recorded as a loss if the asset is retired before being fully depreciated.

If the asset was sold at the end of year 4 for $12,000, Silicon would follow a similar procedure:

Assets =		Liabilities + Equity	+ (Revenues − Expenses)	
Cash	12,000		Loss on Disposal of	
Equipment	− 100,000		Plant Assets	− 8,000
Accumulated				
Depreciation	80,000			

The difference between the amount received for the asset and the asset's book value is a gain or loss. If Silicon had received more than $20,000 for the asset, it would have recorded a gain.

Depletion of Natural Resources

Objective 8
Explain accounting rules for investments in natural resources.

Paper, petroleum, mining, and other companies invest in natural resources. They purchase or lease land that contains timber, oil, or minerals. The cost of the land is primarily for the natural resources it contains.

The amount reported for natural resources on a company's balance sheet is the cost of the asset less depletion. *Depletion* **is the systematic allocation of the cost of natural resources to the periods that benefit from their use.** Assume Silicon purchased land containing minerals on April 1, 1997, for $8 million. The transaction affected the company's accounts as follows:

Assets =		Liabilities + Equity	+ (Revenues − Expenses)
Cash	− 8,000,000		
Mineral Deposits	8,000,000	0	0

The company estimated the land contained 80,000 tons of minerals when it was purchased. Thus, the estimated cost per ton was $100 ($8 million/80,000 tons). During 1997, Silicon mined the land and removed 16,000 tons of the minerals. The cost of the asset consumed during 1997 would affect the company's accounts as follows ($100 × 16,000 tons):

Assets =		Liabilities + Equity	+ (Revenues − Expenses)
Inventory	1,600,000		
Mineral Deposits	− 1,600,000	0	0

The minerals are inventoried until they are consumed or sold. Cost of goods sold should be increased when the inventory is sold. This example assumes the land has negligible value apart from the value of the mineral deposits. If the land is valuable apart from the deposits, the estimated cost of the land should be recorded as a separate asset. Only the estimated value of the deposits should be depleted.

GAAP require that natural resources be reported by companies at their amortized costs. The market values of these resources is not reported on the financial statements, though some companies disclose information about the current value of these assets in notes to the financial statements. For some companies, the market values may be much higher than book values. Companies owning oil and timber reserves, for example, may have experienced dramatic increases in the market values of these resources in recent years because of increasing demand. The market value of a company's stock may reflect the unrecorded value of these assets.

SELF-STUDY PROBLEM 11-2

Banana Boat Co. purchased equipment on January 1, 1997, at a cost of $400,000. The equipment has an expected life of eight years, at which time it is anticipated to have negligible value. The company's management is considering whether to depreciate the equipment on a straight-line, double-declining balance, or sum-of-the-years'-digits basis. The company's tax rate is 30%. For tax purposes, the equipment will be depreciated over seven years using the double-declining balance method, regardless of which method is used for financial reporting purposes.

Required

What effect would each of the three methods have on Banana Boat's net income in 1997? What effect would each method have on the company's cash flows for the year?

The solution to Self-Study Problem 11-2 appears at the end of the chapter.

INVESTMENT IN LEASED ASSETS

Objective 9
Distinguish between operating and capital leases.

In addition to purchasing plant assets, some companies lease assets from other companies. Leasing is common in certain industries, such as airlines. Leases are of two major types: operating and capital. **An** *operating lease* **is a contract that permits one organization to use property owned by another organization for a limited period of time. The costs of operating leases are expensed in the period in which leased assets are used.** For example, assume Silicon paid $60,000 for equipment it leased in 1997. If the leases were accounted for as operating leases, Silicon would record $60,000 of lease expense in 1997. Minimum future payments associated with operating lease contracts must be disclosed by corporations as discussed in Chapter 9.

A *capital lease* **is a contract that permits one organization to use property owned by another organization as though the property had been purchased. Capital leases transfer most of the risks and rights of ownership to the company leasing the assets.** These lease contracts are for most of the useful life of an asset and may provide an option for the lessor to purchase the asset. For accounting purposes, capital leases are treated as purchase contracts. Leased assets are reported on the balance sheet, along with other plant assets.

The amount recorded for leased assets is the present value of future lease payments. Capital leases are a form of financing in which a company acquires the right to use a resource in exchange for payments over a specified period. The payments compensate the owner of the asset for the asset cost and for interest for financing the lease. In substance, the arrangement is the same as a company's borrowing money to purchase an asset. An asset is acquired, and a loan is created that must be repaid with interest.

For example, assume Silicon leased equipment on January 1, 1997. The lease contract called for five annual payments of $3,000. Silicon could have borrowed cash at 9% to purchase the equipment. On January 1, 1997, the leased asset would be recognized by Silicon as the present value of the lease payments. The present value of an annuity of five periods at 9% is 3.88965 (Table 2). The present value of the lease payments would be $11,669 ($3,000 × 3.88965). The lease would affect Silicon's accounts as follows:

Assets =		Liabilities + Equity		+ (Revenues − Expenses)
Equipment Under Capital Lease	11,669	Capital Lease Obligation	11,669	

The transaction is treated as though Silicon purchased the asset and borrowed money to finance the purchase.

Two transactions are necessary at the end of 1997. One of these records depreciation on the leased asset. Assuming straight-line depreciation of $2,334 ($11,669/5), the transaction would affect Silicon's accounts as follows:

Assets =		Liabilities + Equity	+ (Revenues − Expenses)	
Accumulated Depreciation	−2,334		Depreciation Expense	−2,334

The second transaction recognizes the payment of principal and interest on the financing arrangement. Exhibit 11-6 provides a lease amortization schedule.

Exhibit 11-6   Lease Amortization Schedule

a	b	c	d	e	f
Period	Lease Obligation at Beginning of Period	Interest Expense (b × .09)	Lease Payment	Principal Payment (d − c)	Lease Obligation at End of Period (b − e)
1	$11,669	$1,050	$3,000	$1,950	$9,719
2	9,719	875	3,000	2,125	7,594
3	7,594	683	3,000	2,317	5,277
4	5,277	475	3,000	2,525	2,752
5	2,752	248	3,000	2,752	0

The lease is treated as an installment loan. A portion of each payment is treated as interest and a portion is treated as a payment of loan principal. At the end of 1997, this transaction would affect Silicon's accounts as follows:

Assets =		Liabilities + Equity		+ (Revenues − Expenses)	
Cash	− 3,000	Capital Lease Obligation	− 1,950	Interest Expense	− 1,050

Silicon would continue to record transactions at the end of each year. The asset would be depreciated at the rate of $2,334 per year. The principal and interest for the financing arrangement would be recorded according to amounts shown in the lease amortization schedule.

The net result of these transactions is the inclusion of assets and liabilities on the balance sheet for leased assets. By requiring these amounts to be reported, GAAP attempt to increase the comparability between amounts reported by different corporations. For example, assume Lease Airlines leased its aircraft and Purchase Airlines purchased its aircraft. If capital leases were not reported on the balance sheets, Lease Airlines would have far fewer assets and liabilities than Purchase Airlines. Attempts to compare the performances of the two companies would be difficult. The ratio of net income to total assets of Lease, for example, would be much higher than that for Purchase if both had the same amount of net income. Reporting leased assets and obligations makes the two companies' financial statements more comparable.

Japanese companies do not include the asset or liability associated with capital leases on their balance sheets. All leases are reported as operating leases. Thus, for industries in which capital leasing is important, the airline and automobile industries for example, a Japanese company would report lower amounts of assets and liabilities than an identical U.S. company.

INTANGIBLE ASSETS, DEFERRED CHARGES, AND OTHER ASSETS

Objective 10
Explain accounting issues
associated with intangible
assets, deferred charges, and
other assets.

Intangible assets include the cost of legal rights such as copyrights, patents, brand names, and trademarks owned by a company. The purchase price or legal fees associated with securing the rights are recorded as assets. These costs, then, are amortized over the life of the assets, usually on a straight-line basis.

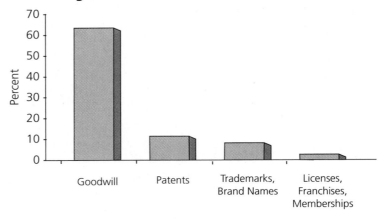

Percentage of Major Corporations Reporting Intangible Assets

Data source: AICPA, Accounting Trends & Techniques, 1994

GAAP require intangibles to be amortized over a period of 40 years or less. A longer amortization period reduces the amount of expense recognized each year relative to a shorter period. As an example, assume Silicon purchased intangible assets for $1 million. By amortizing the assets over 40 years, it would recognize $25,000 of expense each year.

U.S. GAAP do not permit companies to report the estimated market value of their brands, trademarks, and other intangibles as part of their assets. They can report only the cost associated with these items as assets on their balance sheets. Brands and trademarks, however, may be among a corporation's most valuable resources. For example, the Coca-Cola brand name has been estimated to have a value of almost $25 billion.[3] Many companies would report much higher asset and stockholders' equity amounts if the market values of these assets were included. Some countries, such as Great Britain, permit corporations to report the estimated market value of these assets. Therefore, British companies may appear to have higher asset and equity values than their U.S. counterparts.

Another category of long-term assets is deferred charges. *Deferred charges* **are assets resulting when a company prepays expenses that will result in long-term benefits.** These charges typically are amortized over future periods. Start-up costs on new businesses, divisions, or projects often are capitalized and reported as deferred charges. These costs include costs incurred prior to the

---

[3]   Reported in *USA Today*, August 12, 1992.

beginning of operation of a business venture. Typical costs are legal fees, support services, and advertising. These costs are recorded to an asset account such as ORGANIZATIONAL COSTS.

Other assets can include miscellaneous accounts that do not fit under other categories. **Plant assets held for disposal** is an example. If plant assets have been removed from service and a company is attempting to sell them, they are listed as other assets rather than as plant assets. Prepaid and deferred tax charges may be reported as separate items if they are material. Prepaid taxes are current assets. **Deferred tax charges** generally are long-term assets. Both accounts result from differences between financial and tax accounting procedures. These differences can result in liabilities, deferred tax obligations, as described in Chapter 9, or in assets.

Research and development activities are important for many companies. These costs are associated with new-product design and development. Though these costs are likely to benefit future periods, GAAP require these costs to be expensed in the period in which they are incurred. Uncertainty about the periods that benefit from the costs is the rationale for immediate expensing of the costs.

Prepaid pension costs also may be reported as assets. These prepayments result when the value of pension plan assets is in excess of benefit obligations, as described in Chapter 9.

Corporations report other types of assets. Certain assets are important to a specific industry or company. A description of the assets often is provided in notes to the financial statements.

CASH AND ACCRUAL MEASUREMENT

Objective 11
Compare cash and accrual measurement of investing activities.

The statement of cash flows reports the amount of cash flow associated with investing activities. Exhibit 11-7 provides a portion of Coca-Cola's statement of cash flow for 1993.

Investing activities affect both the operating and investing sections of the cash flow statement. Depreciation and amortization expenses (item 3) result from the use of plant assets. But, these expenses do not involve payments of cash and, therefore, are added back to net income. Instead, cash is paid when assets are acquired (item 16), often called **capital expenditures**. Cash is received when plant assets are sold (item 17). These sales may result in gains or losses (item 7) on the income statement, but the gains or losses do not produce cash flows beyond the amount received (item 17). Therefore, gains are subtracted and losses added to net income to compute cash flows from operating activities. Similarly, sales of investments (item 15) result in cash inflows, while purchases of investments (item 14) result in cash outflows. Decreases in (sales of) marketable securities (item 11) or (collections of) receivables (item 13) result in cash inflows. Finance receivables (items 12 and 13) are listed among investing, rather than operating, activities because these activities are not part of Coca-Cola's primary business activities. Lending money to bottling companies or customers is a type of investment in these companies, rather than the result of sales of products to the customers.

Equity income (item 5) is investment income from the equity method. Except for the dividends received from these investments, this income does not in-

Exhibit 11-7   Operating and Investing Sections of Coca-Cola Statement of Cash Flows

Year Ended December 31, (in millions)	1993
Operating Activities	
1. Net income	$2,176
2. Effects of changes in accounting principles	12
3. Depreciation and amortization	360
4. Deferred income taxes	(62)
5. Equity income, net of dividends	(35)
6. Foreign currency adjustments	9
7. Gains on sales of assets	(84)
8. Other noncash items	78
9. Net change in operating assets and liabilities	54
10. Net cash provided by operating activities	2,508
Investing Activities	
11. Decrease in current marketable securities	29
12. Additions to finance subsidiary receivables	(177)
13. Collections of finance subsidiary receivables	44
14. Acquisitions and purchases of investments	(816)
15. Proceeds from disposals of investments and other assets	621
16. Purchases of property, plant, and equipment	(800)
17. Proceeds from disposal of property, plant, and equipment	312
18. All other investing activities	(98)
19. Net cash used in investing activities	(885)

Items have been numbered and minor changes have been made in format to facilitate the discussion.

volve cash inflow. Therefore, the noncash portion of income is subtracted from net income in computing operating cash flows. This income is the result of an investing activity by Coca-Cola. The adjustment is made to cash flow from operating activities, however, because the equity income is included on the income statement.

The primary cash flow results of investing activities are the sale and acquisition of plant assets and investments, including investments in other companies and marketable securities. These are the primary items found in the investing activities section of the cash flow statement. Other items affect the operating activities section because gains and losses on sales of plant assets and investments and depreciation and amortization of long-term assets do not result in cash inflows and outflows. Therefore, the accrual results of operations (item 1) must be adjusted for noncash items to compute the cash flow results of operations (item 10).

CONTROL OF ASSETS

Objective 12
Identify asset control procedures.

Control of assets is an important accounting issue. Accounting records should be compared with results of physical inspections of assets on a regular basis. Accounting records identify the amount of cash, securities, inventories, and plant assets a company should have available. The records provide a basis for determining whether assets are missing and for determining who is responsible for the assets. Internal controls in the accounting system are designed to ensure the proper recording of these assets. Chapter 4 described some of these controls. Physical controls are necessary to protect the assets from theft, misuse, and deterioration. Failure to protect assets results in misstated account balances when recorded assets do not exist.

Control procedures involve independent verification of assets, security over access to assets, and inspection of assets. Cash and securities are especially vulnerable because they are easily concealed and are readily transferable. Safes, vaults, and banks are used to protect these assets. Many securities are registered in the name of the owner, thereby controlling the transfer of the assets. Surprise audits of cash and securities are used to verify their existence. Retail companies often maintain large amounts of cash. Cash is obtained from the sale of merchandise and is needed to make change for customers. Cash registers are used to protect this cash. Sales receipts or cash register tapes provide independent verification of the amount of cash reported by sales clerks. Surprise cash counts can reveal whether employees are using cash for personal benefit, for example, for unreported short-term loans to themselves.

Accounting records identify the amount of cash and securities deposited in bank accounts or invested with brokerage firms and other financial institutions. These institutions provide monthly or quarterly statements of account balances and transactions for the period. Reconciliation of these statements with the company's accounting records verifies the accuracy of the records.

Physical assets, such as inventories and plant assets, should be secured. Storerooms, warehouses, and other facilities protect these assets. Access is permitted only to authorized personnel. Periodic counts verify the accuracy of accounting records. Proper hiring and training procedures can help with asset security. Retail stores often use magnetic tags to prevent shoplifting. More expensive products are kept in locked cases. Display items may be secured so they cannot be removed.

Tools and equipment are the responsibility of specific employees. These employees may be personally liable for loss of tools or equipment. Cars, trucks, and other vehicles are assigned to individuals who are responsible for their use and protection. Major assets may be insured for fire or theft. Guards and surveillance equipment are used to protect inventories and plant assets.

Control is a major management activity in most organizations. Control involves a combination of accounting and other procedures.

SELF-STUDY PROBLEM 11-3

Silicon Co. reported the following transactions, in millions, for the year ended December 31, 1997:

Sale of plant assets with a book value of $22 for $16, reporting a loss of $6.
Sales of securities with a book value of $10 for $14, reporting a gain of $4.
Depreciation and amortization expense for 1997 of $8.
Income from equity investments of $5 and dividends from these investments of $2.
Acquisitions of plant assets of $35.
Acquisitions of long-term investments of $10.
Net income of $50.

Required

Prepare the operating and investing sections of Silicon's cash flow statement, assuming no other activities affected these sections.

The solution to Self-Study Problem 11-3 appears at the end of the chapter.

REVIEW   *Summary of Important Concepts*

1. Investments in cash and securities:
   a. Investing activities provide resources an organization needs to operate. These resources are reported primarily as assets.
   b. Cash and equivalents include bank accounts, currency, checks, some short-term investments, and other ready sources of money.
   c. Marketable securities may be either current or long term depending on management's intention to sell them during the coming fiscal period.
   d. Marketable equity securities are reported on the balance sheet at the lower of cost or market. Losses on these investments are recognized in the period in which a decline in market value occurs. These losses are recognized on the income statement for short-term investments and on the balance sheet for long-term investments.
   e. Corporations report long-term investments in equity securities that represent 20% to 50% of the common stock of another company using the equity method. The owned company's net income is reported as investment revenue by the investor in proportion to the percentage of common stock owned.
   f. Companies controlled by an investor corporation are reported as consolidated subsidiaries. A parent and its subsidiaries are reported as though they were one entity in the parent's consolidated financial statements.
   g. Mergers and acquisitions occur when one company obtains a controlling interest in the common stock of another corporation. Mergers and acquisitions are accounted for by the purchase or pooling of interests method.
   h. Investments in debt securities are recorded at cost. A premium or discount on the securities is amortized over the life of the securities.

2. Investments in plant assets, intangibles, and other assets:
   a. Plant assets are reported on the balance sheet at cost less accumulated depreciation.
   b. Several methods of depreciation are used, including: straight-line, declining balance, sum-of-the-years'-digits, and units-of-production. Most corporations use straight-line depreciation for financial statement purposes. Accelerated methods often are used for tax purposes.
   c. Depletion allocates the cost of natural resources to expense as the assets are consumed.
   d. Operating leases are expensed during the period leased assets are used. The present values of future payments for capital leases are recorded as assets and liabilities.

3. The statement of cash flows reports cash flows associated with investing activities. Cash flow and accrual measures of asset transactions often differ.

4. Control of assets is important to ensure the accuracy of accounting information.

D E F I N E   *T e r m s   a n d   C o n c e p t s   D e f i n e d   i n   T h i s   C h a p t e r*

accelerated depreciation	depletion	operating lease
acquisition	equity method	straight-line depreciation
available for sale securities	goodwill	sum-of-the-years'-digits
capital lease	held-to-maturity debt securities	depreciation
declining balance depreciation	merger	trading securities
deferred charges	minority interest	units-of-production depreciation

S O L U T I O N S

SELF-STUDY PROBLEM 11-1

a. Adam Co. would use the equity method for its investment because it owns 20% to 50% of Smith Co.'s stock. Adam is assumed to have significant influence over Smith. Adam would recognize 35% ($1.75 million) of Smith's income as investment revenue for 1997. The dividends received from Smith ($700,000) would reduce Adam's investment account. After these transactions have been recorded, the book value of Adam's investment in Smith would be $21.05 million ($20 + $1.75 − $0.7).

b. Adam Co. would record the merger as a pooling of interests, assuming all conditions for a pooling were met. Smith's account balances would be combined with those of Adam's at their book value. The stock issued by Adam would be recorded at the book value of Smith's stockholders' equity. Consolidated statements would not be necessary because only one legal entity existed after the merger. Smith would have had no net income and would have paid no dividends for 1997 because it ceased to exist as a separate legal entity at the time of the merger.

c. Adam Co. would report its investment in Smith Co. stock at its market value of $7 per share, for a total of $7 million on June 30, 1997, because Adam has little influence over Smith (the investment is less than 20% of Smith's common stock). It would report the holding loss of $1 million as a reduction in stockholders' equity. The $2 million of dividends would be reported as investment (other) revenue on Adam's income statement. Smith's net income would have no effect on Adam's financial statements.

d. Adam Co. would record the investment at cost since this acquisition is a purchase of greater than 50% interest. Adjustments would be made to Adam's investment account for Smith's net income and dividends in the same manner as under the equity method. 95% of Smith's net income would be added to the investment account, and 95% of Smith's dividends would be subtracted. The investment account would not appear on Adam's consolidated financial statements, however. The statements would report the consolidated results of the two companies as though they were one company. Smith's assets and liabilities would be included on the consolidated balance sheet at their estimated fair market values. Any excess of cost over the fair market value of identifiable net assets would be reported as goodwill.

SELF-STUDY PROBLEM 11-2

Computation of depreciation for 1997 would be:

Straight-line $\ 50{,}000 = \$400{,}000/8$ years
Double-declining balance $\$100{,}000 = \$400{,}000 \times \frac{2}{8}$
Sum-of-the-years'-digits $\ 88{,}889 = \$400{,}000 \times \frac{8}{36}$

Depreciation under each method would reduce net income, after taxes, as follows:

Straight-line $\$35{,}000 = \$\ 50{,}000 \times (1.0 - 0.3)$
Double-declining balance $\$70{,}000 = \$100{,}000 \times (1.0 - 0.3)$
Sum-of-the-years'-digits $\$62{,}222 = \$\ 88{,}889 \times (1.0 - 0.3)$

Use of the straight-line method would produce the highest net income. The choice of method for calculating depreciation on the income statement has no effect on Banana Boat's method for tax calculation. Therefore, it does not affect the company's cash flows. Note that, other than reducing taxes, depreciation does not affect cash flows.

SELF-STUDY PROBLEM 11-3

Silicon Co.
Statement of Cash Flows
For the Year Ended December 31, 1997

(in millions)
Operating Activities

Net income	$50
Adjustments for noncash items:	
Depreciation and amortization	8
Loss from sale of plant assets	6
Gain from sale of investments	(4)
Equity in earnings, less dividends	(3)
Cash flow from operating activities	$ 57

Investing Activities

Sale of plant assets	$16
Sale of securities	14
Acquisitions of plant assets	(35)
Acquisitions of long-term investments	(10)
Cash flow for investing activities	$(15)

EXERCISES

11-1. Write a short definition for each of the terms listed in the "Terms and Concepts Defined in This Chapter" section.

11-2. Archer Co. produces sporting goods equipment. Identify and describe briefly the types of assets Archer is likely to include in its accounting system.

11-3. At the end of its 1996 fiscal year, Hamlet Co. owned the following investments:
   a. $100,000 of bonds of major corporations with maturities of five years or more.
   b. $160,000 of common stock of major corporations.
   c. $75,000 of commercial paper issued by major corporations with maturities of 6 months or less.
   d. $50,000 of bonds that are not readily marketable with maturities of 2 years.
   e. $40,000 of bonds of major corporations with maturities of 12 months or less.
   Determine the amount Hamlet would report as current assets, assuming management plans to sell the bonds and common stock during the next fiscal year. Explain your answer.

11-4. Ophelia Co. owned the following investments at the end of its 1997 fiscal year:
   a.   10,000 shares of the common stock of Claudius Co. Claudius had 1 million shares outstanding.
   b.   2 million shares of the common stock of Polonius Co. Polonius had 3 million shares outstanding.
   c.   300,000 shares of the common stock of Gertrude Co. Gertrude had 1 million shares outstanding.
   d.   400,000 shares of the preferred stock of Fortinbras Co. Fortinbras had 500,000 shares of preferred outstanding.
   Assume each of these investments is properly accounted for as a long-term investment. How would Ophelia account for each type of investment? Explain the purpose of each accounting rule used by Ophelia to account for its investments.

11-5. Macbeth Co. recorded the following transactions during its 1996 fiscal year:
   a.   Purchased 5% of the outstanding shares of Duncan Co. for $300,000 plus brokerage fees of $30,000.
   b.   Purchased 2% of the outstanding shares of Macduff Co. for $400,000 plus brokerage fees of $40,000.
   c.   Received $50,000 of dividends from Duncan Co.
   At the end of 1996, the Duncan shares had a market value of $350,000. The Macduff shares had a market value of $360,000. Macbeth owned no other investments in common stock. The transactions were properly recorded as short-term investments in trading securities. Use the following format to identify the effect of each event on Macbeth's account balances:

Assets =	Liabilities + Equity	+ (Revenues − Expenses)

11-6. Isabella Co. recorded the following transactions during its 1995 fiscal year:
   a.   Purchased 5% of the outstanding shares of Othello Co. for $300,000, plus brokerage fees of $30,000, as a short-term investment.
   b.   Purchased 2% of the outstanding shares of Ferdinand Co. for $400,000, plus brokerage fees of $40,000, as a long-term investment.
   c.   Received $50,000 of dividends from Othello Co.
   At the end of 1995, the Othello shares had a market value of $350,000. The Ferdinand shares had a market value of $360,000. All investments were classified as available for sale.

Isabella owned no other investments in common stock. Use the following format to identify the effect of each event on Isabella's account balances:

Assets =	Liabilities + Equity	+ (Revenues − Expenses)

11-7. In 1991, Chanticleer Co. acquired 40% of Pertelote Co. for $30 million. Pertelote's net income and dividend payments since the purchase are shown below:

Year	Net Income	Dividends
1992	$8,000,000	$3,000,000
1993	7,400,000	2,500,000
1994	8,100,000	3,000,000
1995	8,500,000	3,200,000

At the beginning of its 1996 fiscal year, Chanticleer sold its investment in Pertelote for $42 million. Determine the amount Chanticleer reported on its balance sheet for its investment in Pertelote in 1992 through 1995. How much profit (or loss) did Chanticleer record from its sale of Pertelote in 1996?

11-8. Daedalus Co. purchased 100% of Icarus Co. common stock on June 1, 1996, for $200 million in cash. At the time of the purchase, the fair market value of Icarus's assets was $350 million. The fair market value of its liabilities was $180 million. The transaction was accounted for as a merger using the purchase method. Use the following format to indicate the effect the transaction had on Daedalus's accounts:

Assets =	Liabilities + Equity	+ (Revenues − Expenses)

Explain the meaning of goodwill and how it affects a company's financial reports.

11-9. Castor Co. acquired 100% of Pollux Co.'s common stock during 1997. At the end of the 1997 fiscal year, Pollux's assets had a book value of $80 million and a market value of $93 million. Its liabilities had a book value of $30 million and a market value of $32 million. Castor's assets had a book value of $310 million and a market value of $340 million. Its liabilities had a book value of $130 million and a market value of $140 million. There were no other intercompany transactions during 1997. If Castor exchanged 7 million shares of its common stock for all of Pollux's common stock in a pooling of interests, what amounts would it report on its consolidated balance sheet at the end of 1997 for total assets, total liabilities, and total stockholders' equity? Pollux's common stock was selling at $10 per share at the time of the acquisition.

11-10. Plato Co. sold merchandise to Aristotle Co. on November 1, 1996, at a price of $50,000. The merchandise cost Plato $36,000. Aristotle signed a note to pay Plato the sales price plus interest at an annual rate of 12%. Plato's fiscal year ends December 31. Aristotle paid the note plus interest on April 30, 1997. Use the following format to indicate the effect the transactions related to the sale had on Plato's accounts.

Assets =	Liabilities + Equity	+ (Revenues − Expenses)

11-11. Troilus Co. purchased $400,000 of long-term bonds on May 1, 1995, at maturity value plus accrued interest since January 1. Interest at an 8% annual rate was received in semi-annual payments on July 1, 1995, and January 1, 1996. Troilus's fiscal year ends December 31. The bonds were sold on March 1, 1996, for $430,000, including accrued interest. The bonds were classified as held to maturity. Use the following format to indicate the effect the transactions related to the bonds had on Troilus's accounts:

Assets =	Liabilities + Equity	+ (Revenues − Expenses)

11-12. Cressida Co. purchased delivery equipment on April 1, 1996, at a cost of $200,000. The equipment is expected to have a useful life of seven years and no salvage value. How much depreciation expense would Cressida record in 1996 using the straight-line, double–declining balance, and sum-of-the-years'-digits methods? The company's fiscal year end is December 31. If the units-of-production method is used, how much depreciation would Cressida record? Assume the equipment is expected to be used for 250,000 miles. During 1996, the equipment was used for 60,000 miles.

11-13. Europa Co. purchased a building on March 1, 1980, at a cost of $4 million. For financial reporting purposes, the building was depreciated on a straight-line basis over 372 months at $10,000 per month. The building was sold on October 31, 1996, for $7.2 million. How much gain or loss did Europa record on the sale of the building? Accelerated depreciation was used to record depreciation for tax purposes. As of October 31, 1996, Europa had recorded $3 million of depreciation on an accelerated basis. How much gain or loss did Europa record on the sale of the building for tax purposes? Why would Europa use straight-line depreciation for financial reporting purposes and accelerated depreciation for tax purposes?

11-14. Palamon Co. owns rights to coal reserves in several states. The rights cost the company $140 million. The reserves are expected to produce 50 billion tons of coal. During the company's 1995 fiscal year, 5 billion tons of coal were mined from the reserves. Prior to 1995, 30 billion tons of coal had been mined. How much depletion expense would Palamon record in 1995? At what amount would the company report the coal reserves on its balance sheet at the end of 1995? What effect would the depletion expense have on the company's cash flows in 1995?

11-15. Lancelot Co. leased equipment at the beginning of its 1996 fiscal year. The lease calls for payments of $100,000 per year for five years. Lancelot could borrow to purchase the assets at an annual rate of 11%. What amount would Lancelot report as an asset at the end of 1996 for the lease if it was accounted for as a capital lease? Assume straight-line amortization. What amount would the company report as a liability at the end of 1996 if the lease was accounted for as a capital lease? How much expense would Lancelot report for the lease if it was accounted for as a capital lease? What effect would the lease have on Lancelot's financial statements and related notes if the lease were accounted for as an operating lease? Why might Lancelot prefer to report the lease as an operating rather than a capital lease?

11-16. Franchesca Co. recorded the following transactions during its 1996 fiscal year:
a. Construction costs associated with facilities currently in progress:

Labor	$350,000
Materials	675,000
Utilities	87,000
Tools and special equipment	22,000
Interest on construction loan	94,000

b. The cost of an addition to an existing building was $840,000.
c. The cost of repairs to equipment was $90,000. These repairs are required on a regular basis and do not affect the estimated useful life of the equipment.
How would each of these transactions affect Franchesca's financial statements for 1996? Assume cash had been paid for all costs by the end of the fiscal year.

11-17. The Nestlé Company reported total fixed assets of 24,006 million Swiss francs for the fiscal year ended December 31, 1993. Of this amount, 20,070 million were tangible fixed assets; 3,936 million were investments and other assets, primarily loans to other companies. Notes to the statements disclosed the following:

> Tangible fixed assets are shown in the balance sheet at their net replacement values arrived at as follows:
> —Land: market value prudently estimated.
> —Other tangible fixed assets: replacement new value (the amount which theoretically would have to be invested in order to replace an asset by a similar new asset duly installed and rendering the same service) less the accumulated depreciation calculated on this value.
>   These amounts are recalculated each year.
>   Depreciation is provided on the straight-line method so as to amortize fully the replacement new values of tangible fixed assets over their estimated useful lives, ...
>   Goodwill arising on consolidation, which represents the excess of the purchase cost over the fair value of the net tangible assets acquired, is written off against reserves in the year acquired.

The reported book value of tangible fixed assets on a historical cost basis was 15,390 million Swiss francs. Reserves are a portion of stockholders' equity, similar to paid-in capital in excess of par. What major differences exist in the reporting of these long-term assets by Nestlé and the way they would be reported by a U.S. company? What effect do these differences have on the financial statements of Nestlé relative to a U.S. company?

11-18. Companies sometimes sell fixed assets to other companies or to investors and then lease the assets back. For example, General Motors raised about $650 million by selling machines at GM's Saturn plant and other similar assets to investors. GM leased the assets back and paid investors over a period of 18 years for these arrangements at an effective interest rate of about 9%. Investors who purchased the assets were able to depreciate them for tax purposes. GM incurred heavy losses during the early 1990s from its operating activities. Therefore, the depreciation was of no immediate value to GM because it paid no taxes on its operations. What advantages were available to GM from this arrangement? What effect would you expect this arrangement to have on GM's cash flows, income, and balance sheet? Why?

11-19. At the beginning of its 1997 fiscal year, Madrian Corp. owned 47% of Juvenal Co.'s common stock. Though it has been profitable, Juvenal has had some financial problems in recent years and is highly levered. During 1997, Madrian acquired Homer Co. Among Homer's investments was an investment in 5% of Juvenal Co.'s common stock. Before the end of its 1997 fiscal year, Madrian sold a portion of its investment in Juvenal to reduce its total ownership to 50%. What effect did the sale have on Madrian's financial statements for 1997? Why might Madrian prefer one alternative for accounting for its investment in Juvenal to another?

11-20. Why is accounting information useful as a means of controlling assets and ensuring their security?

PROBLEMS

PROBLEM 11-1   Reporting Investments

During its 1996 fiscal year, Portia Co. purchased 10% of the common stock of Leonardo Co. for $3,470,000, including fees. Also, it purchased 5% of the common stock of Shylock Co. for $2,690,000, including fees. During 1996, Portia received $500,000 of dividends from Leonardo. At the end of the fiscal year, the investment in Leonardo had a market value of $3,100,000. The investment in Shylock had a market value of $2,800,000. Portia owned no other stock investments during 1996. During its 1997 fiscal year, Portia sold the Shylock investment for $2,900,000. The company purchased a 3% investment in Balthasar Co. for $1,930,000, including fees. During 1997, Portia received $500,000 of dividends from Leonardo. At the end of 1997, the Leonardo investment had a market value of $3,350,000 and the Balthasar investment had a market value of $1,940,000. Portia owned no other stock investments during 1997. All of Portia's investments were properly accounted for as long-term investments. All investments were classified as available for sale.

Required   (a) Prepare a schedule calculating the amount Portia would report for long-term investments on its balance sheet at the end of 1996 and 1997. (b) Prepare a schedule calculating the effect of Portia's investment activities on its income for 1996 and 1997.

PROBLEM 11-2   Accounting for Investments

At the end of its 1995 fiscal year, Seuss Co. owned the following investments:

a.   2% of Hermia Co. stock, purchased at a cost of $375,000.

b.   1% of Lysander Co. stock, purchased at a cost of $250,000.

c.   35% of Demetri Co. stock, purchased at a cost of $42 million.

d.   10% of Paxton Co. stock, purchased at a cost of $5,380,000.

Seuss's management expects to sell its investment in Hermia and Lysander during the 1996 fiscal year and has classified these investments as trading securities. It does not expect to sell its investments in Demetri or Paxton during the 1996 fiscal year. The market value of each investment at the end of the 1995 fiscal year was:

Hermia	$	390,000
Lysander		240,000
Demetri		44,300,000
Paxton		5,200,000

During 1995, Seuss received $70,000 of dividends from Hermia and $1,800,000 of dividends from Demetri. Demetri Co. reported net income of $6 million in 1995. Paxton Co. reported net income of $4.8 million. Seuss Co. owned no other stock investments during 1995.

Required Prepare a schedule to determine the amount Seuss would report on its balance sheet for investments at the end of 1995. What effect would these events have on the company's income for 1995?

PROBLEM 11-3 Reporting Consolidations

Penelope Corp. owns 100% of Syrius Corp.'s common stock at the end of 1996. Penelope paid $150 million for Syrius's stock at the beginning of the year. A part of Penelope's assets and Syrius's liabilities is a loan from Penelope to Syrius for $20 million. In addition, Syrius sold goods priced at $8 million to Penelope during 1996. Syrius's cost for these goods was $5 million. Syrius earned net income of $30 million in 1996 and paid no dividends.

Required

(a) Use the following format to describe the effect of the investment transaction on Penelope's account balances:

Assets =	Liabilities + Equity	+ (Revenues − Expenses)

(b) Compute the balance of Penelope's investment in Syrius at the end of 1996 (use the equity method).

(c) Complete the following table to compute the amounts that would be reported on Penelope's balance sheet and income statement for 1996.

(in millions)	Penelope Corp.	Syrius Corp.	Adjustments	Penelope Corp. Consolidated Statements
Total assets	$570	$230		
Total liabilities	234	50		
Stockholders' Equity—Syrius		180		
Stockholders' Equity—Penelope	336			
Liabilities and Stockholders' Equity	$570	$230		
Revenues	$660	$170		
Expenses	(540)	(140)		
Net income	$120	$ 30		

PROBLEM 11-4   Accounting for Investments in Bonds

Pirrus Co. purchased 100 Achilles Co. bonds on April 1, 1997. The bonds pay interest semiannually on March 31 and September 30 at an annual coupon rate of 10%. The bonds sold at an effective yield of 8%. The effect of brokerage fees are included in computing the effective yield. The bonds mature on March 30, 1999, at a value of $1,000 per bond. Pirrus's fiscal year ends on September 30.

Required   (a) Compute the price Pirrus paid for Achilles' bonds. (b) Prepare an amortization schedule for Pirrus's investment. (c) Use the format below to indicate the effect transactions associated with the bonds would have on Pirrus's accounts in 1997, 1998, and 1999, assuming the securities are classified as held-to-maturity securities:

Assets =	Liabilities + Equity	+ (Revenues − Expenses)

PROBLEM 11-5   Comparing Depreciation Methods

Chaucer Co. purchased equipment with an expected useful life of four years. The equipment was purchased on January 1, 1994, for $125,000. It is expected to have a salvage value of $5,000 at the end of four years.

Required   (a) Prepare a depreciation schedule for the asset showing the book value and depreciation expense on the asset each year using the straight-line, double–declining balance, and sum-of-the-years'-digits methods. (b) Which method would you prefer to use for financial reporting purposes if you were manager of Chaucer Co.? Which method would you prefer for tax purposes? Explain. (c) Which method has the greatest effect on cash flow each year? Why?

PROBLEM 11-6   Accounting for Capital Leases

Bath Co. signed a lease contract for equipment on January 1, 1995. The contract called for seven annual payments of $8,000. Bath could have borrowed to purchase the equipment at 10%.

Required   (a) Prepare a lease payment schedule for the asset. (b) Use the following format to identify the effect of the capital lease on Bath's accounts at the time of the contract and at the end of Bath's fiscal year on December 31, 1995. Assume the lease is amortized on a straight-line basis.

Assets =	Liabilities + Equity	+ (Revenues − Expenses)

(c) How much would Bath report on its balance sheet for 1995 as a capital lease asset and as a capital lease obligation?

PROBLEM 11-7   Analyzing Long-Term Assets

American Home Products reported the following information in its 1993 annual report:

(in thousands)	1993	1992
Balance Sheet		
Property, plant, and equipment	$3,460,365	$3,056,893
Less accumulated depreciation	1,400,580	1,279,102
Property, plant, and equipment, net	2,059,785	1,777,791
Goodwill	716,395	708,832
Statement of Cash Flows		
Depreciation and amortization expense	241,068	210,213
Purchase of property, plant, and equipment	(517,912)	(428,109)
Proceeds from sale of assets	13,614	60,341

The company also reported:

> *Property, Plant, and Equipment* is carried at cost. Depreciation is provided over the estimated useful lives of the related assets, principally on the straight-line method.
> *Goodwill* is being amortized on the straight-line method over periods not exceeding 40 years. Accumulated amortization was $636,385,000 and $604,484,000 at December 31, 1993 and 1992, respectively.

Required Answer each of the following questions, assuming no other major transactions occurred that affected the company's long-term assets during 1993:

a. Approximately how much amortization expense did American Home Products record in 1993?

b. Approximately how much depreciation expense did the company record in 1993? What is the approximate average useful life of the company's plant assets? What is the average age of the company's plant assets?

c. What was the net increase in the company's plant assets during 1993? What events account for this increase?

d. Was the net effect of the company's long-term asset transactions on its net income for 1993 greater or less than the effect of these transactions on its cash flows? Explain.

PROBLEM 11-8 Explaining Asset Changes

Intel Corporation reported the following information on its 1993 balance sheet:

(in millions)	1993	1992
Short-term investments (at cost, which approximates market)	**$1,477**	**$ 993**
Property, plant, and equipment:		
Land and buildings	1,848	1,463
Machinery and equipment	4,148	2,874
Construction in progress	317	311
	6,313	4,648
Less accumulated depreciation	2,317	1,832
Property, plant, and equipment, net	**3,996**	**2,816**
Long-term investments (at cost, which approximates market)	**1,416**	**496**

In addition, Intel reported the following information on its statement of cash flows for 1993:

(in millions)	1993
Cash flows provided by (used for) operating activities:	
Net income	$ 2,295
Adjustments to reconcile net income to net cash provided	
by operating activities:	
Depreciation	717
Net loss on retirements of plant assets	36
(other items omitted)	. . .
Net cash provided by operating activities	**2,801**
Cash flows provided by (used for) investing activities:	
Additions to plant assets	(1,933)
Sales and maturities of investments	5
Additions to investments	(1,409)
Net cash used for investing activities	**(3,337)**
Net cash provided by financing activities	**352**

Required   Answer each of the following questions:

a.   What was the primary source used by Intel to finance its investment activities in 1993?

b.   Assume all major transactions affecting plant assets and investments are summarized in the information provided above. Prepare a schedule to explain the change in Intel's plant assets during 1993. Begin with the balance of property, plant, and equipment, net of depreciation, at the beginning of 1993.

c.   Prepare a schedule to explain the change in Intel's investments during 1993.

d.   Did Intel's plant assets increase or decrease during 1993? To what extent does your answer depend on whether the change in plant assets is measured in terms of nominal dollar values, real dollar values, or economic benefits to the company (such as value of goods produced using the plant assets) of plant assets acquired and disposed of during the year.

PROBLEM 11-9   Ethics in Financial Reporting

More Money is a medium-sized bank. The bank's stock is owned primarily by residents in the city where the bank operates. During the 1980s the bank lent money for numerous real estate developments. Much of the loans were used to construct office space by developers who expected to repay the loans from office rent. Aggressive lending and building practices resulted in overbuilding. A downturn in the local economy drastically reduced demand for office space. As a result, many of the buildings were largely empty in 1995. Rent from the facilities was insufficient to pay interest on several of the bank's larger loans. The bank permitted several borrowers to restructure their loans, providing a longer period of repayment and lower interest rates. The market value of the property has decreased approximately 40% since its construction. The bank's 1995 balance sheet reported loans in the bank's long-term investment portfolio of $43 million. This amount was net of a loan loss reserve of $5 million. The bank also included $18 million of property among its assets. This property resulted from foreclosures the bank had made on several loans. The property is valued at the present value of the loan payments, including interest the bank expected from the original borrowers. The bank is collecting rent from tenants and expects to sell the property when real estate values return to higher levels. The bank's total assets were $80 million and total stockholders' equity was $10 million. Its reported profits for 1995 were $6 million. The bank's auditors have questioned its management about its loans and property values. They believe that the current market value of the loan portfolio is about $35 million. They are less sure about the value of the property. The bank's managers have argued that the current market value of the loans is not relevant because they do not expect to sell the loans. Instead, they expect to hold the loans until they mature. Also, they do not plan to sell the property until they can recover the amount the bank invested.

Required   At what value should More Money's loan portfolio be valued? Why? Do you see any ethical problems with the way the bank's managers want to report its assets? What problems may arise for the bank if it reports its loans at their current market value?

PROBLEM 11-10   Exchange of Assets

Garvin Co. purchased manufacturing equipment in July 1992 for $1,600,000. The equipment was depreciated over an expected useful life of five years using the straight-line method. The equipment was assumed to have a residual value of $100,000. In July 1996, Garvin traded the equipment in on the purchase of some new equipment. The new equipment sold for $1,850,000. The seller allowed Garvin a discount of $75,000 for the old equipment. Garvin paid cash for the old and new equipment.

Required   Answer each of the following questions:

a.   Prepare a schedule to determine the gain or loss Garvin should recognize for trading in the old equipment for new equipment.

b.   Use the following format to describe the effect of the trade-in on Garvin's accounts:

Assets =	Liabilities + Equity	+ (Revenues − Expenses)

c.   Calculate the net effect all transactions associated with old equipment had on Garvin's pretax income from 1992 through 1996. Also, calculate the net effect all transactions associated with the equipment had on cash flows for this period. Explain the relationship between the effect on pretax income and the effect on cash flows.

PROBLEM 11-11   Comparing Depreciation Methods

Tax rules permit some assets to be depreciated using an accelerated method during the early years of an asset's life. Once the asset reaches the age that straight-line depreciation produces more favorable tax results, the remaining book value of the asset can be depreciated on a straight-line basis. Pandora Co. purchased equipment on March 1, 1995, at a cost of $1,800,000. The equipment was depreciated for a full year in 1995. It was expected to have a useful life of six years. Tax rules permit the use of the double–declining balance method reverting to the straight-line method when it becomes advantageous to the company.

Required   Determine the amount of depreciation Pandora should take on the asset each year for tax purposes. Assuming a tax rate of 34%, how much would the company save each year in taxes compared to using the straight-line method over the entire life of the asset?

PROBLEM 11-12   Multiple-Choice Overview of the Chapter

1. Short-term investments in marketable equity securities should be accounted for using the:
   a. equity method.
   b. consolidation method.
   c. fair market value method.
   d. cost method.

2. If the market value of a company's portfolio of trading securities is greater than the cost of the portfolio at the end of a fiscal year, the company should report:
   a. a loss on its income statement.
   b. a gain on its income statement.
   c. its investments at cost.
   d. neither a gain nor a loss.

3. Dividends received from investments accounted for using the equity method should be recorded by the investor as:
   a. an increase in investment revenue.
   b. an increase in stockholders' equity.
   c. a decrease in long-term investments.
   d. an increase in long-term investments.

4. Long-term investments in the common stock of another company normally should be accounted for as a consolidated subsidiary if the investor owns an interest of:
   a. more than 50%.
   b. not less than 90%.
   c. not less than 20%.
   d. not more than 50%.

5. The excess of cost over the market value of identifiable net assets acquired in a purchase of another company should be reported as:
   a. a fixed asset.
   b. an intangible asset.
   c. an expense of the period in which the acquisition occurs.
   d. a revenue of the period in which the acquisition occurs.

6. When a company purchases bonds at a premium, amortization of the premium:
   a. increases interest revenue recorded over the life of the bonds.
   b. decreases interest revenue recorded over the life of the bonds.
   c. increases the book value of the investment over the life of the bonds.
   d. is not recorded until the bonds are sold or mature.

7. Horner Co. recorded $20,000 of depreciation on assets acquired at the beginning of 1994. The assets cost $50,000 and had an estimated useful life of five years. The method Horner used for depreciating the assets was the:
    a. straight-line method.
    b. cost recovery method.
    c. sum-of-the-years'-digits method.
    d. double–declining balance method.

8. Avery Co. sold a truck in 1996. At the time of the trade, the old truck had a book value of $10,000. The truck sold for $14,000. As a result of this transaction, Avery should record:
    a. a loss of $4,000.
    b. a gain of $4,000.
    c. a loss of $14,000.
    d. a gain of $14,000.

9. Costs a business incurs prior to beginning operations normally are accounted for as:
    a. expenses of the period in which they are incurred.
    b. expenses of the first year of operations.
    c. deferred charges to be amortized over several years after operations begin.
    d. reductions in revenues over the first five years of operations.

10. Capital expenditures during a fiscal period:
    a. increase the book value of plant assets during the period.
    b. decrease the book value of plant assets during the period.
    c. decrease accumulated depreciation during the period.
    d. decrease total assets during the period.

CASES

CASE 11-1   Comparison of Purchase and Leasing of Plant Assets

Wakefield Co. plans to acquire new equipment on January 1, 1996, the beginning of the company's fiscal year. The equipment costs $2 million. Wakefield can either borrow $2 million from a bank at 10% interest or lease the equipment. A lease would be accounted for as a capital lease. The equipment is expected to have a useful life of four years, which would be the lease period. It would have no residual value at the end of that period. Wakefield normally uses the straight-line method to depreciate its equipment. Lease payments would be $635,000 per year for the four-year lease. If money is borrowed from a bank, one-fourth of the principal, plus interest, would be repaid each year.

Required   As a manager with the company, you have been asked to evaluate the alternatives and to recommend the best choice for acquiring the equipment. Determine the effect of (a) purchasing and (b) leasing the equipment on Wakefield's balance sheet, income statement, and statement of cash flows over the four-year period. Evaluate the alternatives and make a recommendation.

CASE 11-2   Analysis of Investment Activities

Appendix B of this book contains a copy of the 1994 annual report of Nike, Inc.

Required   Review the annual report and write a short report in which you identify each of the following:

a.   Identify the accounting methods used by the company for cash and equivalents, plant assets, intangible assets, and advertising costs.

b.   Identify the cost of each of the company's types of plant assets and the total amount of accumulated depreciation on these assets at the end of 1994.

c.   Explain the change in the company's plant asset accounts in 1994 by an analysis of its investment activities and depreciation reported for 1994.

PROJECTS

PROJECT 11-1   Comparing Types of Assets

Obtain the most recent annual report available for each of three corporations from your library. Look for companies in different industries. Identify the primary types of assets of each company. In particular, determine the relative proportion of current, long-term investment, plant, intangible, and other assets for each company. Provide a graph or diagram to illustrate the comparisons. Write a brief analysis of differences in assets. What explanations can you provide for why the assets are different or are similar?

PROJECT 11-2   Comparing Accounting Methods

Examine the annual reports of five companies. Identify the accounting methods used by each to account for investments in securities, plant assets, and intangible assets. Write a short report identifying and comparing the methods. What effects are the methods likely to have on each company's financial statements?

PROJECT 11-3   Evaluating Mergers and Acquisitions

Use The *Wall Street Journal Index* or a business periodical index to identify a recent acquisition or merger involving a major company. Use the company's annual report or financial information from Moody's manuals or another source to determine the effect of the merger on the company's financial statements. Compare the company's statements of the year before to the year after the acquisition or merger. Determine which method was used to account for the merger. Write a short report describing the method and the effect it had on major items in the company's financial statements, such as total assets, long-term debt, stockholders' equity, net income, interest expense, and cash flows from operating activities.

PROJECT 11-4 Evaluating Capital Leases

Identify a recent article in the *Wall Street Journal* or in a business periodical describing the use of capital leases by a company. Make a copy of the article. Write a memo to your instructor identifying the event and the reasons cited in the article for the company's use of the leases. Attach the copy of the article to the memo.

PROJECT 11-5 Evaluating Asset Control

Identify a recent article in the *Wall Street Journal* or in a business periodical describing a company that has reported an asset control problem. These problems usually involve the discovery of employee or management fraud. Make a copy of the article. Write a memo to your instructor identifying the event and the reasons it occurred. Attach the copy of the article to the memo.

Chapter 12

Analysis of Investing Activities

Investment decisions involve choices managers make in acquiring resources. Managers decide which resources to acquire, how to acquire them, and when to replace them. Managers use financial statement information in making their decisions. These decisions also involve information available to managers that is not available to external decision makers. Regardless of the source of information used in their decisions, managers are concerned about the effects of their decisions on their company's performance as revealed in its financial statements. Investors and other external decision makers use financial statement information to evaluate managers' decisions.

This chapter examines investment decisions made by managers. It considers how financial accounting information is used in making these decisions. Also, it considers how financial accounting information can be used to identify and evaluate these decisions.

Major topics covered in this chapter include:

- Investment valuation
- Comparison of investment decisions
- The effect of investment decisions on risk and return
- The effect of operating leverage on earnings
- Analysis of cash management decisions

CHAPTER

Objectives

Once you have completed this chapter, you should be able to:

1. Explain the importance of investing activities in creating company value.
2. Explain how accounting information can be used to describe the effects of investing decisions.
3. Use accounting information to compare investment decisions among companies.
4. Explain the purpose of segment reporting.
5. Identify the purpose of mergers and acquisitions and the effect they can have on accounting information.
6. Explain why fair market value reporting of assets can be useful.
7. Explain the effect of operating leverage on a company's earnings.
8. Analyze a company's cash management.

THE IMPORTANCE OF INVESTING ACTIVITIES

Objective 1
Explain the importance of investing activities in creating company value.

Investing activities are central to business decisions as illustrated in Exhibit 12-1. Decisions about the amount and types of assets employed by a company are critical to its success and affect most other decisions. Financing activities are necessary to provide money for the acquisition of assets and other resources. The more a company invests, the greater its demand for capital. Operating activities also result from investing activities. Resources are used to produce, sell, and distribute goods and services to customers. The ability of a company to manufacture and sell products depends on the resources in which it has invested. Thus, investment decisions, to a large extent, determine the operating and financing activities of a company. Success depends on how well managers are able to make investment decisions.

Exhibit 12-1   The Role of Investing Activities

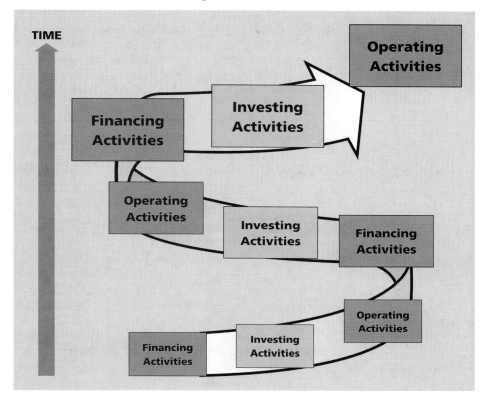

Growth is a primary attribute of successful companies. By investing in assets of the correct amounts, types, and locations, companies create products demanded by customers. A company increases its value through growth. Growth results through investing in the development of new products and new markets. Additional product development, manufacturing, sales, service, and distribution facilities permit a company to create and manufacture new and better products and to sell these to larger numbers of customers in more locations. Thus, greater investment results in a demand for additional financing and provides a basis for greater amounts of operating activities over time, as illustrated in Exhibit 12-1.

Of course, poor investment decisions lead to poor performance. Investing in too many of the wrong assets or in the wrong locations drains a company's resources. Cash will be needed to repay financing and maintain facilities that are not adding to a company's value. Thus, investing decisions focus on whether investments are likely to add value to a company (planning decisions) and whether past decisions have added value (control decisions).

External decision makers also focus on these decisions in evaluating performance and assessing company value. Investors purchase securities rather than using their cash for additional food, clothing, housing, recreation, and other resources that could be consumed in the current period. They forego current-period consumption in exchange for expected future cash flows that can be used to enhance future consumption. Managers decide on the amount of cash to pay out to investors during a period, in the form of dividends, and on the amount of cash generated from current operations to reinvest in the company. Reinvestment adds additional potential value to a company for its investors and other stakeholders. But, this reinvestment adds value only if the new investment permits a company to generate higher earnings.

External decision makers examine the rate of return a company earns on its investments as a basis for evaluating whether management is making good investment decisions. Decision makers consider the types of investments made by managers and the risk added to a company as a result of these investments. Investments in different types of assets and the ability to manage these assets lead to higher or lower value for a company over time. Good investment decisions lead to growth and higher value. In this chapter, we will examine some of the ways external decision makers evaluate investment decisions.

ACCOUNTING INFORMATION AND INVESTMENT DECISIONS

Objective 2
Explain how accounting information can be used to describe the effects of investing decisions.

Accounting information is useful for understanding and evaluating investment decisions. In this section, we will examine this role of accounting. We begin with a comparison of two key measurements used to evaluate investment decisions: return on assets and return on equity.

Accounting Measures of Return

Chapter 10 discussed return on equity as a measure for evaluating financing decisions. Return on assets is a commonly used accounting measure for evaluating investment decisions. An important difference exists between these two measures. Return on equity is affected by how a company chooses to finance its investments. Companies with different capital structures (debt to equity ratios) will exhibit different return on equity values, even if other company attributes are the same. In contrast, return on assets is not affected by financing decisions. It measures performance relative to total investment, regardless of how the investment was financed. Exhibit 12-2 illustrates differences between these two measures.

Exhibit 12-2 provides income statement and balance sheet information for a hypothetical company. Return on equity is the ratio of income (after preferred dividends) to average common stockholders' equity, including common stock and retained earnings. Average common equity usually is calculated as the average of the amount of equity reported at the beginning and end of the fiscal year. Return on equity includes the effects on income available to common stockholders of borrowing (interest expense) and of issuing preferred stock (preferred dividends). Therefore, it is affected by how much debt and preferred stock a company has issued.

Return on assets **is the ratio of the amount of income a company would report if it had no debt or preferred stock to its average total as-**

sets. Average total assets usually are calculated as the average of the amount of assets reported at the beginning and end of the fiscal year. If a company had no debt, it would incur no interest expense. Therefore, interest expense is added back to net income. This calculation is complicated by the fact that interest expense is deductible from income taxes. Therefore, if no interest expense was incurred, no deduction would be made from taxes. To correct for the tax effect, interest expense is added to net income after considering the tax effect. This adjustment is made by multiplying interest expense by 1 minus the tax rate. The tax rate can be estimated as the ratio of income tax expense to pretax income. Preferred dividends are not subtracted from income in computing return on assets, because the measure presumes no preferred stock exists.

Exhibit 12-2 Differences Between Return on Assets and Return on Equity

	1996		**1996**	**1995**
Sales	$10,000	Assets	(g) $9,000	(h) $8,400
Cost of goods sold	4,000	Liabilities	$3,500	$3,300
Gross profit	6,000	Equity:		
Other operating expenses	3,500	Preferred stock	500	500
Operating income	2,500	Common equity	(i) 5,000	(j) 4,600
Interest expense	(a) 500	Liabilities & equity	$9,000	$8,400
Pretax income	(b) 2,000			
Income tax expense	(c) 600			
Net income	(d) 1,400			
Preferred dividends	(e) 200			
Income available for common	(f) $ 1,200			

$$\text{Return on Equity} = \frac{\text{Income Available for Common}}{\text{Average Common Equity}} =$$

$$\frac{\overset{(f)}{\$1,200}}{\underset{(i)\qquad(j)}{(\$5,000 + \$4,600)/2}} = \frac{\$1,200}{\$4,800} = 25\%$$

$$\text{Return on Assets} = \frac{\text{Net Income} + \text{Interest Expense} (1 - \text{Tax Rate})}{\text{Average Total Assets}} =$$

$$\frac{\overset{(d)}{\$1,400} + \overset{(a)}{\$500} [1 - \overset{(c)}{(\$600}/\overset{(b)}{\$2,000)}]}{\underset{(g)\qquad(h)}{(\$9,000 + \$8,400)/2}} = \frac{\$1,400 + \$500 (0.7)}{\$8,700} = 20.1\%$$

In summary, return on assets is the rate of return a company would earn if its total capital consisted of common stock. Return on equity is the rate of return for common stockholders, given that a company's capital structure includes debt and (perhaps) preferred stock. Return on assets measures performance relative to investing activities. Return on equity measures performance relative to investing and financing activities. To assess the effects of financing decisions, one can examine the difference between return on assets and return on equity. If financial leverage is beneficial to a company because it is making good use of debt and preferred stock, its return on equity will be higher than its return on assets. Usually when a company is performing well, its return on equity will be higher than its return on assets. When a company is not performing well, its return on equity often is lower than its return on assets.

Using Accounting Return to Evaluate Investment Decisions

Return on assets and return on equity are useful performance measures because they permit evaluators to assess a company's earnings relative to the amount invested in assets or relative to the amount invested by stockholders. These measures can be compared across companies so that companies of different sizes can be evaluated relative to each other. Also, comparisons can be made over time. As a company invests in new assets, it should be able to generate additional earnings at a rate at least as great as the rate it earns on its existing assets. Thus, if a company's managers are making good investment decisions, the company's return on assets should be relatively high and remain stable or increase over time. High and increasing return on assets are associated with value.

Exhibit 12-3 illustrates the relationship among return on assets, return on equity, and company value. The graph summarizes data for over 900 major corporations. Each dot on the graph represents a portfolio of approximately 90 companies. A **portfolio** is a group of companies. The vertical axis measures return on assets and return on equity. These ratios are expressed as percentages. The horizontal axis provides the ratio of market to book value of common equity. The market value of equity is the price per share of stock times the number of shares outstanding. It is a measure of the value of a company to its stockholders. The book value of equity is the amount of common equity reported by a company on its balance sheet. The ratio of market to book value is an indication of the value of a company to its stockholders relative to each dollar they have invested in the company. For example, a ratio of 1.2 indicates that each dollar invested has produced a market value of $1.20. More valuable companies exhibit higher market to book values. Data in the exhibit are averages of annual returns over a five-year period (1988–1992).

High-value companies are to the right side of the graph, and low-value companies are to the left. Observe that both return on assets and return on equity increase as the values of companies increase (as one moves from left to right). Also, observe that return on equity generally is higher than return on assets. The difference between return on equity and return on assets increases as company value increases. High accounting returns are associated with high company values. When income is high, financial leverage is beneficial, and return on equity is higher than return on assets. When income is low, financial leverage can result in lower return on equity than return on assets. The lowest-value companies in Exhibit 12-3 illustrate this effect. Ordinarily, as return on assets increases, return on equity increases as well.

Exhibit 12-3   The Relation Between Accounting Return and Company Value

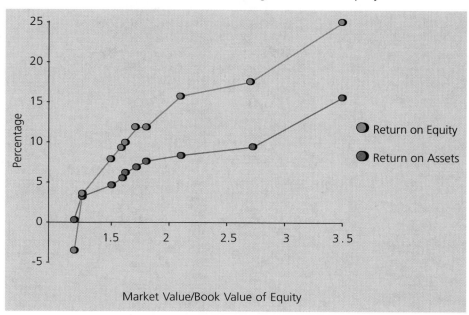

Data source: Compustat Annual Industrial File, 1993.

Accounting Return and Company Value

Company value typically is associated with return on assets. A major reason for this association can be observed from Exhibit 12-4. This exhibit illustrates the relation between return on assets and growth. Companies that report high return on assets are high-growth companies. The exhibit includes both asset and equity growth, measured as percentages on the vertical axis. As return on assets increases, toward the right of the graph, asset and equity growth tend to increase as well. Growth is measured by the percentage change in assets or equity from one period to another: (Y2 − Y1)/Y1, where Y is the relevant variable (assets or equity) in period 1 or 2. For example, if a company's assets increased from $10 million (Y1) at the end of 1996 to $12 million (Y2) at the end of 1997, the company's asset growth for 1997 would be 20% ([$12 − $10]/$10). Data for Exhibit 12-4 are for the same companies as Exhibit 12-3. Growth is measured as the average annual percentage change from 1988 to 1992. Thus, if the total percentage growth for a company was 50% over the five years from 1988 to 1992, the average annual growth would be 10% per year (50%/5 years). As assets grow, equity grows as well. Equity growth is higher than asset growth for high-return (high-value) companies. These companies reinvest earnings and use financial leverage to create stockholder value. Growth, especially equity growth, is much lower for low-return (low-value) companies. These companies must borrow most of the capital they need to finance investment because their earnings are relatively low.

526

Chapter 12

Exhibit 12-4   Return on Assets and Company Growth

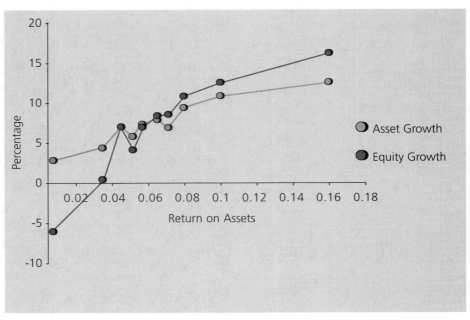

Data source: Compustat Annual Industrial File, 1993.

Accounting Return and Cash Flow

Return on assets also is associated with cash flow from operating, investing, and financing activities as illustrated in Exhibit 12-5. This exhibit illustrates the relation between return on assets and operating, investing, and financing cash flows. The data are for the companies used in the earlier exhibits. Cash flows are divided by average total assets to control for differences in company sizes and to make the cash flows comparable to return on assets (earnings adjusted for interest / average total assets). These ratios are measured on the vertical axis as percentages. Average annual ratios of cash flows to total assets and return on assets are provided for the 1988–1992 period.

Operating cash flows increase as return on assets increases. Net income and operating cash flows tend to move in the same direction. As net income increases, operating cash flows increase for most companies. Thus, high-value companies report high net incomes and high operating cash flows, relative to the amounts invested in their assets. As return on assets increases, toward the right of the graph, the ratio of operating cash flows to total assets also increases.

High-return (high-value) companies invest more of their cash flows in acquiring additional long-term assets than do low-return (low-value) companies. Therefore, cash outflows for investing activities are larger (more negative) for high-return than for low-return companies, as shown in Exhibit 12-5. These payments for resources are consistent with high growth in assets. For a company's assets to grow, it must invest more and, consequently, its cash flow for investing activities will be negative.

Exhibit 12-5   The Relation Between Return on Assets and Cash Flow

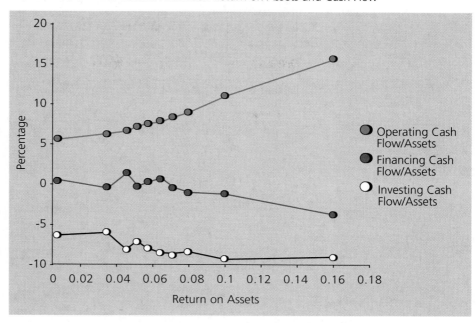

Data source: Compustat Annual Industrial File, 1993.

High-growth companies generate larger amounts of cash from their operating activities to invest than do low-return companies. As illustrated in Exhibit 12-5, high-return companies often are able to take advantage of their high operating cash flows to meet their investment needs and to pay out cash in financing activities. They can repay debt, repurchase stock, or pay dividends. Low-return companies usually depend on additional external financing to help them meet their cash flow needs. Therefore, net cash flow from financing activities typically is higher (more positive) for low-return than for high-return companies.

Other Factors That Affect Investing and Financing Decisions

Factors other than profitability (as measured by return on assets) affect the investing and financing activities of companies, however. The amount of investment required in certain types of assets and the type of financing used to acquire these assets vary across companies, depending on the types of products companies produce and sell. Some companies require large investments in plant assets to produce goods. Automobile, steel, chemical, paper, and other manufacturing companies are examples. Public utilities and some retail companies also require large investments in plant facilities. These companies are examples of capital intensive companies. *Capital intensity* **is the ratio of plant or long-term assets to total assets employed by a company.** Capital intensive companies require large amounts of investment in long-term assets. Often they use long-term debt to finance much of this investment. Therefore, the amount of debt in the capital structure (financial leverage) of these companies often is high relative to other companies.

Exhibit 12-6 illustrates the relation among return on assets, capital intensity, financial leverage, and dividend payout. These ratios are measured as percentages on the vertical axis.

Exhibit 12-6 The Relation Among Return on Assets, Capital Structure, and Asset Structure

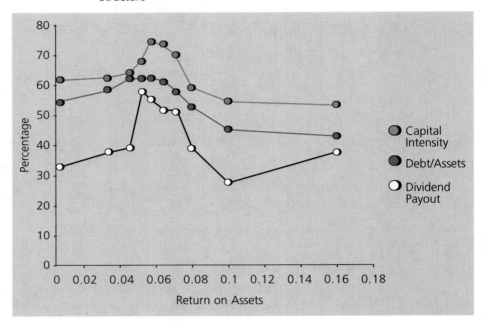

Data source: Compustat Annual Industrial File, 1993.

Data in the exhibit are for the same companies and time periods as in the previous exhibits. Observe that companies in the middle of the graph exhibit higher levels of capital intensity than those at either side of the graph. These are companies with relatively large investments in long-term assets. The higher levels of capital intensity are associated with higher debt to asset ratios and with higher dividend payout ratios.

Debt to assets is an indicator of financial leverage. It provides the same information as the debt to equity ratio. When the ratio is high, as it is for capital intensive companies, the amount of debt in the capital structure is high relative to the amount of equity and relative to total assets. Thus, capital intensive companies have higher proportions of debt and, therefore, are more highly levered than other companies, on average.

Dividend payout is the ratio of cash dividends (for common stock) to earnings. It is a measure of the percentage of earnings paid out to stockholders. Also, it is an inverse measure of the percentage of earnings reinvested in a company. If the ratio is high, a smaller percentage of earnings is reinvested than if the ratio were low. Consequently, as shown in Exhibit 12-6, capital intensive companies pay higher proportions of their earnings as dividends than other companies, on average.

High capital intensity, high financial leverage, and high dividend payout describe a specific segment of companies in our economy. These companies tend to be large manufacturing companies and public utilities. As illustrated in Exhibit 12-6, these companies tend to be in the middle of companies ranked by return measures. They earn a relatively stable return. They operate in industries that permit relatively slow but continuous growth. Operating cash flows are relatively high. Because earnings are stable and cash flows are high, these companies can afford high levels of debt, relative to less stable companies. Their high operating cash flows provide cash to repay debt, to pay interest, and to pay dividends. Because growth is slow, they do not require high levels of reinvestment. Therefore, cash can be paid out to investors in the form of dividends and interest.

In contrast to the high capital intensive companies are those on each side of Exhibit 12-6. These tend to be companies in highly competitive industries. They compete for customers by developing and marketing products with better features and lower costs than those of competitors. Because of the high competitive nature of their markets, some of these companies will do well, while others will not do as well. These companies are less stable than capital intensive companies. Earnings tend to be more volatile. Therefore, they cannot afford as much debt as more-stable companies. High debt and unstable earnings are a combination that spells high risk and potential disaster. These highly competitive companies have opportunities for high growth. If they are able to produce and market products demanded by customers, they can experience rapid sales growth. To take advantage of these opportunities and because they rely on relatively small amounts of debt, they need to reinvest high proportions of their earnings rather than paying dividends. These companies are to the right side of Exhibit 12-6. If these companies are not successful, however, their earnings and cash flows will be relatively small. They will need external financing to support investment in assets that will permit them to become more competitive. These companies are to the left side of Exhibit 12-6. Until they become more competitive, their returns, growth, and value remain relatively low. If they are unable to become competitive, they are likely to be taken over by other companies or to go out of business.

Summary of Accounting Return

In summary, return on assets is a measure of relative company performance. Companies that generate high returns typically are high-growth, high-value companies. They invest large amounts in new assets to provide a basis for producing and selling additional goods and services. Companies in industries that require large investments in long-term assets tend to be more stable than less capital intensive companies. These stable, slow-growing companies are in the middle of the value range. Measures such as return on assets, asset growth, and cash flow for investing are useful for evaluating investment decisions. These measures should be evaluated in relation to the types of industries in which companies operate. Measures such as capital intensity, financial leverage, and dividend payout are useful for describing industry attributes.

The next section demonstrates the use of these measures to evaluate company performance.

SELF-STUDY PROBLEM 12-1

The following information is provided for Zork Co.:

(in millions)	1996	1995	1994
Operating income	$120.0	$110.0	$100.0
Interest expense	20.0	8.0	5.0
Pretax income	100.0	102.0	95.0
Income tax (30%)	30.0	30.6	28.5
Net income	70.0	71.4	66.5
Preferred dividends	7.0	4.0	0.0
Income available for common	63.0	67.4	66.5
Average total assets	800.0	770.0	730.0
Average common equity	250.0	290.0	280.0

Required

Calculate Zork Co.'s return on assets and return on equity each year and evaluate the investing decisions of the company.

The solution to Self-Study Problem 12-1 appears at the end of the chapter.

COMPARING INVESTMENT DECISIONS

Objective 3
Use accounting information to compare investment decisions among companies.

Accounting information can be used to compare investment decisions of different companies. It can be used to answer questions such as: How do investment decisions differ among companies? At what rate are companies increasing their assets? How have companies financed their assets? How well are companies using their assets to generate earnings and cash flows?

Exhibit 12-7 provides accounting information for two retail companies, The Limited, Inc. and Wal-Mart Stores, Inc. A comparison of assets and income reveals that Wal-Mart is several times larger than The Limited. Items are identified in the exhibit for ease of reference. Net income and total assets are identified as (1) Return on assets (2) for the two companies are similar for the three years shown, however. Return on assets and similar ratios are relative measures that can be used to compare companies of different sizes. Both companies have experienced a decrease in return on assets over the three years. Return on equity (3) also has decreased for each company. Return on equity is higher for Wal-Mart because of its greater use of financial leverage, as apparent in its debt to assets ratio. The decreases in returns are associated with declines in values of the companies, as seen in the market to book value of equity ratios (4). Nevertheless, both companies would be located to the far right of the market to book value relation illustrated in Exhibit 12-3. Wal-Mart would be farther to the right (higher value) than The Limited.

We can evaluate the companies in several ways. One is to examine their return on assets and return on equity measures, as in the previous paragraph. Another is to examine their growth rates and patterns. Both companies have

Exhibit 12-7   Selected Accounting Information for The Limited and Wal-Mart

(in millions except ratios)	The Limited				Wal-Mart			
	1994	**1993**	**1992**	**1991**	**1994**	**1993**	**1992**	**1991**
Operating income	701.6	788.70	712.7		4,208.6	3,489.0	2,819.0	
Interest expense	(63.9)	(62.4)	(63.9)		(517.0)	(322.7)	(265.9)	
Other income, net	7.3	19.1	11.5		0.0	0.0	0.0	
Pretax income	645.0	745.4	660.3		3,691.6	3,166.3	2,553.1	
Income taxes	254.0	290.0	257.0		1,358.3	1,171.5	944.6	
(1) Net income	391.0	455.5	403.3		2,333.3	1,994.8	1,608.5	
Current assets	2,220.6	1,784.1	1,532.4		12,114.6	10,197.6	8,575.4	
(1) Total assets	4,135.1	3,846.5	3,418.9	2,871.9	26,440.8	20,565.1	15,443.4	11,388.9
Total liabilities	1,693.8	1,578.9	1,542.1	1,311.8	15,688.4	11,805.9	8,453.7	6,023.4
Common equity	2,441.3	2,267.6	1,876.8	1,560.1	10,752.4	8,759.2	6,989.7	5,365.5
Dividends	130.7	101.7	101.1		298.8	241.4	195.0	
Operating cash flow	448.1	754.1	475.6		2,195.5	1,278.3	1,356.7	
Investing cash flow	(75.5)	(489.6)	(541.8)		(4,486.0)	(3,506.3)	(2,149.9)	
Financing cash flow	(93.3)	(257.0)	86.8		2,298.3	2,209.8	810.8	
Average assets	3,990.80	3,632.70	3,145.40		23,502.95	18,004.25	13,416.15	
Average equity	2,354.45	2,072.20	1,718.45		9,755.80	7,874.45	6,177.60	
Income tax rate	0.394	0.389	0.389		0.368	0.370	0.370	
Interest (after taxes)	38.736	38.123	39.029		326.773	203.304	167.522	
Net income + interest	429.736	493.623	442.329		2,660.073	2,198.104	1,776.022	
(2) Return on assets	0.108	0.136	0.141		0.113	0.122	0.132	
(3) Return on equity	0.166	0.220	0.235		0.239	0.253	0.260	
(10) Debt/assets	0.410	0.410	0.451		0.593	0.574	0.547	
(11) Capital intensity	0.463	0.536	0.552		0.542	0.504	0.445	
(12) Dividend payout	0.334	0.223	0.251		0.128	0.121	0.121	
(7) Operating cash flow/assets	0.112	0.208	0.151		0.093	0.071	0.101	
(6) Investing cash flow/assets	−0.019	−0.135	−0.172		−0.191	−0.195	−0.160	
(8) Financing cash flow/assets	−0.023	−0.071	0.028		0.098	0.123	0.060	
(5) Asset growth	0.075	0.125	0.190		0.286	0.332	0.356	
(5) Equity growth	0.077	0.208	0.203		0.228	0.253	0.303	
(9) Market value of equity	7,156.0	9,065.0	9,768.6		62,067.6	71,287.6	59,748.0	
(4) Market/book value	2.93	4.00	5.20		5.77	8.14	8.55	

Data Source: 1994 annual reports.

exhibited growth in assets and equity (**5**). Growth rates have been higher for Wal-Mart. Growth rates have decreased over the three-year period for both companies. The growth rates of these companies are relatively high compared with the average for companies with similar returns in Exhibit 12-4. Wal-Mart, in particular, has been growing much faster than the average.

The higher growth rates also can be seen in the investing cash flows of the two companies. Both companies have been using their cash flows to acquire new assets (**6**). These investment rates are much higher (more negative cash flow), especially for Wal-Mart, than the averages for companies of similar returns in Exhibit 12-5. The Limited has financed its growth primarily through operating cash flows (**7**). Over time, its operating cash flows as a percentage of assets have been higher than the average in Exhibit 12-5. In contrast, Wal-Mart's operating cash flows as a percentage of assets have been about average. Wal-Mart has paid for much of its growth with additional financing. Its financing cash flows as a percentage of assets (**8**) are higher than the average in Exhibit 12-5. Thus, both companies have enjoyed above-average investment opportunities. Their additional investments have been associated with additional earnings, though they have experienced some decrease in return on assets (**2**) and return on equity (**3**) from 1992 to 1994. These attributes help explain the high, but decreasing, values of the two companies (**4** and **9**). Wal-Mart's higher growth and returns are associated with its higher value (**4**) relative to The Limited.

The Limited's debt to asset ratio (**10**) is low relative to the average for similar companies in Exhibit 12-6. Wal-Mart's ratio is about average. This higher amount of financial leverage for Wal-Mart, during a period in which both companies have performed well, helps explain the higher return on equity and value of Wal-Mart. The capital intensities (**11**) of the two companies are about average for similar companies in Exhibit 12-6. Wal-Mart's dividend payout ratio (**12**) has been below average, while The Limited's payout has been about average. Wal-Mart has had especially good investment opportunities and has used most of its operating cash flows to take advantage of these opportunities. The Limited has had slightly lower opportunities but has had higher operating cash flows than Wal-Mart. Consequently, it has paid out higher dividends.

Observe that a variety of factors are associated with company value. Among these are return on investment, growth (associated with additional investment), and capital structure (the use of financial leverage). The direction of change in these factors also provides information about future prospects. Remember from Chapter 8 that value is determined by expected future cash flows discounted at a required rate of return. Both The Limited and Wal-Mart have exhibited high returns and growth that should result in future cash flows. Thus, the values of these companies are high. As return and growth rates decrease, however, expected future cash flows also decrease, reducing value. Therefore, the values of both companies have decreased from 1992 to 1994.

THE EFFECT OF INVESTING ACTIVITIES ON RISK AND RETURN

By diversifying its investments to permit the production and sale of several types of products, a company can reduce its risk. A company that specializes in one product or location puts all of its eggs in one basket. If that product or location does well, the company does well. Otherwise, it may have difficulty continuing as a business. By producing several products or by operating in several locations, a company has the opportunity to do well even if some products or locations do not succeed. As a result, most large corporations produce a variety of products and operate in many locations. For example, Coca-Cola has enlarged its product line over this century from one soft drink brand to a variety of brands. It has expanded from its local market in the southern U.S. to become a large international company. Approximately 70% of Coke's sales now are made outside of the U.S.

Diversification, by investing in the production and sale of various types of products, can lead to more stable income and cash flow patterns. Stability of cash flows reduces the risk that a company will be unable to meet payments to creditors or to provide for its other cash needs. Also, it increases the probability that a company will be able to pay regular dividends to preferred and common stockholders.

Corporations report information about their various product lines in their annual reports. The following section considers these disclosures.

Segment Reporting

Objective 4
Explain the purpose of segment reporting.

Many corporations invest in a variety of product lines. Corporations disclose information about these lines in their annual reports as *segment information*. Sales, earnings, assets, and other information normally are included for each principal product line. For example, Exhibit 12-8 contains information reported by Coca-Cola in its 1993 annual report.

Exhibit 12-8   Segment Information from Coca-Cola Annual Report for 1993

| (in millions) | Soft Drinks | | Foods | Corporate | Consolidated |
	United States	International			
Net operating revenues	$2,966	$9,205	$1,766	$ 20	$13,957
Operating income	618	2,753	127	(396)	3,102
Identifiable operating assets	1,956	5,809	761	1,280	9,806
Equity income				91	91
Investments				2,215	2,215
Capital expenditures	136	557	30	77	800
Depreciation and amortization	91	172	38	59	360

Corporations report segment information about product lines and geographic areas in which they operate. In addition to the information provided in Exhibit 12-8, Coca-Cola reports the same type of information about its operations in the U.S., Africa, Europe, Latin America, and other locations in its annual report.

Information reported about segments includes operating revenues, operating income, and identifiable operating assets for each segment. These assets are those used specifically by a particular segment. Revenues, income, and assets that are not associated with a specific segment are reported in the "Corporate" column. Total revenues, income, and assets for the company as a whole are reported in the "Consolidated" column.

This information can be used to calculate return on asset ratios by computing the ratio of segment income to assets. For example, the ratio of income to assets for the U.S. soft drink segment would be 31.6% ($618/$1,956). The same calculations for the other segments reveals ratios of 47.4% ($2,753/$5,809) for International soft drinks and 16.7% ($127/$761) for Foods. These compare with a 31.6% ($3,102/$9,806) ratio for the company as a whole. It is apparent that international soft drinks operations are Coke's most profitable segment. The foods segment is relatively small and is providing a much lower return than the other segments.

Coca-Cola has been investing heavily in its international soft drinks segment. Exhibit 12-8 reveals that capital expenditures were much greater in this segment than in any of Coke's other segments in 1993. Capital expenditures far exceed depreciation and amortization expenses for this segment. Therefore, we can conclude that much of this investment is in new assets, rather than in replacement of existing assets. In contrast, Coke's capital expenditures in its foods division were lower than its depreciation and amortization expenses, indicating a reliance on older long-term assets.

Companies choose to diversify in different ways. Coke has diversified primarily by extending its operations internationally. It has invested heavily in foreign operations and holds a dominant market share in many countries. It has not expanded beyond the soft drink and food-related industry, however. Some companies choose to diversify into different kinds of product lines. The Walt Disney Company, for example, operates in the theme parks and resorts, film, and consumer products industries. While all of these industries are entertainment related, they include a wide variety of products. Segment information is useful for identifying the types of products a company produces and sells, where it produces and sells them, and the relative investments and profitabilities associated with these product lines.

Merger and Acquisition Decisions

Objective 5
Identify the purpose of mergers and acquisitions and the effect they can have on accounting information.

Diversification and expansion are primary reasons companies merge with and acquire other companies. These decisions can have a major effect on accounting information. The merger of Time, Inc. with Warner Communications, Inc. to form Time Warner, Inc. illustrates the effect. Time purchased Warner Communications' common stock, completing the $14 billion purchase in January 1990. To finance the acquisition, Time Warner issued $8.3 billion of long-term debt and $5.6 billion of preferred stock. Approximately $8 billion of the additional $14 billion of assets recognized in the merger was goodwill. Depreciation and amortization expenses increased by $600 million as a result of the merger. Interest expense also increased dramatically. Time Warner reported losses of about $750 million from 1989 to 1991 as a result of these additional expenses. Payments for interest and preferred dividends increased by about $1.2 billion as a result of the merger.

As a consequence of the merger, Time Warner's financial performance appeared to deteriorate. Some of this appearance was due to the accounting methods used in the merger. Time's purchase of Warner resulted in a write-up of Warner's assets to fair market value, increasing depreciation expense. The recognition of large amounts of goodwill increased amortization expense, as well. The merged company owned the same assets the separate companies held prior to the merger, however. The additional depreciation and amortization expenses did not affect Time Warner's operating cash flows or its prospects for future cash flows because depreciation and amortization are noncash expenses. In contrast, the additional interest and dividend payments had a real economic effect on the company because they required the outflow of cash. Care must be used when one observes large amounts of goodwill and large increases in depreciation and amortization expense on a company's financial statements. These events may signal that a company's expenses have been inflated relative to its cash flows, resulting in earnings that are artificially low. Comparing net income with cash flow from operating activities can provide an indication of whether earnings are representative of cash flows. The following information for Time Warner illustrates:

(in millions except percentages)	1987	1988	1989	1990
Net income (loss)	$ 578	$ 712	$ (432)	$ (227)
Operating cash flow	932	929	693	649
Total assets	8,296	9,511	24,791	25,337
Goodwill	997	986	9,044	9,073
Assets − goodwill	7,299	8,525	15,747	16,264
Net income/total assets	7.0%	7.5%	− 1.7%	− 0.9%
Cash flow/(assets − goodwill)	12.8%	10.9%	4.4%	4.0%

Time Warner's income decreased dramatically after the merger (1989–1990) relative to the pre-merger totals for Time and Warner combined (1987–1988). At the same time, assets increased dramatically. Therefore, Time Warner appeared to be facing major financial problems after the merger as represented by net income/total assets. Examination of operating cash flows relative to assets excluding goodwill reveals a bit different story, however. Though the company's performance was not as good after the merger as before, the cash flow/(assets − goodwill) ratio suggests that it was not facing imminent financial problems.

Whether investment decisions, such as merger and acquisition decisions, increase a company's value often is unknown for several years. Time merged with Warner because each company owned resources that, in combination, might create additional value. Warner had foreign operations Time considered to be valuable for expanding its own operations into international markets. Warner's movie and TV studios could provide programs for HBO and Cinemax cable channels, owned by Time. The value of the investment decision depended on the ability of the company's management to take advantage of the combined resources. Success would be measured by long-run profitability and cash flows, not by short-run losses.

FAIR MARKET VALUES

Objective 6
Explain why fair market value reporting of assets can be useful.

Some accountants and financial analysts believe that financial statements should report fair market values of assets and liabilities rather than, or in addition to, historical costs. For example, tangible assets, such as inventory and plant assets, might be reported on the balance sheet at their estimated replacement costs at the end of each fiscal year. Such reports would require companies to appraise the value of their assets and liabilities each year. Price indexes for specific types of assets that indicate changes in asset costs during the year might be used for this purpose. Many managers and accountants are concerned, however, that these appraisals are too subjective to provide reliable information. The added cost of providing this information also has been cited as a reason for not reporting current values.

Current Value of Assets and Company Value

Even if assets were adjusted to their current values, a company's balance sheet would not report total company value, however. For example, prior to the Time Warner merger, the two companies reported combined total assets of $9.5 billion. After the merger, total assets were reported at $24.8 billion, an increase of $15.3 billion. Of this amount, only $2.1 billion resulted from an adjustment of previously recognized assets to their fair market values. The remaining $13.2 billion resulted from goodwill and other assets that were previously unrecognized. Even if Warner's assets had been recorded at their fair market value prior to the merger, the financial statement amounts of Time Warner would have been dramatically different from those of Time and Warner prior to the merger.

The amounts reported on the balance sheet, whether considered individually or in total, do not represent the fair market value of a corporation. The value of a corporation is determined by its ability to generate cash flows through its operating activities. Investor assessments of this ability, adjusted for risk, determine the market value of a company's stock.

A company's balance sheet identifies primarily the historical cost of its assets and the source of financial resources used to acquire them. Changes in the composition of assets, liabilities, and equities over time generally is useful information. In addition, information about changes in the relationship between these amounts and a company's net income or cash flows can be useful. This information helps investors and other external decision makers understand how a company is using its resources. It does not tell them what a company is worth. The value of a company typically is different from the value of its separate assets. The ability to manage assets, the value of trained employees, and the value of established markets are not reported on the balance sheet.

Two companies may have identical assets but have different market values. For example, a restaurant may go out of business in a specific location because it cannot generate a profit. New owners may buy the building and equipment and create a successful new business. The difference between success and failure often occurs because of how the assets are managed, not because of the assets themselves. A profitable business will be more valuable than an unprofitable business with the same assets.

Time believed Warner was considerably more valuable than its $5.2 billion market value. Time's management believed Warner's assets, employees, products, and markets would be more valuable in combination with those of Time than they were as a separate company. **Value results from the ability to manage resources, including tangible assets, money, and people.**

Nevertheless, many accountants have argued that financial statements should report the current value of assets and liabilities. This information could enhance the ability of decision makers to compare companies and provide for more equitable measurement of performance. Some countries, such as Great Britain and the Netherlands, permit corporations to use current values as the measurement basis for reporting their assets. Therefore, companies in these countries normally would report higher amounts for their assets than identical U.S. companies. Performance measures, such as return on assets, also are affected.

Financial Assets and Liabilities

One area in which fair market accounting has received special attention is in the reporting of financial assets and liabilities, such as debt and equity securities. Many securities are traded on a regular basis, revealing their current market prices. Changes in market values of notes, bonds, and other debt instruments can be determined from changes in market rates of interest and expected cash flows. Financial instruments are primary assets for many financial institutions. Banks, savings and loans, insurance companies, and other institutions invest heavily in these assets. Cash is provided by depositors or policy owners. Institutions such as banks and savings and loans lend this cash to businesses or individuals. Excess cash is invested in marketable securities until it is needed.

During periods of rapid change in interest rates and other economic conditions, historical costs of financial instruments can be misleading. During the 1980s many savings and loans reported large amounts of financial investments at historical costs. The market values of many of these investments, however, were far below their costs. Therefore, the fair market values of the companies' assets sometimes were less than their liabilities. If fair market amounts had been reported, the companies would have been insolvent (their liabilities would have been greater than their assets).

To illustrate, assume Sly Savings and Loan's assets at the end of 1997 consisted of three financial instruments, each costing $2,000:

1997	Historical Cost	Fair Market Value
Assets	$2,000	$3,000
	2,000	500
	2,000	300
Total assets	6,000	3,800
Liabilities	4,000	4,000
Equity	2,000	(200)

During 1998, the company sold the asset with a market value of $3,000, thereby generating income of $1,000, a return on assets of 16.7% and a return on equity of 50%. It invested cash from the sale in another instrument at a cost of $3,000. Therefore (assuming no changes in the market value of other assets) its financial position at the end of 1998 was:

1998	Historical Cost	Fair Market Value
Assets	$3,000	$3,000
	2,000	500
	2,000	300
Total assets	7,000	3,800
Liabilities	4,000	4,000
Equity	3,000	(200)

Though the company's financial position appeared to be improving and it appeared to be profitable, the company was insolvent. In 1999, the company's liabilities became due and it sold all of its investments at their fair market values. It incurred a loss of $3,200, and it reported its financial position as:

1999	Historical Cost	Fair Market Value
Total assets (cash)	3,800	3,800
Liabilities	4,000	4,000
Equity	(200)	(200)

The company's insolvency now becomes apparent on its historical cost balance sheet. Creditors and owners were misled during 1998 into believing the company was doing well, when, in fact, it was facing a major problem. Many savings and loans and some banks faced this situation in the late 1980s and early 1990s. They were able to hide their financial problems for several years behind historical cost financial statements. These institutions had many loans among their assets that were not paying expected interest. Real estate loans, in particular, often were returning very low yields. In many cases, their market values were far below their historical cost values.

Accounting Methods and Interpretation of Financial Statements

The accounting methods used by companies affect their financial statements. A company's net income, return on assets, and other profitability and risk measures may look very different if it uses one method rather than another. Management may choose among these methods, for example, straight-line versus accelerated depreciation. In other cases, such as purchase or pooling for mergers and acquisitions, a choice does not exist. Unless a transaction can be structured to meet stringent requirements to be a pooling of interests, purchase accounting is required. Nevertheless, the method used may have a major effect on reported accounting numbers. Decision makers should consider the effect of accounting methods on reported numbers when analyzing accounting information.

SELF-STUDY PROBLEM 12-2

The following information was reported by Big Catch Co.:

(in millions)	1997	1996
Depreciation and amortization expense	$ 250	$ 130
Income before interest and taxes	800	500
Interest expense	285	150

(in millions)	1997	1996
Income before taxes	515	350
Income taxes (40%)	204	140
Net income	311	210
Preferred dividends	20	2
Net income available for common stock	291	208
Total assets	9,500	4,800
Intangible assets	2,700	250
Cash flow from operating activities	700	315

Many of the changes that occurred in Big Catch's financial statements resulted from acquisitions of other companies accounted for by using the purchase method. Assume the increase in depreciation and amortization expense, interest expense, and preferred dividends resulted from acquisition activity. Also, assume $900 million of plant assets and the increase in intangible assets (primarily goodwill) resulted from recording assets and liabilities of acquired companies at their fair market values instead of at their book values.

Required

(a) Calculate return on assets and cash flow from operating activities to total assets for 1997 and 1996 as reported. Use the total assets reported in each year as the denominator in these calculations. (b) Calculate these amounts for 1997 after adjusting for the effects of the purchase method on net income, cash flows, and total assets. Assume the income tax rate for 1997 was 40%.

The solution to Self-Study Problem 12-2 appears at the end of this chapter.

OPERATING LEVERAGE

Operating leverage **is the proportion of a company's total expenses that are fixed.** *Fixed costs* **are expenses that do not vary in proportion to sales activity.** *Variable costs* **are expenses that do vary in proportion to sales activity.** Operating leverage is affected by a company's asset composition. Companies with large proportions of long-term assets typically have large fixed costs. As an illustration, assume two companies, Fixed and Variable, are similar except for their asset composition. Exhibit 12-9 provides information for the two companies.

Both companies have the same amount of total assets. Fixed Co. has a larger proportion of long-term assets, however. Long-term assets typically are associated with fixed costs, such as depreciation and amortization of plant and intangible assets, repair and maintenance costs, utilities, insurance, and other costs associated with these assets. Current assets include inventory, short-term investments, and prepaid expenses that are more likely to vary with sales activity.

As a result, Fixed Co. has more fixed costs that are expensed in the first scenario than does Variable Co. Variable Co. has a higher proportion of variable costs that are expensed. Both companies have the same amount of sales. Observe

Objective 7
Explain the effect of
operating leverage on a
company's earnings.

Exhibit 12-9   Comparison of Operating Leverage

	Fixed Co.	Variable Co.
Current assets	$ 400,000	$ 600,000
Long-term assets	600,000	400,000
Total assets	$1,000,000	$1,000,000
First Scenario		
Sales revenue	$ 500,000	$ 500,000
Variable costs, 20% and 60% of sales	(100,000)	(300,000)
Fixed costs	(300,000)	(100,000)
Income before taxes	100,000	100,000
Income taxes, 30%	(30,000)	(30,000)
Net income	$ 70,000	70,000
Return on assets	7.0%	7.0%
Second Scenario		
Sales revenue	$ 700,000	$ 700,000
Variable costs, 20% and 60% of sales	(140,000)	(420,000)
Fixed costs	(300,000)	(100,000)
Income before taxes	260,000	180,000
Income taxes, 30%	(78,000)	(54,000)
Net income	$ 182,000	$ 126,000
Return on assets	18.2%	12.6%

that at a sales level of $500,000, the companies earn the same amount of net income and return on assets.

The second scenario differs from the first because sales are assumed to be $700,000 for both companies. Fixed costs remain the same as in the first scenario, but variable costs increase in proportion to sales. Consequently, Fixed Co. now earns a higher net income than Variable Co. Operating leverage, like financial leverage, provides a magnifying effect on net income. As sales increase, high leverage improves net income. As sales decrease, however, high leverage has a detrimental effect on net income. Net income is more sensitive to changes in sales revenue for Fixed Company than for Variable Company.

Operating leverage is particularly important for certain types of companies. Most major manufacturing companies, utilities, and transportation companies are capital intensive. Large investments have been made in long-term assets. Investments in plant assets are necessary to increase sales and production capacities. If sales do not keep pace with investments, however, these companies will incur costs associated with their excess capacity. As an example, consider the case of Delta Air Lines. About 75% of Delta's assets are long term, particularly airplanes. Delta incurs costs associated with these assets, their operations, and their maintenance. Each flight will incur costs, including the cost of the airplane, maintenance and fuel costs, crew salaries, and landing fees. Delta incurs these costs whether the plane's seats are 30% occupied or 80% occupied. Its costs are largely fixed. Its revenues, however, depend on the number of tickets it sells. Exhibit 12-10 illustrates the effects of high fixed costs on the profits of companies like Delta.

Exhibit 12-10   The Effect of Operating Leverage on Profitability

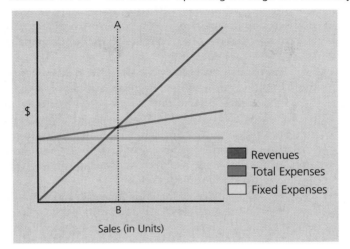

As sales increase (toward the right of the graph), revenues increase in proportion. For example, if Delta sells more seats to passengers, its revenues increase because of higher ticket sales. Total expenses also increase with higher sales. However, the rate of increase in total expenses is not very great for companies like Delta, because many of the expenses are fixed in the short run. Therefore, if Delta can sell enough seats so that it can operate at a level to the right of line AB, it is profitable. If Delta operates to the left of AB, however, it loses money. Many airlines, including Delta, reported losses during the early 1990s because of their high fixed expenses and relatively low sales volumes.

Like many companies, Delta has high operating leverage. If it can increase sales by operating closer to maximum capacity, it can earn relatively high returns. When sales fall and the company is operating well below its maximum capacity, its returns decrease rapidly. Manufacturing companies like automobile and paper companies also are affected by high operating leverage. Operating near capacity normally means relatively high returns. Operating well below capacity normally results in losses. If a company loses market share so that it faces long-term declines in sales, it usually will eliminate excess capacity by selling off assets and closing facilities. By eliminating plant assets and laying off employees, a company reduces expenses and a portion of its investment. Thus, it is able to increase revenues relative to expenses and investment. These changes should increase earnings and return on assets. Managing the amount and type of investment a company makes is a key to success.

CASH ANALYSIS AND MANAGEMENT

Cash is vital to an organization. Without sufficient cash, an organization cannot survive. Managing cash is a vital function. Too little cash and an organization is incapable of meeting its current obligations, replacing assets, or taking advantage of new opportunities. Too much cash also can be a problem unless a company has good opportunities for investing the cash. Cash does not earn a return until it is invested. Therefore, excess cash should be invested. If excess cash will be needed in the near future for other purposes, investments should be short-term. If excess cash will not be needed for other purposes, a company should look for new investment opportunities, repay existing debt, repurchase stock, or pay cash dividends to its stockholders.

Objective 8
Analyze a company's cash management.

The inability to generate cash is the cause of most business failures. Therefore, careful monitoring of cash flows should be a high priority in every business. Operating cash flows should be used to replace current assets, pay dividends, and pay for operating costs. Financing activities provide cash flows for long-term asset purchases. Many companies maintain lines of credit with financial institutions that permit them to borrow on a short-term basis to meet short-term cash flow needs. Financing for major acquisitions normally requires a company to issue new stock or long-term debt.

The statement of cash flows provides information about a company's cash flow decisions. It is valuable for evaluating how a company is obtaining and using cash. Exhibit 12-11 provides summary cash flow information for two companies for 1991 to 1993.

Exhibit 12-11   Analysis of Cash Flows

(in millions)	1993	1992	1991
Vulcan Materials			
Operating	$193.0	$201.1	$183.3
Investing	(103.8)	(110.7)	(98.7)
Financing	(90.9)	(93.7)	(84.2)
Allied Products			
Operating	67.8	12.1	34.5
Investing	63.4	(1.1)	27.6
Financing	(92.2)	(13.0)	(67.3)

For most companies, the amount of cash flow from operating activities is approximately equal to the amount of cash flows for investing and financing activities:

Operating Cash In = Cash Used for Investing + Cash from (or for) Financing

For example, net cash inflows from operating activities for Vulcan Materials in 1993 were $193 million, approximately equal to the total of net cash outflows for investing and financing activities. This relationship is logical because all cash flows result from one of these three types of activities. If a company generated $30 million of cash flow from operating activities and needed $50 million for investing activities, it would need to raise $20 million from financing activities: $30 = ($50) + $20.

The source of cash inflows for Vulcan Materials for the years shown in Exhibit 12-11 was operating activities. These activities provided sufficient cash to meet current operating needs and to provide for the company's investing activities. Excess cash was used to repay debt and to repurchase stock. Therefore, cash was used for financing activities. In contrast, Allied Products relied on operating and investing activities to provide cash inflows from 1991 to 1993, primarily for use by financing activities. Cash generated from operating activities and cash from selling assets was used to repay debt.

Vulcan's cash flows are typical of companies that are performing relatively well. It has been able to generate enough cash flow from operating activities to meet its investing needs. Excess cash has been used to reduce debt and repurchase stock. In contrast, cash flows of Allied Products are typical of companies that are having financial problems. The company issued large amounts of debt during the late 1980s to finance investment and operating activities. It has been unable to generate sufficient cash from operating activities to repay debt and interest. Therefore, it has sold assets to provide needed cash. An examination of cash flows is useful for assessing a company's future earnings and growth prospects. Those for Vulcan were much better in 1993 than those of Allied Products.

SELF-STUDY PROBLEM 12-3

Cash flow information is provided below for two companies in the same industry. Cash outflows are shown in parentheses.

(in millions)	1997	1996	1995
Walnut Corp.			
Operating activities	$417	$358	$353
Investing activities	(141)	(182)	(123)
Financing activities	(126)	(200)	(360)
Pecan Inc.			
Operating activities	817	694	599
Investing activities	(533)	(699)	(532)
Financing activities	(173)	(14)	(83)

Required

Analyze the companies' cash flows for 1995 to 1997.

The solution to Self-Study Problem 12-3 appears at the end of the chapter.

R E V I E W *Summary of Important Concepts*

1. Investing activities are important for determining company value.

2. Evaluation of investment decisions:
   a. Return on assets is a measure used to evaluate investment decisions.
   b. Return on assets is higher on average for high-growth, high-value companies.

3. Through ratio analysis, users of accounting information can compare the investment decisions of different companies to evaluate their relative value.

4. Risk and return:
    a. Diversification through investment in different types of assets, product lines, and locations can reduce a company's risk. Information concerning a company's segments can assist users of the firm's financial information in evaluating risk.
    b. Mergers and acquisitions enable a company to diversify and expand. Care must be used in interpreting accounting information after a major merger or acquisition because of the effect the transaction may have on accounting information.

5. Reporting fair market values for certain types of assets may provide useful information that can prevent decision makers from being misled by historical cost information.

6. Operating leverage, the proportion of a company's total expenses that are fixed, affects the amount and volatility of a company's earnings.

7. The statement of cash flows provides information that can be used to analyze a company's cash management decisions. This information can be used to identify cash flow problems.

D E F I N E   *Terms   and   Concepts   Defined   in   This   Chapter*

capital intensity   operating leverage   variable costs
fixed costs   return on assets

S O L U T I O N S

SELF-STUDY PROBLEM 12-1

1996

$$\text{Return on Assets} = \frac{\$70 + [\$20(1 - .3)]}{\$800} = 10.5\%$$

$$\text{Return on Equity} = \frac{\$63}{\$250} = 25.2\%$$

1995

$$\text{Return on Assets} = \frac{\$71.4 + [\$8(1 - .3)]}{\$770} = 10.0\%$$

$$\text{Return on Equity} = \frac{\$67.4}{\$290} = 23.2\%$$

1994

$$\text{Return on Assets} = \frac{\$66.5 + [\$5(1 - .3)]}{\$730} = 9.6\%$$

$$\text{Return on Equity} = \frac{\$66.5}{\$280} = 23.8\%$$

Zork Co.'s return on assets has increased steadily from 1994 to 1996. Therefore, this information suggests the company has been making good investment decisions that have resulted in additional earnings relative to total investment. Return on equity has been somewhat more erratic. The increase in return on equity from 1995 to 1996 resulted from increased financial leverage. Larger proportions of debt and preferred stock in the company's capital structure permitted it to earn a higher return for its stockholders. Return on assets measures the effects of investing activities. Return on equity measures the effects of both investing and financing activities.

SELF-STUDY PROBLEM 12-2

(a)	1997	1996
Return on assets: [net income + interest expense (1 − .40)] ÷ total assets	5.1%	6.3%
Cash flow to total assets	7.4%	6.6%

(b)	1997
Income before taxes	$ 515
Excess depreciation and amortization ($250 − $130)	120
Restated income before taxes	635
Income taxes, 40%	(254)
Net income as restated	$ 381
Net income as restated plus interest expense [285 × (1 − .40)]	$ 552
Total assets	$9,500
Intangible assets from acquisition ($2,700 − $250)	(2,450)
Write-up of plant assets to fair market	(900)
Total assets as restated	$6,150
Return on assets ($552/$6,150)	9.0%
Cash flow to total assets ($700/$6,150)	11.4%

SELF-STUDY PROBLEM 12-3

Both companies had positive cash flows from operating activities each year. Pecan, Inc. used much more cash for investing activities during the period than did Walnut Corp. Walnut used most of its cash for financing activities. The investing practices suggest that Pecan had better investment options than did Walnut. Investment in these opportunities by Pecan appear to have had a beneficial effect on the company's operating cash flows. Pecan's operating cash flows have been growing much more rapidly than those of Walnut.

EXERCISES

12-1. Write a short definition for each of the terms listed in the "Terms and Concepts Defined in This Chapter" section.

12-2. Why are investment activities critical to the success of a company?

12-3. How do investing activities affect a company's growth?

12-4. What are the conceptual differences between return on assets and return on equity? Which would you use to evaluate investment decisions? Why?

12-5. Some companies distribute most of their earnings to stockholders in the form of dividends. Other companies distribute a small portion of their earnings as dividends or pay no dividends at all. How does a company's dividend policy affect its investment decisions? What does a company's dividend policy signal about its investment opportunities?

12-6. Information is provided below for McDonald's Corporation from its 1993 annual report:

(in millions)	1993	1992	1991	1990
Interest expense	316	374	391	
Pretax income	1,676	1,448	1,299	
Provision for taxes	593	489	439	
Net income	1,083	959	860	
Total assets	12,035	11,681	11,349	10,668

Evaluate McDonald's investing decisions by computing and analyzing its return on assets for 1991 through 1993.

12-7. The following information was reported by McDonald's Corporation in its 1993 annual report:

(in millions)	1993	1992	1991	1990
Cash flow from operating activities	1,680	1,426	1,423	
Total assets	12,035	11,681	11,349	10,668

Evaluate McDonald's investing decisions by computing the ratio of cash flow from operating activities to average total assets for 1991 through 1993. Compare the cash flow ratio with return on assets from Exercise 12-6.

12-8. Companies often invest in assets that will permit them to produce several different product lines. What are the advantages of investing in several product lines as opposed to making larger investments in the production of a single product?

12-9. Segment information is provided below from the 1993 annual report of Vulcan Materials Company:

(in millions)	1993	1992	1991
Operating income:			
Construction materials	$116.7	$ 88.3	$ 41.8
Chemicals	17.4	51.3	42.6
Total	134.1	139.6	84.4
Average assets:			
Construction materials	$707.4	$708.4	$748.4
Chemicals	248.5	226.4	226.1
Total	955.9	934.8	974.5

Evaluate the performance of each of Vulcan's segments and the effect it had on the company's overall performance. If you were a manager at Vulcan, how would this information affect your investment decisions?

12-10. Hockey Co. acquired Puck Co. during 1995. The companies merged to form Hockey Puck Co. The merger was accounted for as a purchase. The fair market value of Puck Co.'s net assets was $38 million. Hockey Co. paid $60 million for the net assets. The merger was financed by the issuance of long-term debt at an interest rate of 12%. Prior to the merger, Hockey Co. had total assets of $90 million and total liabilities of $40 million. Its net income for 1995 was expected to be $10 million. Puck expected net income for 1995 of $4 million. How would the merger affect Hockey Puck's financial statements for 1995? What effect would it have on the use of financial statement information by investors and other external parties?

12-11. During 1991 PepsiCo, Inc. paid over $600 million for acquisitions accounted for by using the purchase method. Other major acquisitions also occurred in 1992 and 1993 amounting to approximately $2,221 million. Of the company's total assets of $23,705 million at the end of 1993, $7,929 million were goodwill. Total assets were $20,951 million in 1992. Net cash flow from operating activities was $2,712 million in 1992 and $3,134.4 million in 1993. Net income was $374.3 million in 1992 and $1,587.9 million in 1993. Interest expense was $586 million in 1992 and $572.7 million in 1993. Evaluate the effect of PepsiCo's acquisitions on the company's performance.

12-12. Anthro Poid is a friend who is planning to be a business manager. In a recent discussion about financial matters, Anthro made the following statement: "A company's balance sheet measures the value of a company's resources. Investors can use this value for pricing the company's stock and for comparing the values of different companies." How would you respond to Anthro?

12-13. At the end of its 1996 fiscal year, Shangri-La Co. owned the following investments:

Investment	Historical Cost	Fair Market Value
A	$650,000	$765,000
B	840,000	730,000

Other assets had a book value of $2.4 million and liabilities had a book value of $1.8 million. Shangri-La's pretax income for 1996 was $400,000 and its tax rate was 35%. If the company sold investment A at the end of 1996 for cash, what effect would the sale have on its financial statements and return on assets? Assume assets are reported on the financial statements at historical cost. What effect would the sale of investment B have on the company's financial statements and return on assets? Compare these amounts to those that would be reported if no investments were sold.

12-14. Selected financial information for two companies is reported below from their 1993 annual reports:

(in millions)	Digital Equipment Corporation	Honeywell, Inc.
Plant assets, at cost	$7,193	$6,783
Depreciation expense	699	575
Net cash outflow for plant assets	481	909

Compare the depreciation policies and investment rates of the two companies.

12-15. Selected accounting information is provided below for two companies:

(in millions)	1990	1991	1992	1993
Total assets:				
Sara Lee	7,636	8,122	9,989	10,862
Warner-Lambert	3,261	3,602	4,077	4,828
Depreciation & amortization:				
Sara Lee	351	394	472	522
Warner-Lambert	120	135	156	170
Capital expenditures:				
Sara Lee	595	522	509	728
Warner-Lambert	240	326	334	347

What trends in asset investments are apparent from examining the data presented above?

12-16. The Ming and Shang companies both increased sales by 30% between their 1995 and 1996 fiscal years. Ming's net income increased 40% as a result of the increased sales. Shang's net income increased 20%. Explain why differences in operating leverage may have resulted in a higher increase in net income for Ming than for Shang. Provide a diagram to illustrate your explanation.

12-17. Maglioni Co. recorded sales revenues of $5 million in 1996. The company incurred expenses of $4.5 million. Fixed costs accounted for $2 million of these expenses. How much net income would Maglioni have reported if its sales had been $4 million? $6 million? Suppose the company's total expenses were $4.5 million in 1996 and fixed costs accounted for $3 million of these expenses. How much net income would Maglioni have reported if its sales had been $4 million? $6 million? What conclusions can you draw from this analysis about the effect of operating leverage on net income?

12-18. The balance sheet and statement of cash flows provide information about a company's access to and use of cash. What differences would you expect to see in the information related to cash on these statements for a company reporting strong financial performance versus a company reporting weak financial performance?

12-19. Information is provided below from the statement of cash flows of Delta Air Lines, Incorporated for 1994:

(in millions)	1994	1993	1992
Net cash provided by operating activities	$ 1,324	$ 677	$ 149
Net cash used in investing activities	(1,510)	(1,327)	(3,039)
Net cash provided by financing activities	308	1,780	2,176

Most of the cash provided by financing activities was from the issuance of long-term debt, the issuance of preferred stock, and from sale and lease-back of fixed assets. Evaluate Delta's cash flows over the three years. What information is communicated about the company's future prospects by its investing and financing activities during this period?

12-20. Florez Co. increased its investment in long-term assets by 20% in the past three years. This investment was financed by rapid increases in cash generated from operating activities. Cash from operating activities also was used to repay about 30% of Florez's long-term debt and to repurchase 10% of its common stock. What effect would you expect these events to have on the company's earnings per share, return on assets, and return on equity?

PROBLEMS

PROBLEM 12-1 Evaluating Accounting Rate of Return

Information is provided below from the 1994 annual report of Wal-Mart Stores, Inc.:

(in millions)	1994	1993
Total assets	$26,441	$20,565
Common stockholders' equity	10,752	8,759
Interest expense	331	
Income before income taxes	3,691	
Provision for income taxes	1,358	
Net income	2,333	

Required   Compute return on assets and return on equity for the company for 1994. What information is provided by the difference between the two ratios? If Wal–Mart's sales and operating income grow during 1995, do you expect return on assets or return on equity to grow at a faster rate? Why?

PROBLEM 12-2   Evaluating Growth

Information is provided below from the 1994 annual report of Wal-Mart Stores, Inc.

(in millions)	Total Assets	Common Equity
1990	$ 8,198	$ 3,966
1991	11,389	5,365
1992	15,443	6,990
1993	20,565	8,759
1994	26,441	10,752

Required   Compute the average annual growth rates for assets and common stock-holders' equity from 1990 to 1994. From this information would you expect the market value of Wal-Mart to be high or low relative to the amount invested by stockholders (book value of equity)? Why?

PROBLEM 12-3   Evaluating Investment Decisions

During 1993, Intel Corporation invested $3,337 million of cash in additional assets. Of this amount, $1,933 million was invested in plant assets. The remainder was invested in securities. The company invested $1,228 million of cash in additional plant assets in 1992. Other information reported by the company in its 1993 annual report includes:

(in millions)	1993	1992	1991
Total assets	$11,344	$8,089	$6,292
Interest expense	50	54	
Income before taxes	3,530	1,569	
Income taxes	1,235	502	
Net income	2,295	1,067	

Required   Compare the results of Intel's investment decisions during 1992 and 1993.

PROBLEM 12-4   Evaluating Investment Decisions

The following information was reported by Intel Corporation in its 1993 annual report:

(in millions except EPS)	Total Assets	Long-Term Debt	Additions to Plant Assets	Net Income	Earnings per Share
1993	$11,344	$426	$1,933	$2,295	$5.20
1992	8,089	249	1,228	1,067	2.49
1991	6,292	363	948	819	1.96
1990	5,376	345	680	650	3.20
1989	3,994	412	422	391	2.07
1988	3,550	479	477	453	2.51

Required   Evaluate Intel's investment decisions for the period from 1989 to 1993.

PROBLEM 12-5   Evaluating Investment Decisions

The following information was reported by PepsiCo, Inc. in its 1993 annual report:

(in millions)	1993	1992	1991
Net income	$ 1,587.9	$ 374.3	$ 1,080.2
Cash flow—operating	3,134.4	2,711.6	2,430.3
Cash invested in other companies	1,011.2	1,209.7	640.9
Cash purchases of plant assets	1,981.6	1,549.6	1,457.8
Cash dividends paid	461.6	395.5	343.2
Total assets	23,705.8	20,951.2	18,775.1

Required   Identify and evaluate PepsiCo's investment decisions over the three years shown above.

PROBLEM 12-6   Analysis of Segment Information

Segment information is provided below from the 1993 annual report of Cooper Industries:

(in millions)	1993	1992	1991
Electrical products:			
Earnings	$ 316.0	$ 295.0	$ 273.4
Assets	1,178.9	1,267.0	1,265.8
Automotive products:			
Earnings	188.9	139.0	145.2
Assets	2,208.8	2,245.5	1,648.9
Petroleum & industrial equipment:			
Earnings	130.4	208.8	310.6
Assets	1,687.5	2,167.8	2,423.5
Total corporate:			
Earnings before taxes	625.4	580.1	668.6
Assets	7,147.8	7,575.6	7,148.6

Cooper also disclosed two smaller segments that are not shown. Total corporate earnings and assets also include general and administrative expenses and assets that were not allocated to individual segments.

Required What effect have these segments had on Cooper Industries' risk and return for the period shown?

PROBLEM 12-7 Analysis of Acquisitions

Fast Burn Co. is considering the acquisition of Plenty Fuel Co. Fast Burn would acquire all of Plenty Fuel's common stock, which if purchased for cash would cost $15 million. The fair market value of Plenty's assets is $18 million, and the fair market value of its liabilities is $6 million. Financial statements for the two companies for their most recent fiscal years reveals:

(in millions)	Fast Burn	Plenty Fuel
Total assets	$30.7	$14.5
Total liabilities	16.9	5.8
Net income	5.6	2.7

To finance the acquisition, Fast Burn would issue additional common stock. The stock could be sold for cash or it could be exchanged directly with Plenty Fuel's current stockholders. Goodwill would be amortized over 10 years. There were no intercompany transactions between the companies.

Required (a) What effect would the acquisition have on Fast Burn's consolidated financial statements and profitability if the acquisition were accounted for as a purchase? (b) What effect would the acquisition have on Fast Burn's consolidated financial statements and profitability if the acquisition were accounted for as a pooling of interests? (c) What effect would the accounting method used (purchase or pooling) have on Fast Burn's cash flows?

PROBLEM 12-8 Comparing Investment Activities

Information is provided below from the 1993 annual reports of The Coca-Cola Company and PepsiCo, Inc.:

(in millions except per share amounts)	Coca-Cola	PepsiCo
Current assets	$ 4,434	$ 5,164
Investments and other assets	3,309	1,757
Plant assets, at cost	5,596	14,250
Plant assets, net	3,729	8,856
Goodwill and intangibles	549	7,930
Total assets	12,021	23,706
Current liabilities	5,171	6,575
Long-term debt	1,428	7,443

(in millions except per share amounts)	Coca-Cola	PepsiCo
Shareholders' equity	4,697	6,338
Net income	2,176	1,588
Interest expense	168	573
Depreciation and amortization	360	1,442
Net cash provided by operating activities	2,508	3,134
Net cash used in investing activities	(885)	(2,771)
Net cash used in financing activities	(1,540)	(303)
Earnings per share	1.67	1.96
Market value of equity	58,102	33,450
Stock price per share	44.625	41.875
Cash from operating activities per share	1.92	3.87

Required Use accounting ratios to compare the investing activities and performances of the two companies for 1993. What important differences exist in the investing and financing activities of the companies? How do these differences affect the risk and return of the companies? How do these differences affect the market to book value of equity ratios and price/cash flow from operating activities ratios of the two companies?

PROBLEM 12-9 Assessing Operating Leverage Effects

Information is provided below from the financial statements of two companies for 1996:

	Jekle	Hyde
Total assets	$30,000	$80,000
Total debt	10,000	50,000
Total equity	20,000	30,000
Sales	28,000	75,000
Operating expense	20,000	60,000
Operating income	8,000	15,000
Interest expense	800	5,000
Pretax income	7,200	10,000
Income taxes (30%)	2,160	3,000
Net income	5,040	7,000
Return on assets	18.7%	13.1%
Return on equity	25.2%	23.3%

Jekle's operating expenses include fixed costs of $5,000. Hyde's operating expenses include fixed costs of $50,000. All other operating expenses vary in proportion to sales for both companies. Assume that during 1996 sales for both companies increased by 20% from the amount reported, to $33,600 for Jekle and to $90,000 for Hyde.

Required (a) Compute the net income Jekle and Hyde would report for 1996 if sales increased by 20%. (b) Compute return on assets for Jekle and Hyde, assuming the increase in sales. (c) Explain why the increase in sales would affect Jekle and Hyde differently and explain which company is riskier.

PROBLEM 12-10   Comparing Operating Leverage

Information is provided below from the 1993 annual reports of Microsoft Corporation and The Limited, Inc. The earnings shown below are operating income, income before interest and taxes.

	Microsoft		The Limited	
(in millions)	Sales	Earnings	Sales	Earnings
1989	804	171	4,648	625
1990	1,183	279	5,254	698
1991	1,843	463	6,149	713
1992	2,759	708	6,944	789
1993	3,753	953	7,245	702

Required   Prepare a graph to illustrate the relationship between each company's earnings and its sales over the five years. Which company has the highest operating leverage? What effect does operating leverage have on the companies' operating income?

PROBLEM 12-11   Comparing Cash Flows

Cash flow information is provided below for two companies in the health care products industry. Cash outflows are shown in parentheses.

(in millions)	1993	1992	1991	Total
Johnson & Johnson				
Operating activities	2,168	2,149	1,675	$5,992
Investing activities	(1,261)	(1,173)	(1,028)	(3,462)
Financing activities	(1,244)	(785)	(873)	(2,902)
Warner-Lambert				
Operating activities	466	636	736	1,838
Investing activities	(759)	(336)	(306)	(1,401)
Financing activities	30	(104)	(195)	(269)

Required   Analyze the companies' cash flows for 1991 to 1993 and for the three years in total.

PROBLEM 12-12   Multiple-Choice Overview

1. Return on assets involves a comparison of average assets with:
   a.   net income.
   b.   net income adjusted for preferred dividends.
   c.   net income adjusted for income taxes.
   d.   net income adjusted for interest expense.

2. High-value companies usually exhibit a:
   a. return on assets greater than return on equity.
   b. return on assets less than return on equity.
   c. return on assets equal to return on equity.
   d. negative return on equity and positive return on assets.

3. A company with good investment opportunities normally can increase its stock-holders' wealth by:
   a. increasing its cash dividend payout rate.
   b. investing in new assets.
   c. reducing the amount invested in new assets.
   d. reducing its rate of return on new assets.

4. A company can reduce the volatility of its net income by:
   a. diversifying its product line.
   b. increasing its financial leverage.
   c. increasing its operating leverage.
   d. investing in projects with high expected returns.

5. In an acquisition accounted for as a purchase, the assets and liabilities of the acquired company are reported on the consolidated balance sheet of the acquiring company at their:
   a. book value.
   b. present value.
   c. estimated fair market value.
   d. original cost.

6. The amortization of goodwill affects the net income and net cash flow from operating activities of the acquiring company as follows:

	Net income	Net cash flow
a.	Yes	Yes
b.	Yes	No
c.	No	Yes
d.	No	No

7. Company A has a higher proportion of fixed to variable costs than Company B. The sales revenues of both companies increased by 10%. You would expect:
   a. Company A's expenses to increase more rapidly than Company B's.
   b. Company A's expenses to decrease while Company B's increase.
   c. Company A's net income to decrease while Company B's increases.
   d. Company A's net income to increase more rapidly than Company B's.

8. Company A and Company B are similar in size and in many other respects. The companies reported the following net cash flow from (used for) investing activities in their 1994 annual reports:

(in millions)	1994	1993	1992
Company A	$(460)	$(350)	$(265)
Company B	200	35	(80)

From this information you would expect:
   a. Company A to be growing more rapidly than Company B.
   b. Company B to be growing more rapidly than Company A.

c. Company B to have better investment alternatives than Company A.
d. Company A to be in greater need of cash than Company B.

9. Relative to Company A, Company B is more capital intensive, has a higher dividend payout, and has a higher debt to asset ratio. Company A's asset growth rate has been larger than B's. From this information, it is likely that:
a. Company A is riskier than Company B.
b. Company B is riskier than Company A.
c. Company A has a higher market value than Company B.
d. Company B has a higher market value than Company A.

10. Which of the following net cash flow patterns is typical of a company with high growth potential and strong financial performance?

	Cash flow from operating activities	**Cash flow from investing activities**
a.	Outflow	Outflow
b.	Outflow	Inflow
c.	Inflow	Inflow
d.	Inflow	Outflow

CASES

CASE 12-1 Analysis of an Acquisition

You are a financial analyst with a major corporation, High Hopes Co. You have been assigned the task of evaluating a potential acquisition candidate, Roll-the-Dice, Inc. Selected accounting information for the two companies is presented below. Information for 1995 and 1994 reports actual company results. Results for 1996 are projected from information available at the beginning of the year.

(in millions)	1996	1995	1994
High Hopes Co.			
Depreciation and amortization expense	$ 13.4	$ 13.1	$ 11.6
Operating income	46.3	42.7	37.5
Interest expense	4.9	5.1	5.5
Provision for income taxes	12.6	11.8	11.0
Net income	28.8	25.8	21.0
Total assets	305.7	292.1	274.8
Total liabilities	125.9	128.0	135.2
Total stockholders' equity	179.8	164.1	139.6
Net cash flow from operating activities	40.4	38.5	32.8
Net cash flow used for investing activities	(14.1)	(12.8)	(9.8)
Net cash flow used for financing activities	(25.3)	(25.7)	(23.0)

(in millions)	1996	1995	1994
Roll-the-Dice, Inc.			
Depreciation expense	$ 5.4	$ 5.2	$ 4.5
Operating income	22.8	19.3	12.9
Interest expense	3.7	3.5	3.0
Provision for income taxes	6.2	4.7	4.2
Net income	12.9	11.1	5.7
Total assets	114.3	111.0	93.4
Total liabilities	35.8	33.2	31.8
Total stockholders' equity	78.5	77.8	73.5
Depreciation and amortization expense	5.4	5.2	4.5
Net cash flow from operating activities	18.7	16.4	14.6
Net cash flow used for investing activities	(13.7)	(7.9)	(18.3)
Net cash flow from (used for) financing activities	(4.5)	(8.6)	3.8

The acquisition, if it were to occur, would result in High Hopes purchasing all of the common stock of Roll–the–Dice at a price of $130 million. To finance the acquisition, High Hopes plans to issue $130 million of long-term debt at 10.7% annual interest. The debt would be repaid in equal installments over 10 years. The fair market value of Roll–the–Dice's assets is $127 million. The fair market value of its liabilities are $37 million. The additional assets would increase depreciation on Roll–the–Dice's current assets from $5.4 million to $7 million. Goodwill from the acquisition would be amortized over 10 years. There are no intercompany transactions between High Hopes and Roll–the–Dice. Assume High Hope's income tax rate is 34%.

Required Prepare summary pro forma income statement and statement of cash flows for High Hopes for 1996, assuming it acquires Roll–the–Dice at the beginning of 1996. What recommendation would you make to High Hope's management concerning the acquisition?

CASE 12-2   Evaluating Investment Decisions

Appendix B of this book contains a copy of the 1994 annual report of Nike, Inc.

Required Review the annual report and write a short report in which you identify each of the following:

a.   What major investment decisions did the company make from 1992 to 1994?

b.   Evaluate the company's growth rates from 1990 to 1994 for its total assets, common shareholders' equity, and net income.

c.   Compute return on assets for the company for 1992 to 1994.

d.   Did the company's market to book value of equity increase or decrease from 1992 to 1994? What factors account for this change?

e.   Compare the return on assets of the company's major geographic areas in 1994.

PROJECTS

PROJECT 12-1   Comparing Investment Decisions

Obtain the most recent annual report available for each of three corporations from your library. Calculate the return on assets for each company for each of the most recent three years. Write a brief report comparing the companies' returns. What explanations can you provide for why the returns were different or similar?

PROJECT 12-2   Comparing Investment Decisions

Obtain the most recent annual report available for each of three corporations from your library. Examine the cash flows associated with investing activities for each company for each of the most recent three years. Write a brief report comparing the companies' investing activities. Explain how the companies' investing decisions affected their cash flows. Explain how each company's investing decisions affected its asset growth.

PROJECT 12-3   Comparing Segment Information

Obtain the most recent annual report available for each of three corporations from your library. Find corporations in the same industry. Examine information reported by each company about its industry segments. Compute return on assets for each segment for each company. Write a short report comparing the segments and their performances for each company.

PROJECT 12-4   Evaluating Cash Flows

Use the annual report of a major corporation to determine the company's net cash flows from operating, investing, and financing activities for the last five years. You may need to use reports from earlier years to obtain some of the information. Prepare a graph to illustrate changes in the cash flows over the five-year period. Write a short report describing the changes and explaining their importance for evaluating the company's performance and investing decisions.

PROJECT 12-5   Comparing Operating Leverage

Use annual reports or other sources of accounting information to identify an example of a company with a high amount of operating leverage and a company with a low amount of operating leverage. Examine the relationship between the sales revenues and operating incomes of each company for the last five years. Graph these relationships and write a short report comparing the operating leverages and operating performances of the two companies.

Chapter 13

Operating Activities

CHAPTER

O v e r v i e w

As discussed in previous chapters, financing and investing activities support operating activities by providing necessary resources. Operating activities create goods and services and market these products to customers. This chapter examines accounting for a company's operating activities. The income statement and statement of cash flows provide information about operating activities. These activities also affect information reported on the balance sheet, as shown in the following illustration:

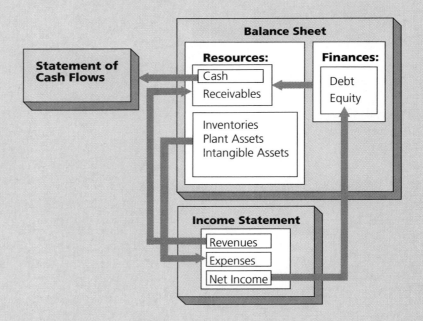

This chapter discusses the contents of the income statement and statement of cash flows and interrelationships among elements of these statements and those of the balance sheet.

Major topics covered in this chapter include:

- Revenues and accounts receivable
- Cost of goods sold and inventories
- Operating income and expenses, other revenues and expenses, and income taxes
- Special income statement items
- Cash flow from operating activities

CHAPTER

O b j e c t i v e s

Once you have completed this chapter, you should be able to:

1. Identify the purpose and major components of an income statement.
2. Identify transactions that affect gross profit.
3. Determine when a company should recognize revenues.
4. Determine the amount of accounts receivable a company should report.
5. Determine the amount of inventories for merchandising and manufacturing companies.

6. Explain the effect of inventory measurement methods on cost of goods sold and inventory.
7. Explain the reporting and measurement of operating expenses.
8. Explain the reporting and measurement of other revenues and expenses.
9. Explain the reporting and measurement of income taxes.
10. Explain the reporting and measurement of discontinued operations, extraordinary items, and accounting changes.
11. Determine net income available for common shareholders.
12. Distinguish primary and fully diluted earnings per share.
13. Compare accrual and cash operating results.
14. Explain the reporting of subsequent events.

REPORTING OPERATING RESULTS

Objective 1
Identify the purpose and major components of an income statement.

The income statement reports the accrual basis results of operating activities for a fiscal period. It includes revenues from sales and services. Expenses associated with production, marketing, distribution, managing, and other functions are subtracted from these revenues to calculate net income. Net income is a primary measure of a company's performance during a fiscal period. It is a measure of the results of operating activities. Therefore, decision makers use net income to evaluate a company's success in providing value for its stockholders and as a basis for forecasting future operating results.

To illustrate the reporting of operating activities, Exhibit 13-1 contains Coca-Cola's income statement from its 1993 annual report. Major items reported on the income statement include operating revenues, gross profit, operating income, income before income taxes, income before changes in accounting principles, net income, net income available to common stockholders, and earnings per share. These items are typical of those reported by most corporations. The following sections examine reporting and measurement issues associated with each of these items.

GROSS PROFIT

Objective 2
Identify transactions that affect gross profit.

Gross profit **is the excess of operating revenues over cost of goods sold.** It represents the difference between the amount a company expects to receive from its sales and the cost of resources consumed in producing or acquiring goods and services that are sold during a fiscal period. Coca-Cola reported gross profit of $8,797 million in 1993 (item 3 in Exhibit 13-1).

Gross profit results from transactions between a company and its customers and suppliers. Suppliers are providers of resources used in producing goods and services. Customers are purchasers of these goods and services. Merchandising and manufacturing companies acquire resources from suppliers and sell goods to customers. Operating transactions of service companies are simpler than those of other companies. These companies sell services that usually do not require large

Exhibit 13-1 Effects of Changes in Accounting Principles

The Coca-Cola Company
Consolidated Statement of Income

Year Ended December 31 (in millions except per share data)	1993	1992	1991
1. **Net Operating Revenues**	$13,957	$13,074	$11,572
2. Cost of goods sold	5,160	5,055	4,649
3. **Gross Profit**	8,797	8,019	6,923
4. Selling, administrative, and general expenses	5,695	5,249	4,604
5. **Operating Income**	3,102	2,770	2,319
6. Interest income	144	164	175
7. Interest expense	(168)	(171)	(192)
8. Equity income	91	65	40
9. Other income—net	16	(82)	41
10. **Income Before Income Taxes**	3,185	2,746	2,383
11. Income taxes	997	863	765
12. **Income Before Changes in Accounting Principles**	2,188	1,883	1,618
13. Effects of changes in accounting principles	(12)	(219)	—
14. **Net Income**	2,176	1,664	1,618
15. Preferred stock dividends	—	—	1
16. **Net Income Available to Common Share Owners**	$ 2,176	$ 1,664	$ 1,617
17. **Income per Common Share**			
18. Before changes in accounting principles	$1.68	$1.43	$1.21
19. Effects of changes in accounting principles	(.01)	(.17)	—
20. **Net Income per Common Share**	$ 1.67	$ 1.26	$ 1.21
21. **Average Common Shares Outstanding**	1,302	1,317	1,333

Minor modifications have been made to the format for presentation purposes. Items have been numbered for reference.

amounts of inventories or transactions with suppliers. The following sections examine accounting for activities that affect gross profit.

Revenue Recognition

Objective 3
Determine when a company should recognize revenues.

Operating revenues result from sales of goods and services to customers. For most companies, sales are linked closely with accounts receivable because sales are made on credit. Therefore, the recognition of revenue affects the recognition of accounts receivable.

Coca-Cola reported net operating revenues of $13,957 million in 1993 (item 1 in Exhibit 13-1). For most companies, revenues are recognized at the time title (ownership) to goods or services is transferred to customers. Title to most goods passes to the buyer at the time of delivery or at the time goods are shipped to the buyer. In many retail companies, revenue is recognized at the time of sale, when customers take possession of goods. Service companies normally recognize revenue at the time services are performed. Manufacturing companies and some merchandising companies often ship goods to customers. A company may assume responsibility for the goods until they are received by the customer. Alternatively, a company may assume responsibility for the goods only until they are transferred to a freight company. The freight term associated with these shipments is **free on board (FOB)**. When goods are shipped **FOB destination**, title to the goods is transferred to the customer when goods are delivered (i.e., the seller pays the shipping costs). When goods are shipped **FOB shipping point**, title passes to the customer when goods are picked up by the shipper (i.e., the buyer pays the shipping costs).

As a general rule, revenue should be recognized when four criteria have been met:

1. a company has completed most of the activities necessary to produce and sell goods or services,
2. the costs associated with the goods or services have been incurred or can be measured reasonably,
3. the amount of revenue can be measured objectively, and
4. the collection of cash from the purchaser is reasonably assured.

A company usually has earned revenue at the time services are performed or goods are transferred. For example, Georgia–Pacific disclosed its revenue recognition policy in its 1993 annual report as follows:

> The Corporation recognizes revenue when title to the goods sold passes to the buyer, which is generally at the time of shipment.

Digital Equipment Corporation reported revenue recognition for sales and services in its 1993 annual report as:

> Revenues from product sales are recognized at the time the product is shipped. Services and other revenues are recognized ratably over the contractual period or as the services are performed.

Certain types of revenues result in recognition problems because the activities that produce the revenues occur over more than one fiscal period. The next section considers long-term contracts, which are a common example of this recognition problem.

Revenue Recognition for Long-Term Contracts. Revenue recognition sometimes requires a company to estimate when revenue has been earned. Revenues earned from long-term contracts often are recognized in proportion to the passage of time. For example, if a company contracts to provide maintenance services over a three-year period for $75,000, it might recognize $25,000 per year. This recognition assumes that approximately the same amount of service is provided each year.

Long-term construction contracts can pose special recognition problems, depending on contract terms. For example, Boeing reported the following revenue recognition policies in its 1993 annual report:

Sales under commercial programs and U.S. Government and foreign military fixed-price contracts are generally recorded as deliveries are made. For certain fixed-price contracts that require substantial performance over a long time period before deliveries begin, sales are recorded based upon attainment of scheduled performance milestones. Sales under cost-reimbursement contracts are recorded as costs are incurred and fees are earned.

The *percentage of completion method* **for long-term contracts recognizes revenues and expenses for long-term contracts in proportion to the amount of the contract completed each fiscal period.** To illustrate, assume Asphalt Co. signs a contract on March 1, 1996, with a local government to resurface its streets. The contract calls for payment of $12 million over 3 years, the expected period to complete the project. At the start of the project, Asphalt expects to earn net income of $2 million from the contract. During 1996, the company incurs $2 million in costs and expects to incur an additional $8 million to complete the project. Therefore, the company assumes that 20% ($2 million/$10 million) of the contract has been completed and recognizes 20% of total contract revenue in 1996:

Revenue recognized in 1996 (20% × $12,000,000)	$2,400,000
Expenses recognized in 1996	2,000,000
Net income in 1996	$ 400,000

A variety of methods are used in practice to estimate the proportion of a contract that has been completed.

If Asphalt incurs more costs than expected, it will earn less profit, assuming the contract does not permit the added costs to be transferred to the government. If costs cannot be transferred, the contract is a fixed-cost contract. If costs can be transferred, it is a cost-reimbursement contract. Assume Asphalt incurred $4 million of costs in 1997. The company revises its estimates and now expects to incur an additional $4.5 million after 1997 to complete the fixed-cost contract. Thus, as of the end of 1997, it expects to incur total costs of $10.5 million and earn a profit of $1.5 million. For 1996 and 1997, the company has incurred a total of 57% of the expected costs ($6.0 million/$10.5 million). Therefore, it has earned revenues for the two years of $6,840,000 (57% × $12 million). Of this amount, $2,400,000 was reported as revenue in 1996. Consequently, revenue and net income for 1997 would be:

Revenue recognized in 1997 ($6,840,000 − $2,400,000)	$4,440,000
Expenses recognized in 1997	4,000,000
Net income in 1997	$ 440,000

The percentage of completion method requires a company to estimate revenues earned each period from a long-term contract. It provides a better matching of revenues and expenses, however, than waiting until the project is completed. **The** *completed contracts method* **recognizes revenue when a long-term contract is completed.** This method should be used only when considerable uncertainty exists about the profits being earned from a project or about the payments being collected.

Long-term contracts provide one example of the need for special revenue recognition methods. A variety of revenue recognition methods are used in different industries because of variations in the earnings process. The following section considers some of these methods.

Other Revenue Recognition Methods. Specific methods of revenue recognition vary across companies, depending on the types of products sold. Following are examples of revenue recognition policies disclosed by companies in various industries in their recent annual reports.

Delta Air Lines:
> Passenger and cargo revenues are recorded as revenue when the transportation is provided. The value of unused passenger tickets is included in current liabilities as air traffic liability.

Walt Disney:
> Revenues from theatrical distribution of motion pictures are recognized when motion pictures are exhibited. Television licensing revenues are generally recorded when the program material is available for telecasting by the licensee and when certain other conditions are met. Revenues from video sales are recognized on the date the video units are made widely available for sale by retailers.
>
> Revenues from participants/sponsors at the theme parks are generally recorded over the period of the applicable agreements commencing with the opening of the attraction.

Marvel Entertainment Group, Inc.:
> Sales of comics are recorded on a date which approximates the retail on sale date. Sales of sports picture cards and confectionary products are recorded upon shipment of products. Sales made on a returnable basis are recorded net of a provision for anticipated returns. Subscription revenues are generally collected in advance for a one year subscription. These revenues are deferred and recognized as income on a pro-rata basis over an annual period. Income from licensing of characters owned by the Company and publication rights is recorded at the time collection is assured.

Revenue recognition methods attempt to estimate the revenue earned during a fiscal period. Recognition also requires estimation of discounts and returns that are expected to reduce the revenue earned in a fiscal period. In addition, these recognition issues affect the amount of accounts receivable reported by a company, considered in the next section.

Accounts Receivable

Objective 4
Determine the amount of accounts receivable a company should report.

Accounts receivable are amounts owed an organization by customers. This account links sales revenue with cash received from customers. A company increases the account when it sells goods or services on credit and decreases it when cash is received from the customer. The balance of this account identifies the amount a company expects to collect from its customers.

Sales Discounts and Returns. Revenues are reported on the income statement net of discounts and net of expected returns. Discounts result when a company sells goods at reduced prices. Prices may be discounted for a variety of reasons. Customers who purchase large quantities of goods often receive discounts from the list price. Also, discounts often are provided as an incentive for early payment of accounts receivable by customers (considered in this section). The amount a company expects to receive from a sale is the amount that should be recorded as revenue.

For example, assume Crunchy Foods Co. sells goods priced at $25,000 to a customer with terms 2/10, n/30 (2% discount if paid in 10 days, net amount due in 30 days, as discussed in chapter 9). The amount of sales revenue and accounts receivable associated with this transaction should be reported as $24,500, net of the discount of $500 ($25,000 × .02). The amount recognized for revenue is the amount Crunchy Foods expects to receive from its customer. The sale and receipt of cash would affect the company's accounts as follows:

Assets =		Liabilities + Equity		+ (Revenues − Expenses)	
Accounts Receivable	24,500			Sales Revenue	24,500
Cash	24,500				
Accounts Receivable	− 24,500		0		0

In practice, many companies recognize receivables and sales revenues at their gross amount, $25,000 in this example. Then, if a customer pays within the discount period, they reduce the amount of revenue through a contra-account, such as SALES DISCOUNTS:

Assets =		Liabilities + Equity		+ (Revenues − Expenses)	
Accounts Receivable	25,000			Sales Revenue	25,000
Cash	24,500			Sales Discounts	− 500
Accounts Receivable	− 25,000				

Sales discounts are subtracted from sales revenues in reporting net operating revenues on the income statement.

Companies also should subtract expected sales returns in computing net operating revenues. Some companies sell merchandise with the expectation that some of the merchandise will be returned from the buyer. For example, publishing companies, such as Marvel Entertainment Group, Inc., often allow returns of books and magazines sold to retail stores. If a retailer does not sell all of its supply of a magazine for the current month, it can return them to the publisher for credit against the amount it owes. College bookstores often return unsold textbooks if they have an oversupply.

As an illustration, assume Textbook Publishing Co. sold $5 million of books during fiscal 1997. It recorded sales revenue and accounts receivable for the $5 million. From past experience, the company estimates that 15% of sales will result in returns in 1998. Therefore, Textbook Publishing should record an adjustment to its revenues and receivables at the end of the 1997 period. The effect of these transactions on the company's accounts would be:

Assets =		Liabilities + Equity	+ (Revenues − Expenses)	
Accounts Receivable	5,000,000		Sales Revenue	5,000,000
Allowance for Returns	−750,000		Sales Returns	−750,000

Both ALLOWANCE FOR RETURNS and SALES RETURNS are contra-accounts. Textbook Publishing would report net accounts receivable and net sales revenue of $4,250,000 on its 1997 financial statements.

Most companies that sell goods and services on credit expect a portion of their accounts to become uncollectible. Estimated uncollectible accounts also affect the amount of accounts receivable reported for a fiscal period as discussed below.

Uncollectible Accounts. Companies sell goods and services in one fiscal period that prove to be uncollectible in another period. To match the loss associated with the uncollectible accounts with the sales that resulted in the uncollectible accounts, companies should estimate the amount of losses they expect from uncollectible accounts at the end of their fiscal years. For example, assume Crunchy Foods has $2 million of accounts receivable outstanding at the end of 1996. It estimates that approximately 3% of these accounts will not be paid by customers. Though the company will make a reasonable effort to collect from its customers, some accounts will not be collectible. The amount estimated to be uncollectible should be recorded as follows:

Assets =		Liabilities + Equity	+ (Revenues − Expenses)	
Allowance for Doubtful Accounts	−60,000		Doubtful Accounts Expense	−60,000

The *ALLOWANCE FOR DOUBTFUL ACCOUNTS* **identifies the amount of accounts receivable a company's management expects is likely to become uncollectible.** The allowance account is a contra-asset account that is subtracted from ACCOUNTS RECEIVABLE. Thus, the accounts receivable amount reported on the balance sheet is shown net of the allowance.

Learning Note Companies refer to the allowance for doubtful accounts by a variety of names, including allowance for uncollectible accounts, allowance for bad debts, or simply allowances.

Once an account is determined to be uncollectible, it is eliminated and the amount is subtracted from a company's accounts receivable balance. For example, assume Crunchy Foods determines on March 12, 1997, that a receivable for the Belly Up Corp. is uncollectible. Belly Up's account balance is $40,000. Crunchy Foods would eliminate the account as follows:

Assets =		Liabilities + Equity	+ (Revenues – Expenses)
Accounts Receivable	– 40,000		
Allowance for Doubtful Accounts	40,000	0	0

An additional expense is not recognized on March 12 because it was part of the doubtful accounts expense estimated on December 31, 1996.

Companies estimate the amount of uncollectible accounts from prior experiences. They may examine current overdue accounts, and they may consider current economic conditions in forming their expectations. Uncollectible accounts increase for most companies during recessionary periods.

A company's credit policies affect the amount of uncollectible accounts it expects. A company can increase its sales by accepting customers with higher credit risks. More uncollectible accounts are likely to result from these sales, however. Therefore, doubtful accounts expense is reported as part of selling expenses because it is a cost of selling goods and services to customers who are unable to pay for their purchases.

Companies report accounts receivable on their balance sheets net of the allowance for returns and the allowance for doubtful accounts. For example, Coca-Cola reported in its 1993 annual report (in millions):

	1993	1992
Trade accounts receivable, less allowances of $39 in 1993 and $33 in 1992	$1,210	$1,055

SELF-STUDY PROBLEM 13-1

Freddy Stair Co. owns and operates dance studios. The company contracts with customers for dance lessons. Customers may pay for their lessons in one of three ways. They may pay $50 at the end of each month. They may pay $550 in advance for the coming year. Or, they may pay $350 at the end of each 6 months.

The following amounts resulted from operating activities for 1997:

Fees collected from customers paying monthly	$120,000
Fees collected from customers paying in advance	55,000
Fees collected from customers paying semiannually	70,000
Total fees collected	$245,000

Of the fees collected in advance, $20,000 are for lessons to be provided in 1998. Customers paying semiannually owe $40,000 for lessons received but not yet paid. Approximately 6% of these fees are likely to be uncollectible. The company recognized revenues of $285,000 in 1997 and reported net accounts receivable of $40,000.

Required

Determine the amount of revenues and accounts receivable Freddy Stair should have reported for 1997.

The solution to Self-Study Problem 13-1 appears at the end of the chapter.

COST OF GOODS SOLD AND INVENTORIES

To generate revenues, merchandising and manufacturing companies must acquire or produce inventories. Inventories are assets reported on the balance sheet. Once goods are sold, inventories are reduced and cost of goods sold is recognized on the income statement. Therefore, the amount reported for inventories on the balance sheet affects the amount reported for cost of goods sold on the income statement. Accounting for cost of goods sold and inventories involves measurement and reporting issues. Reporting rules identify how costs are reported on the income statement and balance sheet. Measurement issues determine how the costs are computed. The following sections examine reporting and measurement issues associated with cost of goods sold and inventories.

Reporting Cost of Goods Sold and Inventory

Objective 5
Determine the amount of inventories for merchandising and manufacturing companies.

Inventories are goods a company intends to sell. Cost of goods sold is the cost of goods a company actually has sold during a fiscal period. Coca-Cola reported cost of goods sold of $5,160 million in 1993 (item 2 of Exhibit 13-1). Inventories for merchandising companies consist primarily of merchandise for sale. Inventories for manufacturing companies include goods for sale, goods at intermediate stages of production, and materials and supplies that will be used in the production process. These inventories are referred to as finished goods, work in process, and raw materials. For example, a note to Coca-Cola's 1993 balance sheet provided the following information.

Inventories consist of the following (in millions):

December 31	**1993**	**1992**
Raw materials and supplies	$ 689	$ 620
Work in process	4	23
Finished goods	356	376
	$1,049	$1,019

The totals from this note are the amounts reported as inventories on the company's balance sheet.

The following sections examine reporting of cost of goods sold and inventories for merchandising and manufacturing companies.

Merchandising Companies. Accounting for merchandise inventory transactions is fairly simple. A company increases the balance of MERCHANDISE INVENTORY when inventory is purchased. It decreases the account balance when inventory is sold. For example, assume Crunchy Foods purchased $50,000 of inventory on May 4, 1996, and sold $20,000 on May 6. These transactions would affect the company's accounts as follows:

Assets =	Liabilities + Equity	+ (Revenues − Expenses)
Merchandise Inventory 50,000	Accounts Payable 50,000	
Merchandise Inventory − 20,000		Cost of Goods Sold − 20,000

The cost of inventory includes the amount paid for the goods themselves plus shipping costs paid by the buyer. Goods in transit between the seller and buyer should be included as part of the buyer's inventory at year end if title to the goods and the risk of ownership have been transferred to the buyer at that time.

In addition to recording purchase and sales transactions that affect financial statements, companies maintain detailed records that describe the inventory item and the quantity purchased and sold. These records provide information for determining the number of units on hand, demand for each item, and when to reorder. These records also are used for control purposes. Periodically, physical counts of inventory are verified against inventory records to determine if theft or misplacement has occurred and to check the accuracy of the accounting records.

Manufacturing Companies. Accounting for inventory transactions of a manufacturing company is more complex. The production process can be viewed as involving three stages. Exhibit 13-2 illustrates these stages for Plastic Container Corporation for 1996.

Exhibit 13-2   Inventories for a Manufacturing Company

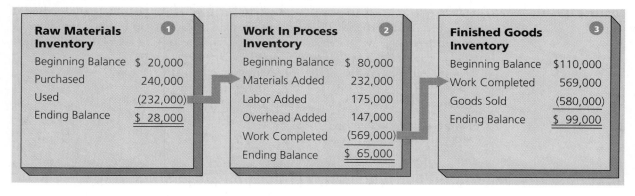

In stage 1, Plastic Container had $20,000 of raw materials available at the beginning of 1996. *Raw materials* **are the physical ingredients of a product, such as chemicals, metals, wood, or components acquired from a supplier.** For example, Plastic Container purchases plastic pellets as raw materials. It heats these pellets and molds them into containers in its production process. Plastic Container purchased $240,000 of raw materials in 1996 and placed $232,000 of the raw materials into production. Therefore, the balance at the end of 1996 was $28,000, as shown in Exhibit 13-2.

These transactions affected the company's accounts as follows:

Assets =		Liabilities + Equity		+ (Revenues − Expenses)
Raw Materials	240,000	Accounts Payable	240,000	
Raw Materials	−232,000			
Work in Process	232,000		0	0

RAW MATERIALS and WORK IN PROCESS are inventory accounts. *Work in process* **consists of goods currently in the process of being manufactured.**

In stage 2, the company had $80,000 of goods already in the production process at the beginning of 1996. These goods were partially completed before 1996 but required additional materials and processing during 1996. Raw materials from stage 1 were added to production during 1996, as previously shown. In addition, $175,000 of **wages and benefits of employees who worked directly in the manufacturing process** were added to the cost of production. These costs are *direct labor* costs. Also, $147,000 of overhead costs were used in the production process. *Overhead* **costs include the costs of supplies ($25,000), utilities ($30,000), depreciation of plant assets ($70,000), and indirect labor ($22,000) used in the production process.** *Indirect labor* **includes the cost of wages and benefits paid to maintenance and supervisory employees who are associated with the production process.** All of these costs were added to work in process inventory during the year. The $569,000 cost of goods completed during 1996 was transferred to FINISHED GOODS INVENTORY. *Finished goods* **are products awaiting sale.** These transactions would affect Plastic Container's accounts as follows:

Assets =		Liabilities + Equity		+ (Revenues − Expenses)
Work in Process	175,000	Wages Payable and Deferred Benefits	175,000	
Work in Process	147,000	Utilities Payable	30,000	
Supplies	− 25,000	Wages Payable and		
Accumulated		Deferred Benefits	22,000	
Depreciation	− 70,000			
Finished Goods	569,000			
Work in Process	− 569,000		0	0

In stage 3, Plastic Container had $110,000 of FINISHED GOODS INVENTORY at the beginning of 1996. Goods completed during 1996 were transferred to finished goods as shown above. The cost of goods sold during 1996 decreased the finished goods inventory account:

Assets =		Liabilities + Equity	+ (Revenues − Expenses)
Finished Goods	− 580,000		Cost of Goods Sold 580,000

Thus, the final step in the process is recognition of COST OF GOODS SOLD.

Observe that companies do not recognize expenses for materials, labor, and overhead used in the production process until goods are sold. These costs become part of the company's inventories until the finished goods are sold. At the time of sale, these product costs are transferred to expense. This accrual accounting procedure matches expenses with revenues in the period in which revenues are recognized. Product costs of goods that are unsold at year end are reported on the balance sheet as part of a company's inventories.

Exhibit 13-3 illustrates the accounting process associated with inventory for merchandising and manufacturing companies.

Exhibit 13-3   A Summary of Inventory Transactions

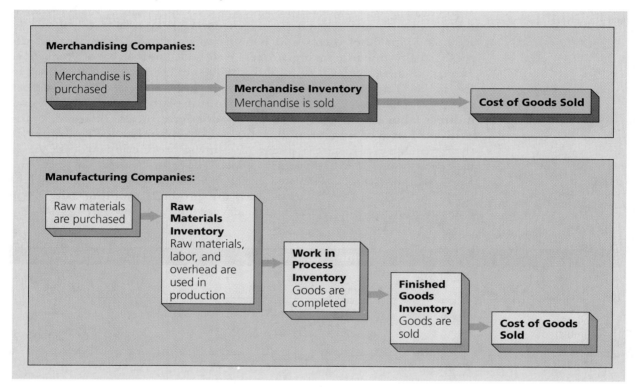

Companies must measure the costs associated with inventory transactions to determine the amount of inventories and cost of goods sold to record for individual transactions and the amount to report on financial statements. The following section examines inventory measurement.

Inventory Measurement

Objective 6
Explain the effect of inventory measurement methods on cost of goods sold and inventory.

In addition to the reporting of inventories discussed in the previous section, measurement of inventories is an important issue for many companies. Estimation issues arise because costs of merchandise, raw materials, labor, utilities, supplies, and other resources change over time. For example, Fair Deal Automobile Co. is a retailer of new cars. In March 1997, Fair Deal purchased six X-14 Flaming Arrows from the manufacturer, all with standard equipment and costing $12,000 each. In May 1997, the company purchased five more X-14 Flaming Arrows with the same equipment. But this time, the cost of the cars to Fair Deal had risen to $12,800 each. In June 1997, Fair Deal sold three of the cars. Should it recognize cost of goods sold of $12,000 or $12,800 for each car?

Fair Deal should have no difficulty in deciding which cost to recognize. Each car was identified in the company's inventory records by the vehicle identification number. Even if all of the cars were the same color, the company must specifically identify which cars were sold and match the cost with sales revenue. Therefore, if it sold two cars that cost $12,000 and one that cost $12,800, it would recognize cost of goods sold and a reduction in inventory of $36,800 in June.

Now consider the example of Fresh Line Markets. The company owns and operates retail grocery stores. It buys canned goods in bulk to take advantage of quantity discounts. In March 1997, the company purchased 100 cases of Caribou Canned Corn for $4.80 a case. Each case contained 24 cans at a cost of $.20 per can. In May 1997, Fresh Line purchased 100 additional cases of corn at $5.28 a case, a cost of $.22 a can. In June 1997, Mrs. Doris Daye purchased 2 cans of Caribou Canned Corn. Should the company record cost of goods sold for the corn at $.20 or $.22 a can?

The First-In First-Out Method. It is unlikely that Fresh Line can distinguish among cans of corn. Even if it could, the cost of identifying each unit would be prohibitive. Therefore, Fresh Line estimates the cost of goods sold. **It assumes those units of inventory acquired first are sold first, known as the** *first-in first-out method,* **or** *FIFO.* For example, assume that the company's inventory contained 30 cases of Caribou Canned Corn at the beginning of March. Each case cost $4.32. It purchased 100 cases at $4.80 in March and 100 cases at $5.28 in May. For the three months ended May 31, the company sold 190 cases of the corn. What would cost of goods sold be for the period and how much inventory would be reported at the end of the period?

Exhibit 13-4 illustrates the assumed flow of merchandise and costs for March through May using the FIFO method.

Exhibit 13-4   FIFO Inventory Flow Assumption

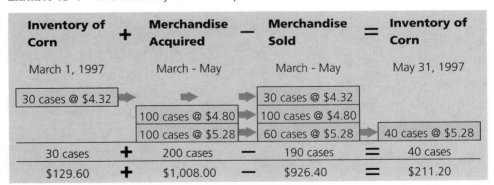

Using the FIFO assumption, Fresh Line would recognize cost of goods sold using the cost of the merchandise acquired first. Therefore, it would recognize 30 cases from beginning inventory plus 100 cases acquired in March and 60 cases acquired in May as being sold. The 40 remaining cases acquired in May would be the company's ending inventory of corn. Cost of goods sold for the three-month period would be $926.40. The inventory balance at the end of May would be $211.20.

Two other inventory estimation methods are common. **One assumes the last units acquired are sold first, the** *last-in first-out method*, **or** *LIFO*. **The other assumes an average cost of units available during a period as the cost of units sold, the** *weighted average method*.

The Last-In First-Out Method. Exhibit 13-5 illustrates the LIFO method for Fresh Line, using the same data as Exhibit 13-4.

Exhibit 13-5   LIFO Inventory Flow Assumption

Inventory of Corn	+	Merchandise Acquired	−	Merchandise Sold	=	Inventory of Corn
March 1, 1997		March - May		March - May		May 31, 1997
30 cases @ $4.32						30 cases @ $4.32
		100 cases @ $4.80		90 cases @ $4.80		10 cases @ $4.80
		100 cases @ $5.28		100 cases @ $5.28		
30 cases	+	200 cases	−	190 cases	=	40 cases
$129.60	+	$1,008.00	−	$960.00	=	$177.60

Using the LIFO assumption, Fresh Line would recognize cost of goods sold using the cost of the merchandise acquired last. Therefore, it would recognize 100 cases acquired in May plus 90 cases acquired in March as being sold. The 10 remaining cases acquired in March plus the 30 cases of beginning inventory would be the company's ending inventory of corn. Cost of goods sold for the three-month period would be $960.00. The inventory balance at the end of May would be $177.60.

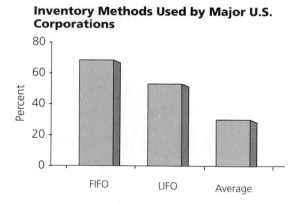

Inventory Methods Used by Major U.S. Corporations

(Data source: AICPA, Accounting Trends and Techniques, 1994)

Fresh Line might use LIFO if it stacks inventory in its warehouse so the most recent cases acquired are placed on display and sold first. This inventory management practice is not likely because the older inventory would eventually spoil. The company is more likely to sell the oldest units first. Nevertheless, the company might use LIFO to measure cost of goods sold. **Estimation methods, such as FIFO and LIFO, are used to measure the amount of inventory reported on a company's balance sheet and the amount of cost of goods sold reported on its income statement. They do not necessarily correspond with the physical flow of goods through a company.** Most companies will sell their oldest goods first to avoid spoilage and obsolescence. They may use LIFO to account for these goods because of tax advantages.

Because the cost of canned corn rose from March to May, cost of goods sold was higher using LIFO than using FIFO. LIFO matches the most recent cost of goods acquired with sales revenue for a fiscal period. FIFO matches the earliest cost of goods in inventory with sales revenue for a fiscal period. In inflationary periods, LIFO often results in higher cost of goods sold and lower net income than FIFO. At the same time, LIFO normally results in lower inventory balances than FIFO:

	FIFO	LIFO
Inventory costs matched with sales on income statement	Earliest Acquired	Most Recently Acquired
Inventory costs remaining on balance sheet	Most Recently Acquired	Earliest Acquired

When used to measure taxable income, LIFO also reduces the amount of income subject to taxation for many companies. Therefore, for these companies, LIFO reduces cash outflow for income taxes. Federal tax regulations require that companies choosing to use LIFO for tax purposes also use that method for financial reporting purposes. Thus, many companies use LIFO in preparing their financial statements so they can use it in preparing their tax returns.

If costs were to decline during a fiscal period, the relationship between FIFO and LIFO would be reversed. LIFO would produce higher net income and lower cash flows because of higher taxes. Therefore, companies whose costs are likely to decline over time normally would not use LIFO. For example, the cost of computer components has declined steadily since the early 1980s. Computer manufacturers seldom use LIFO.

In addition, LIFO can result in higher taxable income if a company sells more inventory than it acquires during a period. For example, assume Plastic Container Corp. uses the LIFO method. At the beginning of 1996, it had an inventory of raw materials consisting of 3,000 tons at a LIFO cost of $400 per ton. During 1996, the company acquired an additional 8,000 tons at a current cost of $700 per ton. Thus, it has 11,000 tons of raw material available for use. If it used 10,000 tons of the raw material to produce goods sold during 1996, the company would be forced to recognize 2,000 tons of materials at a much lower cost of $400 per ton as part of cost of goods sold:

Beginning inventory	3,000 tons	(at $400 per ton)
Inventory purchased	8,000 tons	(at $700 per ton)
Inventory available	11,000 tons	

Inventory sold using LIFO:

	8,000 tons	(at $700 per ton)
	2,000 tons	(at $400 per ton)
Total inventory sold	10,000 tons	

Profits and taxable income will be higher than if the cost of materials used during the current period were the cost of materials purchased during the period. If the company had been using FIFO, the cost of its beginning inventory would have been much closer to the current price of $700 per ton. LIFO results in inventory costs that often are much lower than current costs. Therefore, the amount reported on the balance sheet for inventory often understates the current cost of inventory when LIFO is used. Companies that cannot control their inventory levels may not find LIFO to be a suitable method if they risk dipping into early inventory layers.

Most countries other than the U.S. do not permit the use of LIFO, and there are no tax advantages for the use of LIFO in these countries. Therefore, multinational firms, including large U.S. corporations, normally use FIFO for inventories held in foreign countries even if they use LIFO for similar inventories held in the U.S. Companies can use LIFO for some inventories and FIFO and/or weighted average for others.

Weighted Average Method. A third commonly used inventory estimation method is the weighted average method. As an illustration, Fresh Line's weighted average inventory cost for March through May would be:

Beginning inventory	30 cases × $4.32 =	$ 129.60
Inventory acquired	100 cases × $4.80 =	480.00
	100 cases × $5.28 =	528.00
Total inventory available	230 cases	1,137.60
Average cost per case	$1,137.60/230 =	$4.9461
Cost of goods sold	190 × $4.9461 =	$939.76
Ending inventory	40 × $4.9461 =	$197.84

The average cost method produces cost of goods sold and ending inventory amounts between those produced by FIFO and LIFO.

Companies use inventory estimation methods to determine the cost associated with inventories and cost of goods sold. In addition, GAAP require companies to compare the costs determined from the estimation methods with the current market cost of inventories. If current market costs are below estimated costs, inventories must be written down to current market. The following section describes this process.

Learning Note   A variety of specialized inventory measurement rules have been devised for companies in different industries. Dollar value LIFO, retail LIFO, and retail dollar value LIFO are examples of specialized methods. Though the mechanics of calculating inventory costs differ, the concepts underlying these methods are similar to those presented above.

Lower of Cost or Market Inventory Valuation. GAAP require inventory to be reported at the **lower of cost or market**. The measurement of inventories is complex because the market values of inventories are not always readily determinable. GAAP specify a procedure for computing market value that considers current replacement cost and the amount a company expects to receive from selling inventory less the profit it expects to earn from the inventory. Once market value is determined, the cost of inventory is compared with the market value. If the market value is less than cost, the inventory is written down to market.

For example, assume Plastic Container has inventory costing $100,000 at the end of its 1997 fiscal year. The current market value of the inventory is determined to be $90,000. The inventory would be adjusted as follows:

Assets =		Liabilities + Equity	+ (Revenues − Expenses)	
Inventory	− 10,000		Loss from Revaluation of Inventory	− 10,000

The loss is recognized in the period in which the inventory declines in value. An excess of market value over cost is not recognized through a valuation adjustment, another example of the application of conservatism to accounting measurement.

Comparing Inventory Costs Among Companies

GAAP require companies to disclose the methods used to measure inventories and cost of goods sold. Also, GAAP require those that use LIFO to disclose the effect of using this method on reported inventory value. For example, Coca-Cola disclosed in its 1993 annual report:

> Inventories are valued at the lower of cost or market. In general, cost is determined on the basis of average cost or first-in, first-out methods. However, for certain inventories, cost is determined on the last-in, first-out (LIFO) method. The excess of current costs over LIFO stated values amounted to approximately $9 million and $24 million at December 31, 1993 and 1992, respectively.

The current cost of Coca-Cola's inventory at the end of 1993 would have been approximately equal to its FIFO cost because FIFO results in the most recent inventory costs' being reported on the balance sheet. Thus, if Coca-Cola's LIFO inventories had been reported on a FIFO basis, its cost of goods sold would have been $15 million more in 1993 than the amount reported on its income statement. Beginning inventory would have been $24 million larger than reported, while ending inventory would have been $9 million larger. Therefore, on a FIFO basis the company would have reported $15 million more cost of goods sold ($24 − $9) than the amount reported using LIFO. Decision makers can use this information in comparing the costs of companies using the LIFO method with those using FIFO. For example, Coca-Cola's income could be analyzed for comparison with companies using FIFO by increasing its cost of goods sold by $15 million and then recomputing other income statement amounts.

FIFO, LIFO, and average estimation methods are used by merchandising and manufacturing companies. Manufacturing companies use these methods for raw materials, work in process, and finished goods inventories. Modern manufacturing methods have eliminated large amounts of inventories for some companies. Materials are obtained from suppliers as they are needed, "just-in-time" for inclusion in the manufacturing process. Work in process flows at a rate sufficient to meet orders without accumulating large amounts of work in process or finished goods inventory. Companies using just-in-time manufacturing procedures will report relatively small amounts of inventory. These companies expense almost all manufacturing costs each period as part of cost of goods sold. Therefore, the choice of inventory estimation methods is less important for these companies than for those with large inventories.

SELF-STUDY PROBLEM 13-2

Fashion Mart is a clothing retailer. At the end of 1997, the company reported $8 million of inventory on a FIFO basis. During 1998, the company acquired $30 million of inventory. It reported $10 million of inventory at the end of 1998 on a FIFO basis. If the company had used LIFO, it would have reported $6 million of inventory at the end of 1997 and $7 million at the end of 1998. The company's income tax rate is 30%.

Required

(a) What would the difference have been in Fashion Mart's net income and cash flow from operating activities if it had used LIFO instead of FIFO in 1998? (b) What factors should the company consider in deciding which inventory estimation method to use?

The solution to Self-Study Problem 13-2 appears at the end of the chapter.

OTHER ITEMS AFFECTING NET INCOME

Product revenues result from the sale of goods and services. Product costs result from the acquisition and production of goods and services. Gross profit is the excess of product revenues over product costs associated with the goods and services sold during a period. Items reported on the income statement after gross profit include operating expenses, financial revenues and expenses, and special items. When all of these items are included, the income statement would report the information shown at the top of the next page.

The following sections consider information reported after gross profit on the income statement.

Operating Income

Objective 7
Explain the reporting and measurement of operating expenses.

Operating income **is gross profit minus other operating expenses. Operating expenses include nonproduction costs associated with operating activities during a fiscal period.** These costs are expensed in the period in which they occur. For most companies, most of these costs are associated with

marketing, research and development, and general administrative activities. Marketing costs include advertising, direct selling, and distribution costs. Depreciation of assets used primarily in selling activities and salaries and commissions of the sales force are included in this category. Administrative costs include depreciation of plant assets used in administrative activities, such as office buildings and equipment, and management and office worker salaries. Costs associated with research and development, distribution, marketing, servicing, and general management activities are expensed during the period in which they occur.

Coca-Cola reported selling, administrative, and general expenses of $5,695 million and operating income of $3,102 million in 1993 (items 4 and 5 in Exhibit 13-1):

Year Ended December 31 (in millions)	1993	1992	1991
1. **Net Operating Revenues**	$13,957	$13,074	$11,572
2. Cost of goods sold	5,160	5,055	4,649
3. **Gross Profit**	8,797	8,019	6,923
4. Selling, administrative, and general expenses	5,695	5,249	4,604
5. **Operating Income**	3,102	2,770	2,319

Corporations often summarize their operating expenses as one line on the income statement (item 4). Some operating expenses are reported separately on the income statement, however. For example, GAAP require companies to report separately any unusual or infrequent revenues or expenses that are material in amount. Certain other expenses that are important for a company's operating activities, such as research and development expenses and depreciation expenses, also must be disclosed. They may be reported separately on the income statement or disclosed in notes to the financial statements.

Other Revenues and Expenses

Objective 8
Explain the reporting and measurement of other revenues and expenses.

Other revenues include interest and other income from short-term and long-term investments. Other expenses include interest on short-term and long-term debt. These amounts are accrued. Thus, the amount of revenue reported is the amount earned, regardless of whether cash was received. The amount of expense reported is the amount of liability incurred during the current fiscal year, regardless of whether cash has been paid.

As shown in Exhibit 13-1, Coca-Cola reported interest income of $144 million (item 6) and interest expense of $168 million (item 7) in 1993. Also, it reported equity income of $91 million (item 8) and other income of $16 million (item 9):

Year Ended December 31	1993	1992	1991
5. **Operating Income**	3,102	2,770	2,319
6. Interest income	144	164	175
7. Interest expense	(168)	(171)	(192)
8. Equity income	91	65	40
9. Other income—net	16	(82)	41
10. **Income Before Income Taxes**	3,185	2,746	2,383

Equity income is revenue from investments accounted for using the equity method, as discussed in Chapter 11. These investments are those in corporations over which Coca-Cola has significant influence. Notes to Coca-Cola's statements reveal other income was primarily from the sale of property and investments in other companies.

Items 6 through 9 represent nonoperating revenues and expenses. They are not part of Coca-Cola's primary operating activities. Therefore, they are reported after operating income. The net effect of these items is included in income before income taxes (item 10). The next section examines income taxes.

Income Taxes

A company's income statement reports the amount of income taxes that a company would incur if its pretax income were all taxable in the current fiscal year. Thus, income taxes reported on the income statement are determined primarily by multiplying pretax income times the corporate tax rate. Coca-Cola reported income taxes of $997 million for 1993 on its income statement (item 11 in Exhibit 13-1):

Year Ended December 31	1993	1992	1991
10. **Income Before Income Taxes**	3,185	2,746	2,383
11. Income taxes	997	863	765
12. **Income Before Changes in Accounting Principles**	2,188	1,883	1,618

Objective 9
Explain the reporting and
measurement of income
taxes.

The effective tax rate used by Coca-Cola was 31.3% ($997/$3,185). The U.S. federal statutory rate for corporate income was 35% in 1993. A note to Coca-Cola's statements disclosed that the actual rate was 31.3% after considering the effect of state and foreign tax rates. For example, the company's earnings associated with operations in Puerto Rico were tax exempt.

The amount of income tax liability a company incurs in a fiscal period often differs from the income tax expense it reports on its income statement. This difference results in deferred taxes. Coca-Cola disclosed that its total income taxes for 1993 included:

Current taxes	$1,059 million
Deferred taxes	(62 million)
Total taxes	$997 million

Current taxes of $1,059 million were the company's tax liability for 1993 as computed on its tax return. The difference between the amount reported on the income statement ($997 million) and the amount of liability ($1,059 million) resulted from differences in the amounts of revenues and expenses reported for financial statement and tax purposes.

Coca-Cola's tax liability was greater than its reported tax expense in 1993 (in millions):

Assets =	Liabilities + Equity		+ (Revenues − Expenses)	
0	Income Taxes Payable	1,059	Income Tax Expense	−997
	Deferred Taxes	−62		

This transaction reduced the company's deferred tax liability by $62 million in 1993.

Deferred taxes are affected by timing differences between when revenues and expenses are recognized for financial statement purposes and for taxation purposes. Timing differences result when different accounting methods are used for computing depreciation, employee benefit, inventory, and other costs for financial reporting and for tax purposes.

Companies often use accounting methods for financial statements different from those used for tax purposes. The intent of financial statements is to present fairly a company's financial performance in conformity with GAAP. The intent of tax accounting is to report a company's taxable income. Companies will attempt to minimize their tax obligations by minimizing taxable income consistent with tax regulations. However, companies usually want to present the most positive net income allowable under GAAP. Since tax regulations and GAAP do not always coincide, the amount of income for financial reporting purposes often differs from that for tax purposes.

Companies select accounting methods to help them meet their financial and tax reporting objectives. For example, assume Plastic Container Corp. reported the following information for financial reporting and tax purposes in 1996:

	Income Statement	Tax Return
Revenues	$8,000,000	$8,000,000
Depreciation expense	(1,000,000)	(1,600,000)
Other expenses	(5,000,000)	(5,000,000)
Pretax income	2,000,000	1,400,000
Income taxes (34%)	(680,000)	(476,000)
Net income	$1,320,000	$ 924,000

The company used the straight-line method to compute depreciation on its income statement and used the accelerated method permitted by tax regulations on its tax return. The effect of the difference in accounting methods on the company's accounts would be:

Assets =	Liabilities + Equity		+ (Revenues − Expenses)	
0	Income Taxes Payable	476,000	Income Tax	
	Deferred Taxes	204,000	Expense	− 680,000

A tax difference may result either in an asset or a liability for deferred taxes. If a company's income tax liabilities (tax return calculations) have been less than its income tax expenses (financial statement calculations), it will report a deferred tax liability on its balance sheet. The liability represents expected future tax payments. If its income tax liabilities have been greater than its income tax expenses, it will report a deferred tax asset on its balance sheet. The asset represents expected future tax benefits through reduced tax payments.

The transaction for Plastic Container increased its deferred tax liability by $204,000. In future periods, the accelerated depreciation method used for tax purposes will produce less depreciation expense than the straight-line method used for financial reporting purposes. In those years, the amount of taxes computed on the tax return will be greater than the amount reported on the income statement. For example, assume that in 1997 Plastic Container computes income taxes on its income statement as $800,000 and income taxes on its tax return as $920,000. The effect of the computations on the company's accounts will be:

Assets =	Liabilities + Equity		+ (Revenues − Expenses)	
0	Income Taxes		Income Tax	
	Payable	920,000	Expense	− 800,000
	Deferred Taxes	− 120,000		

The company's deferred tax liability is reduced by $120,000 in 1997. This is the type of transaction reported by Coca-Cola in 1993 on the preceding page.

For many companies, the amount left after income taxes are deducted from pretax income is net income. For other companies, special items that affect net income are reported after income taxes. These items are considered in the following section.

Special Items

In addition to those revenues and expenses that are common to most corporations, special revenue and expense items are reported occasionally. These special items are reported separately from other items and require special disclosure. Separate reporting is required because they affect net income during the current fiscal period but will not affect net income of future periods. Therefore, decision makers should evaluate these items differently from those activities that are expected to affect income in future periods, especially when forecasting future income. Three types of special items may occur: discontinued operations, extraordinary items, and accounting changes.

Objective 10
Explain the reporting and measurement of discontinued operations, extraordinary items, and accounting changes.

Discontinued Operations. Continuing operations are those from which a company expects to derive income in future years. In contrast, *discontinued operations* **are those from which a company will no longer derive income.** Discontinued operations result when a company sells or closes a major component of its operations.

In 1993, Allied Products Corporation reported (in millions):

Discontinued operations (net of tax):	
Income from operations	$ 5.8
Gain on disposition of discontinued operations	5.5
Income from discontinued operations	$11.3

A gain or loss on discontinued operations is reported separately from income from continuing operations. Because the operations have been discontinued, the gain or loss from sale is a one-time event. Also, the income (or loss) from the operating activities of the discontinued operation will not reoccur in future years. Therefore, this income (or loss) is reported separately, as well. Thus, in evaluating Allied Product's earnings for 1993, decision makers should be aware that net income for the year included a one-time gain of $11.3 million that will not reoccur in future years.

A gain or loss from sale of a discontinued operation is reported on the income statement net of income taxes. Like the gain or loss, the income tax effect is a one-time event. If Allied Products had not had a pretax gain on its discontinued operations, it would not have incurred taxes on the gain.

Extraordinary Items. Gains and losses that are both unusual and infrequent are reported as *extraordinary items*. Unusual and infrequent are determined from the reference point of an individual company. What is unusual and infrequent for one company may not be unusual or infrequent for another. Extraordinary items are reported separately on the income statement (net of taxes) to call attention to their special nature. Like discontinued operations, a specific extraordinary item would not reoccur in future years.

As an example, Time Warner reported the following on its 1993 income statement (in millions):

Income before income taxes	$ 81
Income taxes	(245)
Income (loss) before extraordinary item	(164)
Extraordinary loss	(57)
Net income (loss)	$(221)

Time Warner's extraordinary loss resulted from retirement of debt. The tax effect of the extraordinary item was a reduction in taxes of $37 million. Other causes of extraordinary items are losses from natural disasters such as fires, termination of pension plans, and litigation.

U.S. GAAP are more restrictive in defining extraordinary items than GAAP in some other countries. Therefore, extraordinary items are more common and include a broader range of transactions in some foreign corporate reports.

Accounting Changes. *Accounting changes* **are the effects on income due to changes in the application of accounting principles from one fiscal period to another.** Companies report material effects on their income when adopting new accounting standards or changing from one accounting method to another. Coca-Cola reported on its 1993 income statement (in millions):

	1993
10. Income Before Income Taxes	$3,185
11. Income taxes	997
12. Income Before Changes in Accounting Principles	2,188
13. Effect of changes in accounting principles	(12)
14. Net Income	$2,176

An accounting change is reported as a separate item on the income statement, net of tax effects. This reporting requirement calls attention to the change. Consistency is an important attribute of accounting methods. A company should not change accounting methods except when justified by changes in the company's economic circumstances or when necessary to adopt a new accounting standard. A paragraph also is added to a company's audit report to bring attention to a change in an accounting method. This paragraph brings to the reader's attention the inconsistency between accounting methods used in prior years and those used in the current year.

A **change in accounting method** is different from a **change in accounting estimate**. Estimates are required by many transactions. For example, when a company records depreciation expense, it must estimate the remaining useful life of its plant assets. These estimates are likely to change from time to time as additional information becomes available to managers or as conditions change. Changes in estimates do not require special reporting or disclosure. Also, they normally do not have a cumulative effect. Rather, they are prospective. That is, the change considers the current and future periods, not the past.

For example, assume Plastic Container Corp. changed its estimate of the remaining useful life of some of its plant assets from 10 years to 8 years. If the book value of the assets was $100,000 per year, it would record $12,500, instead of $10,000, of depreciation expense each year over the remaining life of these assets. No adjustment would be made to depreciation reported in prior years.

A corporation's net income includes income from continuing operations and adjustments for special items. Net income is the amount earned by both preferred and common stockholders for a fiscal period. The next section considers the adjustment necessary to compute net income earned by common stockholders.

Minority Interest in Income

As discussed in Chapter 5, consolidated financial statements include a parent corporation and its subsidiaries. The parent may own less than 100% of some subsidiaries. For example, if a corporation owns 80% (the majority interest) of another corporation, the remaining 20% is minority interest. The consolidated income statement includes revenues and expenses of the parent and its subsidiaries as though they were one company. **The portion of subsidiary net income attributable to minority interest is reported on the income statement as** *minority interest in income of consolidated subsidiaries*.

As an illustration, Ford Motor Company reported the following information on its 1993 income statement:

(in millions) Year Ended December 31	**1993**
Income before income taxes	$4,003
Provision for income taxes	(1,350)
Minority interest in net income of subsidiaries	(124)
Net income	$2,529

Ford's income statement contained the same kind of revenue and expense items as Coca-Cola's except for the separate reporting of minority interest in income. Observe that the minority interest is subtracted from pretax income in computing net income. It is the portion of net income attributable to owners of subsidiaries rather than to owners of Ford.

Net income (loss) is the remainder after adjustments are made for minority interest in income and special items. It is a measure of the net result of operating activities during a fiscal period. It may not be the amount earned by common stockholders, however, because of dividends paid on preferred stock. The next section considers the computation of net income available for common stockholders.

Net Income Available for Common Stockholders

Dividends on preferred stock are deducted from net income to compute net income available for common stockholders. Preferred dividends represent a claim by preferred stockholders on a company's earnings. This claim almost always takes precedence over the claim of common stockholders. Coca-Cola reported preferred dividends of $1 million in 1991 and net income available for common of $1,617 million (items 15 and 16 in Exhibit 13-1):

Year Ended December 31	**1991**
14. **Net Income**	1,618
15. Preferred stock dividends	1
16. **Net Income Available to Common Share Owners**	1,617

Objective 11
Determine net income available for common shareholders.

Net income available for common is the net result of operating activities for a fiscal period after considering the effects of distributions to suppliers, employees, governments, creditors, and preferred stockholders. It is an accrual measure of the profit earned by common stockholders. It is an estimate of the increase in common stockholder value resulting from a company's performance during a fiscal period. This value also is expressed on a per share basis to provide a means for individual stockholders to estimate the effect of a company's performance on the portion of the company they own.

EARNINGS PER SHARE

Objective 12
Distinguish primary and fully diluted earnings per share.

GAAP require corporations to report net income on a per share basis. By multiplying earnings per share times the number of shares owned, a stockholder can identify the amount of profit attributable to the stockholders' investment. For many companies, this amount is net income divided by the average common shares outstanding during a fiscal period. A weighted average number of common shares is computed by considering the number of months shares of common stock were outstanding throughout a fiscal period. This average is used in the computation because profits are earned throughout the period. For example, assume Marble Slab Corp. had 2 million shares of common stock outstanding at the beginning of 1996. On October 1, 1996, the company issued an additional 1 million shares. The weighted average number of shares would be 2.25 million [(2 million × ¾) + (3 million × ¼)]. If Marble Slab had reported net income of $5 million for 1996, its earnings per share would have been $2.22 ($5 million/2.25 million).

Coca-Cola reported earnings per share of $1.67 in 1993 on 1,302 million average shares (items 20 and 21 in Exhibit 13-1):

Year Ended December 31	**1993**	**1992**	**1991**
17. **Income per Common Share**			
18. Before changes in accounting principles	$1.68	$1.43	$1.21
19. Effect of changes in accounting principles	(.01)	(.17)	—
20. **Net Income per Common Share**	$1.67	$1.26	$1.21
21. **Average Common Shares Outstanding**	1,302	1,317	1,333

Observe that when a company reports special items, such as changes in accounting principles, it must also report separately earnings per share for these items. Thus, in 1993 Coca-Cola reported earnings per share for continuing operations of $1.68 (item 18) and earnings per share for changes in accounting principles of $(.01) (item 19). Separate reporting also is required for extraordinary items and discontinued operations.

Earnings per share is complicated for some companies by the existence of convertible bonds, convertible preferred stock, stock options, or stock warrants. These instruments permit the owner to exchange them for shares of common stock. If an exchange is made, additional shares of common stock will be issued. These companies report two sets of earnings per share numbers, primary and fully diluted earnings per share. *Primary earnings per share* **is earnings per share attributable to common stock outstanding and to common stock equivalents.** *Fully diluted earnings per share* **is earnings per share attributable to common stock after considering all effects of exercising options and warrants, convertible debt, and convertible preferred stock that would reduce earnings per share.**

Instruments that are substantially the same as common stock are considered **common stock equivalents**. For example, stock options and warrants are common stock equivalents because they permit the owner to acquire common stock. Convertible debt and convertible preferred stock are common stock equivalents if they meet certain criteria. If the effect of exercising options and warrants or converting debt and preferred stock is to dilute (reduce) earnings per share, these instruments are referred to as dilutive securities. Primary earnings per share assumes dilutive common stock equivalents were converted to shares of common stock during a fiscal period. Fully diluted earnings per share assumes all dilutive securities were converted to shares of common stock during a period. It represents the minimum amount of earnings per share a company would report if options, warrants, and convertible securities were exchanged for common stock. Fully diluted earnings per share will always be less than or equal to primary earnings per share.

Corporations report primary and fully diluted earnings per share for various categories of income. For example, National Medical Enterprises reported the following information on its 1994 income statement:

	1994	1993	1992
Earnings (loss) per share:			
Primary:			
Continuing operations	$ 1.29	$1.59	$1.27
Discontinued operations	(4.19)	(0.63)	(0.50)
Extraordinary charges	0.00	0.00	(0.17)
Cumulative effect of a change in			
accounting principle	0.36	0.00	0.00
	$(2.54)	$0.96	$0.60
Fully diluted:			
Continuing operations	$1.23	$1.49	$1.19
Discontinued operations	(4.10)	(0.58)	(0.44)
Extraordinary charges	0.00	0.00	(0.15)
Cumulative effect of a change in			
accounting principle	0.33	0.00	0.00
	$(2.54)	$0.91	$0.60

The income statement presents the results of operating activities on an accrual basis. The statement of cash flows presents the cash flow results of operating activities. Differences between the cash flow and accrual measures were considered in detail in Chapter 6. The following section summarizes information reported about operating activities on the statement of cash flows.

CASH FLOW FROM OPERATING ACTIVITIES

Objective 13
Compare accrual and cash operating results.

The statement of cash flows presents the results of operating activities for a fiscal period on a cash basis. Exhibit 13-6 contains information Coca-Cola reported in its 1993 annual report. Like most companies, Coca-Cola uses the indirect format for presenting its statement. This format adjusts net income (item A) for noncash revenues and expenses (items B–I).

Exhibit 13-6

The Coca-Cola Company
(Excerpt from Consolidated Statement of Cash Flows)

Year Ended December 31, (in millions)	1993
Operating Activities	
A. Net income	$2,176
B. Depreciation and amortization	360
C. Deferred income taxes	(62)
D. Equity income, net of dividends	(35)
E. Foreign currency adjustments	9
F. Gain on sales of assets	(84)
G. Other noncash items	78
H. Net change in operating assets and liabilities	54
I. Effects of changes in accounting principles	12
J. Net cash provided by operating activities	2,508
Investing Activities Net cash used in investing activities	(885)
Financing Activities Net cash used in financing activities	(1,540)
Effect of Exchange Rate Changes	(41)
Cash and Cash Equivalents Net increase in cash during the year Balance at beginning of year	42 956
Balance at end of year	998

Minor modifications have been made to the format. Details of investing and financing activities have been omitted. Items have been lettered for reference.

Depreciation and amortization (item B), foreign currency adjustments (item E), other noncash items (item G), and the effects of changes in accounting principles (item I) were expenses recognized in 1993. These expenses did not require cash outflow during 1993. (Other noncash items were miscellaneous items that were not described in detail in Coca-Cola's annual report.)

Equity income (item D) and the gain on sale of assets (item F) were revenues that did not provide cash inflow. Recall from Chapter 11 that a company records equity income when it uses the equity method to recognize a portion of the net income of another company in which it has invested. Dividends received from the equity investment provide cash inflows. Equity income in excess of dividends does not provide cash flow during the period in which the income is recognized. Gains on sale of assets result when the sales price is greater than the book value of the assets. Cash inflows from the sales are reported as cash flow from investing activities. Therefore, the gains do not provide any additional cash flow.

Coca-Cola recorded income tax expense of $997 million on its income statement for 1993 (Exhibit 13-1). Its liability (and required cash payment) for income taxes was $1,059 million for 1993. Thus, cash payments for income taxes were $62 million greater ($1,059 − $997) than income tax expense. The difference of $62 million was the decrease in deferred taxes for the year. Therefore, on the statement of cash flows, Coca-Cola subtracted the decrease in deferred taxes (item C) to account for the additional cash outflow.

Coca-Cola's net change in operating assets and liabilities (item H) were the changes in current assets and liabilities. A note to the financial statements disclosed details of these changes (in millions):

Year Ended December 31,	**1993**
Increase in trade accounts receivable	$(151)
Increase in inventories	(41)
Increase in prepaid expenses and other assets	(76)
Decrease in accounts payable and accrued expenses	(44)
Increase in accrued taxes	355
Increase in other liabilities	11
	$ 54

Changes in these accounts measure the difference between accrual basis recognition of revenues, cost of goods sold, and operating expenses, and cash basis recognition. Recall from Chapter 6 that increases in current assets decrease cash flows and increases in current liabilities increase cash flows.

Coca-Cola's net income of $2,176 million in 1993 (Exhibit 13-1) resulted in net cash flow from operating activities of $2,508 million (item J).

In addition to reporting financial activities for the past fiscal year, corporations report information about events that occurred subsequent to the fiscal year but prior to the time their annual reports are prepared for distribution. The next section considers reporting of subsequent events.

SUBSEQUENT EVENTS

Annual financial statements report the effects of transactions for fiscal years. Thus, if the statements are dated December 31, 1996, they report account balances at this date. The annual report containing the statements usually is published 60 to 90 days after the close of a company's fiscal year. *Subsequent events* **are major economic activities occurring after the close of a company's fiscal year but prior to the time its annual report is printed.** GAAP require companies to disclose information about these activities in notes to their financial statements. The disclosure should identify important facts associated with the event, including the amounts of transactions that have occurred. Common types of subsequent events include changes in debt, litigation, business combinations, discontinued operations, and stock dividends or splits.

Objective 14
Explain the reporting of subsequent events.

These transactions are not included in a company's financial statements for the period prior to the event. They are included in financial statements for the fiscal year ended after the transactions have occurred. Subsequent events are reported in the annual report to inform decision makers of major events that will affect the company's future financial statements.

The final section of this chapter explains some of the major differences in reporting the results of operating activities between U.S. and foreign corporations.

INTERNATIONAL REPORTING OF OPERATING ACTIVITIES

Foreign corporations report much of the same income statement information as U.S. corporations. The formats of the statements often are different, however.

For example, the format used by British corporations to report operating results differs from the format used by U.S. corporations. The information reported and reporting rules, however, are similar. Though differences exist in reporting among companies in different countries, the content usually is similar. Care must be used in making comparisons because of differences in reporting and measurement rules.

Considerable diversity exists in reporting cash flows. Some foreign corporations report a statement of cash flows that is similar to that reported by U.S. corporations. Some report a statement of changes in working capital that explains changes in current asset and liability accounts but does not specifically report cash flows. Others report only an income statement without a cash flow or other statement of operating activities.

SELF-STUDY PROBLEM 13-3

Ben E. King Co. reported the following items on its income statement for 1997:

a. Net operating revenues, $845,000
b. Cost of goods sold, $320,000
c. Selling and administrative expenses, $280,000
d. Research and development expenses, $78,000
e. Net interest expense, $4,000
f. Provision for income taxes, $50,000
g. Current year loss from discontinued operations of $30,000, net of tax of $10,000
h. Loss from sale of discontinued operations of $100,000, net of tax of $30,000

i. Cumulative effect (gain) of change in accounting principle of $120,000, net of tax of $40,000
j. Preferred stock dividends, $60,000

The company had 10,000 shares of common stock outstanding throughout the fiscal year.

Required

Compute each of the following:

1. Gross profit
2. Operating income
3. Income (loss) from continuing operations, before taxes
4. Income (loss) before discontinued operations and cumulative effect of accounting change
5. Income (loss) before cumulative effect of accounting change
6. Net income
7. Net income (loss) available for common shareholders

Earnings per share for:

8. Continuing operations
9. Discontinued operations
10. Net income (loss) before cumulative effect of accounting change
11. Cumulative effect of accounting change
12. Net income (loss)

The solution to Self-Study Problem 13-3 appears at the end of the chapter.

R E V I E W   *Summary of Important Concepts*

1. Revenues and accounts receivable:
    a. Revenues generally are recognized when goods and services are transferred to customers. Revenue recognition methods vary when revenues are earned over long periods (such as long-term contracts), collectibility is not assured, or amounts are not easily estimated.
    b. Accounts receivable are reported net of allowances for doubtful accounts and returns. An expense associated with these amounts is recorded at the end of a fiscal period as an estimate of sales for the period that will not result in cash inflows.

2. Cost of goods sold and inventories:
    a. Merchandising companies report merchandise inventory. Manufacturing companies report raw materials, work in process, and finished goods inventories.
    b. Most companies measure cost of goods sold and ending inventory amounts using FIFO, LIFO, or weighted average estimation methods.
    c. The choice of inventory estimation method affects the amount of net income reported for a period.
    d. Cash flows are affected by the income tax consequences resulting from the choice of inventory estimation method. LIFO generally produces lower income tax obligations.

3. Operating income and expenses, other revenues and expenses, and income taxes:
   a. Gross profit is the excess of net operating revenue over cost of goods sold. Gross profit results from transactions involving customers and suppliers.
   b. Operating income is gross profit minus operating expenses. Operating expenses are period costs not directly related to production or inventory cost.
   c. Financial revenues and expenses are subtracted from operating income to produce income before taxes.
   d. Income tax expense is shown on the income statement as the statutory rate on pretax income for a period. The difference between this amount and the amount of tax obligation computed on a corporation's tax return is deferred tax. Deferred tax results from differences in the recognition of revenues and expenses for financial statement and tax purposes.

4. Special income statement items:
   a. Minority interest in income of consolidated subsidiaries is the portion of subsidiary net income attributable to minority owners of subsidiaries.
   b. Gains and losses associated with discontinued operations, extraordinary items, and accounting changes are reported separately, net of income tax effects.
   c. Dividends on preferred stock are deducted from net income to compute net income available for common stockholders.
   d. Corporations report primary and fully diluted earnings per share for primary categories of net income.
   e. Subsequent events are major economic activities occurring after the end of a fiscal year but before financial statements are printed and made available to decision makers.

5. Cash flow from operating activities:
   a. The income statement reports the accrual basis results of operating activities for a period. The cash flow statement reports the cash basis results of operating activities for a period.

DEFINE   *Terms and Concepts Defined in This Chapter*

accounting changes	fully diluted earnings per share	overhead
allowance for doubtful accounts	gross profit	percentage of completion method
completed contracts method	indirect labor	primary earnings per share
direct labor	last–in first–out (LIFO) method	raw materials
discontinued operations	minority interest in income of	subsequent events
extraordinary items	consolidated subsidiaries	weighted average method
finished goods	operating income	work in process
first–in first–out (FIFO) method		

SOLUTIONS

SELF-STUDY PROBLEM 13-1

	Cash	Revenues	Net Accounts Receivable
Customers paying monthly	$120,000	$120,000	$ 0
Customers paying in advance	55,000	35,000	0
Customers paying semiannually	70,000	110,000	37,600
Total	$245,000	$265,000	$37,600

Receivables for customers paying semiannually include amounts owed of $40,000 less estimated uncollectible accounts of $2,400 ($40,000 × .06).

SELF-STUDY PROBLEM 13-2

(a) (in millions)	FIFO	LIFO
Beginning inventory	$ 8.0	$ 6.0
Inventory acquired	30.0	30.0
Ending inventory	(10.0)	(7.0)
Cost of goods sold	$ 28.0	$29.0
Cost of goods sold, tax benefit (30%)	8.4	8.7
Effect on net income	$ 19.6	$20.3

Fashion Mart's cost of goods sold would have been $1 million greater if it had used the LIFO method. It would have saved $300,000 ($8.7 − 8.4) in taxes if it had used the LIFO method compared with the FIFO method. On an after-tax basis, cost of goods sold would have been $700,000 greater ($20.3 − $19.6) if the LIFO method had been used. Therefore, net income would have been $700,000 less under LIFO than under FIFO. Cash outflows would have been $300,000 lower under LIFO, the amount of additional tax savings.

(b) Fashion Mart should consider the effect of the choice of inventory estimation method on its future cash flows. If the company expects its inventory costs to continue to increase and its sales are relatively stable, LIFO will result in lower income tax obligations than will FIFO. If costs or sales are volatile, LIFO might not be an advantage. For example, if the company sells more inventory than it acquires during a fiscal year, LIFO will result in higher net income and tax obligations than will FIFO.

SELF-STUDY PROBLEM 13-3

Net operating revenues	$845,000
Cost of goods sold	(320,000)
1. Gross profit	525,000
Selling and administrative expenses	(280,000)
Research and development expenses	(78,000)

2. Operating income	167,000
Net interest expense	(4,000)
3. Income from continuing operations, before taxes	163,000
Provision for income taxes	(50,000)
4. Income before discontinued operations and cumulative effect of accounting change	113,000
Discontinued operations:	
Current period loss, net of tax of $10,000	(30,000)
Loss from sale of discontinued operations, net of tax of $30,000	(100,000)
5. Loss before cumulative effect of accounting change	(17,000)
Cumulative effect of change in accounting principle, net of tax of $40,000	120,000
6. Net income	103,000
Less: preferred dividends	(60,000)
7. Net income available for common shareholders	$ 43,000
Earnings per share:	
8. Continuing operations ($113,000/10,000 shares)	$11.30
9. Discontinued operations ($130,000/10,000 shares)	(13.00)
10. Net loss before cumulative effect of accounting change ($17,000/10,000 shares)	(1.70)
11. Cumulative effect of accounting change ($120,000/10,000 shares)	12.00
12. Net income ($103,000/10,000 shares)	$10.30

EXERCISES

13-1. Write a short definition for each of the terms listed in the "Terms and Concepts Defined in This Chapter" section.

13-2. Distinguish between the results of operating activities reported on the income statement and results of operating activities reported on the statement of cash flows. What effect do differences between these statements have on the balance sheet?

13-3. An excerpt of the income statement from the 1993 annual report of General Mills, Inc. is provided below:

Fiscal Year Ended May 31 (in millions except per share data)	1993
Continuing operations:	
Sales	$8,134.6
Costs and expenses:	
Cost of sales	4,297.6
Selling, general, and administrative	2,645.2
Depreciation and amortization	274.2
Interest, net	73.6
Total costs and expenses	7,290.6
	continued

Fiscal Year Ended May 31 (in millions except per share data)	1993
Earnings from continuing operations before taxes	844.0
Income taxes	337.9
Earnings from continuing operations	506.1
Discontinued operations after taxes	0
Net earnings	$ 506.1
Earnings per share:	
Continuing operations	$3.10
Discontinued operations	0
Net earnings per share	$3.10
Average number of common shares	163.1

Write a short explanation of each item presented on the income statement. How much gross profit and operating income did General Mills report for 1993?

13-4.   An excerpt of the income statement from the 1993 annual report of Alcoa is provided below:

For the year ended December 31	1993
(in millions except share amounts)	
Revenues	
Sales and operating revenues	$9,055.9
Other income, principally interest	93.0
	9,148.9
Costs and Expenses	
Cost of goods sold	7,187.0
Selling, general, administrative, and other expenses	603.6
Research and development expenses	130.4
Provision for depreciation, depletion, and amortization	692.6
Interest expense	87.8
Taxes other than payroll and severance taxes	105.6
Unusual items	150.8
	8,957.8
Earnings	
Income before taxes on income	191.1
Provision (credit) for taxes on income	10.3
Income from operations	201.4
Minority interests	(196.6)
Net Income	$ 4.8
Earnings per Common Share	$ .03

Write a short explanation of each item presented on the income statement. How much gross profit and operating income did Alcoa report for 1993?

13-5. Gross profit results from transactions of a company with its customers and suppliers. What types of transactions affect gross profit? How does accounting for timing differences between cash flow and accrual measurements of these transactions affect the financial statements?

13-6. Aracnoid Co. manufactures specialized industrial equipment. The equipment often is sold under credit terms that provide for payment over a two- or three-year period. A substantial prepayment is required before equipment is manufactured. The purchaser accepts title to the equipment at the time it is received. Aracnoid also sells service contracts on the equipment it sells. These multiyear contracts stipulate that Aracnoid will provide periodic maintenance on the equipment and will repair the equipment if it breaks down. How should Aracnoid determine its sales and service revenues?

13-7. On June 1, 1996, Milo Construction Co. signed a contract to construct a building for MiGrain Agricultural Cooperative. The contract called for MiGrain to pay $4 million to Milo for the building, once construction was completed. Milo expected total construction costs to be $3.2 million. By December 31, 1996, the end of Milo's fiscal year, it had incurred costs of $800,000 on the project. How much revenue and profit should Milo recognize for the project for 1996? Assume the company does not pay income taxes. Also, assume little uncertainty exists about the receipt of payment for the project. How would your answer differ if MiGrain was facing serious financial difficulty at the end of 1996 that could lead to bankruptcy?

13-8. New Cleus Co. sold merchandise during its 1995 fiscal year. The total sales price of the merchandise was $30 million. Because of quantity sales discounts, the company billed its customers $28.5 million for the merchandise. New Cleus sells goods to retailers who have a right to return the merchandise if it does not sell within 90 days. New Cleus expects a return rate of 5% of the amount sold. How much revenue should New Cleus recognize for 1995? Justify your answer.

13-9. Karloff Co. reported accounts receivable at the end of 1996 of $3,200,000, net of an allowance of $450,000. During its fiscal 1997 year, it recorded sales of $18,600,000, on credit, and collected $18,750,000 from customers. It wrote off $165,000 of bad debts and estimated that it required an allowance for doubtful accounts at the end of 1997 equal to 3% of its 1997 sales. Use the following format to identify how each of these events would affect Karloff's accounts during 1997.

Assets =	Liabilities + Equity	+ (Revenues − Expenses)

What was the net amount of accounts receivable reported by Karloff on its 1997 balance sheet?

13-10. Rath Bone Co. purchased $860,000 of merchandise on credit during its 1996 fiscal year. At the end of 1995, the company reported accounts payable of $90,000 and merchandise inventory of $55,000. It made payments to suppliers of $847,000 and sold merchandise that cost $900,000 during 1996. Use the following format to identify how each of these events would affect Rath Bone's accounts during 1996.

Assets =	Liabilities + Equity	+ (Revenues − Expenses)

How much merchandise inventory and accounts payable would Rath Bone report on its 1996 balance sheet?

13-11. Sandberg Co. purchased $750,000 of materials on credit during its 1996 fiscal year. $775,000 of materials were placed into production. Other production costs included $540,000 of direct labor and $220,000 of overhead. Finished goods costing $1,600,000 were completed during the year, and finished goods costing $1,580,000 were sold. Use the following format to identify how each of these events would affect Sandberg's accounts during 1996. Record overhead to accounts payable.

Assets =	Liabilities + Equity	+ (Revenues − Expenses)

13-12. Dickinson Co. is a wholesaler of garden supplies. At the beginning of its 1997 fiscal year, the company owned 300 bags of X50 lawn fertilizer at a cost of $8 per bag. During April, May, and June of 1997, the following events occurred:

> Purchased 800 bags on April 1 at $8.25 each.
> Sold 1,000 bags during April.
> Purchased 1,500 bags on May 1 at $8.50 each.
> Sold 1,350 bags during May.
> Purchased 1,200 bags during June at $8.60 each.
> Sold 1,275 bags during June.

How much inventory of X50 would Dickinson report on June 30 and how much cost of goods sold would it report for the product for the three months if it used the FIFO estimation method? How much inventory and cost of goods sold would it report if it used the LIFO method? What would its weighted average cost of inventory have been for the month?

13-13. Some corporations use FIFO to estimate their inventory costs. Others use LIFO. What issues are important to this decision? What effect can the choice have on a company's net income and cash flow from operating activities?

13-14. Sara Lee Corporation reported inventories of $2,280 million in 1993 and $2,160 million in 1992. It used LIFO for much of its inventory. If it had used FIFO, it would have reported inventories of $2,318 million in 1993 and $2,195 million in 1992. Assuming an income tax rate of 34%, what effect did the use of LIFO, instead of FIFO, have on the company's reported net income and income taxes?

13-15. GAAP require companies to report inventories on a lower of cost or market basis. What is the purpose of this measurement rule? What effect does it have on a company's financial statements?

13-16. PepsiCo, Inc. reported a provision for income taxes of $834.6 million on its 1993 income statement. Deferred income taxes increased from $1,682.3 million in 1992 to $2,007.6 million in 1993. The company paid $675.6 million of income taxes in 1993. Use the following format to indicate the effect of these transactions on PepsiCo's accounts:

Assets =	Liabilities + Equity	+ (Revenues − Expenses)

What information is provided by deferred income taxes?

13-17. Allied Products Corporation reported the following information in 1993 (in thousands):

Income from continuing operations before taxes	$ 6,387
Provision for income taxes	(436)
Income from continuing operations	5,951
Income from discontinued operations, net of tax	11,385
Income prior to other adjustments	$17,336

What are discontinued operations? Why did the company report discontinued operations and the related amount of income taxes separately from continuing operations?

13-18. American Brands, Inc. reported net income of $469.8 million in 1993. It reported primary earnings per share of $2.32 and fully diluted earnings per share of $2.29. Distinguish between primary and fully diluted earnings per share. Why were both amounts reported by American Brands?

13-19. Georgia–Pacific Corporation reported a net loss of $124 million in 1993. It reported cash provided by operations of $868 million. Among the adjustments to net income on the statement of cash flows (prepared using the indirect format), the company reported:

> depreciation
> depletion
> amortization of debt discounts and premiums
> amortization of goodwill
> deferred taxes
> gain on sale of assets
> change in receivables, inventories, and payables

Why are these items listed on the statement of cash flows?

13-20. Indestructo Corp.'s fiscal year ends on December 31. In its 1995 annual report, the company reported: "In February 1996, Indestructo issued 10 million shares of common stock, resulting in net proceeds of approximately $500 million." Why is this event reported in the 1995 annual report? What effect did it have on the company's 1995 and 1996 financial statements?

PROBLEMS

PROBLEM 13-1   Interpreting an Income Statement

Income statement information from the 1993 annual report of Unisys Corporation is provided on page 599. Unisys provides computer products and services.

Years ended December 31 (in millions, except per share data)	1993	1992	1991
Revenues			
Sales	$4,705.4	$5,399.5	$ 5,714.6
Services	1,593.1	1,336.4	1,147.4
Equipment maintenance	1,444.0	1,686.0	1,834.1
	7,742.5	8,421.9	8,696.1
Costs and Expenses			
Cost of sales	2,798.7	3,342.8	4,196.8
Cost of services	1,225.2	1,061.6	949.6
Cost of equipment maintenance	820.4	980.1	1,194.4
Selling, general and administrative expenses	1,648.9	1,780.8	2,295.3
Research and development expenses	515.2	535.9	638.9
	7,008.4	7,701.2	9,275.0
Operating income (loss)	734.1	720.7	(578.9)
Interest expense	241.7	340.6	407.6
Other income (expense), net	11.0	55.5	(301.8)
Income (loss) before income taxes	503.4	435.6	(1,288.3)
Estimated income taxes	141.8	139.4	105.0
Income before extraordinary items and change in accounting principles	361.6	296.2	(1,393.3)
Extraordinary items	(26.4)	65.0	
Effect of changes in accounting principles	230.2		
Net income (loss)	565.4	361.2	(1,393.3)
Dividends on preferred shares	121.6	122.1	121.2
Earnings (loss) on common shares	$ 443.8	$ 239.1	$(1,514.5)
Earnings (loss) per common share Primary			
Before extraordinary items and changes in accounting principles	$ 1.46	$ 1.06	$ (9.37)
Extraordinary items	(.16)	.40	
Effect of changes in accounting principles	1.39		
Total	$ 2.69	$ 1.46	$ (9.37)
Fully diluted			
Before extraordinary items and changes in accounting principles	$ 1.48	$ 1.04	$ (9.37)
Extraordinary items	(.11)	.36	
Effect of changes in accounting principles	.94		
Total	$ 2.31	$ 1.40	$ (9.37)

Required   Answer each of the following questions:

a.   How do sales differ from services and maintenance? Why are these amounts shown separately?

b.   What was Unisys's gross profit in 1993? What information does this amount provide?

c.   What was the amount of total operating expenses for 1993?

d.   Why are interest expense, and other income reported after operating income?

e.   Why were the extraordinary items and effect of changes in accounting principles listed separately?

f.   Did Unisys have any dilutive securities outstanding during the three years reported on the income statement? How do you know?

PROBLEM 13-2   Earnings per Share

Refer to the income statement information for Unisys Corporation provided in Problem 13-1.

Required   Answer each of the following questions:

a.   How do primary earnings per share differ from fully diluted earnings per share? Why are both sets of numbers provided by Unisys?

b.   Why did Unisys report extraordinary items and the effect of changes in accounting principles separately in its earnings per share information? Why would investors be interested in this information?

PROBLEM 13-3   Revenue Recognition

Unisys Corporation reported the following information in its 1993 annual report:

> Sales revenue is generally recorded upon shipment of product in the case of sales contracts, upon shipment of the program in the case of software, and upon installation in the case of sales-type leases. Revenue from service and rental agreements is recorded as earned over the lives of the respective contracts.

Required   What is meant by revenue recognition? Why does Unisys use different revenue recognition principles for different types of revenue? What are the critical events for each of these types of revenue?

PROBLEM 13-4   Operating Transactions

Nabokov Co. purchased $4,230,000 of merchandise on credit during its 1996 fiscal year. At the end of 1995, the company reported accounts payable of $870,000 and merchandise inventory of $535,000. It made payments to suppliers of $4,280,000 and sold merchandise that cost $4,060,000 during 1996.

Required   Determine the amount of each of the following items reported on Nabokov's 1996 financial statements: merchandise inventory, accounts payable, cost of goods sold, cash paid to suppliers. Explain the difference between the amounts of cost of goods sold and cash paid to suppliers reported for the period.

PROBLEM 13-5   Inventory Transactions of Manufacturing Companies

O'Neill Co. began its fiscal 1996 year with $870,000 of raw materials inventory, $1,390,000 of work in process inventory, and $620,000 of finished goods inventory. During 1996, the company purchased $3,550,000 of raw materials, and used $3,720,000 of raw materials in production. Labor used in production for the year was $2,490,000. Overhead was $1,380,000. Cost of goods sold for the year was $7,500,000. The ending balance of finished goods inventory was $530,000.

Required   Use Exhibit 13-2 as a format for developing a diagram to show the effect of these events on O'Neill's inventory accounts for 1996.

PROBLEM 13-6 Preparing an Income Statement

Salinger Co.'s accounting system listed the following information for the company's 1997 fiscal year (in millions):

Average common shares outstanding	2.4
Cost of goods sold	$170.3
Extraordinary gain	18.2
Gain on sale of securities	8.6
General and administrative expenses	75.5
Income taxes (34% of pretax income)	
Interest expense	12.0
Interest income	5.9
Loss associated with cumulative effect of accounting change	4.0
Loss from discontinued operations	13.1
Sales of merchandise	320.8
Selling expenses	30.2

Required Prepare an income statement for Salinger Co. for the year ended December 31, 1997. Assume the tax rate of 35% applies to special items as well as ordinary income.

PROBLEM 13-7 Comparing Inventory Estimation Methods

Information (in millions) about total inventory at year-end and cost of goods sold for Axelrod Co. is provided below. Axelrod uses the LIFO estimation method. The company's tax rate is 34%.

Year	LIFO Inventory	Inventory Purchased	FIFO Inventory
1993	$24.2		$27.5
1994	26.3	502.7	30.0
1995	30.2	510.6	34.4
1996	32.8	522.6	37.4
1997	31.4	535.1	35.8

Required Compute the cost of goods sold that Axelrod would report using the LIFO and FIFO methods. (Cost of goods sold = beginning inventory + purchases − ending inventory.) What would be the effect on Axelrod's pretax income and cash flows each year for 1994 through 1997 if the company had used FIFO rather than LIFO? Is the company better off using LIFO or FIFO? Why?

PROBLEM 13-8 Inventory Estimation and Income Control

Kerouac Co. uses the LIFO inventory estimation method. At the beginning of its 1996 fiscal year, the company's inventory consisted of the following:

Units	Unit Cost	Total Cost
8,000	$22.00	$176,000
4,000	23.00	92,000
2,000	32.00	64,000
2,000	34.00	68,000

These units were purchased over several years, during which inventory costs increased rapidly. During 1996, Kerouac produced 20,000 additional units of inventory at an average cost of $36 per unit. The average sales price of units sold during the year was $55.

Required Answer the following questions:

a. What would be Kerouac's gross profit and average gross profit per unit if it sold 20,000, 24,000, 28,000, or 36,000 units during 1996?

b. Assume Kerouac sold 36,000 units during 1996. How many units would it need to produce to minimize the tax effect of its gross profit? How many units would it need to produce to maximize its gross profit?

c. If you were a manager of Kerouac and wanted to control the amount of gross profit reported by the company in 1996, what could you do? If you wanted to develop an accounting standard that could prevent this type of management manipulation of income, what kind of standard might you propose?

PROBLEM 13-9   Computing Accounts Receivable

Erdman Corp. reported accounts receivable of $16.5 million at the end of its 1996 fiscal year. This amount was net of an allowance for doubtful accounts of $1,800,000. During 1997, Erdman sold $56.5 million of merchandise on credit. It collected $57.9 million from customers. Accounts valued at $1,980,000 were written off as uncollectible during 1997. Erdman's management estimates that 4% of credit sales made during 1997 will be uncollectible.

Required Answer each of the following questions:

a. What amount will Erdman report for accounts receivable and the allowance for doubtful accounts for 1997?

b. Why do companies record expenses for uncollectible accounts based on estimates from sales during the prior year rather than recording the expenses when accounts are written off in a future period?

c. What percentage of its 1997 credit sales did Erdman expect to become uncollectible? If this percentage were to increase over several years, what information might it provide to decision makers?

PROBLEM 13-10   The Effect of Accounting Choices

Ginsberg Co. is a recently formed, publicly traded company. On December 31, 1996, the company reported the following information.

a. Sales revenues were $13,680,000. 360,000 units were sold. Credit sales were $10,000,000. Uncollectible accounts associated with 1996 credit sales are estimated to be between 3% and 4%.

b. 140,000 units of inventory were available at the beginning of the year at a unit cost of $10 per unit; 250,000 units were purchased during the year at $10.50, and, later, 150,000 units were purchased at $11.50 per unit.

c. Plant assets included equipment with a book value of $3,375,000 and buildings with a book value of $8,260,000. The equipment has an estimated remaining useful life of between 4 and 7 years. The buildings have an estimated remaining useful life of between 25 and 35 years.

d. Intangible assets cost $1,200,000 and have a remaining useful life of no less than 10 years.

e. The company has the option of adopting a new accounting standard for the 1996 fiscal year. If the standard is adopted for 1996, the cumulative effect of the accounting change, before the tax effect, will be a loss of $1,100,000.

f. The company's tax rate is 34%. Other operating expenses were $6,245,000. Interest expense was $460,000. 500,000 shares of common stock were outstanding throughout the year.

Required Provide pro forma income statements for 1996 showing the minimum and maximum amounts of net income and earnings per share Ginsberg could report under GAAP.

PROBLEM 13-11 Accounting Choice Decisions

Malamud Co. reported sales revenue of $10 million for its 1996 fiscal year. The company uses FIFO for inventory estimation purposes. Cost of goods sold was $3.8 million. If the company had used LIFO, its cost of goods sold would have been $4.5 million. The company reported depreciation expense of $1.2 million on a straight-line basis. If the company had used accelerated depreciation, it would have reported depreciation expense of $1.7 million. Other expenses, excluding income tax, were $3 million. The company's income tax rate was 30%.

Required Compute Malamud's net income as reported and as it would have been reported if LIFO and accelerated depreciation had been used. What effect would the choice of accounting methods have on the company's cash flows from operating activities during 1996 if the same methods were used for both financial reporting and tax purposes?

PROBLEM 13-12 Multiple-Choice Overview of the Chapter

1. The excess of sales revenues over cost of goods sold for a fiscal period is:
    a. net income.
    b. income before taxes.
    c. operating income.
    d. gross profit.

2. Timing differences between sales revenues recognized during a fiscal period and cash collected from customers during the period affects the change in the balance of:
    a. accounts receivable.
    b. unearned revenue.
    c. gross profit.
    d. allowance for doubtful accounts.

3. A transaction to estimate the amount of doubtful accounts expense for a fiscal period would affect the:
    a. accounts receivable and doubtful accounts expense accounts.
    b. allowance for doubtful accounts and doubtful accounts expense accounts.
    c. allowance for doubtful accounts and accounts receivable accounts.
    d. allowance for doubtful accounts and sales revenue accounts.

4. Universal Joint Co. publishes a monthly periodical, *Grease Today*. At the beginning of March, the company's unearned revenues included 1,200 subscriptions at $36 per subscription. During March, the company received 200 new subscriptions at $36

each. The March issue was shipped to all subscribers on March 25. The amount of subscription revenue the company should recognize in March would be:
a. $7,200.
b. $4,200.
c. $3,600.
d. $600.

5. Two companies are identical except that one used LIFO and the other used FIFO. Both companies produced and sold the same amount of goods during 1996. The company that would report the highest net income:
a. would be the company that used LIFO.
b. would be the company that used FIFO.
c. would depend on the change in inventory costs during the year and whether more goods were produced than sold.
d. would depend on the price at which the goods were sold and the cost of the goods at the end of the fiscal year.

6. MacLean Co. reported income tax expense on its 1997 income statement of $3.4 million. The amount of income tax the company owed for 1997, determined on its tax return, was $2.8 million. The change in the company's deferred taxes account for 1997 would be:
a. an increase of $0.6 million.
b. an increase of $2.8 million.
c. a decrease of $0.6 million.
d. a decrease of $2.8 million.

7. Redford Co. reported net income of $40 million for its 1996 fiscal year. The company recorded interest expense of $10 million for the year. Also, it paid preferred dividends of $2 million and common dividends of $5 million. The average number of common shares outstanding for the year was 10 million. The company would report earnings per share of common stock for 1996 of:
a. $4.00
b. $3.80
c. $3.30
d. $2.30

8. McManus Co. reported net income for 1997 of $20 million. The average number of common shares outstanding for the year was 10 million. The company also had convertible bonds outstanding at the end of 1997, though none of the bonds were converted during the 1997 fiscal year. If all the bonds were converted, net income would have increased by $1 million in 1997, and average common shares would have increased by 800,000 shares. McManus would report for 1997:
a. primary earnings per share of $2.00 and no amount for fully diluted earnings per share.
b. primary earnings per share of $2.00 and fully diluted earnings per share of $2.10.
c. primary earnings per share of $2.10 and fully diluted earnings per share of $2.00.
d. primary earnings per share of $2.00 and fully diluted earnings per share of $1.94.

9. Sontag Co. sold plant assets with a book value of $8 million for $10 million during its 1996 fiscal year. The effect of the transaction on the company's pretax income and cash flow from operating activities for 1996 would be:

	Effect on pretax income	Effect on operating cash flow
a.	$2 million	$2 million
b.	$2 million	$0
c.	$2 million	$10 million
d.	$8 million	$10 million

10. Vonnegut Co. sold a subsidiary in January 1997 for a loss of $10 million. The sale of the subsidiary should be reported in Vonnegut's 1996 annual report as:
    a. an extraordinary item.
    b. a discontinued operation.
    c. a subsequent event.
    d. an infrequent, but not unusual, item.

C A S E S

CASE 13-1 Examining Operating Activities

Appendix B of this book contains a copy of the 1994 annual report of Nike, Inc.

Required Review the annual report and answer each of the following questions:

a. What was the primary inventory estimation method used by Nike? If the company had not used LIFO for valuing any of its inventories, what would the effect have been on the company's cost of goods sold and operating income?

b. What was the amount of Nike's allowance for doubtful accounts for 1994? Did the relationship between estimated doubtful accounts expense and net sales change from 1993 to 1994?

c. How much income tax expense did Nike recognize for 1994? How much income tax did the company owe for 1994? What was the primary cause of the difference between income tax expense and income tax payable? How much income tax did Nike pay in 1994?

d. Nike reported "other expenses" of $8.3 million in 1994. What were these other expenses?

e. How much did Nike report for depreciation and for interest expense in 1994? How much cash did Nike pay for depreciation and interest in 1994?

CASE 13-2 Examining Accrual and Cash Flow Measures of Operating Activities

Appendix B of this book contains a copy of the 1994 annual report of Nike, Inc.

Required Review the annual report and answer each of the following questions:

a. What was the absolute and percentage relationship between cash flow from operating activities and net income for Nike for 1992 through 1994?

b.   What were the primary causes of differences between cash flow from operating activities and net income in 1994?

c.   Approximately how much cash did Nike collect from customers in 1994? Approximately how much cash did the company pay to suppliers?

PROJECTS

PROJECT 13-1 Comparing Revenue and Inventory Methods

Obtain the most recent annual report available for each of three corporations from your library. Use companies from different industries. Examine the revenue recognition and inventory estimation methods used by each company. Write a short report comparing the methods used by each company.

PROJECT 13-2 Comparing Income Statements

Obtain the most recent annual report available for each of three corporations from your library. Compare the amounts reported on the income statements of the companies. Which items were most important relative to the companies' total revenues? What differences and similarities did you find in the format and terminology of the reports? What special items were disclosed? Write a short report summarizing your findings.

PROJECT 13-3 Comparing Income Tax Reporting

Obtain the most recent annual report available for each of three corporations from your library. Find corporations in the same industry. Examine the disclosures provided by each company about its income taxes. How much income tax did each company report on its income statement? How did this amount compare with the amount of income tax the company owed on its taxable income? How much income tax did each company pay during the year? How much deferred tax did it report, and how did the balance of deferred taxes change during the year? What explanations are provided about differences between income taxes reported for financial statements and tax purposes? Summarize your findings in a short report.

PROJECT 13-4 Examining Earnings per Share

Find an example of a company that reported primary and fully diluted earnings per share in a recent year. Examine disclosures in the company's annual report about its earnings per share. What types of dilutive securities were outstanding? How did these securities affect the company's earnings per share? Summarize your findings in a short report.

PROJECT 13-5 Examining Cash Flows

Obtain the most recent annual report available for each of three corporations from your library. Compare the amounts reported on the statements of cash flows of the companies. What explanations were provided for differences between net income and cash flow from operating activities? What differences and similarities did you find in the format and terminology of the reports? Write a short report summarizing your findings.

Chapter
14

Analysis of Operating Activities
and Company Value

Through its operating activities, an organization develops, produces, distributes, and markets goods and services. These activities are part of an organization's transformation process. The goal of this process is to create value for those who purchase an organization's products. Effective and efficient creation of value for customers results in profits and value for a company's owners. Operating activities present managers with opportunities, challenges, and uncertainties. Operating decisions are the choices managers make to take advantage of opportunities or to deal with challenges and uncertainties. Accounting information describes the results of operating decisions. It can be used to identify and evaluate management decisions. It can help decision makers understand an organization's economic attributes and how these attributes developed. Also, accounting information can help decision makers form expectations about an organization's economic future.

Many types of analysis of operating decisions are possible. This chapter examines analytical approaches that are useful for interpreting financial accounting information. These approaches consider both accrual and cash flow measures of operating activities. They permit evaluation of companies over time and comparisons among companies. A primary objective of this analysis is determination and evaluation of a company's risk and return and the effect of risk and return on a company's stakeholders. The chapter focuses primarily on the relation between risk and return and the value of a company to its stockholders. Attributes of a company that affect the value of the company for its stockholders also normally affect the value of the company for its creditors, suppliers, employees, and other stakeholders.

Major topics covered in this chapter include:

- The importance of operating results for the creation of company value.
- Attributes of companies that affect their earnings and returns to stockholders.
- The importance of growth for the creation of value.
- The effect of operating activities on a company's risk.
- A summary of accounting information and the evaluation of company value.

Once you have completed this chapter, you should be able to:

1. Explain the importance of return, growth, and risk in determining company value.
2. Analyze a company's financial accounting information to evaluate the strategies used to create earnings and return on assets.
3. Evaluate the effect of a company's use of financial leverage to improve return on equity.
4. Identify company attributes associated with growth in returns and company value.
5. Explain the importance of accrual and cash flow measures of operating results for understanding and evaluating growth and company value.
6. Identify the effect of risk on a company's expected return on equity.
7. Identify causes of risk for a corporation.
8. Analyze a corporation's financial statements to explain the value of the company.

OPERATING RESULTS AND COMPANY VALUE

Objective 1
Explain the importance of return, growth, and risk in determining company value.

A company is valuable when it is able to create high returns for its owners relative to the risk associated with the returns. Chapter 8 described a valuation model in which the present value (PV) of an asset, including a company as a whole, is determined by expected cash flows (C) discounted at a rate of return (R) that is a function of a risk:

$$PV = \sum C /(1 + R)^t.$$

This present value equation is useful for estimating the value of an asset when an investor expects cash flows at specific time intervals (t). Recall from chapter 8 that the equation can be modified for valuing common stocks that have an infinite life and for which the cash flows are expected to grow. The modified equation is:

$$PV = C /(R - G),$$

where G is the expected rate of growth.

This model is more than a conceptual representation. It describes the primary factors relevant for valuing a company. Companies with high expected cash flows relative to the risk associated with these cash flows are more valuable than other companies. Companies that are expected to grow at high rates are more valuable than other companies, as well.

Expected cash flows, growth, and risk are not easy to estimate, however. No specific measures of these variables exist. Various methods have been described in the literature for estimating these variables. A relatively straightforward approximation results from using income-based measures. Cash flows to owners of a company result from the ability of the company to generate profits. Higher profits usually result in higher cash flows that can be used to pay dividends to owners. The amount of dividends paid during a period is less important than the ability to pay dividends in the future, however. Owners often are willing to forego dividends now in order to receive higher dividends or higher value for their stock in the future. Thus, both the level of income and growth in income are important for creating value. As discussed in previous chapters, return on equity is a useful relative measure of income for comparing companies' performances. We should expect that companies with high return on equity and high growth in return on equity will be more valuable than other companies, if the companies exhibit about the same amount of risk.

Risk is uncertainty about expected cash flows. When a company's income is volatile, uncertainty exists about the amount of cash flows investors can expect in the future. If a company's income is stable, owners generally can be more assured about the amount of cash flow they can expect than if income is volatile. Therefore, the volatility of income (or return on equity) is a useful accounting measure of risk. Volatility can be measured by the distribution of return on equity over time. Standard deviation is a commonly used measure of the distribution. A high **standard deviation** indicates high volatility and high risk. (You may wish to refer to Appendix A of chapter 8 for a review of standard deviation.)

Thus, three accounting measures provide a simple means of describing company value: return on equity, growth in return on equity, and volatility (standard deviation) of return on equity. Exhibit 14-1 illustrates the relation between company value and each of these three measures for a large sample of major corporations.[1]

Exhibit 14-1   The Association Between the Value of Common Stock and Return on Equity, Growth, and Risk

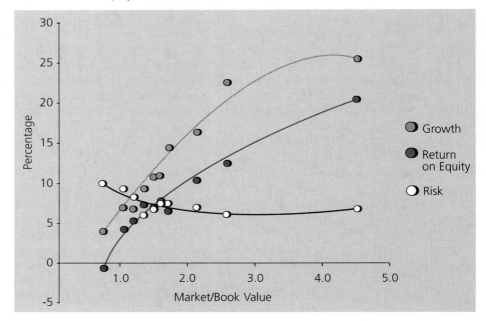

Data source: 1993 Compustat Annual Industrial File.

High-value companies are those with high market values relative to their book values and are toward the right on the graph. When a company's market value is high relative to its book value, the price that owners can obtain for their invest‐ments is high relative to the amount owners invested in the company. Market value is the price per share of common stock of a company times the number of shares outstanding. Book value of equity is total stockholders' equity (minus any preferred stock) as reported on a company's balance sheet.

Return in Exhibit 14-1 is the average annual return on equity (excluding special items such as discontinued operations, extraordinary items, and account‐ing changes). Growth is the average ratio of the change in net income (before special items and after preferred dividends have been subtracted) to common stockholders' equity. For example, a company reporting net income of $10 mil‐lion in 1995, $12 million in 1996 and common stockholders' equity of $20 mil‐lion in 1995 would have a growth rate of 10% = ($12 − $10)/$20. Risk is the standard deviation of return on equity. Trendlines are shown in the exhibit to provide an indication of the average relationships among the variables.

[1]   The sample consists of approximately 900 corporations. Data are averages and standard devia‐tions for 1983–1992. Companies were ranked by the market to book value ratio and grouped into 10 portfolios from low to high value. This sample is used repeatedly in this chapter.

It is apparent from Exhibit 14-1 that high-value companies (those to the right of the graph) are those with high returns, high growth, and low risk relative to low-value companies. The relations presented in the exhibit are average relations for the groups of companies. Exceptions to these general patterns exist. Determination of company value is complex and depends on many factors that are specific to a company. The exhibit provides a general description of company values that is reasonably accurate for a large segment of the economy. It provides evidence of the association between financial accounting information and company values.

The task of valuing companies is not as simple as calculating values for three variables, however. If we want to estimate what the value of a company will be in the future, we must determine what we expect the amounts of these variables to be in the future. Thus, much of the value of financial accounting is in providing information for estimating what is likely to happen in the future. Accounting helps decision makers assess future profitability and cash flows by describing the transformation process of a company that generates profitability and cash flows. The following sections examine economic attributes associated with profitability and expectations about future profitability.

ATTRIBUTES AFFECTING RETURN ON EQUITY

Return on equity is the ratio of a company's income available for common stockholders (net income − preferred dividends) to its average common stockholders' equity. Thus, economic attributes or activities that affect income or equity affect return on equity. Financing, investing, and operating activities affect return on equity as discussed in this section.

Strategies for Creating Profits

Objective 2
Analyze a company's financial accounting information to evaluate strategies used to create earnings and return on assets.

Profits measure the results of operating activities. A company that is successful in transforming resources creates value by generating resources from products it sells. The sold products are more valuable than the resources it consumes in producing and selling its products. You might recall from chapter 1 that profitable companies are effective and efficient. An effective company is one that produces and sells products demanded by customers. An efficient company is one that consumes low amounts of resources in producing and selling its products relative to the resources it generates from sale of its products. Thus, the ability of a company to produce profits can be separated into two components. One is the ability to create sales revenues from the resources (assets) available for manufacturing and selling those products. Effectiveness can be measured as the ratio of sales revenues to total assets. Assets usually are computed as the average of total assets for a fiscal period by adding the beginning and ending amounts of total assets and dividing by 2. **The ratio, sales/average assets, often is referred to as** *asset turnover***; it is a measure of the ability of a company to generate sales from its total investment.** The second component is efficiency, which can be measured as the ratio of earnings to sales. **The ratio, earnings/sales, often is referred to as** *profit margin***; it is a measure of the ability of a company to generate profits from its sales.**

In combination, asset turnover and profit margin are equal to return on assets:

Return on Assets = Asset Turnover × Profit Margin

$$\frac{\text{Earnings}}{\text{Average Assets}} = \frac{\text{Sales}}{\text{Average Assets}} \times \frac{\text{Earnings}}{\text{Sales}}$$

Recall that earnings in the return on assets ratio are defined as net income adjusted for interest expense: Net Income + Interest Expense (1 − Tax Rate). Thus, we can define profit margin as: [Net Income + Interest Expense (1 − Tax Rate)]/Sales.

Return on assets is a measure of operating results that compares a company's earnings with its total investment. This measure ignores the sources of financing used to acquire the company's assets. Thus, interest expense is added back to net income. Companies that are effective (as measured by high asset turnover) and efficient (as measured by high profit margin) are profitable (as measured by high return on assets).

The amounts of asset turnover and profit margin will not be the same for all companies. Even among highly profitable companies, asset turnover will be higher for some and profit margin will be higher for others. These components of return on assets provide useful information about companies' operating activities. To illustrate, consider the following information for two hypothetical companies:

	Margin Co.	**Turnover Co.**
Average assets	$1,000	$800
Sales	800	800
Income (adjusted for interest)	100	80

Return on Assets = Asset Turnover × Profit Margin:

Margin Co.	$100/$1,000	= $800/$1,000	× $100/$800
	0.10	= 0.80	× 0.125
Turnover Co.	$80/$800	= $800/$800	× $80/$800
	0.10	= 1.00	× 0.10

Return on assets for both companies is 10%. The companies use different operating strategies for generating their returns, however. Margin Co. generates a higher amount of income from its sales than Turnover Co. Turnover Co., on the other hand, generates a higher amount of sales from its assets than does Margin Co.

These differences are not necessarily an accident. Operating strategies differ among companies. Some companies require relatively large amounts of investment in assets to produce and sell their products. Utilities and manufacturing companies often require large investments in plant assets, for example. Therefore, their asset turnover ratios often are relatively low compared with companies such as service or retail companies. To generate high returns, companies with low asset turnovers must produce high profit margins.

Profit margins are higher when companies are efficient in controlling costs than when they are inefficient. Therefore, all companies attempt to control costs.

To produce high profit margins, a company must be able to sell its products at a relatively high price compared to the costs of producing and selling the products. To illustrate, consider again two hypothetical companies. Discount Co. and Specialty Co. are both clothing stores. Discount Co. competes by selling its products at low cost. It keeps its production and selling costs low and passes these low costs on to customers in the form of low prices. Its profit margin is relatively low because it must sell its products at low prices. Its asset turnover is high, however, because its competitive prices permit it to sell a lot of its products. Discount Co. is an example of a cost leader. It generates return on assets by high asset turnover.

Specialty Co. sells brand clothing, noted for style and high quality. Also, it provides a high level of customer service. Its prices are relatively high because its customers are willing to pay a premium for its products. Therefore, its profit margin is high. Asset turnover is low, however, because sales volume is low and investment in facilities and inventory is high relative to Discount Co. Specialty Co. is an example of a product-differentiated company. It generates return on assets by maintaining a high profit margin.

Exhibit 14-2[2] provides information about the profit margins and asset turnovers of several major companies.[3] Return on assets is profit margin times asset turnover. Therefore, for example, a return on assets (ROA) of 10% can result from a profit margin of 0.10 and an asset turnover of 1.00, as at point A, or from a profit margin of 0.05 and an asset turnover of 2.00, as at point B. Companies toward the top of the graph exhibit high profit margins. Those to the right of the graph exhibit high asset turnovers.

Observe that Wal–Mart generates return on assets of approximately 15% by high asset turnover and low profit margin. It is a discount store and a cost leader. It competes by selling a high quantity of products at a low cost. The Limited and Nike also generate return on assets of approximately 15%. These companies have lower asset turnovers but higher profit margins than Wal–Mart. They produce and sell name brand merchandise. Coca-Cola also has a return on assets of about 15%. It uses a combination of moderate profit margin and moderate asset turnover to generate this return.

McDonald's and Toys R Us both generate return on assets of about 10%. McDonald's has relatively high profit margin and Toys R Us a relatively high asset turnover. Capital intensive companies, such as Southwestern Bell and Southern Company (utilities), rely on high profit margins. Their asset turnovers are low because of the high level of investment in plant assets. Because they are regulated monopolies, they can command a relatively high price. Utilities provide products required by customers without having to compete with other producers. Wal–Mart, at the other extreme, is in a highly competitive business.

Some companies, Digital Equipment (DEC), Delta Air Lines, International Paper, and Scott Paper, have been relatively unsuccessful in their operating strategies. Both their profit margins and asset turnovers have been low.

Exhibit 14-3 summarizes the discussion of operating strategies.[4] Companies differ with respect to the types and amounts of assets needed to produce and sell their products. They also differ with respect to the types and amounts of compe-

---

[2] Adapted from Clyde P. Stickney, *Financial Statement Analysis: A Strategic Perspective*, Harcourt Brace Jovanovich, 1990, p. 167.

[3] Data are averages for 1983–1992. Data for these periods are used for this sample of companies throughout this chapter.

[4] Adapted from Alfred Rappaport, *Creating Shareholder Value*, The Free Press, 1986, pp. 97–98.

Exhibit 14-2   Trade-offs Between Profit Margin and Asset Turnover

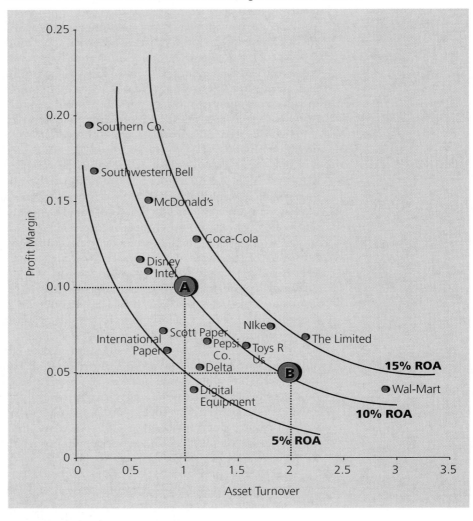

Data source: 1993 Compustat Annual Industrial File (see Exhibit 14-4).

tition they face. Therefore, companies rely on different strategies to generate profits.

A high rate of return on assets results when a company is effective in using its assets to produce and sell large quantities of products and when it is efficient in controlling costs. These attributes can be evaluated by examining the relative amounts of assets and costs of a company. For example, the amount of investment in inventory, accounts receivable, and plant assets can be evaluated by comparing these amounts relative to a company's sales and by examining changes in these amounts over time. Companies should maintain only the amount of investment in assets required by their sales and operating strategies. Efficiency can be evaluated by comparing cost of goods sold and other operating expenses to sales and by examining changes in these amounts over time. Costs should be in line with sales and unnecessary costs should be eliminated.

Exhibit 14-3 Operating Strategies for Creating Profits

Economic Attribute	Competitive Strategy	
	Product Differentiation	**Cost Leadership**
Asset turnover	Low	High
Profit margin	High	Low
Capital intensity	High	Low
Sales	Premium price	Competitive price and high volume
Costs	Necessary costs include research, design, and production costs to ensure quality and product features and costs of high levels of customer service	Cost control is critical; eliminate costs whenever possible
Products	Emphasize features and quality	Standardize design and control cost
Assets	Maintain receivables, inventory, and plant needed for premium products and service	Keep to a minimum and eliminate excess

Enhancing Return Through Financial Leverage

Objective 3
Evaluate the effect of a company's use of financial leverage to improve return on equity.

Return on equity is a measure of operating results that considers the effect of financial leverage on income and investment. Conceptually, we may think of return on equity as return on assets adjusted for the effect of financial leverage:

Return on Equity = Return on Assets × Effect of Financial Leverage.

A company can create higher returns for its owners by financing a portion of its total investment with debt. This use of financial leverage magnifies return on assets. To illustrate, assume the following information for Leverage Company:

Average assets	$1,000
Average common equity	600
Net income	200
Interest expense	50
Income tax rate	35%

Return on assets would be 23.25% [($200 + $50 (1 − .35))/$1,000]. Return on equity would be 33.33% ($200/$600). Thus, return on equity is 1.43 times the amount of return on assets:

Return on equity = Magnification effect of leverage × Return on assets
33.33%   =   1.43   ×   23.25%

Leverage Company's return on equity is higher than its return on assets because of the leverage created by using debt to finance part of the company's assets. By using debt, owners invested only 60% ($600/$1,000) of the amount that would be needed if no debt had been used. Also because of using debt, however, net income was reduced by interest expense on the debt.

Exhibit 14-4 provides information for the 15 companies illustrated in Exhibit 14-2. Observe that profitable companies exhibit high return on assets and are able to leverage this return into high return on equity. Coca-Cola, for example, is able to more than double its return on assets of 14.6% to generate a return on equity of 31.2% by using a relatively large amount of debt. Equity is only about 42.5% of Coke's total capital structure. Recall, however, that financial leverage also reduces return when a company is not performing well. Delta has a lot of debt in its capital structure. Because its return on assets is low (6.4%), the effect of using debt is to reduce return to stockholders. Therefore, Delta's return on equity is lower than its return on assets.

Exhibit 14-4   The Effect of Financial Leverage on Operating Results

	ROE	ROA	Magnification Effect	Asset Turnover	Profit Margin
Coca-Cola	0.312	0.146	2.14	1.126	0.131
DEC	0.032	0.044	0.73	1.101	0.043
Delta	0.045	0.064	0.70	1.168	0.053
Intel	0.117	0.086	1.36	0.725	0.112
International Paper	0.082	0.054	1.52	0.854	0.062
McDonald's	0.190	0.102	1.86	0.688	0.150
Nike	0.208	0.148	1.41	1.867	0.079
PepsiCo	0.210	0.084	2.50	1.237	0.070
Scott Paper	0.116	0.065	1.78	0.854	0.076
Southern	0.129	0.069	1.87	0.347	0.198
SW Bell	0.130	0.068	1.91	0.402	0.170
The Limited	0.289	0.157	1.84	2.135	0.074
Toys R Us	0.174	0.104	1.67	1.528	0.068
Wal-Mart	0.259	0.128	2.02	2.930	0.044
Disney	0.165	0.086	1.92	0.684	0.125

Source: 1993 Compustat Annual Industrial File.

Exhibit 14-5 illustrates the relation between return on equity and return on assets for companies with high or low financial leverage. When return on assets is low, financial leverage has a negative effect on a company's return on equity. When return on assets is high, financial leverage has a positive effect on return on equity.

SELF-STUDY PROBLEM 14-1

Information is provided below from the 1993 annual report of Chrysler Corporation (in millions):

Sales revenues	$43,600
Interest expense	1,104
Income before taxes	3,838
Income taxes	1,423
Net income (before special items)	2,415

Exhibit 14-5   The Effect of Financial Leverage on Return

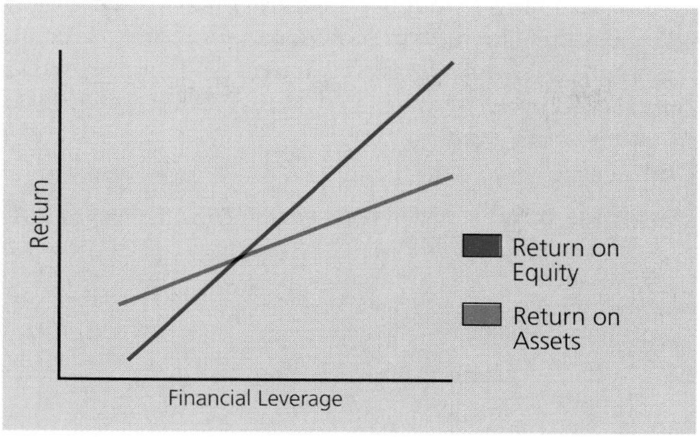

Preferred dividends	80
Average total assets	42,242
Average common equity	7,185

Required

Determine the following from this information: (a) asset turnover, (b) profit margin, (c) return on assets, and (d) return on equity. Evaluate Chrysler's operating strategy and the effect of leverage on the company's return to stockholders.

The solution to Self-Study Problem 14-1 appears at the end of the chapter.

GROWTH IN OPERATING RESULTS

Objective 4
Identify company attributes associated with growth in returns and company value.

Return on equity measures profitability for a period of time. It is a bit like identifying a car as being at the corner of 5th and Elm, traveling at 50 miles per hour. We know where the car was at a particular time and how fast it was going. We might also want to know in which direction the car was headed and whether it was speeding up or slowing down, however, if we want to locate the car at some future time. Growth provides this type of information for a company. Two companies may have the same return on equity at a particular time, say 20%. If one company's growth rate is 10% per year and the other's is -10% per year, we can estimate return on equity for next year as being 22% (20% + (10% × 20%)) for one company and 18% (20% $-$ (10% × 20%)) for the other. Thus, growth of return on equity is useful information.

Growth and Investment Opportunities

Growth results from the ability of a company to produce and sell products that are increasing in demand. If a company can sell more of its products while controlling its costs, its profits and expected future cash flows will increase. To generate higher sales, companies usually must invest in more assets. Consequently, they also must obtain additional financing. A profitable company can provide much of this financing through reinvestment of its earnings. Therefore, growth in sales (operating activities) are associated with growth in assets (investing activities) and growth in equity (financing activities). High-growth companies are usually high-value companies, as illustrated in Exhibit 14-6. Data are for the 900-company sample.

Exhibit 14-6   The Relations Among Growth in Sales, Assets, and Equity and Value

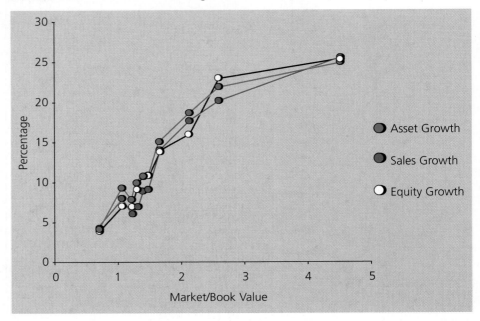

Source: 1993 Compustat Annual Industrial File.

The exhibit demonstrates that sales, assets, and equity all tend to grow at about the same rate for a company but vary considerably for different companies. Growth is the average annual percentage change in sales, assets, or equity for the 1983–1992 period. High growth rates are associated with high market to book value ratios. Growth in sales, assets, and equity is associated with growth in return on equity. Compare Exhibit 14-6 with Exhibit 14-1. Value results from the interaction of financing, investing, and operating activities.

Companies grow when they take advantage of investment opportunities. A company may create opportunities by developing new products or by moving into new markets. High technology companies, like Intel, can grow rapidly by developing products that surpass the capabilities of competitor products. Research and development are critical activities for these companies. Coca-Cola operates in a relatively mature industry. New brands are created to compete with existing brands, but the potential for large increases in sales volume is low. Coke has grown by moving into foreign markets. These markets often are less competitive than the U.S. market.

Another growth option is to obtain opportunities from other companies by merger or acquisition. PepsiCo, for example, has acquired a variety of other companies in the food industry in recent years.

Investment opportunities are more common for certain types of companies than for others and are associated with economic attributes of these companies. Exhibit 14–7 illustrates several attributes of high-value companies. These attributes also are associated with investment opportunities and growth. Data are for the 900-company sample.

Exhibit 14-7 Company Attributes Associated with Investment Opportunities

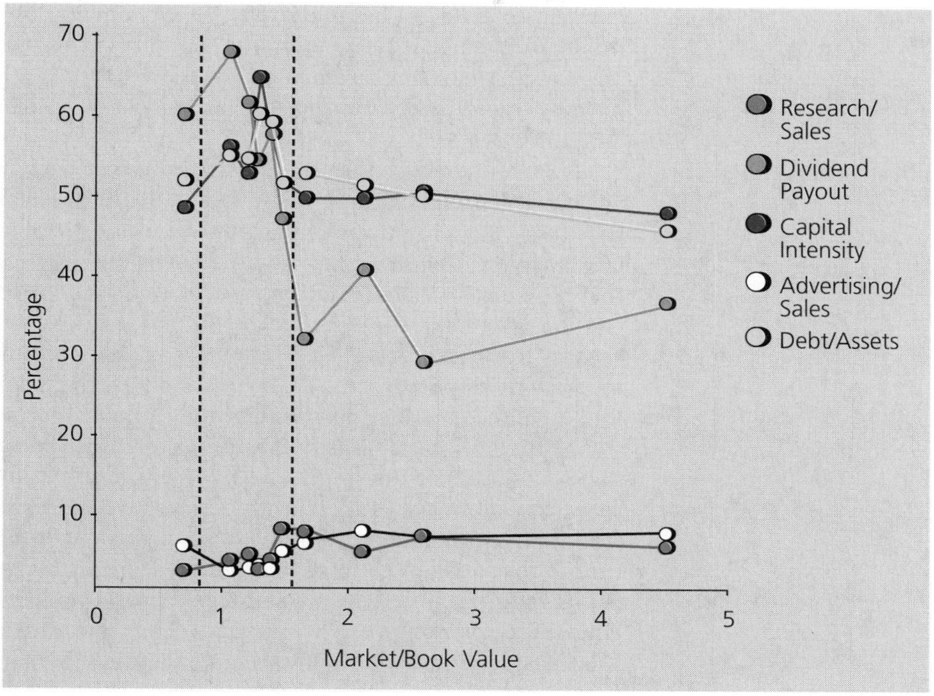

Source: 1993 Compustat Annual Industrial File.

Observe that high-value, high-growth companies (those to the right of the dotted lines) pay relatively small amounts of dividends. These companies depend on operating activities to generate cash flows, which they reinvest in new assets. Thus, their debt to asset ratios are relatively low, as well. High-value, high-growth companies tend not to be capital intensive. They invest heavily in research and development and advertising rather than in plant assets.

Capital intensive companies (those between the dotted lines) tend to be moderate-value companies. Also, they are moderate-growth companies. They pay out relatively large amounts of dividends. Because they must invest heavily in assets, their return on assets tends to be relatively low. Because their earnings are relatively stable, they can support relatively large amounts of debt. Financial leverage is used to boost return so that return on equity is competitive with other companies.

Low-value, low-growth companies are to the left of the dotted lines in the graph. These are companies that have not been successful with their investment opportunities or for which investment opportunities are relatively low. They have generated low earnings and often depend on external financing. They pay relatively high dividends when cash is available because their investment opportunities are limited.

Low-value, low-growth companies are not necessarily poor investments for stockholders. Investors have different reasons for investing. Some investors want their investments to increase in value through growth. Others, however, are interested in steady dividends which often are paid by low-growth companies.

Exhibit 14-8 provides information for the 15 companies examined earlier. The companies are ranked by market to book value. Observe that high-value companies tend to have high-return on equity, low dividend payout, low to moderate financial leverage, and high equity growth. Wal-Mart and The Limited are examples of high-return, high growth companies. Coca-Cola is a high-return but low-growth company and its market value is lower than Wal-Mart or The Limited.

Low-value companies are either those that have performed poorly in return and growth (Digital Equipment, Delta, Scott Paper, and International Paper) or those that have low investment opportunities (Southwestern Bell and Southern Company). Observe that dividend payouts are high for the utilities. Also observe that they use financial leverage to increase return on equity. They provide returns to their owners in the form of steady dividend payments. In contrast, companies such as Toys R Us and The Limited pay low amounts of dividends because of investment opportunities. Other companies, Digital Equipment and Delta, pay low dividends because poor operating results reduce available cash flows.

Exhibit 14-8 also lists bond ratings for those companies that had bonds outstanding. Observe that high-value companies typically have higher bond ratings than low-value companies. Though we have emphasized the use of accounting information to value common stocks in this chapter, the same type of information is relevant to creditors and other decision makers. Most external decision makers are interested in profitability, growth, and risk attributes of companies. The ability of a company to meet its debt requirements or to make payments to suppliers depends largely on the same factors that affect its ability to create value for stockholders. Consequently, the types of information and analysis examined in this chapter are relevant for many user decisions.

Exhibit 14-8   Value Associated with Return, Growth, and Investment Opportunities

	Market/ Book Value	ROA	ROE	Dividend Payout	Debt/ Assets	Capital Intensity	Equity Growth	Bond Rating
Wal-Mart	16.508	0.128	0.259	0.113	0.553	0.432	0.317	Aa1
The Limited	11.121	0.157	0.289	0.174	0.501	0.571	0.338	A1
Coca-Cola	7.001	0.146	0.312	0.468	0.575	0.563	0.039	Aa3
Toys R Us	6.055	0.104	0.174	0.000	0.442	0.530	0.227	Aa3
PepsiCo	4.949	0.084	0.210	0.380	0.701	0.677	0.135	A1
Disney	4.457	0.086	0.165	0.337	0.544	0.572	0.154	Aa3
Nike	4.151	0.148	0.208	0.313	0.360	0.254	0.227	none
Intel	3.946	0.086	0.117	0.004	0.362	0.462	0.208	none
McDonald's	3.546	0.102	0.190	0.162	0.572	0.936	0.136	Aa2
Digital Equipment	1.637	0.044	0.032	0.000	0.297	0.310	0.054	A2
SW Bell	1.590	0.069	0.130	0.677	0.611	0.871	0.037	A1
Delta	1.544	0.064	0.045	0.112	0.672	0.809	0.103	Baa3
Scott Paper	1.460	0.065	0.116	0.158	0.629	0.750	0.046	A3
Southern Company	1.361	0.069	0.129	0.674	0.706	0.887	0.068	A1
International Paper	1.190	0.054	0.082	0.570	0.528	0.759	0.073	A3

Growth and Cash Flow

Several themes have been emphasized throughout this book. These include the importance of financing, investing, and operating activities in the transformation process and the creation of value through the transformation process. Accounting provides information for understanding the process and how value is created. A third theme of importance is the relation between accrual and cash flow measures of the transformation process. Accounting provides both types of information. The income statement provides accrual information. The cash flow statement provides cash flow information, and the balance sheet provides information linking accrual with cash flow measures. It should come as no surprise then that both accrual and cash flow measures and the relation between them provide useful information for understanding return and growth.

Income and cash flow from operating activities tend to move together. Companies reporting large amounts of net income generally report large amounts of operating cash flows. Therefore, high-value companies tend to be those with high operating cash flows. Exhibit 14-9 illustrates the relation among cash flows and company value. The exhibit reports data for the 900-company sample. Cash flows were divided by common stockholders' equity to control for differences in size across companies.

Exhibit 14-9 Cash Flows and Company Value

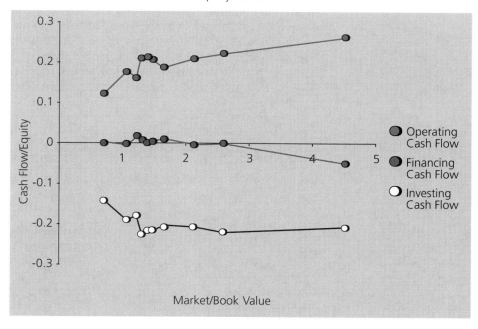

Source: 1993 Compustat Annual Industrial File.

High-value companies exhibit high operating cash flows. These cash flows are used to take advantage of investment opportunities and provide the major source of financing for these companies. Low-value companies generate low amounts of cash flow from operating activities and invest lower amounts of cash (less cash outflow) in additional assets.

Cash flow can pose a problem for high-growth and low-growth companies. High-growth companies often do not generate enough cash flow from operating activities to meet their investment needs. Though income may be high for these companies, their operating cash flows tend to lag income and may not be sufficient to permit the companies to take advantage of their investment opportunities. Thus, to conserve cash for investment, these companies pay low amounts of dividends and rely on external financing to help with cash requirements. A major risk for these companies is that they will borrow heavily to provide cash for investment but the investments will turn out not to be as good as expected. If demand for products does not materialize, these companies become low-growth, low-return companies that face a questionable future.

Low-return, low-growth companies that have not performed well often experience cash flow problems because their operating activities are producing low amounts of cash flows. Both income and cash flow are low for these companies. Low cash flow companies may have difficulty meeting debt requirements and paying their ongoing expenses. If operating cash flows become too low, these companies are forced to liquidate or to merge with other companies. Bankrupt companies generally are in the low cash flow category.

Cash flow poses a special problem for new companies. Income typically is low for these companies until they can establish customers for their products. They rely on external financing to provide cash for their investment opportunities. Operating cash flow is low and tends to lag income. If successful, these companies will grow by reinvesting their earnings and gradually reducing reliance on external financing. If they are not successful, however, they usually are forced to liquidate to pay off creditors. Most bankruptcies occur within the first year of a new company's operations. Failure to secure sufficient financing and poor cash flow are the major causes of business failure for these companies.

Summary of Growth Attributes

Companies can be separated into high- and low-value groups based on the following attributes:

	High-Value Companies	Low-Value Companies
Sales growth	High	Low
Asset growth	High	Low
Equity growth	High	Low
Return on equity	High	Low
Return on assets	High	Low
Operating cash inflow	High	Low
Investing cash outflow	High	Low
Dividend payout	Low	High
Debt /assets or debt /equity	Low	High
Capital intensity	Low	High
Research and development expenditure	High	Low

A specific company may not exhibit all of the attributes of either high-value or low-value companies. Coca-Cola, for example, is a high-value company, but its growth rates are relatively low. These attributes are general tendencies. High- and low-value companies will tend to exhibit the attributes described on page 622.

SELF-STUDY PROBLEM 14-2

Information is provided below from the annual report of Johnson & Johnson:

(in millions)	1993	1992	1991
Sales	14,138	13,753	12,447
Net income before special items	1,787	1,625	1,461
Average assets	12,063	11,199	10,010
Average common equity	5,370	5,353	5,167
Dividends	659	587	513
Depreciation and amortization	617	560	493
Operating cash flow	2,168	2,149	1,675
Average market value of equity	31,062	35,531	31,015

Required

Use the information provided to calculate for 1993 and 1992: (a) return on equi- ty, (b) growth in return on equity [(net income at end of year − net income at beginning of year)/average equity], (c) growth in equity [(average equity for year 2 − average equity for year 1)/average equity for year 1], (d) growth in sales, as for equity, (e) growth in assets, as for equity, (f) (net income + depreciation)/av- erage equity, (g) operating cash flow/average equity, (h) dividend payout (divi- dends/net income before special items), and (i) market/book value of equity. Use the information in (a) to (h) to help explain the change in (i).

The solution to Self-Study Problem 14-2 appears at the end of the chapter.

RISK AND OPERATING ACTIVITIES

Objective 6
Identify the effect of risk on a company's expected return on equity.

The results of operating activities are uncertain. Future operating results often differ from past results. Results are better for some companies but worse for oth- ers. The amount of uncertainty, or risk, associated with companies' operating re- sults varies across companies. Operating results for some companies are relatively stable, changing little from year to year. Utilities, for example, generally are stable because their earnings are regulated. They are permitted to set prices to ensure the rate of return to stockholders remains within a limited range. Highly com- petitive companies often experience wide variations in returns, however. When market conditions are good and a company's products are in high demand, the company's returns are high. But, when market conditions are poor and demand is weak, returns are low.

Exhibit 14-10 provides a general description of the risk and return relation. Return is defined in the exhibit as return on equity. Risk is defined as the vari- ability of return on equity, measured by the standard deviation of return on equity.

Exhibit 14-10   The Relation Between Risk and Return

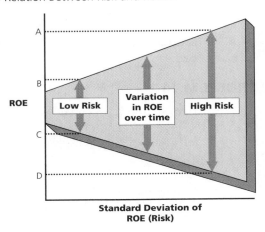

Low-risk companies are toward the left side of the graph, and high-risk companies are toward the right. Return on equity remains relatively stable over time for low-risk companies (as represented by the width of the shaded area). Therefore, investors can be relatively sure of the rate of return the company is likely to earn in the future (between points B and C, for example). Return on equity varies much more for high-risk companies. Consequently, investors are less sure of the rate of return a high-risk company is likely to earn (between points A and D, for example). In some situations, a high-risk company may earn a higher return than a low-risk company during a particular period. This result is represented in the exhibit by points A and B. In other situations, however, a high-risk company may earn a lower return than a low-risk company. This result is represented by points C and D. In general, low-risk companies earn moderate, but stable, returns. High-risk companies, in contrast, earn high and low returns that vary more from period to period.

Causes of Risk

Objective 7
Identify causes of risk for a corporation.

A variety of factors help explain why some companies are riskier than others. Some of these factors can be controlled by a company's management, but many cannot. We can identify some of these factors from the sample of 15 companies examined earlier. Exhibit 14-11 illustrates the relation between risk and return for these companies. Risk is measured by the standard deviation of return on equity, and return is return on equity. Observe that the companies conform to the pattern described in Exhibit 14-10, as illustrated by the shaded area of Exhibit 14-11. High-risk companies fall into a broader range of returns than low-risk companies. Some high-risk companies earn higher returns, but others earn lower returns, than low-risk companies.

A comparison of Exhibit 14-11 with the company data in Exhibit 14-8 reveals that companies toward the bottom of Exhibit 14-11 are low-value companies and those toward the top are high-value companies.

The variability of return on assets and return on equity are related to the variability of sales. Exhibit 14-12 illustrates these relations for the 900-company

Exhibit 14-11   Risk and Return Relation for Selected Companies

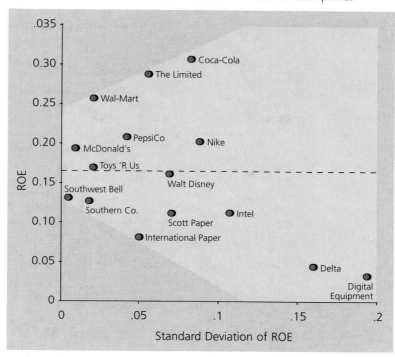

Data source: 1993 Compustat Annual Industrial File.

sample. Companies that exhibit a high standard deviation of sales also generally exhibit a high standard deviation of return on assets and return on equity. When customer market conditions are stable, a company is likely to be low risk. For example, utilities (Southwestern Bell and Southern Company) are low-risk companies as seen in Exhibit 14-11. Because their returns are regulated and their markets are not competitive, these companies face stable market conditions.

Regulation and competition are factors that affect the stability of customer markets. Competition results from product and market conditions. Some companies produce and sell products that must compete with similar products sold by other companies. Sales are affected by the price and features of these products. General economic conditions are more favorable to some products and industries than others at different times. Therefore, market conditions are more favorable for certain companies than for others during a specific period.

Many companies suffered from poor economic conditions during the early 1990s. Most industrial nations faced a recession during this period in which the general level of economic activity was relatively low. Companies that depend heavily on industrial production and a high level of business activity to prosper performed poorly during this period. A decrease in business demand for major computer systems hurt companies like Digital Equipment, along with other major companies like IBM. A decrease in business travel affected most major airlines, including Delta. A decrease in demand for packaging and office products affected paper companies, including International Paper and Scott Paper.

Exhibit 14-12   Variability of Sales and Return

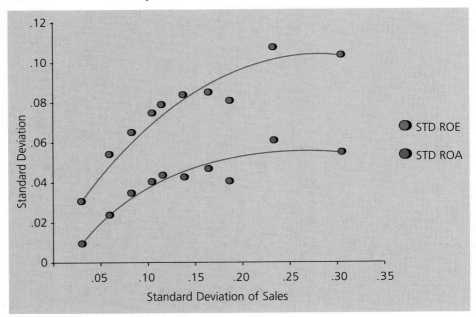

Other companies were less affected or perhaps positively affected by the economic recession. Discount stores and fast food restaurants prospered during this period as many consumers switched to buying low-cost products. Wal-Mart, McDonald's, PepsiCo (parent of Pizza Hut, Kentucky Fried Chicken, and Taco Bell), and Toys R Us are all low-cost, high volume producers, relative to other companies in their industries. Products such as soft drinks were not especially affected by the recession.

Companies such as Delta, Digital Equipment, International Paper, and Scott Paper are in competitive industries. Until the early 1980s, airlines were regulated so that fares and control over routes were not highly competitive. Deregulation stimulated greater competition, however; and several major airlines (Eastern and Pan Am) were forced out of business. Airlines and many other companies that performed poorly during the late 1980s and early 1990s were companies with high fixed costs. As passenger demand decreased, airlines were forced to cut prices to attract customers. Therefore, sales revenues decreased, but many airline costs (airplanes, maintenance, fuel, employees) could not be reduced substantially, at least in the short run. Manufacturing companies, such as paper companies, require large investments in production facilities. As demand for products decreases, these companies also are forced to cut prices to attract customers. Many of their costs cannot be eliminated, however. Thus, earnings of companies with high operating leverage (high fixed costs) are likely to be low when economic conditions are poor. Over several years, these companies can restructure their operations to eliminate unneeded facilities and employees. These changes take time and are costly to accomplish, however.

Because capital intensive companies require large amounts of investments, their asset turnover ratios often are relatively low. To create returns, these companies rely on high profit margins. When economic conditions are good, these companies can generate high profit margins because it is difficult for other companies to enter their markets. High levels of investment produce a barrier to entry into some industries. It is difficult for a new company to enter the automobile or paper industries, for example, because of the large amount of investment necessary to begin companies in these industries. Thus, if demand is high, capital intensive companies can maintain high prices and still sell most of the goods they produce. When economic conditions are bad, however, profit margins and returns are low for these companies.

Interest rates also affect demand for many products. When interest rates charged by banks and other financial institutions are low, consumers borrow more heavily to purchase homes, automobiles, major appliances, and other goods. Therefore, the sales of companies in these industries are sensitive to the level of interest rates. During the early 1990s, the federal government reduced interest rates to stimulate increased economic activity. As the economy began to recover, the government increased interest rates to prevent high demand from creating a major increase in inflation. Automobile and home sales were spurred by low interest rates but slowed as interest rates increased with the economic recovery.

Risk also is affected by management decisions. Some companies are able to maintain a high level of performance, even in poor economic and highly competitive conditions, by continuing to produce innovative and high-quality products. Others can maintain performance by eliminating unnecessary costs and reducing product prices. Digital Equipment and IBM suffered during the 1980s and 1990s from highly competitive markets in which low-cost personal computers replaced larger systems in many businesses. Poor performance for these companies resulted from the failure of managers to adapt quickly to changing market conditions. Walt Disney Company suffered, at least temporarily, from an investment in Euro-Disney that produced low returns during the early 1990s.

Investment decisions affect performance and risk. Good investments usually result in steady growth and increased earnings. For example, Coca-Cola has benefited from large foreign investments. Sales have increased internationally, while domestic sales have remained relatively stable. Coke faced a relatively mature market in the U.S., with little growth potential. Coke has increased its growth potential by entering new markets. In contrast, poor investments often lead to unstable earnings as companies attempt to improve poor performance. Digital Equipment has invested heavily in changing its product lines to make them more competitive. During this transition, low profits and high restructuring costs have reduced the value of the company.

Financial leverage is another factor that affects risk. Managers decide on the mix of debt and equity to finance their investments. Reliance on debt can increase return on equity when a company's sales and return on assets are high. High levels of debt also increase risk, however. If a company's sales and return on assets are low, financial leverage results in lower return on equity.

Exhibit 14-13 describes the relation between financial leverage and risk. The exhibit separates companies with low financial leverage (low debt/assets) from those with high financial leverage (high debt/assets). Data are for the 900-company sample. The relation between the standard deviation of return on assets and the standard deviation of return on equity is presented for each group of companies.

The variability in return on equity is larger for the high–financial leverage companies than for the low-leverage companies for the same amount of variability in return on assets. For example, compare the standard deviation of return on

Exhibit 14-13   The Effect of Financial Leverage on Risk

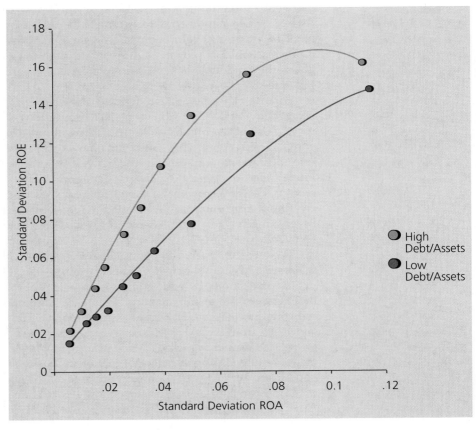

Source: 1993 Compustat Annual Industrial File.

equity for high- and low-leverage companies that have a standard deviation of return on assets of 0.04. The standard deviation of return on equity is 0.11 for high-leverage companies compared to 0.07 for low-leverage companies. Thus, the variability of return on equity is about a third higher for these high-leverage companies.

Thus, a variety of factors affects a company's risk. Some of these factors are not controllable by a company's management: general economic conditions, competition, and interest rates. Other factors are controllable: research and development, expansion to new markets, new investment, and financial leverage. These factors affect the stability of a company's sales and earnings. Also, they affect future earnings and uncertainty about these earnings.

ACCOUNTING INFORMATION AND COMPANY VALUE

Objective 8
Analyze a corporation's financial statements to explain the value of the company.

Throughout this book, we have considered the importance of accounting as a source of information for helping decision makers understand and evaluate company activities. Decision makers can understand performance if they can interpret accounting information about a company's transformation process. The balance sheet, income statement, and cash flow statement, along with related notes, are important for understanding the financing, investing, and operating activities in a company's transformation process.

Exhibit 14-14 summarizes the types of information available from a company's financial statements. The ability to identify and interpret this information will permit you to evaluate the financial performances of most companies.

These measures normally are used in one of two ways. One approach is to compute measures for different companies as a basis for comparing the companies. Strengths and weaknesses and expectations about future performance can be assessed in making investment decisions. Sometimes, measures for a particular company are compared with the average for a particular industry or set of companies. A second approach is to compute measures at different times to determine whether a particular company's performance is improving or whether the company's risk is changing.

The analysis of a company's performance is complex. The factors described in Exhibit 14-14 are not exhaustive of all factors that might be important for a specific decision. Instead, they provide a conceptual description of the types of accounting information considered by decision makers in evaluating a company's performance. An understanding of the concepts underlying these accounting measures provides a starting point for reading and interpreting a company's financial statements.

SELF-STUDY PROBLEM 14-3

Information is provided below for two companies, Sara Lee Corporation and Vulcan Materials Company, from their 1993 annual reports. The values are averages and standard deviations for the 1989–1993 period.

	Sara Lee	Vulcan
Return on equity	0.217	0.145
Return on assets	0.083	0.091
Debt/assets	0.685	0.359
Asset turnover	1.502	1.022
Profit margin	0.055	0.089
Operating cash/equity	0.290	0.277
Sales growth	0.070	0.015
Asset growth	0.171	0.025
Equity growth	0.180	0.021
Dividend payout	0.409	0.522
Investing cash/equity	0.214	0.150
Capital intensity	0.635	0.724
Standard deviation of ROE	0.020	0.050
Standard deviation of Sales	0.190	0.038

Required

Use the information to assess the value of each company. Which company do you believe is more valuable? Why? The market/book value of one of the companies was 2.4 and that of the other was 3.3 in 1993. Which company had the higher ratio?

The solution to Self-Study Problem 14-3 appears at the end of the chapter.

Exhibit 14-14 Accounting Information Useful for Evaluating Company Value

Accounting Information	Importance	Calculation
1. Return on equity	Ability to create value for its stockholders from its operating activities	(Net income* − preferred dividends) / average common equity
a. Return on assets	Ability to create value from total investment	[Net income* + (interest expense (1 − tax rate))]/average assets
(1) Asset turnover	Ability to generate sales from total investment	Sales/average assets
(2) Profit margin	Ability to generate profit from sales	[Net income* + (interest expense (1 − tax rate))]/sales
b. Financial leverage	Use of debt to increase return to stockholders	Debt/assets or debt/equity
c. Operating cash flow	Source of cash for new investment and payments to stockholders	Net operating cash flow/equity
2. Growth in ROE	Direction and amount of change in future ROE	(Income at time 2 − income at time 1)/equity at time 1
a. Growth in sales	Increased demand usually results in higher return	(Sales at time 2 − sales at time 1)/sales at time 1
b. Growth in assets	Increase in investment is basis for additional sales	(Assets at time 2 − assets at time 1)/ assets at time 1
c. Growth in equity	Reinvestment of earnings increases value in company for stockholders	(Equity at time 2 − equity at time 1)/ equity at time 1
d. Dividend payout	Reinvestment of earnings increases value in company for stockholders	Dividends/net income
e. Investing cash flow	Reinvestment of operating cash increases value in company for stockholders	Net cash flow for investing
f. Capital intensity	Growth potential usually higher for less intensive companies	Long-term assets/total assets
g. Research and development	Growth potential is usually higher for innovative companies	Research and development expenses/ sales
3. Risk	Uncertainty about returns to stockholders	Standard deviation of ROE
a. Variability of ROA	Volatility of earnings excluding effects of financial leverage	Standard deviation of ROA
b. Variability of sales	Volatility of demand for products	Standard deviation of sales
(1) Market conditions	Sensitivity of sales to general economy	General levels of economic growth and interest rates
(2) Competition	Ability to control demand and prices	Types of products, capital intensity, regulation
(3) Innovation	Ability to develop new and better products	Research and development expenses/ sales
c. Financial leverage	High leverage increases volatility of earnings	Debt/assets or debt/equity

Net income usually is defined as income before special items (discontinued operations, extraordinary items, and accounting changes) in this analysis.

R E V I E W *Summary of Important Concepts*

1. A company's market value is affected by its return, growth, and risk attributes.
   a. Return can be measured by return on equity.
   b. Growth can be measured by the change in net income relative to equity.
   c. Risk can be measured by the variability (standard deviation) of return on equity.

2. Return on equity is affected by return on assets and by financial leverage.
   a. Return on assets is profit margin times asset turnover. Companies may use different strategies to create return on assets. A cost leadership strategy results from low prices and cost control, resulting in low profit margin and high asset turnover. A product differentiation strategy emphasizes product quality or features and is associated with high profit margin and low asset turnover.
   b. Financial leverage magnifies return on assets. Return on equity is return on assets times the effect of financial leverage. When a company is performing well, return on equity is higher than return on assets.

3. Growth results when a company takes advantage of investment opportunities by acquiring additional assets.
   a. An increase in assets usually is associated with an increase in sales and equity. More assets provide for greater capacity to produce and sell products. An increase in equity results from higher net income that is reinvested to acquire additional assets.
   b. Certain types of companies often have greater investment opportunities than others. Growth companies are often less capital intensive, have lower financial leverage, pay out less dividends relative to earnings, and spend more on advertising and research than other companies.
   c. High-value, high-growth companies create cash from sales activities and reinvest much of the cash in additional assets. They use their cash to take advantage of investment opportunities rather than paying large amounts of dividends.

4. Risk results from uncertainty about future earnings and operating cash flows.
   a. High levels of competition for a company's products often results in high risk. Utilities and other regulated companies are generally low risk.
   b. Capital intensity, operating leverage, and financial leverage are other attributes that affect risk.

5. Accounting information is useful for assessing return, growth, and risk attributes. Therefore, it is useful for evaluating company value.

D E F I N E *Terms and Concepts Defined in This Chapter*

asset turnover   profit margin

SOLUTIONS

SELF-STUDY PROBLEM 14-1

(a) Asset turnover = sales/average assets = $43,600/$42,242 = 1.03

(b) Profit margin = [net income + interest (1 − tax rate)]/sales =
[$2,415 + $1,104 (1 − ($1,423/$3,838))]/$43,600 = $3,110/$43,600 = 0.0713

(c) Return on assets = asset turnover × profit margin = 1.03 × .0713 = 0.0735 or
= [net income + interest (1 − tax rate)]/average assets = $3,110/$42,242 = 0.0735

(d) Return on equity = (net income − preferred dividends)/average equity =
($2,415 − $80)/$7,185 = 0.325

Chrysler's return on assets of 7.35% was relatively low compared with many other companies discussed in this chapter. Neither its asset turnover nor its profit margin were high. Given the capital intensive nature of Chrysler operations, one would expect the company to rely on profit margin as an operating strategy. The company used its very high financial leverage to generate a high return on equity of 32.5%, however. Chrysler's assets were 5.88 times ($42,242/$7,185) its common stockholders' equity. This large amount of debt provided a high magnification effect that resulted in a high return on equity.

SELF-STUDY PROBLEM 14-2

	1993	**1992**
a. Return on equity	0.3328 = 1,787/5,370	0.3036 = 1,625/5,353
b. Growth in ROE	0.0302 = (1,787 − 1,625)/5,370	0.0306 = (1,625 − 1,461)/5,353
c. Growth in equity	0.0032 = (5,370 − 5,353)/5,353	0.0360 = (5,353 − 5,167)/5,167
d. Growth in sales	0.0280 = (14,138 − 13,753)/13,753	0.1049 = (13,753 − 12,447)/12,447
e. Growth in assets	0.0771 = (12,063 − 11,199)/11,199	0.1188 = (11,199 − 10,010)/10,010
f. (Net income + depreciation)/equity	0.4477 = (1,787 + 617)/5,370	0.4082 = (1,625 + 560)/5,353
g. Operating cash flow/equity	0.4037 = 2,168/5,370	0.4015 = 2,149/5,353
h. Dividend payout	0.3688 = 659/1,787	0.3612 = 587/1,625
i. Market/book value	5.7844 = 31,062/5,370	6.6376 = 35,531/5,353

The decrease in market to book value can be explained, partially, by the decrease in growth in equity, sales, and assets. Return on equity, growth in ROE, operating cash flow/equity, and dividend payout did not change much between 1992 and 1993. The decrease in the sales growth rate could signal a decrease in future earnings growth. Though ROE is relatively high, the growth rates in ROE, equity, sales, and assets are relatively low compared with other companies discussed in this chapter. Johnson & Johnson is similar to Coca-Cola in its ROE, growth, and market to book value ratios. Both are high-return but low-growth companies. Other factors, such as changes in the general economy, also may explain some of the decrease in company value. These factors cannot be assessed from the information provided.

SELF-STUDY PROBLEM 14-3

Sara Lee's return on equity was much higher than Vulcan's, though Vulcan's return on assets was higher. The difference can be explained by Sara Lee's higher financial leverage. Its debt to asset ratio is almost double that of Vulcan. Sara Lee is using financial leverage effectively to generate higher returns for its stockholders. Growth rates also are higher for Sara Lee for assets, sales, and equity. Operating cash flow to equity is about the same and relatively high for both companies. Operating cash flow/equity is almost twice return on equity for Vulcan. Investing cash flow/equity is considerably higher for Sara Lee. Vulcan is more capital intensive and its dividend payout ratio is higher. These ratios suggest that Vulcan is a slow growth, capital intensive company. It is reinvesting at a lower rate than Sara Lee. Its investment opportunities are not as good. Therefore, it is paying a higher dividend rate to its stockholders. The standard deviation of return on equity is relatively low for both companies, though it is lower for Sara Lee than for Vulcan. In contrast, the standard deviation of sales/assets is higher for Sara Lee. Thus, though its sales are more volatile, its earnings are less volatile than Vulcan's. One explanation for this difference would be that Vulcan has relatively high fixed operating costs. Therefore, it is less capable of keeping its expenses in line with sales, as sales change.

All of these factors suggest that, though both companies are performing well, Sara Lee is the higher value company. Sara Lee's market/book value in 1993 was 3.3. Vulcan's was 2.4.

EXERCISES

14-1. Write a short definition for each of the terms listed in the "Terms and Concepts Defined in This Chapter" section.

14-2. What is a company's economic environment? How does this environment affect the company's performance? You have accepted a position as local manager of a fast food franchise, specializing in Tex-Mex cuisine. Identify economic factors that are likely to have an influence on the success of your franchise. Which factors do you consider to be most important?

14-3. Return on assets and return on equity are measures of performance. Explain the difference between the two measures.

14-4. Explain why the growth and variability of earnings should affect the value of a company's common stock.

14-5. The following is information from the 1993 income statement of Rubbermaid, Inc.:

Years Ended December 31, (in thousands except per share amounts)	1993	1992	1991
Net sales	$1,960,207	$1,805,332	$1,667,305
Cost of sales	1,285,949	1,200,651	1,102,685
Selling, general, and administrative expenses	328,741	310,410	307,780
Realignment costs*		27,500	
Other charges (credits), net:			
Interest expense	7,787	7,561	8,300
Interest income	(4,921)	(4,923)	(5,889)
Miscellaneous, net	768	(2,700)	(8,158)
	3,634	(62)	(5,747)
Earnings before income taxes	341,883	266,833	262,587
Income taxes	130,470	99,907	99,937
Net earnings	$ 211,413	$ 166,926	$ 162,650
Net earnings per common share	$ 1.32	$ 1.04	$ 1.02

Costs to realign and integrate certain operations

How much did sales grow from 1991 to 1992 and from 1992 to 1993? Restate each item on the income statement (except earnings per share) as a percent of net sales. What important changes occurred in Rubbermaid's relative expenses and income over the three-year period? What conclusions can you draw about the company's economic environment? What conclusions can you draw about the company's operating leverage? Are most of its costs fixed or variable?

14-6. Information from the 1993 income statement of General Mills, Inc. is provided below:

(in millions)	1993	1992	1991
Sales	$8,134.6	$7,777.8	$7,153.2
Net earnings	506.1	495.6	472.7

Calculate profit margin for General Mills for each of the three years. What information do these amounts provide about the company's operating activities over the three years?

14-7. Selected information from the 1994 annual report of Home Depot, Inc. is provided below:

(in millions)	1994	1993
Net sales	$9,238.7	
Interest expense	30.7	
Net income	457.4	
Total assets	4,700.8	$3,931.7
Income tax rate	37.9%	

Calculate Home Depot's profit margin, asset turnover, and return on assets for 1994. Use earnings plus interest adjusted for taxes in your computations. In comparison with the companies shown in Exhibit 14-2, what strategy does Home Depot appear to be using to generate profits?

14-8. Selected information from the 1993 annual reports of American Brands, Inc. and Philip Morris Companies, Inc. is provided on the next page. Both companies are in the tobacco and consumer products industry.

(in millions)	American Brands	Philip Morris
Net sales	$13,701	$60,901
Interest expense	244	1,391
Income before special items	668	3,658
Total assets, 1993	16,339	51,205
Total assets, 1992	14,919	50,014
Income tax rate	38%	42%

Compare the operating strategies of the two companies by calculating profit margin, asset turnover, and return on assets. Which company appears to be doing the better job with its strategy?

14-9. Summarize the primary differences between cost leadership and profit differentiation strategies. How can these strategies be used to improve return on assets and profitability? In particular, how would you expect the choice of strategy to affect the components of return on assets reported by companies using these strategies?

14-10. The following information was taken from the 1993 annual report of Unisys Corporation (in millions):

Net income	$565.4
Interest expense	241.7
Preferred dividends	121.6
Average total assets	7,534
Average common equity	896
Income tax rate	28%

Calculate return on assets and return on equity. What conclusions can you draw about the effect of financial leverage on return to common stockholders?

14-11. Information is provided below from the 1993 annual report of Rubbermaid Inc.:

(in thousands)	1993	1992	1991
Net earnings	$211,413	$164,095	$162,650
Net cash from operating activities	287,396	176,896	249,165
Net cash from (for) investing activities	(207,870)	(138,086)	(119,980)
Net cash from (for) financing activities	(74,218)	(69,637)	(53,362)

Evaluate Rubbermaid's performance over the three years presented. Would you characterize the company as growing, stable, or declining? Is it surprising that the change in net earnings differs from the change in net cash from operating activities over the period? Which measure of operating activities is more stable? Why?

14-12. The following information was reported by Delta Air Lines in its 1994 annual report:

(in millions)	1994	1993	1992
Net income (loss) available to common	$ (519)	$ (1,112)	$ (525)
Net cash from operating activities	1,324	677	149
Common shares outstanding	50.5	50.1	49.7
Total assets	11,896	$11,871	$10,162
Total common stockholders' equity	1,467	1,913	1,894

Evaluate Delta's performance over the three-year period. Calculate earnings per share and cash flow per share. Would you expect the company's stock price to have increased or decreased over the three years? If you were a creditor or owner of Delta, would you be concerned about the company's declaring bankruptcy in the near future?

14-13. Tin Roof Construction is a producer of modularized homes. The homes are constructed in components that can be assembled into a variety of models that vary in price. The company's strategy is to create high volume through low cost. Explain how Tin Roof's sales and net income are likely to be affected by changes in the general level of interest rates in the economy.

14-14. Companies can be separated into high- and low-value groups based on a variety of attributes. Complete the table below by indicating whether the value of each attribute indicates a high- or low-value company. The first item is prepared as an example.

Attribute	Magnitude of Attribute	Expected Company Value
Asset growth	High	High
Capital intensity	High	
Debt/assets	Low	
Dividend payout	Low	
Equity growth	Low	
Investing cash outflow	High	
Operating cash inflow	Low	
Research and development expenditure	High	
Return on assets	Low	
Return on equity	High	
Sales growth	High	

14-15. Regulation and competition are factors that affect the volatility of a company's income. Explain why each factor is important and how it affects company risk and return. Should you expect higher risk companies to earn higher returns? How do actual returns differ from expected returns?

14-16. Companies vary with respect to operating and financial leverage. Explain how each of these factors affects a company's risk and return. Draw graphs that show revenues on the horizontal axis and return on assets (for operating leverage) or return on equity (for financial leverage) on the vertical axis. Illustrate the effects of operating and financial leverage by drawing lines on the graph to indicate these effects for two companies, one with high leverage and the other with low leverage.

14-17. Accounting reports provide a variety of information for evaluating a company. For each accounting number in the following list, write the letter from the description in the right hand column that indicates the type of information provided by the number.

Accounting Information	Description
_____ Asset turnover	a. Ability to create value for its stockholders from its operating activities
_____ Profit margin	
_____ Dividend payout	b. Ability to create value from total investment
_____ Financial leverage	c. Ability to generate sales from total investment
_____ Growth in assets	d. Ability to generate profit from sales

Accounting Information	Description
_____ Growth in equity	e. Use of debt to increase return to stockholders
_____ Growth in sales	f. Source of cash for new investment and pay-ments to stockholders
_____ Growth in ROE	
_____ Operating cash flow	g. Direction and amount of change in future ROE
_____ Investing cash flow	
_____ Return on assets	h. Increased demand usually results in higher return
_____ Return on equity	
_____ Variability of sales	i. Increase in investment is basis for additional sales
_____ Variability of ROA	
_____ Research and development	j. Reinvestment of earnings increases value in company for stockholders
	k. Reinvestment of operating cash increases value in company for stockholders
	l. Growth potential is usually higher for innovative companies
	m. Volatility of earnings excluding effects of financial leverage
	n. Volatility of demand for products

14-18. Information is provided below from the 1993 annual reports for two companies. Use this information to compare the risks of the companies.

	Sara Lee Corporation		Unisys Corporation	
(in millions)		Stockholders'		Stockholders'
Year	Net Income	Equity	Net Income	Equity
1993	704	3,551	565.4	1,017.5
1992	761	3,382	361.2	541.8
1991	535	2,550	(1,393.3)	342.1
1990	470	2,292	(436.7)	1,907.0
1989	410	1,915	(639.3)	2,452.9
1988	325	1,575	680.6	3,526.1

PROBLEMS

PROBLEM 14-1   Explaining Market to Book Values

Information is provided below from the 1993 annual reports of Johnson & Johnson and Vulcan Materials Company.

	Johnson & Johnson	Vulcan Materials
Return on equity	26.8%	14.5%
Growth in earnings	4.5%	−1.0%
Standard deviation of ROE	5.2%	5.0%
Market/book value	5.6	2.3

Data are annual averages and standard deviation for the 1989–1993 period.

Required   Use the information provided to explain why Johnson & Johnson's market to book value is over twice as high as that of Vulcan Materials.

PROBLEM 14-2   Product Demand Analysis

You have been hired as a marketing manager for Astro Whiz Appliance Co. The company manufactures major home appliances, such as refrigerators, stoves, and dishwashers. The company has been in existence for only a few years. It has not paid much attention to market demand in the past because it has been able to sell as much as it produced, largely because of special features of its appliances that made them energy efficient. The company is considering the addition of production capacity and has become concerned about demand for its products. Part of your job is to provide top management with demand information. The president of the company, Myrtle Whiz, has asked you to prepare a memo describing the factors you believe the company should consider in its product demand analysis.

Required   Write a memo to President Whiz identifying the factors and explaining how they might affect the company's sales revenues.

PROBLEM 14-3   Comparing Operating Strategies

Companies' operating strategies often result in differences in the following attributes: (a) asset turnover, (b) profit margin, (c) capital intensity, (d) sales price per unit, (e) types of products, and (f) amount invested in assets.

Required   Discuss the types of competitive strategies a company might use and how the strategy would affect each of the attributes listed above. What factors are likely to affect the strategy selected by a company?

PROBLEM 14-4   Comparison of Profit Margins

Information is provided below from the 1994 annual reports of Microsoft Corporation and Wal-Mart Stores, Inc. Neither company reported any preferred stock outstanding.

(in millions)	1994	1993	1992	1991	1990
Microsoft:					
Net income	$1,146	$ 953	$ 708	$ 463	$ 279
Stockholders' equity	4,450	3,242	2,193	1,351	919
Wal-Mart:					
Net income	$ 2,333	$1,995	$1,608	$1,291	$1,076
Stockholders' equity	10,752	8,759	6,990	5,366	3,966

Required   Calculate return on equity for each company for 1990-1994. Evaluate the performances of the companies during this period with respect to return, growth, and risk.

PROBLEM 14-5   Return Analysis

Information is provided below for three companies from their 1993 annual reports.

(in millions)	Allied Products	Chrysler	CSX Corp.
Net sales	$218.0	$43,600	$8,940
Interest expense	6.4	1,104	298
Pretax income	6.4	3,836	633
Income taxes	0.4	1,423	274
Preferred dividends	2.0	80	0
Average total assets	238.3	42,242	13,235
Average common equity	46.0	7,185	3,078

Required   (a) Calculate asset turnover, profit margin, return on assets, and return on equity for each company. (b) Evaluate the relationship between asset turnover and profit margin and between return on assets and return on equity for the companies.

PROBLEM 14-6   Assessing Operating Strategies

Discount Shoes and Elegant Footwear are both retail shoe companies. Both have outlets in major cities throughout the U.S. Discount Shoes uses a cost leadership strategy, and Elegant Footwear uses a product differentiation strategy.

Required   Answer each of the following questions:

a.   What differences would you expect to observe between the two companies with respect to the location and design of their stores, the types of products they sell, and the types of service they provide?

b.   Compare the companies' sales revenues, cost of goods sold, operating expenses, accounts receivable, merchandise inventory, and plant assets based on the strategies they use to generate profits.

PROBLEM 14-7   Evaluating Investment Opportunities

Information is provided below from the 1993 annual reports of Sara Lee Corporation and Warner-Lambert Company:

(in millions)	1993	1992	1991	1990	1989
Sara Lee					
Total assets	$10,862	$ 9,989	$ 8,122	$ 7,636	$ 6,523
Common stockholders' equity	3,551	3,382	2,550	2,292	1,915
Sales	14,580	13,243	12,381	11,606	11,718
Warner-Lambert					
Total assets	$4,828	$4,077	$3,602	$3,261	$2,860
Common stockholders' equity	1,390	1,528	1,171	1,402	1,130
Sales	5,794	5,598	5,059	4,687	4,196

Required   Calculate the annual growth in assets, common equity, and sales for each company for 1990–1993. Evaluate the growth of each company and the effect the company's growth rates are likely to have on the values of the companies.

PROBLEM 14-8   Evaluating Growth and Value

Information is provided below for Vulcan Materials Company and Intel Corporation from their 1993 annual reports.

	Vulcan Materials	Intel
Total assets	$1,079	$11,344
Long-term debt	102	426
Long-term assets	776	5,542
Net income	88	2,295
Dividends	46	391

Required   Calculate the following ratios for each company: long-term debt/total assets, long-term assets/total assets, dividend payout. Evaluate the companies from these ratios with respect to growth and value.

PROBLEM 14-9   Evaluating Company Value

Information is provided below for two companies, Johnson & Johnson and Warner-Lambert, from their 1993 annual reports.

	Johnson & Johnson	Warner-Lambert
Return on equity	0.333	0.400
Return on assets	0.146	0.140
Debt/assets	0.545	0.712
Asset turnover	1.150	1.200
Profit margin	0.150	0.057
Operating cash/equity	0.389	0.097
Sales growth	0.068	0.073
Asset growth	0.082	0.170
Equity growth	0.026	0.094
Dividend payout	0.369	0.421
Investing cash/equity	0.226	0.546
Capital intensity	0.574	0.540

Required   Use the information to assess the value of each company. Which company do you believe is more valuable? Why? The market/book value of one of the companies was 5.2 and that of the other was 6.5 in 1993. Which company had the higher ratio?

PROBLEM 14-10   Multiple-Choice Overview of the Chapter

1. Wool Sweater Co. reported sales of $10 million in 1993 and $12 million in 1994. Also, it reported gross profit of $5 million in 1993 and $4.8 million in 1994. From this information, you could conclude:
   a. The company was more effective and efficient in 1993 than in 1994.
   b. The company was more effective and efficient in 1994 than in 1993.
   c. The company was more effective in 1994 than in 1993 but was more efficient in 1993 than in 1994.
   d. The company was more effective in 1993 than in 1994 but was more efficient in 1994 than in 1993.

2. The effect of changing economic conditions on demand for a company's products affects:
   a. the company's risk and return.
   b. the company's risk but not its return.
   c. the company's return but not its risk.
   d. neither the company's risk nor its return.

3. A company's profit margin is the ratio of its earnings to:
   a. total assets.
   b. total liabilities.
   c. operating income.
   d. operating revenues.

4. If Alpha Co. has higher operating leverage than Beta Co., an equivalent increase in sales for both companies should result in:
   a. a greater increase in operating income for Alpha than for Beta.
   b. a greater increase in operating income for Beta than for Alpha.
   c. the same increase in operating income for Alpha and Beta.
   d. an increase in operating income for Beta but a decrease for Alpha.

5. Chrysanthemum Co. reported a profit margin of 2% and an asset turnover of 5% for its 1994 fiscal year. The company's return on assets for the year was:
   a. 2%.
   b. 2.5%.
   c. 3%.
   d. 10%.

6. Green Co. reported a profit margin of 2.0 and an asset turnover of 7.0 during 1995. Blue Co. reported a profit margin of 4.0 and an asset turnover of 3.0 during the same period. From this information, you would expect that:
   a. Green Co. is more capital intensive than Blue Co.
   b. Blue Co. is more capital intensive than Green Co.
   c. Blue Co. is in a more highly competitive industry than Green Co.
   d. Blue Co. earned a higher return on assets than Green Co.

7. The difference between a company's return on assets and its return on equity can be explained by the company's:
   a. operating leverage.
   b. variability of sales.
   c. financial leverage.
   d. profit margin.

8. A company whose standard deviation (variability) of return on equity is high is likely to be:
    a. a high value company.
    b. a poor investment.
    c. a large, stable company.
    d. a high-risk company.

9. Company A and Company B are similar in most respects and both reported approximately the same amount of net income in recent years. Company A's operating cash flows have been consistently less than its net income, while Company B's operating cash flows have been consistently greater than its net income. Therefore, you should expect:
    a. Company A is growing faster than Company B.
    b. Company B is growing faster than Company A.
    c. Company A is facing greater financial problems than Company B.
    d. Company B is a higher value company than Company A.

10. Bankruptcy often results because a company:
    a. cannot earn enough to pay dividends to its stockholders.
    b. has more liabilities than its equity.
    c. earns a low profit margin.
    d. cannot make payments to its creditors.

C A S E S

CASE 14-1   Analysis of an Investment

You are an investment analyst. Some of your clients have talked with you about an investment they are considering in a new company, Mountain Top Resorts. This company will construct and rent condominiums to tourists on Snowshoe Mountain. The total investment required for the project is $5,000,000. Individual investors are expected to invest not less than $100,000 each. They could borrow up to this amount at 10% annual interest. The development will contain 50 units that will cost $70,000 per unit to construct. Land for the development will cost $250,000. $300,000 will be held in reserve for first-year operating costs for the year beginning January 1, 1996. The remaining investment capital will be used for furnishings, streets, parking lots, sidewalks, and landscaping. Buildings will be depreciated over a 20-year period. Other depreciable assets will be depreciated over 5 years. Straight-line depreciation will be used. Based on an analysis of similar developments in the area: Units should rent for an average of $1,000 per week. Each unit should rent for a minimum of 25 weeks per year. Each unit is expected to rent for 30 weeks per year. Maintenance and operating costs are expected to average $100 per unit-week for 52 weeks. Management costs will be $250,000 per year. A reserve fund will be established with annual reinvestments of profits of $200,000 for future repair and replacement of property. Remaining profits will be distributed to investors in proportion to their investments. The company is not subject to income tax.

Required   (a) Calculate the net income and cash flow to investors from operating activities expected from the project in 1996, assuming average rental of 25 and 30 weeks. Assume cash flows are equivalent to revenues and expenses except for depreciation. Which is more relevant to the investment decision, net income or cash flow? Why? (b) Assume investors could expect to receive net cash flows from their investments for 10 years at the amounts expected for 1996. At the end of 10 years they expect to be able sell their investments for $2 million. What is the present value of the cash flows assuming 25-week and 30-week average rentals each year? (c) What effect does the company's operating leverage have on its expected operating results? (d) Would you recommend that your clients invest in Mountain Top Resorts? What factors are important to this decision other than those considered above?

CASE 14-2   Making an Investment Decision

A friend has given you a hot tip on an investment opportunity in a business venture. You would have to invest $20,000 in the business for a 10% ownership share. The business would import goods from South America and sell them in several large cities in the U.S.

The total investment in the company will be $500,000, including debt of $300,000 at 12% interest. The investment will be used to acquire merchandise, equipment, and facilities, and to cover initial operating costs. Expected sales each year will be $1,000,000, though sales could be as low as $700,000. Annual expenses include wages of $100,000 plus sales commissions of 15% of sales, transportation costs of 8% of sales, cost of goods sold of 30% of sales, depreciation of $80,000, insurance and miscellaneous costs of $30,000, and interest. The debt will be repaid along with interest in equal annual installments over a five-year period. The business will operate for five years and then be liquidated. The expected liquidation value is $200,000, after repayment of debt. $100,000 will be reinvested each year for asset replacement and upkeep. Remaining cash flows will be distributed to the owners.

Required

1. Prepare an income statement for the company for the first year assuming (a) expected sales and (b) minimum sales.

2. Calculate return on assets, return on equity, profit margin, and asset turnover for results based on (a) and (b) above.

3. Determine the annual debt payment and prepare an amortization schedule for the first two years.

4. Prepare a cash flow statement for the company based on (a) and (b) in part 1 above, assuming all cash flows are approximately equal to revenues and expenses except depreciation. Also, calculate the cash distribution to owners.

5. Assuming that you require a 12% return on your investment, would you invest in this business if annual sales are $1,000,000? If annual sales are $700,000?

6. Assess the company's risk and return prospects. Should you invest in this company?

CASE 14-3   Analysis of Operating Activities

Appendix B of this book contains a copy of the 1994 annual report of Nike, Inc.

Required   Review the annual report and answer each of the following questions: (a) Compute profit margin, asset turnover, return on assets, the financing effect of leverage, the income effect of leverage, and return on equity for the company for 1992–1994. (b) Evaluate the changes in these amounts over the three-year period. (c) What strategy does the company appear to be following to generate profits? (d) Compare the company's net income and cash flow from operating activities for 1992–1994 and explain differences in the amounts and patterns you identify.

PROJECTS

PROJECT 14-1   Comparing Profit Margins and Asset Turnovers

Obtain the most recent annual report available for each of three corporations from your library. Use companies from different industries. Calculate the profit margins, asset turnovers, and return on assets for each company. Write a short report comparing the ratios and summarizing the information they provide the companies.

PROJECT 14-2   Comparing Operating Leverages

Obtain the most recent annual report available for each of three corporations from your library. Prepare a graph illustrating the relationship between operating income and operating revenue for each company using data for the last five years. Use your graph to determine which company appears to have the highest operating leverage and which has the lowest. What can you conclude about the relative risks of the companies? Summarize your findings and conclusions in a short report.

PROJECT 14-3   Comparing Return on Equity

Obtain the most recent annual report available for each of three corporations from your library. Find corporations in the same industry. Calculate return on assets, earnings leverage, capital structure leverage, and return on equity for each company. Write a short report comparing the results. What effect does financial leverage have on return on equity for each company? Which companies have the highest and lowest financial leverages? What effect does financial leverage have on the risks of the companies?

PROJECT 14-4   Comparing Net Income and Cash Flow

Use an annual report or other source of accounting information to identify the net income and cash flow from operating activities of a company for a five-year period. Graph the relationship between net income and cash flow for the five years. Write a short report comparing the company's net income and cash flow. Explain any concerns raised by your analysis about the company's financial condition or operating results.

PROJECT 14-5   Analyzing Business Failure

Use a business periodicals index or the *Wall Street Journal Index* to identify a recent company that went bankrupt or was liquidated. Use the company's annual report or other sources of accounting information to determine the company's total assets, total liabilities, net income, and cash flow from operating activities for the five years prior to the bankruptcy or liquidation. Graph these amounts for the five-year period. Write a short report summarizing any results from your graph that might have been useful for forecasting the company's financial problems.

Appendix A

Sources of Information About Companies and Industries

Many college and public libraries contain publications that provide information about companies and industries. The following listing describes some of the publications you may find useful. The listing is not comprehensive. Check with your librarian for other publications that may be available in your library.

Industry Classification

- The *Standard Industrial Classification Manual* categorizes companies by standard industrial classification (SIC) code. Companies with the same classification codes produce similar products. Other reference materials often use SIC codes to identify companies and industries.

Indexes to Journal and Newspaper Articles

- *Predicasts F&S Index* identifies and summarizes articles from more than 750 publications about products, industries, and companies.
- The *Business Periodicals Index* identifies articles in major business journals by topic.
- The *Accounting and Tax Index* identifies articles in accounting and business journals associated with accounting topics.
- The *Wall Street Journal Index* identifies articles from *The Wall Street Journal* by company and topic.
- The *New York Times Index* identifies articles from *The New York Times* by company and topic.

Business Periodicals

- *Forbes* provides descriptive articles on many companies and industries. Special issues provide summary information for large companies.
- *Fortune* provides descriptive articles on many companies and industries. Special issues provide summary accounting information for large U.S. and foreign companies.
- *Business Week* provides general coverage of a wide variety of business issues, including selected industries and companies.
- *The Wall Street Journal* provides daily coverage of major events related to specific companies and industries.
- *Barron's* provides various economic and financial indicators.

Financial Services

- *Standard & Poor's Corporation Records* provides information on over 6,000 companies.
- Standard & Poor's *Industry Surveys* provides detailed analysis of over 50 industries.
- Standard & Poor's *Stock Reports* provides concise descriptions of major corporations.
- *Moody's Industrial Manual, Moody's Bank and Financial Manual, Moody's Public Utilities Manual, Moody's Transportation Manual,* and *Moody's Municipal & Government Manual* provide detailed information about major organizations of each type. These manuals are published annually.
- *Value Line Investment Survey* provides analysis and commentary on major industries and companies.

Computer Services

- *Dow Jones Information Services* provide on-line computer access to news, financial, and economic indicators.
- *National Automated Accounting Research System (NAARS)* provides computer access to news, financial statement, and other accounting information for major corporations.
- *Compact Disclosure* provides accounting and other information on over 13,000 corporations.

Government Economic and Industry Publications

- A variety of economic indicators are provided in government publications such as *Survey of Current Business, Economic Indicators,* and the *Federal Reserve Bulletin.*
- The Department of Commerce publishes economic censuses of various types of industries, such as retail, wholesale, service, and manufacturing. It also publishes *U.S. Industrial Outlook,* providing an analysis of prospects for major industries.

Industry Ratios

- Industry averages for a variety of ratios and other accounting measures are available in *Standard & Poor's Analysts Handbook,* Robert Morris Associate's *Annual Statement Studies,* Dunn & Bradstreet's *Industry Norms & Key Business Ratios,* and the Department of Commerce's *Statistical Abstract of the United States.*

Appendix B

Nike, Inc.
Financial Report

FINANCIAL HISTORY

(in thousands, except per share data and financial ratios)

	1994	1993	1992	1991	1990	1989	1988
Year Ended May 31:							
Revenues	$3,789,668	$3,930,984	$3,405,211	$3,003,610	$2,235,244	$1,710,803	$1,203,440
Gross margin	1,488,245	1,543,991	1,316,122	1,153,080	851,072	635,972	400,060
Gross margin %	39.3%	39.3%	38.7%	38.4%	38.1%	37.2%	33.2%
Net income	298,794	365,016	329,218	287,046	242,958	167,047	101,695
Net income per common share	3.96	4.74	4.30	3.77	3.21	2.22	1.35
Average number of common and common equivalent shares	75,456	77,063	76,602	76,067	75,668	75,144	75,278
Cash dividends declared per common share	.80	0.75	0.59	0.52	0.38	0.27	0.20
Cash flow from operations	576,463	265,292	435,838	11,122	127,075	169,441	19,019
Price range of common stock							
High	74¾	90¼	77⅜	54½	41½	19⅞	13¼
Low	43⅛	55	35⅛	26	19	11 9/16	7
At May 31:							
Cash and equivalents	$ 518,816	$ 291,284	$ 260,050	$ 119,804	$ 90,449	$ 85,749	$ 75,357
Inventories	470,023	592,986	471,202	586,594	309,476	222,924	198,470
Working capital	1,208,444	1,165,204	964,291	662,645	561,642	419,599	295,937
Total assets	2,373,815	2,186,269	1,871,667	1,707,236	1,093,358	824,216	707,901
Long-term debt	12,364	15,033	69,476	29,992	25,941	34,051	30,306
Redeemable Preferred Stock	300	300	300	300	300	300	300
Common shareholders' equity	1,740,949	1,642,819	1,328,488	1,029,582	781,012	558,597	408,567
Year-end stock price	59	72½	58	39¾	39¼	19	12⅛
Market capitalization at May 31	4,318,800	5,499,273	4,379,574	2,993,020	2,942,679	1,417,381	899,741
Financial Ratios:							
Return on equity	17.7%	24.5%	27.9%	31.7%	36.3%	34.5%	27.4%
Return on assets	13.1%	18.0%	18.4%	20.5%	25.3%	21.8%	16.7%
Inventory turns	4.3	4.5	3.9	4.1	5.2	5.1	5.0
Current ratio at May 31	3.2	3.6	3.3	2.1	3.1	2.9	2.2
Price/Earnings ratio at May 31	14.9	15.3	13.5	10.5	12.2	8.6	9.0
Geographic Revenues:							
United States	$2,432,684	$2,528,848	$2,270,880	$2,141,461	$1,755,496	$1,362,148	$ 900,417
Europe	927,269	1,085,683	919,763	664,747	334,275	241,380	233,402
Asia/Pacific	283,421	178,196	75,732	56,238	29,332	32,027	21,058
Canada, Latin America, and other	146,294	138,257	138,836	141,164	116,141	75,248	48,563
Total Revenues	$3,789,668	$3,930,984	$3,405,211	$3,003,610	$2,235,244	$1,710,803	$1,203,440

All per common share amounts have been adjusted to reflect the 2-for-1 stock split paid October 5, 1990. The Company's Class B Common Stock is listed on the New York and Pacific Exchanges and trades under the symbol NKE. At May 31, 1994, there were approximately 77,000 shareholders. Years 1993 and prior have been restated to reflect the implementation of Statement of Financial Accounting Standard No. 109 – Accounting for Income Taxes (see Notes 1 and 6).

MANAGEMENT DISCUSSION AND ANALYSIS

Highlights

• In fiscal 1994 revenues decreased for the first time in seven years, slipping 4% from the record $3.93 billion for fiscal 1993. On a positive note, however, fiscal year 1994 began with record first quarter revenues and ended with record fourth quarter revenues. For the first time in the Company's history, two $1 billion revenue quarters were achieved in the same fiscal year.

• Net income also decreased for the first time in seven years, declining 18% to $298.8 million (or $3.96 per share), from the record $365.0 million (or $4.74 per share) earned in fiscal 1993. Decreased revenues and increased selling and administrative expenses were the primary factors.

• Fiscal 1994 was the second-best revenue year and third-best net income year in the Company's history. Momentum, slowed after the record first quarter, was regained in the fourth quarter, and a 10% increase in Futures orders indicates renewed growth heading into the first six months of fiscal 1995.

Results of Operations

A decrease in revenues and increased selling and administrative expenses were the primary factors in reduced earnings for fiscal 1994, while increased revenues and improved gross margins, offset partially by increased selling and administrative expenses, were the highlight of earnings growth in fiscal 1993. Despite a sluggish economy in the United States and abroad, the Company has been able to sustain its worldwide market share. The Company faces a mature market in the United States, where industry sources expect growth rates to range between 3 and 5%. The Company's international markets are less mature, however, and offer more potential for future growth. Accordingly, the Company has continued to invest in international infrastructure in order to prepare for that future growth, resulting in an increase in selling and administrative expenses as a percentage of revenues. Through its aggressive worldwide marketing efforts and international infrastructure spending, the Company hopes to exceed those underlying market growth rates and thereby continue to increase its worldwide market share. However, until economies in the U.S. and Europe show full recovery, the Company may not realize those growth rates.

The 4% decrease in 1994 revenues was attributable to both U.S. and international footwear along with U.S. apparel. The U.S. footwear revenue decline of 5% was attributable to a 2% decrease in pairs shipped and a 3% decrease in average sales price per pair. The most notable reason for the decrease was a 22% decline in basketball category revenue, offset partially by increases in cross-training, outdoor, and women's fitness categories. International revenues declined $45 million (3%) overall from 1993, composed of a $51 million (5%) decrease in international footwear revenues and a $6 million (2%) increase in international apparel revenues. International revenues decreased as a result of poor economies in Europe, negatively impacting operations and currency translation of revenues. This was partially offset by increases in revenues from Asia and Latin America, primarily as a result of the acquisition of NIKE's Japan distributor during the third quarter of fiscal 1994. The 15% growth in 1993 revenues as compared to 1992 was primarily attributable to an increase of 24% in international footwear and apparel revenues and a 13% increase in U.S. footwear revenues. Increases in international revenues were a result of gains in market share, expansion of the 1993 international market for sports and fitness products, and the establishment of NIKE-owned operations in place of independent distributors in order to control all aspects of the business, while U.S. footwear was up due to increases of 10% in pairs shipped and 3% in average selling prices. Other brands include Cole Haan,® Tetra Plastics, Sports Specialties (acquired during fiscal 1993) and i.e.™ (discontinued during fiscal 1994). The breakdown of revenues follows:

(in thousands)

Year Ended May 31,	1994	% CHG	1993	% CHG	1992	% CHG
United States footwear	$1,868,900	(5)%	$1,968,500	13%	$1,744,200	4%
United States apparel	338,500	(6)	360,500	(2)	368,500	13
Other brands	225,300	13	199,800	26	158,200	17
Total United States	2,432,700	(4)	2,528,800	11	2,270,900	6
International footwear	998,200	(5)	1,049,100	21	867,500	33
International apparel	358,800	2	353,100	32	266,800	27
Total International	1,357,000	(3)	1,402,200	24	1,134,300	32
Total NIKE	$3,789,700	(4)%	$3,931,000	15%	$3,405,200	13%

Gross margin remained level at 39.3% for fiscal 1994 and fiscal 1993, and increased from 38.7 % in fiscal 1992. Steady gross margin performance reflects a solid U.S. inventory position resulting from strong inventory management and the Company's innovative advance order Futures Program. Strong consumer demand and internally controlled close-out distribution channels also contributed to improved margins. Consolidated global NIKE brand margin increased for fiscal 1994 over both fiscal 1993 and 1992, but was reduced by decreases from other brands. International gross margin for fiscal 1994 was consistent with 1993, experiencing close-out sales in the first half of the year and a resulting improved inventory/lower close-out position in the second half. Partially offsetting the second half improvement was the effect of changing from royalty arrangements (100% margin) to normal wholesale margin operations in new NIKE-owned subsidiaries. International gross margin experienced a decline in fiscal 1993 due to poor European economies resulting in higher close-out sales. The Company continues to place strong emphasis on inventory management, minimizing foreign exchange risk, and production sourcing in order to maximize gross profit.

Total selling and administrative expenses as a percentage of revenues were 25.7% in 1994 compared to 23.5% in 1993 and 22.4% in 1992. Increases in the percentage over 1993 are primarily attributable to lower revenues, with increases in total expense primarily attributable to new NIKE-owned international operations and other planned growth in international infrastructure. Increases in 1993 expenses over 1992 were primarily attributable to the Company's aggressive worldwide advertising campaigns along with increases in operations, most significantly in work force. The Company expects to continue to invest in growth opportunities and therefore, expects selling and administrative expenses during fiscal 1995 to increase slightly as a percentage of revenues.

Consolidated interest expense decreased $10.5 million from 1993 as a result of scheduled repayment of $50 million of long-term debt, reduced average short-term borrowings and lower interest rates. The 1993 reduction of $5 million from 1992 was a result of lower borrowings and interest rates. During 1995, given increased NIKE-owned operations and increasing interest rates, the Company expects average interest expense to exceed 1994 levels.

Cash generated by operations increased cash available for investments resulting in increased interest income, which is included in other income/expense, in fiscal years 1994 and 1993. Other expenses for fiscal 1994 include approximately $7 million of non-recurring specific obligations related to the shutdown of certain facilities in conjunction with the consolidation of European warehouses.

The Company's effective income tax rate increased to 39.1% from 38.6% in fiscal 1993 and 36.9% in fiscal 1992, reflecting the higher overall rate due primarily to the 1% increase from the Omnibus Budget Reconciliation Act of 1993, which was retroactive to January 1, 1993. Additionally, the Company adopted Financial Accounting Standards Board (FASB) Statement 109 "Accounting for Income Taxes" during the first quarter of fiscal 1994, which required application of the 1% increase to deferred taxes. Partially offsetting these increases was the Company's decision to permanently reinvest foreign earnings overseas, resulting in a decrease in tax expense. See further discussion in Notes 1 and 6 to the Consolidated Financial Statements. The Company anticipates the effective tax rate for fiscal 1995 will approximate the rate in fiscal 1994.

The results of consolidated operations were negatively affected by strengthening of the U.S. dollar in comparison to foreign currencies. Generally, a stronger U.S. dollar will result in lower translation of operating results in these consolidated statements than would a weaker U.S. dollar.

Worldwide orders for athletic footwear and apparel scheduled for delivery between June and November 1994 are approximately $1.8 billion, 10% higher than such orders in the comparable period of the prior year. These orders are not necessarily indicative of total revenues for subsequent periods because the mix of advance orders and "at once" shipments may vary significantly from quarter to quarter and year to year. Additionally, as international operations continue to shift to a greater emphasis on Futures orders, this mix again may vary. Finally, exchange rate fluctuations can also cause differences in the comparisons.

The Company's international operations are subject to the usual risks of doing business abroad, such as the imposition of import quotas or anti-dumping duties. In this regard, the European Union (the "EU") has imposed quotas that restrict the importation into the EU of footwear manufactured in The People's Republic of China (the "PRC"). Such quotas are applicable throughout all of the Member States that comprise the EU. The Company has been closely monitoring EU quota proposals for the past several years and has had contingency plans in place. While such quotas have required the Company to limit the quantities of footwear sourced in the PRC, they have not had a material adverse impact on the Company's business.

The Company has learned that the EU Commission, at the request of the European footwear manufacturers, might initiate an anti-dumping investigation covering footwear imported from the PRC, Indonesia and Thailand. The Company has recently been advised that such a complaint has been submitted to the EU Commission. However, as of the date of this report, the complaint has not been made public. The Company is unable to predict to what extent its footwear will be covered by such an investigation, or the likelihood that the EU Commission will ultimately impose anti-dumping duties on any of the Company's footwear imports. If the EU Commission were to impose such duties, it is possible that the Company would be forced to shift some production from the PRC to other countries in order to maintain competitive prices. The Company believes that it is prepared to deal effectively with any such duties that may arise and that any adverse impact would be of a short-term nature.

The Company continues to closely monitor international trade restrictions and to develop contingency plans. The Company believes that its major competitors would be similarly impacted by any such restrictions.

Liquidity and Capital Resources

The Company's financial position remains extremely strong at May 31, 1994. Cash and equivalents increased $228 million (78%) as a result of a record $576 million in cash provided by operations, offset partially by cash used for planned financing and investing activities and the repurchase of Company stock. Working capital at May 31, 1994, increased $43 million over May 31, 1993, resulting from higher cash and equivalents and accounts receivable partially offset by decreased inventories and increases in current liabilities. The Company's current ratio was 3.2 at May 31, 1994, compared to 3.6 at May 31, 1993, decreasing primarily due to the addition of NIKE-owned subsidiaries with assets substantially equivalent to liabilities.

Inventory levels have decreased $123 million since May 31, 1993, primarily due to reductions in U.S. footwear, U.S. apparel and European inventories, offset partially by the additions of new NIKE-owned subsidiaries. In general, reductions are a result of strong inventory management in relation to anticipated revenue levels. Additionally, relative to May 31, 1993, a larger volume of inventory representing orders scheduled for delivery to retailers during the next quarter was received from factory sources subsequent to year-end. Accounts receivable increased $36 million due to the addition of NIKE-owned subsidiaries, offset partially by reductions in other regions in relation to fourth quarter revenues.

Cash provided by operations was a record $576 million in 1994 compared to $265 million and $436 million in 1993 and 1992, respectively. The increase in the current year is a result of decreased inventory levels, offset partially by decreases in net income and non-cash charges. The 1993 decrease was primarily a result of increased inventory levels, offset partially by increases in net income and non-cash charges.

Additions to property, plant and equipment for fiscal 1994 were $95 million, with the most significant component related to the consolidation of European apparel warehouses, which began and was substantially completed during fiscal 1994. Additions to property, plant and equipment of $97 million and $106 million in fiscal 1993 and 1992, respectively, related to the expansion of existing U.S. headquarters and U.S. and international warehouse facilities to satisfy increased capacity needs, along with investments in management information systems and new NIKE retail locations. Anticipated capital expenditures for fiscal 1995 approximate $130 million, with the primary components consisting of the consolidation of European footwear warehouses. Funding is expected to be provided primarily by operations.

Current liabilities increased $109 million, with much of the increase due to the addition of new NIKE-owned subsidiaries which added operationally related debt, including notes and accounts payable and accrued liabilities. The reduction in current portion of long-term debt is due to the retirement of two $25 million notes at the beginning of fiscal 1994.

Additional investing activities in 1994 included the acquisition of certain international distributors, including Japan, and in 1993 included the acquisition of Sports Specialties, which designs and markets licensed headwear.

During fiscal 1994, the Company announced that the Executive Committee of its Board of Directors, acting within limits set by the Board, authorized a plan to repurchase a maximum of $450 million NIKE Class B Common Stock over a period of up to three years. Funding has, and is expected to continue to come from operating cash flow in potential combination with occasional short- or medium-term borrowings. The timing and the amount of shares purchased will be dictated by working capital needs and stock market conditions. As of May 31, 1994, the Company had repurchased 2.8 million shares at a total cost of $140.1 million.

Dividends per share of common stock for fiscal 1994 rose $.05 over fiscal 1993 to $.80 per share. Dividend declaration in all four quarters has been consistent since February 1984. Based upon current projected earnings and cash flow requirements, the Company anticipates continuing a dividend and reviewing the amount during the second quarter board meeting. The Company's policy continues to target an annual dividend in the range of 15% to 25% of trailing twelve-month earnings.

The Company's commercial paper program, rated A1 by Standard and Poor's Corporation and P1 by Moody's Investors Service, requires the support of committed and uncommitted lines of credit. No amounts were outstanding under this program at May 31, 1994 and 1993. Additionally, no amounts were outstanding at May 31, 1994 and 1993, under a committed $300 million multiple option credit facility. See Note 4 of the Consolidated Financial Statements for further details concerning the Company's short-term borrowing. NIKE's debt-to-equity ratio was consistent, with ratios of .4:1, .3:1 and .4:1 at May 31, 1994, 1993 and 1992, respectively.

Management believes that funds generated by operations, together with currently available resources, will adequately finance anticipated fiscal 1995 expenditures, with the potential exception of the stock repurchase program discussed above.

FINANCIAL REPORTING

Management of NIKE, Inc. is responsible for the information and representations contained in this report. The financial statements have been prepared in conformity with the generally accepted accounting principles we considered appropriate in the circumstances and include some amounts based on our best estimates and judgments. Other financial information in this report is consistent with these financial statements.

The Company's accounting systems include controls designed to reasonably assure that assets are safeguarded from unauthorized use or disposition and which provide for the preparation of financial statements in conformity with generally accepted accounting principles. These systems are supplemented by the selection and training of qualified financial personnel and an organizational structure providing for appropriate segregation of duties.

An Internal Audit department reviews the results of its work with the Audit Committee of the Board of Directors, presently consisting of three outside directors of the Company. The Audit Committee is responsible for recommending to the Board of Directors the appointment of the independent accountants and reviews with the independent accountants, management and the internal audit staff, the scope and the results of the annual examination, the effectiveness of the accounting control system and other matters relating to the financial affairs of the Company as they deem appropriate. The independent accountants and the internal auditors have full access to the Committee, with and without the presence of management, to discuss any appropriate matters.

REPORT OF INDEPENDENT ACCOUNTANTS

Portland, Oregon
July 5, 1994

To the Board of Directors and
Shareholders of NIKE, Inc.

In our opinion, the accompanying consolidated balance sheet and the related consolidated statements of income, of cash flows and of shareholders' equity present fairly, in all material respects the financial position of NIKE, Inc. and its subsidiaries at May 31, 1994 and 1993, and the results of their operations and their cash flows for each of the three years in the period ended May 31, 1994, in conformity with generally accepted accounting principles. These financial statements are the responsibility of the Company's management; our responsibility is to express an opinion on these financial statements based on our audits. We conducted our audits of these statements in accordance with generally accepted auditing standards which require that we plan and perform the audit to obtain reasonable assurance about whether the financial statements are free of material misstatement. An audit includes examining, on a test basis, evidence supporting the amounts and disclosures in the financial statements, assessing the accounting principles used and significant estimates made by management, and evaluating the overall financial statement presentation. We believe that our audits provide a reasonable basis for the opinion expressed above.

Price Waterhouse

NIKE, INC. CONSOLIDATED STATEMENT OF INCOME

(in thousands, except per share data)

Year Ended May 31,	1994	1993	1992
Revenues	$3,789,668	$3,930,984	$3,405,211
Costs and expenses:			
Cost of sales	2,301,423	2,386,993	2,089,089
Selling and administrative	974,099	922,261	761,498
Interest expense (Notes 3, 4 and 5)	15,282	25,739	30,665
Other (income)/expense, net (Notes 1, 9 and 10)	8,270	1,475	2,141
	3,299,074	3,336,468	2,883,393
Income before income taxes	490,594	594,516	521,818
Income taxes (Note 6)	191,800	229,500	192,600
Net income	$ 298,794	$ 365,016	$ 329,218
Net income per common share (Note 1)	$ 3.96	$ 4.74	$ 4.30
Average number of common and common equivalent shares (Note 1)	75,456	77,063	76,602

The accompanying notes to consolidated financial statements are an integral part of this statement.

NIKE, INC. CONSOLIDATED BALANCE SHEET

(in thousands)

May 31	1994	1993
Assets		
Current assets:		
Cash and equivalents	$ 518,816	$ 291,284
Accounts receivable, less allowance for doubtful accounts		
of $28,291 and $19,447	703,682	667,547
Inventories (Note 2)	470,023	592,986
Deferred income taxes (Note 6)	37,603	23,499
Prepaid expenses	40,307	42,452
Total current assets	1,770,431	1,617,768
Property, plant and equipment, net (Notes 3 and 5)	405,845	377,995
Goodwill (Note 1)	157,187	159,579
Other assets	40,352	30,927
Total assets	$2,373,815	$2,186,269
Liabilities and Shareholders' Equity		
Current liabilities:		
Current portion of long-term debt (Note 5)	$ 3,857	$ 52,985
Notes payable (Note 4)	127,378	108,165
Accounts payable (Note 4)	210,576	135,701
Accrued liabilities	181,889	138,563
Income taxes payable	38,287	17,150
Total current liabilities	561,987	452,564
Long-term debt (Notes 5 and 12)	12,364	15,033
Non-current deferred income taxes (Note 6)	18,228	31,978
Other non-current liabilities (Note 1)	39,987	43,575
Commitments and contingencies (Note 11)	—	—
Redeemable Preferred Stock (Note 7)	300	300
Shareholders' equity (Note 8):		
Common Stock at stated value:		
Class A convertible – 26,679 and 26,691 shares outstanding	159	159
Class B – 46,521 and 49,161 shares outstanding	2,704	2,720
Capital in excess of stated value	108,284	108,451
Foreign currency translation adjustment	(15,123)	(7,790)
Retained earnings	1,644,925	1,539,279
Total shareholders' equity	1,740,949	1,642,819
Total liabilities and shareholders' equity	$2,373,815	$2,186,269

The accompanying notes to consolidated financial statements are an integral part of this statement.

NIKE, INC. CONSOLIDATED STATEMENT OF CASH FLOWS

(in thousands)

Year Ended May 31,	1994	1993	1992
Cash provided (used) by operations:			
Net income	$ 298,794	$365,016	$329,218
Income charges (credits) not affecting cash:			
Depreciation	64,531	60,393	47,665
Deferred income taxes and purchased tax benefits	(23,876)	4,310	8,222
Other non-current liabilities	(3,588)	19,847	9,992
Other, including amortization	8,067	12,951	9,355
Changes in certain working capital components:			
Decrease (increase) in inventory	160,823	(97,471)	115,392
Decrease (increase) in accounts receivable	23,979	(62,538)	(74,430)
Decrease (increase) in other current assets	6,888	(5,133)	(6,239)
Increase (decrease) in accounts payable, accrued			
liabilities and income taxes payable	40,845	(32,083)	(3,337)
Cash provided by operations	576,463	265,292	435,838
Cash provided (used) by investing activities:			
Additions to property, plant and equipment	(95,266)	(97,041)	(106,492)
Disposals of property, plant and equipment	12,650	5,006	4,065
Acquisition of subsidiaries:			
Goodwill	(2,185)	(52,003)	—
Net assets acquired	(1,367)	(25,858)	—
Additions to other non-current assets	(5,450)	(3,036)	(7,494)
Cash used by investing activities	(91,618)	(172,932)	(109,921)
Cash provided (used) by financing activities:			
Additions to long-term debt	6,044	1,536	45,901
Reductions in long-term debt including current portion	(56,986)	(5,817)	(3,467)
Decrease in notes payable	(2,939)	(2,017)	(194,668)
Proceeds from exercise of options	4,288	7,055	4,159
Repurchase of stock	(140,104)	—	—
Dividends – common and preferred	(60,282)	(53,017)	(43,760)
Cash used by financing activities	(249,979)	(52,260)	(191,835)
Effect of exchange rate changes on cash	(7,334)	(8,866)	6,164
Net increase in cash and equivalents	227,532	31,234	140,246
Cash and equivalents, beginning of year	291,284	260,050	119,804
Cash and equivalents, end of year	$ 518,816	$291,284	$260,050

NIKE, INC. CONSOLIDATED STATEMENT OF CASH FLOWS

(in thousands)

Year Ended May 31,	1994	1993	1992
Supplemental disclosure of cash flow information:			
Cash paid during the year for:			
Interest (net of amount capitalized)	$ 11,300	$ 20,800	$ 29,200
Income taxes	189,800	235,200	184,100
Supplemental schedule of non-cash investing activities:			
The Company had a like-kind exchange of certain			
equipment during the year as follows:			
Cost of old equipment	$ 24,057	—	—
Accumulated depreciation	(14,502)	—	—
Cash received	652	—	—
Book value of new asset	$ 10,207	—	—
The Company acquired new NIKE subsidiaries			
during the year as follows:			
Assets acquired	$ 124,966	—	—
Less: cash paid	(3,552)	—	—
Liabilities assumed	$ 121,414	—	—

The accompanying notes to consolidated financial statements are an integral part of this statement.

NIKE, INC. CONSOLIDATED STATEMENT OF SHAREHOLDERS' EQUITY

(in thousands)

	Common Stock				Capital In Excess Of Stated Value	Foreign Currency Translation Adjustment	Retained Earnings	Total
	Class A		Class B					
	Shares	Amount	Shares	Amount				
Balance at May 31, 1991	27,438	$164	47,858	$2,712	$ 84,681	$ (4,428)	$ 949,660	$1,032,789
Stock options exercised			214	1	9,118			9,119
Conversion to Class B Common Stock	(519)	(3)	519	3				—
Translation of statements of foreign operations						5,114		5,114
Net income							329,218	329,218
Dividends on Redeemable Preferred Stock							(30)	(30)
Dividends on Common Stock							(44,515)	(44,515)
Cumulative effect of change in accounting for income taxes (see Notes 1 and 6)							(3,207)	(3,207)
Balance at May 31, 1992	26,919	161	48,591	2,716	93,799	686	1,231,126	1,328,488
Stock options exercised			342	2	14,652			14,654
Conversion to Class B Common Stock	(228)	(2)	228	2				—
Translation of statements of international operations						(8,476)		(8,476)
Net income							365,016	365,016
Dividends on Redeemable Preferred Stock							(30)	(30)
Dividends on Common Stock							(56,833)	(56,833)
Balance at May 31, 1993	26,691	159	49,161	2,720	108,451	(7,790)	1,539,279	1,642,819
Stock options exercised			167	1	6,287			6,288
Conversion to Class B Common Stock	(12)	—	12	—				—
Repurchase of Class B Common Stock			(2,819)	(17)	(6,454)		(133,633)	(140,104)
Translation of statements of international operations						(7,333)		(7,333)
Net income							298,794	298,794
Dividends on Redeemable Preferred Stock							(30)	(30)
Dividends on Common Stock							(59,485)	(59,485)
Balance at May 31, 1994	26,679	$159	46,521	$2,704	$108,284	$(15,123)	$1,644,925	$1,740,949

The accompanying notes to consolidated financial statements are an integral part of this statement.

NIKE, INC. NOTES TO CONSOLIDATED FINANCIAL STATEMENTS

Note 1 - Summary of significant accounting policies:

Basis of consolidation:

The consolidated financial statements include the accounts of the Company and its subsidiaries. All significant intercompany transactions and balances have been eliminated. To facilitate the timely preparation of the consolidated financial statements, the accounts of certain international operations have been consolidated for fiscal years ending in April.

Recognition of revenues:

Revenues recognized include sales plus fees earned on sales by licensees.

Advertising:

Advertising production costs are expensed the first time the advertisement is run. Media (TV and print) placement costs are expensed in the month the advertising appears.

Cash and equivalents:

Cash and equivalents represent cash and short-term, highly liquid investments with maturities essentially three months or less.

Inventory-valuation:

Inventories are stated at the lower of cost or market. Cost is determined using the last-in, first-out (LIFO) method for substantially all U.S. inventories. International inventories are valued on a first-in, first-out (FIFO) basis.

Property, plant and equipment and depreciation:

Property, plant and equipment are recorded at cost. Depreciation for financial reporting purposes is determined on a straight-line basis for buildings and leasehold improvements and principally on a declining balance basis for machinery and equipment, based upon estimated useful lives ranging from three to thirty-two years.

Goodwill:

At May 31, 1994 and 1993, the Company's excess of purchase cost over the fair value of net assets of businesses acquired was $157,187,000 and $159,579,000, respectively, net of amortization of $25,025,000 and $22,181,000, respectively. This excess is being amortized on a straight-line basis over five to forty years. Goodwill amortization expense was $7,018,000, $5,083,000 and $4,818,000 for the years ended May 31, 1994, 1993 and 1992, respectively, which is included in other income/expense.

Other non-current liabilities:

Other non-current liabilities include amounts with settlement dates beyond one year, and are primarily composed of long-term deferred endorsement payments of $33,586,000 and $38,328,000 at May 31, 1994 and 1993, respectively. Deferred payments to endorsers relate to amounts due beyond contract termination, which are discounted at various interest rates and accrued over the contract period.

Endorsement contracts:

Accounting for endorsement contracts is based upon specific contract provisions. Generally, endorsement payments are expensed uniformly over the term of the contract after giving recognition to periodic performance compliance provisions of the contracts.

Foreign currency translation:

Assets and liabilities of international operations are translated into U.S. dollars at current exchange rates. Income and expense accounts are translated into U.S. dollars at average rates of exchange prevailing during the period. Adjustments resulting from translating foreign functional currency financial statements into U.S. dollars are taken directly to a separate component of shareholders' equity. Foreign currency transaction gains and losses are included in income.

Forward exchange contracts:

The Company enters into forward exchange contracts in order to reduce the impact of foreign currency fluctuations on primarily non-U.S. purchases of inventory. Gains or losses on these transactions are matched to inventory purchases and charged or credited to cost of sales as such inventory is sold.

Income taxes:

   Deferred income taxes are recognized for timing differences between income for financial reporting purposes and taxable income. Income taxes are provided currently on financial statement earnings of international subsidiaries expected to be repatriated. The Company intends to determine annually the amount of undistributed international earnings to invest indefinitely in its international operations.

   In June 1993, the Company adopted Statement of Financial Accounting Standards No. 109, Accounting for Income Taxes (FAS 109). The adoption of FAS 109 changes the Company's method of accounting for income taxes from the deferred method (APB 11) to an asset and liability approach. Previously the Company deferred the past tax effects of timing differences between financial reporting and taxable income. The asset and liability approach requires the recognition of deferred tax liabilities and assets for the expected future tax consequences of temporary differences between the carrying amounts and the tax bases of other assets and liabilities.

   The Company's Consolidated Balance Sheet has been restated for the effects of the FAS 109 adoption. See Note 6 for further discussion.

Net income per common share:

   Net income per common share is computed based on the weighted average number of common and common equivalent (stock option) shares outstanding for the periods reported.

Reclassifications:

   Certain prior year amounts have been reclassified to conform to the 1994 presentation. These changes had no impact on previously reported results of operations or shareholders' equity.

Note 2 – Inventories:

   Inventories by major classification are as follows:

(in thousands)

May 31,	1994	1993
Finished goods	$465,065	$587,081
Work-in-progress	2,915	3,951
Raw materials	2,043	1,954
	$470,023	$592,986

The excess of replacement cost over LIFO cost approximated $19,367,000 at May 31, 1994, and $22,542,000 at May 31, 1993. During 1994 and 1992, certain inventory quantities were reduced resulting in liquidations, which were not material, of LIFO inventory quantities carried at different costs prevailing in prior years as compared with the cost of those years' purchases.

Note 3 – Property, plant and equipment:

   Property, plant and equipment includes the following:

(in thousands)

May 31,	1994	1993
Land	$ 59,761	$ 50,851
Buildings	154,731	152,368
Machinery and equipment	317,782	296,680
Leasehold improvements	54,383	46,611
Construction in process	52,428	24,522
	639,085	571,032
Less accumulated depreciation	233,240	193,037
	$405,845	$377,995

Capitalized interest expense relating to construction of the Company's world headquarters and other projects was $270,000, $767,000 and $636,000 for the fiscal years ended May 31, 1994, 1993 and 1992, respectively.

Note 4 – Short-term borrowings and credit lines:

Notes payable to banks and interest bearing accounts payable to Nissho Iwai American Corporation (NIAC) are summarized below:

| | Banks | | | | NIAC | |
| | U.S. Operations | | International Operations | | | |
(in thousands)	Borrowings	Interest Rate	Borrowings	Interest Rate	Borrowings	Interest Rate
May 31, 1994	$6,462	4⅞%	$120,916	4¾%	$118,274	4⅔%
May 31, 1993	$4,597	4½%	$103,568	8⅓%	$57,542	3½%

At May 31, 1994 and 1993, NIKE had no outstanding borrowings under its $300 million unsecured multiple option facility with sixteen banks, which matures on November 30, 1995. This agreement contains optional borrowing alternatives consisting of a committed revolving loan facility and a competitive bid facility. The interest rate charged on this agreement is determined by the borrowing option and under the committed revolving loan facility is either the Prime Rate or London Interbank Offered Rate (LIBOR) plus .30%. The agreement provides for annual fees of .125% of the total commitment. Under the agreement, the Company must maintain, among other things, certain minimum specified financial ratios and balances. Domestic subsidiaries had $6,462,000 and $4,597,000 outstanding at May 31, 1994, and May 31, 1993, respectively, under unsecured, uncommitted short-term credit agreements.

Ratings for the Company to issue commercial paper, which is required to be supported by committed and uncommitted lines of credit, are A1 by Standard and Poor's Corporation and P1 by Moody's Investor Service. At May 31, 1994 and 1993, there were no balances outstanding under these arrangements.

The Company has outstanding loans at interest rates at various spreads above the banks' cost of funds for financing international operations. Certain of these loans can be secured by accounts receivable and inventory.

The Company purchases through NAIC substantially all of the athletic footwear and apparel it acquires from non-U.S. suppliers. Accounts payable to NIAC are generally due up to 115 days after shipment of goods from the foreign port. Interest on such accounts payable accrues at the ninety day LIBOR rate as of the beginning of the month of the invoice date, plus .30%.

Note 5 – Long-term debt:

Long-term debt includes the following:

(in thousands)

May 31,	1994	1993
8.45% unsecured term loan, due July 1993	$ —	$25,000
7.90% unsecured term loan, due June 1993	—	25,000
9.43% capital warehouse lease, payable in quarterly installments through 2007	9,098	9,628
Other	7,123	8,390
Total	16,221	68,018
Less current maturities	3,857	52,985
	$12,364	$15,033

Amounts of long-term maturities in each of the five fiscal years 1995 through 1999 respectively, are $3,857,000, $3,536,000, $1,210,000, $976,000 and $898,000.

Note 6 – Income taxes:

Income before income taxes and the provision for income taxes are as follows:

(in thousands)

Year Ended May 31,	1994	1993	1992
Income before income taxes:			
United States	$318,367	$372,996	$317,560
International	172,227	221,520	204,258
	$490,594	$594,516	$521,818
Provision for income taxes:			
Current:			
United Sates			
Federal	$121,892	$126,071	$ 91,652
State	23,832	26,425	22,306
International	64,034	74,866	68,337
	209,758	227,362	182,295
Deferred:			
United States			
Federal	(12,931)	1,741	11,030
State	(1,868)	1,229	200
International	(3,159)	(832)	(925)
	(17,958)	2,138	10,305
	$191,800	$229,500	$192,600

During fiscal 1994 the Company determined approximately $56,000,000 of its undistributed international earnings were permanently reinvested in certain international subsidiaries. This resulted in a reduction of $12,800,000 in the 1994 provision for deferred income taxes.

On August 10, 1993, the Omnibus Budget Reconciliation Act of 1993 was signed into law, raising corporate rates 1%. This resulted in an increase of approximately $7,200,000 in tax expense, computed as the impact of the 1% applied retroactively to earnings from January 1, 1993, and also to deferred taxes in accordance with FAS 109.

As discussed in Note 1, the Company adopted FAS 109 during the first quarter of the current year. The Company has elected to report the cumulative effect of the FAS 109 adoption as of May 31, 1987. The cumulative effect of $3,207,000 has been recorded as a reduction in common shareholder's equity for each of the years subsequent to 1987. There was no impact on the results of operations previously reported for the years 1987 through 1993. The adoption of FAS 109 had no effect on income taxes, the provision for income taxes, and the effective tax rates for the years ended May 31, 1993 and 1992.

As of May 31, 1994, the Company has utilized all foreign tax credits.

Deferred tax liabilities (assets) are comprised of the following:

(in thousands)

May 31,	1994	1993
Undistributed earnings of international subsidiaries	$ 16,405	$ 28,182
Acquired tax benefits	5,554	6,421
LIFO inventory	2,504	2,681
Acquisition basis adjustment	1,361	1,793
Depreciation	2,896	1,883
Tax reserves and accrued liabilities	332	2,835
Inventory reserves	1,744	—
Other	1,213	855
Gross deferred tax liabilites	32,009	44,650
Allowance for doubtful accounts	(6,795)	(6,900)
Inventory reserves	(13,071)	(5,272)
Deferred compensation	(6,724)	(5,006)
Tax reserves and accrued liabilites	(10,592)	(7,156)
Tax basis inventory adjustment	(7,100)	(9,321)
Depreciation	(1,408)	(949)
Other	(5,694)	(1,567)
Gross deferred tax assets	(51,384)	(36,171)
	$(19,375)	$ 8,479

A reconciliation from the U.S. statutory federal income tax rate to the effective income tax rate follows:

Year Ended May 31,	1994	1993	1992
U.S. Federal statutory rate	35.0%	34.0%	34.0%
State income taxes, net of federal benefit	3.2	3.3	3.0
Tax benefit from permanent reinvestment of international earnings	(2.6)	—	—
Impact of rate increase	1.5	—	—
Other, net	2.0	1.3	(.1)
Effective income tax rate	39.1%	38.6%	36.9%

During 1982, the Company purchased future tax benefits for $15,277,000. Tax benefits of $5,554,000 in excess of the purchase price have been recognized as of May 31, 1994 and are classified in non-current deferred income taxes.

Note 7 – Redeemable Preferred Stock:

Nissho Iwai American Corporation (NIAC) is the sole owner of the Company's authorized Redeemable Preferred Stock, $1 par value, which is redeemable at the option of NIAC at par value aggregating $300,000. A cumulative dividend of $.10 per share is payable annually on May 31 and no dividends may be declared or paid on the Common Stock of the Company unless dividends on the Redeemable Preferred Stock have been declared and paid in full. There have been no changes in the Redeemable Preferred Stock in the three years ended May 31, 1994. As the holder of the Redeemable Preferred Stock, NIAC does not have general voting rights but does have the right to vote as a separate class on the sale of all or substantially all of the assets of the Company and its subsidiaries, on merger, consolidation, liquidation or dissolution of the Company or on the sale or assignment of the NIKE trademark for athletic footwear sold in the United States.

Note 8 – Common Stock:

The authorized number of shares of Class A Common Stock no par value and Class B Common Stock no par value are 60,000,000 and 150,000,000, respectively. Each share of Class A common Stock is convertible into one share of Class B Common Stock. Voting rights of Class B Common Stock are limited in certain circumstances with respect to the election of directors.

The Company's Employee Incentive Compensation Plan (the "1980 Plan") was adopted in 1980 and expired on December 31, 1990. The 1980 Plan provided for the issuance of up to 3,360,000 shares of the Company's Class B Common Stock in connection with the exercise of stock options granted under such plan. No further grants will be made under the 1980 Plan.

In 1990, the Board of Directors adopted, and the shareholders approved, the NIKE, Inc. 1990 Stock Incentive Plan (the "1990 Plan"). The 1990 Plan provides for the issuance of up to 4,000,000 shares of Class B Common Stock in connection with stock options and other awards granted under such plan. The 1990 Plan authorizes the grant of incentive stock options, non-statutory stock options, stock appreciation rights, stock bonuses, and the sale of restricted stock. The exercise price for incentive stock options may not be less than the fair market value of the underlying shares on the date of grant. The exercise price for non-statutory stock options and stock appreciation rights, and the purchase price of restricted stock, may not be less than 75% of the fair market value of the underlying shares on the date of grant. No consideration will be paid for stock bonuses awarded under the 1990 Plan. The 1990 Plan is administered by a committee of the Board of Directors. The committee has the authority to determine the employees to whom awards will be made, the amount of the awards, and the other terms and conditions of the awards. As of May 31, 1994, the committee has granted substantially all non-statutory stock options at 100% of fair market value on the date of grant under the 1990 Plan.

The following summarizes the stock option transactions under the 1980 Plan and 1990 Plan for the three fiscal years ended May 31, 1994:

	Shares (in thousands)	Option Price Per Share($)
Options outstanding May 31, 1992:	1,955	4.75 to 65.38
Exercised	(322)	4.75 to 65.50
Surrendered	—	—
Granted	491	56.25 to 82.13
Options outstanding May 31, 1993:	2,124	4.75 to 82.13
Exercised	(161)	4.75 to 56.25
Surrendered	(101)	20.41 to 82.13
Granted	492	50.13 to 56.88
Options outstanding May 31, 1994:	2,354	4.75 to 56.88
Options exercisable at May 31:		
1993	665	4.75 to 65.38
1994	917	4.75 to 38.25

In addition to the option plans discussed previously, the Company has several agreements outside of the plans with certain directors, endorsers and employees. As of May 31, 1994, 1,018,000 options with exercise prices ranging from $.417 per share to $76.25 per share had been granted. The aggregate compensation expenses related to these agreements is $5,670,000 and is being amortized over vesting periods from October 1980 through October 1998. The outstanding agreements expire from February 1998 through September 2005.

The following summarizes transactions outside the option plans for the three years ended May 31, 1994:

	Shares (in thousands)	Option Price Per Share($)
Options outstanding May 31, 1992:	235	4.75 to 43.25
Exercised	(20)	4.75
Surrendered	—	—
Granted	50	56.25 to 76.25
Options outstanding May 31, 1993:	265	4.75 to 76.25
Exercised	(6)	4.75 to 12.50
Surrendered	(20)	71.75 to 76.25
Granted	30	48.13 to 51.00
Options outstanding May 31, 1994:	269	4.75 to 51.00
Options exercisable at May 31:		
1993	156	4.75 to 43.25
1994	193	4.75 to 56.25

Note 9 - Benefit plans:

The Company has a profit sharing plan available to substantially all employees. The terms of the plan call for annual contributions by the Company as determined by the Board of Directors. Contributions of $8,500,000, $10,300,000 and $8,800,000 to the plan are included in other expense in the consolidated financial statements for the years ended May 31, 1994, 1993 and 1992, respectively.

The Company has a voluntary 401(k) employee savings plan. The Company matches a portion of employee contributions vesting that portion over 5 years. Company contributions to the savings plan were $3,503,000, $3,150,000 and $2,296,000 for the years ended May 31, 1994, 1993 and 1992.

Note 10 - Other income/expense, net:

Included in other income for the years ended May 31, 1994, 1993 and 1992, is interest income of $19,064,000, $15,377,000 and $11,892,000, respectively. During fiscal year 1994 the Company recognized $7,060,000 in non-recurring specific obligations associated with the shutdown of certain facilities in conjunction with the consolidation of European warehouses.

Note 11 - Commitments and contingencies:

The Company leases space for its offices, warehouses and retail stores under leases expiring from one to fifteen years after May 31, 1994. Rent expense aggregated $37,677,000, $33,195,000 and $23,935,000 for the years ended May 31, 1994, 1993 and 1992, respectively. Amounts of minimum future annual rental commitments under non-cancellable operating leases in each of the five fiscal years 1995 through 1999 are $30,412,000, $28,189,000, $25,917,000, $19,971,000, $18,130,000, respectively, and in aggregate $252,923,000.

Lawsuits arise during the normal course of business. In the opinion of management, none of the pending lawsuits will result in a significant impact on the consolidated financial position.

Note 12 - Fair value of financial instruments:

The Company estimates the fair value of its monetary assets and liabilities based upon the existing interest rates related to such assets and liabilities compared to the current market rates of interest for instruments of a similar nature and degree of risk. Cash and equivalents and notes payable to banks approximate fair value as reported in the balance sheet. The fair value of long-term debt is estimated using discounted cash flow analyses, based on the Company's incremental borrowing rates for similar types of borrowing arrangements. The fair value of the Company's long-term debt at May 31, 1994, is approximately $12,016,000, compared to a carrying value $12,364,000. The fair value of the Company's foreign currency exchange contracts (see Note 1) is estimated based generally on rates from quoted markets. The fair value of such contracts is $13,183,000 less than the stated amount.

Note 13 - Industry segment and operations by geographic areas:

The Company operates predominantly in one industry segment, that being the design, production and marketing of athletic and casual footwear, apparel and accessories. During 1994, 1993 and 1992, sales to one major customer amounted to approximately 14% of total sales in those years. Information about the Company's operations in the United States and international markets is presented below. Inter-geographic revenues and assets have been eliminated to arrive at the consolidated amounts. Expenses and assets not identifiable with the operations of a specific geographic segment have been listed separately.

(in thousands)

Year Ended May 31,	1994	1993	1992
Revenues from unrelated entities:			
United States	$2,432,684	$2,528,848	$2,270,880
Europe	927,269	1,085,683	919,763
Other international	429,715	316,453	214,568
	$3,789,668	$3,930,984	$3,405,211
Inter-geographic revenues:			
United States	$ 3,590	$ 3,583	$ 7,265
Europe	—	—	—
Other international	8,092	9,350	9,076
	$ 11,682	$ 12,933	$ 16,341
Total revenues:			
United States	$2,436,274	$2,532,431	$2,278,145
Europe	927,269	1,085,683	919,763
Other international	437,807	325,803	223,644
Less inter-geographic revenues	(11,682)	(12,933)	(16,341)
	$3,789,668	$3,930,984	$3,405,211
Operating income:			
United States	$ 344,632	$ 401,096	$ 356,589
Europe	124,242	177,716	173,175
Other international	65,894	65,236	51,602
Less corporate, interest and other income (expense)			
and eliminations	(44,174)	(49,532)	(59,548)
	$ 490,594	$ 594,516	$ 521,818
Assets:			
United States	$1,171,948	$1,347,507	$1,095,180
Europe	490,465	429,660	453,794
Other international	273,236	128,080	79,862
Total identifiable assets	1,935,649	1,905,247	1,628,836
Corporate cash and eliminations	438,166	282,216	244,025
Total assets	$2,373,815	$2,187,463	$1,872,861

Glossary

A

accelerated depreciation an accounting method that allocates a larger portion of plant asset cost to expense early in the asset's life than does the straight-line method.

account a record of increases and decreases in the dollar amount associated with a specific resource or activity.

accounting an information system for the measurement and reporting of the transformation of resources into goods and services and the sale or transfer of these goods and services to consumers.

accounting changes the effects on income of changes in the application of accounting principles from one fiscal period to another.

accounting cycle the process of analyzing transactions, recording transactions in the journal and ledger accounts, and preparing financial reports from the ledger.

accounting information system the specific part of the management information system responsible for identifying financial resources, tracking their transformation, determining their costs, and describing the results in financial reports.

accounting standard an official pronouncement establishing acceptable accounting procedures or financial report content.

accounts payable amounts owed by an organization to its suppliers.

accounts receivable amounts of cash to be received in the future from credit sales to customers.

accrual basis an accounting system in which revenues are recognized (recorded) when earned and expenses are recognized (recorded) when incurred.

accrued expenses expenses recognized prior to the time cash is paid for resources consumed.

accrued revenues revenues recognized prior to the time cash is received for goods and services sold.

accumulated depreciation the sum of all depreciation expense recorded on fixed assets since their acquisition.

acid-test ratio see quick ratio.

acquisition an economic event in which one company acquires a controlling interest in another company, which continues to exist as a separate legal entity.

allowance for doubtful accounts an account that identifies the amount of accounts receivable a company's management expects is likely to become uncollectible.

amortization the process of systematically allocating a cost to expense over a period of time.

annuity a series of equal payments over a specified number of equal time periods.

appropriation of retained earnings a transfer of a portion of retained earnings to a separate account to restrict its use.

articulation the relationship among financial statements in which the numbers on one statement explain numbers on other statements.

asset turnover the ratio of operating revenues to average total assets during a fiscal period; it is a measure of the ability of a company to generate sales from its total investment.

assets resources controlled by an organization and available for its use in the future.

attestation affirmation by an auditor as to whether financial statements are presented fairly in conformity with generally accepted accounting principles and are reliable representations of an organization's economic activities.

audit a detailed examination of an organization's financial reports and supporting documents; also, a verification process to ensure that information provided by an accounting system is reliable.

audit committee members of a corporation's board of directors who discuss the audit and its findings with the independent auditors.

audit opinion see audit report.

audit report a statement of the auditor's belief about the fairness and reliability of accompanying financial information.

authorized shares the maximum number of shares a corporation can issue without receiving approval from stockholders and the state to amend its charter.

available for sale securities those marketable securities a company may sell but that it does not buy and sell on an on-going basis.

B

balance sheet the financial report commonly used to report the amounts of assets, liabilities, and owners' equity.

bond a certificate of debt issued by an organization that represents an amount owed to a creditor.

book value the net dollar amount reported for an account on an organization's financial statement.

business organizations organizations that sell goods and/or services with the intention of earning profits.

business risk uncertainty associated with a company's financing, investing, and operating activities that affects the amount and timing of its cash flows.

C

capital resources invested by owners in a business; sometimes used to refer to resources provided by owners and to resources provided by creditors.

capital expenditures amounts paid for the purchase, lease, and construction of plant assets.

capital intensity the ratio of plant or long-term assets to total assets employed by a company.

capital lease a contract that permits one organization to use property owned by another organization as though the property had been purchased. Capital leases transfer most of the risks and rights of ownership to the company leasing the assets.

capital stock see common stock.

capital structure the way a company chooses to finance its assets and operating activities.

cash basis an accounting system in which revenues are recognized when the related cash is received and expenses are recognized when the related cash is paid.

cash flow the amount of cash received by an organization (cash inflow) or the amount of cash paid out by an organization (cash outflow) during a certain period of time.

cash flow to current maturities of long-term debt ratio the ratio of net cash flow from operating activities to current maturities of long-term debt; this ratio measures the sufficiency of cash to meet current debt payments.

certified public accountant (CPA) an accountant who has passed a rigorous exam and has been granted a license to practice by a state or territory of the U.S.

chart of accounts a list of account titles and their numbers used by an organization in its accounting system.

charter the legal right granted by a state permitting a corporation to exist.

commitment a promise to engage in some future activity that will have an economic effect.

common stock the ownership rights of investors in a corporation.

compilation financial statements prepared by an independent accountant for a client from the client's accounting records.

completed contracts method an accounting method that recognizes revenue when a long-term contract is completed.

conceptual framework a set of objectives, principles, and definitions to guide the development of new accounting standards.

consolidated financial statements a report of the combined economic activities of two or more corporations owned by the same stockholders.

contingency an existing condition that may result in an economic effect if a future event occurs.

contra account an account that offsets or reduces the amount of another account; sometimes referred to as a valuation account.

contracts legally binding agreements for the exchange of resources and services.

contributed capital the amount of direct investment by owners in a corporation.

control the evaluation of organizational activities and modification of these activities to achieve organization goals.

convertible bonds bonds that can be converted into shares of the issuer's stock.

corporation a legal entity separate and distinct from its owners.

cost accounting those functions necessary to accumulate and report a company's costs.

cost management strategies and methods to reduce costs and increase competitiveness.

cost of goods sold the cost incurred by an organization to acquire or produce the inventory that was sold during a specific period.

cost of services sold the cost of material, labor, and other resources consumed directly in producing services sold during a period.

coupon rate of return see nominal rate of return.

creditor a person or organization who loans financial resources to an organization.

credits bookkeeping entries that decrease asset or expense account balances and increase liability, owners' equity, or revenue account balances.

current assets cash or other resources management expects to convert to cash or consume during the next fiscal year, or operating cycle (if longer than a year).

current liabilities obligations management expects to pay during the next fiscal year or operating cycle (if longer than a year).

current ratio see working capital ratio.

D

data base a physical or electronic arrangement of data that allows the data to be retrieved and manipulated systematically.

date of declaration the date a corporation's board of directors announces that a dividend will be paid.

date of payment the date dividends are mailed to recipients.

date of record the date used to determine the recipients of a dividend.

debentures bonds that are unsecured by specific assets.

debits bookkeeping entries that increase asset or expense account balances and decrease liability, owners' equity, or revenue account balances.

debt covenants see loan agreements.

debt financing results when a company obtains financial resources from creditors.

debt to equity ratio the ratio of total debt to total stockholders' equity; this ratio is a measure of capital structure and is sometimes called debt to net worth. Net worth is total assets minus total liabilities.

debt to total assets ratio the ratio of total debt to total assets; this ratio is a common measure of capital structure. It also is known as debt total capitalization (liabilities plus stockholders' equity) and as simply the debt ratio.

debtors those with obligations to an organization.

declining balance depreciation an accounting method that allocates a multiple of the straight-line rate times the book value of an asset to depreciation expense.

deferred charges assets resulting when a company prepays expenses that will result in long-term benefits.

deferred expenses expenses that have not yet been incurred but for which cash has been paid.

deferred revenues revenues that have not yet been earned but for which cash has been collected.

deferred tax liability an estimate of income taxes that the company will pay in the future related to income it already has earned.

depletion the systematic allocation of the cost of natural resources to the periods that benefit from their use.

depreciation the process of allocating the cost of fixed assets to expense over the accounting periods that benefit from the asset's use.

depreciation expense the cost of fixed assets recognized as being consumed during a fiscal period.

direct labor wages and benefits of employees who work directly in the manufacturing process that are added to the cost of production.

discontinued operations major lines of business or segments from which a company will no longer derive income.

discussion memorandum a document that identifies accounting issues and alternative approaches to resolving the issues that may lead to an accounting standard.

dividend payout ratio the total cash dividend for a fiscal period divided by net income for the period; this ratio is a common measure of the relative amount of dividends paid by a corporation during a fiscal period.

dividends distributions of assets, usually cash, to stockholders from a corporation's profits.

dividends per share the ratio of dividends on common stock to the average number of shares of common stock outstanding; this ratio is a measure of dividend payment decisions.

double-entry bookkeeping a systematic method for recording the effects of transactions in an accounting data base where each transaction is recorded in two or more accounts.

E

earnings per share a measure of earnings performance of each share of common stock during a fiscal period; computed by dividing net income by the average number of shares of common stock outstanding during a fiscal period.

effective business an organization that meets customer needs by producing or providing goods and services that customers demand at a price they are willing to pay.

effective rate of return the actual return earned on an investment or incurred on a liability.

efficient business an organization that produces or provides goods and services at reasonable cost relative to the selling prices of its products.

equity financing the issuance of stock as a means of raising capital for a corporation.

equity method an accounting method that requires an investor company to recognize revenue from an investee company's net income in proportion to the investors' ownership.

expenses decreases in assets or increases in liabilities from producing and delivering goods or providing services that constitute the primary operating activities of an organization.

exposure draft a document that describes a proposed accounting standard.

extraordinary items gains and losses that are both unusual and infrequent.

F

financial accounting the process of preparing, reporting, and interpreting accounting information that is provided to external decision makers.

financial leverage the use of debt to increase a company's earning performance; the ratio of debt to equity in a company's capital structure.

financial revenues and expenses see other revenues and expenses.

financing activities the methods an organization uses to obtain financial resources from financial markets and how it manages these resources.

finished goods products awaiting sale.

first-in first-out (FIFO) method an accounting method for estimating inventory cost that assumes those units of inventory acquired first are sold first.

fiscal period any period of time for which operating results are collected and reported; could be a day, week, month, quarter, year, etc.

fixed assets see property, plant, and equipment.

fixed costs expenses that do not vary in proportion to sales activity.

foreign currency translation the process of converting the financial results of operations that occur in a foreign currency into U.S. dollars for financial reporting purposes.

form 10-K reports annual registration statements filed by corporations with the SEC.

fully diluted earnings per share earnings per share attributable to common stock after considering all effects of exercising options and warrants, convertible debt, and convertible preferred stock that would reduce earnings per share.

future value the amount an investment is worth or the amount of a liability that is owed at some time in the future.

G

generally accepted accounting principles (GAAP) the standards developed by professional accounting organizations to identify appropriate accounting and reporting procedures.

generally accepted auditing standards (GAAS) procedures used in conducting an audit to help auditors form an opinion about the fairness and reliability of the audited statements.

going concern an organization that can be expected to continue to operate into the foreseeable future.

goodwill the excess of cost over the market value of identifiable net assets resulting from the purchase of one company by another.

governmental and nonprofit organization one whose purpose is to provide goods or services without the intention of making a profit.

gross profit the difference between the cost and selling price of goods or services sold to customers during a period.

H

held-to-maturity debt securities securities for which an investor has the intent and ability to hold the securities until they mature.

historical cost the purchase or exchange price of an asset or liability at the time it is acquired or incurred.

I

income from operations the excess of gross profit over operating expenses.

income statement a commonly used financial statement that measures profit (net income) by subtracting the cost of resources consumed from the prices of goods and services sold for a certain period of time.

indirect labor the cost of wages and benefits paid to maintenance and supervisory employees who are associated with the production process.

information facts, ideas, and concepts that help us understand the world.

intangible assets long-term legal rights resulting from the ownership of patents, copyrights, trademarks, and similar items.

interest the cost of borrowed money; the return earned by a creditor.

interest expense the cost associated with borrowing money during a fiscal period.

interest payable an amount owed to creditors for the use of the creditors' money during a fiscal period.

internal control an organization's plan and the procedures it uses to safeguard its assets, ensure reliable information, promote efficiency, and encourage adherence to policies.

investing activities the selection and management of resources that will be used to develop, produce, and sell goods and services.

investors owners and creditors who provide money to an organization with the expectation of earning a return.

issued shares the number of shares that have been sold by a corporation to investors.

J

journal a book or computer file for recording transactions in the order in which they occur.

L

last-in first-out (LIFO) method an accounting method for estimating inventory cost that assumes the last units of inventory acquired are sold first.

ledger a book or computer file for summarizing account balances.

liabilities obligations owed by an organization to its creditors.

limited liability characteristic of a corporation in which shareholders are not personally liable for the debts of a corporation.

liquid assets resources that can be converted to cash in a relatively short period.

liquidity the extent to which an organization has sufficient cash and other liquid assets to pay current obligations.

loan agreements restrictions placed on a company's economic activities by its creditors.

long-term investments investments in securities that will not mature during the coming fiscal year and that management does not plan to convert to cash during the coming year.

long-term liabilities obligations not classified as current liabilities.

M

managerial (or management) accounting the process of preparing, reporting, and interpreting accounting information for use by an organization's internal decision makers.

manufacturing companies organizations that produce goods they sell to consumers, to merchandising companies, or to other manufacturing companies.

market any location or process that permits the exchange of resources.

market rate see effective rate of return.

marketable security a financial instrument (usually a stock or bond) that can be readily sold in an organized market.

materiality criteria for establishing the importance of a transaction or of a potential misstatement in financial statements.

merchandising companies organizations that sell to consumers goods that are produced by other companies.

merger an economic event that occurs when companies combine their resources and operations so only one legal entity continues to exist.

minority interest the portion of a subsidiary's stockholders' equity owned by shareholders other than the parent corporation.

minority interest in income of consolidated subsidiaries the portion of subsidiary net income attributable to minority interest.

moral hazard the condition that exists when agents (e.g., managers) have access to information that is not available to principals (e.g., stockholders) and are in a position to use the information to make decisions that are in the best interest of the agents, but not in the best interest of the principals.

mutual agency a legal right that permits a partner to enter into contracts and agreements that are binding on all members of a partnership.

N

net cash flow the difference between cash inflows and cash outflows during a specific period of time.

net income the difference between revenues and expenses for a period; also called net earnings.

net loss the result when expenses are greater than revenues for a period.

nominal rate of return the rate of interest paid on an investment or liability.

nonbusiness organizations governmental or nonprofit organizations, including civic, social, and religious organizations.

notes payable contracts with creditors that affirm the borrower will repay the amount borrowed plus interest at specific dates.

O

operating activities the use of resources to design, produce, distribute, and market goods and services.

operating expenses costs of resources consumed as part of operating activities during a fiscal period that are not directly associated with specific goods or services. Most operating expenses are period costs because they are recognized in the fiscal period in which they occur.

operating income the excess of gross profit over operating expenses.

operating lease a contract that permits one organization to use property owned by another organization for a limited period of time. The costs of operating leases are expensed in the period in which leased assets are used.

operating leverage the proportion of a company's total expenses that are fixed.

organization a group of people who work together to develop, produce, and/or distribute goods or services.

other assets a general category of assets that sometimes includes long-term investments in other companies, noncurrent receivables, fixed assets held for sale, prepaids not expected to be consumed in the next fiscal period, and long-term legal rights such as patents, trademarks, and copyrights.

other revenues and expenses revenues and expenses that are not directly related to a company's primary operating activities.

outstanding shares the number of a corporation's shares currently held by investors.

overhead production costs other than direct materials and direct labor.

owners' equity the amount of the owners' investment in an organization; legally, the amount of assets remaining after all creditor claims have been satisfied.

P

paid-in capital in excess of par value the excess of the sales price of stock sold by a corporation over its par value.

par value the value assigned to each share of stock by a corporation in its corporate charter.

parent corporation a corporation that controls another corporation, normally by owning more than 50% of the other corporation's common stock.

partnership a business owned by two or more persons, with no legal identity distinct from that of their owners.

percentage of completion method an accounting method that recognizes revenues and expenses for long-term contracts in proportion to the amount of the contract completed each fiscal period.

period costs all costs except those incurred to manufacture or acquire a product and prepare it for sale. These costs are reported as expenses in the period in which they occur.

periodic measurement estimated results of financing, investing, and operating activities recorded during a particular period.

planning the development of organizational goals and the development of strategies and policies to achieve these goals.

plant assets see property, plant, and equipment.

preemptive right the right of stockholders to maintain the same percentage of ownership when new shares are issued.

preferred stock stock that has a higher claim on dividends and assets than common stock.

prepaid rent an asset representing the cost of a rented resource to be consumed in the future.

present value the amount an investment is worth or the amount of a liability that is owed at the beginning of a time period.

primary earnings per share earnings per share attributable to common stock outstanding and to common stock equivalents.

primary market the market in which new (or original) issues of stocks and bonds are sold.

principal the amount of a loan that must be repaid.

product costs costs incurred to manufacture or acquire a product and distribute it to customers. These costs are expensed in the period the goods with which they are associated are sold.

profit the difference between the price received for goods or services sold and the total cost to the seller of all resources consumed in developing, producing, and selling those goods or services during a particular period; another name for net income or net earnings.

profit margin the ratio of a company's earnings to its operating revenues, it is a measure of the ability of a company to generate profits from its sales.

property, plant, and equipment long-term, tangible assets that are used in a company's operations.

proprietorship a business owned by one person, with no legal identity distinct from that of the owner.

proxy a document that authorizes management to cast votes for its stockholders at a stockholders' meeting.

proxy statement information distributed to stockholders about matters that will be considered at a corporation's annual stockholders' meeting.

Q

quick ratio the ratio of cash plus marketable securities and receivables to total current liabilities; this ratio measures the sufficiency of current cash-generating assets to meet current obligations. This ratio is a more conservative form of the current ratio.

R

raw materials the physical ingredients of a product that are used in the manufacturing process.

retail companies see merchandising companies.

retained earnings the portion of cumulative net income that has been reinvested in an organization.

return of investment an amount received by investors that is paid from the amounts the investors originally invested.

return on assets the ratio of net income plus interest expense adjusted for taxes to average total assets.

return on equity the ratio of net income minus preferred dividends to average common stockholders' equity; this ratio is a measure of return on investment by common stockholders.

return on investment the amount of profit earned by a business that could be paid to owners; also see return on assets.

revenues increases in assets or decreases in liabilities from selling goods or providing services that constitute the primary activities of an organization.

review an examination by an independent accountant of a client's financial statements to provide assurance they appear to be in good order.

risk uncertainty about an outcome, such as the return on an investment.

S

secondary market a market in which investors sell to each other.

service companies organizations that sell services rather than goods.

shareholders' equity see stockholders' equity.

source documents the original records of specific transactions, such as sales invoices, receipts, and shipping documents.

stakeholders those who have an economic interest in an organization and those who are affected by its activities.

stated rate see nominal rate of return.

statement of cash flows a financial statement that reports events that resulted in cash inflows and outflows for a fiscal period.

statement of stockholders' equity a financial statement that provides information about changes in stockholders' equity accounts for a corporation during a fiscal period.

stock certificates of ownership in a corporation.

stock dividends shares of stock distributed by a company to its current stockholders without charge to the stockholders.

stock market an organization established to facilitate the trading of shares of corporate securities; examples include the New York Stock Exchange, the American Stock Exchange, or the Tokyo Stock Exchange.

stock options legal rights that permit the holder, often an employee of the grantor, to purchase a specified number of shares of a company's stock at a predetermined price.

stock split the issuance by a corporation of a multiple of the number of shares of stock outstanding prior to the split.

stock warrants legal rights that permit the holder to purchase additional shares of the issuer's stock at a future date at a prescribed price.

stockholders owners of a corporation.

stockholders' equity claims by owners of stock to the resources of a corporation.

straight-line depreciation an accounting method that allocates an equal amount of the cost of a plant asset to expense during each fiscal period of the asset's expected useful life.

subsequent events major economic activities occurring after the close of a company's fiscal year but prior to the time its annual report is printed.

subsidiary a corporation controlled by other corporations, normally by ownership of more than 50% of the subsidiary's common stock.

subsidiary ledger a collection of a related group of accounts, such as all accounts receivable or all accounts payable, that are subcategories of a general ledger account.

sum-of-the-years'-digits depreciation an accounting method that allocates depreciation according to a fraction, n/N, in which n is remaining life of the asset at the beginning of the period and N is the sum of the years of the expected useful life of the asset.

system a set of interrelated activities or processes that work together to achieve a goal.

T

times interest earned ratio the ratio of income before interest and taxes to interest expense; this ratio measures the sufficiency of current income to cover interest requirements.

trading securities those marketable securities a company buys and sells on an on-going basis.

transaction an event that increases or decreases an account balance.

transaction analysis the process of evaluating a transaction to determine its effect on specific accounts.

transformation process a cycle that begins with the acquisition of capital from investors and creditors. This capital is invested in facilities, equipment, people, and other resources needed to create goods and services. Organizations use these resources in developing, producing, distributing, and selling goods and services. Selling goods and services results in the inflow of additional financial resources so that the cycle can continue. An organization's success in the transformation process determines its profitability.

translation adjustment gains or losses resulting from translating the operations of a company's foreign subsidiaries into U.S. dollars for purposes of reporting consolidated financial statements.

treasury stock stock a corporation sold to its investors and then repurchased from them; this stock can be reissued.

U

unearned revenues obligations to provide goods or services in the future, usually because cash has been received for the goods or services.

units-of-production depreciation an accounting method that produces a level amount of depreciation expense per unit of output, rather than per fiscal period.

V

variable costs expenses that vary in proportion to sales activity.

W

warranty a promise by a seller to repair or replace defective products or to service products over a period of time.

weighted average method an accounting method for estimating inventory cost that assumes an average cost of units available during a period as the cost of units sold.

withdrawals distributions of assets, usually cash, to a proprietor or partner.

work in process goods currently in the process of being manufactured.

working capital the amount of current assets minus the amount of current liabilities.

working capital ratio the amount of total current assets divided by the amount of total current liabilities; this ratio is a measure of the ability of a company to meet its current obligations.

Y

yield to maturity see effective rate of return.

Index